American Writing Today

Edited by
Richard Kostelanetz

American Writing Today

Edited by
Richard Kostelanetz

The Whitston Publishing Company
Troy, New York
1991

Acknowledgments

Alfred A. Knopf, Inc. for permission to reprint poetry excerpts from *Selected Poems of Langston Hughes* (copyright © 1959 by Langston Hughes), and "Song for a Banjo Dance" from *The Weary Blues* by Langston Hughes (copyright © 1926 by Alfred A. Knopf, Inc.; renewed 1953 by Langston Hughes).

New Directions Publishing Corp. for permission to reprint poetry excerpts from *The Collected Shorter Poems* by Kenneth Rexroth (copyright © 1966, 1963, 1962, 1952, 1949, 1944, 1940 by Kenneth Rexroth; (copyright © 1956, 1951, 1950, 1944 by New Directions Publishing Corp.); from *New Poems* by Kenneth Rexroth (copyright © 1971, 1973, 1974 by Kenneth Rexroth, copyright © 1974 by New Directions Publishing Corp.).

The Estate of Charles Olson for permission to reprint poetry excerpts from *The Distances* by Charles Olson (copyright © 1951, 1952, 1953, 1954, 1955, 1956, 1957, 1958, 1959, 1960, 1961 by Charles Olson); from *Pleistocene Man: A Curriculum for the Study of the Soul* by Charles Olson (copyright © 1968 by Charles Olson); from *Maximus Poems* by Charles Olson (copyright © 1960 by Charles Olson).

Farrar Straus & Giroux, Inc., for permission to reprint poetry excerpts from *For the Union Dead* by Robert Lowell (copyright © 1956, 1960, 1961, 1962, 1963, 1964 by Robert Lowell); from *Near the Ocean* by Robert Lowell (copyright © 1963, 1965, 1967 by Robert Lowell); from *For Lizzie and Harriet* by Robert Lowell (copyright © 1967, 1968, 1969, 1970, 1973 by Robert Lowell); from *The Dolphin* by Robert Lowell (copyright © 1973 by Robert Lowell); from *History* by Robert Lowell (copyright © 1967, 1968, 1969, 1970, 1973, by Robert Lowell); from *Day by Day* by Robert Lowell (copyright © 1975, 1976, 1977 by Robert Lowell).

Gary Snyder for permission to reprint poetry excerpts from *RIPRAP & Cold Mountain Poems* by Gary Snyder (copyright © 1958, 1959, 1965 by Gary Snyder); from *Myths & Texts* by Gary Snyder (copyright © 1960, 1978 by Gary Snyder); from *Six Sections from Mountains and Rivers Without End Plus One* by Gary Snyder (copyright © 1957, 1958, 1959, 1960, 1961, 1962, 1963, 1964, 1965, 1966, 1967, 1968, 1969, 1970 by Gary Snyder); from *Regarding Wave* by Gary Snyder (copyright © 1967, 1968, 1969, 1970 by Gary Snyder).

Donald Hall, Allen Ginsberg, Richard Kostelanetz, Tom Ockerse, and Mary Ellen Solt for poems quoted in the context of their own expositions.

Contents

Preface

> The critic will soon find, and constantly, that [John] Milton is a more rewarding and suggestive poet to work with than Blackmore. But the more obvious this becomes, the less time he will want to waste belaboring the point.
>
> —Northrop Frye

American Writing Today intends to be a comprehensive critical survey of the past forty years of American poetry and fiction; an earlier edition, in two volumes available only abroad, was meant as well to complement earlier anthologies in the Voice of America's Forum series. The chapters are based upon a series of broadcasts that were produced for Voice of America in 1980. Most contributors to the book wrote fresh essays at that time while others reviewed transcripts of their talks; yet others participated in symposia that appear here in transcript form. The bibliography concluding this book was written especially for its pages.

In some of the following chapters, major contemporary writers talk about themselves; others are discussed by experts on their work. Individuals identified with certain general tendencies, such as science fiction, alternative publishing, or feminist criticism, discuss those developments in the context of their own work. Since no one was told what to write or how to approach his or her subject, one attraction of this anthology should be variousness in style and diction, in structures as well as interests. In this age of the decision-making panel, it pleases me to report that no one else was responsible for selecting the individual commentators and for moderating the symposia. Since this edition restores several essays that the publisher (USIA) cut against my wishes, I am now wholly responsible for editing this book.

As the earlier VOA books on American literature were done fifteen and more years before, this had to include chapters on writers who should have been discussed before but were not: Saul Bellow,

Gertrude Stein, Edmund Wilson, Kenneth Burke and Langston Hughes. Secondly, given the assignment to making a book that would be "acceptable" now and nonetheless survive for fifteen more years (and behind that, given the current peculiarities of U. S. literary politics), it became very, very difficult to include individual chapters on anyone born after 1932 (John Updike). Thus, younger writers with individual chapters are here not to talk about themselves but to be experts on new developments or to participate in symposia on general developments. One way that *American Writing Today* differs from other critical anthologies of its sort, not only those in the VOA series, is stylistic variety in the essays, for if only to reflect the pluralism of America I very much wanted to avoid giving any impression that they emerged from a single machine.

I should add that doing the original edition of this book involved more nuisance than it was worth. When the folks at the USIA first approached me, I did not see that they needed me initially to get the participation of writers they could not get themselves. Once they had the material in hand, their mood changed. Certain essays were dropped from the final book. As my own name did not appear on the title page of the final proofs, I had to hold onto them until my contact at USIA assured me in writing that it would be in its appropriate place. (The fact that it took him months to deliver this letter speaks volumes, as they say.) One virtue of this American edition is restoring these previously omitted essays.

I am thankful to Jean Goode for contracting this first American edition and then to several dozen colleagues, American writers all, for reaffirming their participation. (Some even provided new information for their essays or biographical notes.) Certain quotations from writers' works were excluded at the implicit request of publishers refusing to give permission for fair use in a critical context. Perhaps this refusal reflected a suspicion that such quotations would not confirm claims made on their behalf. Any scholar choosing to discuss these writers in the future should be forewarned about their publishers, much as you would advise a newcomer to your city not to patronize the most dangerous neighborhoods. Otherwise, every effort has been made to identify the holders of copyrighted material. If any error or omission has occurred, it will be corrected in future editions, providing that written notification is provided in writing to the author and the publisher.

For initial assistance in preparing this book for the printer I'm grateful to Sarah Gleason; and for concluding assistance in organizing the contributors' proofs and then proofing the entire manuscript himself, I owe a big debt to Ophir Finkelthal. This new edition is dedicated to Jerome Klinkowitz.

Richard Kostelanetz
New York, New York

Introduction

Richard Kostelanetz

America ended World War II the beneficiary of unrivaled good fortune. Its lands were unscathed, its home populations unharmed. It had also become the residence of many of Europe's most prominent refugee intellectuals. In the late 1930s Albert Einstein and John von Neumann, the two most consequential minds in modern mathematics, came to live in the United States and to stay to their deaths. So did the artists Hans Hofmann, L. Moholy-Nagy, Piet Mondrian, Joseph Albers, and Marcel Duchamp. In the wake of European troubles also came the composers Arnold Schönberg and Igor Stravinsky, the architects Walter Gropius and Ludwig Mies van der Rohe, and the sociologists Hannah Arendt and Herbert Marcuse, all of whom also stayed here and contributed to American culture. Major European writers, by contrast, tended to reside in America only during the war, most of them returning home as soon as they could: the French surrealist André Breton, the Nobel Prize-winners Maurice Maeterlinck and Thomas Mann, the Swede Sigrid Undset, the Austrian Hermann Broch, the Frenchmen Jules Romains, André Maurois, St. Jean-Perse, and Claude Lévi-Strauss, the Czech Franz Werfel, the Hungarian Ferenc Molnar, and the Spaniard Jorge Guillén. Though the work that most of these immigrants wrote contributed to their native cultures, their presence here helped bring American culture out of provincial isolation. Indeed, by the end of the war, America had become what it had never been before—a cultural center for the world, and its prominence would remain. It is indicative that after 1945 its best artists and thinkers were rarely expatriates, "alienated" from their homelands, but full-time residents of the United States.

From the perspective of 1980, we can see clearly that there were two *boom* periods in post-World War II American culture; there were two eras in which a large amount of major work was produced and important new names initially appeared. The first boom occurred immediately after the war and continued until the early 1950s. This would be the era of Jackson Pollock's and Willem de Kooning's best paintings, Aaron Copland's most lasting music, Martha Graham's greatest dance, and, in literature, the early works of Norman Mailer, Ralph Ellison, Robert Lowell, and Saul Bellow. In contrast, the half-dozen years immediately in the wake of this boom were perceived as a time in which, culturally, "nothing is happening."

The second boom began around 1959 and ran through the 1960s. This would be the era of pop and then minimalism in visual art, the music of John Cage and the choreography of Merce Cunningham, and, in literature, the emergence of Joseph Heller, John Barth, Thomas Pynchon, and Vladimir Nabokov, among others. Here began the emergence of intermedia, or arts that intrinsically integrated more than one art: happenings, kinetic environments, the theater of mixed means, visual poetry, text-sound, etc. The 1960s was a time for the success of art and literature that seemed more audacious and more advanced than that of the previous era.

One needs to understand at the beginning that the American literary scene does not have a central continuous establishment located in the capital city and intimately connected to the government. Washington, D. C. has never had much of a cultural community. The U. S. government did not establish a literary agency until the founding of the National Endowment for the Arts in the early 1960s, and NEA literature still does not have much consequential impact. While it is true that New York City is the center of American commercial publishing and thus the center of U. S. literary export (particularly to Europe), it is by no account the center of literary creation. Major American writers have always lived all over the country, scarcely in touch with the centers of power, let alone each other. William Faulkner, we remember, lived most of his life in Oxford, Mississippi; Ernest Hemingway, after living abroad, traveled between Key West, Florida, and Ketchum, Idaho. The poets William Carlos Williams and Wallace Stevens spent most of their lives, respectively, in Rutherford, New Jersey, and Hartford, Connecticut.

Instead of looking for a center in American literature, let me suggest that we notice numerous mini-establishments distributed around the country. Each has its generals and its foot soldiers, as well as its camp followers, with varying degree of power and numbers. Some of these groups are organized around specialized literary interests—science fiction or avant-garde writing. Most are organized around some kind of minority affiliation, which may be geographic, ethnic, racial, academic, or sexual. Thus, we hear, for instance, of "Southern writers," "Jewish writers," "black writers," "Black Mountain poets," and "woman writers." It is true that alliances and allegiances within each group tend to be tenuous and irregular—writers being by nature indepedent spirits—and that literary groups tend to be cliques within the sociological category (e.g., not every writer living in the South is a "Southern writer"). Nonetheless, it can be observed that these groups exist, with varying degrees of cohesiveness and power, and that each tends to develop a literary ideology based upon its particularity. That is, Southern writers are likely to say that there is somethir.g important about coming from the South, and Black Mountain poets tend to make grand claims for the arts school that they attended. Each group develops an ideology in part to present its works to that segment of the American public that cares about literature. Thus, in the American literary scene as a whole, groups and ideologies compete with one another in a continual flux, where everyone is winning readers and yet no group finally wins everybody.

It should also be understood that this book is devoted to *literature*, which is to say those works of imaginative art that will survive the present. One distinction that is sometimes lost in some current discussions is that between art and pop. They have always inhabited separate domains, intending to reach audiences of different dimensions, extending from separate traditions, and seldom interacting (or resembling each other) at their creative origins. Pop, simply, is art for the millions; and the aural, visual, and literary arts each have their popular genres. Just as pop music derives from modern music, so do both journalism and pop-song lyrics relate to literature, and commercial art to painting. Essentially, all pop forms are more direct in their communication, more universally accessible, less innovative in form, less complex in ideas, more clichéd, more conducive to collaborative production, more subservient to both recognizably transient fads and mediumistic conventions. Just as newspapers and magazines are meant to be quickly discarded, so, by design, are both posters and pop records.

Art, unlike pop, is not limited to the demands of the mass market, or by established structural conventions, or by available materials; so that pop strives to emulate (or imitate) the creative freedom of art, rather than vice versa. All pop is, by definition, intended not for the few, as is more serious art, but for the many (which may, however, include "the few"); so that pop at its most successful is many times more commercial than art. The essential pop medium for writing is the newspaper, which is explicitly designed to be read today and discarded tomorrow; and much of the writing that appears in lowest-period "mass" paperbacks is similarly pop. Especially if it is at its beginnings unfashionable, the work of great art is appreciated at first by a few, who in turn communicate their enthusiasm to increasingly wider circles.

In part because of the educational boom of the 1960s, book publishing became more profitable than ever before. Thus, expanding diversified corporations, called "conglomerates," began to regard publishing houses as attractive plums to add to their corporate trees. By the end of the decade, Random House had been purchased by RCA; Bobbs-Merrill became a division of ITT; and Holt Rinehart Winston, itself the product of mergers, became a division of CBS. These conglomerates were not book-lovers desiring to publish the best books and somehow make enough money to continue their prestigious mission but absentee-owners insisting that the book-publishing company produce greater and still greater profits. The same editors who two decades ago might have looked for a classic literary work were now scrambling for the "big book," the pop blockbuster, that would sell millions of copies and earn considerable profits for their conglomerates. Meanwhile, in order to maximize financial returns on their investment, the conglomerates insisted that their book divisions publish less of those kinds of books not likely to return a profit. Those drastically reduced categories inevitably included poetry, "literary" novels, works of literary criticism, books by unknowns.

By the mid-1970s noticeably less *literature* was being published by the larger commercial houses. In the wake of their default emerged new small publishers based on the traditional model—book-lovers essentially trying to sell enough past books to do a new one. I call them "alternative publishers" because they emphasize those works that the commercial publishers are likely to dismiss as too limited in audience appeal. That is, whereas commercial publishers make decisions primarily to earn money, alternative publishers do things largely for love, which may be aesthetic love, spiritual love, political love, or empathy. Also, whereas the commercial publishers are, as noted before, centered in New York, alternative publishers are distributed across the country. The analogues in American theater have been "off-

Broadway" and, more recently, "off-off-Broadway."

As a result, by the end of the 1970s, one could safely generalize that most of the consequential poetry and much of the important fiction, particularly by writers under 40, were published not by the commercial houses but by these new alternative publishers. At first, one scarcely heard of this literary drift, in part because the prominent "book reviews" were beholden to the commercial publishers who advertised in their pages; but by now, awareness of this shift is common knowledge. One index of the change is the fact that librarians specializing in contemporary literature are nowadays more inclined to order new titles from alternative publishers.

One fact that intellectuals abroad find hard to understand is the large number of serious writers in America—the battalion of people creating poetry and fiction out of the most estimable traditions of modernist literature. Their numbers have doubled in the past decade. There are thousands of publishing poets—not part-time versifiers, but people who consider poetry their principal vocation and thus devote much of their lives to the writing of poetry. (Needless to say, most of them earn most of their incomes doing something else.) After all, the profession is open to individuals of all classes, from all regions and all ethnic and religious backgrounds. There are nearly as many fiction-writers. One reason for this increase in numbers is the sharp increase, in the past two decades, of the numbers of school classes or "workshops" devoted to some kind of "creative writing." In courses of this kind, instead of writing research papers, as they might in a standard academic class, students produce stories and poems for professorial adjudication.

By the end of the 1950s at some colleges a student could "major" in creative writing—make it his undergraduate speciality; and one could take even a master's degree (customarily an M.F.A.—a Master of Fine Arts) and in a few places a doctorate in creative writing. (Just as a doctorate in philosophy requires the completion of an acceptable book-length research paper, so these creative-writing doctorates require a full-length book of poetry and fiction.) The simplest index of the impact of this creative-writing revolution is this: whereas few notable American writers born before 1925 ever took a writing course, most of those born after that date took at least one or two; those born after 1940 may have majored in creative writing and perhaps taken a graduate degree in it as well. Most publishing writers born after 1950 appear to have an M.F.A.

What an advanced degree in creative writing qualified its recipient to do was, of course, teach creative writing in an ever-increasing dissemination. By the 1970s, there were creative-writing courses in the junior colleges, in the high schools. Needless to say perhaps, most people taking those courses did not become committed poets and fictioners; many of them became more receptive to the sophisticated appeals of first-rate poetry and fiction. Thanks in part to these creative-writing courses, the audience for the best American writing today continues to increase. Indeed, poets in America today have more readers than any English-language poets ever had before.

It is scarcely surprising that most American writers nowadays earn most of their living by teaching. Those who write commercially successful books can live off their royalties, and others write prose articles for remunerative magazines. Famous poets often give readings of their work, especially at universities, where fees can exceed a thousand dollars for a single performance. Someone like myself, who has taught only twice, tends to do several things, such as writing articles, curating exhibitions, organizing broadcasts, giving "illuminated demonstrations" of my creative work, editing anthologies, and selling copies of my books that the original publishers have allowed to go out of print. However, I am single and live modestly, with the annual income of a laborer. If I needed to support a family, I too would probably become a full-time teacher.

The increasing number of writers is partially responsible for another peculiar characteristic of American writing today—the diversity of partially acceptable styles. It is possible to have, in some circles, a literary reputation based entirely on realistic fiction and, in other circles, on more experimental fiction. In the literary bookstores and on the college reading lists, informal writers appear to coexist peaceably with formal ones, urban with rural, experimental with conservative, each one sure that his or her approach should be primary, often to the exclusion of all others. One by-product of this diversity is an atmosphere of opportunity, so that an incipient writer coming of age in the 1980s knows that literally anything can be done, if it is persuasive and successful on its own terms.

Conversely, if there is no literary center, then there are no powerful groups that can award universally recognized badges of merit and promotion. Then, too, it becomes very hard for a newcomer to stand out from the pack. This I take to be the principal reason why the following selection of individuals has remarkably few writers under 40. This absence distresses me in principle, for much of the second half of my book *The End of Intelligent Writing: Literary Politics in America* (1974, 1977), was devoted to a favorable survey of younger writers. However, in making selections for this project, I had to balance my own enthusiasms against my responsibilities for, first, portraying the entire post-World War II period (and thus inevitably favoring writers who have often been known for at least half of it), and second, including writers whose books would be available to foreign readers, if not in their local literary bookstore, then at least in their local American Cultural Center. Both these criteria ruled against individual programs devoted to some of my favorite contemporaries; so some of them appear in the symposia. Nonetheless, it has been my hope to produce the strongest possible survey, one that would be interesting to read from beginning to end and that will hopefully survive the 1980s as the best book of its kind.

Bibliography*

Fleming, Donald and Bernard Bailyn, editors. *The Intellectual Migration: Europe and America 1930-1960*. Cambridge, Massachusetts: Harvard University Press, 1969.

Kostelanetz, Richard. *The End of Intelligent Writing: Literary Politics in America.* Mission, Kansas: Sheed & Ward, 1974, 1977.

—. *Master Minds*. New York: Macmillan, 1969.

---

* The remaining bibliography for this chapter appears as the concluding chapter.

Edmund Wilson

Lewis M. Dabney

Critic, portraitist, reporter, and historian, Edmund Wilson remains a central figure in the contemporary American literary scene. He is a guide to the artistic and social movements of the jazz age and the depression. He is an interpreter of the 19th-century heritage, and of the connections among personality, social history, politics, and literature. His fiction, poetry, and plays, his accounts of languages and traveling can still instruct, amuse, and move. Wilson was the last of the great journalists who wrote for the educated man-in-the-street as well as the literary and learned world before the age of the media and the specialization of intellectual life. His versatility and range, his sound intelligence and taste, his dramatic imagination and what W. H. Auden called the "elegant clarity" of his style enabled him to command an audience for 50 years. A spokesman for the new writing of the 1920s, from Proust and Joyce to Hemingway and Fitzgerald, in the 1930s Wilson turned to political journalism and chronicled the Marxist heroes in *To the Finland Station*. As his literary generation faded after World War II, he took on new interests, learning Hebrew and Russian, investigating the Dead Sea Scrolls, the New York State Indians, 19th-century soldiers and statesmen. *Patriotic Gore*, his account of Civil War personalities and their writing, is often called a classic, and his posthumous letters and journals sustain our interest in the man and his times.

Wilson's 20th-century career was built on the individualism and idealism of the 19th century, when literature was the natural language of communication. Born into the educated professional class in Red Bank, New Jersey, in 1895, he was the son of a brilliant trial lawyer whose dinner-table discourses affected the critic's style, and who, in the "gilded age" of the millionaires and corrupt bosses, passed on to him a patriotism that looked back to the republic of

Lincoln. The senior Edmund Wilson—the son signed himself "Jr." in his early work—adhered to the values of the Protestant-Puritan tradition, teaching the boy to admire effort, energy, commitment, and to fear laziness and mediocrity. The father's family were orthodox Presbyterians, while Wilson's mother's people, descended from the New England Mathers, "had scrapped the old-time religion and still retained a certain animus toward it." Like the classic American writers, Wilson carried on the Puritan tradition by rebelling against it, and like other critics from the Romantics on, he transferred to literature the passion and piety of a faith undermined by science.

Readers of his autobiographical essays know that his boyhood was difficult, for his mother was deaf and his father suffered from depression and hypochondria. The boy's companions were his relatives and the books on the shelves of the family libraries. The French critic Taine was one of his first models. "He had created the creators themselves as characters in a larger drama of cultural and social history," Wilson writes. George Bernard Shaw was the intellectual hero of his adolescence, and when reading Shaw at 17, he lost his faith, a "revelation in reverse" that was encouraged by distaste for evangelical preachers and admiration for his Greek teacher. At the Hill School and Princeton University Wilson absorbed the education of the gentleman-amateur, which at its best fostered sound judgments and the ability to express oneself, to assimilate great figures of the past, and to find one's way around in new terrain. What he cherished from his college years was an exposure to what Matthew Arnold called "the best that is known and thought," and in that setting of football and torchlight parades, memorialized in Fitzgerald's *This Side of Paradise*, Wilson read Plato, Dante, and Flaubert. Christian Gauss's courses introduced him to Renan, Michelet, and Sainte-Beuve, giving him the perspective on 19th-century French culture which is the point of departure of *Axel's Castle* and *To the Finland Station*. Like other major writers of the 1920s, Wilson was liberated from a provincial English culture by the Continental aesthetic. He acquired a new model in Henry James and on a summer trip abroad began making the record of conversations, scenes, and thoughts to which, like Pepys and the Goncourts, he would add throughout his life.

He also admired the racy journalism of H. L. Mencken and James Huneker. This was the great age of reporter-writers, and when he graduated, Wilson got a job on a New York newspaper, for he was bored with the scene in which he had grown up. World War I broke the cocoon of privilege, thrusting the young man with all his humanistic baggage into the modern world. Not wanting to be an officer like his friends, he went to war as an enlisted man in the hospital corps, and a few months tending the wounded and burying the dead in France made him a permanent skeptic as regards the myths that rationalize men's wars. A soldier's perspective on the class structure of the army prepared him to side with labor in the depression, even as he learned to appreciate the variety of American life. Returning to New York to take up a literary career, Wilson was drawn to the glitter of the metropolitan scene and the romanticism of bohemia. His books capture the milieu in which, as "a man of the twenties," he came of age, one of "drinks, animated conversation, gaiety, brilliant writing, uninhibited exchange of ideas." The personal world of his journals in *The Twenties* and its sequel *The Thirties* complements the reporting on the jazz age and the depression that first appeared in *The New Republic* and is gathered together in *The American Earthquake*. In the novel *I Thought of Daisy* (1929) a "symphonic structure" out of Proust and Joyce is imposed on the conventional materials of a young man's attempt to come of age.

The major work of Wilson's youth was the book reviewing that was collected in *The Shores of Light* or built upon in *Axel's Castle* and in the latter essays of *The Triple Thinkers* and *The Wound and the Bow*. No other American critic has had such importance in a vital literary scene as he did when he adjudicated the new writing of his countrymen and interpreted the international Modernist movement. Wilson helped launch Hemingway, seeing his originality and power, and deserves some credit for Fitzgerald's development to *The Great Gatsby*. Celebrating *Ulysses*, which made everything else, Wilson said, "look brassy," he cultivated the "usable past" in essays on Poe, James, and Crane. Although some of his judgments of poetry have been questioned, he was an astute interpreter of the early Eliot and one of the first to see Yeats as the greatest of modern poets, whose lyric voice kept the muse alive in a scientific, democratic world. Alert to stylistic experiments, from Stein's emulation of Cubism to Lawrence's account of sexual experience, he discussed them in the context of Freud's influence, the philosophy of Alfred North Whitehead, the effects of the world war.

Working in the 19th-century tradition of the reviewer-critic, he accepted a responsibility to give the gist of a book or tell the story. He believed he should also "be able to see the author's development in the context of the national literature and the national literature in relation to other literatures," and he learned "to pursue a line of thought through pieces on miscellaneous and more or less fortuitous subjects," making weekly journalism serve his higher aims. His first job was at *Vanity Fair*, the most literate of fashion magazines, but by mid-decade he had moved to *The New Republic*, where Herbert Croly's vision of "the promise of American life" complemented Wilson's ambitions for American writing. There his book reviews and social reportage appeared along with the serial versions of *Axel's Castle* and *To the Finland Station*. In this forum Wilson carried on the work of Mencken and Van Wyck Brooks, those prophets of the renascence of the 1920s who never escaped the provincialism of the old America. While Mencken kept on denouncing the philistines and Brooks elaborated upon our artistic failures, the younger man spoke for the generation that was creating a literature for what Dos Passos skeptically called "the American century." In dramatic monologue, dialogue, and polemic he entertained readers while instructing them about cultural issues. Mediating between "highbrow" and "lowbrow," he also criticized the doctrinaire "Humanism" of Irving Babbitt and Paul Elmer More, and the susceptibility of his own contemporaries to political and religious myths.

Axel's Castle, which made the young critic's reputation, is both a celebration and a critique of the modern masters. He saw that Proust, Joyce, Eliot, Yeats, Valéry, and Stein, whom he named symbolists, had common techniques and values, that like the Romantics in their time, they had "disintegrated the old mechanism and revealed to the imagination a new flexibility and freedom." To Maxwell Perkins he wrote of his intention to give "popular accounts that will convince people of their importance and persuade people to read them." The result was a map of this artistic and intellectual terrain that remains useful after 50 years of specialized scholarship. As he lived with these writers, however, he grew skeptical of them as "guides to life," at any rate for Americans. The escapist strain in Yeats, Eliot's spiritual weariness, and the narcissism of Valéry seemed a luxury after the stock market crash, and a brief nervous breakdown in 1930 only increased Wilson's impatience with Proust's hypochondria. He continued to revere the life-affirming Joyce and would promote *Finnegans Wake* as eagerly as *Ulysses*, but his Proust chapter breaks in two when a remarkable paraphrase of *Remembrance Of*, capturing its themes and power in 30 pages, is succeeded by an attack on the author's perversities. Attempting to grasp their relationship to Proust's moral genius, to match what Wilson would call the wound and the bow, he found historical perspective in Marx and was able to sum up Proust's world as "the Heartbreak House of capitalist culture."

The moral values of *Axel's Castle*, then, are at odds with its aesthetic ones. The book reflects the conflict between the avant-garde and its bourgeois public, a creative tension that could not survive the economic transformations of the depression. Wilson's detractors are right that he did not fully assimilate Modernism. His activist temperament and Protestant-American heritage made him uneasy with the "resignationism" which the Modernist, it seemed to him, derived from the *fin-de-siècle*, when Villiers de L'Isle-Adam's Axel rejected life. Wilson hoped to reconcile the Modernists' imaginative freedom with the social responsibility of Shaw and Anatole France. His own literary idealism was now to be visited on the great Marxists, men who had imposed their ideals on the world. Yet he could compare the moral insight of Lenin to that of Proust for Soviet readers in 1935. For American intellectuals of the 1930s and their heirs he made the politics of the left compatible with high culture.

* * * * *

The lasting reportage and history Wilson produced in the 1930s reflect the experience of his contemporaries as they moved through radical aspiration to disenchantment with Stalin's Russia. The same week that *Axel's Castle* appeared in 1931, he was urging fellow writers to help "take Communism away from the Communists and apply it to American conditions," and though he was too much the individualist to become a Communist like some of his friends, for several years he led the leftward movement of the intelligentsia. His survey of the country in the depression, *The American Jitters*, is as powerful as the vivid partial accounts of Steinbeck, Agee, and others, for he finds ways to confront what was happening—some of them anticipate the methods of the "new journalists"—that press readers to consider what was to be done. He sets the dedication of the Empire State Bulding off against the suicides of unemployed workers. He describes the world of those who do have jobs, from the Detroit assembly lines, where a sudden silence means that someone has lost a finger, to the 110-degree heat at Hoover Dam, to the bleak winter streets of Lawrence, Massachusetts, where immigrant workers face the powerful owners of the textile mills. The hopelessness of rural poverty, the impersonal pressures of New York, and the wasteland of southern California all underscore the bankruptcy of a system where "everybody is out for himself and devil take the hindmost, with no common purpose and little common culture to give life stability and sense." Free now to voice the artist's distaste for a commercial civilization, eager to resume the struggle which his father's American generation had lost in the gilded age, Wilson found in Marxism a weapon. "It gave us a new sense of power," he wrote many years later, "to find ourselves still carrying on while the bankers, for a change, were taking a beating."

The classic study of revolutionary Marxism that is still for some readers Wilson's major work was begun in 1934 but not finished until 1940. Before he could go far with *To the Finland Station,* he had to see the Soviet Union for himself, and in the version of his journal published after a five-month tour in 1935 the pilgrim fights off a skepticism that is more fully documented in *Red, Black, Blond, and Olive,* Wilson's accounts of his travels in four civilizations. The Moscow Trials of 1937-38 showed him, as they did others, how far Stalin's Russia was from "the first truly human culture" which the great Marxists had intended to create. *Finland Station* remains a monument to the "revolutionary will" of the early 1930s as well as to those 19th-century men and women who asserted themselves against the world to bring an idea into being. Wilson recreates the whole intricate movement of socialist life, its assumptions and counter-assumptions, its actions and stallings, between the French Revolution and the October Revolution of 1917. Dismissing Hegel's dialectic as a religious myth, he derives the force of Marxism from Protestantism and Romanticism, the age of reason, the idea of progress, the moral heritage of Judaism.

He conceived the book as a three-act drama, seeing Michelet, Marx, and Lenin as its central figures. The Lenin portrait is not quite in focus, for Wilson was working with partially censored sources, and his admiration for the Russian statesman clashed with his knowledge of what had happened to the revolution. Nor could he transfer his idealism to Trotsky, despite the man's heroic qualities. The only character Wilson idealizes is Michelet, whose *History of France* showed the American how to act in the present by writing about the past, how to unite research with creative empathy and narrative skill. Michelet went directly to the sources and reported on them for his readers, "without allowing either the journalistic or the academic formulas to come between first-hand knowledge and us." Wilson's tribute suggests how he learned to integrate his own skills as a reporter, an interpreter of texts, a storyteller, and a dramatist, by focusing on historical materials. He came into full possession of his powers in *Finland Station,* a process fired by the revolutionary idea.

Marx dominates the book, and Wilson's heroic portrait remains a convincing account of Marx's intellectual and moral power. His Marx is a philosopher, a scientist, an artist—in *Das Kapital* "the poet of commodities"—a Promethean figure combating the dehumanization of society through the profit motive. He is also the paterfamilias of the picnics in Soho and "the great secular rabbi of the nineteenth century," who hoped that the bourgeoisie would have cause to remember his carbuncles. Wilson incorporates the history of Communism with a human life he shared to the point of breaking out in boils of his own. With a sensitivity to unconscious motives derived from Freud, he shows how the struggle of Marx's life colored his cruel account of the historical process. "Only so sore and angry a spirit, so ill at ease in the world," he concludes, "could have recognized and seen into the causes of the wholesale mutilation of humanity, the grim collisions, the uncomprehended convulsions, to which that age of great profits was doomed." Here is the theme of the wound and the bow in Wilson's literary essays. The agony of the artist—"the romantic agony" as his friend Mario Praz calls it—is wedded to a Marxist vision of historical necessity.

The intellectual experience of the 1930s is applied to criticism in *The Triple Thinkers* and *The Wound and the Bow,* necessary reading for anyone concerned with the origins of imaginative literature in personality and social history. Life and art are here better correlated than in *Axel's Castle,* partly because Wilson is no longer exploring an avantgarde but returning to writers who had formed his taste in youth, to whom he brings a Modernist perspective. The first collection coordinates his education in Marxism with his interest in biography and his aesthetic judgments. He assesses Shaw's political ideas along with his dramatic art, "a music of ideas, or rather, a music of moralities." The famous Freudian reading of *The Turn of the Screw* is accompanied by a shrewd analysis of James's point of view on European and American society. The portraits of Housman and John Jay Chapman resemble the work of a gifted painter whose empathy with his subjects enables him to probe issues important to himself, project his own malaise, define his code. Rescuing Chapman from obscurity, Wilson is fortified by the artistic and political integrity of this spiritual ancestor in the

1890s, a link to his father's world. He is saddened to find in the brilliant, bitter scholarship of Housman's later years the thwarted psychic energies of the poet of *The Shropshire Lad*. If the early Freudianism of the *Turn of the Screw* essay is dated, the study of Housman illustrates the suggestiveness, moral authority, and polish of Wilson's lasting criticism, that of a man interpreting his peers.

At the end of *The Triple Thinkers* art is called a victory of the intelligence over "some ache of disorder, some oppressive burden of uncomprehended events," and seven writers are viewed in this perspective in *The Wound and the Bow*. The influential monographs on Dickens and Kipling take the abandonment each suffered in childhood as a source of the power of his fiction. Dickens's memory of fear and helplessness became a powerful instrument to expose the corruption of Victorian England, while Kipling's talent was partly thwarted, Wilson believes, by the nature of man's adjustment to authority. Seeing such a psychic strain in the work of a contemporary, Hemingway, he shows how it yields social insight when artistically controlled. His long essay on Turgenev, written many years later, relates the novelist's clear vision of Russian society to his struggles with a tyrannical mother, who oppressed her sons as she did her serfs. Such studies do not pretend to exhaust their subjects and offer successor critics no formulae. Wilson does not explain exactly how the wound relates to the bow, and his experience, imaginative sympathy, and reading contribute as much as an acquaintance with Freud. He enables us to understand people of another time and place as though they were our contemporaries. He projects a conviction that the human spirit, so quick to bruise, is not easily crushed, that the artist-hero can make comprehensible and bearable the world that politics has failed to change.

* * * * *

Of the second half of his career it has been said that Wilson came to critical maturity as he lost his subject and was no longer the interpreter of a vital contemporary culture. He achieved an extraordinary compensation as a latter-day encyclopedist whose synoptic mind, curiosity, and enthusiasm carried him through the literatures of the past and into the corners of the modern world. His own personality, his aesthetic, political, and moral values became as important to his readers as his ability to understand what he wrote about. There was a letdown, however, in the morally discouraging years of World War II. He had resisted American entry into the conflict, remembering the First World War and wary of an alliance with Stalin's Russia. Meanwhile he saw the shared values of the literary community of the 1920s eroded by Hollywood, the Luce magazines, the big book clubs; and the deaths of F. Scott Fitzgerald, Sherwood Anderson, and John Peale Bishop brought home Wilson's role as a survivor in a darkened world. Collecting Fitzgerald's fragmentary work in *The Crack-up*, promoting *The Last Tycoon* in *The Shock of Recognition*, Wilson documented a national tradition through the comments of writers on each other's contributions, opening up the 19th-century world described in *Patriotic Gore*. Despite these sustaining loyalties, in the postwar years his buoyant, determined temperament remained subject to depressions, marks of something like a crisis of middle age.

He had married Mary McCarthy, who in her 20s was already established in the New York literary world, and they left the city to settle on Cape Cod. They had a son, Reuel, Wilson's second child—he had a daughter, Rosalind, by Mary Blair—and McCarthy and he each produced a book of stories, *The Company She Keeps* and *Memoirs of Hecate County*. *Hecate County* is a purge of accumulated disappointments with art, politics, book clubs, romance, and social life. No longer trying to crowd his material into the form of a novel, as in *I Thought of Daisy*, he develops his themes in separate modes, mixing macabre fantasy with realism and satire against a shadowy exurban background. Scenes and people are as meticulously described as in Wilson's reportorial writing, yet arbitrarily appear and disappear like the magical properties manipulated by one of his characters in a nightclub act. In "The Princess with the Golden Hair," which caused the book to be banned in New York, the narrator's pursuit of a bourgeois dreamgirl is played off against his affair with a working-class woman, drawn from the Anna of Wilson's journals. Some, like John Updike, still admire his sexual frankness, while others dislike what they consider an exploitative relationship or are uncomfortable when the author of *To the Finland Station* and *Patriotic Gore* takes notes on his encounters like a naturalist, as someone said, at the zoo of himself. This marks the effort of a man of the 1920s to cast off "Puritan" inhibitions while he falls back on the Puritan sense of sin to describe a corrupted world. The world of *Hecate County* is going to hell in a hack, and the devil finally comes on stage in the guise of an 18th-century French philosophe, to boast of his triumphs in the age of Hitler and Stalin.

The book suggests the difficulties of Wilson's private life. The years with McCarthy were turbulent, and what became a collision of literary egos ended, in 1946, in divorce. But with Elena Thornton, an equally strong-minded, independent woman, he achieved a lasting domestic accord, and while he exorcized his demons in *Memoirs of Hecate County*, he was already reasserting his own code in the memoirs of teachers, family, and friends completed in the 1950s. Written after their subjects' deaths and scattered through various volumes, these essays have a special place in American autobiography, for they illustrate what Alfred Kazin calls Wilson's gift of "articulating his life without telling it." In them he appears at the side of the stage, a foil to people whose values he admires, who are described with all the warmth, the generosity, the nurturing responsiveness that can only be implicit in his criticism. He pays tribute to the civilizing influence of learning ("Mr. Rolfe," "Christian Gauss as Teacher of Literature") and to the creative life ("Edna St. Vincent Millay," "Paul Rosenfeld"), while making whole chapters of American cultural history available to his countrymen. Most important as autobiography is his account of his father, whose neurotic hypochondria had oppressed Wilson's boyhood. In "The Author at Sixty" he sees his father's malady as a mark of psychic energies repressed in the corrupt America of the gilded age and can do justice to the senior Edmund Wilson's old-fashioned integrity vis-à-vis the corporations and the government, as well as his ways as a talker and inquiring traveler. Thus he creates a model for his own later years. In one of those powerful concluding passages that distinguish Wilson's essays, the continuity from father to son is represented by an old stone house that has come down in the family, the solidity and beauty of which reassure the critic despite his isolation in the America of the 1950s and, by extension, the isolation of American literary life. "I may find myself here at the center of things," he writes, "since the center can be only in one's head, and my feelings and thoughts may be shared by many."

From the end of World War II to his death in 1972 Wilson was a regular reviewer and travel-writer for *The New Yorker*, roles that overlapped as he commented on the writers of countries he visited and on the societies from which his literary subjects came. The reviews of 30 years are collected in "chronicles" (*Classics and Commercials, The Bit Between My Teeth*), which Leon Edel groups with Wilson's important books, but what he chronicles is his own reading rather than the new writing of the time, for the two no longer coincide as in the work of *The Shores of Light*. In the 1940s Wilson addressed the contemporary scene to object to fads, from detective stories and best sellers to the cult of Kafka among the intellectuals, finding relief in British comedy and satire, in Jane Austen and Swift, Thackeray and Evelyn Waugh. His own satirical instincts, never long dormant, color the verse as well as the reviewing of his middle years. He could take note of significant new talent in the 1950s and 60s—his was the best account of Lowell's *Imitations*—but he gave more space to his great contemporaries, Malraux, Auden, and Pasternak, and often returned to the literary world of his youth, contributing to the revival of interest in the 1920s, retrieving partly forgotten figures like James Branch Cabell, clarifying the careers of Swinburne and Oscar Wilde on the basis of new scholarship. His later criticism is more conversational than *The Triple Thinkers* and *The Wound and the Bow*. He savors text, milieu, and personality with an art of quotation from anecdotes and letters like that in *Patriotic Gore*.

Russian literature was a continuing preoccupation in these decades. In the 1930s he had begun learning the language to read Pushkin, and after World War II his interest was fostered by his wife Elena, who was half-Russian, and by Nabokov and other friends. As a Westerner Wilson believed he could see aspects of the classics that Russians missed. He could comment on the national character in the mirror of art, in 19th-century fashion, balancing what he liked about this people against their susceptibility to authoritarian rule, against the masochism he found in even so great a writer as Solzhenitsyn. He admired the moral force of *Doctor Zhivago* and discovered the whole ritual of the Orthodox Church in this novel, only to have this disowned by Pasternak, whose authority Wilson, not being a New Critic, gladly accepted. The essays collected in *A Window on Russia* show the generalist's strengths and limitations vis-à-vis specialized scholars. Passing over the literature of the revolutionary and post-Stalinist periods, Wilson sees how the exotic, impenetrable aspects of old Russia reveal themselves in Gogol's prose, and he opens up the worlds of the Westernizers Pushkin and Turgenev, elegant stylists who "taught Russia how to know herself."

The restless explorer of literatures was also himself in motion, for travel was as much a part of Wilson's life as reading, and he interpreted unfamiliar ways of living with the same pleasure he took in telling people about books they hadn't read. The volume of his travel writing increased when he felt himself less at home in his own country, declaring that he did not belong to the America of *Life* magazine, resenting what seemed an imitation of Soviet repression in the McCarthy years. He was generally disappointed on revisiting western Europe. His books record the Old World's loss of political and cultural authority through the half-century since he had seen London crowds celebrate the advent of World War I. On the other hand, in Israel, Hungary, French Canada, Haiti, and among the Iroquois and Zuñi Indians, he found vital communities surviving on the margins of the imperial state, minority civilizations not yet taken over by mass culture. Had he lived until 1980, Wilson would surely have learned Polish to explore the classic literature of that country along with the work of the dissident intelligentsia. He was impressed with the cohesive role of religion for such minorities, and the more intense passages in his travel journalism reflect the power of communal belief and ritual. Anthropologists testify to the authority of Wilson's extraordinary account of the Zuñi Shalako, a fusion of magic and theater with religious purpose and sustained physical energy. When *Apologies to the Iroquois* turns from the life of this tribe in white America to the Little Water Ceremony, an able, sympathetic reporting job becomes an artistic recreation of a rite of rebirth, through which the secular individualist fortifies himself in the face of intellectual isolation and old age.

Wilson could only momentarily enter into a nonliterate culture, but Judaism engaged his imagination and intellect over many years. The Jews were the people of the Book, spiritual ancestors of the Puritans from whom he descended. Their God was not perverse and full of surprises like the God of Calvin; their ritual appealed to him as the Christian mythology did not. *A Piece of My Mind* and *Patriotic Gore* amusingly recall how Lowell, Chapman, and Calvin Stowe, Harriet Beecher's husband, identified with the Chosen People to the point of imagining themselves of Hebrew descent. Wilson's "Judaizing" phase took him from his portrait of Marx as a Jewish prophet through the later years when he learned Hebrew, traveled in Israel, absorbed the scholarship about the Dead Sea Scrolls. In the Arnoldian tradition he tried to balance the "transcendent observation" he associated with the Graeco-Roman heritage. In Israel he drily noted that the Bible promises the Lord's people not only their own lands but also the houses and cities of others, and he took the Dead Sea Scrolls as a challenge to the exclusiveness of both Judaism and Christianity. The moral vitality of Jewish culture, however, powerfully drew him and gave weight to his narrative and dramatic account of the discovery of the scrolls and the ancient Essene sect, a book that invests the disputes of the scholars and the values of a utopian community in the desert two thousand years ago with the same high excitement. As progressivism failed Wilson, as he took a long view of the human struggle, he sought the strength of Hebraism for his own work. In the later years he tacked up a phrase from the Torah in his study and used it as a grace over the orange juice at breakfast. *Hazayk, hazayk, venit-hazayk,* he said, telling the editor that this helped him "jack up my waning powers."

* * * * *

Wilson's major effort to understand the life of his own country is *Patriotic Gore,* an affirmation of American character and society in the test of the Civil War as well as a critique of the mythologies through which the war is popularly seen. Conceived in the late 1940s and completed in 1961, the book consists of a series of portraits, most of which were tried out in *The New Yorker*—interpretations of the letters, speeches, diaries, memoirs, reports, and apologetics that describe the crisis, and the novels and poems that register its effects. "Everyone speaks in character in such a way that one can almost hear their voices," he states in introducing these studies in which what people say of each other, of themselves, and what he can intuit from their prose is distilled in the light of his reading and his 20th-century experience. The book combines the study of personality with a Critic's Tour of Neglected Works and a moral history of the culture.

The long internal struggle with the Puritan heritage that spills over into Wilson's writing about the Jews is an organizing theme of *Patriotic Gore* and converges with the politics of his travel writing, for he sees the Puritan sense of mission and purpose creating the mythology of American expansion. In his preface—at the time notorious—Lincoln and Lenin are compared as idealists who helped bring to birth the bureaucratic states of the Cold War, which have gobbled up everyone from the American Indians and the secessionist South to the Hungarian revolutionists. By making imperialism and big government a single enemy, Wilson offends the pieties simultaneously of progressivism and of the right, and in Mark Twain's later vein he likens nations at war to sea slugs ingurgitating their own kind to the accompaniment of righteous noises. Implicit is his own experience from the 1930s through World War II to the moment before the

Vietnam War, but his perspective goes back to World War I, when he had invoked the Gettysburg Address in an epitaph, "American Soldiers," ironically commenting on the crusade to make the world safe for democracy:

> All stubborn and obscene, they toiled in pain.
> Go, countryman of theirs. They bought you pride.
> Look to it the Republic leave not vain
> The deaths of those who knew not why they died.

Although the polemical vision fades into the background of this discursive, pluralistic book, it colors two major portraits. Vice-President of the Confederacy Alexander Stephens is retrieved from obscurity to make the case against concentration of power, for he had combated what Jefferson Davis, like Lincoln, thought necessary wartime abridgements of civil liberty, and as a political prisoner after the war, he had a foretaste of modern despotism that intensified his defense of his principles. Stephens's antagonist and the Caesar of the book is Lincoln, who had begun with the same political views, had started as a free-thinker, but in the crisis imposed the religious mythology of New England on the consolidation of the state. This is a partial portrait of the man who was central to the whole American myth on which Wilson had been raised, one *Patriotic Gore* takes seriously enough to try to overturn. Admiring his poetic imagination, command of language, precise intelligence, and driving will—there is nothing of the sentimentalized folk hero here—Wilson stresses Lincoln's ignorance of the technological capitalism that was already transforming the Union sanctified by blood. Lincoln did not understand the historical process which he molded as a statesman and justified as a prophet, and which his death helped to mythologize. Robert Penn Warren put this well in a tribute to *Patriotic Gore*, calling Wilson's Lincoln a Hegelian hero who can see into the surface of the moment but cannot see into its death. This is scarcely the view of the hero in history that animates *Finland Station*. Wilson refuses to give to Lincoln the faith he had given to Lenin and Marx.

Meanwhile, Wilson traces the reverberations of the Civil War in varied lives, circling around the same events, seeing how people's stories and their values intertwine. He moves from the North to the South and back again, and from prophets of the war to statesmen, soldiers, observers, and postwar writers who function as a chorus. This is the structure of epic, but he distributes his space as he likes, lingering with obscure statesmen and writers to whom he would once have paid less attention than to those utopian socialists whose experiments are dispatched in a few pages of *Finland Station*. That book takes unity and momentum from the revolution toward which it moves, and it is a young man's book, impatient to change the world. In *Patriotic Gore* the aging Wilson's resistance to central authority, his concern with enduring rather than making history, are matched to a new savoring of experience. The dialogue between these books is extraordinary in an age of broken careers and cultural discontinuities. Both bring the individualism of the 19th century into the 20th, the heroic personality into the age of the anti-hero.

The literary history in *Patriotic Gore* is also social history. Discovering *The Valley of Shadows*, Francis Grierson's remarkable account of the mood of the Middle West before the Civil War, Wilson tells of its author's career as a music critic and pianist upon the European concert stage, of his mysticism, his death as an impoverished storekeeper in Los Angeles. At an old-fashioned lecturer's leisurely pace he goes through the novels of Cable, Stowe, and DeForest, taken as genre paintings that reveal the life of a period. He portrays another brilliant "wounded" artist, Ambrose Bierce, and develops the thesis that American prose was reshaped by men who, like Lincoln and Grant, "had to convince and direct," "had no time to waste words." Although he considers the war a disaster for the republic, he prefers this "war style" to the sometimes florid eloquence of prewar literature and oratory and to the elaborate mannerisms of Adams and James, which Wilson relates to their youthful roles as spectators of the conflict.

The larger portraits are what Lowell had in mind in calling this book an American Plutarch. Almost all are of Northerners—the Stowes, Grant, Sherman, Justice Holmes—familiar, two-dimensional presences here seen afresh and dramatized like personalities of fiction and the stage. Wilson's Grant has been a favorite of readers, interweaving the testimony of contemporaries with the qualities of the *Personal Memoirs* to retrieve Grant's reputation from his failures as President. Wilson shows the general's humanness, modesty, and lack of illusions about his historical role even as he shows how that role was reshaped in the postwar years, when Grant eventually found himself hobnobbing with Kaiser Wilhelm:

For the boy from the two-room cabin, who had not wanted

to go to West Point and who had hoped that it might be abolished in order that he might not have to finish there, who had had, he said, "a horror" of the Mexican War in which he had been forced to serve, believing it to be "most unjust," who had taken to drink and, discharged from the army, had gone to clerking in his brothers' leather store, who could not bear the sight of blood nor even face a steak not well done, and who said that he much preferred farming to fighting—this man had found himself, in his forties, the most conspicuous figure in what had been up to that time the most destructive war in history and afterwards at the head of the formidable state which this war had consolidated: the equal, the sympathetic colleague, of the master of that other great new state which had consolidated the German principalities.

There is more of the critic himself in Wilson's portrait of Supreme Court Justice Oliver Wendell Holmes, who was four times wounded on the field but carried the standard of the old republic through the postwar industrial transformation and into the America of the second Roosevelt. The great judge is not sentimentalized. Admiring his patriotism as well as the dissenting opinions on labor and free speech that made him a hero to liberals, Wilson shows how the war destroyed Holmes's social ideals along with his religion and left a Hobbesian view of state power to sustain his philosophy of law. The spiritual energy of Calvinism survived in the work in which Holmes aimed to "touch the superlative." This portrait draws on Wilson's early loss of faith and political disappointments, his loyalty to his country and his profession. When Americans look for greatness in their public men, it can provide them a standard against the image-making of the pollsters and the media.

* * * * *

Patriotic Gore did not, as some hoped, help Wilson to the Nobel Prize, but it led to official recognition in the form of one of President Kennedy's Freedom Medals, an appropriate award for someone whose single aim, he once said, was "not art or science but the improvement of America." Financial awards followed, but he refused to behave as a respectable monument. Harassed by the Internal Revenue Service over taxes, he struck back in *The Cold War and the Income Tax*. He also criticized current clichés and jargon, and ridiculed the heavy-handed editing sponsored by the Modern Language Association. His dislike of the pedantry and ostentation that made great literature less accessible brought him into conflict with Nabokov over the Russian's translation of *Eugene Onegin*. If it was amusing when each of these friends claimed a superior knowledge of the other's native tongue, it was sad to see them demolishing one another in the magazines, sacrificing the intellectual companionship and mutual admiration that make their long correspondence so vital. For Wilson anger had become something of a tonic, which kept him from relaxing too much, sustained his vigor when his major work was behind him.

To visit the man in the mid-1960s, when he was editing his journals, was to find him looking back to what Dos Passos had said to Cummings in 1925, or what Gertrude Stein had really thought of Fitzgerald and Hemingway, while Wilson addressed the world around him with an intent curiosity that brought to mind Henry James's injunction to be one of those on whom nothing is lost. Kazin has pictured Wilson among the intellectuals on the beach at Cape Cod, looking out of place yet somehow the center of attention. He was more at home in upstate New York, in the old stone house where he had been spending summers since the early 1950s. He had his friends etch their poems with a stylus on the windows, and the place was a centerpiece of life as a work of art as well as a base of operations for forays into the Indian country and Canada. The journal in *Upstate* shows him absorbed in the landscapes and the village life, in a round of country expeditions and visits to and from friends. He sometimes succumbed to pessimism as he considered the danger of nuclear war and the decline of literate culture or observed the deterioration of his body, worn out by a malaria acquired in Haiti, radical dentistry, and drinking too much. Yet he continued to write vigorously about books and travel, filling in the corners of the American literary landscape, completing his work on the Russians, exploring new interests. Although he acknowledged he was too old to start learning Chinese, he devoured the volumes of Balzac during his last winter, in preparation for a long article.

The porousness and receptivity which could incorporate so much were checked by the integrity of character, the consistency of vision, that make Wilson's work a unity. Delmore Schwartz once likened him to a son of the heroes of Henry James, "who has had his moral experience" among the symbolists and in the Soviet Union rather than in the Italy of Milly Theale or the France of Lambert

Stretcher. Schwartz saw how an individualism drawn from the old American life sustained Wilson's cosmopolitan education and career. An internationalist like Eliot, Pound, and Hemingway, Wilson was also a patriot who took his country's limitations as a challenge. Another continuity in his writing is the historical point of view, which joins his notebooks and travel journalism, his autobiographical essays and his book reviews. *To the Finland Station* and *Patriotic Gore* are histories of consciousness, which put us in touch with the past through the minds of people who write, an activity that is as useful, and no more subjective, than studying artifacts and material culture. Wilson writes admiringly of the great historians—of Francis Parkman in *O Canada*, Michelet and Marx in *Finland Station*, Gibbon and Macaulay in his letters and journals. His books remind professors of literature and history of their heritage from a time when these were the central concerns of educated men rather than separated fields in the academy, a time when the creative artist and the social commentator were often the same person.

In university English departments his place has too often been a marginal one, for Wilson was an empiric who resisted theory, and he offered no convenient formulation of his methods, which were various. He appreciated literature and encouraged people to read it while he defined the conditions in which it had emerged and explored the author's personality. He confessed himself bored by *explication de texte*, and the New Critics sometimes dismissed him as a popularizer. His background and standards, however, marked him as elitist for the literary left that emerged from the 1960s, and he has been easy for post-structuralist theorists to ignore, since his insights into psychology and history, anthropology and the study of language, draw on his own experience and depend on the particular case. A master of detail, he sometimes makes sweeping generalizations but is not really interested in developing them. He is best described in James's words about Sainte-Beuve: "He was the student, the inquirer, the observer, the active, indefatigable commentator, whose constant aim was to arrive at justness of characterization."

His readers were spread through the professions, the academy, government, and the New York intellectual world, from the days when this centered in *Partisan Review* to those of *The New York Review of Books*. The New York critics learned from him and magnified his influence, valuing his ability to connect the spheres of art and politics, to mediate between the humanistic tradition and the culture of

Modernism, Marx, and Freud. Lionel Trilling recalled how, at a political affair of the 1930s (both men then being Marxists), Wilson asked about his work on Arnold. "He actually thought that a book on Matthew Arnold would be interesting and useful. He wanted to read it," Trilling writes, stressing the "liberating effect" that only Wilson could have had, "with his involvment in the life of the present which was so clearly not at odds with his natural and highly developed feeling for scholarship." This same sense of the utility of learning and the commmunity of those who write and read is available in Wilson's books. They were produced in stages through the magazines, and not all their ambivalences and contradictions were ironed out, but they communicate the vitality of the times, the issues, and the man, the pulse of Emerson's "man thinking." They show that one can simultaneously be a scholar, an artist, and an activist.

In a generation of great creators Wilson was the artist of the actual, whose imagination responded to the constraints of fact, of positive evidence. Best in Wilson's fiction are the accounts of particular people and places, and by his middle years the critic was as engaged with the personalities and milieux of writers as with their work. The theme of the wound and the bow enabled him to deal with literature in terms of the life behind it in a way that joined his psychological interest to his vision of the artist as a moral hero. He could draw on his own experience in understanding Dickens's boyhood abandonment and its effects, Marx's alienation and his impulse of human solidarity, Holmes's skepticism and sense of calling. Such characterizations are also strongly rooted in the documents with which he is working. Wilson continually quotes from these, and as he seeks the essence of a book or person, the reader comes to terms with the material, entering into other periods and lives, into the creative effort of civilization.

"We have to take life—society and human relations—more or less as we find them, and there is no doubt they leave much to be desired," Wilson wrote to Louise Bogan when she was recovering from a nervous breakdown in 1931. "The only thing we can really make is our work. And deliberate work of the mind, imagination, and hand, done, as Nietzsche says, 'notwithstanding,' in the long run remakes the world." This is the spirit of Arnold and Carlyle, but it was also the high tide of confidence of the 1920s, when a group of creative minds remade American literature. Young Wilson saw himself as a catalyst within this group, and to look back on their work and personalities, as the expanding store of letters, papers, and biographies encourages us to do, is to find the man and his influence at many turnings. His later years belied Fitzgerald's remark that there are no second acts in American lives. The world might not be remade, but the republic of letters was extraordinarily various, and as artists could make use of psychic pain, so civilizations could resist erosion. While others adapted themselves to mass communications or the academy, Wilson cantankerously went his own way, and he completed his career as he began it: a writer addressing readers about personal interests and values. He continued to work when old age forced him to eat, sleep, and work in the same room, for writing was part of his definition of himself. *Scribo ergo sum* could have been his motto.

The notices of his death called him the last man of letters, on the premise that a technological age cannot foster a writer for whom literature, in all its forms, is the natural record of human experience and aspiration. As Wilson's stature becomes clearer, it is tempting to take him as an anachronism, a monument with a certain irrelevance. He would have considered this an abuse of the historical method, and he certainly did not see himself as the end of a tradition. He believed that standards could be sustained within the marketplace and that the life of "thought and creative instinct and fellowship" would last as the authority of the classics did. Looking back to his college years, he remembered that "you read Shakespeare, Shelley, George Meredith, Dostoevsky, Ibsen, and you wanted, however imperfectly and on however infinitesimal a scale, to learn their trade and have the freedom of their company." Wilson succeeded, and his work continues to make it easier for others to do so.

Bibliography

By Edmund Wilson:

Axel's Castle: A Study in the Imaginative Literature of 1870-1930. New York and London: C. Scribner's Sons, 1931.

The Triple Thinkers: Ten Essays on Literature. New York: Harcourt Brace, 1938; revised edition, New York: Oxford University Press, 1948.

To the Finland Station: A Study in the Writing and Acting of History. New York: Harcourt Brace, 1940.

The Wound and the Bow: Seven Studies in Literature. Boston: Houghton Mifflin, 1941; revised edition, New York: Oxford University Press, 1947.

Memoirs of Hecate County. Garden City, New York: Doubleday, 1946; revised edition, London: W. H. Allen, 1958.

Classics and Commercials: A Literary Chronicle of the Forties. New York: Farrar, Straus, 1950.

The Shores of Light: A Literary Chronicle of the Twenties and Thirties. New York: Farrar, Straus and Young, 1952.

Red, Black, Blond, and Olive: Studies in Four Civilizations: Zuñi, Haiti, Soviet Russia, Israel. London: W. H. Allen, 1956; New York: Oxford University Press, 1956.

The American Earthquake: A Documentary of the Twenties and Thirties. Garden City, New York: Doubleday, 1958.

Apologies to the Iroquois. New York: Farrar, Straus and Cudahy, 1960.

Patriotic Gore: Studies in the Literature of the American Civil War. New York: Oxford University Press, 1962.

The Bit Between My Teeth: A Literary Chronicle of 1960-65. New York: Farrar, Straus and Giroux, 1965.

The Dead Sea Scrolls, 1947-1969. New York: Oxford University Press, 1969.

A Window on Russia: For the Use of Foreign Readers. New York: Farrar, Straus and Giroux, 1972.

Letters on Literature and Politics. Edited by Elena Wilson. New York: Farrar, Straus and Giroux, 1977.

About Edmund Wilson:

Aaron, Daniel. Introduction to *Letters on Literature and Politics*, by Edmund Wilson. New York: Farrar, Straus and Giroux, 1977.

Dabney, Lewis M. Introduction to *The Viking Portable Edmund Wilson*. New York: Viking Press.

French, Philip, editor. *Three Honest Men: Edmund Wilson, F. R. Leavis, Lionel Trilling, a Critical Mosaic*. Manchester, England: Carcanet New Press, 1981.

Paul, Sherman. *Edmund Wilson: A Study of Literary Vocation in Our Times*. Urbana: University of Illinois Press, 1965.

Wain, John, editor. *Edmund Wilson: The Man and His Work*. New York: New York University Press, 1978. (Including essays by Alfred Kazin, Larzer Ziff, Peter Sharett, Helen Muchnic, John Wain, and John Updike.)

Gertrude Stein

Richard Kostelanetz

> *I found myself plunged into a vortex of words, burning words,*
> *cleansing words, liberating words, feeling words, and the words were*
> *all ours and it was enough that we held them in our hand to play with*
> *them; whatever you can play with is yours, and this was the beginning*
> *of knowing; of all Americans knowing, that it could play and play with*
> *words and the words were all ours all ours.*
>   Gertrude Stein,
>   "American Language and Literature" (undated)

Though Gertrude Stein died over three decades ago, her books have survived her; and by now, more than a century after her birth, February 3, 1874, these extraordinary writings are finally winning the recognition they deserve. No longer the epitome of inscrutable preciosity in modern literature, she is now ranked among the greatest inventors, whose best writings still seem very, very contemporary. It is hard for a reader today to believe that Stein belonged by birth to the generation of Theodore Dreiser (b. 1871), Stephen Crane (b. 1871), H. L. Mencken (b. 1880), and Eugene O'Neill (b. 1888). At a time when readers of literature have successfully assimilated the innovations of, say, Faulkner and Pound, most of Stein's works still seem very, very strange. If you were not otherwise informed, you would initially suspect that they were written yesterday. Their sole peer in this respect is James Joyce's *Finnegans Wake*.

Critics have long acknowledged Gertrude Stein's perspicacity as an art collector, but only recently have her literary achievements begun to be widely honored. In the past few years several publishers have reissued over two dozen volumes of her prose, plays, and poems, most of which had been out of print for years; for the first time ever, nearly all of Stein's writings are readily available. Her plays are frequently produced, while some have become popular; sympathetic critical books are appearing after decades of scholarly neglect. A few years ago *Rising Tides* (1973), a fresh anthology of "20th Century American Woman Poets," opened not with Marianne Moore or Edna St. Vincent Millay, as one might expect, but with Gertrude Stein.

Back in 1926 she wrote, in her inimitable style, "For a very long time everybody refuses and then almost without a pause almost everybody accepts. In the history of the refused in arts and literature the rapidity of the change is always startling. Now the only difficulty with the *volte face* concerning the arts is this: When the acceptance comes, by that acceptance the thing created becomes a classic." She continued, "And what is the characteristic quality of a classic. The characteristic quality of a classic is that it is beautiful. . . . Of course it is beautiful but first all beauty in it is denied and then all the beauty of it is accepted." In her familiarity with the distinctive career of avant-garde art, Stein implicitly predicted that by the centenary of her birth her own much-scorned scribblings would be regarded as, yes, beautiful and classic.

It is perhaps a tribute to the originality and integrity of her more difficult writings that they, in contrast to other dimensions of her achievement, have taken so long to be recognized. Back in the 1930s Stein became a celebrated eccentric, thanks mostly to *The Autobiography of Alice B. Toklas* (1933) that became a best-seller and then to her highly publicized U. S. lecture tour in the wake of the book's success. For the next decade her most conspicuous activities would be reported in the newspapers, often with whimsy, rarely with undiluted cultural respect. This exploitation of her personality was, like her art collection, merely incidental to what she considered her primary interest, which was her writing. From 1902, when she began her first novel, to her death 44 years later, Stein wrote steadily, producing some of the most extraordinary books in modern literature—books so original they still strike many literate people as "unreadable."

It is wise to divide Stein's books into two groups—the simple ones and the more difficult ones: and although these terms are themselves too simplistic to provide much crucial insight, they have their truth. The *simple* books are those enjoyed by moderately sophisticated readers of realistic fiction: not only *Q. E. D.* (1950) and *Three Lives* (1909), but the two autobiographies, *The Autobiography of Alice B. Toklas* and *Everybody's Autobiography* (1937), and then the later novels like *Ida* (1941) and *Brewsie and Willie* (1946), in addition to the later memoirs, such as *Paris, France* (1940) and *Wars I Have Seen* (1945). And these remain her most popular works. Nearly everything else can justly be considered *difficult*. However, the fact that these works are frequently dismissed as "inscrutable" does not mean that they cannot be understood.

One reason why even experienced readers find Stein's prose so difficult is that they expect elements that simply are not there. In her fictions they look for full-bodied characters but instead find only caricatures; instead of comprehensive descriptions, they find repetitious declarations. Instead of plots that come to a climax, there is uninflected narrative. In her essays they expect developed definitions and instead find circuitous, indefinite encirclings around an ostensible subject; in lieu of representation, they find abstraction. Even those readers accustomed to the classic modernists—to Joyce, Proust, Eliot, et al.—often find Stein's work opaque, largely because her innovations are not like theirs. What readers often miss is that an understanding and appreciation of Gertrude Stein starts with her style. Whereas Pound, among others, experimented primarily with literary structure, Stein concentrated on language. "I like writing," she once wrote. "It is so pleasant, to have the ink write it down on the paper as it goes on doing."

Gertrude Stein was almost incapable of writing a common sentence. Even in personal letters she was continually shifting the order of words so that the syntactical parts of a sentence fall in unusual places. Adverbs that conventionally come after their verbs now appear before, as do prepositional phrases. The object of a clause becomes the subject (i.e., "the ink write it down"), and both adjectives and prepositions have ambiguous referents. Some parts of speech are omitted, while others are duplicated. All these essentially mechanical devices enabled her to express rather simple sentiments in remarkably striking forms: "William Aspinwall Bradley our agent came to stay. After a little while I asked him to go away, not because he was not a pleasant guest because he was but because after a time they are part of the way we live every day or they are not and I prefer them to be not." In some of Stein's works the sentences are usually short; in others they are alarmingly long. From sentences of every length, she usually removed all internal punctuation, thus increasing the possibility of ambiguous comprehensions. She favored participles as well, in part to create a sense of interminable continuity. Reading Stein is the best preparation for reading more Stein, for nobody teaches readers how to read Stein better than Stein herself.

Another device of hers is the use of a severe limitation, such as writing a piece with words of only one syllable or severely restricting the vocabulary of a passage (and thus necessitating the repetition of those few words):

> Very fine is my valentine.
> Very fine and very mine.
> Very mine is my valentine very mine and very fine.
> Very fine is my valentine and mine, very fine very mine
>   and mine is my valentine.

Always responsive to linguistic possibilities in mundane experience, she once wrote prose that intentionally imitated the rhythms that her dog made while lapping water; other passages imitated sounds in the street or waves hitting the shore or a background of streams and waterfalls.

Early in her career, Stein assimilated a primary strategy of experimental art—doing the opposite of convention. If most writers strive for variety in expression, she would repeat certain words and phrases in numerous, slightly different clauses. ("It's not all repetition," she once told a reporter. "I always change the words a little.") If literate writers customarily strove to display a rich vocabulary along with allusions and other literary connotations, she confined herself to common words and their immediate meanings. She avoided myth and most kinds of metaphor. In lieu of balanced sentences, she decided to explore imbalance. Instead of instilling emotion through rhetoric and flowery language, she kept her prose generally free of adjectives and adverbs. Typically, she eschewed not only the naturalism then fashionable in fiction writing but the symbolism favored by French poets. As an American individualist, she was neither a Surrealist nor a Dadaist, neither a Futurist nor a Constructivist, to cite several European terms that are erroneously applied to her work. Always, Gertrude Stein was something else.

The key to her genius is that she could turn these counter-conventional attitudes to literary advantage, as in transforming a limited vocabulary into something astonishingly evocative. To portray an imprisoning relationship she wrote:

> In working when she did what she did she worked all
> she worked and she did all she did when she did what she
> did. She did what she did and she worked. She felt what
> she felt and she did what she did and she worked. She did

> what she did and she felt what she felt when she was doing
> what she did when she worked. She felt what she felt when
> she did what she did when she worked. She worked when
> she did what she did. She felt what she felt, when she did
> what she did. She worked when she did what she did and
> she felt what she felt when she worked, when she did what
> she did.

Repetition was only one of Stein's stylistic ideas, as the attempt to emancipate language from conventional syntax led swiftly (and logically) to a more radical effort to separate language from context. In short pieces written around 1911 and collected as *Tender Buttons* (1914, and subsequently reprinted, *in toto*, in the 1946 edition of the *Selected Writings of Gertrude Stein*), the texts often have no apparent relation to their subtitles; yet the rhythms of the words or their taste (especially if read aloud) relate to one's experience of that declared subject. An example is "Custard," which reads in its entirety:

> Custard is this. It has aches, aches when. Not to be.
> Not to be narrowly. This makes a whole little hill.
> It is better than a little thing that has mellow real
> mellow. It is better than lakes whole lakes, it is better than
> seeding.

In "Salad Dressing and an Artichoke" Stein writes:

> Please pale hot, please cover rose, please acre in the red
> stranger, please butter all the beef--steak with regular fed
> faces.

According to her friend Alice B. Toklas, it was one of Stein's aims "to describe something without mentioning it." Another close friend, the composer Virgil Thomson, finds that, "Each description is full of clues, some of them easy to follow up, others put there for throwing you off the scent." One of her critics, Donald Sutherland, shrewdly suggests, "One has to give her work word by word the deliberate attention one gives to something written in italics."

In later Stein, such as "Preciosilla" (1926) and certain chapters of *Geography and Plays* (1922), adjacent words have even less syntactical relation to each other:

> Lily wet lily wet while. This is so pink so pink in
> stammer, a long bean which shows bows is collected by a
> single curly shady, shady get, get set wet bet.

But, especially if this passage is read aloud, one can hear unities in diction, rhythm, and alliteration, as well as coherences in more subtle qualities like timbre, density, and other nonsyntactic kinds of relatedness.

> In the win all the band beagles which have cousin lime
> sign and arrange a weeding match to presume a certain
> point to exstate to exstate a certain pass lint to exstate a lean
> sap prime lo and shut shut is life.

In passages like these Stein achieved a scrupulously nonrepresentational prose—language that is intended to be appreciated simply as language, apart from anything else; and those I quoted above strike me as beautiful and really quite classic. As Sherwood Anderson put it, "She is laying word against word, relating sound to sound, feeling for the taste, the smell, the rhythm of the individual word." Thanks to her experimental attitude toward the mechanics of prose, Stein created not one original style but a succession of them, all of which are highly personal and thus eventually inimitable. As Sutherland testifies, "Though many other things attach me to Gertrude Stein, what really holds me is her overwhelmingly rhetorical agility."

What Stein did was recapitulate in language the history of Modernist painting. Her initial scrambling of syntax could be considered an appropriate literary analogy for painterly Cubism, which likewise scrambled the viewer's perspective upon an identifiable subject. As in painting, such techniques not only distort the representation of the worldly reality but they also flatten the work's form (by diffusing the traditional ways of focusing in time and space). As Cubism brought the reorganization of visual space, so Stein reorganized the frame of literature. Another analogy is the history of atonal music, as composers who avoided the tonics and dominants of classical harmony found other ways of organizing musical sound. All these developments gave mediumistic qualities more prominence than they had before; and just as Cubist painting forces the viewer to pay closer attention to two-dimensional composition, so Stein's sentences always call attention to themselves as language. What you read is most of what there is.

The next step, in both post-Cubist painting and her own writing, was the elimination of an outside subject, once again in order to emphasize the essential properties of the artist's medium. If the materials indigenous to painting are paint and two-dimensional canvases, the mediumistic writer dealt with words and words alone, as in this marvelous passage from "A Sweet Tail (Gypsies)":

> Able there to ball bawl able to call and seat in a tin a tin whip with a collar. The least licence is in the eyes which make strange the less sighed hole which is nodded and leaves the bent tender.

Like the Modernist painters, Stein was interested not in new ideas and new subjects but in new perspectives, new perceptions, new forms, and new mediumistic possibilities; yet the kinds of perceptual shifts that an experienced viewer makes before an abstract painting are rarely made in perusing print. As nonrepresentational prose makes no pretenses about referring to any reality beyond itself, it need not be "interpreted." What you read is all there is.

Whereas Pound and Eliot initially thought of themselves as poets who also dabbled in essays and plays, Stein's primary medium was prose; only later did she turn to poetry and drama. This might explain why those poets' plays tend to be fairly conventional as drama; Stein's plays and opera librettos, by contrast, represent a radical departure in the history of dramatic writing. As in her prose, Stein made theatrical advances by emphasizing certain dimensions while totally neglecting others. Her scripts say nothing about costumes, timing, scenery, phrasing, decor, or direction. Many lack any sense of plot, protagonist, character development, conflict, or denouement. Her texts are customarily printed as just a series of unattributed lines (which are occasionally extended into short paragraphs), so that even when the head of the text announces the play's characters, it is frequently hard to tell which passage belongs to which character. Stein further confuses dramatic exposition by violating the fundamental conventions of dramatic organization. Thus, her plays have any and all numbers of scenes and acts, while a "Scene II" sometimes follows "Scene III" which had followed an earlier "Scene II." Early in *Four Saints in Three Acts* she writes: "Repeat First Act." No theatrical texts written before were ever like these.

An extreme example that, nonetheless, exemplifies Stein's playwriting is "A Curtain Raiser," which was written in the 1910s:

> Six,
> Twenty,
>   Outrageous
> Late

Weak.
>   Forty.
More in any wetness.
Sixty three certainly.
Five
Sixteen
Seven.
Three
More in orderly. Seventy-five.

That is the *entire* text, which typically emphasizes verbal style to the neglect of everything else. To the critic Donald Sutherland, these evocations of sound and image are plays rather than fictions because they are designed to be performed and because they present "movement in space, or in a landscape." They are organized not as narratives but as a series of joyous moments, each of which is as important as every other. Rather than telling "what happened," they are happening. Sutherland continues: "These plays of hers do not tell you anything. They merely present themselves, like a drama or a circus or any play that is really a stage play." Though a text like Stein's allows its director enormous liberties, the verbal style still bestows particular qualities upon the final production. Stein became the historical precursor of a popular contemporary practice of writing scripts so unorthodox in form that the performances they generate would necessarily be comparably eccentric.

Stein also wrote poems, most of which appeared in two books, *Before the Flowers of Friendship Faded Friendship Faded* (1931) and *Stanzas in Meditation* (1956). Her poems are as nonrepresentational as her most abstract prose, completely eschewing subject and yet observing selected conventions of poetry—meter, alliteration, and consistent diction. They exemplify what Stein once called "really writing."

I wish now to wish now that it is now
That I will tell very well
What I think not now but now
O yes oh yes now.
What do I think now
I think very well of what now
What is it now it is this now
How do you do how do you do
And now how do you do now.
This which I think now is this.

As Stein's poems are scarcely appreciated by either critics or anthologists, they remain the most neglected dimension of her writing.

Almost from the beginning of her professional career, Stein wrote essays about the world around her. Just as her perceptions are invariably original, so the best of these essays are stylistically remarkable. The earliest efforts of note were the "portraits" of Matisse and Picasso, which emphasize certain points not by elaboration but by repetition. (Thus, Matisse is "expressing something struggling," while Picasso is "certainly working" and "completely charming.") From portraits she moved eventually into "geographies," as she called them, or portraits of places, which mix detail with impressions, going around their subjects rather than at them. Some of these were reportedly done by Stein's concentrating upon a particular subject and then writing down whatever flashed into her head, for she hoped to record in print the characteristic image and sound of her subjects. As she put it, her aim was "exactitude in the description of inner and outer reality." Beginning in 1922 with an essay called "An Elucidation," Stein also began to write prolifically about her own work; but rather than providing simple, Aristotelian guidance (and compromising certain previous integrities), she pursued her ealier stylistic predilection and wrote essays that explain by example—elucidating *within* the essay, rather than through it or by it. Nonetheless, in this respect too, the best preparation for reading Stein is Stein herself.

Another source of Stein's continuing importance is her influence on younger artists—not only those she knew personally, like the composer Virgil Thomson and the writers Ernest Hemingway, Thornton Wilder, and Sherwood Anderson, but the many creative people who read and assimilated her work. Hemingway reveals Stein's influence particularly in his use of a mundane vocabulary, outright repetitions, and syntactical shifts, such as placing the adverbs after the verb instead of prior to the verb or after the object (e.g., "He poured smoothly the buckwheat batter"). In my judgment, Stein probably influenced William Faulkner's use of excessively long sentences and John Dos Passos's penchant for dropping parts of speech, as well as E. E. Cummings's syntactical shiftings, Samuel Beckett's uninflected prose, and Norman Mailer's habit of impersonating Alice B. Toklas—speaking of himself not as "I" but as "Mailer" or "Aquarius."

Adventurous young authors customarily ignore the recently dominant figures to discover present possibilities in previously neglected precursors. The declining influence of Faulkner and Pound accompanies the rise of Stein, who is presently having another round of influence. Unlike before, however, it is now the more radical works that seem most alive. I see and hear their influence in the nonrepresentational poetry of John Ashbery, Clark Coolidge, and Bruce Andrews, among others. Andrews, a young poet-critic, once told me: "Repetition seems like a very personal mark that does not open doors for us, but the idea of nonsyntactical organization stands ready for any of us to use. Once syntax is abandoned or attenuated and need no longer function as the organizing principles for the signifiers, there is a tremendous and unprecedented freedom in the ways words can be organized." I also hear Steinian aesthetics in the modular music of Philip Glass, Steve Reich, Terry Riley, and Meredith Monk, in which fixed motifs—modules—are repeated through a succession of otherwise changing relationships.

One reason why Stein's writings seem so contemporary is that they suggest further possibilities in literary art; another is that they force even experienced readers to readjust—to stretch, if not expand—their perceptual capabilities. Reading a lot of Stein induces you to pay closer attention to the language of English sentences. Three and four decades ago, when writers praised Gertrude Stein, they were talking about works which were not commmonly available. Fortunately, that is no longer true. Readers of the world are finally free to discover what Stein knew all along—that she was as a writer indeed "a genius" and that her best books are spectacularly original.

As a literary inventor she ranks with Ezra Pound and Walt Whitman; but unlike them, she made decidedly innovative contributions to not just one genre or two, but several. In American literary history she has had no equal as an avant-garde person-of-letters.

Bibliography

Anthologies of Gertrude Stein's Works:

Haas, Robert Bartlet, editor. *A Primer for the Gradual Understanding of Gertrude Stein.* Los Angeles: Black Sparrow, 1973.

Kostelanetz, Richard, editor. *The Yale Gertrude Stein*. New Haven, Connecticut: Yale University Press, 1980.

Meyerowitz, Patricia, editor. *Gertrude Stein: Writings and Lectures, 1909-1945*. London: Peter Owen, 1967.

Van Vechten, Carl, editor. *Selected Writings of Gertrude Stein*. New York: Random House, 1946.

About Gertrude Stein:

Mellow, James. *Charmed Circle: Gertrude Stein & Company*. New York: Praeger, 1974.

Sutherland, Donald. *Gertrude Stein: A Biography of Her Work*. New Haven, Connecticut: Yale University Press, 1951.

The Double Life of Vladimir Nabokov

Carl R. Proffer

Vladimir Nabokov had two tongues. The poems, stories, plays, and novels which he wrote in Russian between 1917 and 1940 established his place as one of the best Russian writers of the 20th century. With the publication of his first English-language novel, *The Real Life of Sebastian Knight* in 1941, Nabokov became an American writer; and in the remaining 36 years of his career he created a series of works in American prose and poetry—including *Lolita, Pale Fire,* and *Ada*—so brilliant in their style that John Updike and many others could confidently call Nabokov the most important living American writer. Nabokov himself insisted on being called an American writer, even though he did not arrive in the United States until he passed 40. And without a cursory look at this path—his life—it is difficult to understand his Russian novels or his American novels properly.

Nabokov was born in 1899 in St. Petersburg, Russia, into a wealthy aristocratic family. His father was a prominent liberal political figure, as well as a scholar. V. D. Nabokov was a member of the Provisional Government set up by the first (February) Revolution of 1917, but after the Bolshevik *coup d'état* in October, the Nabokov family emigrated. Vladimir, the eldest son, and his brother attended Cambridge University from 1919 to 1922, graduating with honors. Language presented no problem because English was spoken in the Nabokov household, along with Russian and French, from the time Nabokov was a small child.

After graduation from Cambridge, Nabokov moved to Berlin, then one of the major centers of Russian émigré life and culture. While he took a variety of odd jobs during the next two decades—ranging from teaching English to teaching tennis—Nabokov never considered himself anything but a writer. He regularly published poetry in the émigré periodicals. His first novel, *Mary,* came out in 1926 and was followed by a series of ever more complex and original ones, among them *The Defense, Glory, Despair, Invitation to a Beheading,* and *The Gift.* It was in Berlin that Nabokov's father was killed by a Fascist goon in 1922, that he was married to Vera Sonim, and that his only son, Dmitri, was born. But in the late 1930s Nabokov and his family moved ahead of Hitler to France, and soon, barely a step ahead of the Nazis, they left Europe for America.

The Nabokovs sailed into New York Harbor on May 28, 1940. After many difficulties, Nabokov got a series of academic jobs— teaching first Russian and then Russian literature at Wellesley. He was also a research fellow in Harvard's Museum of Comparative Zoology, where he practiced professionally his life-long hobby of lepidopterology, the study of butterflies, a hobby which spilled over profitably into his prose. His final position was at Cornell, where he taught Russian and world literature to ever increasing numbers of students, even before the success of *Lolita* in 1958. *Lolita* enabled Nabokov to retire from teaching, and in 1960 he and his wife visited Europe and decided to stay. From then until his death in 1977 Nabokov lived in Montreux, Switzerland, a place of residence which he insisted not be ascribed to any Americaphobia, but to research requirements (especially art museums) and the desire to be near family members still living in Europe. (Nabokov kept his American passport to the end of his life.) During the prolific years in Montreux, apart from the original works which Nabokov wrote, including *Ada, Transparent Things,* and *Look at the Harlequins!,* Nabokov accomplished or oversaw the transference into English of nearly all of his Russian prose, including such collections as *Tyrants Destroyed* and *A Russian Beauty.*

He also worked in the opposite direction: he translated *Speak, Memory* and *Lolita* into Russian. His books, both Russian and American, became extremely popular all over the world, and he was very widely translated. Scores of scholarly books and dissertations were written about him in English, German, and French. Moreover, beginning with the "third wave" of Russian emigration in 1973-74, Nabokov's original Russian-language books, by now bibliographical rarities, were almost all reprinted in Russian and became popular among the new émigrés. One of the most peculiar aspects of Nabokov's Russian and American books is that for all of their importance and widespread availability across the world, not one of them has ever been allowed to appear in his native country. In Soviet histories of literature he is a non-person.

There are several reasons why such an illustrious writer is totally banned in the U. S. S. R. His liberal democratic family background is the least important of these. Nabokov's failure to *return* to his homeland is more important: Party literary policy requires public repentance of any émigré who is to be mentioned favorably or printed. Even more significant was the very fact that Nabokov achieved so many successes—not only with readers, but with critics, and not only in Russian, but in English. It is a Soviet article of official faith that he who emigrates severs his roots and dies in desolation. Without the great breast of the motherland, they argue, talent has no sustenance. But Nabokov's works were translated into dozens of languages and influenced a whole generation of writers. Since every new success was a blow to the ridiculous Soviet dogma, he has never been forgiven by the commissars of culture.

And finally, both the Russian Nabokov and the American Nabokov are banned in totalitarian countries for reasons intrinsic to his works. Neither in manner nor matter is he acceptable to the communal mind. Above all his works celebrate individual freedom. In the postscript to the Russian *Lolita* (banned from Russia), Nabokov wrote: "Freedom of spirit! The whole breath of humanity is contained in these words." When asked about his politics, he was terse as usual: "My desires are modest. Portraits of the head of government should not exceed a postage stamp in size. No torture and no executions." The detail, the particularity of things, is especially important to Nabokov. The tiny postage stamp of his example carries immense weight, as anyone who has lived in a totalitarian country understands. Thoroughfares and public buildings lined with massive images of the leader or leaders are sure signs that the public is thoroughly controlled.

In the elegantly blunt introductions to his later books Nabokov repeatedly urged readers not to consider him in social or political terms. He insisted on being read as an artist, not as a commentator on current events. In part this was Nabokov's rebellion against the centuries-old Russian tradition of "relevant" literature; novels and poems and plays devised and discussed as vehicles of persuasion. But in part the "rejection of relevance" was Nabokov's natural predisposition, combined with the absolute liberty he had living and writing in the Western tradition.

Of course, Nabokov did use political themes, and if we examine them in terms of the novels or stories of which they are parts, we are not violating his injunctions. To some extent one should see Nabokov's fictional totalitarian worlds as fairy-tale realms, even when, as in *Bend Sinister* (1947), they have many things in common with Nazi Germany or Communist Russia. *Bend Sinister*'s Padukgrad is a fantasy locale, with fantasy names and a language invented, like everything else, by Nabokov. He specifically draws our attention to the author's special role as sole god and creator, and to the "imaginariness" of the character's lives. But this novel was only a first and tentative flight into the fairy-tale freedom which marked Nabokov's later English works (beginning with *Pale Fire*) and which Nabokov had already brilliantly achieved in his 1936 Russian novel *Invitation to a Beheading*. Let us take this book as a representative of Nabokov's first career and examine it more closely, before considering a representative work from his second career.

Invitation to a Beheading describes the sentencing, incarceration, and apparent execution of a man named Cincinnatus. The setting is an unnamed, run-down country which seems to be somewhere between East and West Europe. The book has puzzled many readers and generated many purely political interpretations. As is often the case with Nabokov's novels, the book is not what it seems most likely to be.

The surface story seems solid enough: Cincinnatus lives in a society which tolerates only transparent openness and predictability. Anyone who is different (opaquely closed, unpredictable, inventive) is shunned—and when different enough he is beheaded. But society requires the victim's warm endorsement of all the conventions of the extermination process. (This is the source of much macabre wit.) Finally, the appointed hour of the joyous execution comes, festively witnessed, blood to act as cement for the collective society. The final paragraphs are ambiguous, but readers from totalitarian nations, especially Russians, tend to see *Invitation to a Beheading* as an obvious allegory for their own country. Indeed, in the mid-1960s, the novel was typed up in multiple copies and circulated in *samizdat* in the U. S. S. R., the first of Nabokov's works to be spread that way. But Nabokov's main purpose was not to show the banal evils of police states.

The setting of the novel is not only unrealistic in the sense that it isn't modelled on any specific society—it is outside *any* earthly society. The central theme of the novel is one of Nabokov's favorites; the supremacy of imagination. This theme is conveyed partly through patterns of opposed images, including here vs. there, we vs. I, matters vs. spirit, translucence vs. opacity, mortality vs. immortality, and, of course, prison vs. freedom.

The narrator of the novel imagines a future world. Its futurity, its science-fiction nature, is indicated by the presence of such strange things as the "sabayon" they drink, the electric hearse, swan-shaped electric "wagonets," and vehicles called spring-powered "clocklets." This imagined world is so far in the future that matter itself has worn out—people have even become transparent (and as they get closer to death they become almost invisible). Nothing is new, because the Last Inventor died long, long ago.

The narrator's hero, and alter-ego, the writer Cincinnatus, senses that his mode of existence is special and strange—in fact, though he never states it precisely this way, he is dimly aware that he is a character in a work of art. His crime is "gnostic turpitude"—i.e., he sees the novel's material world as (someone else's) fantasy. And at the end when Cincinnatus' own mind makes the final liberating leap, he realizes that imagination makes him free to do anything, including walk away from his executioners. All through the story he keeps dreaming of a radiant world, another dimension, and wondering how to "slide into" this other dimension. In the final paragraphs he achieves this.

Like his creator, Cincinnatus is a writer. But he is a beginner, he only senses "what one must do for a commonplace word to come alive and to share its neighbor's sheen, heat, shadow . . . so that the whole line is live iridescence." The ordinary world cannot abide his criminal opacity (secrecy, originality). Cincinnatus feels a special kinship with the huge live moth that visits his cell because, for the moth (in Russian, "night butterfly"), the night *is* day. And it is important that Nabokov sends this night butterfly to Cincinnatus immediately after Cincinnatus has written the word "death"—and then crossed it out. (For the writer, cancelling the word is equivalent to cancelling the reality of the word.) Nabokov expects the reader to know that for centuries the butterfly has been a symbol of immortality. The fabulous life cycle of the butterfly, with its bizarrely different stages of existence, made it a natural symbol. Of course, Nabokov knew the lore of each lepidopteron, and only an expert such as Nabokov could choose the specific lepidopteron which appears in Cincinnatus' cell. Described in beautiful and precise detail, it is the Great Peacock Moth (*Saturnia Pyri*), unmistakable because it is as large as a man's hand, the largest lepidopteron in all Europe, a truly spectacular and extraordinary creature that few people ever see.

It is appropriate that this symbol of immortality appear to (and be protected by) Cincinnatus just before he goes out to what appears to be death, but what is actually the long dreamed of transition into another dimension—the soul taking flight into immortality. At the end of the novel Cincinnatus goes to be with other immortal fictional characters ("where, to judge by the voices, stood beings akin to him"), as Nabokov leaves him, having completed the novel and returned to the non-creative state. In the last paragraph of *Invitation to a Beheading*, as Nabokov puts down his pen and ceases thinking about that world, the world of Pierre the executioner and the other phantoms whirlingly disintegrates.

Invitation to a Beheading has a claim to being the most universal of Nabokov's Russian novels, and arguably, along with *The Gift*, his highest Russian achievement. Because of the richness of *Lolita, Pnin, Pale Fire,* and *Ada,* it is more precarious to attempt a ranking of the American novels—but certainly one can say that *Lolita* is his *most American* novel. After the completion of *Lolita* Nabokov moved in new directions, expanding his world beyond the known "real" world into other worlds—not exactly science fiction ones (although science fiction magazines and critics have adopted him), but certainly realms where reference to normal geography and chronology is of a minimal assistance to the reader (as in *Pale Fire* and *Ada*).

The furor over *Lolita* now seems faintly ridiculous, but 25 years ago community standards were quite different. D. H. Lawrence and Henry Miller were still regarded as pornographic or "erotic classics," and because of Humbert Humbert's perverse passion, Nabokov's book was classified the same way—and first printed in France by the notorious Olympia Press. The barriers soon fell. Those who bought *Lolita* to be titillated were disappointed, and now it seems almost chaste. "Nymphet" has entered the language. "Lolita" has become an eponym—which I have seen used on restaurants, rest-rooms, a coffee liqueur, and boutiques (not the loftiest of Nabokov's contributions to culture, but one he no doubt found amusing).

Humbert Humbert, like many of Nabokov's heroes before, suffers from an excruciatingly extreme passion. Often a Nabokov character's monomania dooms him, whether it be chess (*The Defense*) or locating the perfect double and committing the perfect murder (*Despair*). The extreme pressures under which Nabokov's heroes act

are revelatory of character. Thus Humbert Humbert is an outsider
socially and sexually; he never really tries to understand American
life, or any life outside his own passion. He is the controlling consciousness, the ostensible teller of the tale, and many readers—both in
English and in Russian translation—made the elementary error of
equating Nabokov with the narrator. A second common and equally
breath-taking mistake was to conclude that Humbert's perversion is
glorified. Obviously Humbert tries to present nympholepsy in the
best possible light; but in spite of himself (and because of Nabokov the
moralist), it is clear to a reasonably careful reader that Humbert, even
leaving aside the fact that he is a madman and a murderer, is responsible for destroying Lolita's childhood. Indeed, all of Nabokov's negative characters unwittingly reveal the truth about themselves and
their ideals—to anyone not blind to details or to common moral
values.

Lolita is such a complex work, with so many things happening
simultaneously, that it was bound to mislead some readers, especially
those not accustomed to truly modern fiction. In my own Keys to Lolita
and in Appel's Annotated Lolita many of the camouflaged meanings
and allusions are explained. No doubt in the future similar books will
be written about all of Nabokov's novels. Some critics disapprove of
fiction which can be explicated in such detail. But one should not
forget that Nabokov's novels can be read with enjoyment and profit
without any such guides—they are far more accessible works than,
say, Joyce's novels. I do not understand why one should hold it against
Nabokov that successive generations of readers keep discovering new
dimensions in his fiction. Such thinking is reductive and amounts to
special pleading for ignorance.

Anyone can read Lolita, Pale Fire, or Ada; but the reader who has
a good knowledge of English or French or Russian literature, and who
understands the many explicit and hidden allusions, will understand
much more. The reader who has a good knowledge of botany and
zoology will understand more still. (In Ada the characteristics or
histories of trees, plants, or insects play important roles in characterization; thus, for example, the major female characters are named after
genera of orchids.) The same can be said of readers who have other
kinds of special information, ranging from European painting to
chess. This is not intellectual snobbery, as some argue, but merely the
writer's use of all of nature's riches and human culture, including
masterpieces created by great artists, as materials for new worlds of

the imagination. Thus an intonation from Jane Austen or the etymology of the word "orchid" are as much valued parts of "reality" as a drill-press or a party-leader.

Perhaps again the concept of imagination is the key to most of Nabokov. If one does not have or respect imagination, it is hard to appreciate Nabokov. He celebrates it, he celebrates liberty, language, love, and beauty. He asserts the sanctity of individual human life. He prizes wit and his own wit is always directed against those who by normal moral standards deserve it—people who do not love, destroyers of freedom, preachers of mediocrity, anyone who maims or kills to force his ideas on other human beings, people who are ignorant of themselves or the physical and intellectual world around them. Of course, Nabokov has no sermons. He loathed propaganda fiction. But these noble values are constants in his world.

And his world is very large. It circles the globe. It includes the Far West of the United States (*Lolita*), the Far East of Russia (*The Gift*), the Far North of the imagination (*Pale Fire*), the Riviera; it includes deserts and beaches, mountains and American and Siberian forests, Russian estates and American campuses, Baltic spas and California motels, and still other worlds, the beautiful fantasy worlds of Zembla or the anti-world of *Ada* where other worlds—mainly American and Russian—are mixed together geographically and historically in amusing and revivifying ways.

And, finally, there is Nabokov's "Other World." This level of his work is just now being revealed, but the first discoveries that have been made promise to change everyone's way of looking at Nabokov. The theme of time is a fairly constant one in Nabokov, and the ability of man to overcome time through memory and imagination is explored in many of his works (notably in *The Gift* and *Ada*). In his dissertation on *Ada*, Brian Boyd shows that important characters in the novel who die actually live on in other forms and subtly influence the behavior of the living. This study was written just before the author's widow Vera Nabokov tantalized readers, in her introduction to Nabokov's collected poetry in Russian, by saying that the major overlooked theme of his work was the "other-worldly" theme. And now W. W. Rowe has provided readings of several Nabokov works which attempt to demonstrate that he repeatedly refuses to let characters "die" completely but instead has them shift to some other plane or mode of existence, from which they are able to observe and gently bear on the fates of the living. Clearly, there are still many things in

Nabokov which will continue to puzzle and delight his readers and his re-readers.

Bibliography

By Vladimir Nabokov:

Mary. Translated by Michael Glenny in collaboration with the author. New York: McGraw-Hill, 1970. (First published in Russian in 1926.)

The Defense. Translated by Michael Scammell and the author. New York: Putnam, 1964. (First published as "The Luzhin Defense" in Russian in 1930.)

Despair. Translated by the author. New York: Putnam, 1969. (First published serially in Russian in 1934.)

The Gift. Translated by Dmitri Nabokov and Michael Scammell in collaboration with the author. New York: Putnam, 1959. (First published serially in Russian in 1937.)

Invitation to a Beheading. Translated by Dmitri Nabokov in collaboration with the author. New York: Putnam, 1959. (First published in Russian in 1938.)

The Real Life of Sebastian Knight. Norfolk, Connecticut: New Directions, 1941. (First work originally written in English.)

Bend Sinister. New York: Holt, 1947. (First work written in the U. S.)

Speak, Memory: An Autobiography Revisited. New York: Putnam, 1966. (First published in the U. S. as *Conclusive Evidence* and in London as *Speak, Memory* in 1951.)

Lolita. Paris: Olympia Press, 1955; New York: Putnam, 1958.

Pnin. Garden City, New York: Doubleday, 1957.

Pale Fire. New York: Putnam, 1962.

Pushkin, Aleksandr. *Eugene Onegin.* Four Volumes. New York: Bollingen Series / Pantheon Books, 1964. (Translator, editor, author of the commentary.)

Ada, or Ardor: A Family Chronicle. New York: McGraw-Hill, 1969.

Transparent Things. New York: McGraw-Hill, 1972.

A Russian Beauty and Other Stories. Translated by Dmitri Nabokov and Simon Karlinsky in collaboration with the author. New York: McGraw-Hill, 1973.

Strong Opinions. New York: McGraw-Hill, 1973. (A collection of interviews and other personal statements.)

Look at the Harlequins!. New York: McGraw-Hill, 1974.

Tyrants Destroyed and Other Stories. Translated (first 12 stories) by Dmitri Nabokov in collaboration with the author. New York: McGraw-Hill, 1975.

About Vladimir Nabokov:

Appel, Alfred, editor. *The Annotated Lolita*. New York: McGraw-Hill, 1970.

Field, Andrew, compiler. *Nabokov: A Bibliography*. New York: McGraw-Hill, 1973.
(A complete list of Nabokov's works in all genres and in all translations through 1971.)

Proffer, Carl R. *Keys to Lolita*. Bloomington: Indiana University Press, 1967.

Mason, Bobbie. *Nabokov's Garden: A Guide to Ada*. Ann Arbor, Michigan: Ardis, 1974.

Schuman, Samuel, compiler. *Vladimir Nabokov: A Reference Guide*. Boston: G. K. Hall, 1979. (An annotated listing of all writings about Nabokov in English through 1977.)

Henry Miller: Dreaming and Writing

Jay Martin

In many ways, Henry Miller should scarcely seem like a contemporary writer. Born in 1891, he would more naturally be regarded as a contemporary of Hemingway, Fitzgerald, and Faulkner. Parts of his work, including his representation of sexuality and even his style, now seem somewhat dated, if not old-fashioned. He could easily be subjected to the kind of treatment which bright young British reviewers used to visit upon the previous generation: "How charming to remember those more innocent days when Henry Miller's stories appeared in the once crisp but now, alas, yellowed pages of Samuel Putnam's *New Review*." Miller himself, beginning in the 1950s, strived to achieve the image of a wise old man meditating on Partington Ridge like some Tibetan sage.

What keeps him our contemporary is neither what once made him scandalous nor what later made him a cult hero. These made him appear different from us—more lusty and unconcerned, or more meditative and untroubled, either ahead of us or behind us, but not contemporary with us. These made him seem like a deliciously rebellious friend or an all-knowing grandfather. But what makes him resemble us now, what makes him seem to duplicate ourselves, is Miller's closeness to his dream life and to the universal language of dreams that speaks to us in the present tense. In back of Miller's portrayal of sex, beneath his claims of sagacity, is the man who learned how to become a writer by imitating his dreams—he has been writing from the wellspring of his dreams all these years. The surface of his work may be antiquated, but the pure strain of unconscious creativity that lies beneath the surface keeps him our contemporary.

We talk about "dreaming our lives away", but as Henry Miller once remarked, anyone who has experienced a really good dream "never complains of having wasted his time. On the contrary, he is delighted to have partaken of a reality which serves to heighten and enhance the reality of everyday."[1] After years of futile efforts to become a writer, Miller, as I shall show, at last released his creativity by dreaming his life into art. He made his literary intentions clear in *The Cosmological Eye*: "My aim in writing is to establish a greater REALITY. I am not a realist or a naturalist; I am for life, which, in literature, it seems to me, can only be attained by the use of dream and symbol."[2] Certainly in his personal experience, and even more completely in his fiction, Miller attempted to open himself up to the influence of the impulsive, unconscious, archaic, magical, symbolic, and mythical—and he learned to do this first by surrendering himself to his dreams.

I shall argue that there are three sorts of dreams, representing three stages, involved in Miller's creativity and, by extension, in the creative process more generally. The first stage, where creativity is blocked is represented and epitomized by an anti-creative, traumatic dream of self-dissolution: what Heinz Kohut calls a "self-state dream."[3] Second, there is the familiar dream based on conflict, which, in the creative process, seems to come to focus especially in the clash between id and superego. Finally, prior to the release of creativity, there occurs what I call a "creative dream"; this comes, typically, at the conclusion of the dream series outlined above, and has as its manifest function and latent meaning the restoration of the self to a wholeness through art. In the case of his dreams of 1932-33, Miller, like any creative artist engaged in the process I am describing, dreamed his way not toward personal health but artistic accomplishment. He was not concerned with a personal cure but with an artistic breakthrough.

The book in which lay the origin of Miller's other books, then, was the one which he called "Dream Book." He got the idea of recording his dreams in late September 1932, recorded the first dream in early October, and continued to record dreams until the end of 1933. This book still remains unpublished in manuscript, though some of it, transformed, went into the chapter of *Black Spring* titled "Into the Night Life." This "Dream Book," this "log of dreams,"[4] was crucial in Miller's development. In retrospect, the compilation was so honest that it made Miller himself uncomfortable. "It is all spiced with humor, but murderous humor," he told the French surrealist Raymond Queneau in 1950. "As I reread it, I have the impression that it belongs rather in the files of some psychoanalytic journal. The general public is not ready for such naked transcriptions of the dream plasma."[5] Once deposited in the Henry Miller Collection in the UCLA research library, where it might be inspected by scholars, the "Dream Book" was removed from the archives by Miller before his death and now is not available for public inspection of any kind.[6]

Whatever discomfort his exposure of his secrets in the "Dream Book" later caused him, during 1932 and 1933 composition of the dream book was a necessity for Henry Miller. Consider his situation. In New York, where he had grown up, he had wished to be a Writer, and he had written several journalistic articles, a dozen *fin de siècle* prose poems, some criticism, and two unpublished novels so bad that even friends and lovers of Miller's could not find anything to praise in them. Everything he produced was wooden, dull, dead.

Then, while he was struggling to get his recent experiences recorded—in the book that was eventually to be called *Tropic of Cancer*—he felt that he could free his vision and the approach to his material by adopting the understanding and point of view of the dreamer. Thus, he decided to set forth on the laborious project of recording, meditating upon, and—possibly—understanding his dreams. He began a notebook, wrote "Dream Book" on the first page, and went to sleep. This was a new kind of "work" for a Brooklyn boy, a tailor's son, who had worked and failed at every other kind of job in the world. Perhaps he was intended for dream work? That was indeed, as it turned out, the very work, perhaps the only work, for which he *was* suited.

The two godparents who presided over the birth of the dream book were Friedrich Nietzsche and Sigmund Freud. In early 1933, as the dream book was getting well-started, Miller wrote in another notebook, one he was keeping for a possible study of D. H. Lawrence:

> . . . let us now turn to psychological facts. "At night all leaping fountains speak with a louder tone; my soul too is a leaping fountain"—says Zarathustra. *"Into the night-life seems to be exiled"*—these are the famous words from Freud's *Interpretation of Dreams*—"into the night-life seems to be exiled what once ruled during the day." This sentence contains the entire modern psychology.(!) Its great idea is the stratification of the psyche. . . . [Our primitive organization is] revealed by the dream, revealed by the child, revealed by psychosis as a still existing psychic reality.[7]

Miller was trying to learn how to write a new, revolutionary—if need be, psychotic—kind of literature, and he was influenced by Nietzsche's commitment to the truth-telling capacity of the irrational, as well as by Freud's main postulates concerning dreams: (1) that the content of any dream is the fulfillment of a wish, (2) that dreams take the place of actions, (3) that dream distortions could be interpreted, and (4) that sexual impulses reaching back into childhood are the decisive factors in repression, which the dream lifts.[8]

For Miller, the implications of this last postulate were crucially important. The idea that he derived from it was that the child— originally healthy, then sexually wounded—survived in the dream. If that child could be found, Miller believed, then his own authentic being could guide him toward re-becoming the artist he had been by nature. "Every child at play," Freud wrote in "Creative Writers and Daydreaming" (1907), "behaves like a creative writer, in that he creates a world of his own, or rather, re-arranges the things of his world in a new way which pleases him."[9] Miller wanted to rearrange his world through recapturing his childhood and understanding the origins of his sexual impulses and fixations. He proceeded through interpreting his dreams. In order to write literature he would first write psychology and attempt, as he told Anaïs Nin, "to give name to the nameless."[10] Miller possessed a remarkably clear sense of the relation between dreaming and acting. In dreams, he wrote in his notebook, "everything has logic behind it, everything that is said or done is said or done purposively, has meaning, significance. The paranoic lives and then dreams his action through. Or he dreams and then lives his actions out."[11] Clearly Miller wanted to dream acutely and deeply enough that he could "act out" his associations in literature. He was also instinctively aware that, as the psychoanalyst Harold Blum has said, "the dream is not only a normal regression, but . . . especially illustrative of unconscious personality organization."[12] He was determined to map his "personality organization" and then to re-map (and perhaps remake) it artistically.

Miller recorded very few dreams from his youth and he says that he remembered very few dreams. But he did have one dream which recurred frequently during a 60-year period, between his early 20s and well into his 80s. In 1977 he told it this way to an interviewer:

> The one dream I have—I think it's very significant about me and my relation to my world around me . . . is this dream. It recurred—it stopped now, but it had recurred— for many years. I would never know when to expect it. The dream begins: I might be shaving myself and looking in the

mirror, and suddenly there's a different man: it isn't my
face—it's somebody else looking back at me. And then I go
crazy. I don't know what I do, but I know the next thing is
I'm in the insane asylum and I don't remember anything
that goes on there except that I'm there quite a long while,
it seems to me, and I'm dying to get out. And one day I
manage to escape. I'm always climbing a high wall and
dropping over into freedom . . . escaping the asylum. But
when I do, and I land on my feet, I look to the right and left,
and there I see a couple coming toward me. They look like
friendly people; and I wave . . . [as if to say:] 'Hello!'—
'Come on!', like I'm glad to meet someone, talk to them. I
begin to talk and they shake their heads: no comprehension—'No compris,' you know what I mean? Then a terrible
sense of devastation overtakes me. Then I know I am really
nuts, you know that? But then the dream ends, fortunately.
So maybe that's where I'm at now—that I'm really nuts, but
I have accepted it, do you see what I mean?[13]

In many ways this dream recapitulates the neurotic conflicts that
operated in 1932 when Miller started to compose his dream book. In
very general terms this is what Heinz Kohut calls a "self-state dream,"
a concise expression and metaphoric summary of the condition of
one's psychic being. In the mirror of his unconscious, where Miller
looks to discover the self that he believes to be his, his mirror-
reflection, he discovers that he has deceived himself: the identity that
he perceives in the mirror is not the one he believed he possessed, and
the disjunction between himself—now understood to be a false,
deceptive self—and his double drives him into a frenzy. Literally, he
feels his self to be split into two from within, between a false self that
is his and a true self that is possible to achieve. His only sanity consists
in his desire for restitution, escape from the asylum. Alternately, he
must experience regression in splitting. Capacity for restitution and
reunification of the self seems to be available through going "outside"
the bad introject that has made his doppleganger alien to his authentic
self. On going outside, he goes, of course, toward object-love, which
has its origin in relation to parents. Almost immediately upon his
going outside, over the wall of self, then, undisguised parent figures
appear. The only trouble is that the loved objects reflect Miller's
damaged psyche as little as does his double in the mirror. They are
foreign, alien: they do not even understand English, the language in
which he wants to write books in order to give expression to his sense
of self. This old couple speaks French, only a slight displacement from

Miller's parents, both of whom spoke German primarily; Miller's parents always opposed his desire to become a writer—they could not "understand" him. Splitting, by way of bad introjections or alien projections, gives him no way to restore the self by seeing it mirrored from within or without—and, at the end of the dream this lack of hope for restoration brings on the "terrible sense of devastation," a psychotic state of the self, in which the self seems crazy even to itself.

Perhaps Miller's own dream, then, tells us more than any explicit confession could of how it felt to be Henry Miller—from the inside. But if this self-state dream expressed his illness, the dreams that he recorded during 1932-33 were meant to cure him. They were not, of course, "meant" to do so consciously; rather, in the dream book is exhibited an interplay between dreams that describe the self by pointing to its traumas, as opposed to dreams in which the fundamental wish comes to be to inspect and eventually to undo the traumas that the self-state dreams describe.

I take the "Dream Book," then, as offering a fairly coherent series of dreams, which increasingly reflect Miller's wishes to restore his self to identity with its mirror image and to rid himself of the distorted introjections and projections that are first caused by and later perpetuate his splitting. The fundamental theme or preoccupation of these dreams is that the self is troubled (attacked, punished, embarrassed, etc.), usually by some intrusive sexual material, but the self can imagine achieving wholeness by subjecting libidinous impulses to the control of aesthetic form. Repression has previously dissolved or fragmented the self; now sublimation might replace repression and work toward creative restoration.

In a short paper, such as this one, I cannot quote and analyze Miller's dreams at length, but I can at least given an account of the issues involved in them. Certainly, early on in the dream book, many elements seem to refer to what the psychoanalyst Otto Rank called the "Birth trauma," and it is not coincidental that Rank was Anaïs Nin's analyst and that Miller was studying his books during this period. In the very first dream that he recorded, Miller sees himself "caught in the teeth of a billiard ball" until "the shell of the ball falls apart just like an egg that is being hatched, and out I step." Behind this suggestion that birth itself is damaging is the belief that the castrating mother means to maim him by controlling him. The name that he gets is "Gottlieb Leberecht Müller,"[14] meaning that he must be a good, right-living boy who always obeys his mother. The same theme is present in the third dream he recorded, concerning "Aunt Annie Heller, deaconess of the old Presbyterian Church on Driggs Avenue." In a reversal of the expected situation, the strict religious deaconess behaves whorishly while Miller himself has to curb her provocative behavior. Forced to look at her vagina, he imagines it as something else: "By some magic she has but to touch it and it is transformed—like the little Japanese papers which one puts in a glass of water, which open up before your eyes into magnificent and astounding shapes."[15]

We can see, I think, that Miller's defense against sexuality was to try to turn it into art. This pretense that sex could really be made into something else had been the trouble with his earlier works. Now, in 1932, however, he was trying to learn how to bring sex itself directly into his work instead of disguising it. This would mean, eventually, that he would have to give up the desire to make art, and so he would move toward the full conception of *Tropic of Cancer*, as anti-art art. But for the time, in his dreams, it was enough to try to let his sexual impulses appear in relatively undisguised form. This is what began to happen early in January 1933. On January 25, 1933, he had two dreams. In the first, mother is "groaning and threatening to kill father" and to turn her son into a homosexual, in defense against which he fantasizes about committing incest with her. In the second dream of that night, he goes into "mother's room" and, exposed to ridicule because he is dressed only in his nightshirt, he confesses to her and all his relatives that he has committed adultery with Anaïs Nin,[16] who is clearly a transference mother. Obviously, mother, castration fears, and his superego development were closely connected. The picture of Miller's youth that begins to emerge from these dreams—one that is confirmed by later dreams—is of early childhood experience in which he was over-stimulated sexually by his mother, only to be thrust away when he responded with his own sexual overtures. Clearly, he was being asked to be simultaneously the object of stimulation and also to exercise strict control over his own impulses. The resulting feelings of self-imposed impotence were vividly expressed in dreams of late January and early February; the predominating metaphor in these is that of an amusement park, and especially the normally powerful sexual image of the giant roller coaster. Here, the roller coaster is immobile, useless. In associations to these dreams Miller stressed the frustrating and sexually unattainable aspects of the symbol of the roller coaster: "The image of the roller coaster is strong and recalls my lonely walks in the evening at Coney Island, where with a drawing

pad under my arm and a note-book in my pocket I would stand gazing
at all these crazy things.... I liked Coney Island particularly in winter
when it was deserted and these objects stood out gaunt and ridiculous,
useless as though images or objects Dali writes of."[17]
     At last, by means of his dreams and his examination of them,
Miller became able to represent his greatest fear—of castration—
directly in a dream of February 7:

> she reaches for a pair of scissors lying on the table. It is a
> huge pair, very blunt, rusty, old. She is cutting the string
> which is attached to a condom inside her, a condom that
> she has inserted herself without my knowing it; as she cuts
> the string I am in a sweat for fear she will cut my penis off;
> in fact, as she cuts away I seem to feel it is my penis, as
> though the string attached to the condom were a fibre of
> my body....[18]

By looking directly at his fear he masters it: the pain is "quite bearable"
and "simply makes [him] nervous."
     Miller's fears and the conflicts that grew out of them were
clearly on a preverbal level, but his dreams gave him images by which
to fuse his anxieties with his capacity for speech, and thus give his fears
meaning. His dreams, then, have a goal, an "intention" of sorts—and
once he was able to deal comfortably with his sexuality in his dreams,
he could learn to do so in art. By this means he arrived at the central
dream of the series, in which he reconstructed his recurring state-of-
the-self dream, by transforming it into a dream of the state-of-his-
artistic-capacity.
     In this central dream he is in a "strange house" and, with
Michael Fraenkel (the Boris of *Tropic of Cancer*) makes a discovery
"down in the cellar" of a "piece of art, a huge Japanese screen." At first,
Miller feels guilty because this "piece of art" he has "discovered" is
being sold for too high a price, especially since he has done nothing but
carry "pieces of it upstairs . . . to be examined." But at last he discovers
that his art work is truly wonderful. As the screen is rubbed with a rag
"marvellous pieces unfold themselves to the eye, pieces of decoration
such as I have never seen before, seemingly incredible in color and
design." And at the same time, "a society woman, very proper, very
ritzy, clad in a sheath-like gown of expensive nature, gets down on the
floor, and lifting her dress up over her backside so as to expose herself
fully, grovels lasciviously on the floor, remarking at the same time that
she is doing this to show that she is not too hoity toity, that there is

nothing she wouldn't do for the sake of art, etc."[19]

This dream clearly begins with the suspicion that this creative talent is worth nothing; anything would be too much for what he will bring up "accidentally" from the "cellar" of his unconscious. Besides, this piece of art is only a "screen," a defense against exposing himself as a narrow, intolerant man whose excessive reaction formation against homosexual impulses is all too apparent. Yet, a crucial alteration in perception occurs in this central dream. What he has brought up from "downstairs" turns out to be really valuable and, what is more, astonishingly beautiful.

So in the midst of the expression of his conflicts and anxieties, then, Miller did manage to use his dreams to achieve a solution to conflicts through art and to heal the splits from within and without that had earlier blocked his creativity almost completely. Now, this central dream suggests he *could* bring up a book with many episodes (a screen with many pictures) from his unconscious, even a book like *Tropic of Cancer*; and despite its exhibition of male and female sexuality, the expression and exposure would be justified by its artfulness. He could well join with the lady in saying that there was nothing *he* "wouldn't do for the sake of art."

As Miller was to write in his notebook in 1933, he started with a clinical interest in his dreams; then, from therapy, he moved to an interest in his dreams as fantasy materials; and finally he understood his dreams as the process of creative transformation itself. Undoubtedly, he made his way toward the restoration and creative reinvigoration in a "transformative dream," a creative counter-part and answer to the "self-stated dream." And so he began the creation of a body of work which, because it is so continuously and so deeply and richly informed by the stimulus and presence of the "creative dream" at its core, still seems meaningful to us.

Notes

[1] Henry Miller, *Big Sur and the Oranges of Hieronymous Bosch* (New York: New Directions, 1956), p. 56.

[2] "Biographical Note," *The Cosmological Eye* (Norfolk, Connecticut: New Directions, 1939), p. 363.

[3] *The Restoration of the Self* (New York: International Universities Press, 1977).

[4] Henry Miller to Dante Zaccagnini, February 8, 1950, in Henry Miller Collection, Special Collections, UCLA Library, Los Angeles, California.

[5] Henry Miller to Raymond Queneau, August 3, 1950, in Henry Miller Collection.

[6] The "Dream Book" was bound by Miller, supplied with a title page done in watercolors, and dedicated to Anaïs Nin. It was contained in the Special Collections at UCLA under the call number 110/2, box 10. There is a second version, with additions, marked "Dream Book" (1933); and still one more retyped version, to which earlier dreams are added, which I call below "Dream Book," revised version.

[7] Quoted from manuscript for "Brochure," Vol. 2 (notebook bound in red), in the section "Soul & Destiny (Gottfried Benn)," n.p., UCLA Special Collections.

[8] See Sigmund Freud, *The Interpretation of Dreams*, Vols. 4-5, Standard Edition, translated by James Strachey et al., (London: The Hogarth Press, 1953 [1900]), passim.

[9] Sigmund Freud, "Creative Writers and Day Dreaming," *Jensen's 'Gradiva' and Other Works*, Vol. 9, in Standard Edition, translated by James Strachey et al. (London: The Hogarth Press, 1959 [1907]), pp. 143-4.

[10] For an understanding of *Daseinsanalyse*, see chiefly, M. Boss, *Psychoanalysis and Daseinsanalysis*, translated by L. B. Lefebre (New York: Basic Books, 1963). For Miller's comments on psychology, see Henry Miller, *Letters to Anaïs Nin*, edited by Gunther Stuhlman (New York: Putnam, 1965), p. 23 (letter of February 12, 1932).

[11] "Dream Book," p. 10.

[12] Blum, "The Changing Use of Dreams in Psychoanalytic Practice: Dreams and Free Associations," *International Journal of Psycho-Analysis*, Vol. 57 (1976), pp. 315-24. On the relation between dreams and acting out, see Doryann Lebe, *The Dream in Clinical Practice*, edited by Joseph Natterson (New York and London: Jason Aronson, 1980), pp. 209-23.

[13] Connie Goldman, "Interview with Henry Miller," "Options" (771220), 1978, National Public Radio, Jay Martin Collection.

[14] "Dream Book" (1933) and "Novel Based on Dreams" (Manuscript titled "At Night all Leaping Fountains Speak With a Louder Tone," p. 12), in University of California, Los Angeles Special Collections Library. This and subsequent quotations by permission of Henry Miller.

[15] "Dream Book," revised version: "Old Dreams #3."

[16] "Paris Notebooks," Vol. 2, Clichy, 1933, pp. 130-32. Manuscript in UCLA, Special Collections, call number 110/2, box 25.

[17] "Dream Book," revised version: pp. 2-3. Notes inserted into "Brochure," 1932-3, Vol. 1, pp. 196 (verso), 197 (verso), 1-2, manuscript in UCLA Special Collections. "Dream Book," revised version: p. 3: comment on dream of January 31, 1933.

18 "Dream Book," p. 4.
19 "Dream Section," pp. 3-4, UCLA Special Collections.

Bibliography

By Henry Miller:

Henry Miller on Writing. Edited by Thomas H. Moore. New York: New Directions,
    1964.
The Rosy Crucifixion: Sexus. New York: Grove Press, 1965.
The Rosy Crucifixion: Nexus. New York: Grove Press, 1965.
The Rosy Crucifixion: Plexus. New York: Grove Press, 1965.
A Henry Miller Reader. Edited by Lawrence Durrell. Revised edition. New York:
    New Directions, 1969.
The Air-Conditioned Nightmare. New York: New Directions, 1970.
Tropic of Capricorn. New York: Ballantine, 1974.
Tropic of Cancer. New York: Ballantine, 1975.

About Henry Miller:

Gordon, William A. *The Mind and Art of Henry Miller.* Baton Rouge: Louisiana State
    University Press, 1967.
Martin, Jay. *Always Merry and Bright: The Life of Henry Miller.* Santa Barbara,
    California: Capra Press, 1978.
Wickes, George. *Henry Miller.* Minneapolis: University of Minnesota Press, 1966.

Langston Hughes: Black America's Poet Laureate

Larry Neal

James Mercer Langston Hughes was born in Joplin, Missouri, on February 1, 1902. He was one of the most prolific writers in American literary history. His plays, poems, and anthologies have found a permanent place in this nation's literary canon, and his work continues to inform Afro-American literature and theater. For several generations of Afro-American artists, his work has vividly illustrated the creative possibilities of the culture and consciousness of black culture.

Hughes came from a separated family; and by the time he was 13, the young boy had lived in Buffalo, Cleveland, Lawrence (Kansas), Mexico City, Topeka (Kansas), Colorado Springs, and Kansas City, before returning to Cleveland for high school. He started writing verses there, and fortunately, his creative talents were encouraged by a perceptive teacher. Then in 1921 he went to live with his father in Mexico, where Langston taught English in two Mexican schools. His first prose piece was published while he was still in Mexico. Called "Mexican Games," it appeared in the *Brownies Book*, the innovative children's series edited by the distinguished black scholar-activist W. E. B. DuBois.

1921 was an important year in the young poet's life; for it was the year in which Langston Hughes's classic poem, "The Negro Speaks of Rivers," was published in the *Crisis* magazine, the official organ of the NAACP (National Association for the Advancement of Colored People). The poem was dedicated to DuBois:

> I've known rivers:
> I've known rivers ancient as the world and older than the
>   flow of human blood in human veins.
>
> My soul has grown deep like the rivers.

I bathed in the Euphrates when dawns were young.
I built my hut near the Congo and it lulled me to sleep.
I looked upon the Nile and raised the pyramids above it.
I heard the singing of the Mississippi when Abe Lincoln
     went down to New Orleans, and I've seen its muddy
     bosom turn all golden in the sunset.

I've known rivers:
Ancient, dusky rivers.

My soul has grown deep like the rivers.[1]

The poem was enthusiastically received by a broad cross-section of the poetry-reading public. Its young writer became famous, and a major literary career was launched. Along with Claude McKay's defiant sonnet "If We Must Die," it is still the most widely recited poem in Afro-American literature. Specifically what is it about the poem that has engaged so many diverse audiences? And what is its special meaning in the context of the Afro-American cultural matrix?

Well, for one thing, the poem is not complex. Its lyricism is direct and honest, without being simplistic in the pejorative sense. Langston makes a mythic unity between the souls of black people and the timeless rivers of life. The first three lines meditate upon the order of the world as perceived through the image of the river. Thus, the speaker declares that his spirit is godlike and antecedent to the birth of the human race. Hughes's concept of the soul is decidedly Platonistic. The "I" of the first three lines exists in some strange, prehistoric, metaphysical dawn.

But with the line "I bathed in the Euphrates when dawns were young," he introduces the reader to actual history. He evokes the image of a universal and ancient black humanity that actively contributes to the building of civilizations. The poem celebrates the American Negro's African origins as the poet identifies with the myriad of workers who labored to build the pyramids.

Then abruptly the images leap forward into modern history where the poet hears the "singing" of the Mississippi and associates it with the Union conquest of the Confederacy and the abolition of slavery in the United States. Now all of the rivers of the poem converge in the speaker's evocation of the Mississippi, which has a special place in the American ethos. The Mississippi, called by the Indians the "Father of Rivers," is the mightiest and most legendary river on the North American continent. Throughout the poem, the speaker is a witness to history. The poet asserts the oneness of his soul with that of the river. Thus, in the tradition of Afro-American spirituals, he has been baptized in the river: and this baptism has conferred upon him a knowledge of his universality and ancestral continuity—a continuity which extends backward into the cosmic past where the rivers were "older than the flow of human blood in human veins."

What we have here is a compressed epic rendered in highly lyrical terms. Despite the obvious universality of the poem, it must not be forgotten that its speaker is a representative of the Negro race.

The "I" of the poem is not the modern, severely alienated "I" of T. S. Eliot's love-song for Prufrock. The comparison may seem somewhat invidious; but the contrast is nonetheless interesting. In Eliot the weight of the years is burdensome for the speaker while Langston's speaker, who is as old as time itself, attempts to occupy a meaningful place at the center of the human universe. The voice in Langston's poem is not simply speaking for himself alone. Rather, his is the collective voice of a people striving to define themselves against a background of political and social oppression. The lyric gestures towards the epic form in that it attempts to express the collective ethos of a profoundly spiritual people. Langston's career, like James Joyce's, especially centers around his attempt to interpret the "soul" of his race.

And for Langston, the soul of his race was best illuminated and manifested in the folklore and musical culture of Black America. For as Professor George Kent notes in an essay on Langston Hughes and the Afro-American folk and cultural tradition: "The folk forms and cultural expressions were themselves definitions of black life created by Blacks on the bloody and pine-scented Southern soil and upon the blackboard jungles of urban streets, tenement buildings, store-front churches, and dim-lit bars. . . ."[2]

Thus, it was this particular vision that led Langston Hughes to attempt a poetic translation of the entire universe of black music. In his poetry and prose one hears the cadences of working-class black people. Langston became a poet who was intimately familiar with the possibilities of "ordinary" black speech and its attendant rhythms. He became interested in the folk tales with their wry humor and wisdom. As for the musical form called the blues, he understood that the bittersweet songs popularized by artists like Bessie Smith, Ma Rainey, Blind Lemon Jefferson, and innumerable others expressed compelling attitudes towards life. These songs, built upon the complex vagaries of the human condition—the mysteries of love, hate, chaos, and economic dislocations—were the stuff of great literature. In his first autobiography, *The Big Sea*, he put it this way:

> I tried to write poems like the songs they sang on Seventh Street (in Washington, D. C.)—gay songs, because you had to be gay or die; sad songs because you couldn't help being sad sometimes. But gay or sad, you kept on living and you kept on going. Their songs—those on Seventh Street—had the pulse beat of the people. . . .[3]

So it is that in Langston's poetry we discover a special kind of attitude towards Afro-American music. And at the core of his poetic strategy is an attempt to *reveal* the ethos of black America as symbolized in black music. Thus, he was not merely concerned with the aesthetic surface of the music. He was not a musicologist. It appears that Langston's intention was to look behind or beneath that surface to the lives of its creators: Langston knows that the musician is not merely an entertainer and that the music does not spring from the same ground as European classical music. Rather, the music stands as a metaphor for the actual conditions of black people in America. In a poem entitled the "Trumpet Player" he gives us this vision:

> The Negro
> With the trumpet at his lips
> Has dark moons of weariness
> Beneath his eyes
> Where the smoldering memory
> Of slave ships
> Blazed to the crack of whips
> About his thighs.

Like the blues singer, Langston is urged to keep alive the painful memories of the ancestral past. He probes beneath the vibrant music to the memory of the slaves' "middle passage" from Africa with its well-known horrors. In the next stanza the Negro musician is seen having altered his African identity by taming down his head of "vibrant hair." Ever aware of irony and what Ralph Ellison called the "American joke," the poet describes the slicked down hair as glowing like a "crown." The music is a kind of contradiction:

> The music
> From the trumpet at his lips

> Is honey
> Mixed with liquid fire.
> The rhythm
> From the trumpet at his lips
> Is ecstacy
> Distilled from old desire—

We learn that these old desires are essentially a longing for a transcendent freedom.

> Desire
> That is longing for the moon
> Where the moonlight's but a spotlight
> In his eyes,
> Desire
> That is longing for the sea
> Where the sea's a bar-glass
> Sucker size.

The poet always sees life in Harlem with a double consciousness. In one context, Langston is the romantic in love with the glorious beauty of his people. And whenever possible, he celebrates the intrinsic spiritual values which give the culture its tone and texture. But he rarely eschews the tough-mindedness of the folk sensibility with its acid-like cynicism. This essential toughnesss of spirit leads him to remind us of the terrible price black people have paid in quest of the urban El Dorados. There is a terror lurking beneath the music:

> The Negro
> With the trumpet at his lips
> Whose jacket
> Has a *fine* one-button roll,
> Does not know
> Upon what riff the music slips
> Its hypodermic needle
> To his soul—

At what point in the musician's encounter with the mystery and the elegance of his art does he become addicted like a common junkie? And at what point does the artist risk the loss of his identity by giving into the rigorous demands of his craft? How does one maintain balance and grace in the ritual journey through the river's fire? In the last stanza the poet gives the answer:

> But softly
> As the tune comes from his throat
> Trouble
> Mellows to a golden note.

Yes, pain is transformed into art. The troubles, the "bad air," are distilled into a compelling and transcendent art form. As in the blues, the troubles are syncopated into a dance beat.

Ralph Ellison's now famous eloquent definition of the blues is pertinent here. Ellison writes that the "blues is an impulse to keep the painful details and episodes of a brutal experience alive in one's aching consciousness, to finger its jagged grain, and to transcend it, not by consolation of philosophy but by squeezing from it a near-tragic, near-comic lyricism. As a form the blues is an autobiographical chronicle of personal catastrophe expressed lyrically." And this is the attitude which informs most of Hughes's blues-oriented poems.

There is a decidedly religious side to Langston's sensibility. This sense of religious ecstasy occurs when the poet tries to express the sensual energy of the music. We especially note this tendency in such pieces as, "Jazzonia," "Song for a Banjo Dance," "When Sue Wears Red," "Spirituals," and "Tambourines." In "Jazzonia," for example, the images of the Harlem cabaret with its dancing girl are juxtaposed against images of the Biblical Eve and the Cleopatra of classical literature:

> Oh, silver tree!
> Oh, shining rivers of the soul!
>
> In a Harlem cabaret
> Six long-headed jazzers play.
> A dancing girl whose eyes are bold
> Lifts high a dress of silken gold.
>
> Oh, singing tree!
> Oh, shining rivers of the soul!
>
> Were Eve's eyes
> In the first garden
> Just a bit too bold?
> Was Cleopatra gorgeous
> In a gown of gold?
>
> O, shining tree!
> Oh, silver rivers of the soul!

> In a whirling cabaret
> Six long-headed jazzers play.[4]

This poetic sensibility is clearly not in a strict Puritan mode. Here, there is a kind of agreement between the sacred and profane— a merger, so to speak, between the sensual and the spiritual. We can also perceive this kind of linkage in the poem, "When Sue Wears Red":

> When Susanna Jones wears red
> Her face is like an ancient cameo
> Turned brown by the ages.
>
> Some with a blast of trumpets,
> Jesus!

This image is highly saturated with internal cultural meanings. There is a kind of racial in-joke involved in its strategy. What Langston does here is riff off on the stereotypical idea that Negroes, as a race, especially like the color red. Bright, primary colors are generally associated with the dressing styles of the black working classes. But the color red, with all of its symbolic overtones, occupies a special place in Afro-American folkways. And Langston, who had a keen ear and eye for folk humor, has lent archetypal weight to the in-house jokes black Americans make about themselves concerning the color red. Langston's red, as used here, symbolizes both royalty and passionate love:

> When Susanna Jones wears red
> A queen from some time-dead Egyptian night
> Walks once again.
>
> Blow trumpets, Jesus!
>
> And the beauty of Susanna Jones in red
> Burns in my heart a love-fire sharp like pain.
>
> Sweet silver trumpets,
> Jesus!

Those joyous shouts that punctuate the poem are essentially double-entendres which function to merge the sacred and profane. The speaker of the poem could either be in church or on a street corner in Harlem. The point is that the beauty of the brown-skinned Sue evokes an ecstatic outburst which can, by a subtle shift in intonation, either express Sue's holiness and regalness, or her passionate sensuality. There is a special exuberance of spirit associated with Afro-American culture. And Langston was not prudish about celebrating it. In "Song for a Banjo Dance," the poet urges the dancer to:

> Get way back, honey,
> *Do that low-down step.*
> Walk on over, darling,
> Now! Come out
> With your left.
> Shake your brown feet, honey,
> Shake 'em, honey chile. [Italics mine][5]

Again there is the double-entendre on the words "low-down step." As used here the words are a description of the choreography of the dance, but they also convey overtones of the erotic. Nonetheless, Langston's eroticism is *never* prurient or voyeuristic. His work always strives to celebrate both the joys and the suffering of life.

Stylistically Langston's poetry is characterized by a robust, direct tone, and by a kind of unadorned, uncontrived eloquence which springs from the actual feel and smell of *real* life. This is why he is the most popularly read and memorized poet in the Afro-American community.

Langston's poetic voice is essentially saturated by the emotional ethos of the blues. His artistic power resides in his skillful rendering of the complex nuances of black, urban speech:

> **Boogie: 1 a.m.**
>
> Good evening, daddy!
> I know you've heard
> The boogie-woogie rumble
> Of a dream deferred
> Trilling the treble
> And twining the bass
> Into midnight ruffles
> Of cat-gut lace.

Langston's poetry rarely exhibits the kind of complexity and density of thought that is often encountered in poetry in the tradition of Pound and Eliot. Despite the absence of cabalistic strageties for literary scholars to gnaw on, a line such as the "boogie-woogie rumble/ of a dream deferred" carries a great deal of lyric clout. Just what does "the boogie woogie" rumble have to do with a "dream deferred"? And just what dream was deferred? Langston's poem "Harlem" gives part of the answer:

> What happens to a dream deferred?
>
> > Does it dry up
> > like a raisin in the sun?
> > Or fester like a sore—
> > And then run?
> > Does it stink like rotten meat?
> > Or crust and sugar over—
> > like a syrupy sweet?
> >
> > Maybe it just sags
> > like a heavy load.
>
> *Or does it explode?*

So the dream of democracy that has been deferred grumbles and rumbles on into the small hours of the Harlem morning. Most of the characters in this montage of deferred dreams persistently question the contradictions of the dream. They are adroitly and eloquently walking the thin line between spiritual self-assertion and despair:

> **Dream Boogie: Variation**
>
> Tinkling treble,
> Rolling bass,
> High noon teeth
> In a midnight face,
> Great long fingers
> On great big hands,
> Screaming pedals
> Where his twelve-shoe lands,
> Looks like his eyes
> Are teasing pain,
> A few minutes late
> For the Freedom Train.

In Langston's blues aesthetic, music is always symbolic of the larger human dilemmas in the social environment. Rarely do we find the musicians in Langston's poetry depicted as creating art devoid of social meaning and human significance. For the people in Langston's poetry the music is clearly, to quote Kenneth Burke, "equipment for living":

> Little cullud boys with fears,
> frantic, kick their draftee years
> into flatted fifths and flatter beers . . .

These lines are from a poem called, "Flatted Fifths." Its title refers to the music of Charlie Parker and Dizzy Gillespie which was notable for the uniquely creative manner in which the flatted fifth was employed in jazz improvisation. To the chagrin of musicians like the drummer Max Roach, that music came to be known as "bebop," and its adherents and fans were called "be-boppers." Thus the poem opens with the lines: "Little cullud boys with beards / re-bop be-bop mop and stop." Here is Langston's attempt to imitate the rhythmic figures of the new urban black music. This is consistent with Langston's aesthetic urge to coax his words as close as possible to actual songs. Like the poetry of Paul Lawrence Dunbar, James Weldon Johnson, Walt Whitman, and Carl Sandburg, Langston's work displays a very compelling emotional quality when read aloud. The aim of this kind of poetry is the lyrical evocation of the working person's struggle to realize the American "dream." And Langston, as the poet laureate of his people, sought persistently to maintain an urgency of voice. He either cursed the dream as nightmare or he celebrated the strength and tenacity of the people as they brought a special brand of folk humor to exploding the illusions of the dream. But through all of this Langston truly believed in the possibility of the dream's realization:

Laughers

> Dream singers,
> Story tellers,
> Dancers,
> Loud laughers in the hands of Fate—
>   My people.
> Dish-washers,
> Elevator-boys,
> Ladies' maids,
> Crap-shooters,
> Cooks,
> Waiters,
> Jazzers,
> Nurses of babies,
> Loaders of ships,
> Rounders,
> Number writers,
> Comedians in vaudeville

And band-men in circuses—
Dream-singers all,—
    My people.
Story-tellers all,—
    My people.
Dancers—
God! What dancers!
    Singers—
God! What singers!
Singers and dancers.
Dancers and laughers.
    Laughers?
Yes, laughers ... laughers ... laughers—
Loud-mouth laughers in the hands
        Of Fate.[6]

Notes

[1] Langston Hughes, *Selected Poems* (New York: Knopf, 1959).   All other poetry quoted in this chapter except where noted is taken from this anthology.

[2] George Kent, *Blackness and the Adventure of Western Culture* (Chicago: Third World Press, 1972).

[3] Langston Hughes, *The Big Sea* (New York: Knopf, 1940).

[4] Stephen Henderson, *Understanding the New Black Poetry* (New York: Morrow, 1973). This critical anthology contains many exciting ideas about the aesthetics of Afro-American poetry.

[5] Henderson.

[6] Henderson.

Bibliography

The Weary Blues. New York: Knopf, 1926.
Fine Clothes to the Jew. New York, Knopf, 1927.

The Big Sea. New York: Knopf, 1940.
Shakespeare in Harlem. New York: Knopf, 1942.
One-Way Ticket. New York: Knopf, 1949.
Simple Speaks His Mind. New York: Simon and Schuster, 1950.
Montage of a Dream Deferred. New York: Henry Holt, 1951.
I Wonder as I Wander. New York: Rinehart, 1956.
The Langston Hughes Reader. New York: Braziller, 1958.
Selected Poems. New York: Knopf, 1959.
The Best of Simple. New York: Knopf, 1959.
Ask Your Mama: 12 Moods for Jazz. New York: Knopf, 1961.
Something in Common, and Other Stories. New York: Hill & Wang, 1963.
The Panther and the Lash. New York: Knopf, 1967.

About Langston Hughes:

Emanuel, James A. *Langston Hughes.* New York: Twayne, 1967.
Henderson, Stephen. *Understanding the New Black Poetry.* New York: Morrow, 1973.
Kent, George. *Blackness and the Adventure of Western Culture.* Chicago: Third World Press, 1972.
Wagner, Jean, *Black Poets of the United States.* Translated from the French by Kenneth Douglas. Champaign: University of Illinois Press, 1973.

Kenneth Burke

Richard Kostelanetz

For me, his life is a design, gives me satisfaction enough, always from the viewpoint of an interest in writing. He is one of the rarest things in America: He lives here, he is married, has a family, a house, lives directly by writing without having much sold out.
William Carlos Williams
"Kenneth Burke" (1929)

In May 1975, the American Academy and National Institute of Arts and Letters had their annual simultaneous meeting in which new members were inducted and standing awards disbursed. The same polite applause followed every announcement until a swell of hand-clapping greeted an elderly, compactly built, short man whose name, while scarcely known to the general public, has long commanded the highest respect in the literary trade. Simply, Kenneth Burke is a writer whom other writers enormously respect. The award he received was cast in gold; its title: "Distinguished Service Medal."

There has not been anyone quite like him in American literature since Ralph Waldo Emerson; and Burke's activity, like Emerson's, falls into several categories and yet transcends any of them in its total scope. Burke has published one novel, *Towards a Better Life* (1932); a book of short stories, *The Complete White Oxen* (1924; augmented edition, 1968); and enough poetry to fill a *Collected Poems 1915-1967* (1968). He also did an early translation of Thomas Mann's "Death in Venice" that some people prefer to those more recently available. There are three big books ostensibly of literary criticism, *Counter-Statement* (1931), *The Philosophy of Literary Form* (1941), *Language as Symbolic Action* (1966), and then six more titles that are about something else—sociology a bit, pedagogy a bit less, "theorizing" a bit more: *Permanence and Change* (1935), *Attitudes Toward History* (1937), *A Grammar of Motives* (1945), *A Rhetoric of Motives* (1950), *A Rhetoric of*

Religion: Studies in Logology (1961), and *Dramatism and Development* (1972). These last books are so diffuse, so leavened, so unsystematic that they are not "philosopy" in any formal sense but something else—something thoroughly idiosyncratic; Burkology.

Born Kenneth Duva Burke in Pittsburgh, on May 5, 1897, he went to public high school (where one classmate was the literary critic Malcolm Cowley) and then to Ohio State for a semester. Since his father had meanwhile taken a job in Hoboken, he went to live with his parents in nearby Weehawken, commuting by ferry and subway to Columbia for another year, before dropping out of college completely, not because he disliked it but because academic rigamarole kept him from taking the advanced courses he wanted. Instead, he went to live in Greenwich Village in a house that was filled with young artists and writers, the painter Stuart Davis and the novelist Djuna Barnes among them; and within a few years, his poems and essays were appearing regularly in literary journals.

Married in 1919, he had his first child in 1922, the year he moved to a farm on Amity Road in Andover, New Jersey, and he has lived there ever since. Initially he commuted by bicycle, train, ferry, and trolley to New York City and its literary scene, working for spells as an editorial assistant at *The Dial*, the most consequential literary magazine of the period, and then for a full year ghostwriting a book on drug addiction for the Rockefeller Foundation. Unlike Cowley, among other writers of his "lost generation," Burke never went to Europe. He remembers that he had planned to go since the middle 1920s, but always a crisis got in the way. "A kid was born, or something around here had to be fixed. Suddenly I discovered that everyone was coming back here," which is to say that World War II had begun. Not until the 1970s, after his second wife's death, did Burke finally get to Europe, visiting Italy, France, England, and Spain, mostly to give lectures and participate in conferences. This absence may explain why so little of his writing has been translated into other languages or why so few European intellectuals know his name. A second reason is that in his styles of writing and thinking Burke has always been egregiously American.

Just after the New Year 1981, I went to visit Burke in Andover, which is a small town in New Jersey's northernmost county. "Rustic" is scarcely the word for his compound of renovated barns, small farmhouses, garages, and outhouses. Electricity and telephones did not come here until the late 1950s, and running water came just to his own house a decade later. Central heating has not yet been discovered on this property. Burke is probably the last major American writer to have read mostly by kerosene light.

Burke greeted me with a ready smile, his booming, rustic, distinctly American voice inviting me into his kitchen, which is the warmest room in the house. With piles of books and papers all over the other ground-floor rooms, this is clearly the home, within a farmhouse, of a literary bachelor. "Everything gets lost around this goddam place about ten minutes after I get it," he told me. "If you can't find something right away, it is ridiculous to look for it." Bookcases fill most of the walls. At one end of the space is a manual typewriter; at another end is a piano with handwritten scores of melodies that had recently been coming into Burke's head. On the mantelpiece is a certificate from the American Academy of Arts and Letters. The medal itself is in a vault. "It's gold, you know," he reminded me.

His hair has thinned considerably in recent years, and what remains is stark white. Around his mouth is a trim Van Dyke beard. The day we met he wore farm clothes—corduroys, a gray sweater over a flannel shirt that was open at the neck, a jacket with pens in the handkerchief pocket, and sensible walking shoes. He puts on his glasses only to read. To go outside in the snow, he merely donned an overcoat and cap—no gloves or earmuffs for him. He speaks in vigorous bursts, punctuated by pauses for breath, in a slangy style that I would characterize as "informal American." He likes to talk, to tell stories and jokes, and to laugh heartily at his own humor. Often brilliant by the sentence, he can become more confusing over larger units.

As usual, he has been working on his books, arising at dawn and working through the afternoon, cooking his own meals and then doing household chores and watching television in the evening. There are four books near completion: one on Shakespeare, another on devices, a third based on lectures he gave recently at SUNY-Buffalo, and "A Symbolic of Motives" that completes the trilogy begun with *A Grammar*. He has also been working not on the memoirs that some people think he should write—his memory is keen and his anecdotes vivid—but on an intellectual autobiography that he hopes will summarize his thinking. On the side he continues to write essays and occasional poems for the American cultural magazines that have always been his principal forum. Within the past few years some of the former have appeared in *Kenyon Review*, *American Imago*, and the

Journal of the American Academy of Religion, among others. Nearly all of his non-fiction books are not sustained expositions but collections of previously published essays.

* * * * *

He is a critic for the adventurous; you take from him what you can get, and only later realize how much it was.
Robert Martin Adams
New York Review of Books (1966)

One reason why Burke is not better known is that his books are as uncompromising as his life-style and speech. There is no way that anyone, even an aggressive publisher, can sell them (or him) to a large audience. His books are disorganized; they are filled with unfamiliar words, at times of his own invention (e.g., "dramatism," "logology," "socioanagogic"). They abound with explanations that do not explain, elucidations that do not elucidate, clarifications that do not clarify. His characteristic structural device is the digression. As Howard Nemerov put it, "His mind cannot stop exploding."

Some of his sentences are brilliant, if not aphoristic: literature is "equipment for living." "Nothing can more effectively set people at odds than the demand that they think alike." "Form in literature is the arousing and fulfillment of desires." His metaphors are outrageous—who else in an essay about John Keats and his Grecian Urn would compare a literary critic to "a radio commentator broadcasting a blow-by-blow description of a prize-fight," or the Teutonic prose of Kant and Hegel to "the shifting of cars in a freight yard"? Burke loves to refer familiarly to earlier works of his, if not quote from them at length, less out of egomania than out of impatience to get onto his next urgent point. He is intellectually unpredictable even to those who think they know him well, while his use of evidence is at times capricious. In truth, Burke's eccentric style is profoundly American; no European thinker could write like this, even if he tried.

Wayne Booth, a University of Chicago professor who is one of Burke's closest readers, warns that he "invents problems that are essentially beyond solution and then claims to solve them by using principles that can be assumed only as part of his invention. His whole enterprise is impossibly, shockingly ambitious; yet it finally frustrates intellectual ambition by undermining all solutions." In truth, all his ideas cannot be completely summarized in an article; a monograph is scarcely spacious enough. No summary can substitute for the experience of reading the Burkean text itself; in that sense, his work is closer than most expository writing to the art of poetry. For now, it is best to identify certain themes.

One is that a work of art is an organic collection of "strategies" or rhetorical devices that "aim" to affect readers in certain discernible ways, so that the first task of literary criticism is identifying "a generating principle, in terms of which you can account for all the work's most important developments." A second theme is that narrative usually functions as a "symbolic action" for a mythic base; in literature, the principal ritual ("the arousing and fulfilling of an audience's expectations") portrays various forms of rebirth. A third related idea is that in creating a literary work the writer suffers a ritual of personal purification through the articulation of subconscious conflicts. When he or she succeeds artistically, the work relates to his or her life by offering model strategies for "encompassing situations." Thus, on the one hand, the analysis of a writer's language can be understood as revealing his deepest psychology; on the other, Burke echoes the Aristotelian idea of poetry as cathartic to its audience, the work thus requiring the "completion" or fulfillment of the expectation it creates.

Analysis of "symbolic action," that characteristic Burkean epithet, thus involves the study of the relation of the work both to its author and to its readers, for Burke has developed an interesting, illuminating way of regarding literary works as reflecting and providing strategies for life. Another Burkean theme is that the critical tools developed in literary analysis can also be applied to non-literary expository texts to reveal their imaginative, "dramatistic" organization. As Stanley Edgar Hyman put it, "Anyone reading him for the first time has the sudden sense of a newly discovered country in his own backyard."

As a critic of literature, Burke believes that it is better to trust the tale than the teller, and in the following passages is a glimpse of his analytic style:

> By charting clusters, we get out clues to the important ingredients subsumed in "symbolic mergers." We reveal, beneath an author's "official front," the level at which a lie is impossible. If a man's virtuous characters are dull, and his wicked characters are done vigorously, his *art* has

> voted for the wicked ones, regardless of his "official front."
> If a man talks of *glory* but employs the imagery of *desolation*,
> his *true subject* is desolation.

Thus, it is the ultimate aim of Burkean literary criticism to prepare readers' minds better to understand imaginative literature.

The keystones in his literary criticism are extended essays, many of them over 10,000 words in length, on such classic subjects as Shakespeare's plays, Goethe's *Faust*, Coleridge's "Kubla Khan," and Keats's "Ode to a Grecian Urn," as well as St. Augustine's *Confessions* and Hitler's *Mein Kampf*. It is in these essays that he demonstrates his capacity for spectacularly attentive and systematic reading of a verbal text. When I asked him how this was done, he produced a copy of a book he had once reviewed, Harold Bloom's extended critical essay on Wallace Stevens. On every page are perhaps 20 inked annotations. Key words are underlined, vertical lines trace connections. On the blank pages in the back of the book and even on the fly leaves are more extensive notes, some of them referring to the book in general and others to particular passages. This is the kind of critical artifact that should be on permanent display in every university library.

One quality these major essays have is the use of several sorts of critical tools, most of them drawn from intellectual domains outside literature; for within the profession of literary criticism, Burke has exemplified the principle of "all there is to use"—all the analytic equipment that is available. These essays are also so dense and suggestive with insights and hypotheses, as well as digressions, that they, unlike most literary criticism, can be profitably reread time and time again with increasing comprehension. As early as 1941, W. H. Auden identified Burke as "unquestionably the most brilliant and suggestive critic now writing in America." In *Modern Literary Criticism* (1977), a huge person-by-person survey, Elmer Borklund credits Burke with "a body of work which in sheer size and complexity is unmatched by the efforts of any critic since Coleridge," which is to say that for quality, variety, quantity, and originality Burke has no equal.

Because of his emphasis upon reading a literary text in a complex and thorough way, Burke was regarded as a principal figure of the so-called New Criticism that seemed so dominant in the 1950s, while his interest in psychology made him an exemplary Freudian critic as well. Nonetheless, his long-standing concern with the encompassing structural elements in literature relate him to today's fashions in sophisticated literary criticism. One reason why Burke has survived professionally is that current interests keep abreast of him. To Harold Bloom, the Yale literary theorist and critic, "Kenneth Burke seems to me the strongest living representative of the American critical tradition. My own criticism, since it changed in about 1967 or so, owes more to Burke than to any other figure. Burke, rather than Foucault or Derrida, provides for central American critics their inevitable ideas of the Negative and its uses."

The best guide to Burke's literary thinking remains the penultimate chapter of Stanley Edgar Hyman's *The Armed Vision* (1949); the most useful introduction to Burkology are the two paperback anthologies that Hyman coedited with Barbara Karmiller, *Perspective by Incongruity* (1964) and *Terms for Order* (1964). The best summary of "dramatism," or Burkean sociology, is Burke's own contribution to the *International Encyclopedia of the Social Sciences* (1967). The closest semblance of an intellectual biography is Armin Paul Frank's *Kenneth Burke* (1969).

Perhaps the surest index of the variousness and richness of Burke's writing is the richness and variousness of the works that they have clearly influenced—not only literary criticism but sociology as well, for sociologists, like literary critics, have found in his books fertile ideas that could be developed and formalized into well-known theories. Burke's analytical method of "perspective by incongruity" has visibly informed Erving Goffman's books, beginning with *The Presentation of the Self in Everyday Life* (1959), while Hugh Dalziel Duncan wrote several books, including *Communication and Social Order* (1962), on the Burkean theme that art is the base of all communication (in contrast to Durkheim, among others, who defined religion as the base). Burke is also cited at the beginning of Robert K. Merton's work on the bureaucratic personality, C. Wright Mills's essay on the vocabulary of motives, and Harold Garfinkel's essay on degradation ceremonies. Sociologists such as Marvin D. Scott identify Burke as an American precursor to French structuralist theory.

Burke is also the major influence behind Stanley Edgar Hyman's *The Tangled Bank* (1961), which is a brilliant and monumental analysis of the artistic strategies in the writings of Karl Marx, James G. Fraser, Sigmund Freud, and Charles Darwin. Burke's notion of the myth of purpose, passion, pain, and perception, as well as of narrative rebirth, inform his friend Ralph Ellison's classic novel, *Invisible Man* (1951). "Kenneth's analysis of how language operates in society has been very important to me," Ellison said recently. "He remains one of the most useful authors for the writer, or for anyone interested in how language shapes, directs and achieves human motives." These examples hardly expire an exhaustive catalogue, for there is no one else for whom the epithet *seminal* is more appropriate. Nonetheless, precisely because Burke's writings cannot be reduced to a few accessible doctrines, there has never been a school, let alone a class, of Burkites.

Burke may not be writing his memoirs, but anyone who has seen him recently knows that he can look back proudly on 60 years of writing, publishing mostly in literary magazines and then in a dozen books (that are, to their credit, *all* indicatively still in print), of lecturing to scores of audiences, of influencing professionals in several fields, of siring a loyal clan, of living a literary life with unfailing integrity. It is not surprising that he earned more applause than anyone else at the American Academy.

Bibliography

By Kenneth Burke:

Counter-Statement. Berkeley: University of California Press, 1968. (First edition 1931).
The Philosophy of Literary Form: Studies in Symbolic Action. Berkeley: University of California Press, 1973. (First edition 1941)
A Grammar of Motives. Berkeley: University of California Press, 1969. (First edition 1945)
A Rhetoric of Motives. Berkeley: University of California Press, 1969. (First edition 1950)
Language as Symbolic Action: Essays on Life, Literature and Method. Berkeley: University of California Press, 1966.

About Kenneth Burke:

Frank, Armin Paul. *Kenneth Burke*. New York: Twayne, 1969.
Rueckert, William H. *Kenneth Burke and the Drama of Human Relations*. Minneapolis: University of Minnesota Press, 1963.
—, editor. *Critical Response to Kenneth Burke: 1924-1966*. Minneapolis: University of Minnesota Press, 1969.

Kenneth Rexroth

Donald Hall

Among Kenneth Rexroth's lesser accomplishments, he appears as a character in two famous novels. James T. Farrell put him in the *Studs Lonigan* trilogy (1932-35), where he is a kid named Kenny working in a drugstore. With more creative denomination, Jack Kerouac called him Rheinhold Cacoethes in *The Dharma Bums,* that 1958 Beat Generation testament, where he is the figure we recognize: anarchist, leader of San Francisco's literary community, and poet.

For decades he has written lines like these, setting human life in a context of stone:

> Our campfire is a single light
> Amongst a hundred peaks and waterfalls.
> The manifold voices of falling water
> Talk all night.
> Wrapped in your down bag
> Starlight on your cheeks and eyelids
> Your breath comes and goes
> In a tiny cloud in the frosty night.
> Ten thousand birds sing in the sunrise.
> Ten thousand years revolve without change.
> All this will never be again.

One thing that is without change is that everything changes. Like many of the greatest poets—Wordsworth, Keats, Frost, Eliot—Rexroth returns continually to one inescapable perception. Maybe this elegiac vision of permanent stone and vanishing flesh derives from the great private event of his middle years—the death of his first wife Andrée in 1940 after 13 years of marriage. Her name and image return decades after her death.

But Rexroth is not limited to elegy; he is the most erotic of modern American poets, and one of the most political. The great

public event of his young life was the execution of Sacco and Vanzetti.
Years after the electrocution he wrote "Climbing Milestone Mountain":

> In the morning
> We swam in the cold transparent lake, the blue
> Damsel flies on all the reeds like millions
> Of narrow metallic flowers, and I thought
> Of you behind the grille in Dedham, Vanzetti,
> Saying, "Who would ever have thought we would make
> 	this history?"
> Crossing the brilliant mile-square meadow
> Illuminated with asters and cyclamen
> The pollen of the lodgepole pines drifting
> With the shifting wind over it and the blue
> And sulphur butterflies drifting with the wind,
> I saw you in the sour prison light, saying,
> "Goodbye comrade."

In Rexroth's poems the natural world, unchanged and changing,
remains background to history and love, to enormity and bliss.

As a young man, Rexroth was a Wobbly—an Industrial Worker
of the World, or IWW—and he studied Marxism as a member of a John
Reed Club. Later he became anarchist and pacifist, ideologies which
his mature philosophic poems support with passion and argument.
His politics of the individual separates him from the mass of Americans—and obviously from Stalinists—and yet joins him to all human
beings; it is a politics of love—and Rexroth is the poet of devoted
eroticism. "When We With Sappho" begins by translating from a
Greek fragment, then continues into a personal present:

> " . . . about the cool water
> the wind sounds through sprays
> of apple, and from the quivering leaves
> slumber pours down . . . "
>
> We lie here in the bee filled, ruinous
> Orchard of a decayed New England farm,
> Summer in our hair, and the smell
> Of summer in our twined bodies,
> Summer in our mouths, and summer
> In the luminous, fragmentary words
> Of this dead Greek woman.
> Stop reading. Lean back. Give me your mouth.
> Your grace is as beautiful as sleep.
> You move against me like a wave

That moves in sleep.
Your body spreads across my brain
Like a bird filled summer;
Not like a body, not like a separate thing,
But like a nimbus that hovers
Over every other thing in all the world.
Lean back. You are beautiful,
As beautiful as the folding
Of your hands in sleep.

This passionate tenderness has not diminished as Rexroth has aged.
His latest book includes the beautiful "Love Poems of Marichiko,"
which he calls a translation from the Japanese; however, a recent
bibliography lists the translation of Rexroth's "Marichiko" *into* Japanese: in the middle of his eighth decade, the poet has written his most
erotic poem.

His work for 40 years has moved among his passions for the
flesh, for human justice, and for the natural world. He integrates these
loves in the long poems and sometimes in briefer ones like "Lyell's
Hypothesis Again":

Lyell's Hypothesis Again

*An Attempt to Explain the Former
Changes of the Earth's Surface by
Causes Now in Operation
Subtitle of Lyell: Principles of Geology*

The mountain road ends here,
Broken away in the chasm where
The bridge washed out years ago.
The first scarlet larkspur glitters
In the first patch of April
Morning sunlight. The engorged creek
Roars and rustles like a military
Ball. Here by the waterfall,
Insuperable life, flushed
With the equinox, sentient
And sentimental, falls away
To the sea and death. The tissue
Of sympathy and agony
That binds the flesh in its Nessus' shirt;
The clotted cobweb of unself
And self; sheds itself and flecks
The sun's bed with darts of blossom
Like flagellant blood above

The water bursting in the vibrant
Air. This ego, bound by personal
Tragedy and the vast
Impersonal vindictiveness
Of the ruined and ruining world,
Pauses in this immortality,
As passionate, as apathetic,
As the lava flow that burned here once;
And stopped here; and said, 'This far
And no further.' And spoke thereafter
In the simple diction of stone.

———

Naked in the warm April air,
We lie under the redwoods,
In the sunny lee of a cliff.
As you kneel above me I see
Tiny red marks on your flanks
Like bites, where the redwood cones
Have pressed into your flesh.
You can find just the same marks
In the lignite in the cliff
Over our heads. *Sequoia
Langsdorfii* before the ice,
And *sempervirens* afterwards,
There is little difference,
Except for all those years.

Here in the sweet, moribund
Fetor of spring flowers, washed,
Flotsam and jetsam together,
Cool and naked together,
Under this tree for a moment,
We have escaped the bitterness
Of love, and love lost, and love
Betrayed. And what might have been,
And what might be, fall equally
Away with what is, and leave
Only these ideograms
Printed on the immortal
Hydrocarbons of flesh and stone.

The poet writes best when his passions coalesce.

It is the strength of Rexroth's language that it proscribes nothing. He uses words from the natural sciences and from mathematics,
as well as philosophical abstractions which modern poetic practice is

supposed to avoid. If he sometimes aims to speak in "the simple diction of stone," he refuses the temptation to purity: this same brief poem uses classical reference, scientific terminology and Latin taxonomy, earth-history, the "flagellant blood" of Christianity, and intimate common speech: "tiny red marks on your flanks / like bites. . . ."

In "Lyell's Hypothesis Again" we hear Rexroth's characteristic rhythm—swift and urgent, slow and meditative, powerful; his line hovers around three accents, mostly seven or eight syllables long. (Much of his poetry is strictly syllabic.) It is remarkable how little Rexroth's line has changed over 40 years, in a world of poetic fashions. This steadfastness or stubbornness recalls his patience over publication: he did not publish a book of poems until 1940, when he was 35 years old, although he had been writing since the early 1920s. Later, in *The Art of Worldly Wisdom* (1949), he collected and published work from his Cubist youth. Some had appeared in Louis Zukofsky's *An Objectivists' Anthology* (1932).

When we try to describe a poet's style, it can be useful to name starting points, but that is not easy with Kenneth Rexroth. He has said that Tu Fu was the greatest influence on him; fair enough, but there is no analogy between the Chinese line, end-stopped, with its count of characters, and Rexroth's run-in enjambed syllabics. In temperament and idea Rexroth is close to D. H. Lawrence, about whom he wrote his first major essay in 1947. But Lawrence's best poems take off from Whitman's line—and Rexroth's prosody is as far from Whitman's as it can get. Perhaps there is a bit of William Carlos Williams in his enjambed lines; maybe Louis Zukofsky. We could say, throwing up our hands, that he is a synthesis of Tu Fu, Lawrence, and Mallarmé. To an unusual extent, Rexroth made Rexroth up.

* * * * *

He was born in Indiana in 1905 and spent most of the 1920s in Chicago's Bohemia—poet, painter, and autodidact. Late in the decade he moved to San Francisco where he has lived much of his life, moving down the coast to Santa Barbara only in 1968. He was the poet of San Francisco even before Robert Duncan, Philip Lamantia, Kenneth Patchen, and William Everson (Brother Antoninus). For decades he has advocated the poetry of the West, the elder literary figure of the city where poetry came to happen: Jack Spicer, Philip Whalen, Michael McClure, Lawrence Ferlinghetti, Lew Welch, Joanne Kyger. . . . His influence on the young is obvious, clearest in Gary Snyder, who is worthy of his master. When young writers from the East arrived in the 1950s—Allen Ginsberg, Jack Kerouac, Gregory Corso—they attended gatherings at Rexroth's house, and it was Rexroth who was catalyst for the 1955 Six Gallery reading that was the public birth of the Beat Generation.

Later, alliances altered. . . . Talking about Kenneth Rexroth, it is easy to wander into the history of factionalism, for he has been partisan, and few polemicists have had a sharper tongue. Inventor of *"The Vaticide Review"* (apparently referring to *The Partisan Review*, but it can stand in for all the quarterlies), he wrote in 1957 of poet-professors, "Ninety-nine percent of them don't even exist but are androids manufactured from molds, cast from Randall Jarrell by the lost wax process." On the west coast he has been a constant, grumpy presence. If the West has taken him for granted, the East has chosen to ignore him, perhaps because he has taken potshots at the provincial East forever and ever. The *Harvard Guide to Contemporary American Writing* (1979), which purports to cover the scene since 1945, will do for an example: the poetry critic quotes *none* of Rexroth's poetry but sputters about his "intemperate diatribes." Nor does Rexroth make the *New York Review of Books* shortlist of Approved Contemporaries. Which is a pity, because he is better than anyone on it.

Taste is always a fool—the consensus of any moment; contemporary taste is the agreement of diffident people to quote each other's opinions. It reaffirms with complacency reputations which are perceived as immemorial, but which are actually constructed of rumor, laziness, and fear. As a writer ages and issues new volumes, he or she is reviewed as if the writing had remained the same, because it would require brains and effort to alter not only one's past opinion but the current professional assessment.

Perhaps the consensus of our moment, product largely of the East and the academy, is especially ignorant, especially gullible. Or perhaps it is only—in the matter of Kenneth Rexroth—that the tastemakers are offended by Rexroth's morals. In fact they *ought* to be because the ethical ideas that Rexroth puts forward with such acerbity are old-fashioned and individual—anathema to the suburban, Volvo-driving, conformist liberalism of the academy. He stands firm against technocracy and its bureaus and hierarchies, to which the university is as devoted an institution as General Motors. Rexroth's morals derive in part from Indiana before the First World War, in part from centuries of oriental thought, and in part from the radical non-Marxist thinking of late 19th-century Europe.

He has not been wholly without attention. James Laughlin of *New Directions* has been his loyal publisher who keeps his poetry in print. Morgan Gibson wrote a book about him which lists many reviews and articles about his poetry; a magazine called *The Ark* devoted a 1980 issue to his work; his reading aloud to music, which is superb and innovative, can be heard on several tapes and records.

Still, he should be acclaimed as one of the great poets of our literature because he has written poems like "The Signature of All Things."

> My head and shoulders, and my book
> In the cool shade, and my body
> Stretched bathing in the sun, I lie
> Reading beside the waterfall—
> Boehme's "Signature of all Things."
> Through the deep July day the leaves
> Of the laurel, all the colors
> Of gold, spin down through the moving
> Deep laurel shade all day. They float
> On the mirrored sky and forest
> For a while, and then, still slowly
> Spinning, sink through the crystal deep
> Of the pool to its leaf gold floor.
> The saint saw the world as streaming
> In the electrolysis of love.
> I put him by and gaze through shade
> Folded into shade of slender
> Laurel trunks and leaves filled with sun.
> The wren broods in her moss domed nest.
> A newt struggles with a white moth
> Drowning in the Pool. The hawks scream,
> Playing together on the ceiling
> Of heaven. The long hours go by.
> I think of those who have loved me,
> Of all the mountains I have climbed,
> Of all the seas I have swum in.
> The evil of the world sinks.
> My own sin and trouble fall away
> Like Christian's bundle, and I watch
> My forty summers fall like falling
> Leaves and falling water held
> Eternally in summer air

Deer are stamping in the glades,
Under the full July moon.
There is a smell of dry grass
In the air, and more faintly,
The scent of a far off skunk.
As I stand at the wood's edge,
Watching the darkness, listening
To the stillness, a small owl
Comes to the branch above me,
On wings more still than my breath.
When I turn my light on him,
His eyes glow like drops of iron,
And he perks his head at me,
Like a curious kitten.
The meadow is bright as snow.
My dog prowls the grass, a dark
Blur in the blur of brightness.
I walk to the oak grove where
The Indian village was once.
There, in blotched and cobwebbed light
And dark, dim in the blue haze,
Are twenty Holstein heifers,
Black and white, all lying down,
Quietly together, under
The hugh trees rooted in the graves.

—————

When I dragged the rotten log
From the bottom of the pool,
It seemed heavy as stone.
I let it lie in the sun
For a month; and then chopped it
Into sections, and split them
For kindling, and spread them out
To dry some more. Late that night,
After reading for hours,
While moths rattled at the lamp—
The saints and the philosophers
On the destiny of man—
I went out on my cabin porch,
And looked up through the black forest
At the swaying islands of stars.
Suddenly I saw at my feet,
Spread on the floor of night, ingots
Of quivering phosphorescence,
And all about were scattered chips
Of pale cold light that was alive.

Starting from his reading in a Christian mystic (Jacob Boehme, 1575-1624), he writes vividly of the natural world, he refers to *Pilgrim's Progress*, he ranges out into the universe of stars and focuses back upon the world of heifers and minute phosphorescent organisms. It is a poetry of experience and observation, of knowledge and allusion, and finally a poetry of wisdom.

This poem comes from the *Collected Shorter Poems* (1967). There is also a *Collected Longer Poems* (1968); they are five in number, including "The Phoenix and the Tortoise," a 30-page meditative philosophic poem from the early 1940s, and "The Dragon and the Unicorn," from the second half of the same decade, which describes European travel and argues on a high level of abstraction. Best of the long poems is the latest, "The Heart's Garden, the Garden's Heart" (1967).

There is also a collection of verse plays. There are many volumes of prose: *An Autobiographical Novel* (1966), several volumes of essays both literary and political, and a rapid polemical literary history called *American Poetry in the Twentieth Century* (1971). In addition, Rexroth has translated from Latin, Greek, French, German, Spanish, Swedish, but it is his work in Chinese and Japanese which is deservedly best known—beginning with *One Hundred Poems from the Chinese* (1956). Certainly his verse translations remain among the best work in an age of translation.

But if we look for the best, we look to his own poems. To end with, here is a lyric from his *New Poems* of 1974:

Your Birthday in the
California Mountains

A broken moon on the cold water,
And wild geese crying high overhead,
The smoke of the campfire rises
Toward the geometry of heaven—
Points of light in the infinite blackness.
I watch across the narrow inlet
Your dark figure comes and goes before the fire.
A loon cries out on the night bound lake.
Then all the world is silent with the
Silence of autumn waiting for
The coming of winter. I enter
The ring of firelight, bringing to you
A string of trout for our dinner.
As we eat by the whispering lake,
I say, "Many years from now we will

Remember this night and talk of it."
Many years have gone by since then, and
Many years again. I remember
That night as though it was last night,
But you have been dead for thirty years.

Bibliography

By Kenneth Rexroth:

The Art of Worldly Wisdom. Prairie City, Illinois: Decker Press, 1949.
100 Poems from the Chinese. New York: New Directions, 1956. (As translator)
An Autobiographical Novel. Garden City, New York: Doubleday, 1966; reprinted,
      Santa Barbara, California: Ross-Erickson, 1978.
The Collected Shorter Poems. New York: New Directions, 1967.
The Collected Longer Poems. New York: New Directions, 1968.
American Poetry in the Twentieth Century. New York: Herder & Herder, 1971.
The Rexroth Reader. Edited by Eric Mottram. London: Cape, 1972.
New Poems. New York: New Directions, 1974.
The Morning Star. New York: New Directions, 1979.

About Kenneth Rexroth:

Gardner, Geoffrey, editor. "For Rexroth" Issue. *The Ark* (New York), Vol. 14 (1980).
      (With tributes by W. S. Mervin, William Everson, James Wright and others.)
Gibson, Morgan. *Kenneth Rexroth.* New York: Twayne, 1972.
Parkinson, Thomas. "Kenneth Rexroth, Poet." *The Ohio Review,* Vol. 17, No. 2
      (Winter 1976).

Saul Bellow

Ihab Hassan

There may be some truths which are, after all, our friends in the universe.

Saul Bellow

Praise now comes as naturally to Saul Bellow as the light of day. A Nobel laureate in 1976, winner of three National Book Awards, two Guggenheim Fellowships, one Pulitzer Prize, and many other honors, he fills our expectations of a major novelist and aligns himself with the central tradition of Western literature; for his achievement, though deep in the American grain, appears more and more universal in its apprehensions of reality.

Adhering intuitively to "the axial lines of existence," Bellow's quest for that reality has taken him through many climes of his life and our age. Born in 1915 in Lachine, Canada—he was the fourth and last child of Russian Jewish emigrants from St. Petersburg—he came with his parents to Chicago in 1924, settling down on Division Street. Like Augie March, fictive Chicagoan, free-style and city bred, Bellow has remained faithful to the genius of that place though he traveled far to Stockholm and Paris, Kyoto and Jerusalem. A literary intellectual, read widely in history and philosophy, sociology and anthropology, he yet refuses to render the rough texture of American experience into abstract schemes or parodic games. A Jew by birth, who grew up speaking Yiddish and Hebrew, French and English, he maintains both his Old World heritage and complex New World fate without constraint to his vision.[1] In this, he incarnates the authority of the classic European realists—Cervantes, Balzac, Dickens, Tolstoy—as well as those American moderns—Dreiser, Faulkner, Hemingway—whom he admires best

Bellow's work changes, develops over four decades, but his

fidelity to some vital concerns, some "friendly truths" or Heraclitean "essence of things," gives that work continuity, marking it with the seal of an original temper.[2] For the center of that novelistic temper is not fashionably "hollow"; nor, despite all our "distractions," does the center break. Quite the contrary: "Out of the struggle at the center has come an immense, painful longing for a broader, more flexible, fuller, more coherent, more comprehensive account of what we human beings are, who we are, and what this life is for," Bellow declares in his Nobel speech.[3] The center, then, radically affirms being or what few novelists now dare to name: spirit, soul.[4] But what else does that "comprehensive account" include?

It includes, of course, everything we ascribe to the real: knowledge, love, freedom, death, power, morality, society, all the various joys and afflictions of being human, and language itself which takes us to the edge of what we can grasp. I put knowledge first because, increasingly, Bellow appears as a cognitive, even a gnostic, writer who carries his epistemological investigations to their imaginative limits in his quest for reality. All else seems mere "distraction," "harassment," "frenzy," "dissolution by detail," "sheer noise," in a world much "too much with us."[5] Since mind has become the active human environment even more than nature, the true "revolution" must also be noetic, spiritual: "It will have to do with the internal state."[6] Thus Bellow, to the consternation of conventional critics, challenges in his later work narrow and tedious acceptations of rationality.

Yet Bellow would have scarcely impressed us as a major author on the strength of his gnostic motive alone; the density of history, the quiddity of culture, the particularity of meaning, always mediate his vision, which recovers for us the value of flesh and bone. Struggling with the obdurate facts of America, of contemporary life really, his imagination refuses to abdicate. For Bellow sensed before all the "new journalists" that the "facts themselves are not what they once were and perhaps present themselves to the imagination of the artist in a new way."[7] The imaginative discovery of these new facts makes Bellow, like so many of his heroes, a Columbus of the near at hand. But this mariner sails not only the shallows of American society; he must also navigate inward, secret seas.[8] And returning from his fictive voyage, more quest than voyage, he testifies in that novel speech which we call style.

The character of Bellow's evolving style, like that of his social perceptions, partly derives form the situation of the serious writer whose feelings must run counter to the dominant culture, for whom art and authority must remain disjunctive. Thus the most affirmative of American novelists must also dissent, giving scope to his opposing self when the world attempts to seduce or dissolve that self as mass society and modernist thought, respectively, threaten to do. Resolutely, sometimes crankily, Bellow resists both seduction and dissolution on behalf of his readers as well as himself. "One can seduce the public by giving them precisely what they want. Or, with the authority of art, one can risk their displeasure by telling them what is really in their hearts and hope that somehow or other, one will get through," he remarks.[9] It is, of course, the latter stance that Bellow has tried to maintain from the start, despite all his misgivings about the authority of art.

This stance—simultaneously one of search and avoidance, openness and resistance—also characterizes so many of Bellow's heroes, who become outsiders, rebel-victims to various degrees. The quest for true knowledge may lead them to know love or death, may end all too humanly in qualified failure or conditional success; yet it remains always an aspect of their moral, indeed of their metaphysical freedom; for some truths act on the side of life, Bellow insists. Such truths come not from sundry ideologues—"reality instructors" as he calls them—but from hints, persistent intuitions, secret promptings that the heroes themselves experience.

Yet Bellow's heroes are nothing ethereal. If they come finally to wisdom or humility, they often begin in bitter humiliation. Plaintive, crotchety, querulous, they cultivate their quotidian defeats in the spirit of hope, longing for a harmony on the other side of innocence. There is something in them of Gimpel the Fool, the title character in the story by Isaac Bashevis Singer which Bellow translated from the Yiddish. But there is also much in them of the American Adam, struggling not on rolling plains or high seas but amid the inexhaustible illusions of cities to fulfill his fate. The illusions jingle with money. The conflicts of class, the tensions of race, the tacit discriminations of power, respond variously to the sound of money as do sex, fame, and happiness, or whatever else stirs the vain heart. As a character in "A Father-to-Be" says: "money surrounds you in life as the earth does in death."[10] And that may be finally the point: money, ground and agent of American illusions, seems no less changeful and pervasive than death, coin of all substitutions.

Bellow's career, I have intimated, undergoes changes of another kind. With characteristic severity of mind, if not habitual modesty, Bellow considers his early works "errors—perhaps inevitable errors, but errors nonetheless. . . ."[11] This is perhaps too little to say about such works as *Dangling Man* (1944) and *The Victim* (1947). True, these novels seem somewhat constrained, inhibited in their artistic as well as their moral energy, which Bellow ascribes to his timidity before the ruling—Flaubertian, Jamesian—models of his day. But then, beginning with *The Adventures of Augie March* (1953), his "primitive prompter" breaks through, opening wide the forms of fiction, sweeping before it cultural stereotypes, including that of the American Jew. Leaving "complaint" behind, Bellow turns to comedy "as more energetic, wiser, and manlier."[12] Though he now believes *Augie March* to have been an extravagant book, it remains a generative work, creating a bold, new style capable of both rendering and comprehending American experience. The work, in any case, points to two outstanding subsequent achievements: *Henderson the Rain King* (1959), perhaps Bellow's finest novel, and *Humboldt's Gift* (1975).

But what of his *œuvre* more concretely? I can give it but the most cursory attention in these pages.[13] His first novel, *Dangling Man*, seems closer to the introspective manner of Kafka or Dostoyevski than of Dreiser. Its hero, Joseph, betrays the ironies of existential man, caught between metaphysical absurdity and social regimentation in wartime America. With the acerbic naïveté that constitutes his character, Joseph confronts various possibilities of freedom—to be, to act, to suffer, to understand—only to escape freedom in the army he finally joins. Alienation, he senses, is a fool's plea, for the world lies within us. Yet he laments: "Who can be the earnest huntsman of himself when he knows he is in turn a quarry? Or nothing so distinctive as quarry, but one of a shoal, driven towards the weirs."[14] In the end, Joseph admits: "I had not done well alone."[15] Turned inward upon itself, pale in style and thinly dramatic—much of the work takes the form of a diary—*Dangling Man* established a certain anxious mood of post-war society rather than the measure of its author's gifts.

The Victim carries the mummery of guilt, dread, and self-vindication farther. Addressing itself overtly to anti-Semiticism in America, the novel spins around two antagonists, Kirbee Allbee and Asa Leventhal—one Gentile, the other Jew, weird doubles—to tell a universal fable of human ambiguities. Who is his brother's keeper? Reversal presses upon reversal. It is Allbee, for instance, who poses as the aggrieved party and cries: "'Know thyself'! Everybody knows but nobody wants to admit."[16] In the final irony, the two antagonists become identified, self and other suddenly one, as Leventhal looks at the back of Allbee's neck, feeling that foreign presence as his own. Thus Leventhal realizes that "everything, everything without exception, took place as if within a single soul or person."[17] Yet racial prejudice and sacramental reconciliation account only for part of the novel's meaning; the practical context is money, success, status, all the deadly urges of a vast competitive order, which Bellow knows how to articulate. At once dour, ironic, and compassionate, the book stands as a landmark of Jewish fiction in America.

But it was *The Adventures of Augie March* that jolted its author into fame. Recovering the generous picaresque form, the novel shapes the multitudinous experiences of the hero into a language of the self seeking a special destiny. Augie's character, as Herzclitus thought, is his fate, a fate balanced within the concentric circles of his Jewish family, his boisterous city (Chicago), and his country, still brash before the turn of the century. Humorous and headlong, the narrative carries Augie through many episodes, erotic encounters, shady dealings, the ins and outs and dead ends of the American dream. Innocent in some ways to the end, and perhaps a trifle the *schlemiel*, he can still say: "I did have opposition in me, and great desire to offer resistance and to say 'No'!"[18] Thus Augie remains open to the highest bid of freedom and call of experience. Conceiving of himself as a "servant of love"—a neophyte, that is, in the luminous mystery of responsiveness, acceptance—he tries always to align himself with the "axial lines" of existence: "Truth, love, peace, bounty, usefulness, harmony."[19] Yet Augie is no latter-day Candide. He recognizes "worldwide Babylonishness"; he experiences that darkness which no human evades. Still, after all his tribulations, hearing a servant girl laugh, he thinks: "That's the animal *ridens* in me, the laughing creature, forever rising up"—and so refuses "to lead a disappointed life."[20] We can see how this big, comic book restores wonder and a certain blatancy to fiction and, despite its excesses, sets an example to postwar novelists intent on accommodating, as Bellow put it, "the full tumult, the zaniness and crazed quality, of modern experience."[21]

In *Seize the Day* (1956), however, Bellow returns to the leaner form of the novella and writes a brief masterpiece on the human encounter with error and death. Lost to himself on the streets of New York, Tommy Wilhelm feels the agonizing necessity "to translate and translate, explain and explain," without understanding, without knowing the crazy from the sane, the wise from the fools.[22] Moneyless, wifeless, all too mortal, Wilhelm still finally achieves an insight into things: against the pretender-soul, full of the world's cunning, he affirms the true-soul, released in vast and selfless sorrow. Failure ceases to be a personal matter, and death no longer appears to him the ultimate degradation, apotheosis of all errors.

Of all Bellow's novels, *Henderson the Rain King* possesses perhaps the largest, the freest sense of life. Set in Africa and frankly conceived as a quest romance (Bellow had never visited that continent), the novel raises action and desire to the level of wisdom. Henderson's heart constantly cries: "I want, I want, I want." Yet he commits himself to an ideal of service that men like Albert Schweitzer and Wilfred Grenvell once embodied, an ideal that he finally comes to understand before a sacred lioness, in a moment of pure being. Gigantic, rich, spiritual, a strange amalgam of vehement forces, Henderson is driven toward a life of heroic failures and clownish quests, seeking salvation at 55, and betraying in his great suffering, Gentile face, "like an unfinished church," all "the human passions at the point of doubt."[23] His quest, above all, is for knowledge, reality. "The physical is all there, and it belongs to science. But then there is the noumenal department, and there we create and create and create," he reflects.[24] Despite the archaic haze of fertility rituals, ceremonial hunts, and totemic cults through which Henderson's spirit flashes, truth comes to him first in blows, then in stillness, redeeming error, awakening his soul from his sleep. Death stalks him, mirrored in the cosmic coldness of an octopus' eye. But so does life, some powerful magnificence not human, at sunrise. Henderson learns to conjugate: "He wants, she wants, they want."[25] The African adventure, sometimes too conjured and colorful, still sharply reflects back upon Western civilization, its style magical and comical at once, joyful in its knowledge that chaos does not run the whole human show.

After *Henderson the Rain King,* the various movements of the 1960s—mainly "distractions" in Bellow's view—begin to press on American consciousness and so to challenge the artist to a new perception of his role in culture. Bellow meets this challenge unevenly in his two subsequent novels. *Herzog* (1964), a quasi-epistolary work, mixing action, introspection, and rememberance, bristling with perceptions as well as ideas, sets itself against current notions of alienation and revolution but ends by giving the reader an uneasy sense of its major characters. For Herzog remains an equivocal creation of pain. Lucid at times, biting with the double edge of irony and self-pity, ranging in his intelligence over the entire field of culture, he is a prisoner of himself, though he finally claims: "*I am pretty well satisfied to be, to be just as it is willed, and for as long as I may remain in occupancy.*"[26] This is not entirely convincing. Bellow, we know, means Herzog comically to exemplify the shame and impotence of privacy, a refined masochism of the heart.[27] Yet the exemplification aspires also to its own refutation; the ideas of freedom and personal choice in the novel seem plaintively unresolved.

This plaintive note—in Bellow, it implies always some unique admixture of feeling, refractoriness, and questing spirit—becomes almost sour in *Mr. Sammler's Planet* (1970). Its aged, one-eyed hero, however, claims to witness more than to judge. A survivor of pogroms and wars, a connoisseur of Bloomsbury and an acquaintance of H. G. Wells, a friend to civilization, he moves through brutal New York streets and wonders about the future of the earth, of the race, viewing the spectacle from "the place of honor," which is "outside." "Is our species crazy?" Can it endure "futurelessness"?[28] Sammler juxtaposes past and present, Europe and America, imagination and science, the earth and the moon, decency and rage of every kind, and ends by endorsing ancient pieties, the "civil heart." For greatness without models is to him inconceivable, and "One could not be the thing itself—reality."[29] Written in a new, laconic, elliptic style, the novel, like all Bellow's works, remains on the side of man, that "animal of genius." Yet its primness of vision inhibits its capacity to perceive or prophesy.

In *Humboldt's Gift*, however, Bellow recovers the amplitude of his vision, which the style reflects in disciplined ebullience and taut vigor. All of his vital concerns are here again: history, a nightmare during which Humboldt tries "to get a good night's rest"; America, "God's experiment," with its dislike of "special values" and suffering; Chicago, "a cultureless city pervaded nevertheless by Mind"; art and power, imagination and science; love, marriage, divorce, sex; money, "the dollar as the soul's husband"; the defence of the individual against insidiuous distractions; the whole "Intellectual Comedy of the modern mind."[30] Other concerns appear even more acute, more inward with the ethos of this late book: the question of death; the possibility of reincarnation and immortality; the place of the "imaginative soul" in a phenomenal world; boredom, "a kind of pain caused by unused powers"; the invisible but "real life" which flows, "between here and there"; "Being" and "Knowledge" united, manifest in "projections of the cosmos," in "the signature of spiritual powers."[31]   Thus gnostic meditations, no less than social comedy and the existential farce of self-awareness, qualify the efforts of Charlie Citrine to comprehend the legacy of Humboldt, a brilliant, failed, suicidal poet, modeled in part on Delmore Schwartz. The legacy is that of imagination in America and, beyond that, of the noumenal human gift. To that end, Citrine—himself an aging, celebrated writer—consults various exemplars of spirit, from Plato to Hegel, Houdini, and Rudolf Steiner. But in the end, as always, it is in his own resources that Citrine finds the way, between innocence and corruption, toward that stillness Valéry invokes when he says: "[il] *trouve avant de chercher*" [he finds before seeking].[32] This is Citrine's gift. It is also, preeminently, Bellow's own, which no lapses or *longeurs* in this major work can revoke.

How, then, may we receive so large, so crucial, a gift? Bellow is not an experimental writer in the postmodern sense, though no two novels in his *œuvre* seem styled or felt alike. And his affirmative stance, at times nearly ostentatious, may ignore some darker reaches of the spirit and so lend itself to popular simplicities. Yet in refusing disappointment on behalf of us all, he defends human sense and presence as Herzog does in his letter to God.[33] Certainly Bellow, despite a certain impatience which could narrow his judgment, possesses distinct "clairvoyance about discovering issues, questions, problems before they are seen by most others."[34] More mindful, perhaps, than any contemporary American novelist, he claims for knowledge, imagination, and spirit their place in creation, without fracturing our being. In assigning to his heroes the task of self-creation, of awakening the soul to itself amidst time's miseries, he proves himself a new gnostic; but this gnostic holds no contempt for the world or its infinite particulars, slights neither nature nor history. Heir of a central vision and art's high mystery, Saul Bellow joins those generous forebears, among them our native Transcendentalists, who believe that the universe could deliver itself to our listening.

Notes

[1] Though the inflections of Yiddish speech, the twists of the Jewish joke, the wisdom and weight of Hebrew history all find their way into Bellow's work, he is right to protest the label of "Jewish writer": "I find the label intellectually vulgar, unnecessarily parochializing and utterly without value—especially since, from a personal point of view, it avoids me both as a writer and as a Jew," he remarks (Joseph Epstein, "Saul Bellow of Chicago," *The New York Times Book Review*, 9 May 1971, p. 12). Earlier, Bellow also said: "For us the pain of Shylock may be greater than for others because we are Jews, but it has fundamentally the same meaning discovered in Job or Lear. . . ." ("The Jewish Writer and the English Literary Tradition," *Commentary*, October 1949, p. 366).

[2] See "Saul Bellow," in George Plimpton, editor, *Writers at Work: The Paris Review Interviews*, Third Series (New York: Viking Press, 1967), p. 196; and Saul Bellow, "A World Too Much With Us," *Critical Inquiry*, Vol. 2, No. 1 (Autumn 1975), p. 9.

[3] Saul Bellow, "The Nobel Lecture," *American Scholar*, Vol. 46, No. 3 (Summer 1977), pp. 324-25.

[4] "The sense of our real powers, powers we seem to derive from the universe itself, also comes and goes. We are reluctant to talk about this because there is nothing we can prove, because our language is inadequate, and because few people are willing to risk talking about it. They would have to say, 'There is a spirit,' and that is taboo." Bellow, "The Nobel Lecture," p. 325.

[5] This theme, which runs through all Bellow's fiction, also informs his essays from the start. See, for instance, "Distractions of a Fiction Writer," in Granville Hicks, editor, *The Living Novel* (New York: Macmillan & Co., 1957); Sanford Pinsker, "Saul Bellow in the Classroom," *College English*, Vol. 34, No. 7 (July 1973); "Man Underground," in John Hersey, editor, *Ralph Ellison* (Englewood Cliffs, New Jersey: Prentice-Hall, 1974); "Machines and Storybooks: Literature in the Age of Technology," *Harper's Magazine*, August 1974; as well as "A World Too Much With Us" and "The Nobel Lecture" cited previously.

[6] Rosette C. Lamont, "Bellow Observed: A Serial Portrait," *Mosaic*, Vol. 8. No. 1 (Spring 1974), p. 252. For an interesting statement on the cognitive theme in Bellow, see also Brigitte Scheer-Schäzler, "Epistemology as Narrative Device in the Work of Saul Bellow," *Saul Bellow and His Work: Proceedings of a Symposium at the Free University of Brussels*, (Brussels, Belgium, December 10-11, 1977).

[7] Saul Bellow, "Facts That Put Fancy to Flight," *The New York Times Book Review*, 11 February 1962, p. 28.

[8] Or as Bellow puts it: "This society with its titanic products conditions but cannot absolutely denature us. It forces certain elements of the genius of our species to go into hiding. In America they take curiously personal, secret forms." "The Sealed Treasure," *The Times Literary Supplement*, 1 July 1960, p. 414.

[9] Epstein, "Saul Bellow of Chicago," p. 14.

[10] Saul Bellow, *Seize the Day and Other Stories* (New York: Viking Press, 1956), p. 123

[11] Epstein, "Saul Bellow of Chicago," p. 12.

[12] *Writers at Work,* p. 188. See also pp. 182-184 for a discussion of his development.

[13] For a fuller account of Bellow, see Ihab Hassan, *Radical Innocence* (Princeton: Princeton University Press, 1961); Irving Malin, editor, *Saul Bellow and the Critics* (New York: New York University Press, 1967); John J. Clayton, *Saul Bellow* (Bloomington: Indiana University Press, 1968); Brigitte Scheer-Schäzler, *Saul Bellow* (New York: Frederick Ungar, 1972); Nathan A. Scott, *Three American Moralists: Mailer, Bellow, Trilling* (Notre Dame, Indiana: University of Notre Dame Press, 1973); Sarah Blacher Cohen, *Saul Bellow's Enigmatic Laughter* (Urbana: University of Illinois Press, 1974); Earl Rovit, editor, *Saul Bellow: A Collection of Critical Essays* (Englewood Cliffs, New Jersey: Prentice-Hall, 1975.)

[14] Saul Bellow, *Dangling Man* (New York: Vanguard Press, 1944), p. 119.

[15] Bellow, *Dangling Man* p. 190.

[16] Bellow, *The Victim* (New York: Viking Press, 1956), p. 227.

[17] Bellow, *The Victim,* p. 169.

[18] Saul Bellow, *The Adventures of Augie March* (New York: Viking Press, 1953), p. 117.

[19] Bellow, *The Adventures,* p. 454.

[20] Bellow, *The Adventures,* p. 536.

[21] Epstein, "Saul Bellow of Chicago," p. 13.

[22] *Seize the Day,* pp. 83-84.

[23] Saul Bellow, *Henderson the Rain King* (New York: Viking Press, 1959), p. 131.

[24] Bellow, *Henderson,* p. 167.

[25] Bellow, *Henderson,* p. 286.

[26] Saul Bellow, *Herzog* (New York: Viking Press, 1964), p. 340.

[27] *Writers at Work,* pp. 193-94.

[28] Saul Bellow, *Mr Sammler's Planet* (New York: Viking Press, 1970), pp. 73, 75, 92.

[29] Bellow, *Mr. Sammler's,* p. 149.

[30] Saul Bellow, *Humboldt's Gift* (New York: Viking Press, 1975), pp. 4, 162, 69, 340.

[31] Bellow, *Humboldt's,* pp. 362-63, 199-200, 460, 404, 485.

[32] Bellow, *Humboldt's,* p. 73.

[33] Bellow, *Herzog,* pp. 325-326. In many of his public pronouncements, Bellow also tries to avoid the extremes of optimism and pessimism, "the black and white of paranoia." See, for instance, "The Sealed Treasure," p. 414; "Some Notes on Recent American Fiction," in Marcus Klein, editor, *The American Novel Since World War II* (New York: Fawcett Publications, 1969), pp. 169-70, 173-74; and "The Nobel Lecture," p. 324.

[34] Joseph Epstein, "A Talk With Saul Bellow," *The New York Times Book Review,* 5 December 1976, p. 92.

Bibliography

By Saul Bellow:

Dangling Man. New York: Vanguard Press, 1944.
The Victim. New York: Viking Press, 1947.
The Adventures of Augie March. New York: Viking Press, 1953.
Seize the Day and Other Stories. New York: Viking Press, 1956.
Henderson the Rain King. New York: Viking Press, 1959.
Recent American Fiction. Washington: Library of Congress, 1963.
Herzog. New York: Viking Press, 1964.
The Last Analysis. New York: Viking Press, 1965.
Mosby's Memoirs and Other Stories. New York: Viking Press, 1968.
Mr. Sammler's Planet. New York: Viking Press, 1970.
Humboldt's Gift. New York: Viking Press, 1975.
To Jerusalem and Back. New York: Viking Press, 1976.

About Saul Bellow:

Hassan, Ihab. *Radical Innocence.* Princeton, New Jersey: Princeton University Press,
        1961.
Malin, Irving, editor. *Saul Bellow and the Critics.* New York: New York University
        Press, 1967.
Tanner, Tony. *Saul Bellow.* Edinburgh: Oliver & Boyd, 1965.

Ralph Ellison's Vision of *Communitas*

Nathan A. Scott, Jr.

From the time of its first appearance in the spring of 1952 Ralph Ellison's *Invisible Man* has been thrusting itself forward, ever more insistently with the passage of each year, as the commanding masterpiece in the literature of contemporary American fiction—and, now that it has had a career of more than a quarter-century, its priority of place appears indeed to have been solidly consolidated. For no other text of these past years has so lodged itself in the national imagination as has Ellison's great book: it stands today as the pre-eminent American novel of our period, and all that I want here to try to do is to suggest something of what it is that accounts for the kind of powerful claim it continues to exert upon us.

Ours is, of course, a period marked by an efflorescence of fictional talent on the American scene more notable surely than any comparable British or European insurgency. Yet, in its representative expressions, it is a talent, for all its variety and richness, that—in such writers as William Gass, John Barth, Donald Barthelme, and Ronald Sukenick—often chooses to dwell (as the title of a book on recent American fiction by the English critic Tony Tanner says) in a "City of Words." Bellow, Styron, Malamud, and a few others, in their commitment to the traditional arts of narrative, remain sufficiently unreconstructed as to conceive the novel to be a mode of feigned history, but they, though retaining a large and devoted readership, do not carry the day and do not embody what Matthew Arnold called "the tone of the centre." For those who are advancing the new poetics of fiction take it for granted (as William Gass says) "that literature is language, that stories and the places and the people in them are merely made of words as chairs are made of smoothed sticks and sometimes of cloth or metal tubes," and thus, since "there are no events but words in fiction,"[1] they think of the novelistic craft as simply an affair of putting words together in new and surprising combinations—which record nothing other than the event of the writer's having done certain interesting things with language itself. So charmed is the new literature with its own verbal universe of metaphor and metonymy that it refuses any deep involvements with the empirical, verifiable world of actual fact, preferring instead what Conrad long ago called the "prolonged hovering flight of the subjective over the outstretched ground of the case exposed." And thus it forswears the kind of intentionality that looks toward finding new stratagems wherewith to give a liberating "shape and . . . significance to the immense panorama of . . . anarchy which is contemporary history": which is perhaps to say that it does not seek (in Yeats's great phrase) to hold "reality and justice in a single thought."

The kind of *dandysme* which reigns now has in recent years been denominated by literary academicians specializing in *Tendenz* as "post-modernism," but a part of the immense appeal that belongs to a figure like Ralph Ellison is surely an affair of his fidelity to the ethic of classic modernism. For the great masters of this century—Joyce and Lawrence and Mann and Faulkner—were indeed proposing to do what T. S. Eliot in his famous review of *Ulysses* (in the issue of *The Dial* for November 1923) described as Joyce's intention: namely, to give a "shape and . . . significance to the immense panorama of . . . anarchy which is contemporary history." *The Magic Mountain* and *The Death of Virgil, Women in Love* and *The Sun Also Rises, The Sound and the Fury* and *Man's Fate* are books that strike us today as having a remarkable kind of weight and contemporaneity, because they are, as it were, taking on the age: with a fierce kind of audacity, they seem to be intending to *displace* a daunting world, to clear a space for the human endeavor, and thus to keep open the door of the future. In short, their rites and ceremonies and plots and arguments are organized toward the end of envisaging new forms of life for the soul, and it is just in this that one element of the genius of 20th-century modernism lies.

Now it is in this line that Ralph Ellison stands. Immediately after *Invisible Man* first appeared in 1952, the astonishing authority of its art quickly brought it to the forefront of the literary scene, and this at a time when, under the new influence of Henry James, so many representative American writers of the moment such as Jean Stafford, Frederick Buechner, Isabel Bolton, Monroe Engel, and Mary McCarthy—were choosing to seek their effects by the unsaid and the withheld, by the dryly ironic analogy and the muted voice. In the early

1950s Ellison, like Faulkner and Penn Warren, was particularly notable for being unafraid to make his fiction howl and rage and hoot with laughter over "the complex fate" of the *homo Americanus*: indeed, the uninhibited exhilaration and suppleness of his rhetoric were at once felt to be a main source of the richness of texture distinguishing his extraordinary book. Yet the kind of continuing life that his novel has had is surely to be accounted for in terms not of sheer verbal energy alone but, more principally, in terms of the cogency of systematic vision that it enunciates. And though something like this has frequently been remarked, what is most essential in the basic stress and emphasis of the novel has just as frequently been misreckoned, no doubt largely because the book has so consistently been construed as having an import related exclusively to the experience of black Americans.

The protagonist of *Invisible Man* is, of course, a young black man (unnamed) who must pick his perilous way through the lunatic world that America has arranged for its Negro minority. In the beginning, he is what the white masters of the Southern world in which he grows up were once in the habit of calling "a good Negro": he has cheerfully accepted all the promises of that Establishment, so much so that the oily-tongued and cynical president of his college, Dr. Bledsoe, has singled him out as his special ward. But, unhappily, on a certain day he unintentionally exposes a visiting white trustee from the North to the local Negro gin-mill and to the incestuous entanglements of a Negro farmer's family in the neighborhood—and, as a result, he is ousted from the college, as a punishment for his having allowed a donor of the institution to see what visiting white patrons are not supposed to see.

He then moves on to New York, there to journey through the treacherous byways of an infernally labyrinthine world, as he seeks to make contact with whatever it is that may authenticate his existence. The executive powers ordain that, being black, he shall be "invisible," and thus his great central effort becomes that of wresting an acknowledgment, of *achieving* visibility. He gets a job in a Long Island paint factory, and there he becomes involved—again, inadvertently—as a scab in labor violence. Soon afterward, however, he is taken up by "the Brotherhood" (i.e., the Communist Party), after he is heard to deliver an impassioned and a quite spontaneous speech one winter afternoon as he finds himself part of a crowd watching the eviction of an elderly Negro couple from their Harlem tenement flat. The assignment he is given by his new confreres is that of *organizing* the sullenness of Harlem. But he soon discovers that the Negro's cause is but a pawn being used by "the Brotherhood" to promote its "line." So, after the Brotherhood engineers a furious race riot in the Harlem streets, he in utter disillusionment dives through a manhole, down into a cellar, for a period of "hibernation." He has tried the way of "humility," of being a "good Negro"; he has tried to find room for himself in American industry, to become a good cog in the technological machine; he has attempted to attach himself to leftist politics—he has tried all those things by means of which it would seem that a Negro might achieve visibility in American life. But, since none has offered a way into the culture, he has now chosen to become an underground man. All his reversals have been due to the blackness of his skin: so now, at last, he decides to stay in his cellar where, by way of a tapped line, he will steal the electricity for his 1,369 bulbs from Monopolated Light and Power and dine on sloe gin and vanilla ice cream and *embrace* "The Blackness of Blackness."

Yet Ellison's protagonist, unlike so many of his counterparts in black fiction, is in the end by no means one *merely* wounded. True, he twice tells us, in the accent of Eliot's *East Coker*—first in the Prologue, and again at the end of his narrative—that his "end is in ... [his] beginning." And so it is, for his last state—since it is an underworld, a place of exile, of dislodgment and expatriation—is in a way his first. But it is an underworld that *he* has *illuminated*. "Step outside the narrow borders of what men call reality and you step into chaos ... or imagination," he says. When, that is, you step outside the domesticated and the routinized, you may step into chaos, since the definition of the world, as he has discovered, is possibility—the very infiniteness of which may be defeating unless by dint of a feat of imagination some transcendence can be realized. And since, as it would seem, the protagonist-narrator conceives art itself to be the definition of such a transcendence, he—amidst the misrule and confusion of a demented world—has undertaken to form the lessons he has learned into a story, to "put it [all] down," and thereby (like another young man who became an artist) to forge in the smithy of his own soul the uncreated conscience of his native land. His story ends in a cellar, because, having constantly been told that it is in some such novel that he belongs, this *eiron* [ironist] has chosen mockingly to descend, then, into a harlem basement where, if he cannot have visibility, he can at least have *vision*—and where he can produce out of his abysmal pain a poetry that, as he says, "on the lower frequencies . . . [may] speak for you"—*le lecteur.*

The book presents, as Alfred Kazin has suggested, one of the most engaging studies in recent literature in "the art of survival."[2] And in relation to everything with which its young anti-hero must reckon Ellison displays a notable mastery. His reader finds himself, indeed, utterly immersed in all the concrete materialities of black experience: one hears the very buzz and hum of Harlem in the racy, pungent speech of his West Indians and his native hipsters; one sees the fearful nonchalance of the zoot-suiter and hears the terrible anger of the black nationalist on his streetcorner platform; and all the *grotesquerie* in the novel's account of a dreary little backwater of a remote southern black college has in it a certain kind of empirically absolute rightness. The book is packed full of the acute observations of the manners and idioms and human styles that comprise the ethos of black life in America, and it gives us such a sense of social fact as can be come by nowhere in the manuals of academic sociology—all this being done with the ease that comes from enormous expertness of craft, from deep intimacy of knowledge, and love.

Yet, deeply rooted as the novel is in the circumstances of Negro life and experience, it wants on its "lower frequencies" to speak about a larger condition, and, indeed, when Ellison is taken (as he customarily is) to be a barrister seeking on behalf of the black multitudes to impose a certain radical affidavit on the American conscience, what is most deeply prophetic in the testimony brought forward by his book is by way of being obscured. Nor is it at all inapposite to consider the authorial performance conveyed by *Invisible Man* as reflecting a prophetic intention, at least not if one thinks of prophetism in something like the terms proposed by the anthropologist Victor Turner.

Professor Turner's theory of culture, based in large part on his extensive field-researchers amongst the Ndembu people of northwest Zambia, entails an elaborate scheme which he has developed in numerous writings but most fully in three notable books, *The Forest of Symbols* (1967), *The Ritual Process* (1969), and *Dramas, Fields, and Metaphors* (1974). His starting point is the concept of the "liminal phase" advanced by the Belgian ethnographer Arnold van Gennep in his classic work of 1909, *Les rites de passage.* Van Gennep, in working out the logic of "transition" rites, remarked three phases into which they invariably fall and which he identified as, first, separation, then margin (or *limen*, the Latin signifying "threshold"), and then reaggregation. That is to say, the neophyte first undergoes some detachment or dislocation from his established role in a social structure or cultural polity—whereupon he finds himself as novice in a "liminal" situation in which he is neither one thing nor another, neither here nor there, neither what he was nor yet what he will become. Then, in the third phase, the passage is completed by his reincorporation into a social or religious structure: no longer is he invisible by reason of his divestment of status and role, for, once again, he finds himself with acknowledged rights and obligations vis-à-vis those others who with him are members one of another in whatever body it is to which they jointly belong.

Now Professor Turner is careful to remark that "liminars" are, in most human communities, by no means the only *déclassés*, for always there are various "outsiders" (shamans, monks, priests, hippies, hoboes, gypsies) who either by ascription or choice stand outside the established order, just as there are also various kinds of "marginals" (migrant foreigners, persons of mixed ethnic origin, the upwardly and downwardly mobile) who may be "simultaneously members . . . of two or more groups whose social definitions and cultural norms are distinct from, and often even opposed to, one another."[3] But, though at many points he is strongly insistent on these distinctions, at many others he seems to be treating "outsiderhood" and "marginality" as merely special modes of "liminality," and it appears for him to be the decisive antipode to "aggregation."

What Professor Turner is most eager to remark, however, is the wrongheadedness of regarding liminality as a merely negative state of privation: on the contrary, as he argues, it can be and often is an enormously fruitful seedbed of spiritual creativity, for it is precisely amidst the troubling ambiguities of the liminar's *déclassement* that there is born in him a profound hunger for *communitas*. And Professor Turner prefers the Latin term, since he feels "community" connotes an ordered, systemized society—whereas the liminar's yearning is not for any simple kind of social structure but rather, as he says, for that spontaneous, immediate flowing from *I* to *Thou* of which Martin Buber is our great modern rhapsode.[4] Which is to say that the liminar thirsts for *communitas*: this is what the naked neophyte in a seclusion lodge yearns for; this is what the dispossessed and the exiled dream of; this is what "dharma bums" and millenarians and holy mendicants and "rock" people are moved by—namely, the vision of an *open* society in which all the impulses and affections that are normally bound by social structure are liberated, so that every barrier between *I* and *Thou* is broken down and the wind of *communitas* may blow where it listeth.

Moreover, Victor Turner conceives it to be the distinctive mission of the prophet to lift *communitas* into the subjunctive mood: he is the liminal man *par excellence* whose special vocation, as a frontiersman dwelling on the edges of the established order, is to puncture "the clichés associated with status incumbency and role-playing"[5] and to fill for his contemporaries the open space of absolute futurity with a vision of that unanimity, that free unity-in-diversity, which graces the human order when men give their suffrage to the "open morality" (as Bergson would have called it) of *agape*.

Now it is when *Invisible Man* is regarded in its relation to the experiential realities addressed by Victor Turner that its special kind of prophetic discernment may perhaps be most clearly identified. True, its narrator is a young black man encumbered with all the disadvantage that American society has imposed on his kind. But his very last word to the reader—*mon semblable, mon frère!* [my fellowman, my brother]—records his conviction that, "on the lower frequencies," he, in the story he tells about himself, is speaking about a condition that embraces not just his ancestral kinsmen but the human generality of his age. Which suggests that what is most essentially problematic in his situation is not merely his blackness but, rather, something else, and it is this which needs now to be defined.

One of Ellison's critics speaks of how frequently his novel is by way of coming to an end and then having once more to start itself up again,[6] and something like this is surely the case: at least, it may be said that the persistent rhythm of the novel is an affair of the protagonist's drifting into a relation with one or another of the various trustees of social power and then either digging in his heels or taking flight, when the connection threatens to abrogate his freedom. After he is expelled from his college, he takes to New York the various letters of introduction Dr. Bledsoe has provided, and it is his eventual discovery of the cruel dispraise that these sealed letters from the malignant old man have actually conveyed that leads him to think: "Everyone seemed to have some plan for me, and beneath that some more secret plan." And so indeed it is: wherever he turns, he finds himself dealing with those—whether it be Bledsoe or Mr. Norton or the Reverend Homer A. Barbee or the owner of the Long Island paint factory or Brother

Jack—who are eager to map out a design for his life and to convert him into a kind of automaton of their own schemes. They may be agents of religion or education or industry or radical politics, but, at bottom, they are (as Tony Tanner says) "mechanizers of consciousness"[7]—and each is prepared to say something like what Bledsoe says in reference to his college: "This is a power set-up, son, and I'm at the controls." In fact, this young *picaro* does at last himself realize that all his various proctors and patrons have been "very much the same, each attempting to force his picture of reality upon me and neither giving a hoot in hell for how things looked to me." But he is unflagging in his refusal of obedient service to the organizers and manipulators: he wants to be free of that great alien force that we call Society. So, in the logic of the novel, his exemplary role is related not merely to the disinherited American Negro but, far more basically, to that "disintegrated" or "alienated" consciousness which, as Hegel reminds us in the *Phenomenology of Mind*, is distinguished by its antagonism to "the external power of society" and which, in the modern period, is not simply here or there—but everywhere.

Yet, in his liminality, Ellison's young knight does not choose merely to pour scornful laughter on the social establishment, in the manner of Rinehart, for, isolated though he is, he remains totally in earnest. There comes a moment when, though having separated himself from the Brotherhood, he is nevertheless one hunted by the partisans of the West Indian black nationalist, Ras the Exhorter, who conceives the interracialism of the Brotherhood to be a fearfully mischievous confusion of "the blahk mahn" and who is unrelenting in his pursuit of him who has been one of its chief spokesmen in Harlem. So, by way of hurriedly arranging a scanty disguise, our principal purchases some darkly tinted spectacles and a flamboyant hat, and immediately he is mistaken on the streets for a man named Rinehart of whom he has never heard—and whom he never sees. One evening there suddenly emerges from a Lenox Avenue subway exit a large, blowsy prostitute reeking with "Christmas Night perfume" who for a moment takes him to be her Man: "Rinehart, baby, is that you?.... Say, you ain't Rinehart, man . . . git away from here before you get me in trouble." And, as he swings on, a few moments later he is hailed by a couple of hipsters who take him to be Rinehart the numbers man: "Rinehart, poppa, tell us what you putting down." Then a group of zoot-suiters greet him: "Hey now, daddy-o." And again, in an Eighth Avenue tavern he is taken to be Rinehart by the barkeeper: "What

brand you drinking tonight, Poppa-stopper?" Some larcenous policemen expecting a pay-off summon him from their patrol car to a curb
and, when he denies that he is Rinehart, the response flung back at him
is—"Well, you better be by morning." Then, again, outside a storefront
church he is greeted by two aging, pious drones as "Rever'n Rinehart,"
and they offer him assurances about how zealously they are collecting
money for his building fund. And, after many such encounters, he
begins to marvel at this extraordinary personage—"Rine the runner
and Rine the gambler and Rine the briber and Rine the lover and
Rinehart the Reverend." Indeed, he is at once fascinated by the
virtuosity of this remarkable changeling—and, in a way, unhinged by
the abyss of infinite possibility opened up by his glimpse of the
"multiple personalities" worn by this black Proteus.

But, no, not for him the way of this wily rascal who deals with
the intractabilities of social circumstance by simply mocking them in
the cultivation of an extravagant histrionism. No, Ellison's protagonist is a liminar who, though separated from the established orders of
the world, is yet not estranged from himself. And thus he yearns for
an authentic existence, not for Rinehart's world of no boundaries at all
but for something like a New Jerusalem, where no man is an island and
where Love is the name behind the design of the human City.

He is unable to descry at any point on the horizon the merest
prospect, however, of this Good Place. And so at last he descends into
an underground world. He is floundering about one night through
Harlem streets inflamed by the savage race riot that has been carefully
orchestrated by the Brotherhood itself, and, in his abstracted anguish
at the sheer futility of this lunatic paroxysm, he stumbles into some
black *enragés* who, being suddenly angered by the sight of his brief-
case, are about to set upon him, when he lifts the cover of a manhole
and plunges down into a coal cellar below. There he finds a narrow
passage that leads into a "dimensionless room," and this he elects to
occupy as the site of his "hibernation."

This liminar in his cellar bears no resemblance, however, to that
bilious and exacerbated little cipher whose portrayal in Dostoyevsky's
Notes from the Underground has made him one of the great modern
archetypes of the Underground Man. Ellison's hero has been "hurt to
the point of abysmal pain, hurt to the point of invisibility," not only by
American racism but by all those "mechanizers of consciousness"—by
Bledsoe as well as by Mr. Norton, by Brother Jack as well as by Ras the
Exhorter—whose great "passion [is] to make men conform to a pat-

tern." Yet, in his hibernation, he realizes that, for all the vehemence with which he has taken a stand "'against' society," he still wants to defend "the principle on which the country was built." As he says, "I defend because in spite of all"—though "I sell you no phony forgiveness"—"I find that I love." He harbors no love for those who are moved by a "passion toward conformity," for, as he insists, "diversity is the word." "Life is to be lived, not controlled. . . ." So the dream by which he is enheartened in his basement room is the dream that we shall "become one, and yet many": it is the dream of *communitas*. And it is in the eloquence with which the novel projects this vision for the human future that it proves (in the terms I have taken over from Victor Turner) its prophetic genius—and its special relevance to the American situation of our own immediate present. For, given the furious assertiveness that distinguishes the various racial and ethnic particularisms making up our national society today, ours (as one thoughtful observer has recently remarked) is a country representing something like "pluralism gone mad." One of our great needs as a people is to recover a sense of common purposes and of a common destiny that overrides our "atomized world of a thousand me-first . . . groupings" of one kind or another.[8] And it is the remember in this connection that Ellison's novel brings that gives its testimony just now a special poignance.

"Who knows," says the nameless protagonist—"Who knows but that, on the lower frequencies, I speak for you?"

Notes

[1] William H. Gass, *Fiction and the Figures of Life* (New York: Vintage Books, 1972), pp. 27, 30.

[2] Alfred Kazin, *Bright Book of Life: American Novelists and Storytellers from Hemingway to Mailer* (Boston: Little, Brown and Co., 1973), p. 246.

[3] Victor Turner, *Dramas, Fields, and Metaphors* (Ithaca, New York: Cornell University Press, 1974), p. 233.

[4] See Victor Turner, *The Ritual Process* (Ithaca, New York: Cornell University Press, 1977 [paperback edition]), p. 127.

[5] *Ibid.*, p. 128.

[6] See Marcus Klein, *After Alienation: American Novels in Mid-Century* (Cleveland and New York: World Publishing Co., 1964), pp. 107-109.

[7] Tony Tanner, *City of Words: American Fiction, 1950-1970* (New York: Harper & Row, 1971), p. 53.

[8] Meg Greenfield, "Pluralism gone Mad," *Newsweek*, 27 August 1979, p. 76.

Bibliography

By Ralph Ellison:

Invisible Man. New York: Random House, 1952.
Shadow and Act. New York: Random House, 1964. (Essays)

Ellison's short stories, essays, articles, and reviews have appeared in such periodicals as the *American Review, Horizon, Nation, Negro World Digest, Partisan Review, Quarterly Review of Literature,* and *Saturday Review,* as well as in numerous anthologies.

About Ralph Ellison:

Covo, Jacqueline. *The Blinking Eye: Ralph Waldo Ellison and His American, French, German and Italian Critics, 1952-1971.* Metuchen, New Jersey: Scarecrow Press, 1974. (Bibliography)

Gottesman, Ronald, editor. *Studies in Invisible Man.* Columbus, Ohio: Merrill, 1971.

Hersey, John, editor. *Ralph Ellison: A Collection of Critical Essays.* Englewood Cliffs, New Jersey: Prentice-Hall, 1974.

Reilly, John M., editor. *Twentieth Century Interpretations of The Invisible Man.* Englewood Cliffs, New Jersey: Prentice-Hall, 1970.

The Sly Modernism of Isaac B. Singer

Richard Burgin

Without being a literary theoretician or ever wishing to be, Isaac Bashevis Singer has found himself ensconced in various controversies concerning the aims of fiction. He is, for instance, aesthetically at odds with those fictionists who feel the urge to impart an "important" social, political, or philosophical message in their work. He has said, "The moment something becomes an 'ism' it is already false." More important, perhaps, is his commitment to character, plot, and clarity; to, as Henry Miller said, "returning literature to life," which has informed all Singer's fiction from *Satan in Goray* (English edition 1955) and his first major novel *The Family Moskat* (English edition 1950), to his recent collection of stories *Old Love* (English edition 1979). Singer's position dramatizes one of contemporary fiction's central debates which is being rather furiously waged in universities and literary journals across the country. To sum up briefly, we have those writers (and the critics sympathetic to them) who constitute the avant-garde and essentially conceive of fiction as a great chain of being (or, in a sense, as a branch of science) in which the writer believes that fiction is a constantly evolving entity and that if one is not contributing to its evolution, then that seriously undermines the validity of the writer's work. There are, of course, writers who are ambivalent about this issue or consider it a pseudo-issue, but increasingly one feels a sense of polarization between the experimentalists and those writers who continue to work with plots, character developments, and a strong sense of the mechanisms and operations of society.

Curiously one of the principal literary and spiritual progenitors of the experimentalists, Jorge Luis Borges, could scarcely be more conservative in his literary tastes. Not only has he read none of today's avant-gardists (his very poor eyesight may have something to do with this) but he considers Joyce and Beckett not of the first rank, and Kafka much inferior to Henry James. A list of Borges's favorite "modern" authors would certainly include De Quincey, Robert Louis Stevenson, Chesterton, Emerson, and Frost. More importantly, he feels that since we live in a world of infinite or at least indeterminate time, the concept of an avant-garde is illusory, a misnomer based on a misunderstanding of man's relation to time. Though one can scarcely imagine a more different writer, Singer's metaphysics are quite close to Borges's and are likewise crucial to understanding his work and its sly modernism.

Sartre noted in an essay on Faulkner that every writer's style reveals his metaphysics, and in a less than obvious way this is also true of Singer. Consider his prefatory note to *Passions* (1975) in which Singer precisely and simply states his aesthetics:

> While obscurity in content and style may now be the fashion, clarity remains the ambition of this writer. This is especially important since I deal with unique characters in unique circumstances, a group of people who are still a riddle to the world and often to themselves—the Jews of Eastern Europe, specifically the Yiddish-speaking Jews who perished in Poland and those who emigrated to the U.S.A. The longer I live with them and write about them the more I am baffled by the richness of their individuality and (since I am one of them) by my own whims and passions.

In Singer's case we are dealing with a writer who adheres scrupulously to the goals of clarity and specificity, writing about only what he knows through some form of direct experience. This is a seminal reason why there is a certain degree of confusion on the question of his modernity or his contemporary relevance. For Singer is a writer, in an age of cultivated ambiguity, who *wants* us to perceive the epiphanies, doubts, and ambivalences of his characters. The other key term in his brief statement of aesthetics is "riddle"—for that is finally what the universe is for Singer. What he wants us to understand about his characters is their attempts to comprehend the structure and *modus operandi* of a universe that resists understanding. It is one of his special strengths that his characters are not disembodied creations who merely represent metaphysical problems or their author's obsessions, but instead are invariably imbued with exceptional vitality and credibility. One could say without exaggeration that Singer feels and is able to dramatize characters in the same natural way that Kant saw the World in Ideas. The apparent contradiction, then, is of a writer who composes lucid, direct sentences about people and situations he knows, but whose metaphysics, like Kafka's and Borges's, are rooted in and have never escaped from, the interminable riddles of the modern world. It is clarity, then, in the service of illuminating our essential riddle of existence. Let us not forget that Kafka and Borges employ very similar techniques.

One other reason why Singer has adopted many of the stylistic features of 19th-century fiction is that he feels the work of that period is vastly superior to that of the 20th century. He therefore adopted as his masters Tolstoy, Dostoyevsky, and Flaubert, who expressed their social, psychological, and philosophical conceits in a "natural" way through their characters' relations to each other and through their particular situations in a concrete social milieu. Yet Singer's sensibility is more "modern" than these writers', to whom he is frequently compared.

To understand this more fully, we must return to the notion of social structure, which the avant-garde often treats negatively or else with the assumption that it is too amorphous to portray. For these writers, the family, society's fundamental structure, is generally fractured and uncommunicative at best, and more often a procession of horrors—a never-to-be-reconciled nightmare. But in many of his stories, novels, or memoirs, Singer invariably returns to 10 Krochmalna Street in Warsaw where he grew up. In the celebrated memoir of his childhood, *In My Father's Court*, the entire book is set in this neighborhood. Despite the tensions that existed in his family, especially the conflicts between his father's unwavering devotion to Judaism and the more worldly interests of his children, the overpowering feeling that emerges in grand dimensions from *In My Father's Court* is the essential goodness of his parents. Certainly Singer's fiction demonstrates a real awareness of man's capacity for weakness and simple cruelty. What distinguishes his fiction from the work of many experimentalists is that man is always seen in a definite context of family and society that even world war (and Singer has written about both of them) does not destroy. This sense of continuity ultimately forms a basis for the deeper mystery of human character that clarity always provides.

When Singer moves from the family, or from man in society, and considers our cosmic structure, his contradictory attitudes are even more difficult to unravel. Though he has characterized our knowledge of the universe as "a little island in an ocean of nonknowledge," Singer nonetheless affirms his belief in God. (Here he may differ slightly from Borges for whom this question, like infinity itself, is beyond our attempts at description.) But Singer has nonetheless described his God as, "a silent God . . . perhaps a petty God, an amnesiac, perhaps a cruel God." In the last analysis he is certain only that we have too little information to know or even to criticize this God who speaks in a language of incomprehensible deeds.

In his most recent collection of stories, *Old Love,* Singer pursues these concerns while broadening his thematic range, dealing explicitly for the first time with homosexuality and bisexuality in "Two," with sado-masochism in "Not for the Sabbath," and even with incest in "The Bus." Despite this emphasis on the sexually aberrational aspect of human behavior, as well as the exotic locations (Brazil, Spain, Israel), we are, however, firmly in the fictive world of Singer. After all, as the darker side of human sexuality has always been a preoccupation of Singer, these stories are an extension of an on-going concern, rather than an exploration of completely new terrain.

The situations in this collection are various, but Singer's tone of voice or style is consistent, as are his aesthetics. Let me consider one of Singer's stories, "The Bus," from his recent collection. A closer look at the story may help clarify some of the points I've been trying to make about Singer's approach to fiction and therefore his elusive metaphysics (if we take Sartre's dictum about style to be true, as I do). Also this may help us understand the sly modernism of Singer I mentioned earlier.

The story begins (as Tolstoy recommended fiction should) in the middle; that is we are immediately in a crisis the narrator finds inexplicable:

> Why I undertook that particular tour in 1956 is something I haven't figured out to this day—dragging around in a bus through Spain for twelve days with a group of tourists. We left from Geneva. I got on the bus around three in the afternoon and found the seats nearly all taken. The driver collected my ticket and pointed out a place next to a woman who was wearing a conspicuous black cross on her breast. Her hair was dyed red, her face was thickly roughed, the lids of her brown eyes were smeared with blue eyeshadow, and from beneath all this dye and paint emerged deep wrinkles. She had a hooked nose, lips as red as a cinder, and yellowish teeth.

> She began speaking to me in French, but I told her I
> didn't understand the language and she switched over to
> German. It struck me that her German wasn't that of a real
> German or even a Swiss.

In these opening lines the reader is confronted with what we might call two fields of tension: the continuity of concrete detail and the world of deception, ambiguity, and misconception. The concrete information given the reader is chronological time: it is around three in the afternoon in 1956; a definite place—Spain—and a vivid description of Madame Weyerhofer, one of the long story's protagonists. But every time information is given, it is immediately undermined. The narrator knows he is on a bus, but does not know why. He is pointed to a seat next to a woman flaunting an ominous sign (the black cross), and everything about this woman's appearance seems elusive at best or perhaps completely meretricious (dyed hair, rouged face, a use of German that seems suspect).

Though she wears a cross, Celina Weyerhofer soon discloses that she is Jewish, that she is, in fact, a former inmate of a concentration camp. Her husband, a Swiss bank director who is sitting across from her, compelled her to convert to Christianity because, as she explains, "He hates me."

Since the rules of the bus require passengers to exchange seats daily, he soon gets to know her husband whom his wife has characterized as a pathological liar and latent homosexual. He in turn describes his wife's pathology to the narrator.

As the tale grows more dense it also becomes more bizarre. We soon realize that "The Bus" is not going to be a study of the Weyerhofers, for the narrator meets a Mrs. Metalon from Istanbul whose adolescent son Mark, a genius who could do logarithms at the age of five, is scheming to get her married again, this time to the narrator. With a minimal degree of structural complication, Singer increases the complexity of his story without sacrificing any of its narrative energy.

When the bus arrives in Spain, the narrator is assigned a hotel room without a bath, and Mark invites him to use his mother's. By accident, while looking for the Metalon's room, he knocks on the wrong door and ends up in Mrs. Weyerhofer's room. She tells him that the bath is merely a pretext for Mrs Metalon to seduce him. Later, on the bus, after she has once again delayed the trip with one of her shopping excursions, she goes even further to discredit Mrs. Metalon.

> ". . . By the way, I want you to know that this boy, Mark,
> who wants so desperately for you to sit next to that Turkish
> concubine, is not her son."
> "Then who is he?"
> "He is her lover, not her son. She sleeps with him."
> "Were you there and saw it?"
> "A chambermaid in Madrid told me. She made a mistake
> and opened the door to their room in the morning and
> found them in bed together. . . ."
> The narrator ponders the possibility.
> "Who knows what she told me might have been the truth.
> Sexual perversion is the answer to many mysteries. . . ."

What the narrator is dealing with is a set of truths or realities represented by the Weyerhofers and the Metalons, each of whom denies the other's credibility and assures the narrator that his or her truth is the one in which to believe. This is a recurring, indeed, almost archetypal situation in contemporary fiction from the masters of undermined or contradicted truth—Conrad, Faulkner, Kafka, Borges, Beckett, Calvino—to their numerous disciples. What makes this theme unique in "The Bus" is that Singer has built it unpretentiously through the personalities and detailed situations of each of the characters. Like Kafka, the more he elaborates, the more cleary he writes and the more mysterious his situations become. The narrator's own motives and passions are unknown even to himself. He yearns for Mrs. Metalon one moment, but when he has a chance to sleep with her, his passion cools.

Effortlessly the bus begins to assume symbolic dimensions; but like Kafka's castle, it is a multiple symbol or, one might say, an overdetermined one. The bus is at once a symbol of human desire, consciousness, a search for reality, and also an escape from it. Of course, these categories are hardly mutually exclusive; indeed, a central theme of the story is their interrelationship. Consciousness must always desire, and when that fails (one recalls James Agee's line, "Desire fails, everything's a prayer"), one begins the inevitable progression of self-doubt, of looking for solace in faith; one becomes in effect like Samuel Beckett's Watt who relentlessly tries to rationalize, if only by naming, what is in the closed world of language, which can never penetrate, much less illuminate, the thing-in-itself, the inexplicable. In just this way, Singer's narrator in "The Bus" confronts man's essential dilemma, here discreetly raised to metaphysical proportions: the problem of now knowing.

As Beckett's characters wait for Godot, uncertain if he will ever arrive, Singer's characters, like Kafka's land surveyor in search of the Castle, are always moving. In the case of "The Bus" there is a clear destination for the narrator's trip (as there is for the land surveyor), but it is a place Singer treats with far less importance or mystification than Kafka does his Castle. It is, in fact, completely demystified, simply a place one can find on a map. Nevertheless, the narrator never reaches it, for unable to unravel his own tangled motives, he ultimately gets off the bus and takes a train to Biarritz. In the train's diner, incredibly, he encounters Mrs. Weyerhofer who has finally left her husband after denouncing him in front of the other bus passengers as a "Nazi, homosexual, sadist."

During their brief, acerbic conversation on the train the narrator asks her, "Why did you keep the bus waiting in every city?"

> ". . . I don't know," she said at last. "I don't know myself. Demons were after me. They mislead me with their tricks."

The narrator looks out the window meditatively.

> A nocturnal gloom hovered above the landscape, an eternity that was weary of being eternal. Good God, my father and my grandfather were right to avoid looking at women! Every encounter between a man and a woman leads to sin, disappointment, humiliation.

Shortly after his reflection the narrator announces, "I'm finished, gastronomically and otherwise."

But the last word of the story is left for Madame Weyerhofer.

"Don't rush," she said. "Unlike the driver of our ill-starred bus, the forces that drive us mad have all the time in the world."

Singer's bus, then, is another "little island in an ocean of nonknowledge." In fact, it is far too elusive to constitute even a tiny island, and accordingly the narrator vacates it. Both the theme and its treatment place Singer spiritually akin to Borges, Kafka, Beckett, and Nabokov, for whom the problem of knowledge itself replaces the essential concerns of Tolstoy, Dostoyevsky, and Flaubert. This theme and its particular kind of modernism are not unique to "The Bus." We find it in the novels *Enemies, A Love Story*, Singer's most recent novel *Shosha*, and to a substantial degree in *The Magician of Lublin*. Moreover we find it in many of his stories from "Gimpel the Fool" to much of *Old*

Love. Indeed, the problem of knowledge is literally spelled out in the last sentence of the title story of *A Crown of Feathers* (1970): ". . . If there is such a thing as truth it is as intricate and hidden as a crown of feathers."

I am somewhat baffled by those critics who relentlessly stress Singer's devotion to traditional literary and "moral" values while ignoring the meanings that are apparent behind the surface simplicity of his style and his natural storyteller's gift. (Remember Joyce, Faulkner, Kafka, Borges, and Nabokov are all good, almost obsessive storytellers.) The time in which, as F. R. Leavis suggested, literature should be tested against life has passed for many of the readers of today, particularly those with an academic affiliation or orientation. Certainly the merit of literature should not depend on examining its particulars vis-à-vis the particulars of one's notion of life. Neither, however, does a self-contained system of words that has meaning only in relation to itself (not unlike Beckett's Watt who always names things but never understands them) offer us a hueristic alternative. Mastery of form and its varieties are what separates one artist from another but only, to my mind, if one's command of form is suffused by a sensibility that illuminates our experience instead of avoiding it.

Seen in this context, "The Bus," like most of Singer's fiction, reveals a writer who manages to dramatize eternal paradoxes in a wholly contemporary fashion without making us overly aware of it. To my knowledge few fictionists have this special gift, and few have demonstrated it so often.

Bibliography

By Isaac Bashevis Singer:

Novels

The Family Moskat. Translated by A. H. Gross. New York: Knopf, 1950.
Satan in Goray. Translated by Jacob Sloan. New York: Noonday Press, 1955.

The Magician of Lublin. Translated by Elaine Gottlieb and Joseph Singer. New York: Noonday Press, 1960.

The Slave. Translated by the author and Cecil Hemley. New York: Farrar, Straus and Cudahy, 1962.

The Manor. Translated by Joseph Singer and Elaine Gottlieb. New York: Farrar, Straus and Giroux, 1967.

The Estate. Translated by Joseph Singer, Elaine Gottlieb, and Elizabeth Shub. New York: Farrar, Straus and Giroux, 1969.

Enemies, A Love Story. Translated by Aliza Shevrin and Elizabeth Shub. New York: Farrar, Straus and Giroux, 1972.

Shosha. Translated by Joseph Singer and the author. New York: Farrar, Straus and Giroux, 1978.

Collections of Short Stories

Gimpel the Fool and Other Stories. Translated by Saul Bellow, Isaac Rosenfeld, and others. New York: Noonday Press, 1957.

The Spinoza of Market Street. Translated by Martha Glicklich, Cecil Hemley, and others. New York: Farrar, Straus and Cudahy, 1961.

Short Friday and Other Stories. Translated by Joseph Singer, Roger H. Klein, and others. New York: Farrar, Straus and Giroux, 1964.

The Seance and Other Stories. Translated by Roger H. Klein, Cecil Hemley, and others. New York: Farrar, Straus and Giroux, 1968.

A Friend of Kafka and Other Stories. Translated by the author, Elizabeth Shub, and others. New York: Farrar, Straus and Giroux, 1970.

A Crown of Feathers and Other Stories. Translated by the author, Laurie Colwin, and others. New York: Farrar, Straus and Giroux, 1973.

Passions and Other Stories. New York: Farrar, Straus and Giroux, 1975.

Old Love. New York: Farrar, Straus and Giroux, 1979.

Memoirs

In My Father's Court. Translated by Channah Kleinerman-Goldstein, Elaine Gottlieb, and Joseph Singer. New York: Farrar, Straus and Giroux, 1966.

A Young Man in Search of Love. Illustrated by Raphael Soyer. Garden City, New York: Doubleday, 1978.

About Isaac Bashevis Singer:

Allentuck, Marica, editor. *The Achievement of Isaac Bashevis Singer.* Carbondale: Southern Illinois University Press, 1970.

Buchen, Irving H. *Isaac Bashevis Singer and the Eternal Past.* New York: New York University Press, 1968.

Kresh, Paul. *Isaac Bashevis Singer: The Magician of West 86th Street.* New York: Dial Press, 1979.

Malin, Irving, editor. *Critical Views of Isaac Bashevis Singer.* New York: New York University Press, 1969.

—. *Isaac Bashevis Singer.* New York: Frederick Ungar, 1972.

Rosenblatt, Paul and Gene Koppel. *A Certain Bridge: Isaac Bashevis Singer.* Tucson: University of Arizona, 1971.

Siegel, Ben. *Isaac Bashevis Singer.* Minneapolis: University of Minnesota Press, 1969.

The American Land, Character, and Dream in the Novels of Wright Morris

David Madden

One senses in Wright Morris's novels the abiding presence of his Nebraska childhood. But he is no regionalist in the narrow sense. He writes about Nebraska only as it represents conflicting extremes in American land and character. Landscapes, houses, and inhabitants on the great plains become metaphors of the American dream. "The emptiness of the plain generates illusions that require little moisture, and grow better, like all tall stories, where the mind is dry." Standing in the wasteland of the present, dreaming of a heroic past, some men and women become blighted victims of the "poison of the Great American Myth." Bringing into focus a representative part of America, Morris has sought the meaning of the legends, myths, and realities of America as they survive and prevail today in the minds of common people.

In *The Field of Vision* the question is posed: Did one live on the plains in spite of the fact that the conditions were terrible? "No, one lived there *because* of it. Only where fools rushed in were such things as heroes bred." These conditions, says Morris, produced "the power to transform. . . . The budding hero found it more than enough." In Morris's early books the reader may perceive that the plains, despite their adverse effects, produced a breed of men both positively and negatively charged. In Lone Tree, Nebraska, the American dream and the American East-West conflict have become fossilized. With its imagination responding to the magnet of the fabled West, the frontier that no longer exists, and with its back turned toward the industrial East, Lone Tree is a perfect manifestation of an American tendency to build great technological complexities but to gaze in the direction of dreams. "There never was a people who tried so hard—and left so little behind as we do. There never was a people who traveled so light—and carried so much" (*The Inhabitants*).

In *The Territory Ahead*, a literary study, Morris focuses on what he conceives to be the major fault in American writers of genius and in their imitators: the inability to transform through imagination, technique, and conception the raw material of experience, with the result that the writer becomes trapped in a mythic past unable to move on to the territory ahead—the living present. In the faults of the masters whom he discusses, Morris recognizes his own. In his first six novels Morris is immersed in the raw material of his past; in all the others he is moving toward the territory ahead. "Since he must live and have his being in a world of clichés, the writer will know it by the fact that he has not been there before. The true territory ahead is what he must imagine for himself. . . . It seems to be the nature of man to transform—himself, if possible, and then the world around him—and the technique of this transformation is what we call art. . . . Both talent and imagination are of little value" without the conception that transforms.

A central, recurring theme in Morris's novels—around which many other themes resolve and through which his vision is often focused—is the relationship between the hero and his witness. The hero is the character whose effect on the other characters is the concern of the novel; usually he is not the main character in the ordinary sense, and his is not the dominant point of view. The witnesses are those characters who become in some way transformed as a result of their relationship with the hero, whose powers derive from audacity and improvisation. He (or she) makes the act of transformation possible, but before that act can occur, the witnesses must achieve imagination and compassion.

My Uncle Dudley (1942), Morris's first novel, is a wryly humorous chronicle of an odyssey which The Kid—the unnamed adolescent narrator—and his Uncle Dudley make across country in an old Marmon touring car with seven men who share expenses. The car is a gasoline raft afloat on an asphalt river. In the wagon treks westward, survival of the fittest was physically determined; but this spiritual journey of The Kid and Dudley is primarily a matter of moral survival. For The Kid, the campfire and the jail offer two views of the American land and character. Having discovered the land and a few of its heroes, The Kid can then set out alone in search of one of its products—himself.

In *The Man Who Was There* (1945) Morris offers three views of

Agee Ward (perhaps The Kid as a young man). The first is Agee's own view as he returns to the home place. A painter passionately in search of a myth, Agee tries to escape captivity in the nostalgia of the past by processing the past, by transmuting it as myth into the formal, conceptual realm of art. Two witnesses resurrect the hero through visions invoked by psychological ordeals that their memories and intuitions of Agee inspire.

If "an epic is how you feel about something," the episodes, names, and dates in Morris's books are part of one great epic—the epic of the American consciousness: the only wide-open spaces we have left. Like The Kid and Agee Ward, Morris attempts to discover America first, to enter into the "collective memories of the pioneer American past." Morris asks Crèvecoeur's "disquieting and perennial question": What is an American? For Morris the answer lies some-where on the farms and in the small towns of the Midwest, roots of American strength that flower in the East.

In *The Inhabitants* (1946), an experimental use of photographs with texts, the emphasis is on the land and on the artifacts used by the inhabitants; in *The Home Place* (1949), fiction but with photographs, on the inhabitants themselves; and in the novel *The World in the Attic* (1948), on what the land and the people signify to one man: Clyde Muncy (alias The Kid and Agee Ward), writer and self-exiled Nebras-kan, who is nearing middle age—the returning Creative Native. In both *The Inhabitants* and *The Home Place*, as well as in a later non-fictional work, *God's Country and My People* (1970), Morris juxtaposes prose epiphanies with his own stark photographs of landscapes, houses, and artifacts (very seldom of people, never of faces) in such a way that they enhance each other's different effects. Morris is con-cerned with America's "appalling and visible freedom to be blighted." Although the rural way of life is narrow, it seems to win, at least, on its own ground, represented by the old folks. Before the old rural way is lost, Americans need to *look* at it, to assimilate the best of it. In *The World in the Attic* the Muncys represent the urban way in which "the new is obsolete on its appearance." Morris insists that Americans need to go home again and that, in order for Americans to come of age, they must. Drawn back by nostalgia, the promise of the past, Muncy reacts with nausea, the present failure of the dream.

In *The Works of Love* (1952) the American dream proves real but hollow. In the great American desert of the plains, the American dream of success both flowered and withered: "In the dry places, men begin to dream. Where the rivers run sand, there is something in man that begins to flow." Men like Will Brady, who thrive on dreams, often welcome ready-made ones. In one view of the American dream, anything and everything is possible for everyman. But since the Nebraskan and the American past are both mythic and real, the concept of the American dream, based on the clichés of the past, conflicts with the often nightmarish realities of American life. Contrary to reality, Will succeeds as easily as the myth promises. But Morris shows that, once translated into reality, the dream becomes like the "giant brooding" statue of Abraham Lincoln in Chicago—soft green with corrosion. Will does not witness the real heroism out of which the storybook idea of success was fabricated, an idea which is worshipped by men who seek compensation for their own emotional and spiritual lacks.

In Will Brady, Morris has created an archetypal character who symbolizes the American myth of the dream of success, an outgrowth of the myth of the pioneer spirit. He exemplifies the American character and spirit as it has failed; but, in the manner of its failing, it has somehow succeeded in emotional and mystical works of love from "The Wilderness" of the great plains to "The Wasteland" of the great city.

The microcosm of family and home in suburban Philadelphia is the focus for two close observations on middle-class manners on the American scene. Mrs. Ormsby and Mrs. Porter of *Man and Boy* (1951) and *The Deep Sleep* (1953) are the first of Morris's female forces to be observed in direct action. Archetypal mothers, they reject the defunct male West and "make do" in the East. In the house, run by Mrs. Ormsby's and Mrs. Porter's principles, the wilderness and the wasteland meet.

In *Man and Boy* the house is overtly ruled by a "momarchy." A feature editorial recently proclaimed that "Mother had, singlehanded, saved a good part of the nation for the quail." Her son, Virgil, missing in action, "had been missing, some people would say, for a good many years." It is Mother who christens the ship named after her son, a national hero. Mother is a bewitcher who creates public ceremonies in which transformations are possible; her husband's imagination and compassion achieve private transformations in impersonal love and in a vision of permanence.

In *The Deep Sleep* revelations produce resurrections. For son-in-law Webb, the artist intent upon getting the well-composed picture, the Porter house "brought the conflicting forces together and gave them shape. It added up to more than the sum of the separate lives." Webb is faced with the challenge of making sense of the lives of the inhabitants of this house. By the end of the day (the day of the preparations for the funeral of his father-in-law, the Judge, whom he loved and respected), Webb achieves compassion for his mother-in-law, who had seemed, characteristically, to lack feeling.

The urban novels deal with the problematic question: How does one escape captivity in the mythic past to live in the everyday present? In these novels, Morris develops attitudes and techniques for confronting the persistent enigma of his Nebraskan background. Produced by the Midwest, Lawrence, the hero of *The Huge Season* (1954), represents the American dream and character: the audacity and tenacity of his grandfather, who built an empire in the barbed-wire business, come out, in future generations, only in Lawrence, champion tennis player and bullfighter. Perhaps his failure to achieve physical and spiritual conquest over himself symbolizes both the failure of the mythic West and of the 1920s. Foley, his main witness, wonders: "Did they lack conviction? No, they had conviction. What they lacked was intention." Because the hero lived so bewitchingly in the present and killed himself when he saw he had no future as a perfect hero, the witnesses, a gallery of fossils in the present, are captive in the past, unable to light out for the territory ahead. "The shot that killed Lawrence had crippled all of them." With its youthful rites of vitality, the 1920s promised more than the individuals, even Lindbergh, could deliver, at least consistently. But in Foley's imagination it is "a permanent scene, made up of frail impermanent things." Foley does achieve this moment of truth and begins to bury the past.

The lovers in *Love Among the Cannibals* (1957) and *What a Way to Go* (1962) do not go beyond the cannibalistic sexual level where, Morris suggests, everything else begins. Sex is the new frontier, and the Greek and Cynthia are a new species of audacious female; they persuade the male that, on the sexual frontier, where one may start from scratch, "the real McCoy" is still possible.

Morris has observed that one of the most obvious traits of the American character is the ability or the impulse to improvise: "the passion, sometimes the mania to *make it new*." As a massive culture, America is unique in history, remaining "as a *process*, changing its shape and its nature daily, before the world's eyes." For the artist, improvisation becomes experimentation. "If you live in a world of clichés, as I do," says Horter, middle-aged writer of popular song lyrics in *Love Among the Cannibals*, "some of them of the type you coined yourself, you may not realize how powerful they can be." But Mac, who writes the music for their songs, points out that the phony is all one has, it *is*, as opposed to what was or is yet to be; and one must make it real. Horter attempts to transform, to make new the fluctuating clichés of American life.

Professor Soby in *What a Way to Go* is encumbered by his past; in the spontaneous response to the wisdom of the body, Cynthia teaches Soby that sex is one means of living contentedly in the immediate present. On ancient ground (Venice and Greece) wisecracking Cynthia is the nerve center of the lively present; as she helps him get to the simplicity of the Greeks, Soby brings the dead mythic past alive again in his imaginative field of vision.

Warren Howe, middle-aged television scriptwriter in *Cause for Wonder* (1963), deliberately re-experiences his own past. He returns to a castle in Austria, where a madman of his youth still audaciously improvises upon moments in the lives of his guests to cause perceptions and transformations. This novel demonstrates the simultaneity of past and present in mental time and space: past and present in both America and Europe are the ambience of self-discovery. Even forgotten moments of the past are preserved in the creative memory that reconstructs as it resurrects. Howe contemplates as he experiences it the human nature of time and space, which are coexistent dimensions of each other. "If you live in the present," he discovers, "you can't help but be ahead of your time." The usable past is "the here and now." Morris shows how the moment of individual creative vision synthesizes memory and immediate perception, time and space.

Boyd and McKee, as hero and witness in *The Field of Vision* (1956) and *Ceremony in Lone Tree* (1960), represent two opposed sides of the American dream. There comes a point when this relationship must end; the witness must wake from the spell, and the hero must free himself of dependence on the witness. Severance begins in *Field* at a Mexican bullring and is accomplished, for better or worse, in *Ceremony* on native ground, the sanded navel of the world.

None of Morris's characters is capable of achieving the ideal state through all of what, for Morris, are the three ways of self-transcendence: love, imagination, and the heroic. *The Field of Vision* develops the theme that the hero-witness relationship may result both in transforming and in transfixing the hero as well as the witness. Boyd's trouble is that his acts always give off more heat than light, and what has beguiled his witnesses is their hope that the hero will someday make the light they feel hopelessly incapable of making for themselves. When the witnesses realize that, because of the hero's acts, they are, like Scanlon, trapped in the past and unable to function, they back out of his magnetic field. The world may love a fool, but to remain bewitched by him can mean paralysis; the past may be alive, but the present is dead. And present reality, offering only what one can know, without glorious promises, is all one has to work with.

Morris's chief purpose in *Ceremony in Lone Tree* is to free his characters from the past in the midst of an actual conflict between past and present, under the threat or promise of the future. *Ceremony* conveys a sense of past and present in weird coexistence; living and dead "fossils" on the scene parallel immediate things. Lacking a mythic past or a folk tradition that sustains rather than cripples them, and lacking the creative hero that should follow an era of raw experience, the witnesses (and the defunct hero) are caught up in a complex problem of identity that is especially acute in *Ceremony*. Aware that something is ending in Lone Tree, the characters wildly improvise on new selves.

Like Agee and Muncy, Boyd, the audacious amateur, can almost transform the American land and dream into art; he can impose upon the past a semblance of order and meaning. But his shaping imagination is stunned by the senseless fragmentation of the present. The motherly owner of the motel near the atomic proving grounds, eager for Boyd to see the great show, writes WAKE BEFORE BOMB beside his name. Boyd wonders: "How did one do it?" Since neither past nor present is creatively alive, what is lost if one doesn't wake? When the bomb of the past explodes, its light may reveal the extent to which Boyd (and the American dream expressed in him) has failed. "The past, whether one liked it or not, was all that one actually possessed. . . . The present was the moment of exchange—when all might be lost. . . ."

In *One Day* (1965) Morris makes public and private events impinge significantly upon each other in the immediate present on the American scene; he parallels the trivial events of every day with a single, enormous, historical event (the assassination of President

Kennedy) of a single day. Each character is so stimulated by a frightening present to immerse, if not immolate himself, in memories of a haunting, distant past, that the events of the day, even the assassination, pale. The veterinarian Cowie, as Morris's voice, wonders: "Who could say when this day had begun, or would ever end?" Morris suggests an answer in the way he restructures time and space in his characters' various fields of vision. Never has Morris's technique of using one day as a time and point-of-view device had such complex thematic significance. The conceptual power that distinguishes him from many of his contemporaries finds its consummation and justification in that day. Consistent with his increasing interest in the immediate American scene, Morris relates various manifestations of the fluctuating American character to that still point where the trigger found the center of vision and the dance stopped for a moment. X marks the spot where the American character revealed itself to itself and to all the world. Confronted with a senseless human act, Americans immediately attempt to understand the perpetrator. Morris depicts the blighted hero of the American dream surrounded by beguiled witnesses. To excite on almost every page a laughter that turns to acid in the mouth is a near miracle of creation. *One Day* burns with a demonic vision that would be tragic were Morris's comic impulse not so responsive, his humanity not so inclusive. It is a cross-eyed vision that looks in one direction with a Sophoclean and in another with an Aristophanean glance. At the intersection between the two flash such images as Americans see in their nightmares. *One Day* raises the question: After such knowledge, how does Morris manage the compassion that forgives?

In Orbit (1967), like most of Morris's novels, examines the human nature of time. Morris contemplates volatile images of the present as they presage the future. Instead of describing artifacts that are imbued metaphysically with the past, Morris sets in orbit objects that exist only for the present. As in most of his novels, the time span is one day, but here Morris intermingles everyday events with a natural and a public human event that affects only one representative American small-town cosmos. The task of imaginative synthesis is mainly the reader's.

The structure of this short novel visibly expresses the theme. Each character, except the last, opens with a brief scene in which Jubal, a wandering motorcyclist, encounters one of the other characters. Morris evokes the pathos of the isolation from each other of similar minds by showing how separate lives plug into a common current of feeling and perception unaware. Tableaux and events are even funnier from the reader's complex viewpoint.

In this new variation of the hero-witness relationship, the weird behavior of the witnesses, whose gestures Jubal misinterprets, sets off impulses in him. We see here more clearly than in earlier novels the ways in which suppressed but wild people affect the hero. The witnesses have an inner disposition to produce, then respond to the hero. Morris shows the beneficial effects of losing one's mind now and then. He subordinates the action of events to psychological epiphanies. Psychological effects on the characters are more violent than the actual encounters. Compared with all his witnesses, Jubal, Morris suggests, is stable.

In Orbit shows the interaction of sexual, psychological, intellectual, mechanical, and natural forces. Their paths crisscross by chance and finally converge in a tornado. The controlling energy is Morris's conceptual power which compresses chaos into a pattern and gives these forces life as well as symbolic value. Morris opens and closes the novel with a catalytic poetic image of Jubal riding his motorcycle. Jubal responds to the immediate moment spontaneously with speed, and the spectacle of his response affects the "ordinary people who encounter him." The image of the motorcyclist expresses the nature of the contemporary American character and scene; most of our experiences are moments in motion, seeming to have no relevant past. The natural and the anti-natural are the opposing forces Morris depicts. In his novels Morris often stresses the irony of the American's persistent suppression of the natural desire to expose oneself to risk. The motorcycle and the twister storm as complementary forces are juxtaposed. The motorcyclist and the twister are supernatural and natural forces which happen on Pickett "as luck would have it." More than any other Morris novel, *In Orbit* illustrates the concept of a novel as a tissue of images, over which lingers finally a single charged image. In his selection and controlled condensation and juxtaposition of images, Morris achieves the dynamism of the dance.

In *The Fork River Space Project* (1977) Dahlberg, a house painter and one-time writer of semi-science fiction, and Harry Lorbeer, a plumber and proprietor of the space project, change the lives of Kelcey, an aging writer of "humorous fantasy-type pieces," and his young second wife, Alice. This short novel is Kelcey's witty and lyrical meditation on a constellation of images that revolve around two mysterious and suspenseful questions: Did the population of Fork River, Kansas, vanish in a twister or a space ship? Are Dahlberg and Harry planning a space trip and will Alice go with them? In different ways Harry and Dahlberg become heroes to Kelcey and Alice, their witnesses. Alice's response is to become Dahlberg's lover, Kelcey's is to transform himself through his imagination.

Two major motifs that characterize the American experience throughout history are the "great expectations" aroused by the land-scape and its prospects for spiritual and physical development and the long "ceremony of waiting" for those expectations to come to pass. Ultimately, space is the territory ahead that Huck Finn set out for at the end of Twain's classic. In each of his novels Morris has been heading for that space where imagination, mystery, and awe make everything possible. *The Fork River Space Project* is told in the first person, a point of view perfectly suited to a book that demonstrates the power of the imagination, leavened with lucid intelligence, abundantly and com-plexly image-laden, thought-provoking, and poetically suggestive. Through his imagination, expressed in a witty, paradoxical, punning style, Kelcey ponders the nature of human perception and experiences intuition in rarefied moments that Morris embodies in charged im-ages. Kelcey meditates on people, situations, concepts, images. The reader's active participation as collaborator is built into the structures of Morris's style.

Two of Morris's novels are brief meditations on old age. Floyd Warner, an old man who has no real future, experiences the past in *Fire Sermon* (1971) and his own last moments in the present in *A Life* (1973). Morris makes his eleventh trip back to the home place—a ritualistic compulsion to re-experience the past while capturing the spirit of the immediate present. The old man wants to go home to the house his favorite sister's death has left vacant. But he also wants his orphaned 11-year-old nephew, born and raised in California, to know where he came from. While the old man's life is full but stagnating, the boy's is empty. The reader and the characters feel the presence of people who are dead or distant.

Warner drives an old Maxwell coupe, pulling a bullet-shaped trailer in which two hitchhikers, Joy, a radical groupie, and Stanley, a Weatherman, demonstrate the latest works of love before the bugged eyes of the boy. We see events through the mingled visions of the boy and his uncle. The highway dead-ends in the future, with a brief fire stop in Chapman, Nebraska, parched navel of the world. As the house burns, the boy runs away with Joy and Stanley. In *A Life*, Warner journeys alone to visit a farm of his early childhood. He dies, almost willingly, at the hands of another hitchhiker, a modern Indian. Both novels have a static quality in spite of Morris's usually dynamic style.

Morris's style is at its meditative best, though, in *Plains Song: For Female Voices* (1980), which deals with three generations of women (and their men) on the home place, once again. It is a quietly lyrical celebration and an excruciatingly poignant lamentation. Morris makes us feel that up from the flat windy American plains rises everybody's song—a plain song, a plaintive song, at moments almost unbearable, but absolutely unforgettable. In singing of the unfulfilled promise of the great plains experience, Morris fulfills his own promise as an American writer.

Wright Morris's achievement is that he has been able to project upon the literary firmament a many-faceted, serio-comic view of the American dream, landscape, and character. In vision and content, he is, I believe, the most thoroughly American contemporary writer. Although he has nominal affinities with a number of American writers, past and present, Morris has little in common with the raw material, themes, styles, or techniques of his immediate contemporaries. He alone, it seems, has maintained, throughout a large body of work, a constant, though always refocusing, view of his characters and of the world they inhabit.

Bibliography

By Wright Morris:

Novels

My Uncle Dudley. New York: Harcourt, Brace, 1942.
The Man Who Was There. New York: C. Scribner's Sons, 1945.
The World in the Attic. New York: C. Scribner's Sons, 1949.
Man and Boy. New York: Knopf, 1951.
The Works of Love. New York: Knopf, 1952.

The Deep Sleep. New York: C. Scribner's Sons, 1953.
The Huge Season. New York: Viking Press, 1954.
The Field of Vision. New York: Harcourt, Brace, 1956.
Love Among the Cannibals. New York: Harcourt, Brace, 1957.
Ceremony in Lone Tree. New York: Atheneum, 1960.
What a Way to Go. New York: Atheneum, 1962.
Cause for Wonder. New York: Atheneum, 1963.
One Day. New York: Atheneum, 1965.
In Orbit. New York: New American Library, 1967.
Fire Sermon. New York: Harper & Row, 1971.
A Life. New York: Harper & Row, 1973.
The Fork River Space Project. New York: Harper & Row, 1977.
Plains Song: For Female Voices. New York: Harper & Row, 1980.

Short Stories

Real Losses, Imaginary Gains. New York: Harper & Row, 1976.

Photographic Works

The Inhabitants. New York and London: C. Scribner's Sons, 1946. (Reminiscences)
The Home Place. New York: C. Scribner's Sons, 1948. (Fiction)
God's Country and My People. New York: Harper & Row, 1968. (Reminiscences)
Love Affair—A Venetian Journal. New York: Harper & Row, 1972. (Travel)
Wright Morris: Structures and Artifacts: Photographs, 1933-1954. Lincoln: University
      of Nebraska Press, 1975.

Criticisms, Essays, Anthologies

The Territory Ahead. New York: Harcourt, Brace, 1958. (Criticism)
A Bill of Rites, Bill of Wrongs, or Bill of Goods. New York: New American Library,
      1968. (Essays)
Wright Morris: A Reader. New York: Harper & Row, 1970. (Novels, short stories,
      criticism)
*About Fiction: Reverent Reflections on the Nature of Fiction with Irreverent Observations
      on Writers, Readers & Other Abuses.* New York: Harper & Row, 1975. (Criti-
      cism)
Earthly Delights, Unearthly Adornments: American Writers as Image Makers. New York:
      Harper & Row, 1978. (Criticism)

About Wright Morris:

Crumb, G. B. *The Novels of Wright Morris: A Critical Interpretation.* Lincoln: University of Nebraska Press, 1978.
Howard, Leon. *Wright Morris.* Minneapolis: University of Minnesota Press, 1968.
Knoll, Robert E., editor. *Conversations with Wright Morris.* Lincoln: University of Nebraska Press, 1977.
Madden, David. *Wright Morris.* New York: Twayne, 1964.

Theodore Roethke:
The Darker Side of the Dream

Karl Malkoff

The poetry of Theodore Roethke like the work of most contemporary writers, fits easily into traditions that do not strictly respect national or even linguistic boundaries. The student of Roethke's verse has greater need of familiarity with Baudelaire and Neruda than with Longfellow; technically, at least, that verse has more in common with Odysseus Elytis' than with Robert Frost's. And yet, at the very core of his vision, Roethke remains the quintessentially American poet.

To some extent, this is a result of Roethke's sensitivity to the American landscape. Born in Saginaw, Michigan, in 1908, he grew up on his father's floral establishment: rows of greenhouses, acres of virgin forest. And he spent the last 15 years of his life, from 1948 to 1963, as a Professor of English at the University of Washington, in the Pacific Northwest. From the "Greenhouse Poems" early in his career to the "North American Sequence," which appeared in a posthumous volume, stone and stream, earth and sky, and the abundance of living things they support, are crucial to his work. But Roethke's "naturalism" masks concerns still more vital to the American shape of his poetry.

A tortured man—with psychological characteristics both paranoid schizophrenic and manic-depressive—he used his madness, his tenuous sense of self, to become a spokesman for us all. He articulated what is generally repressed: the struggle of the naked self to persist in its existence, of the isolated man to become part of something greater than himself. This is the specifically American tradition to which Roethke belongs. It contains the Transcendentalists—Emerson, Thoreau, Hawthorne, Melville—whose sense of the connections between spirit and matter place the isolated individual amid a great chain of being; it contains William Carlos Williams, who realized man's helplessness "unless the individual raise himself to some approximate co-extension with the universe."[1] And it contains Theodore Roethke.

Although *Open House* (1941) was Roethke's first collection of poems, it was not until his second volume, *The Lost Son and Other Poems* (1948), that he discovered his true voice. It was then that he discovered the Greenhouse. In his earlier work, Roethke, who was in a sense the first of the Confessional poets, had attempted to explore the workings of his psyche and to make it the chief source of his poetry. But although he was able to converse about his experience well enough, he had not learned how to communicate his feelings to his readers in print. The breakthrough came when he realized that the plants of his childhood world shared with him his most pressing concerns: the struggle to come into being and to endure. "Cutting (*later*)" is characteristic of these "Greenhouse Poems":

(One stanza of four lines, another of seven, are
both excluded at the publisher's request.)

The struggle of the shoot is the struggle of the saint; it is the strenuous journey of man's spirit. But what is most important about Roethke's insight is that he does not anthropomorphize the plants; rather he looks within himself for those qualities he shares with the vegetable world: the tensions of growth, the sensuousness of being. By abandoning his exclusively human perspective, the poet is able to see beyond the plant's apparent passivity. Freed of a human sense of time and motion, Roethke perceives the cuttings' immense power. More important still, he perceives himself not as an exile from the natural world but very much—beneath the surface at any rate—part of it. This is no sentimentalizing of pretty flowers. Nor is it the Romantic's apprehension of a Force in Nature. It is simply an ackowledgment of kinship. It is a way of not being alone.

Nonetheless, this is a poetic rather than a philosophical break-through. The genius in Roethke's discovery of the Greenhouse was that what he had really found was a concrete language—one that could be experienced by sense as well as mind, and one that, curiously enough, was perfectly suited to represent the life of the spirit. It saved the poet from abstraction; it brought his words to life.

In the title poem of *The Lost Son* Roethke put to use in more ambitious form the lessons of the "Greenhouse Poems." The problem with those poems, as their author discovered almost at once, was that they were limited to single perceptions, or flashes of insight. They were short, imagistic; they could not bear the weight of a more com-prehensive vision. With the help of critic Kenneth Burke, a friend and colleague of Roethke's when they both taught at Bennington College in the late 1940s, he constructed a broader framework within which he could trace the birth, growth, and survival of the self. He made use of Jungian archetypal patterns: the descent into the underworld, the victory of light over darkness. But the key to the success of this kind of developmental poem (a series of which, beginning with "The Lost Son," was collected by Roethke in *Praise to the End!* [1951]) remains the use of sensuous glimpses of the natural world as emblems of an inner life.

Responding to the loss of his father—which is also the loss of God, the loss of the larger whole in which the self may participate—Roethke calls on his talismans:

(Three lines about a snail, bird and worm
excluded at the publisher's request.)

Wordsworth, Keats, or Shelley might very well have invoked a bird or two—but surely not snail or worm. That is Roethke's touch. Of natural forces, he prefers those that are small; like him, they are puny in the face of the universe. But they endure; they have secrets Roethke must discover. In Jungian terms, atavistic states of mind are useful in providing buttresses against surges of anxiety. That is, when the psyche is under siege, regressive modes of experiencing reality are effective backstops against annihilation.

In the heart of "The Lost Son" Roethke descends into his own peculiar underworld. Homer, Virgil, and Dante have done it before, but Roethke's verse is again clearly recognizable. His underworld is very much like a womb from which he will be reborn; and it has more than an accidental resemblance to the Greenhouse.

(Nine lines about roots, moss, mildew and fish nerves
excluded at the publisher's request.)

By the poem's conclusion, Roethke has been reborn, has at least partially been compensated for the loss of the father (his own father died when the boy was quite young), by experiencing almost mystically his sense of comradeship with nature. In an open field consciousness expands (as reflected in the lengthening, then contracting lines of the poem) to find itself at one with its surroundings.

(Three stanzas, each with five lines, about
light, stillness and the spirit, excluded
at the publisher's request.)

It is, of course, only a temporary victory over aloneness, over the burdens of liberation from the past, from oppressive authority (both of which are embodied by the father). In the Jungian pattern there must be frequent regressions, frequent returns into the darkness, in order for growth to take place. This thought in itself is apparently of some comfort to one, like Roethke, who lives in constant fear of somehow being drawn back into primal ooze.

In the early 1950s the emphases in Roethke's concerns shifted. In part this was a consequence of his having married in 1952 the beautiful Beatrice Heath O'Connell. The sensual, musical, loving "Words for the Wind," from the collection of that title (1959), bears witness to this new dimension of his life.

(Eight lines about loving another excluded
at the publisher's request.)

A less metaphysical, but no less significant, form of isolation had been,
it seems, successfully dealt with.

But most of the changes in Roethke's obsessions came from that
most imposing of all difficulties for the ego: the spector of its own
extinction. Until this point in his life, most of Roethke's attempts to
defend himself against annihilation had been directed towards the
fear of a regression so complete there could be no return. But while he
had effectively avoided that fate—even his psychotic episodes had
become part of a repetitious, and therefore comforting, pattern—he
now faced a threat that was certain to be realized. "Dream of a
woman," he wrote in "The Pure Fury," "and a dream of death." This
was the dichotomy of his emotional life. In addition to whatever
comfort Beatrice may have provided—and most of his more cheerful
poems of the 1950s involved her—Roethke turned to philosophy and
theology, to the Eastern mystics and the religious existentialists. Paul
Tillich's *The Courage to Be* in particular seems to have granted Roethke
solace, and he rewarded it by converting one of its paragraphs into the
first stanza of "The Pure Fury."[2]

In some ways, this aspect of Roethke's career takes him furthest
from an American tradition if we can so describe the shifts from sense
to intellect, from the falling back to one's roots in native soil to a more
existential embracing of one's isolation—though it might be more
accurate to see that Roethke had modified and expanded, rather than
abandoned, his approach to experience. In any case, it is at this time
that the great Irish poet William Butler Yeats began to exert his
influence on Roethke's verse. More and more, he found himself
writing poems whose frames of reference were philosophical rather
than emotional; and when dealing with ideas, who better to adopt as
spiritual father than the author of "Among School Children" and
"Sailing to Byzantium"?

When intellect dominates, the possibilities of merging with the
oneness of being diminish. Roethke is now thrown back on a clearly
existential position, on the absurd triumph. As he concludes "The
Dying Man" sequence, his tribute to Yeats,

(Three lines, beginning
"he dares to live"
excluded at the publisher's request.)

The self in isolation may come to terms with its terror, but it cannot banish it. In fact, it begins to create a split in his poetry. There are those poems that are the voice of the conscious self attempting to come to terms with its aloneness and with its lack of meaningful modes of action. And there are those poems which continue the poet's efforts to become part of something greater than himself. Although generalizations of this sort can be misleading, it seems fair to say that the former poems tend to have regular meters and rhyme schemes; informed by intellect, they are organized by intellectually proposed patterns. The latter poems employ free verse; here intellect becomes subordinate, and such bodily function as breath and pulse determine the poems' rhythms.

　　To go a step further, in the patterned poems the breaking down of the boundaries of the poet's consciousness is experienced as a loss of the self, while in the freer formed poems that same breakdown is a joyful escape from the tyranny and isolation of the ego. Compare, for example, the lines describing Roethke's moment of illumination in the field with the lines below, from "In a Dark Time."

(Three lines, beginning
"Dark, dark my light,"
excluded at the publisher's request.)

While "The Lost Son" describes the coming of light and the promise of future comfort, "In a Dark Time" portrays darkness and a sense of terror that only the formal elements of the poem prevent from deteriorating into panic.

　　If Roethke had been a philosopher, he no doubt would sooner or later have had to come logically to terms with the contradiction. The same experience, arbitrarily, can be either the salvation or the destruction of the self. But he was a poet; his job was to present, to re-enact, rather than interpret. In Roethke's work we are given rare glimpses of that contradiction before it has been rationalized into a political or social philosophy. The freedom to reshape reality sets the scene again for Adam's Fall; the dread of that new Fall is a heavy burden.

If we wish to trace broad patterns in Roethke's verse, we can say the following. At the start of his career, he turned toward the microcosm, toward the world of plants and small animals, as a means of supporting the self. In mid-career, he often preferred existential stances, facing the abyss without shield. And near the end of his career—and his life—he turned at last to what had been conspicuously missing from his previous work: he turned to the macrocosm, to the North American continent.

As in "The Lost Son" and its companion poems, the struggle to be born and reborn, to bring light to darkness, to become a part of the greater whole, predominate in the "North American Sequence." But now the perspective is not that of a child but of an aging man. The landscape shift from the nooks and crannies of the Greenhouse to the vastness of the mid and far west.

(Eight lines from
"Journey to the Interior,"
beginning "In the long journey"
excluded at the publisher's request."

Roethke's America seems to exist in mythical rather than historical time. The exception lies in the allusions to pollution and the despoilation of the continent scattered throughout. But you will look in vain for traces of our political, economic, or social history. Even the pollution is seen rather from the point of view of nature—for nature has its own kind of "history"—than of society. For the journey of the spirit, of the psyche, is eternally the same, and Roethke is able to embody its motions almost as effectively in this visual, adult world as he did in the child's world of touch and smell. For example, in "Meditation at Oyster River" he communicates the powerful longing for renewed movement after a period of stagnation with these images of the Tittebawasee River approaching its spring thaw:

(Eight long lines, beginning
"And the midchannel"
excluded at the publisher's request.)

In the end, Roethke brings past and present together into one image of eternity. In "The Rose" Roethke is able to conflate the private imagery of his childhood with a symbol persistent in the Western tradition from Dante through T. S. Eliot.

(Seven lines, beginning
"And I think of roses"
excluded at the publisher's request.)

But such moments are no more than temporary stays against confusion. Roethke, although only in his 50s, was dying. The price of confronting the chaos within, the price of ecstasy as well as pain, had been great. With a bad heart, shot full of medication, he was "dying inward like an aging tree."

Theodore Roethke died of a heart attack while swimming in a neighbor's pool. He had created one of the unmistakable voices in modern American poetry. He had significantly expanded the vocabulary men use to express their relation to the rest of nature. And he had dealt with painful honesty with the struggles of the liberated self to endure its freedom.

Notes

[1] *Imaginations* (New York: New Directions, 1971), p. 105.
[2] See my *Theodore Roethke: An Introduction to the Poetry* (New York: Columbia University Press, 1966), p. 131.

Bibliography

By Theodore Roethke:

Open House. New York: Knopf, 1941.
The Lost Son and Other Poems. Garden City, New York: Doubleday, 1948.
Praise to the End! Garden City, New York: Doubleday, 1951.
The Waking: Poems 1933-1953. Garden City, New York: Doubleday, 1953.
Words for the Wind. Garden City, New York: Doubleday, 1958.
The Far Field. Garden City, New York: Doubleday, 1964.
The Collected Poems of Theodore Roethke. Garden City, New York: Doubleday, 1966.

About Theodore Roethke:

Blessing, Richard Allen. *Theodore Roethke's Dynamic Vision.* Bloomington: Indiana University Press, 1974.
Malkoff, Karl. *Theodore Roethke: An Introduction to the Poetry.* New York: Columbia University Press, 1966.
Mills, Ralph J., Jr. *Theodore Roethke.* Minneapolis: University of Minnesota Press, 1963.

Charles Olson: Against the Past

Charles Olson was one of the founders of the post-World War II avant-garde that began at Black Mountain College in the 1950s. Nonetheless he had an abiding interest in the past, particularly in discovering the permanent tradition before what he termed (usually contemptuously) "the Socratic universe of discourse." By that he meant all those ideas, images, and syntactical patterns that religion, philosophy, and art have accumulated in the West since Classical Antiquity. In his early work, especially in much of *In Cold Hell, In Thicket* and *Maximus Poems*, he thought he had located such a tradition in the Mediterranean culture of the Second Millenium BCE, in the Hittite Empire, Ugarit and other now-vanished civilizations.

However, by the 1960s in the two sequels to his *Maximus Poems*, he had come to believe that the Ice Age, the Pleistocene Era (from roughly 100,000 to 10,000 BCE), contained the true beginnings of the cultural and artistic condition that he had previously been looking for in the Second Millenium. It was the culture of this era that he wished to see active and informing, not only in his own work but in other poets' as well.

So I think it would be useful to examine, chronologically, Olson's interest(s) in the past, starting with Ezra Pound (for it certainly was from Pound that Olson got the idea of exploring and researching the past from a fresh perspective) and concluding finally with a discussion of the Pleistocene as it affects his poetry and his development as a poet. Of all American writers in this century Olson, it would be fair to say, is unique in conducting this investigation of the distant past (not the Homeric Age nor the Italian Renaissance familiar to readers of Pound's *Cantos*) and in marshalling linguistic, archeological, and geological evidence and sources more like a scholarly specialist than the conventionally imaged man of letters. In any case, we should remember that Olson's interest in the past was not for its own sake, was not scholarly in that sense; rather it sprang from his hatred and distrust of the present, especially the political and economic distortions of modern capitalism. (We should remember that before becoming a poet Olson had a promising career in government service before resigning his position as an Assistant Secretary of the Treasury in 1945.) Like Pound, Olson hoped the past would serve as measure for the present, but he goes much further in trying to reinvent and revivify past cultural conditions often loosely called "primitive" or "ethnopoetic," then using them to break the bonds of Western discourse so as to rebuild the present along lines that Olson saw were useful in the distant past.

Olson's main interest in Ezra Pound, his "master" at least in the 1940s, was in finding a poet who could teach him how to write, how to distill himself and "the American experience" into verse. But in 1951, in "I, Mencius, Pupil of the Master . . ." he criticizes Pound because, as he says, the Master was "embraced by the demon he drove off": the "clank of rhyme" which Pound had used in his translation of the Confucian Odes. Pound's teaching (quoting from the same poem) Olson characterized as follows:

> . . . he
> who taught us all
> that no line must sleep,
> that as the line goes so goes
> the Nation! . . .
> —*The Distances*

The word "line" here, it would be well to note, means more than simply line of verse. Rather Olson is playing with some of the same ideas Pound had earlier presented in Canto 45, the so-called usury canto: "with usura the line grows thick." The poet's line, then, "controls" the nation by controlling the language and checking by its firmness and precision the "bad" lines generated by a usurious capitalism. It also serves as visible measure of what economic and social justice a nation has managed to achieve for itself.

In his famous essay of the 1950s "Human Universe," Olson moves to dispel the classical world of discourse which shapes and encloses thought:

> ... the Greek went on to declare all speculation as enclosed in the "UNIVERSE of discourse." It is their word, and the refuge of all metaphysicians since—as though language, too, was an absolute, instead of (as even man is) instrument. . . .
>
> We stay unaware how two means of discourse the Greeks appear to have invented hugely intermit our participation in our experience, and so prevent discovery. They are . . . logic and classification, and it is they that have so fastened themselves on habits of thought that action is interfered with, absolutely interfered with, I should say.
>
> —*Selected Writings*

These ideas appear in even more stinging terms in his later book or fascicle, *Pleistocene Man* (1967):

<pre>
                 WHY   I   HATE
        Greeks   &   Italians
                                   [The Vatican since Dante]

[Grecian since
  the earliest Renaissance
   —including in fact Thomas Aquinas at least]   is

        the Classical ——— Representational, either one

     THE STATE   ——————   COLORED
                            TELEVISION
</pre>

What Olson is doing here is not only writing off Western/Classical Antiquity, but also its epigones and successors in art, religion, politics, and technology. If the modern world sprang whole from the mind of Greece and Rome like Athena from Zeus' headache, then it is now time to put it back where it belongs—in the den with the television set and the Harvard Classics.

His view of the present is no better. America is not a possible home at present for democracy and real civility. Rather, Olson's America is a place with certain features reminiscent of the nightmares of Mailer's novel *American Dream*, where the Mob, the Church, Big Business, and their political lackeys, the Kennedys and the Nixons, desperately try to run the show. He gives an instance of this in *Pleistocene Man*:

$1,000,000 for example of
$3,000,000
paid to Castro in 1960 was it—1961?
   WAS DIRECTLY FROM THE MOB, BOSTON
raised over the phone over night by—for Robt.
      Kennedy—by Cardinal Cushing

A few years ago too many Americans used to scoff at such notions as this. They dismissed them as mere crankiness, probably because of their unconscious faith in what their European education had tended to inculcate in them about the ethics of public life. However, after Watergate such innocence is harder to come by.

Olson sees Europe as no better off, as the two poems to Rainer Gerhardt in *The Distances* show, where he addresses that continent as follows:

> You could not see, your eyes got small,
> you could not defecate, you were small
> you could not,
> therefore you died

What does Olson offer instead? As he says, he considers the study of the Pleistocene crucial, "a curriculum for the study of the soul" as he subtitles his little volume *Pleistocene Man*. There he defines the Pleistocene as:

> . . . my impression is that [it is] the unusual
>
> whichever end you take, either the "beginnings," at this end, of, say, 4000 Before Christ. . . .
>
> Pleistocene's almost like poetry. In fact it *is* poetry, Pleistocene, in that simplest *alphabetic* sense, that you can learn the language of being alive—in that most elementary way which is so easily taken for granted (or used as though it were only elementary)—that with which you are the most familiar—as though you were learning to read and write for the first ime.

If this sounds nebulous (and it is not all that nebulous), it is because Olson saw in Pleistocene another virtue besides its own intrinsic value, for it offers its student a powerful way to achieve "negative capability." To quote his definition, threading through Keats's words:

"all that irritable reaching after fact and reason . . . man
must stay in this condition of"—gee, I forgot even the
words—"confusion, ambiguity"—he's better there—"and
that I call *Negative Capability*."

—*Poetry and Truth*

In other words, studying the Pleistocene helps us rid ourselves of old
habits of thought inherited from the classical world of discourse. It
leads us away from logic and classification. Not necessarily towards
their opposites—but simply *away* from them. Pleistocene may be
considered as a cultural deconditioning whereby we learn to recognize within ourselves the "bad" civilization and "bad" poetics that have
brought us to our present situation. We see ourselves against a
different background, a different tradition, from that which we are
told the past offers. Olson reverses Plato's parable of the cave. Our
attention is fragmented by the sun of primeval ignorance, not knit
up and made whole by the light of reason. As the Ramones, a new-
wave punk-rock group, put it: "The great news is / we have no mind
to lose."

Through the Pleistocene we can re-establish that contact between nature and art where "as the line goes, so goes the Nation!" The
universe becomes ours again by extension as we see words become
flesh (the art of the logos). If we break the Pleistocene down, as Olson
sometimes did, into the canonical (primary information, such as site
reports of excavations at such touchstones of his as Mt. Carmel or Ras-
Shamra, for example) and the methodological (how this information
was arrived at in the first place and what attitudes it required the
investigator—archaeologist, linguist, whatever—to have), it is the
methodological, Olson would maintain, that ultimately proves the
more valuable. After we have stopped looking at cave paintings,
reading excavation reports, and getting chronologies and blood-types
straight (the "canonical"), the habits of learning and reporting, the
consideration of how things were done naturally and on a human
scale in the Pleistocene (the "methodological"), are what will remain
and re-shape our attention in all spheres of endeavor.

Generally speaking, the Pleistocene exists as surprise, "discovery," as something other than logic and classification. One can never
predict where it will crop up, or guess beforehand what it will have to
tell us; instead, it must be experienced and imagined as well as learned
intellectually. The Pleistocene will never be grasped as a rounded
organic whole, since it is supposed to attack, modify, and re-train the

poetic sensibility. This must happen on a very primary level. Olson compares it to learning "to write and write for the first time." Teaching it, he observes, "could just as properly be teaching primary school or pre-school, pregrade." It could even take the form of just looking at filmstrips or picture books like the medieval *Mutus Liber* or "silent book" (*Pleistocene Man* and *Poetry and Truth*).

The Pleistocene offers a view of man as naked where he must take himself and his world down off the glacial ice and fashion a home—a polis—for himself, out of his own head, unaided except by memory. And how well he acts on the basis of that knowledge is the test of his survival, of his mindedness. Pleistocene, according to Olson, "is conceivably a direct continuance . . . of Paleolithic into the hands of the earliest 'Civilization creators'" in Europe and the Near East principally (*Pleistocene Man*).

In the *Maximus Poems* he describes this renewal of the mind as follows:

> that all start up
> to the eye and soul
> as though it had never
> happened before

And again in "Letter 6":

> There are no hierarchies, no infinite,
>   no such many as mass, there are only
> eyes in all heads,
> to be looked out of

The Pleistocene is part of what allows Olson to get behind the classical persona and reach himself in order, as he says in *Maximus III*, "to write a Republic in gloom on Watch-House Point." As he puts it in the Beloit lectures (1969):

> How do you, how as a person, not only a poet, does one live
> one's image, rather than use it simply for writing—writing
> has been a three hundred year problem in English and now
> is broken. And now we are determined to make our image
> of a union of ourself, I think, and have no other choice,
> whether we like it or not. An obdurate or, as I say, an
> archaic time or condition.
>   —*Poetry and Truth*

That energy which can go into the person as well as the poem, then, does not have to pass through the refining fire of the past or of past habits of thought. If that energy requires new categories for thought and feeling, it will devise them as needed. And discard them as well. This approaches what Olson earlier called "proprioception"—which may be defined here, nonmedically, as awareness of self while using the self as the only absolute measure or reference. In his Buffalo seminars in the early 1960s, Olson used to call for the revival of the middle voice: that condition of the verb which is neither active nor passive but between, which defines action in relation to the actor and its effects on him and others. In this way writing becomes an extension of life, not a masquerade for it.

What is the condition of the self when it writes? Olson believed it was dark and that by illuminating itself it illuminated the world?

> That our . . . condition inside is dark . . . think of yourself as
> an impediment of creation . . . . that the unknown is rather
> your self's insides . . . that we become sure in the dark, that
> we move wherever we wish in the six directions with *that*
> light . . . I mean literally, that to *light that dark* is to have come
> to whatever it is I think any of us seeks. . . .
> —*Poetry and Truth*

The contrast with the ancients' attitude toward the poetic self is instructive and startling. There, the soul is inspired to write by gods who provide words and theme. The poet trains himself by formal education and experience to be a fit vehicle for the Muses' inspirations. For Olson, however, the process of composition is a journey within towards inner light, where each person is a cosmic sum which contains all the possibilities and contraries between light and dark, between material impotence and godlike creation.

This is how Olson could approach the myths as credible wholes—not as stories needing reinterpretation in the light of recent history or one's own psychobiography—as, for example, Pound and Joyce did in their treatment of Odysseus. For most writers, following past tradition, myth has been either metaphor or allegory; for Olson it was literal, "like theology" (*Poetry and Truth*). For Olson myth conveys information of importance: the compact expression of lived experience over generations, not of a single lifetime. It preserves what is necessary for tribal and cultural survival while it scants the personal and the unique. How many historical Agamemmons and Priams were there whose stories got squashed down, summarized in the oral memory, until only the smooth pebble of the myth was left? Yet all we know, perhaps all we will ever need to know of them—if indeed they ever were—is contained in their myths. For myth remarks the salient, while it forbears repetition. Myth can survive from generation to generation, since like the genes it is the carrier and repository of true knowledge. Myth conserves for reasons of survival, not decorousness, not out of past habits of thought brought mindlessly forward. It constitutes the oral encyclopedia and is not employed merely for preserving the cultural niceties.

Olson attempts in *Maximus*, his long, still only partially published epic, to let out the light of himself through myth and by doing so make "the Republic on Watch-House Point" something necessary for our survival as well as his. Maximus/Olson reminds us not only of the poet's titanic body (he was nearly seven feet tall and quite brawny), but also recalls the historical Maximus of Tyre, a Hellenized Semite of the second century CE who was also a survivor—of the pre-Greek, pre-Roman past of the Second and Third Millenia. Here, we see something of Olson's chosen position in the tradition. He was a poet who came to discover a past behind the accepted past of the European-American tradition, a tradition within the tradition if you like, and who then became its inventor, prophet, spokesman, although not a member of it except spiritually. He attempted to recall the rest of us to it, to an older, more wholesome, responsive way of thinking and feeling. In this he opened a future in terms of poetry and experience for himself and others. In *Maximus* Olson assumes a new state of mind (which in fact is a reversion to one from our common past) for which his long poem stands as both example and guide.

Bibliography

By Charles Olson:

Call Me Ishmael. New York: Grove Press, 1958.
The Maximus Poems. New York: Jargon/Corinth Books,1960.
The Distances. New York: Grove Press, 1961.
Selected Writings. Edited by Robert Creeley. New York: New Directions, 1967.
Pleistocene Man: A Curriculum for the Study of the Soul. Buffalo, New York: Institute
     of Further Studies, SUNY, 1968.
Poetry and Truth: The Beloit Lectures and Poems. Edited by George F. Butterick. San
     Francisco: Four Seasons Foundation, 1971.
Muthologos: The Collected Lectures and Interviews. Edited by George F. Butterick. San
     Francisco: Four Seasons Foundation, 1977.
The Fiery Hunt and Other Plays. Edited by George F. Butterick. San Francisco: Four
     Seasons Foundation, 1977.

About Charles Olson:

Butterick, George F. *A Guide to the Maximus Poems of Charles Olson.* Berkeley: Uni-
     versity of California Press, 1978.
Charles Olson special issue. *Boundary 2* (SUNY-Binghamton), Fall 1973/Winter
     1974.
Charters, Ann. *Olson, Melville: A Study in Affinity.* San Francisco: Oyez, 1968.

Source and Reference Material:

Seelye, Catherine, editor. *Charles Olson and Ezra Pound: An Encounter at Saint Eliza-
     beth's.* New York: Grossman/Viking, 1975.
Cambridge Ancient History Series. Second revised edition. Volumes 1 and 2.

Bernard Malamud

John Ashmead

Bernard Malamud has been a teacher of writing since 1940, first in New York high schools and at Oregon State College, presently at Bennington College in Vermont. He is a Jewish-American writer who has won over seven awards for individual short stories plus a National Book Award for his first collection of stories, *The Magic Barrel* (1958). His later novel, *The Fixer* (1967), won another NBA, and he was elected president of American P.E.N. in 1979. The critical response to his work has been a study in paradox. He has had a book of essays written in his honor. Yet, when delivered as addresses at Oregon State College, the essays carried a tone of reservation. Leslie Field spoke of a marginal Jew; Ihab Hassan felt a knot of resistance on reading him; Leslie Fiedler found him timid, pedantic, squeamish—but all praised him mightily.

Yet there is general agreement that Malamud has woven a striking series of narratives with a gift for the mad, the bleak, the charming, and the absurd. From his experiences in a grocery-store-owning family during the depression of the 1930s, and his education (English B.A., City College of New York, 1936; English M.A., Columbia University, thesis on Hardy, 1942) he has developed a remarkable insight into the complexities of society. He has been able to combine the knowledge he has acquired from his wide reading and teaching in American and Western literature and mythology, from his East European Ashkenazic heritage, and from extensive travel—Italy in 1956-57, Russia in 1965—to develop a striking perspective of life. It is as if, in my view, our culture had suddenly given birth to a Jewish-American neo-Hawthorne, and without Hawthorne's lamentable sexual repressiveness. Malamud, I think, gave us the clue to solving the difficulties critics and readers have at times had with his work in his *Paris Review* interview recorded in 1974 at age 60 (No. 61 [1975]):

"In my books I go along the same paths in different worlds." This sentence is usually interpreted to mean that each successive work has a similar route through a different universe, but the sentence can also mean that each individual work contains these different worlds. Three such worlds which can be reckoned with here are the world of Western humanism and its mythology, the world of Jewish-American and Yiddish culture, and finally, least noted by Malamud's critics though stressed by Malamud himself, the world of 19th-century American Romanticism.

Malamud has said "The mythological and symbolic excite my imagination." And in his first novel, *The Natural* (1952), a somewhat incongruous member of that American fictional sub-genre, the baseball novel, we find heroic batter Roy (*le roi*, the king) Hobbs under the tutelage of Pop Fisher (father figure and Grailritual Fisher King). Pop seeks the Pennant (Grail) with the aid of a special bat (lance) called Wonderboy for his team, the Knights. Critics have joyously identified in the novel the Perilous Bed, the Loathly Lady, and the Lady of the Lake (a protector of the orphan or near-orphan hero Malamud invariably favors in his long fiction). They have also found the Wasteland to be regenerated by the new king, and even comic attributes of Chrétien de Troyes' Lancelot of the Cart. (Since some authorities would have it that Chrétien was a converted Jew, we might speculate on this Lancelot as the first Arthurian *schlemiel!*) Though Jewish-American critics such as Leslie Fiedler have dismissed this first novel as almost irrelevant to Malamud's development—it contains no obvious references to Yiddish culture—at its turning point, when Roy Hobbs plays a magical prank on his tormentor, bookie Gus Sands, we can see role and fuction (slot and filler in strict structural terms) of the Yiddish *vitzler*, or prankster, tale: the challenge of the joker, the foil's reaction, and the retort or prank—in this case pulling the owed silver dollars out of Gus's ears and nose.

Though Malamud has often expressed his admiration for Mark Twain, it is odd that no critic I know of has mentioned the structural resemblances of *The Natural* to Mark Twain's *A Connecticut Yankee in King Arthur's Court*, a similar mythic and pastoral mingling of modern and Arthurian myth. Corrupt Judge Goodwin Banner in *The Natural* is as much Twain's Merlin as he is any villainous authority figure from Kafka. And Twain's novel also is dominated by its terminal wasteland.

In *The Assistant* (1957) Malamud appealed to a growing critical and popular interest in Jewish-American fiction with a novel which achieved a much more fused version of his three worlds. Roy Hobbs had been a suffering Jewish-American hero or Job figure manqué, but to show a virtue by its absence is no simple task. This second orphan hero, Frank Alpine, with his many oblique links to St. Francis of the hills (the world of Western humanism), is a far more convincing quest figure. The wasteland, even prison, of the grocery and its owner, Morris Bober, whom Frank first robs and then serves—both have a vitality that undoubtedly stems from Malamud's own family grocery. Here too we find a much better worked out linkage of the seasonal year to the plot (as in Thoreau's Walden). Father-figure Morris Bober dies shoveling snow, and it is springtime when Frank has some new hope of being accepted by daughter Helen Bober. Frank is a favorite Malamud type, the cuckold *schlemiel*, reaching his culmination when he takes a Chaplinesque pratfall into Morris Bober's grave. The Jewish-American idiom of Morris Bober has been much praised (it is curious, however, that he never thinks in this idiom), especially as he explains Jewish suffering, and the value of suffering, to Frank.

There could be no complaints about Malamud's treatment of the Jewish-American world in *The Assistant*, and several times it was called the best Jewish-American novel to date (though critic Ihab Hassan somewhat irreverently referred to the hero's circumcision as a symbolic castration). One or two critics have spotted Malamud's use of the Horatio Alger success story, the "making it" narrative: Roy Hobbs had whittled a better bat, and now Frank Alpine invents a better minestrone soup. More striking is the great Romantic theme of naïve apprentice—the "assistant"—as in Hawthorne's "My Kinsman, Major Molineux." The apprentice ultimately is not a weakling, but a typical romantic-period figure who is about to change his own life and who has some potential for social revolution—an element often overlooked by Malamud's critics.

In both *The Natural* and *The Assistant* Malamud had made some striking, if still tentative and even awkward, juxtapositions of what linguists might call register—a realistic, serious register next to a fantastic, absurdly comic, or even preternatural register. In his first great short story collection, *The Magic Barrel* (1958), he showed how far he had gone beyond such Hawthorne models of the type as "David Swan, A Fantasy" (in which an apprentice nephew travels to join a grocer uncle). In "The Lady of the Lake" (a quest-myth role) Isabella (named after a Stendhal heroine) in a nude bathing scene (as Venus Anadyomene) first reveals the concentration camp number tattooed on her breast (the Jewish holocaust); her narrative and its garden *mise-en-scène* have structural echoes of Hawthorne's "Rappacini's Daughter," which is also set in Italy. Susskind in "The Last Mohican" (first of the Fidelman stories) is part Yiddish *shnorrer* (outrageous beggar) and part Cooper's Uncas—at least he can run like Uncas. Kessler, the retired egg candler of "The Mourners," in a poignant ending recites the Kaddish with his landlord; Kessler's role and several of his functions go back to Melville's most famous Isolatoe, *Bartleby the Scrivener*. "The Magic Barrel" shows marriage broker Salzman finally offering his whore-daughter as a bride to the atheistical future rabbi Leo Finkle who accepts her, in this Chagall-tinted story, hoping to convert her and himself. Her costume has a faint allusion to that of Hester in *The Scarlet Letter*. These solidly fused and economically unified stories succeed by a mastery of scene, in which synagogues can change men's lives, in which *rachmones*—compassionate, unstinting charity and Jewish peoplehood—can exist as values even in a wasteland.

Malamud's next long fiction, *A New Life* (1961), centers again on a migratory orphan apprentice who leaves his cellar prison for a master's degree in English and a teaching post across the continent in Cascadia College, Oregon. Malamud said he had learned from Chaplin "the snap" of comedy, and his cuckold *schlemiel* hero, Lev (heart) or Levin (lightning; also the hero of Tolstoy's *Anna Karenina*) teaches his first class with his fly open. In *The Natural* Malamud had two vampires (Harriet Bird and Memo Paris); here there are four, one of whom is named Avis Fliss (*avis*, Latin for bird, and Fliss using the "fl" phonestheme also found in words such as flutter, flap, fly, etc.). In *The Assistant* there had been three varieties of father, and so there are in *A New Life*. Even Levin is doubled, with a predecessor in office and bed. Though this apprentice is forced out of teaching, he brings about some changes in Cascadia's grotesque English Department, and he himself goes beyond Frank Alpine to both physical and emotional fatherhood—an essential patriarchal part of Jewish *menschlichkeit*. The critics who disappointedly find little Jewishness in *A New Life* seem to have overlooked this crucial value.

Now that we have good structural analyses of the American Western in both French and English, it is hard to make much sense of Leslie Fiedler's charge that *A New Life* is a failed travesty Western. Though there are some possible echoes of Mark Twain's westward-bound tenderfoot narrator of *Roughing It*, the emotional plot structure (leaving aside the slapstick) is that of Hawthorne's *Scarlet Letter*: Levin as adulterous intellectual dimmesdale, Pauline Gilley as Hester (with a forest passion scene), and her impotent husband as Chillingworth. Malamud himself has stressed Levin's fantasies of giving bread to those who are starving, but what has most impressed readers and critics is his defiant response when asked why he is taking off with an older, unreliable woman, pregnant by him, and with two children not his own, into a professionless future—"Because I can, you son of a bitch."

Idiots First (1963), a short story collection, resembles *The Magic Barrel* but in a more bleak tone. Where rough comparisons are possible, we can sense that the Job-like sufferings of the hero of "Angel Levine" affect positively both himself and those with power over him; in "Idiots First" the *schnorrer* Mendel of the title story succeeds in sending his 39-year-old idiot boy to an 81-year-old uncle, but there is little or no enlightenment of Joycean epiphany as Mendel then looks for his waiting angel of death. In "A Choice of Professions" the cuckold *schlemiel* teacher Cronin rejects love from a reformed prostitute and betrays her, in sharp contrast to the title story of *The Magic Barrel*. And "The Jewbird," a Yiddish-American descendant from Poe's Raven, is rejected by his Jewish host, a violation of the sanctity of Jewish peoplehood so often affirmed in *The Magic Barrel*.

Beginning with a 1961 article by Jewish-American novelist Philip Roth in *Commentary* (the magazine which has most encouraged the flowering of Jewish-American fiction), Malamud was criticized for writing about Jews as metaphors, located only vaguely (at times) in the depression of the 1930s. Perhaps in reaction, Malamud wrote *The Fixer* (1966), a novel which starts almost as a documentary based on the Mendel Beiliss case (1911-1913), in which Beiliss was charged with an alleged Jewish ritual murder of a Russian Christian child. (Beiliss was acquitted but died embittered, feeling he had not received proper recognition.)

In *The Fixer* Yakov Bok (goat or scapegoat, unbending iron, Christ), an orphan quest hero and cuckold *schlemiel*, leaves his faithless wife Raisl and seeks a new life in Kiev. There, not admitting he is Jewish, he escapes *shtetl* (Jewish quarter) life and has a brief Horatio Alger success. But he is falsely accused of ritual murder, imprisoned, degraded, abused, and almost as a Jewish existentialist, he calls both God and Job inventions. But he goes on to learn to accept his sufferings and even accepts fatherhood of Raisl's illegitimate child.

Malamud had dissociated himself from activist Jewish extremists, but in the fantastic register ending of *The Fixer* Bok strikes a new note when he says, "You can't sit still and see yourself destroyed." And after a fantastic debate with the Tsar, Bok kills him.

In its evocation of *shtetl* life and culture (Malamud had heard tales of the Beiliss case when he was a boy), Malamud reminds us of the virtues of Ashkenazic Jewry, with its stress on humble lives and doing. (The other branch, Sephardic, stressing elitist intellectuality, is perhaps best represented by Bellow's novel *Herzog*, in which it is very difficult to know whether Herzog meant to shoot his wife but very easy to encounter letter after intellectual letter addressed to a wide range of modern thinkers.) Recent criticism has perhaps unfairly regarded *The Fixer* as a somewhat thinner narrative than was thought at first, but it remains Malamud's greatest critical and popular success.

Pictures of Fidelman (1969) brought together six Italian stories (of seven projected—a fantasy involving Keats and Fidelman was not used) in a picaresque narrative centering on its quest hero, who borders on a *luftmensch* (illusionist): Chapter 1. Failed painter, failed historian of Giotto, but finally compassionate towards *shnorrer* and last Mohican Susskind; Chapter 2. Failed painter but successful seducer of his landlady painter; Chapter 3. Successful copyist while prisoner in a whorehouse; Chapter 4. Successful painter of madonna and child turned pimp and prostitute (a painting which he destroys), but a failure in love; Chapter 5. Failed earth sculptor; Chapter 6. Successful glass sculptor and homosexual. Chapter 4 strongly resembles the structure of Henry James's "The Madonna of the Future" (itself based in part on Washington Allston's real life failure to complete *Belshazzar*). Chapters 5 and 6 suggest the conclusion of Hawthorne's "The Artist of the Beautiful": ". . . the reward of all high performance must be sought within itself, or sought in vain."

But the archetype of *Fidelman*, as is usually the case for all American novels about Italy, is Hawthorne's *The Marble Faun* (1860), in which an American learner comes to artistic and personal maturity in Italy. (Some details echo *The Marble Faun*: the name Donatello, the woman painter who paints herself, the second-rate painter whose copies are masterpieces). Admittedly the most ragged of Malamud's works, with some slapstick sequences better suited to an X-rated film, *Fidelman* still has many wildly comic and moving passages, with a strong intermittent stress on peoplehood, compassion, love.

Malamud's method of shifting back and forth among his three worlds has a danger of overloaded fantasy and symbol—such is the near disaster of his one thesis novel, *The Tenants* (1971). (In "The Girl of My Dreams" from *The Magic Barrel* the writer-hero fails because of just this fault, perhaps prophetically.) *The Tenants* has a plot derived from Poe's "William Wilson," in which the two doubled, opposite characters kill each other. Here white Jewish writer Lesser is doubled against black anti-Semitic writer Willie Spearmint (Shakespeare), the former writing a novel about writing a novel, and the latter concentrating on the black experience. Each is on his own grail quest, for perfect form, for perfect material, in the wasteland of a nearly abandoned tenement. The white Jewish heroine rejects both for impotently failing to acknowledge her existence (an echo of Henry James, *The Beast in the Jungle*?), which she sees as more valuable than the art of either. In a fantastic register ending, Willie castrates Lesser, as Lesser brains Willy with an axe. Compassion, *rachmones*, is the concluding word of the book. This was Malamud's third fictional attempt to cope with Black-Jewish relations; it has received almost as much critical attention as *The Fixer*, but this attention seems more a reflection of the troubled 1960s than of the innate merit of the novel.

Compassion is a dominant theme of Malamud's third collection of short fiction, *Rembrandt's Hat* (1973). The best story, "The Silver Crown," is about a Mellvillean-Yiddish confidence man, or rather confidence rabbi, who persuades people to give money for imaginary silver crowns to cure sick relatives towards whom they have been uncompassionate. Malamud's message, like that of Melville, is that it is better to have confidence. This collection ends with a talking horse who modulates into a centaur—about as wild a story as Malamud has ever done.

Malamud's next novel, *Dublin's Lives* (1979) took Malamud over five years to write, twice as long as any previous novel. It continues the intricate weaving of his three worlds, perhaps with a new overlay of donnishness. Biographer Dubin is a quest hero, a Jewish near-orphan in search of his elusive subject, D. H. Lawrence. En route he encounters a Lady of the Lake (and forest) half his age, Fanny Bick (named for a Jane Austen heroine). He woos her in part with his Horatio Alger Presidential Medal for biography, and unknown to his wife Kitty, they go secretly to Venice together, where Fanny almost immediately cuckolds our *schlemiel* with a gondolier.

Dubin returns to his wife Kitty, who soon also cuckolds him with a neighbor. But after a fortunate fall from Eden, signalled by a snowy wasteland sequence (the seasonal framework follows Thoreau's *Walden*—Thoreau had been one of Dubin's biographical subjects), Dubin again links up with Fanny, and encourages her to become an apprentice lawyer. Young daughter Maud, who has acknowledged her Jewish heritage, is pregnant by a man about Dubin's age (who had taken her to Venice, such is Malamud's liking, as we have seen, for multiple parallel plots). Son Gerald, a draft evader in Sweden and a true *schlimazel* (fool), has ineptly signed on with the KGB in Russia and now wants out. He must be protected by father Dubin, and Maud must be helped to have her illegimate child. Here we can sense that Dubin's fatherhood has gone well beyond that of Levin in *A New Life*, for this is compassionate fatherhood towards the new generation, represented by his son, daughter, and young mistress. Dream and surreal sequences shift us among the three worlds of Malamud: Western literature, Jewish-American themes and roles, 19th-century American Romanticism. The novel ends in a fantastic register, in Dubin's Chaplinesque dash from the bed of Fanny to the bed of Kitty, while Roger Foster, young lover of Fanny and the obvious new Fisher King, waits watching in the wings—a sadly comic eternal quadrangle.

Malamud's last finished novel is *God's Grace* (1982). It treats both the original Holocaust, and a new imagined Holocaust of the future. For several decades the Holocaust to Malamud has been the mark of man's inhumanity to man. *God's Grace*, we might argue, goes one step further, treating the Holocaust as God's inhumanity to man.

Its hero, Calvin Cohn—rabbi manquee and paleologist, son of a rabbi-cantor, has been doing underseas research when the Djanks and the Druzhkies (Yanks and Russians) launch an atomic Holocaust and destroy all other humans. Calvin has many shadings: Adam / Abraham / Parsifal / Romeo / Prospero / Robinson Crusoe / Gulliver / Ahab. His Eve and Juliet is Mary Madelyn, a chimpanzee. An albino ape appears (an oblique Moby Dick?), with other apes as Yahoos from *Gulliver's Travels*, and with the chimpanzee Buz as Isaac / Caliban / and man Friday to Cohn's Robinson Crusoe. And there is even an Arthurian spear, left over, perhaps from *The Natural*, used to harpoon the albino ape.

Calvin, the only surviving human on Cohn's Island, turns into an overachiever, and even un-Job like defier of God. But Esau, the chimpanzee hunter, kills and eats infant baboons, disregarding the First of Calvin Cohn's Seven Admonitions about cherishing life. Calvin has treated the chimpanzees as his inferiors; as a *schlemiel* lecturer he has imposed his Admonitions and teachings on them, rather than encouraging them to learn for themselves. In effect, overachieving Calvin Cohn has eaten from the tree of hubris rather than knowledge.

The novel concludes with the Abraham/Isaac story (*Genesis* 22). In this version, Buz, Cohn's surrogate chimpanzee son, takes the part of Abraham, and white-bearded Cohn, with no saving ram in the thicket as in *Genesis*, plays the part of Abraham's son Isaac and the Jewish gorilla, George, says *Kaddish*.

This complex novel baffled its first reviewers and readers. One difficulty is that *God's Grace* does not fall into a clear genre category; is it science fiction or an allegory? As often in Malamud's work, we gain a deeper insight if we think of it as both Jewish and American in its literary origins, for it is not only Old Testament Biblical in subject, but it strongly partakes of an Americanized Biblical genre that goes back to the days of the Colonies and the Early Republic—the Jeremiad, the warning to prevent future disaster.

Malamud's last but unfinished work is *The Tribe*. This novel concerns itself with the adventures of a Russian Jewish peddlar Yozip among the western Indians. Its *schlemiel* hero Yozip becomes a marshal, is kidnapped by a tribe of Indians and has a dialogue with an Indian chief (whose Indian peace pipe gives Yozip heartburn) about obtaining his freedom.

When we look at Malamud's work as a whole, we see a migratory fiction (which has inevitably combined its three worlds). It is a record of great journeys by humble people, from East Russia and its *shtetls*, to the New York East Side, to the West Coast, with all the stresses of lost relatives, broken homes, desperate struggles for economic and educational success, along with the selfishness, madness, compassion, and peoplehood that such migrations foster. The historian Toynbee once argued that all great epics—*The Iliad*, *The Odyssey*, *The Aeneid*, *Beowulf*—stem from just such great folk wanderings. Though no single work of Malamud deserves the term "epic," perhaps we may borrow a great Sanskrit literary concept, *resonance*, and suggest that, taken as a whole, his work, like the Western films of John Ford, has just such an epic resonance.

Bibliography

By Bernard Malamud:

The Natural. New York: Harcourt Brace, 1952; London: Eyre and Spottiswoode, 1963.
The Assistant. New York: Farrar, Straus and Cudahy, 1957; London: Eyre and Spottiswoode, 1959.
The Magic Barrel. New York: Farrar, Straus and Cudahy, 1958; London: Eyre and Spottiswoode, 1960. (Short fiction, National Book Award)
A New Life. New York: Farrar, Straus and Cudahy, 1961; London: Eyre and Spottiswoode, 1962.
Idiots First. New York: Farrar, Straus & Co., 1963; London: Eyre and Spottiswoode, 1964. (Short fiction)
The Fixer. New York: Farrar, Straus and Giroux, 1966; London: Eyre and Spottiswoode, 1967. (National Book Award)
Pictures of Fidelman: An Exhibition. New York: Farrar, Straus and Giroux, 1969; London: Eyre and Spottiswoode, 1970. (First chapter in *The Magic Barrel*, two more chapters in *Idiots First*)
The Tenants. New York: Farrar, Straus and Giroux, 1971; London: Eyre Methuen, 1972.
Rembrandt's Hat. New York: Farrar, Straus and Giroux, 1973; London: Eyre Methuen, 1973. (Short fiction)
Dubin's Lives. New York: Farrar, Straus and Giroux, 1979.
God's Grace. New York: Farrar, Straus and Giroux, 1982.
The Stories of Bernard Malamud. New York: Farrar, Straus and Giroux, 1983.

About Bernard Malamud:

Bernard Malamud (1914-1986), as one of three best-known Jewish-American writers, has attracted a formidable array of criticism. We can list only a few such items here.

For bibliography see Joel Salzberg, *Bernard Malamud; a Reference Guide* (Boston, Massachusetts: G. K. Hall & Co., 1985). A recent short life is Jeffrey Helterman, *Understanding Bernard Malamud.* (Mathew J. Bruccoli, editor, *Understanding Contemporary American Literature.* Columbia, South Carolina: University of South Carolina Press, 1985).

Collections of critical essays are: Harold Bloom, editor, *Bernard Malamud.* (*Modern Critical Views.* New York: Chelsea House Publishers, 1986), a recent survey.

Leslie A. Field and Joyce W. Field, editors, *Bernard Malamud and the Critics* (New York: New York University Press, 1970), somewhat out of date but best on Malamud and the use of myth. Richard Astro and Jackson J. Benson, *The Fiction of Bernard Malamud* (Corvallis: Oregon State University Press, 1977), includes Donald

Risty, "A Comprehensive Checklist of Malamud Criticism." Leslie A. Fiedler's theory of the travesty Western is clearer in an earlier version, "Malamud's Travesty Western," *Novel*, Vol. 10 (1977).

A few more specialized studies are: Glenn Meeter, *Bernard Malamud and Philip Roth: A Critical Essay* (Grand Rapids, Michigan: William B. Eerdmans, 1968), which distinguishes between two major types of Jewish-American fictions; and Robert Ducharme, *Art and Idea in the Novels of Bernard Malamud, Toward the Fixer* (The Hague and Paris: Mouton, 1974), excellent on the wasteland motif. But I have found the more specialized works that follow more helpful than the straightforward histories: Sol Gittleman, *From Shtetl to Suburbia: The Family in Jewish Literary Imagination* (Boston: Beacon Press, 1978); Melvin J. Friedman, "The Schlemiel: Jew and Non-Jew," *Studies in the Literary Imagination*, Vol. 9, No. 1 (1976); Josephine Zadovsky Knopp, *The Trial of Judaism in Contemporary Jewish Writing* (Urbana: University of Illinois Press, 1975); Wesley A. Kort, *Shriven Selves, Religious Problems in Recent American Fiction* (Philadelphia: Fortress Press, 1972), pp.90-115 on Malamud; Allen Guttmann, *The Jewish Writer in America, Assimilation and the Crisis of Identity* (New York: Oxford University Press, 1971); Ruth R. Wisse, *The Schlemiel as Modern Hero* (Chicago and London: University of Chicago Press, 1971)—probably the best of this group; and Sanford Pinsker, *The Schlemiel as Metaphor, Studies in The Yiddish and American Jewish Novel* (Carbondale and Edwardsville: Southern Illinois University Press, 1971). Two of the best single articles on Malamud I have found are by the German critic Peter Freese: "Bernard Malamud," in Martin Christadler, editor, *Amerikanische Literatur der Gegenwart in Einzeldarstellungen* (Stuttgart: Alfred Kramer Verlag, 1973), and Peter Freese, *Die amerikanishe Kurzgeschichte nach 1945* (Frankfurt am Main: Athenäum, 1974).

I am indebted also to Toby Blum-Dobkin, *Yiddish Folktales About Jesters: A Problem in Structural Analysis and Genre Definition* (New York: YIVO Institute for Jewish Research, 1977), which enabled me to locate the pattern in *The Natural*. So far as I know, there are no systematic studies of Malamud and American Romantic writers.

Jack Kerouac

John Tytell

Every so often a writer appears who so aptly captures the music of his moment, the attitudes and aspirations of his time, that he becomes the voice of a generation. Jack Kerouac was such a writer.

Kerouac's story is one of the more anomalous in the history of American letters. Like Poe, Melville, or Faulkner, he did much of his early work in anonymity, under adverse conditions, and with little encouragement. When the book for which he is best known, *On the Road*, appeared in 1957—six years after he had written it—it aroused considerable consternation and controversy among the book reviewers and literary critics who helped shape popular taste. They deplored the delirious manners and reckless mores of headstrong characters who seemed able to sacrifice conventional bonds and obligations for the sake of excitement. The critics labeled it hedonistic, nihilistic, and blatantly onanistic.

On the Road provoked concern among the critics because the generation Kerouac understood, and to some extent predicted, was still unfathomable to the older custodians of literary culture. Kerouac's prose style was rhapsodically lyrical and as expansive as Whitman in a time of cultural contraction. The flamboyancy of Kerouac's public statements did not win him admiration among those in power in literary circles. His declaration that spontaneity was his method and that vision his object was treated with the same condescension that most romantic attitudes received in the 1950s. His argument that revising his work was anathema—a function of conditioning, a concession to popular taste or editorial inhibition, a betrayal of intuition and immediacy—was dismissed by those who regarded revision as the sacred foundation of literary practice. Mystical Buddhist remarks about the intentions of his art outraged staid commentators like Norman Podhoretz (soon to become editor of the influential magazine *Commentary*), anxious academics, and that part of the audience that insisted on reason and decorum in art and a conventional moral attitude. The uproar caused by Kerouac's novel and by Beat writing, such as Ginsberg's *Howl* and Burroughs's *Naked Lunch*, now seems out of proportion, but at the time the conflict cut across the literary standards of a culture, just as it heralded the conflict of generations that would occur in the United States in the 1960s. Apparently some taboo had been threatened, some nerve in the cultural nexus had been exposed, some tacit agreement between artist and audience had been spurned. Kerouac's critics saw him as the leader of a group of young barbarians storming the literary citadel.

Indeed, Kerouac was a leader. He became the spokesman of a generation without actively seeking that role; the Beat cataclysm which followed was the result of the expression of a group of writers who applied a radical perspective to a culture which they felt had failed to emerge from the blindness of 1950s conformity. To their credit, some of the critics saw the importance of *On the Road*. Malcolm Cowley, the eminent historian of the Lost Generation, recognized the vitality of Kerouac's work when he recommended the publication of *On the Road* to Viking Press. When the book did appear, six years after Kerouac wrote it, Gilbert Millstein greeted it in the pages of *The New York Times* as an "historic occasion," comparing it to Hemingway's *The Sun Also Rises* as a sign of generational expression.

What was this new generation and how did Jack Kerouac, a young man from a small factory town in Massachusetts, come to play such a dominant role in forming it?

The Kerouacs were a provincial, French-Canadian family. Leo Kerouac, Jack's father, owned a printing business that failed in 1936 when the Merrimack River flooded the town of Lowell and swamped his shop. Subsequently, Leo was forced to find work setting type when and where he could. He was generous and gregarious; his wife, Gabrielle Ange, was stolid, practical, domestic, and firmly Catholic. She worked in factories and, throughout her son's childhood, offered him dependable emotional support. That childhood had been traumatized by the death, when Jack was four, of his older brother Gerard, who died from a rheumatic heart condition; but the family was a close one, and Jack was taught traditional Catholic virtues. In high school he achieved recognition as an athlete, as a runner and as a swift fullback on the football team. He was offered athletic scholarships by

Notre Dame, a Catholic university, and by Columbia University, and he chose Columbia despite his mother's objections. That was a turning point for him.

For Kerouac, the country boy, New York City represented the shock of sophistication and tremendous energy. The life of the city served to excite Kerouac in a way that his classes did not, though he had some prominent teachers—Raymond Weaver, who rediscovered Melville for America and introduced Kerouac to gnosticism, the poet Mark Van Doren, who helped get his first novel published, and the distinguished critic Lionel Trilling. After breaking a leg in a football game, Kerouac, who had written over a million words (twice the number in *War and Peace*) during his teenage years, decided to concentrate on writing. The accident became a point of departure for him: he started reading Shakespeare and working on a long novel, *The Town and the City*, contrasting the stability and warmth of his hometown to the fragmenting dissonances of city life.

When Kerouac stopped playing football, the university discontinued his scholarship. The Second World War had begun and Kerouac joined the Navy. What happened next is a symptom of his personality. Unable to tolerate the arbitrary discipline of basic training, he flung his rifle to the ground one morning at drill and walked to the base library where he was apprehended. After months of observation, the Navy psychiatrists diagnosed him as a paranoid schizophrenic, and he was discharged. Still patriotically intent on contributing to the war effort, he signed on a merchant vessel delivering ammunition and bombs to England.

Late in 1944, he returned to the Columbia campus and met Allen Ginsberg, another Columbia student, and William Burroughs, a Harvard graduate living in the area. The three young men all had an interest in writing. Burroughs became his informal mentor in modern letters, introducing Kerouac to writers like Céline, Cocteau, and Kafka, and books like Spengler's *Decline of the West* and Wilhelm Reich's *The Cancer Biopathy*. Charmed by Burroughs's abilities as a raconteur, Kerouac encouraged his older friend to write, accurately predicting that he would complete a novel one day and call it *Naked Lunch*. One of Burrough's friends, a Times Square hipster named Herbert Huncke, introduced the group to drugs. Soon Kerouac was experimenting with marijuana and benzedrine, living part of the time in an apartment near Columbia with Burroughs, Ginsberg, and several other friends, and part of the time with his parents in Queens.

Leo Kerouac was suffering from stomach cancer; his son tended to him, writing at night in the kitchen while his mother worked in a shoe factory.

Kerouac was still applying himself to *The Town and the City* when a young man named Neal Cassady began to correspond with him from a reformatory in New Mexico. Cassady was to become the subject of Kerouac's two most ambitious novels, *On the Road* and *Visions of Cody*. His example would galvanize Kerouac with the recognition of a kinetic form spontaneous and supple enough to simulate the extraordinary energies which Cassady exemplified. A railroad brakeman who read Proust, Cassady had been freed of ordinary notions of responsibility when, as a child, he had been raised on skid row in Denver by an alcoholic father. Riding freight trains, sleeping in hobo camps with his father, stealing cars for joy rides as an adolescent, in and out of reform schools and prison, Cassady became, for Kerouac, the prototype of the Rimbaudian adventurer. He was "consumed by the disease of overlife" as Kerouac would write in his poem about the French poet. Even Cassady's speech patterns embodied his excitement: he would talk in a series of staccato bursts as if his enormous energies were about to erupt volcanically through his mouth. The raw vigors of his stream-of-consciousness delivery helped turn Kerouac away from the literary language and stylistic artifice of *The Town and the City* to a more natural style. Kerouac, still working on his first apprentice book, had been imitating the voices of Fitzgerald, Hemingway, and Thomas Wolfe—but he began to hear a voice that would tune him into the actual registers of American speech.

Cassady visited Kerouac in New York in 1947 and he left an indelible impression. In Cassady, Kerouac recognized a restlessly consuming part of himself that could not be satisfied by writing alone, which was frustrated by the burden of familial responsibility that Kerouac retained to the end. Cassady began sending Kerouac tirading letters from Denver, encouraging him to discover the American landscape through the fortunes of the open road.

Kerouac spent parts of the next few years pursuing Cassady's trail, allowing himself to be lured from the worktable in his mother's kitchen in Queens into the new world which became his subject—a hip carnival of bohemian artists, intellectuals, underground figures. These were the people who disowned the grey-flannel-suit culture of the postwar era, who denied the atmosphere of rampant careerism and the political repression of the Cold War and McCarthy periods. Instead of sobriety, respectability, and affluence, their priorities were pleasure and freedom of expression. They danced, listened to jazz, read Henry Miller, lived for adventure. They were the "mad generation" that Allen Ginsberg later eulogized in *Howl* and that was to become Kerouac's subject in *On the Road*:

> the only people for me are the mad ones, the ones who are mad to live, mad to talk, mad to be saved, desirous of everything at the same time, the ones who never yawn or say a commonplace thing but burn, burn, burn like fabulous yellow roman candles exploding like spiders across the stars.

It was a generation in absolute revolt from the unprecedented pressure for conformity, from bureaucratic regimentation, from the smiling dullness of the Eisenhower years. And it was this underground generation, seeking mystical experience and searching for ecstasy rather than security, that began to simmer during the frozen 1950s. With *On the Road*, Kerouac helped make it boil.

Kerouac was working as a construction laborer in Denver in order to feel Cassady's hometown when his first novel, *The Town and the City*, was accepted by Robert Giroux. Later, Kerouac would live with Cassady and his wife near San Francisco, working on the Southern and Pacific as a railroad brakeman just as Cassady did. Kerouac did everything he could to open himself to the opportunities Cassady presented. All this time Kerouac was writing *On the Road* but did not want to repeat the traditional form he had used in *The Town and the City*. Back in New York City, he was supporting himself by writing script synopses for Twentieth-Century Fox, when he received a sprawling 40-page letter from Cassady—a torrential, single, unpunctuated sentence. The letter provided a recognition, the penultimate insight he needed to express the Cassady story. Kerouac sustained a euphoric momentum during three weeks in April 1951, keeping himself awake with cups of coffee, composing *On the Road* in a single, streaming paragraph onto 16-foot rolls of Japanese drawing paper which he fed into his typewriter and taped together to form a 250-foot scroll.

Allen Ginsberg has commented on the formal breakthrough of the original manuscript:

An attempt to tell completely, all at once, everything on his mind in relation to the hero Dean Moriarty, spill it all out at once and follow the convolutions of the active mind for direction as to the "structure of the confession." And discover the rhythm of the mind at work at high speed in prose.

Even in the compromised published form, *On the Road* is now considered a classic modern American novel, free of pre-imposed patterns, characteristically American in its search for a fluid, unshaped life. Reacting to the embalming stagnation of the 1950s, Kerouac had dangerously proposed a more joyously exciting alternative. He did it in a novel that still had some traditional elements and a redefined form, the picaresque narrative which used a rogue as a hero, an outsider whose conflicts with the symbols of authority would define the nature of power in his culture.

The story of *On the Road* tells how Dean Moriarty (Cassady) and Sal Paradise (Kerouac) career from coast to coast and finally to Mexico in a search for what is important in life and the reasons to live it. Of course, the question is never posed quite so bluntly, but such a concern becomes the thematic tissue of the quest in the novel. Moriarty, a protagonist at once Dionysian and Nietzschean, exists as a response to the stultifying sources of cultural asphyxiation that made the 1950s so bland. Instead of seeking a reasonable adjustment, Dean's particular ability is to become tremendously excited by life in an affirmative "wild yea-saying overburst of American joy." His infectious enthusiasms contradicted the gloomy Spenglerian view of the future expressed by many of Kerouac's friends, especially Burroughs. Instead of accepting despair, Dean acts with passionate abandon. However, this energy, although admirable, is mindless and narcissistically devouring. Representing the momentum of energy for its own sake, Dean seems maddened by the urge to be everywhere at the same time, to love several women, to conduct various searches while fulfilling none. So the negative, some might say demonic, aspects of Dean play their role in elevating the character from simply a figure based on Neal Cassady to something much larger in scope. And Kerouac, through the figure of his narrator, Sal Paradise, tries to offer a check on Dean's exuberant anarchism; indeed, one of the bases for scenic organization in the novel is the way in which other characters find fault with Dean after an episode. Sal is inevitably drained by Dean's propulsions of irresponsibility; like Kerouac, Sal is an outsider, an imperfect man in an alien world, brooding, seized by moments of self-hatred. The refrain in *On the Road* of "everything is collapsing" is a reminder of the effects on himself of disorder of Kerouac's own vision of uncontained release. Clearly the endless celebrations, the pellmell rushing from one place to the next, create an hysteria that makes Sal want to withdraw from the world. This conflict between the needs of self, as expressed by Dean, and the need to escape self, as expressed by Sal, becomes the pivot of Kerouac's fiction.

During the next six years, *On the Road* would be rejected by several publishers for what they misconstrued as structural looseness and tabled by the editors at Viking who realized the power of the story but who wanted a more conventionally presentable manuscript. That period, from 1951 to 1957, became Kerouac's ultimate test as a writer. He alternated his time between the familiar security of his mother's apartment and restless trips to Mexico or California. For most of this period, Kerouac was supported by his mother, and she did not understand the nature of his struggle as a writer. Often, when far from home, he subsisted on pennies a day and lived as a vagabond. But what is most important about this time of deprivation and penury is that Kerouac did not stop observing and recording, that he wrote a series of fictions that departed from the traditional writing of the day and added new dimensions to his own style: *Visions of Cody, Doctor Sax, Maggie Cassidy, The Subterraneans, Tristessa.*

The most ambitious novel of this dark period, when Kerouac was writing for himself alone without hope of publication or support, is his masterpiece, *Visions of Cody.* Also about Cassady, this novel was begun when Kerouac started removing certain sequences from *On the Road* and then elaborating on them. Experimental in form, Joycean in texture, rhythmically inspired by the jazz music he loved, *Visions of Cody* was such a departure from conventional notions of what a novel should be that it remained unpublished in full until 1972, a full three years after Kerouac's death. The freedom of conception and the imaginative range of this novel makes it the best example of Kerouac's ideas on spontaneous prose: his abandonment of conscious control, what he called "an undisturbed flow from the mind." Kerouac compared this kind of writing to orgasm and maintained that the writer's purpose should be to discover "wild form," to purify the mind so that words could pour freely with complete honesty. In *Visions of Cody* the removal of grammatical and syntactical inhibitions, the use of the vernacular, the puns and metaphysical flights, the rambling sentences and stream-of-consciousness passages, the digressive crowd-ing of impressions as well as anecdotes, tall tales, drug fantasies, drawings, letters, a long transcription of a taped conversation with Cassady, imitations of Tom Sawyer and of Bloom's trial in *Ulysses*—that is to say, the Shandyean profusion of the novel leaves the reader giddy and prepared to accept Kerouac's epiphanies, his attempt to make a myth out of the Cassady story and the conjunctions of the Beat brotherhood.

During what I have called the dark period of Kerouac's career, he was also writing poems influenced by jazz and blues, and a long and still unpublished manuscript on Buddhist practice. His involve-ment with Buddhism anticipated (and, with his novel *The Dharma Bums*, actively contributed to) the growing interest in Eastern religion that occurred in the United States in the 1960s. Psychologically, Buddhism helped Kerouac to weather his most depressing years, a time when he felt that even though he was writing some of the best fiction in America, it was unpublishable and unwanted. Kerouac's own meditation and study in Buddhist scripture confirmed some of his most cherished ideas about spontaneity in writing and shifted the Beat emphasis from world weariness to the exaltation of renunciation and beatitude. This shift from despair to joy is most evident in the two best fictions Kerouac wrote in his final period, *The Dharma Bums* and *Desolation Angels*.

It is clear that the publicity caused by *On the Road* and Beat writing from 1957 to 1959, the harshness of his detractors, and the tension caused by television appearances all affected him badly. He had been the burning unknown of the 1950s. Before the literary maelstrom caused by *On the Road*, his friend the poet Gary Snyder had suggested that Kerouac become a fire lookout, and Kerouac spent several seasons on the tops of the highest mountains in the American northwest, a solitary sentinel absorbed in the majesty of nature, living like a modern Thoreau. Suddenly he was catapulted to celebrity. Like Scott Fitzgerald, he was the nucleus of a literary movement that had captured a generation; as it had been for Fitzgerald, the fame sub-verted his sense of himself. He began to drink heavily, to withdraw from his friends and the world. His last years were spent isolated and angry, and his last books, *Big Sur* and *Vanity of Duluoz*, show the strains of a man tired of living and writing.

Now, more than a decade after his untimely death in 1969, Kerouac's reputation in the American literary pantheon is changing.

Originally dismissed as merely the chronicler of the Beat phenomenon, he is receiving both appreciation as a master of style and recognition as a major figure in contemporary literature. In Europe interest in his work has always been pronounced. In the United States almost all of his 19 books are in print; *On the Road* still sells 50,000 copies annually. Just in the last few years there has been a biography by Dennis McNally published by Random House; *Jack's Book*, an anthology of biographical material edited by Barry Gifford and Lawrence Lee; a play on Kerouac's life by Martin Duberman; a four-hour radio broadcast on Kerouac by CBC in Montreal; and a Hollywood film on his life. Kerouac's influence on contemporary writing is still strong; his books are still in the stores and being read; and, a quarter of a century after *On the Road*, there is a critical revival concerning his work.

Bibliography

By Jack Kerouac (in order of composition):

The Town and the City. New York: Harcourt, Brace, 1950.
On the Road. New York: Viking Press, 1957.
Scattered Poems. San Francisco: City Lights, 1971.
Visions of Cody. New York: McGraw Hill, 1972.
Doctor Sax. New York: Grove Press, 1959.
Maggie Cassidy. New York: Avon Books, 1959.
The Subterraneans. New York: Grove Press, 1958.
Tristessa. New York: Avon Books, 1960.
The Dharma Bums. New York: Viking Press, 1958.
Big Sur. New York: Farrar, Straus, 1962.
Desolation Angels. New York: Coward-McCann, 1965.
Vanity of Duluoz. New York: Coward-McCann, 1968.

About Jack Kerouac:

Charters, Ann, editor. *A Bibliography of Works by Jack Kerouac.* New York: Phoenix
    Book Shop, 1967.
Holmes, John Clellon. *Nothing More to Declare.* New York: Dutton, 1967.
Tytell, John. *Naked Angels: The Lives & Literature of the Beat Generation.* New York:
    McGraw Hill, 1976; paperback edition, 1977; Japanese translation, Tokyo:
    Kinokunika Shoten, 1978; German translation as *Prophetan der Apokalypse,*
    Vienna: Europa Verlag, 1979.

An Interview with Allen Ginsberg

VOA: What are you working on right now?

Ginsberg: Well, several things. A little song that I've been writing the last few weeks trying to get one word right in it. I've been writing music and I've been studying work on English poets, by Campion, 15th-century singers. And I wrote:

Love Forgiven

Straight and slender
Youthful tender
Love shows the way
And never says nay

Light & gentle—
Hearted mental
Tones sing & play
Guitar in bright day

Voicing always
Melodies, please
Sing sad, & say
Farewell if you may

Righteous honest
Heart's forgiveness
Drives woes away,
Gives Love to cold clay

I was reading Ezra Pound and Louis Zukofsky, on music related to poetry. And I was beginning to listen to phrasing like "guitar in bright day," "and never says nay," and trying to get those speech cadences into a little poem and then find the melodies that fit the tones. You know that when we talk, we talk in cadences (da-ta-dah, da-da da-ta-da) and we talk in tones. So the vowels have different pitch or tone-like melody. So from natural speech cadences, from the rhythms of every-day talk, we can extrapolate little songs. So I've been interested in that. The teachers of attentiveness and care to sound, cadence, vowel, length, and time in poetry are contemporary poets like Robert Creeley, or great elders, like William Carlos Williams, Pound, or Zukofsky, who recently died. They studied Provençal and Renaissance minstrels, singers, Thomas Campion, John Dowland, Shakespeare (who wrote things to be sung). In fact, all of the great English poets up to the 16th century wrote songs for singing, just as Bob Dylan does now. We're getting back to classical lyric actually sung rather than just written down on a piece of paper and read by the eye from the page without opening your mouth. You see, my father (Louis Ginsberg) was a poet. . . .

VOA: Yes. He wrote in the traditional form.

Ginsberg: He thought he did. He was writing traditional-looking lyrics but he wasn't singing, you see. He was writing in forms originally intended for song. English song got forgotten after the 17th century and poetry got to be more and more speech. Look how English poetry goes to the sonorities of Milton, oratory, then to the sort of witty parlor talk of Alexander Pope, and then through the oratory and intellectual brilliance of Shelley, and then through the ordinary babble of the Victorians, back to the 20th century when Pound and Williams said, let's try to write the way we talk, let's find the cadences of actual speech. But by the 1950s and 60s, black Americans had influenced poetry so much that American poets were beginning to sing blues and then folk music. . . .

VOA: You mean the influence from Langston Hughes?

Ginsberg: No, more from Leadbelly: "Write me a letter, send it by mail, send it in care of the Birmingham Jail."

VOA: Unfortunately, one of his images, the Rock Island Line, was abandoned just this week.

Ginsberg: Industrial civilization seems to be homogenizing everything and bringing us to a kind of apocalyptic end-of-the-world nuclear explosion, on the way killing off Rock Island Line, old housing, fine restaurants—as Ezra Pound pointed out about World War I, "Of one thing you can be sure, that war is the destruction of good restaurants"—and whales, dolphins, and many hundred thousand species, possibly including poets sooner or later.

　　　　Well, as speech and song fell away from each other, people talked more abstractly and bureaucratically in their poetry, and the Industrial Revolution homogenized and stereotyped language. As people lost the handcrafts, attentiveness, and direct care—to their shoes and their houses and their sinks and their gardens—they were fed all over the world with cans and plastic hot dogs and hamburgers and soft drinks, were fed cigarettes and nicotine and sugar and whatever else drives you mad, were fed television, were fed Communism, were fed capitalism, and were fed the State. In other words, all were fed large mental-bureaucracy monopolies, either way you put it, either side of the Iron Curtian the same: and as people were fed police-state mentality, things got more reduplicated and homogenized and standardized. And anybody who stepped out of line got to be thought to be crazy, all over the supposedly cultivated, sophisticated world. So that industrial people no longer have any sense of grounding, often no longer have any sense of relation to their own speech, no longer take pleasure in their own mouths as you will find pleasure taken in the talk style of provincial places like Wales or presumably Azerbaidzhan or certain parts of Brooklyn or New Jersey (as William Carlos Williams took pleasure in the speech of Rutherford). As speech and thought become homogenized with television, radio, newspapers, people are less and less in the middle of their own language, less and less aware of what they're saying and tend to repeat stereotypes, the gossip that they read in the newspapers, as their "philosophy of life." Gossip on television gets taken as somebody's "philosophy of life." So it's a kind of a sleep-walking civilization at this point. There's no longer any individual contact possible with your food, where your food comes from to begin with, with the earth.

The same thing happened to poetry as happened to politics—poetry got separated from the body and politics got separated from real people's bodies actually. So that it was possible to have vast holocausts like the Nazi concentration camps, or the Belgian slaughter of Blacks in the Congo at the beginning of the 20th century, or the vast concentration camps and Gulags in Russia, or the vast massacres that the United States committed in Central America and elsewhere, as the half-million "reds" killed with the U.S.-backed overthrow of Sukarno in Indonesia 1965-1966. So what we have now is a fragmented social universe and the creation of apocalyptic or world-destroying weapons. I think the United States is now contemplating building the biggest thing ever built in the history of man, bigger than the Wall of China, some kind of monstrous nuclear arsenal in the deserts of Utah, an underground Tower of Babel costing 30 to 100 billion dollars; the MX system it's called.

We're further and further away from the preservation of our own bodies. History does approach what the Western Christian Bible prophesied—fire and brimstone coming from the sky. Brimstone is sulphur fumes actually; you see brimstone as you fly into Denver. There's a vast smog the color of human dung, made of "brimstone" or sulphur fumes, over all the great industrial cities. Even in Athens the Parthenon rots. Things once most dear and most cared for are now eaten away by our acid rains.   Acid rain is brimstone, literally! "Brimstone" means the sulphur fumes, sulphur gas, watery sulphur in the atmosphere, sulphur smog!

So what's to do about that? Poetry at least can get back to the body, back to the human voice, to actual personal feelings, and express what is not expressed by governments, by governments' organs of propaganda, by the monopolized mass media. It's a rare instance where a voice like mine will go over a government radio talking about how my own government's policies collaborate with the Russian government's policies, to create a world of brimstone and destruction.

I think that the human voice penetrates through and shatters all of the steely metal pyramids of Time. I think the human voice will outlast them, if there are any human ears left to hear the voice. The reason is that though you can build an architectural thing like an MX system or a giant missile or a giant Empire State Building or a Sphinx or a Wall of China, still, certain human tones reoccur over and over again and their cadences are permanent. You have "Aah." That particular tone lasts longer than metal because it is built into the body. The sigh of release of anxiety, "aaaah," that can be heard millenially, even before the Sphinx was built, and will be heard after the nuclear arsenals here at Rocky Flats, Colorado, and all plutonium factories have dissolved.

VOA: This is what you are talking about in another place as inspiration.

Ginsberg: Yes. Poetic inspiration has always been thought about abstractly. People think that somebody gets goofy and runs around with a bunch of flowers, waving it in smog clouds. But what *inspiration* means is a state of breathing that is unimpeded, unobstructed breath! Unanxious breath where the body tingles and seems hollow and the truth of feeling emerges in articulate, clear, precise language. Truth of feeling will always stay, is what I'm trying to say. "Only emotion endures" in poetry. That is, an emotion that is "objectified" by being put out into the air, in the shape of cadenced words, does endure. So that little tags of Sappho were translated by Catullus in the Roman times, and those were retranslated by English poets in Elizabethan times, and those affect the poets of today—little rhythms out of Sappho like the hendecasyllabic da-ta-da-ta da-ta-ta-da-ta da-da— because they're built into the body and have to do with a certain kind of majesty that the body has when it's breathing properly and in full majestic possession of its own seat.

VOA: You three—Ginsberg, Burroughs, and Kerouac—while, I suppose, crudely said to be lumped into the same school, the "Beat Generation" of writers, really write in different fashion.

Ginsberg: Oh, totally. Gregory Corso, too!

VOA: Burroughs refines and refines and refines.

Ginsberg: Yes.

VOA: And Kerouac was a child of spontaneity.

Ginsberg: He was an old bard of spontaneity. Remember that notion of spontaneity is one of the most ancient bardic forms from Homer's day on. Homer wasn't written down, and much of Homer was improvised and sung. The tradition of spontaneous bardic improvisation is the oldest and most classical form of poetics in the world. Back to the Australian aborigines if you need to go back for a real authoritative antiquity. It's only since Westerners started writings things down in the first millenium and printing them later on in the second thousand years A.D., that things began to get kind of homogenized and that people thought that poetics was writing. Poetics had hardly anything to do with writing from Magdalenian years—24,000 B.C.—to Gutenberg's printing press invention.

VOA: What is poetics?

Ginsberg: It's cadences of human speech, concentrated musical tones of human speech with pictures in it, a mode that can be improvised and always was. This very ancient tradition still exists in America in the form of blues. Perhaps our major treasury of poetry is blues lyrics, calypso, ballad, country-Western, and folk music.

Kerouac was picking up rhythms from modern blues musicians and singers and then returning these sounds to mainstream American white literary practice, using basic cadences of our own actual Americanese speech as distinguished from English speech. It's an old argument anyway—as every nation, every culture has to learn to talk its own talk, to create its own national literature. Poetry's got to be written in its own spoken language, just as in every century,

Wordsworth to Pound, the literary language is renovated by reference to the actual talk of the day: Wordsworth saying that poetry
should be written as real men speak, Pound the same, Williams the
same, Kerouac the same. If you're actually writing not officialese or
hand-me-down rhythms, but your own rhythms, it happens that
those breathings break through the monotonous rhythms of mass
media, or government syntax, the monotone of bureaucratese. What
you hear instead is the freshness of somebody talking for real to
another real person, rather than a scared bureaucrat trying to write
a text that nobody can object to, that can't get him into trouble with
the newspapers. So you have actual speech as against a manipula-
tive speech that hides the point rather than gives it out freely. So that's
where the ancient, careful tradition of handcrafts and body-to-
body, one-to-one relationship with people and with poems differs
from the modern, industrial, homogenized, mass-produced speech.
That's how poetry has kept track of the human breath, human inspiration, human heartbeat, all through these millenia, despite all
the political and social and cultural interrogations and inquisitions
and McCarthyisms and Gulags and atrocities by all governments
on the human body and on people's thoughts. Poetry still does retain
that original freshness of frank thought, telling out what you really
think.
VOA: You told what you really thought, but I don't think the world
was ready for it, but it was not the cadences so much that bothered
people as the vocabulary of it.
Ginsberg: Yes, we're referring probably to "Howl," "Kaddish," and
my later poems.
VOA: Yes.
Ginsberg: Actually, I think that my poetry did move the world
maybe half an inch, which is about as far as any individual person can
desire to move anything, even himself.
VOA: It moved poetics.
Ginsberg: Well, poetics moved quite a bit because you've got to
remember that once people realized how real poetry was, they realized how unreal the Vietnam war propaganda was. Having realized
that, they began to realize that the Vietnam war propaganda was just
a lot of bad poetry or bad theater, so to speak, that war politics was like
a made-up language to entertain or convince. So that the anti-war hero
Abbie Hoffman did coin this very funny aphorism: "You do have the
right to shout 'Theater!' at a crowded fire," meaning we do have the

right to say that this nuclear holocaust that's coming up is the paranoic theater of the billion-dollar theater-producers of the Pentagon and Kremlin. Like the whole public notion of nuclear energy is bought and paid for with a lot of "poetry" printed in the newspapers and broadcast on television. In the year 1978, the U.S. nuclear industry spent 470 million dollars propagandizing nuclear energy, and the anti-nuclear industry (Ralph Nader and friends) spent only four million dollars—which means that the whole poem of nuclear "respectability," the whole image of nuclear public "acceptability" was made up. It's an art work to promote an image, a political image, just like it's an art work to counter it with an individual voice by saying, well, the image built by 470 million dollars is a fake art work, a self-interested image costing 470 million dollars.

All public speech is images, all public speech is speech, and, as such, it is just talk. Poetry is talk.

So what's the alternative now? What's the alternative to this 20th-century, apocalyptic horror scene? I would say, for one thing: some form of free and easy decentralization of thought-form stereotypes, breaking through stereotype language, for a fresh look into the space around us, is necessary. I would say that one proper form to cause that breakthrough is art. Art in the guitar hand of Bob Dylan or John Lennon has had a world-penetrating and waking influence. Song has reached all through the world, reached through the conditioned reflexes of masses frightened by the governments. Art gets through the whole earth. I think meditation practice is free and it's cheap and doesn't require chilams or bongs or pills or electricity as a way of taking stock of all the automatic responses that we're conditioned to (or perhaps we condition ourselves; I won't lay the blame on anyone.) At the moment I'm concerned with song, poetry, the articulation of my own feelings in natural cadences, in relation to awareness of breathing. So I was proposing poetry or art in one form or another, and meditative practice, as well as perhaps farming and sports and healthy labor, as ways of getting out of this blockade of hyperrationalistic paranoia that the world has delivered itself into politically. I mean we're in the midst of a giant cold war, a war of images, and practically everybody that's listening has thought that certainly, inevitably, there is going to be a nuclear holocaust within our lifetime or soon after!

VOA: Leslie Fiedler said that he doesn't worry about this at all because the military doesn't want to be put out of business and they'll save us by not doing that. What do you think?

Ginsberg: I don't think the military are that sane. Civilization isn't that sane! Well, I wrote a long poem called "Kaddish" about my mother who *died* in the mad house, and I've met human beings who *do* go insane and who *do* commit suicide—put themselves out of business!

VOA: Many poets have done that. You're lumped in with the Confessional poets, and certainly some of them were at the core of madness.

Ginsberg: Yes, but is the suicide rate among poets any higher than the suicide rate among politicians or Wall Street brokers? It might be lower, for all we know. Actually poets who commit suicide write about themselves so you know their lives in a very fresh, frank way, whereas most generals commit suicide without getting a chance to tell their story to the ear of God.

VOA: Or perhaps you take yourself out of the Confessional school because you are not mad?

Ginsberg: Oh, I was in a "mad house" for a while when I was young, except that when I got out, they gave me a certificate saying I was never really mad, just sort of average neurotic.

VOA: What do you think?

Ginsberg: Oh, average neurotic, I would say. I felt relatively sane at the time.

I have written a long poem called "Plutonian Ode." For the last couple of years I've been working on it, finishing it this year, and I'll read a few lines of that—a taste of what it's about. It's sort of a challenge to the robotic fear-mentality of the nuclear bombs, was written the night before I was arrested for blocking a train full of plutonium wastes from going out of the Rockwell Corporation Rocky Flats Plutonium-Bomb-Trigger Factory right near Boulder, Colorado. So it's about plutonium itself and says:

> . . . Yeah monster of Anger birthed in fear o most
> Ignorant matter ever created unnatural to Earth! Delusion
>   of metal empires!
> Destroyer of lying Scientists! Devourer of covetous Gener-
>   als, Incinerator of Armies & Melter of Wars!
> Judgment of judgments, Divine Wind over vengeful na-
>   tions, Molester of Presidents, Death-Scandal of Capital
>   politics! Ah civilizations stupidly industrious!

Canker-Hex on multitudes learned or illiterate! Manufactured Spectre of human reason! O solidified imago of
practitioners in Black Arts
I dare your Reality, I challenge your very being! I publish
your cause and effect!
I turn the Wheel of Mind on your three hundred tons! Your
name enters mankind's ear! I embody your ultimate
powers!
My oratory advances on your vaunted Mystery! This
breath dispels your braggart fears! I sing your form
at last
Behind your concrete & iron walls inside your fortress of
rubber & translucent silicon shields in filtered cabinets
and baths of lathe oil,
my voice resounds through robot glove boxes & ingot cans
and echoes in electric vaults inert of atmosphere,
I enter with spirit out loud into your fuel rod drums underground on soundless thrones and beds of lead
O density! This weightless anthem trumpets transcendent
through your hidden chambers and breaks through
iron doors into the Infernal Room!
Over your dreadful vibration this measured harmony
floats audible, these jubilant tones are honey and milk
and wine-sweet water
Poured on the stone block floor, these syllables are barley
groats I scatter on the Reactor's core,
I call your name with hollow vowels, I psalm your Fate
close by, my breath near deathless ever at your side
to Spell your destiny, I set this verse prophetic on your
mausoleum walls to seal you up Eternally with Diamond Truth! O doomed Plutonium.

The Bard surveys Plutonium history from midnight lit
with Mercury Vapor street lamps till in the dawn's
early light
he contemplates a tranquil politic spaced out between
Nations' thought-forms proliferating bureaucratic
& horrific arm'd, Satanic industries projected sudden with
Five Hundred Billion Dollar Strength
around the world same time this text is set in Boulder,
Colorado before front range of Rocky Mountains
twelve miles north on Rocky Flats Nuclear Facility in
United States on North America, Western Hemisphere
of planet Earth six months and fourteen days around our
Solar System in a spiral Galaxy
the local year after Dominion of the last God nineteen
hundred seventy eight

Completed as yellow hazed dawn clouds brighten East,
    Denver city white below
Blue sky transparent rising empty deep & spacious to a
    morning star high over the balcony
above some autos sat with wheels to curb downhill from
    Flatiron's jagged pine ridge
sunlit mountain meadows sloped to rust-red sandstone
    cliffs above brick townhouse roofs
as sparrows waked whistling through Marine Street's
    summer green leafed trees.

VOA: Do you know, when I read the earlier version of that in *Rolling Stone*, I didn't hear this sarcasm. I didn't read it in the poetry the way you read it.

Ginsberg: Well, the sarcasm is more joy. It's "jubilant," jubilation above and beyond the fear of the bomb. In other words, everybody's scared. Everybody's scared because it seems serious, and they got all these guys working there for billions of dollars, and they're going to spend another hundred billion dollars to put the big bombs, the MX system, in a bed underground in the middle of the desert. Everybody takes it so seriously, scared of death naturally, but, on the other hand, it's a big mystique, a big mystery thing. They drive everybody off their rocker a little bit by having something so big, so horrible, that it's going to blow up the earth. Everybody's supposed to be scared of it. Well, screw that! And screw the people that are trying to scare everybody. I mean the worst thing that happens is you die. No point in finally going crazy and trying to bomb everybody out, out of fear of being bombed. Well, I'm not making sense. It's just that the government's situation is maniacal, and the human heart is not maniacal. The human heart is basically humorous.

VOA: Is there a poetry boom? Have you seen any growing interest in poetics?

Ginsberg: All over the world. In 1979 in Europe there were a lot of international poetry readings, big crowds! In Rome with the Russian Yevtushenko, whom I've known many years, there were Romanian poets and Johannes Schenck, a German, and many French poets and Italian poets and Uruguayan poets and a whole bunch of American poets like Burroughs, Gregory Corso, and myself, and Diane di Prima and Anne Waldman, LeRoi Jones, Ted Berrigan, Peter Orlovsky, and other people who teach here in Boulder, Colorado, at Naropa Institute. With three nights of poetry in a row, there was a lot of wildness and disruptive anarchy, but we finally got the people together with the poetry by the second and third nights. And the third night I think the *New York Times* said 10,000 people were there, the *Republica*, a newspaper there, said 15,000, and I think the *Corriera dela Sera*, the big respectable Rome newspaper, said 20,000 people came to the beach at Ostia to hear four hours of poetry, like starting at nine in the evening and going on till one in the morning. Why? Because it's individual people saying what they know from their own tearful heart-voice.

VOA: This was not a Tower of Babel there, although all of these languages. . . .

Ginsberg: Well, I think there were agent-provocateur elements of the Tower of Babel there, yes, but Peter Orlovsky was playing his banjo so joyfully at the end that everybody got up and danced and then rushed on the stage after the show was over. So about five minutes after 1:30, after the poetry was all over, the stage collapsed, there were so many people on it looking for autographs and happy that we were able to bring poetry out of the chaos of those nights.

Right now because of the need for real speech, feeling, heart; because of the threat of robotic communication, there's been an increasing awareness of the delicacy of poetry as both public speech and private. We had an anti-draft rally here on the University of Colorado campus, where I read poems, reread a poem called "America," improvising new lines to a 25-year-old poem. There were a thousand people out there listening to a poem, a thousand students. It's a tremendous lot of people listening to one poem. The key is when poetry returns to actual speech, then people can listen to it because you're talking to them.

VOA: You're also abandoning those classical allusions.

Ginsberg: No, not really.

VOA: There was allusion in that "Plutonian Ode," wasn't there?

Ginsberg: There's lots of classical allusions. It was an ode to Pluto, god of the Underworld, god of wealth, as it turns out. He's like the Rockefellers—the god of wealth and metals underground, Lord of Hades, the father of the Eumenides. The Eumenides are the Furies that come back and revenge themselves on you when you do something unmindful to the earth like fill it up with radioactive wastes. So Pluto is the right god to address this to, Lord of Hades, Lord of Death. It's a funny thought here! The Rockefeller group is the single largest purveyer of nuclear fuel, single largest in the industry. So the Rockefellers are a sort of Plutonian monopoly; they do have this association with Pluto, Hades, underworld wealth!

Plutonium: people don't know much about it; it's a man-made element, an element like iron, oxygen, hydrogen, copper, and gold, but made for the first time by man, alchemized. There's "something new under the sun." Men have made a new element! But it's a very deadly poisonous element, unstable. You know, you put too much in it, and it's got to come apart. It takes a long time to come apart, and as it comes apart, it gives off radioactive bullets, so-to-speak, that go like a truck through your DNA cells, or through your genes, you see, so it's quite dangerous. And it lasts. The half-life is 24,000 years, and the full life before plutonium becomes physically inert is 240,000 years. That's before the Garden of Eden and way beyond that. We'll never see the end of it!

Burroughs has a line: "Selling the ground from under unborn feet." Governor Jerry Brown made some speech of that sort, saying that we have no right to poison the earth for generations to come. Our own grandchildren, our future, future, future descendents, we're leaving them with our problem. We're leaving our garbage behind for our grandchildren to take care of. It doesn't make sense. Something's mad about that. It's unnatural for a family to lay a trip like that on the unborn children; we give them a problem that we can't solve and keep building the problem. So where can this truth be found but in a poem? Or what is that knowledge but a poem? What is the understanding of that but a poetic understanding? It certainly is not a political understanding because they haven't understood it yet, and they're still building plutonium, destroying the upper atmospheres, assassinating the whales and the Amazon Forest, and wrecking the earth. What will happen? Who knows? It's really amazing, it's really interesting to live nowadays. It's interesting to live as long as you're not on the banks of the Ganges vomiting in the mud or on the Cambodian border weighing ten pounds and looking up with giant pupils into the void eyes of nurses—brown-skinned, starving, ribs sticking out, skinny. Ah, a lot of suffering! So who can get out of it? Everywhere there's suffering now, everywhere, more and more difficult, more and more tears. So what can you do about that? I don't know.

VOA: You mentioned a while ago, too, another influence on you who told you about the direction of your work and perhaps changed you, and I'll ask you, did he? That's William Carlos Williams.

Ginsberg: I didn't see him often, though we were in neighboring towns, but he had an enormous moral impact, moral influence, and aesthetic influence. I sent him all my rhymed poems, and he reacted lukewarmly. He was a great innovator in American measure of cadenced free verse, and here I was sending him the same old da-ta da-ta da-dah. But he answered, "In this mode perfection is basic." After that, I took him some other poems that I had written in my notebook that weren't "poems," just prose writings, notebook jottings, journal-thoughts, and reveries, looking out of a window. I'll read one, written in 1947: "The Bricklayers' Lunch Hour." (I wrote it not far from here, down in Denver. Kerouac said in those years, "Down in Denver, down in Denver, all I did was die.")

> Two bricklayers are setting the walls
> of a cellar in a new-dug-out patch
> of dirt behind an old house of wood with brown gables
>   grown over with ivy
> on a shady street in Denver. It is noon
> and one of them wanders off. The young
> subordinate bricklayer sits idly for
> a few minutes, after eating a sandwich
> and throwing away the paper bag. He
> has on dungarees and is bare above
> the waist. He has yellow hair and wears
> a smudged but still bright red cap
> on his head. He sits idly on top
> of the wall on a ladder that is leaned
> up between his spread thighs, his head
> bent down, gazing uninterestedly at
> the paper bag on the grass. He draws
> his hand across his breast and then
> slowly rubs his knuckles across the
> side of his chin, and rocks to and fro
> on the wall. A small cat walks to him
> along the top of the wall. He picks
> it up, takes off his cap, and puts it
> over the kitten's body for a moment.
> Meanwhile, it is darkening as if to rain
> and the wind on top of the trees in the
> street comes through almost harshly.

That is just looking out of my window and describing what I see there. So I divided those little prose things into lines that looked like William Carlos Williams's modern poetry lines and sent about eight or nine such notations to him. And he wrote back immediately, "This is it! Do you have any more of these? I shall see that you get a book."

Thus he pointed my attention to where I was actually writing with
my own talking tone of voice and my own speech, rather than in an
archaic literary mode. The alternative I had sent him was. . . .

VOA: Da-ta-da-ta-da. . . .

Ginsberg: It was:

> ˘ ´ ˘ ´ ˘ ´ ˘ ´
> If money made the mind more sane,
> Or money mellowed in the bowel
> The hunger beyond hunger's pain,
> Or money choked the mortal growl,
> Or made the groaner grin again,
> Or did the laughing lamb embolden
> To lull where has the lion lain,
> I'd go make money and be golden.

Well, that's witty and it's pretty but it's not true. It is not real talk, and
I like Williams's real speech, so that's why I shifted to verse forms that
allow real, modern talk.

Bibliography

By Allen Ginsberg:

Howl, and Other Poems. San Francisco: City Lights, 1956.
Kaddish and Other Poems, 1958-1960. San Francisco: City Lights, 1961.
Reality Sandwiches. San Francisco: City Lights, 1963.
Planet News, 1961-1967. San Francisco: City Lights, 1968.
The Fall of America: Poems of These States, 1965-1971. San Francisco: City Lights, 1973.
Mind Breaths: Poems, 1972-1977. San Francisco: City Lights, 1978.
Allen Verbatim: Lectures on Poetry, Politics, Consciousness. New York: McGraw-Hill,
     1975.
Plutonian Ode, Poems 1977-1980. San Francisco: City Lights, 1982.
Collected Poems. 1947-1980. New York: Harper & Row, 1984.
White Shroud, Poems 1980-1985. New York: Harper & Row, 1986.
Howl, Annotated. New York: Harper & Row, 1986.
Gifford, Barry, editor. *As Ever: The Collected Correspondence of Allen Ginsberg and Neal
     Cassady.* Berkeley, California: Creative Art Books, 1977.

About Allen Ginsberg:

Mortz, William J. *The Distinctive Voice: Twentieth Century American Poetry.* Glenview, Illinois: Scott, Foresman, 1966.

Dowden, George and Laurence McGilvey, editors. *A Bibliography of the Works of Allen Ginsberg.* San Francisco: City Lights, 1971.

Kraus, Michelle P. *Allen Ginsberg: An Annotated Bibliography, 1969-1977.* Metuchen, New Jersey, and London: Scarecrow Press, 1980.

Tytell, John. *Naked Angels: The Lives and Literature of the Beat Generation.* New York: McGraw-Hill, 1976.

Portuges, Paul. *The Visionary Poetics of Allen Ginsberg.* Santa Barbara, California: Ross-Erikson, 1978.

Joseph Heller's Fiction

Walter James Miller

Consider a novel that has been described like this. It is fat, overlong, experimental in structure, intricate in texture. It abounds in allusions, symbols, allegory. It's surrealistic, Dadaist, absurdist, Dantean. Its message is savagely radical: it satirizes cherished notions from the value of the family to the viability of God.

Offhand you would say it sounds like an avant-garde work doomed to be admired—perhaps exegesed—by a small following. You would be unprepared to hear these additional facts. *Catch-22*, as it's called, enjoys worldwide popularity. Its author, Joseph Heller, is the greatest-selling writer of serious fiction in American history. Since *Catch-22* appeared in 1961, it has helped create such a demand for innovative fiction that America-at-large suddenly recognized another experimental writer of Heller's own generation—the long-neglected Kurt Vonnegut—and made best-sellers too out of younger innovators like Thomas Pynchon, E. L. Doctorow, and Robert Coover. Many anomalies for which *Catch-22* prepared the public include this: Heller's second and third novels—*Something Happened* (1974) and *Good as Gold* (1979)—differ so radically from the first, they could have been written by two other innovators.

How could Heller perform such a miracle: producing avant-garde art that appeals to a mass audience? He got history and humor to work hand in hand. In the 1960s many Americans were beginning to question the morality of Uncle Sam's military ventures in Southeast Asia. Increasingly they were doubting the wisdom, even the motives, of many business, professional, and governmental leaders. As the number of citizens suspecting that a rationalist society might be irrational grew and grew, so did the sales of *Catch-22*. Seemingly an attack on the military-industrial complex of World War II, in which Heller had flown 60 combat missions, the novel actually aims, through highly original use of anachronisms, to expose the entire power system of the postwar world. Heller even foresaw many of the emerging crises of our times. *Catch-22* provides not only a catch-phrase to describe modern frustrations, but also Scripture, complete with prophecy and identification of Satan, for the new counter-culture.

But Heller's sense of timing would have availed him little, given the unorthodoxy of his approach, if he had not seduced his reader with black humor and absurdist wit. Step by step the reader braving Heller's strange terrain is rewarded with irreverent gags that promise shocking revelations. "Nately had a bad start. He came from a good family." "All over the world, young men were dying for what they had been told was their country."

Apparently Heller's own disenchantment began with his early experiences as an author. After the war he studied literature and writing at New York, Columbia, and Oxford Universities. By 1949, aged 26, already published in several leading magazines, he was regarded as one of America's most promising fiction-writers.

But then he stopped writing. For more than four years. Why? With his now well-known penchant for staring right through appearances, he came to realize that what he had learned to write—and what editors were so eager to buy—was trivial, formulaic, replicating. He turned his back on the traditional short story, with its unalloyed "realism." Its rationalist structure, its assumptions of continuity in situation and character, its neat resolutions apparently did not square with his own experiences. As soldier, university teacher, advertising writer, citizen—he's an indefatigable student of current events—he had lost confidence in surface meaning, what we smugly call cause-and-effect, determinacy. Realism photographs only outer reality. He had to find a structure and a style faithful to the absurdities he detected inside events, behind beliefs and policies.

Long immersion in the classics, from Homer to Dostoyevsky, and in innovators like Joyce and Faulkner, had not suggested any new approach he could use now. Then in 1953 his reading of Louis-Ferdinand Céline's *Journey to the End of Night* provided a leaven that made sense of Heller's literary and personal background. "Céline did things with time and structure and colloquial speech I'd never experienced before. I found those experiences pleasurable," he recalls. "It was unlike reading Joyce, who did things I'd never seen but that were not pleasurable." Art should enlighten the broadest possible audience, Heller maintains, but to do so it must also entertain. Five weeks later he was launched on a second literary career—this one genuine, continuous, self-renewing.

One reason *Catch-22* took eight years to write is that Heller had a full-time job and could invent new fictional maneuvers only by night. Another is that he felt impelled to work everything he knew, from his sensations of air combat in 1944 to his disgust with the politics of 1960, all into one cycloramic canvas.

Ostensibly, the story focuses on the exploits of the 256th Squadron, operating from the Mediterranean isle of Pianosa to bomb the Nazis' Gothic Line in Italy and installations in France. Yossarian, the main character in a cast of 60 well-defined individuals, earns a captaincy and a medal because he dared a second run over a well-armed, now fully alerted, target. But whenever he nears the number of missions he must fly to earn a tour of non-combat duty, his ambitious superiors keep raising that number far beyond the official Army requirement. They want to build up the best record of any unit. That's easier with seasoned veterans like Nately and Yossarian than with the green recruits who would replace them. Likely to die not for his country but for his colonels, finding all avenues of appeal blocked by those same commanders, Yossarian tries to escape the trap by feigning illness, even insanity. Obviously a crazy airman must be grounded. But there's a catch. He must ask to be grounded, and anyone asking to be excused from combat duty thereby proves he's not crazy. He "would be crazy to fly more missions and sane if he didn't, but if he was sane he had to fly them. If he flew them he was crazy and didn't have to; but if he didn't want to he was sane and had to." *Catch-22* becomes the master symbol, its many variations representing loopholes in the law that mean the powerful can take away the rights of their fellow citizens. Realizing that the Establishment itself has become Evil Incarnate, Yossarian deserts, following a long line of American dropouts, real and fictional, who decide to obey the Higher Conscience: Henry David Thoreau, hero of his autobiographical *Civil Disobedience*, Mark Twain's Huckleberry Finn, Ernest Hemingway's Lieutenant Henry.

Actually, Heller crams into 1944-1945 telling samples of American history from the crowding of the Indians off their own land in the 1800s to the controversies rampant in the Eisenhower Administration (1953-1961). Flashbacks were old tools when Heller used them to uncover corruption in, for example, the medical profession; what was new was his technique of creating fictional events in one period of time (World War II) that parodied actual events that would not occur until a later period (the 1950s). Senator Joseph McCarthy's 1954 anti-Communist battle cry, "Who promoted Major Peress?" is analyzed as an absurd question, "Who promoted Major Major?" Because his first name is Major, an IBM machine reads that as his rank. Heller's answer to McCarthy is typically symbolic. No one is guilty of promoting the Communist Peress; a machine, an organization operating automatically, did it. And the implications of Secretary of Defense Charles Wilson's blooper, "What's good for General Motors is good for the country and vice versa," are dramatized as Lieutenant Milo Minderbinder's black-market policy: "What's good for M&M Enterprises is good for the country." Black-market tactics become Heller's symbol for free enterprise itself; it upholds the consumer's freedom to pay high prices or starve. Some of Heller's anachronisms involve such accurate extrapolations, from conditions rampant when he was writing, that they prepared readers for life in the 1960s and 1970s: like scandals in the U.S. agricultural programs and in the Vietnam war.

Heller's overall time-structure was one of his technical experiments making humor necessary as an inducement. Soon after Yossarian sees, or thinks, of someone or something, he/Heller shies away from this experience, spiraling back over previous action, spiraling so that all events past-present-future are revealed in simultaneity. This recycling continues so long as Yossarian is at the mercy of the "spinning reasonableness" of *Catch-22*. But as soon as he takes definite steps to break out of the vicious cycle, the action becomes linear. Thus the novel's "story-line" resembles the path of a homing aircraft that circles an airport several times before it gets "on the beam" and flies straight in.

Shying, spiraling in the first 38 chapters determines the way, for example, Yossarian's most traumatic experience is revealed to us. Eight times he recalls the dying of Snowden, a gunner wounded over Avignon. Each time we get further details before Yossarian shies. Not until he is close to resolving his problem can he bear, in Chapter 41, to recall the entire scene. Some early readers, even some critics, missed the psychological validity behind this kind of narration. They saw instead only repetition and thought Heller inept.

Psychological reality also guides Heller when he has characters "feel" their way through crises not by thinking in words but by reliving, or reflecting on, archetypal situations. After Yossarian sabotages a mission, he copes with guilt feelings. Walking across the isle, he sees a soldier eating a pomegranate. This reminds the reader of Persephone, who lost her innocence by tasting pomegranate in Hades. Yossarian enters a forest, itself a classical symbol of descent into the shadow side of existence. In sudden darkness he's frightened by burgeoning mushrooms. We know by now that for an airman, they suggest exploding flak and so, especially since they spring here out of black Hades, death itself. Limp and pale, they suggest impotence, dread reward for him anxious over guilt. But Yossarian flees out onto the beach, a margin between two worlds, and enters the Mediterranean. In a ritual of baptism he swims until he feels clean. The scene especially signifies when we realize that Yossarian has been identified earlier, through allusions, with the protagonist of T. S. Eliot's *The Waste Land*: until now, Yossarian has feared death by water, that is, rebirth through baptism. Neither Yossarian nor the reader need verbalize these experiences as I have verbalized them here; the same symbols that work subliminally for the character work for the reader to reflect change of mood from anxiety to peace.

Yossarian "thinks" his way through another crisis while sitting naked in a tree, where Milo visits him. Through a combination of Yossarian's remarks, our own associations, and the chaplain's reflections on this tableau, we see Yossarian as Jesus on the cross and Adam at the tree, Milo the businessman as Satan.

Even characters whom we know only from the outside develop in terms of allusion and allegory. Since Major de Coverley's first name is never pronounced, we suspect he represents divinity; in some religions God's name is unutterable. But inevitably we think of a famous prude in English literature, Sir Roger de Coverley, and we find the name apt for the major. "Roger" is an Air Force code word for "Received and understood." To "roger" a woman means, in British slang, to have one's will of her; this resonates with ironies in Heller's overall situation.

Alerted that Heller characterizes through tag-names, we quickly grasp the nature of Nately (natally, suggesting newly-born, innocent, conscious of genealogy), of Luciana (who brings light into Yossarian's room), of Wintergreen (survival is his talent). Alerted that Heller describes through cultural allusions, we understand characters like Milo and Dobbs all the better if we recognize certain lines about them as parodies of Eliot, Whitman, Tennyson, Shakespeare.

Heller achieves his most memorable effects through surrealistic or expressionistic distortion. Since Milo's black-market operations are international in scope, they inevitably ally him with his counterparts in the Nazi war machine. These dealings take priority over declared national policies; as part of his "contracts" with the Germans, Milo bombs his own squadron. A congressional investigation clears him once he proves the transaction made a tidy profit for free enterprise. Heller thus dramatizes what he sees as the truth behind international cartels. They make a mockery of patriotism; they aid the enemy; businessmen may use the chaos of war to increase their power over (to fight) their own people. Heller's hospital scenes include a man so completely bandaged that no one has ever seen, heard, or touched the person inside. He seems to represent the *thing* that war reduces a man to. Or is the Soldier in White some sinister listening apparatus? Heller intensifies the nightmare quality of surreal situations by alternating them with realistic narration. For sheer descriptive power, metaphoric intensity, and poetic cadences, his realistic battle scenes are unsurpassed in the literature of war.

Catch-22, then, shows the individual in the clutches of monolithic organizations like armies, cartels, governments. Heller's next two novels deal with variations on the same theme. But they differ in that Heller gives greater attention to family relations as intermediate between the individual and his organization, and he popularizes other avant-garde techniques that suit his new situations.

In *Something Happened* Robert Slocum, a minor executive, gropes for status in the dark labyrinths of a giant corporation. Again, the struggle for power within the organization (army, corporation) consumes more energy than does the struggle to achieve the organization's declared goals (winning a war, serving the customer). While Yossarian ultimately rejects any deal that forces him to collaborate with cynical leaders, Slocum learns to play the power game, accepting its hypocrisies, treacheries, unremitting anxieties. Slocum learns by practising on his family. If the British say that the Battle of Waterloo was won on the playing fields of Eton College, then Heller seems to say that the Battle of Corporate Success is won on the testing-grounds of the patriarchal household. Slocum uses any tactic necessary to manipulate his wife, children, and mother, keeping human relations at a distance so he can concentrate on "real" goals: for example, to be the man who makes a three-minute speech at the company's annual convention.

One of his sons sweetly dramatizes an alternative way of life. A superb runner, the boy has no trouble staying ahead of his competitors. But he hates competition and likes to be with people, so when he's running, for the sheer joy of it, he often waits for the others to catch up to him! By degrees, the system, represented by the school track-coach, and ultimately the father too must crush this deviant—that is, humane—child.

Snuffing out a child, who represents man's future with his hope for integrity regained, is part of continuously symbolic action. Slocum has so little sense of self, he takes on characteristics of the person he's with; his wife knows he's been with Kagle if Slocum comes home limping like Kagle. Again, tag-names signify. Executives are named Green, Black, White, Brown; Gray figures near the end. Slocum's other son, an autistic child, prefers lifeless objects, mechanical sameness. Named Derek, connoting "derrick," he serves as an extension of one aspect of his father.

Here Heller's technique is so daring, it's no exaggeration to say that only the author of *Catch-22* could have risked it. His audience had learned to trust his experiments. In order to focus on the dehumanized, obsessed but tranquilized state of mind of a character who, to paraphrase Coleridge, must rise as the condition of not falling, Heller gives us nothing but Slocum's interior monologue. And that monologue is flat, monotonous, dogged, paranoiac. Two passages will illustrate not only the even, drily arithmetic style; they show too the parallels between Slocum's family life and corporate life, the way his need to control is based on fear engendered by hierarchism. On page 17 Slocum thinks: "In my department, there are six people who are afraid of me, and one small secretary who is afraid of all of us. I have one other person working for me who is not afraid of anyone, not even me, and I would fire him quickly, but I'm afraid of him." On page 355, Slocum thinks: "In the family in which I live there are four people of whom I am afraid. Three of these four people are afraid of me, and each of these three is also afraid of the other two. Only one member of the family is not afraid of any of the others, and that one is an idiot."

Not even Kafka would risk using such Kafkaesque techniques for 500 pages without relief. But Heller succeeds in getting the reader to agree that small samples no longer suffice. If such conditions pervade our culture, then art depicting them may defeat its purpose unless it haunts us with equal pertinacity.

In *Good as Gold* Heller continues to study the links between person, family, and gigantic organization. In addition to devising a new novelistic structure, he invents a new way of studying character and again blends realism with black humor and surrealism. Professor Gold is something of a cross between Slocum and Yossarian. Like Slocum, Gold wants to rise—this time, it's in the government—and for most of the novel, he is willing, like Slocum, to sacrifice family, friends, his humanity. But unlike Slocum, when Gold finally faces the question "How much lower would he have to crawl to rise to the top?" he turns his back on the abyss and rejoins family, profession, heritage. Like Yossarian, he first considers joining the power elite but then flees it. Like the airman and unlike the business executive, the professor is brilliant, so Heller is free once again to use his towering talents as a wit.

But Gold is more than a new combination of options open to an individual poised on a low rung in the hierarchy. He's an original study of the way a citizen may choose a national celebrity as his model for success. Jewish Professor Gold decides he will "out-Kissinger" Kissinger, who rose from Harvard professor to become the first Jewish U.S. Secretary of State. The more Gold imitates what (he thinks) Kissinger had to do to get to the top, the more Gold hates Kissinger and Gold. Gold's analysis of Kissinger's character helps Gold change his own. Heller develops a new form of satire: he criticizes a public figure by studying someone who imitates him. He concludes that such leaders are not worthy to serve as role models for anyone with a spark of conscience. Our leaders serve as models of what not to follow.

Gold lives with his wife and children, visits other relatives, and teaches in New York. The New York side of Gold's life Heller handles with satiric realism. Because Gold's review of the President's book *My Year in the White House* pleases the White House, Gold commutes on weekends to Washington hoping to attain a major government post. Gold's Washington side—serving on a commission, having an affair with the daughter of a powerful but anti-Semitic public figure— Heller handles as surrealism. Near the crisis he blends the two settings, two modes. A surrealistic situation that Gold's complicated life might well create in Washington is superimposed on his realistic experiences as he jogs around a track in New York.

In this book Heller especially exploits the sentence that undoes its own work. Its syntax symbolizes the double talk of the public official. "All of us," a White House aide tells Gold, "want you working with us as soon as possible after the people above us decide whether they want you working here at all. . . . In Washington, . . . you rise quickly and can't fall very far. . . . Do whatever you want as long as you do whatever we want. We have no ideas, and they're pretty firm. . . . This administration will back you all the way until it has to."

Fidelity to his subject matter leads Heller to adopt a different method for each novel. Still, I hope he someday spirals back to the consistently multi-level approach of what remains his greatest work: *Catch-22*. This could occur naturally. I think the complex combination of black humor with allegory, symbolism, and allusion, which makes his first novel a work of Dantean dimension, occurred to Heller as a summational approach. As he once said, "Everything I knew at the time is in *Catch-22*." Surely he will sometime feel the need for another encyclopedic synthesis of everything he "knows." For that, he may well have to circle back and around before coming in for a landing.

Bibliography

By Joseph Heller:

Catch-22. New York: Simon and Schuster, 1961; London: Cape, 1962.
We Bombed in New Haven, A Play. New York: Knopf, 1967.
Catch-22: A Dramatization. New York: Delacorte Press, 1973.
Something Happened. New York: Knopf, 1974.
Good as Gold. New York: Simon and Schuster, 1979.

About Joseph Heller:

Kostelanetz, Richard. "The American Absurd Novel." *The Listener*, 13 May 1965; *The New York Times Book Review*, 6 June 1965. Reprinted in *Twenties in the Sixties*. Westport, Connecticut, and London: Greenwood Press, 1979.
Miller, Walter James, and Bonnie E. Nelson. *Joseph Heller's "Catch-22."* New York:

Monarch Press/Simon and Schuster, 1971.
Scotto, Robert M., editor. *Joseph Heller's "Catch-22": A Critical Edition.* New York: Dell Publishing Co., 1973.

Frank O'Hara and His Poetry:
An Interview with Kenneth Koch

VOA: A triumvirate of poets—John Ashbery, Kenneth Koch, and Frank O'Hara—are often referred to as the New York School. Here we'll talk to Kenneth Koch about the work of Frank O'Hara (1926-66).

Mr. Koch, we're always in danger of being perhaps gossipy when we ask one friend to talk about another. One surprising thing about Frank O'Hara, I found, was the smattering of published works during his lifetime, although he seemed to write like water flowing downhill.

In the introduction to the book, *The Collected Poems of Frank O'Hara,* John Ashbery said: "One of his most beautiful early poems, 'Memorial Day 1950,' exists only because I once copied it out in a letter to Kenneth Koch, and Kenneth kept the letter." Why was O'Hara so seemingly negligent about his work?

Koch: I don't know. At the time Frank died, I had no idea how much he had written. When he died, I, Larry Rivers, and a few other friends went into his apartment and got all his manuscripts out. Then another poet and friend, Bill Berkson, and I went through all the manuscripts and catalogued them. I was astonished at the number of poems and at the quality of some of the poems that I had never seen. Frank kept them all in cardboard boxes. Every one was dated.

He didn't always write as easily as water flowing downhill, although I think he usually wrote rather quickly. On a number of the manuscript pages there are revisions—things crossed out and other things written in. They are often very radical revisions, in which lines and ideas are changed enormously. Some of his poems he worked on for days and even for weeks, for example, "Second Avenue." I remember that he and I were writing long poems at the same time: I was writing a poem called "When the Sun Tried to Go On" and Frank was writing "Second Avenue." We used to call each other up every day and read what we had written over the telephone. We inspired each other. Frank went on writing it for a long time.

Why didn't he publish a lot of work? For one thing, it wasn't easy for any of us to publish our work practically up to the time of Frank's death. Frank is a very famous poet now and his work has received the National Book Award. A lot of magazines have been eager to publish any poem of his. But we were all amassing quite a collection of rejection slips even into our 30s. So, first, it wasn't easy for him to publish his poems. Secondly, Frank had very, very high standards for his work although he knew it was good. I never knew how good he knew his poetry was until after his death when I read all his manuscripts; there were certain poems that I had not seen before, or there were certain poems that when I read them all together I saw that Frank had some idea, as a great poet would, that there was something in his work that was very good. But I remember having a talk with him when we were both in our middle 30s. I talked about so-and-so being great and someone else being great, and Frank said, "Listen. I think we can think about ourselves being great when we have done as much as Wallace Stevens or William Carlos Williams." I think he is as good as those poets, but I think it was hard to see it then when I hadn't seen all his work. And it was hard for him to see it because it is hard to see all one's own work. Then also he seemed to be always more interested in writing than publishing, in writing something new.

About the speed of his writing, he was terribly busy. Once he left his appointment book at my house, a little blue book, and I couldn't help looking at it. Almost every day for a month he had an appointment for lunch, dinner, cocktails, at night going to the theater, the opera, the ballet, and so on, or even sometimes an appointment for breakfast. This was along with working full-time at the Museum of Modern Art, where he not only had a job but sometimes had to write catalogues at home. And he spent a lot of time at painters' studios. Frank wrote a number of poems at his office at the museum on his lunch hour or when there would be a lull in the work for ten minutes. It was very often as though he were ready to write a poem, to be bursting with a poem, and whenever he had a moment, he would write it.

One extraordinary thing about Frank was that he could write with other people in the room. If he had an idea while people were there, he would just go and sit down and say, "Excuse me a minute."

And he would write a poem. The strangest example of this I can remember was at a party in East Hampton. There were about 40 people in the room, and Frank sat down in the corner of the room with the typewriter and wrote a rather good poem. He did this without the slightest pretension. I tried to do that, too, but with no success.

If someone interrupted Frank when he was writing, he would put the interruption in the poem. If someone came up and said, "Frank, can I open the window?"—that phrase might get into the poem.

Another way Frank wrote was to music. He would turn on some music or be listening to music on the radio and write a poem inspired by the music. It was as though the poetry was all there in his head and some stimulus—music, something a friend said, or even just some free time—would start if off.

VOA: This seems contrary to many of the things I have read that said that painting was the springboard for much of his art. He got inspiration everywhere.

Koch: He seems to have been inspired by everything that was full of life, energy, excitement, and force. But, no, it wasn't just painting.

VOA: Let's go back to the beginning of Frank O'Hara's work, his early poems. How did he start writing poetry?

Koch: I don't know what made Frank decide to be a poet, and I don't know that anybody knows that about anybody. He began to write poetry when he was quite young. There are good poems by Frank from his late teens. Very early on, his work was very sophisticated and very good.

There is one which he wrote, I think, in his early 20s, that is about being a poet. The title is from Coleridge, "Autobiographia Literaria." It is characteristic of Frank's dash and humor to take the title of this momentous work and do something of his own with it.

(Example excluded at
the publisher's request.)

It is very much like Frank in that it is very ironic about himself.
He is making fun of the pretentious literary attitude that says, "Yes, I
used to be very lonely and sad and nobody liked me, and now I'm a
wonderful person." Yet, at the same time, it is clear that the irony is
there because it is so exaggerated: hiding behind a tree and crying that
he was an orphan, and then the exaggeration of calling himself the
center of all beauty and asking everyone to marvel at this. At the same
time, I believe it. I recognize the feelings. It seems to me to be lyrical
and true at the same time it is funny.

"Today" is another early poem, which was also in that letter
that John Ashbery sent to me in Paris in 1950. This poem is characteristic of Frank's early work in its energy, its excitement, its use of excla-
mations, more particularly perhaps in its love of ordinary but sort of
dazzling words, and in its praise of plain, ordinary things as opposed
to officially poetic things.

(Example excluded at
the publisher's request.)

Frank was in his very early 20s when he wrote this I remember
being influenced by it, although at first I didn't like it because it was
about things that seemed to be too trivial. Later, my own poetry
became full of perals, jujubes, and aspirins: they're not only odd
things, they're odd words.
VOA: With beaches and biers he was probably writing in the
imagery of World War II.
Koch: Yes, February 1950. Frank was in the Navy in World War
II.
VOA: About the cross-influences of the New York poets: Did this
environment, the city, mean a lot to you?
Koch: It meant a lot to me that we were all in the same place,
wherever the place was. I don't think we would have been very happy
in a smaller town, given our voracious appetites for culture, conver-

sation, excitement, and other people. I don't know whether it was specifically New York; it is hard for me to say anything that would really be true about the city at that time. The important thing for me was that we were together in a city that could sustain us.

I suppose there are some general things that one shares in New York: that sort of dizzying anonymity, the feeling of freedom, the "availability of experience," as Marianne Moore says in a poem about New York, the feeling of excitement and nervousness. Frank liked New York an awful lot. He writes about it very directly, praises it, and is very excited by it. He writes more than John or I write about it certainly—about the experiences that we shared with one another. We were together a lot with Larry Rivers and Jane Freilicher, always in their studios and the studios of other painters. So we shared that whole painting scene. Whatever the painters gave us artistically, which was certainly something, I think we probably gave it back to them just as much. They also gave us their company and their social life. They usually had lofts as apartments and studios. They had openings, which were occasions for parties. They worked hard all day and so had some reason to be happy at night. They could actually make some money from their work and we couldn't. The other poets who were around that we knew of were, as I said in my poem "Fresh Air," always thinking about "the myth, the missus, and the midterms." They seemed to be sort of stuffy, precious, academic types, who were writing symbolically about things.

VOA: And you were the iconoclasts?

Koch: I don't know what the word means for me since I wasn't brought up to have any idols that I know of. So I don't know that I was destroying any idols. Frank certainly was not boring, if that's what you mean. Iconoclastic? I don't know. It seems to me that an iconoclast is someone who is really seriously oppressed by the official system in such a way that he has to rebel against it. Perhaps that's a revolutionary, not an iconoclast. An iconoclast may make the mistake of taking the ideas that are opposed to him too seriously and being overconcerned with destroying them, whereas maybe the best thing to do instead of destroying all the Fords is to build a good Chevrolet— which is what I think Frank did.

VOA: Was his poetry founded on a surrealistic or Dadaist approach?

Koch: No, it was not founded on surrealism or Dada. Frank read the French poets and knew them, but his poetry is not surrealistic. It seems to me the surrealist attitude—trusting the unconscious more than the conscious, doing automatic writing, saying whatever comes into your head, using accident in your poems, bringing in material from dreams—all those things that were programmatic for the surrealists (that is, you had to do them if you were going to be a card-carrying surrealist, so to speak), these characteristics have by now become a natural and almost instinctive part of the work of many poets writing in English. You can find them in poets who are not of the "New York School." But whereas a good deal of surrealist poetry tends to stay in this world of dreams and the unconscious and magic, Frank's poetry very clearly comes back to what would be considered ordinary reality. It always ends up back on the streets, back with the taxicabs, and most of all back with his emotional attachments in this life. I can demonstrate that point very clearly with a poem called "Sleeping on the Wing."

Since it is hard to understand a poem the first time you hear it, I think it might help if I say something about it before I read it. It is a poem about going to sleep. Frank says in the beginning that maybe one goes to sleep to avoid a great sadness. Anyway he goes to sleep and has a dream about flying—a rather common kind of dream—and Frank in the poem finds himself way up high in the air, feeling very free and above everything. But then he thinks about something in his waking life, about a friend, that brings him back to consciousness and he wakes up. Although the poem uses certain kinds of very quick and perhaps seemingly non-rational verbal techniques that the surrealists either used or invented, it is not a surrealist poem at all because the whole idea of the poem is that you come back from that to something else.

(Example excluded at
the publisher's request.)

VOA: Can you characterize the changes from those early poems, "Today" and "Autobiographica Literaria"—changes that were wrought on Frank O'Hara while he approached "Sleeping on the Wing"?

Koch: Well, he got older and had more experiences. Frank experienced things strongly. He wrote this in 1955, at age 29. I don't really know how to account for the change in Frank's work. You can say that there was a general change in that the early poems seem almost sheer exuberance in trying out all kinds of different forms and styles. Later, after he had been in New York for a while, there are some poems about suffering, pain, and anger expressed in a direct, angry way. Then there are the poems that seem to express in a rather quiet, calm way a kind of wisdom that he seems to have gotten from both his exuberance and his suffering, but it never was a static wisdom. Frank was always changing and always moving. He was always writing about what was really there in his feelings, in front of him. He always used the words that he really spoke. He used words from books, of course, but there is always something very natural-seeming about his language. He put the names of friends in poems, the names of streets, the names of radio programs, anything, just because it was there. It was very radical of Frank, and it goes along with a whole tradition which has been very important in modern poetry beginning probably with Whitman, a tradition of using the spoken language and writing about ordinary things. Frank takes it even further than Wallace Stevens and William Carlos Williams did, I think. He doesn't at all turn things into literature, although what he writes is literature, of course.

As for the difference between his early and late poetry, well, his work is always about what is most immediate to him and his experience, but I think that when he went to Harvard and then to the University of Michigan as a graduate student, in those early days what seems to come out most strongly in the poems is what he was reading, his excitement about poetry, and then friends, and what was happening, too. What was important in the poems later on seemed increasingly to be his feelings, his relationships to people and the situations that he found himself in. So there is always terribly close attention being paid to what is really there, what's exciting, what's interesting, what's strong, what means something, but the subject changes. Towards the end of his life Frank wrote what I think are some of the most beautiful love poems of the century. One of those, called "Poem," when I first read it, when I too was in my late 30s, I didn't understand very well. Now it seems to me to show a tremendous knowledge of love and relationships between people, and at the same time it is very quiet. It is an odd kind of love poem because it is not a poem written at the beginning of love or the end of love but in the middle. It's written apparently in the middle of a quarrel or is about that situation.

(Example, beginning
"Hate is only one"
excluded at the publisher's request.)

VOA: We have seen that Frank O'Hara used natural language—it's quite evident in these poems—and he used the naturalness of his environment—it's also there. What was so special about Frank O'Hara?

Koch: Well, that is a hard question. What is special is the work that he wrote. I find the language always exciting; I find the music of the poems exciting. In a lot of his poems he seems to be just talking, so that a naïve person might say, "But what's the subject?" He doesn't announce a subject. He's just talking with someone, talking with himself, talking with the reader, talking to a friend, and the subject is the feeling or the situation that has caused him to talk. That is a rather original way to organize a poem.

VOA: Sort of musing out loud?

Koch: I wouldn't say "musing" because musing suggests some sort of self-indulgent way of talking or thinking that is not going to end up as anything original. What original results have ever come from musing? No, Frank is musing in the midst of a hurricane. He called one of his books *Meditations in an Emergency*. The paradox is that he really is thinking all the time, but the situation he is in is more dramatic than those in which a person is usually able to think—at least to think so subtly and imaginatively.

About the relation of art and life in his work, I think it would be wrong to say that his poetry is realistic; it's rather than he uses very real-seeming materials to make something extraordinary.

VOA: Frank O'Hara was very close to art. He worked in the Museum of Modern Art in New York City. What influence did this kind of exposure have?

Koch: He knew all about the painters that he dealt with at the museum before he was a curator there: he was involved in art the minute he came to New York so that it wasn't the job that gave him his familiarity with art. I guess he liked some aspects of his job at the Museum because he was very good at it. It took up an enormous amount of his time, but perhaps that was all right. Boris Pasternak in his autobiography *Safe Conduct* said something to the effect that life distracts us with things that seem necessary for us to do so that it (life) can get on with its real work. Obviously Frank's real work was writing poetry, and—I'm speculating—it's possible that it was good for Frank to have a job that kept him very busy, that those were conditions under which he wrote poetry well.

VOA: Pasternak was important to both you and Frank O'Hara. Frank wrote a critical essay on him.

Koch: Yes, I like that essay. It's a long one, called "Zhivago and his Poems." And I remember another thing about Frank and Pasternak. John Ashbery, Frank, and I all liked Pasternak's early poetry very much, which we read in translation, of course, and his early prose works like *Letters from Tula*, *Aeriel Ways*, and *Safe Conduct*. He got the Noble Prize for *Dr. Zhivago*, and then the Russian government would not allow him to go to Stockholm. Frank and I were at a bar the night we got the news. I went home to go to bed, and at three in the morning Frank called on the phone, "Kenneth, we've got to do something." And I said, "What about?" "About Pasternak obviously. We've got to show him he has some support from us." We must have been 28 years old then, and Pasternak had surely never heard of us. Frank said, "We have to let him know that we stand behind him and that we appreciate his early work, too." I asked, "Well, what should we do?" "I think we should send him a cablegram." I said, "Do you think it will get through?" And Frank said, "It might, and I think we should send it." I said, "Do you think it will get him in trouble?" "No, I don't think so." So we composed a cablegram; it took us about a half hour to get the words right to say that we loved his work and that we liked the early stuff as well as *Dr. Zhivago*. And we sent it. And that's all we heard of it. I don't know that he got it. He certainly did not know who the people were who sent it to him or how to get in touch with us. But this was not at all arrogant on Frank's part. He felt that he and we all worked in the community of artists, and, of course, he was perfectly right.

VOA: The humanness of Frank O'Hara, reflected in his appreciation of Boris Pasternak's work, seems to be reflected all through his later works. Perhaps you have one more poem to leave us with.

Koch: This is a poem inspired by another Russian poet, Vladimir Mayakovsky, and it's called "A True Account of Talking to the Sun at Fire Island." Fire Island is a place full of beaches off the coast of Long Island in New York where Frank would sometimes go in the summer to spend the night or a week or two—to swim. It also happens to be the place where he was killed by a beach buggy when he was 40 years old while spending the weekend. (That, of course, doesn't have anything to do with this poem.) Mayakovsky wrote a poem entitled something like "A True Account of an Extraordinary Experience that Happened to Vladimir Mayakovsky." In Mayakovsky's poem the sun comes in the window, invites itself for tea, and talks to Mayakovsky about his poetry. This is Frank's poem.

(Example excluded at
the publisher's request.)

VOA: That is a portrait of his poetry and a portrait of his life.
Koch: It's a beautiful poem.

Bibliography

By Frank O'Hara:

The Collected Poems of Frank O'Hara. New York: Knopf, 1971.
The Selected Poems of Frank O'Hara. New York: Knopf, 1974.
Early Writing, 1946-1951. Bolinas, California: Grey Fox, 1977.
Poems Retrieved. Bolinas, California: Grey Fox, 1977.
Standing Still and Walking in New York. Bolinas, California: Grey Fox, 1975.
Art Chronicles 1954-1966. New York: Braziller, 1975.

About Frank O'Hara:

Perloff, Marjorie. *Frank O'Hara: Poet Among Painters.* New York: Braziller, 1977.
Berkson, Bill, and Joseph LeSueur, editors. *Homage to Frank O'Hara.* Bolinas, California: Big Sky, 1977; Berkeley, Creative Arts, 1980.
Ashbery, John. Preface to *The Collected Poems of Frank O'Hara.* New York: Knopf, 1971.

Irvin Faust on His Novels

I think it would be useful and informative to discuss briefly my origins as a writer of fiction:

To begin with, I am not a "trained" writer in the sense of the traditional English or literature major in college. To be sure, American writers come from a variety of backgrounds and developments, but mine seems to be even more singular. I was trained in physical education at CCNY (City College of New York), with a minor in biology. I began a teaching career in Harlem in 1949 and discovered I needed a different, more effective way of reaching my students. I found this in the guidance and counseling movement then being developed at Teachers College of Columbia University and returned to graduate work at that institution. I still had not done any writing except for term papers, but at Columbia I came under the wing of a magnificent teacher named Raymond Patouillet, who became my adviser in the doctoral program. It was he, in the mid-1950s, who suggested that I had a flair for putting words on paper and that an experimental case study I had submitted to his course might be the basis for a doctoral thesis. It was. Although unorthodox, my series of case studies was accepted and subsequently published by Teachers College under the title of *Entering Angel's World* (1963).

I was now a guidance counselor in a public high school, finding my new career in education satisfying and productive. This was the early 1960s. Encouraged by Patouillet, I thought I could make the jump from case study to short story, so I took a class at Columbia with the second great teacher in my 25 years of school, full-time and part-time: the novelist and short story writer, R. V. Cassill. In Cassill's class I wrote my first piece of fiction, a story called "Into the Green Night." Cassill liked it, as did my wife Jean, a splendid and tough-minded critic, and I sent it out to the little magazines where so much good serious fiction appears in this country. As I remember, approximately 21 magazines turned it down; the twenty-second accepted it: *The*

Carleton Miscellany, then edited by Reed Whittemore at Carleton College in Minnesota. I was now writing evenings and weekends and I produced two more stories which *Carleton Miscellany* published. Other small magazines began to take my stories, among them *The Transatlantic Review* and the *Paris Review.*

I began to get the letters which are so familiar to writers beginning to publish in the literary quarterlies: an editor for a major publisher has read a story or two and wonders if I have a novel.... No, I don't have a novel, I would respond, but I do have enough stories for a collection.... Please contact us when you have a novel.... Of course; novels make money; stories do not. Which tells us something about art and commerce in the world of letters.

However, a courageous editor named Robert Loomis, at Random House, liked my stories enough to get past the "novel" hang-up, and because of him (and his wife Gloria, who is now my agent), *Roar Lion Roar and Other Stories* was published in 1965. Very well received, it came out in England and France and in paperback, and over the years several of the stories have been anthologized. Random House did not lose money, has even collected some modest return on its "gamble."

The stories range over a number of themes which have intrigued me in the American scene. They explore a variety of Americans and their "adjustment" to that scene.

It is my conviction that we perform, relate, understand and often live and die according to the artifacts and phenomena of our culture. Thus, the movies, radio, sports, television, newspaper heroes are all channels through which and in which my characters function, and succeed or fail. In "Into the Green Night" Armand has his great internal transformation in a movie theater which has become for him practically a place of sanctuary and worship. (The movie palace is called, quite fittingly, The Oasis.) In "Philco Baby" Morty has made his transistor radio a live thing resting in his pocket, and the friends it delivers to his ear sustain him. Alas, life in New York has come to imitate (and, I fear, to mutilate) art as we see the young minority men of the city carrying their portable monsters everywhere and listening rather vacantly to the homogenized beat of rock and roll; the size of their radios may be merely a symbol of *machismo*; the basic insecurity and need I wrote of still exists.

In "Roar Lion Roar" the unschooled Puerto Rican boy finds meaning and dedication in the Ivy League fortunes of the Columbia football team. In the end he gives his life for his beloved Lions, who are unaware that he exists. The loner, the outsider, in the great city, is a theme that has continued to intrigue me, and I could find no more classic case than the aristocratic school juxtaposed against the recently-arrived immigrant who is trying desperately to become "American."

I still had not written, or gotten the idea that I could sustain, a novel; indeed, I was not sure that I ever would. As Salinger said, perhaps I was a sprinter, not a miler. I discovered I could be both during the Cuban missile crisis of 1962.

In that week, and through its aftermath, I observed in my fictive processes a curious reaction: a sense of liberation rather than fear or panic. The novelistic button had been pushed, and I sat down to begin *The Steagle*, which I finished in about eleven months. (I've since learned that if I go much beyond a year with my novels, they're in trouble.) This book, the title of which refers to a wartime professional football team, digs into another aspect of American life which takes my interest in popular culture one step further: the interplay of fantasy and reality. The line between them is blurred in the novel, as it sometimes is in our everyday world, and for a week Harold's childhood fantasies become his functioning realities. The challenge was to sustain the intensity, the fever, and to fuse his inner and outer lives so that something coherent could emerge. I'm reasonably satisfied that this occurred, and every now and then when I see on television the film that was made from the book, I get the curious feeling that fantasy is translating into reality several times over.

Incidentally, *The Steagle* also pursues the idea of the Jewish "outsider" who, like my other gazers-at-the-window, wants with a terrible urgency to become the "American" of his dreams, the WASP hero personified by the lads who fought for Andy Jackson, TR, Wilson, and finally FDR. He never did exist, of course, except in their minds, but that has only made him all the more admirable. I should note that the protagonist of my last novel, *Newsreel* (1980), is a Jew who, despite a liberal background, worships General Eisenhower, precisely because the general enabled him to *become* the American of his dreams in World War II; together, they literally destroyed the would-be assassin of that dream, Hitler. The war, naturally, was a great dividing line and catalyzer in my own life and appears a number of times in this role in my novels. None of my work is autobiographical, but like a character actor, I have used critical events and turning points in my own background in building the lives of my fictional people.

After *The Steagle* was launched, I was affected again by the events of the time: student turmoil of the late 1960s. However, because I always write against the grain, my imagination was gripped by the possibility of a policeman protagonist who was, in essence, a triple agent, almost like the old Czarist provocateurs. This was *The File on Stanley Patton Buchta*, my worst title. (I had now put stories aside and was preoccupied with the novel, although I continued to work in a high school on a full-time basis.) Buchta is a gentile, a typically attractive American boy of middle-European background, who drifts and plays his games until personal tragedy catalyzes him, at least for the moment—much the way America drifts and plays games, until events such as unrestricted submarine warfare in 1916-17, Pearl Harbor in 1941, or Tet in 1968 finally jolt us into action. *Buchta* was one of my two "lost" books in that it was—in my judgment—incorrectly perceived. Maybe it will one day get a second chance.

At this point my work departed into a new and personally fascinating direction: historical fiction with a contemporary interplay.... I had always been an avid reader of history and I became, in 1969, intrigued with a Revolutionary War hero named Marinus Willett, whose life encompassed the colonial period, the beginnings of the nation, and its early development. I traced every lead on him that I could find in and around the city and, without digesting the material, plunged into an historical novel. It grew for 600 pages, then died; it's still on the shelf. But it taught me two things: how to research, and to know that for me historical material had to be either pre-absorbed or absorbed after reading in order for the fusion of past and present to occur.

The movement for all of this to work came during a Memorial Day parade in which two survivors of the Spanish American War were marching. Presto! For years I had been reading about this war and its causes; now I plunged into new research, plucked my main character out of that parade, and began *Willy Remembers*. I raced through it in nine months, weaving the war of 1898 into the events of Willy's life, as well as our national life. Again I wrote against the grain and cast Willy as a narrow-minded, highly bigoted German-American who had loved just three things in his 93 years: his two sons and America. As the work progressed and I knew I was on a "streak," Willy literally took over and in his quasi-senile way commented on the American scene with what I think is more accuracy than clear-headed commentary could have provided. Of all my books, *Willy Remembers* has the most powerful internal engine; it wrote itself with more purity than any of the others. (The original title was *President Dewey*, referring to the boomlet for Admiral Dewey in 1900. It was thought, however, and I agreed, that the reference would be confused with Thomas E. Dewey, the two-time presidential candidate of the 1940s. *Willy Remembers* was my wife's suggestion, and a splendid one. It's probably my best title.)

Willy appeared in 1971. My passion for history continued and was tapped once again by events, this time Nixon's trip to China. Some years earlier I had gotten interested in the Boxer Rebellion, an early imperialist invasion of China in 1900, and had read a good deal about it. At that time I wrote a short story on the subject but it failed, and the Boxer Rebellion was tucked away somewhere in my fictional subconscious. Nixon's trip triggered renewed interest; I returned to my research and began to work on a novel that thematically would resemble a Chinese puzzle, a box within a box within a box. The result, and to me a satisfying one, was *Foreign Devils*, which structurally is my best book. Here again I weave history into the present, but because I enjoy stretching with each book, I introduced a parodistic element. My novel within a novel about the Boxers is written by a Richard Harding Davis type, a war correspondent whose purple prose was devoured by the penny-press readers of the early 1900s. I could thus comment on sophomoric America stretching its muscles and still be true to a recognizable type. Somehow, the compartmentalization, the fusion, the parody, the commentary—all of it worked, at least for me; meeting my self-imposed deadline of a year or less also told me it had worked.

Now came the second of my "lost" children. After finishing *Foreign Devils*, I returned to the America of my lifetime. I had an idea that I could do it justice through the eyes of that national phenomenon, the stand-up comedian. By now (1974) there seemed to be very little to laugh at or about in this country, and to me that made the projected protagonist even more appealing; a burnt-out case who, however, had had some magnificent innings. I decided to match structure to character and completely broke up time sense and continuity; I also hit on the idea of having the comic do a wise-cracking commentary on his own life. The result of all this was *A Star in the Family*, which pretty much achieved what I set out to do. But as far as the reading world was concerned it died aborning. *Star* appeared during the height of the

Lenny Bruce explosion, and critics and public alike mistook it for another book about, or using, Lenny. Which could not be further from the actual fact. My comic, Bart Goldwine, was more in the traditional mode of a Milton Berle, a Jerry Lester, a Harvey Stone. . . . Above all, he was not politically or socially controversial; in fact, he subscribed to the traditional America of his youth. I think the fate of *Star* is instructive in viewing the state of serious American fiction. As a writer I think I have something to say; at the very least, I have a particular vision of the world I'd like to share, a vision that some readers have, in fact, found sympathetic and/or informative. All I ask, really, is that a book be born decently and live whatever life it can on its own merits. I discovered that in the marketplace this will not always occur, that a serious work can be aborted for inappropriate reasons (and another book can be successful for the wrong reasons). The fate of *A Star in the Family*, even more than *Buchta*, told me that the world of letters is indeed a chancy one, with obstacles and twists the impractical fictional mind does not dream of as it sets down the first word of a book.

I did not mourn too long. I returned to my yellow pads (I write all first drafts in longhand) and produced two novels which did not please me. This took place between 1976 and 1977. They came fast, perhaps *too* fast, and are now in the trunk. One of these days I'll go back to them.

In 1978 I returned to World War II. Not to write about the war, but finally to come to grips with what it meant to my generation. After eleven months I produced a book that ran in traditional chronological time from 1946 to 1968, that dealt with a man who had been raised to heroism by the war and afterwards could never stop reaching for that kind of apogee. The title, after a number of changes, was *Newsreel*. It is, to my mind, my most complete book, probably because, although not autobiographical, it deals with subjects I experienced myself. It is also the best I have done with women, previously not my strong point—along with so many other male American writers. In any case, *Newsreel* is my statement on where middle-aged America is today: clinging to the old, assaulted by the new, even suspecting that the new may have some validity, clutching frantically for a simpler time (the simplest of which was the War), yet still wanting to grow and do the *right* thing. *Newsreel* was my eighth book, my seventh work of fiction, my sixth novel. I guess I've been producing. . . .

Where do I go from here? Right now I'm pausing. I continue

to work full time as Director of Guidance and Counseling in a public high school. This double life pays off in each area: I think I'm an effective counselor, and I've produced a book almost every two years on the average, after starting late. I consider myself a writer in the old, European tradition: the professional man who is also the literary man (Chekov, Malraux). I rather think, too, that I'll soon return to the short story, my first love. Or perhaps the novella, a form I've tinkered with, but never with any sense of completeness. I also suspect that I may have a talent for teaching the writing of fiction—to the degree that such a thing is possible. I taught a workshop at the University of Rochester in the summer of 1978 and discovered that my counseling training helped me to open new writers to receive whatever gift they had. I should like to do more of that.

On the other hand, the fictive mind has a way of turning things around. If a novelistic idea strikes, the above fancy thoughts will instantly evaporate, and I'll be off and running. If I'm lucky and the subconscious has been properly cooking, it will be another roller-coaster ride for twelve months or less, the hot and the cold, love-hate experience I think of as the "streak."

Clearly, the compulsive writer, and I am certainly one, has no other choice.

Bibliography

By Irvin Fasut:

Roar Lion Roar and Other Stories. New York: Random House, 1964.
The Steagle. New York: Random House, 1965.
The File on Stanley Patton Buchta. New York: Random House, 1970.
Willy Remembers. New York: Arbor House, 1971.
Foreign Devils. New York: Arbor House, 1973.
A Star in the Family. Garden City, New York: Doubleday, 1973.
Newsreel. New York: Harcourt Brace Jovanovich-Bruccoli Clark, 1980.

About Irvin Faust:

Bruccoli, Matthew J. "Faust on Faust." In *Conversations With Writers*. Edited by M.
    J. Bruccoli. Vol. 2. Detroit: Gale-Bruccoli Clark, 1978.
Campenni, Frank. "Irvin Faust." In *American Novelists Since World War II*. Edited by
    Jeffrey Helterman and Richard Layman. Detroit: Gale-Bruccoli Clark, 1978.
Kostelanetz, Richard. "'New American Fiction' Reconsidered." In *Twenties in the
    Sixties*. Westport, Connecticut, and London: Greenwood Press, 1979.

Short Story Writing

A Conversation among Carol Emshwiller, Kenneth Gangemi, Richard Grayson, and Richard Kostelanetz.

Kostelanetz: Our subject is the short story in America, and with me are four first-rate writers who have had their short stories collected into books.

Joy in Our Cause is the title of Carol Emshwiller's first collection of stories, and to introduce her let me quote what she writes about herself: "Somehow, I didn't come to writing until I was almost 30. My first child was born shortly after I started writing, so all my writing life I've fought, sulked, shouted and screamed, and sometimes tried to be good about not having time to write."

Our second fictioner, Richard Grayson, was born in New York in 1951 and still lives there. He has published over 150 stories in American literary magazines, and the title of his first collection is *With Hitler in New York* (1979).

The other writer with us today has published both short fictions and sustained narratives, which is to say novels or travelogues. Kenneth Gangemi, who was born in 1937, has published two novels, one called *Olt* (1969) and the other called *The Interceptor Pilot* (1975, 1980). Gangemi has also published one collection of poetry titled *Lydia* (1969) and a memoir of travelling in Mexico entitled *The Volcanoes from Puebla* (1979). His one book exclusively of short fiction is *Corroboree* (1976).

A central question is what is the short story and how is it different from a novel or novella? Is that difference primarily one of length?

Grayson: Well, I'm not sure that I can always tell. It's difficult. I remember once teaching a course in the novel, where one of the texts was called *Twelve Short Novels*, and it included Melville's "Bartleby the Scrivener," which I always thought of as a short story. I think it's one of those things that I can't tell you what it is, but I know a *short story* when I see one, and I know a *novel* when I see one.

Kostelanetz: I tried to suggest, in an introduction I wrote many years ago to an anthology of short fiction called *Twelve from The Sixties* (1967), another way to make the distinction: the short story has one narrative line: a novel has two or more. In the latter there is a greater complexity of narrative activity.

Emshwiller: I think something's different about a really long work, even if it only has one major scene or one major thing happening in it. It seems to me there's difference other than length. Perhaps length itself does give a different feel to a work. Certainly one gets to know the characters and/or the author better.

Kostelanetz: Kenneth Gangemi, your one published novel, *Olt* is 55 pages in length and slightly over 12,000 words.

Gangemi: When I finished it, I called it a cycle of three stories. However, for practical and commerical reasons, the publishers called it a novel. In retrospect, I think that they did the right thing.

But when we talk about these definitions now, I think the time or the era should be a factor. These definitions at the turn of the century were very fixed, I think, and definite. In 1950, much less so. And this year, 1980, I think the definitions have become shorter and almost very hard to state in many cases. Perhaps in 1990, or by the year 2000, these definitions will no longer be used except in literary scholarship.

Kostelanetz: You mean there'll just be "prose" and "non-prose"?

Gangemi: Not quite that simple, but people won't worry too much about whether something is a long short story or a novella, or about what is a short story. I don't think many people will ask that question in 20 years.

Kostelanetz: In my anthology of 1960s short fiction that I mentioned before, I suggested there were three phases in a formal evolution of the modern short story. I called them the *arc* story, which has a climax in the middle and then an unraveling; the *epiphany* story, which I associate with James Joyce, where near the end of the narrative there's an event which jells everything into place; and then the *flat* story, where the theme is present from the beginning and the story just goes on, with neither a climax nor an epiphany. Now, the historical precursor in my mind for the last was Chekhov's "A Boring Story." It seems to me that what Jorge Luis Borges, the Argentinian writer, was doing in his most famous pieces was a flat story. Most of Donald

Barthelme's stories are flat stories as well. And my argument at the
time was that the flat story was the dominant form of the '60s. Is that
still true today?

Emshwiller: Yes, I would think that most contemporary stories
are flat stories. I also don't make these distinctions so much in my
mind. I don't even think about them. But I would wonder if there isn't
a form called the orgasmic form, as opposed to the flat form.

Kostelanetz: What does "orgasmic" mean?

Emshwiller: It would mean that the prose itself as well as the
"actions" of the story would simply increase in tempo to a climax and
then slow down. But it would be neither the arc, exactly, nor the
epiphany form.

Kostelanetz?   In one of your best stories, "Autobiography," where
is the climax?

Emshwiller: That's flat, and most of my work is flat; but "Lib," if
you remember it, is obviously an orgasmic story. It may sound flat.
She's simply climbing the stairs, but as she goes up, she talks about
sliding down the bannister which is the orgasmic part of it. The prose
speeds up and there are words and images suggestive of orgasm.
Anyway, whether it seems so or not to you, I tried to use an orgasmic
form. I think perhaps the stories have to be read aloud sometimes for
people to see what you're trying to do. Maybe they don't sound like
orgasms unless you read faster when you get to the right point. I don't
know.

Gangemi: I think you're quite correct in saying that the flat story is
certainly what is being done today. I generally use the term "story"
only when I'm talking to someone else about a piece of fiction. When
I'm reading it myself, I hardly think of the form. And I'm surprised
that more people don't simply refer to something as "a piece of fiction."
That seems to include everything.

Kostelanetz: It is your position, then, that these categories within
fiction are irrelevant and indeed are going to disintegrate.

Gangemi: I figure that if I don't use the terms now, I'm just getting
a little ahead of the game.

Grayson: The epiphany story would seem to me a story maybe of
the '40s or '50s.

Kostelanetz: Well, I was thinking of James Joyce, classically, but
also it seems to me that Flannery O'Connor's stories are very much
epiphany stories.

Grayson: I think I write mostly flat stories. I am conscious of working in one of these three modes, although I never really defined it as such.

Kostelanetz: Have you ever written an arc story?

Grayson: A story in a classical mode?

Kostelanetz: Yes.

Grayson: Yes, I think so. I think some of those have been my least successful.

Kostelanetz: Why is that?

Grayson: Because I don't feel quite comfortable with the form. This is what I was told—a story should have a beginning, a middle and an end—but do they have to be in that order?

I agree with Kenneth that I'd like to see more use of the term "pieces of fiction" or just "fictions," rather than stories, because a lot of the stories I read and enjoy don't fit these definitions. Take Borges's fictional essays—are they really stories?

Kostelanetz: It seems to me Borges writes fictions in the form of essays. When he writes about a man who has discovered in his encyclopedia that there are 13 pages about an imaginary world, he's conning you, within the artifice of writing an essay, with the pretense to truth of an essay; but in its ultimate effect, the piece of prose is a story.

Emshwiller: Well, I think, as Kenneth said, the idea of length is breaking down. I think also the differences between an essay and a story, and the differences between an autobiography and a story, are all breaking down, and everything's bunching up together.

Kostelanetz: I try to argue something else. Maybe I'm big on distinctions, coming out of a critical activity, but it seems to me that a poem is about compression of imagery and effect, that fiction is about extension and narrative and, therefore, about linear activity, and that an essay pretends, or at least tries, to be a description of something outside itself, a definition of something outside itself.

Emshwiller: I feel that I've used poetic forms to such a degree in some of my works that, though they are definitely prose, they are almost poems.

Kostelanetz: Carol, one piece of yours has a title which indicates an essayistic form. It's called "Autobiography," so the reader thinks you will relate the life, from beginning to end, of Carol Emshwiller. But instead, the piece is a series of very evocative paragraphs that relate in a nonlinear fashion various perspectives on your life. Would you call this an autobiography in a fictional form?

Emshwiller: Yes, I guess you could.

Kostelanetz: I think that "Autobiography" is an essay, a great essay. It's not a fiction. You'll remember that I anthologized it in *Essaying Essays* (1975).

Emshwiller: And I consider it a short story very definitely.

Kostelanetz: Well, then let me ask whether you wanted the piece to be real and true to you?

Emshwiller: Yes.

Kostelanetz: Now that, it seems to me, is an essayistic motive.

Emshwiller: I also would like to write essay-short stories that are real essays but that are definitely short stories, too. I want them to be real and true but I also want them to read like a short story. I use the same techniques that I use in my stories. In fact, I consider my "Autobiography" an essay-poem-story, but mainly a story.

Kostelanetz: Kenneth Gangemi, does this distinction mean anything to you? You've written both books of fiction and books of poetry.

Gangemi: Yes, I have, and I think about the distinctions often, and they are very useful. I would say I think of the three separate categories as being poetry, prose poetry, and prose, with gray areas in between. And they're very useful in describing writing. Now, you asked, "What is a poem?" Partly it's the appearance on the printed page—more or less traditional.

Kostelanetz: That is, the horizontal lines whose ends fall short of the available space.

Gangemi: Yes, exactly. Sometimes you have to describe a piece of writing as prose but like prose poetry. That term has been applied to my own book *Olt*, and when you say that, you do tell something about. . . .

Kostelanetz: . . . about the quality of the language, the style of the language?

Gangemi: Yes, and the density of it. You mentioned compression before. So if you describe a book of poetry as bordering in many poems on prose poetry, then you're saying that it's not as compressed as poems really ought to be.

Kostelanetz: Yes. It seems to me, Richard Grayson, one of the qualities of your fiction that I like is the density of the language. My sense is that every sentence is working for you. Does that make it poetry?

Grayson: I don't think it's ever been compared to poetry. When I am working in a prose poem form, I usually think of that as something apart from a story. The language in a prose poem is the overriding concern.

Kostelanetz: If language is, as you say, not your overriding concern, then what is?

Grayson: I think telling a story, the old-fashioned sense of a story.

Kostelanetz: And your story begins then in your own mind with people?

Grayson: My stories do, yes—people and events.

Kostelanetz: Another quality I like in your stories is the illusion of autobiography. You talk very intimately about yourself.

Grayson: Or about a character called "Richard Grayson."

Kostelanetz: Right.

Grayson: There's difference, of course, and that's been going on in short stories and longer fiction for a long time.

Kostelanetz: But I remember a critical article was written about you not too long ago, where someone tried to pull the stories together to characterize their author Richard Grayson. Of course, that critic was way off base becasue he was in effect characterizing the person you've created in the stories in the character named Richard Grayson. Are they genuine autobiography?

Grayson: If I give that away, then I lose the illusion of the stories. Obviously they're autobiographical. To a certain extent they would have to be. And then I like to throw in things which are fiction.

Kostelanetz: In one story you've portrayed yourself dating the daughter of a celebrity.

Grayson: Well, that actually did happen, but the story came off a lot better than life, as it usually does. That's the beauty of writing short stories because you can take life and turn it around so that everything works, so that you do say the things that you should have said at the time which you couldn't think of.

Kostelanetz: So in effect you've rewritten your personal experience.

Grayson: Yes.

Kostelanetz: Carol Emshwiller, have you used your name?

Emshwiller: I don't think I've used my own name.

Grayson: You've used your husband's name.

Emshwiller: Oh, that's true, his first name, and I've used real people. That's true. My feeling about it is that I would even incorporate into my own life things that are not true about it. Not in my story "Autobiography," but in other stories I certainly incorporate anything I want to from anyplace I want to. But I never "name" myself, and when I used my husband, that story was also all true, I think.

Kostelanetz: Kenneth Gangemi, is your book *The Volcanoes from Puebla* fiction?

Gangemi: No, it's nonfiction. And I may be the only one of the three of us who has written a first-person nonfiction narrative like that.

Kostelanetz: It's a travelogue, a memoir of your trip to Mexico.

Gangemi: Yes. It's basically a travel book. But my publisher, Marion Boyars, describes it as a literary travel book.

Kostelanetz: One quality of that book is that you create the impression, which is essentially fictitious, that everything in it happened in 1961 or '62.

Gangemi: I'm careful not to give dates in the book, but now and then a date pops out when it's unavoidable. The book is based upon notebooks compiled in 1962 and '63, when I lived in Mexico. But I took a long trip to Mexico in 1974. And when I came back and wrote the complete book, I updated everything to 1974. But it didn't take much updating because the country had changed very little during that time.

Kostelanetz: How did your own work in fiction evolve, Carol Emshwiller?

Emshwiller: Evolve? It's in the middle of evolving, I guess, right now.

Kostelanetz: Where did you come from?

Emshwiller: I came from the pulps. I started out as the lowest, pulpiest science fiction writer you could have. And then I tried to get out of it. I wrote myself up to the top of that field, and then I tried to get out of it by myself. But I found I couldn't. I went and studied with Kenneth Koch and Kay Boyle, and then I found that I could get out.

Kostelanetz: What's the difference between science fiction and what you do now?

Emshwiller: Oh, a lot of difference. You can't be flat in pulps. Well, you can because I still do it every now and then. I can sell something to a science fiction magazine, and it's sometimes very flat. But usually you have to have an epiphany.

Kostelanetz: You mean there are conventions to which you feel subservient?

Emshwiller: Oh, absolutely, and it's so tight, cut-and-dried, that you know, most of the time anyway, exactly how to form your story.

Kostelanetz: And the fiction you've done since is not so subservient to convention.

Emshwiller: No, the point of the fiction that I've done since is exactly to break all the rules that I know about or to find completely new ways.

Grayson: Don't you think it's unusual, though, that in a field like science fiction where the content of the stories is so limitless, that you're so restricted in form to the conventional narrative?

Emshwiller: Absolutely. I've thought of that, and my husband Ed Emshwiller, who used to be an illustrator for science fiction magazines, also was always fighting the fact that he had to be so conventional in his illustrations.

Kostelanetz: Richard Grayson, how long have you written short stories?

Grayson: I've written stories, I suppose, since I was 13 or 14. I'm a graduate of one of the writing programs of America. Most, I guess, or many young writers today come out of degree programs.

Kostelanetz: I pointed out in my introduction to this book that one of the things that distinguishes America from other countries is the proliferation of these creative writing classes, not only on the college and university level, but on the high school level, and even the post-college extracurricular adult level. This doesn't happen anywhere else in the world. And so the question always arises, particularly from people outside the U.S.: Are all these writing classes good for you?

Grayson: I don't know that it's good for writing in general. I think it does have value. I've found it helpful to me in some areas. We had writing workshops, and we had to turn in stories.

Kostelanetz: So it made you work. But if you had started writing at 13, you'd been working for a while before you took a college writing course.

Grayson: I think before these workshops exposed me to certain experimental writers, such as the people we have here today, I was writing pretty much formula-type stories, things that I had seen in magazines like *Redbook, The New Yorker*. In school I learned that there are many different kinds of fiction, and I wanted to experiment with a lot of different modes.

Kostelanetz: Now, did you experiment through your college writing program?

Grayson: I think so. I'm still experimenting.

Kostelanetz: When did you get your degree?

Grayson: I got my degree, a Master of Fine Arts, in 1976, so that's four years ago.

Kostelanetz: Has your writing changed since you've gotten your degree?

Grayson: I hope so. I think it would have changed had I never been in a program. If for various reasons there were a continuing program that I would never get out of, I think it would have changed. I think basically I developed my own sense of criticism, incorporating perhaps the values of my teachers or fellow students at the time.

Kostelanetz: Kenneth Gangemi, did you get a creative writing degree as an undergraduate?

Gangemi: No, I got an engineering degree.

Kostelanetz: Then how did you get into writing literature?

Gangemi: I started to read contemporary literature in college. Deciding to write myself came after reading books that were intensely meaningful to me.

Kostelanetz: Did you take a writing course at college?

Gangemi: One winter when I was ski-bumming up in Stowe, Vermont, I met a young man a couple of years older than I was, a fellow ski bum, who was a writer. I think he was about 22, and he had sold a couple of stories to magazines. He was the first writer I ever met whom I could relate to, who was roughly my own age, and not one of these older men that you see on book jackets. I figured that if he could do it, I could do it. And I thought about trying to become a writer for a couple of years, and after two or three years I actually did it.

By this time I was out in San Francisco, working as an engineer, and I quit my job and enrolled in creative writing at San Francisco State College, as it was then called, and started.

Kostelanetz: Oh, so you went through a course as well?

Gangemi: I went for just one term. And that was okay, that much exposure. But I can't recommend it much longer than that. I think it's basically a harmful influence. Your work becomes derivative. It improves in some ways, but worsens in others. It takes years to get rid of the bad habits you pick up.

Kostelanetz: But, as Richard Grayson said, it got you going.

Gangemi: Yes. He put it perfectly. They give you exercises, and they're due in a week or two, and you have to sit down and write. It may not be what you want to write, but it does get you writing. The courses are valuable for that.

Kostelanetz: What were your initial writings like?

Gangemi: Terribly derivative, based upon fiction, mostly short stories I had read before. I thought I was giving my stories a new twist, or doing them slightly differently, but that was not true. However, I see the short story as being very valuable for beginning writers because it's something they can handle. When you're starting out, it's very difficult to begin a novel, a big book, a big manuscript. It was certainly too much for me. But a short story, especially one that's between 10 and 20 pages long, that is possible. You can do one in a couple of weeks or even a few days. This might be the greatest benefit of the short story today, a form for beginning writers in which to learn how to write.

Kostelanetz: Was it the form you favored as a beginner?

Gangemi: Yes.

Kostelanetz: Then how did you evolve into your book of poems?

Gangemi: The poetic images in *Lydia* were leftovers from the prose. They were too poetic. When they came into my mind, I wrote them down, but they didn't fit into the prose narrative of *Olt* so I put them aside, into an envelope. After a while I accumulated quite a bit of these poetic phrases and lines and groups of lines. And I accumulated so many that one day after I finished *Olt*, I took out these envelopes and spread out the little bits of paper and saw that there was the beginning of a book of poetry there.

And that's also how *Corroboree* came to be written. I had many lines of prose that were too bizarre, too surreal. They were nonsense lines.

Kostelanetz: That came from *Olt* as well?

Gangemi: Yes, leftover bits of prose. They didn't fit into the relatively straight narrative that *Olt* was. But after a while there was such an accumulation that, when I spread them out, an order began to present itself, and that was the beginning of another book.

Kostelanetz: It seems to me that your work is very much based on the sentence as the unit.

Gangemi: Oh, yes. I still work with scissors and little slips of paper, sometimes only a phrase. Then the paragraphs are all arranged in what appears to be the best order.

Kostelanetz: And this is quite different from the way Richard
Grayson works, I think.

Grayson: I think I work in either paragraphs or clumps of two or
three paragraphs together, in almost scene form.

Kostelanetz: Carol Emshwiller, you spoke about coming out of
the science fiction magazines. Where do your stories appear now?

Emshwiller: Every now and then, in science fiction magazines,
but mostly in literary magazines.

Kostelanetz: Now, by literary magazines you mean magazines, in
roughly six-by-nine-inch format, that come out of universities or
university communities around the U.S.?

Emshwiller: No, not necessarily the universities. Well, *New Directions* and *Tri-Quarterly, Transatlantic Review*—those are not all university magazines.

Kostelanetz: So we've then separated mass magazines, or magazines with art-directed covers, from literary magazines and from
science fiction magazines, which are called "pulps" because they are
printed on pulpier newsprint paper, whereas the slick magazines
have slick paper, by definition. But you now consider literary magazines your principal outlet.

Emshwiller: Mainly, now, yes.

Kostelanetz: Richard Grayson?

Grayson: When I started writing stories, I decided where could I
go with them. I didn't just want to keep them in a drawer. I saw how
various writers marketed their work, and I noticed that certain writers
seemed to find a home for their stories in as many outlets as possible,
and that's what I tried to do.

   I have never got up to the echelon of the mass, slick magazines,
and most of my stories have appeared in little magazines, but I'd say
mostly not those connected to a university.

Kostelanetz: Since you've published so many stories, let me ask if
you still have unpublished stories.

Grayson: Well, ones that I've been writing recently and stories
which I consider unpublishable.

Kostelanetz: Richard Grayson, do you keep a list of places to
publish?

Grayson: Yes, although I keep it on index cards, so it's in a box, and
I end up spending a lot of money on things like postage and mailing
envelopes and Xeroxing the stories in case the editors lose them or
they come back with coffee stains on the front page.

Kostelanetz: Well, one argument I made in my own book, *The End of Intelligent Writing*, was that there were fewer places to publish stories than there had been in the past. I remember ten years ago everybody was decrying the disappearance of the *Saturday Evening Post* and the other mass magazines that published stories. But it seems to be that quite the opposite is true now in America, that there are more places to publish stories now than there were ten or 20 years ago.

There is also a second phenomenon to consider: the number of people writing stories has increased drastically in part because of the creative writing programs. A fiction editor of a literary magazine will say, "We publish two stories in an issue, and I receive 300 stories from which I can select only two." Since there are so many people writing stories, getting them into print is a competitive business.

Well, let me go back. Who reads literary magazines?

Emshwiller: I do.

Grayson: The writers who have stories in them. A writer was telling me the other day that he just hoped that his story in a little magazine would be read by the other writers who had stories in the same issue and might notice his work—that was the best he could hope for.

Kostelanetz: For him the initial line of communication is the other people in the same magazine.

Grayson: Yes.

Kostelanetz: Is that bad?

Gangemi: No, it's something. It's a beginning.

Kostelanetz: We hear a lot about the short story in America today, and a question arises of whom do you think is particularly good?

Gangemi: Every now and then somebody turns out a good short story. I read a lot of little and big magazines, and there's a lot of stories being published but not much of very high quality.

Grayson: Well, Donald Barthelme seems to have inspired the most imitators, more people who are writing Barthelme-like stories. I've been accused of that, too.

Kostelanetz: Why is that? Is his work particularly powerful?

Grayson: I think when Barthelme started writing his kind of story, it got exposure from appearing in *The New Yorker*, a slick magazine with a fairly large circulation. A lot of people noticed the stories and were impressed by the unusual quality of them—that they were fragmented by the language and fictional modes of the story, questions and answers, or just dialogue.

Emshwiller: I have also been accused several times of writing like him, and for a long time I never read him. I thought I was taking a completely unique direction all by myself. I think that we writers were being influenced, at least I was, by Kenneth Koch and by modern poetry, and I was reading lots and lots of poetry.

Kostelanetz: As was Barthelme.

Emshwiller: Exactly. I heard him on the radio one day; I turned him on while I was writing. And I was writing the same story that he was reading over the radio, and he had never published it. I had to scrap the story I was working on, and finally I realized that I really had to read him and change my style.

Kostelanetz: It seems to me that he was writing, as you say, very much in the contemporary mode in its fragmentation, very much influenced by poetry, as were others: but his stories became prominent because they appeared so regularly in *The New Yorker*, which is a magazine that, for better or worse, gives the largest American circulation for short fiction.

He's really a *New Yorker* phenomenon, much as historically James Thurber was a *New Yorker* phenomenon—doing what lots of other people were doing but doing it with more visibility because of the magazine's incomparable circulation.

Kostelanetz: Carol, you spoke about your own reading as being more poetry than fiction. Is that still true?

Emshwiller: Well, I certainly don't read much of the people you mentioned. I would much rather read somebody like Robert Coover or Walter Abish. I find that the authors who were just mentioned write what seems like case histories, even if they're well done.   Their characters I can find just as well in psychology case histories, and I feel there's a problem there, almost like artists had with photographers. But now that writers have to contend with the reality of the case histories, I am not sure that the case histories aren't much more interesting than what Cheever and Flannery O'Connor were doing.

Kostelanetz: You mean the psychological case histories are more fun to read as characterizations.

Emshwiller: Yes, that's right.

Kostelanetz: Just as they say sociology is better to read than sociological fiction, because it has more truth and less garbage.

Emshwiller: So I don't have any interest in reading these people.

I would rather read people who are trying to do more things technically. I also like Beckett, my favorite—my absolute favorite of anybody.

Kostelanetz: Kenneth Gangemi, who do you particularly like
among the current fiction writers?

Gangemi: On the second page of *Corroboree*, there's a list of influences. The list is in alphabetical order, so the first name is Fernando
Arrabal. He's very uneven, but he has written some stunning short
pieces of prose. Not stories, just pieces. Another name is John Collier,
who is very underrated nowadays. He has written some of the finest
stories I have ever read.

Kostelanetz: When did he write?

Gangemi: In the 1930s, '40s, '50s.

Kostelanetz: In America? And you're reading, of course, now
from the second page of *Corroboree*.

Gangemi: Right, the list of influences which I included as sort of an
avant-garde introduction to the book, just a simple list. I think it does
serve as a kind of introduction, using a minimum of words. I also have
Stephen Leacock and Edward Lear here. They are basically nonsense
writers but they have also written short pieces of prose that are
marvelous. Raymond Queneau is also listed here. Now some of his
work is episodic, and his books have been called novels for the same
reason that my book *Olt* was called a novel. It's really not.

Kostelanetz: And one of his most famous books contains 99
descriptions of the same scene.

Gangemi: Yes. *Exercises in Style.* Marvelous book. I also have Erick
Satie listed here. He has written short pieces of nonsense prose that are
excellent, even though he's mostly regarded as a composer.

Kostelanetz: What sort of work are you doing now, what kinds of
writing?

Gangemi: I'm working on a second book of poetry. And when
that's finished, I'll turn to a novel.

Kostelanetz: Do you have any unpublished books?

Gangemi: No, not after *The Interceptor Pilot* appears in English this
year. *Clippings* is, I suppose, an unpublished book: but since I didn't
write a word of it, I can't regard it as *my* unpublished book. It's my
compilation perhaps, something I've put together from passages I
found already in print: but it's not a book I've written.

Kostelanetz: You tend to assemble bits in your writing process, to
begin with.

Gangemi: Yes.

Kostelanetz: Richard Grayson?

Grayson: I'm working on stories at the same time I am trying to write a novel.

Kostelanetz: Have you written novels in the past?

Grayson: Not good ones, only unpublishable ones.

Kostelanetz: Ones that you ought to keep unpublished.

Grayson: I'd like to keep them unpublished, yes. One of the problems of writing stories in America today is that you can't make money doing it. I've just come from a literary agent who said, "You must write a novel," and so I guess I must. I also want to write a novel.

Kostelanetz: Well, Carol Emshwiller published her book of short stories with Harper & Row as well—before a novel.

Emshwiller: Yes, before a novel. I also got the same story for a long time that, well, we'll do your short stories as soon as you do a novel. And finally they said, "Oh, well, we guess you're never going to do that novel," so they did the short stories.

Kostelanetz: Have you done a novel since?

Emshwiller: No.

Kostelanetz: What are you working on now?

Emshwiller: Short stories. I have a short story collection just about ready.

Kostelanetz: Why haven't you written a novel?

Emshwiller: Well, partly it's the interrupted life I've had with the three children. Maybe there is more of a chance for it now, maybe not. I don't know, maybe I'm just a short story writer, but I feel quite differently having had a whole year to myself last year and being able to write. I think I'll be able to expand a little bit.

Kostelanetz: Do any of you teach fiction?

Grayson: I teach, but I don't teach creative writing. What I teach usually is generally writing to college freshmen or I've taught remedial writing for people who are on a low level of literacy, or I've taught English as a second language to people who are just learning English, and I've taught literature.

Emshwiller: I'm about to take over a writing class at NYU. And I think that the main thing is to be supportive. Encouragement is the most important thing: to try to send them off with feelings that they want to write more rather than to discourage them.

John Updike's America

Jerome Klinkowitz

As a full-time professional, John Updike has been writing in America since 1954, the year he graduated from Harvard and sold his first short story to *The New Yorker* magazine. His one-third century tenure as a literary artist is remarkable not only for its artistic success, but for the fact that such a vocation is still financially possible—in Updike's case, by virtue of a reliably supportive publisher and ready magazine market. As fellow novelist Joseph Heller had to remind students (in *Paris Review*, Winter 1974) in the prime of his own commercial popularity, "even if every word a writer writes is published, he will almost surely have to supplement his income, usually by teaching, or perhaps by marrying money." John Updike is one of the very few artistically important writers in America today who has not been forced to rely on either of Heller's options. The business of writing fiction is his very life.

Living and writing in America have formed the substance of Updike's published work. The great majority of his nine novels and six short story collections published in hardcover to date take for their subjects the lives of relatively average people: kids growing up in small towns with ambitions of moving to the big city, young married couples finding their first small apartments and jobs, maturing men and women enjoying relative affluence in the suburbs and (as the one-third century ripens) going through separation, divorce, and remarriage. For Updike the scheme is vaguely autobiographical, and although to keep things mundane he almost always makes his protagonist's job something other than being a writer, the self-consciously artistic language of these fictions more than compensates for the business-like action described. Harry "Rabbit" Angstrom of *Rabbit, Run* and *Rabbit Redux* is a typesetter, and most of the boys in Updike's stories who have hopes of becoming great artists grow up to find themselves commerical illustrators, animators, or photographers. But the language in which Updike characterizes their thoughts and behavior, and the way he arranges and rearranges their stories—all bespeak a self-conscious artistry. Their lives, it seems, are Updike's own life of fiction.

Best known as a regular *New Yorker* contributor, most highly honored for his novel *The Centaur* (National Book Award for Fiction at home, *Le prix du meilleur livre étranger* in France), and most popular with the reading public for his novels *Rabbit, Run* and *Couples,* Updike frequently reflects on his own work in ways that offer several clues to his method as a writer. His first novel, *The Poorhouse Fair* (1959), was written in 1957 as a visionary statement of American life as it might be two decades later; two subsequent editions (1964 and 1977) have contained new and revealing forewords by the author, reflecting how America's ongoing history has variously confirmed or contradicted his suspicions. *Rabbit, Run* (1960) had its sequel eleven years later in *Rabbit Redux.* A brief memoir, "The Dogwood Tree: A Boyhood" (1962), was preserved in Updike's first collection of nonfiction, *Assorted Prose* (1965). And in 1969 the author thought back on what he hoped would be no less than the first half of his life in the long poem *Midpoint.* Memoir and poem are rich with biographical correspondences, inviting readers to assemble an American middle-class saga from his 15 books of fiction. But the best reharvesting of this work has been done by Updike himself, in two paperback originals which reprint, rearrange, and reintroduce short stories from his six hardcover collections and sheaf of uncollected work: *Olinger Stories* (1964) and *Too Far To Go: The Maple Stories* (1979).

"Olinger" is the name Updike invents for the fictional town which vaguely corresponds to his birthplace, Shillington, Pennsylvania, where he spent a self-admittedly sheltered boyhood in the 1930s and '40s. Like William Faulkner's mythical Yoknapatawpha, Olinger's ecology, sociology, and demographics conform closely enough to the author's own home grounds to satisfy readers who demand a "real life story," yet allow sufficient latitude for the writer's essentially imaginative work. "The Maples," Richard and Joan, are a fictional couple Updike wrote about from 1955 through 1976. Their biographical match-ups with the Olinger stories and with the Updikes' own marriage (1953-1976) are numerous, although Richard comes from a town just across the nearby West Virginia border (where Rabbit Angstrom, fleeing a place very much like Olinger and its neighboring city, met a dead end in a murky lovers' lane). Even closer are the comparisons these Maples stories invite with Updike's treatment of American married life in his later novels, just as Olinger serves as a background for most of the earlier ones. By Updike's own choice *Olinger Stories* and *Too Far to Go* have become the center of his fictional and visionary world.

At the heart of these two books, in turn, stands Updike's most important and most characteristic story, "Pigeon Feathers." First published in *The New Yorker* for August 19, 1961, it gave its name to Updike's widely praised collection the next year. It was made the centerpiece of *Olinger Stories* (from which edition the following quotations come), and by reference to theme and technique, it provides the informing principle of nearly all the Maples stories gathered up in 1979. In "Pigeon Feathers" Updike creates David Kern, a 14-year-old protagonist with a boyhood somewhat like his own, whose family's ten-mile move from town out into the country causes things to be "upset, displaced, rearranged." In the Foreword to *Olinger Stories*, Updike remarks how "This strange distance, this less than total remove from my milieu, is for all I know the crucial detachment of my life." Physical separation is the boy's first problem; cut off from school friends, town life, and familiar surroundings, he finds himself isolated as never before. But Updike's story leads to stirrings of a deeper alienation. Rummaging through his mother's dusty college books, David chances upon H. G. Wells's *Outline of History* and reads that author's account of Jesus, of how "he had been an obscure political agitator, a kind of hobo, in a minor colony of the Roman Empire." The boy, though never a religious zealot, is at once distanced from the familiar emotional center of his life. Characteristically, Updike frames this loss in carefully shaped language: "It was as if a stone that for weeks and even years had been gathering weight in the web of David's nerves snapped them and plunged through the page and a hundred layers of paper underneath." It is not the thoughts (in a conventionally religious sense) but rather the simple existence of such a book which, "if true, collapsed everything into a jumble of horror." Far more than a challenge of faith, Wells's book has prompted in David "an exact vision of death: a long hole in the ground, no wider than your body, down into which you are drawn while the white faces above recede." The threat is nothing less than "extinction," which Updike phrases in visionary terms: "a tide of clay had swept up to the stars; space was crushed into a mass."

Shaken loose from the familiar beliefs of his childhood, in themselves little more than comfortable habits, David re-evaluates the texts of his life. Dictionaries, the Bible, sermons, and Sunday school instructions—all are catastrophically dismissed. "He hated everything about them but the promise they held out, a promise that in the most perverse way, as if the homeliest crone in the kingdom were given the Prince's hand, made every good and real thing, ball games and pert-breasted girls, possible." Like Harry Angstrom in *Rabbit, Run*, David cannot find adequate words to counter this vision—not from his mother, not from his minister, not from any of the conventional sources upon whom one is supposed to rely. All he has are "dread" and "fear," the key terms from Updike's reading of Kierkegaard. And so David, who is created in turn by Updike's language, fashions a new world of values from natural details: the subtle radiance of barnlight, the smell of old straw, the "ragged infinity" of the natural world in which even the feathers of pigeons, nuisance birds he slaughters at will, are marvels of creation. As David buries these birds he is "robed in this certainty: that the God who had lavished such craft upon these worthless birds would not destroy His whole Creation by refusing to let David live forever."

This consistent scheme of narrative repeats itself throughout the selections from *Olinger Stories*. A young, sensitive protagonist is by spatial displacement led into a reordering of personal judgment. Particular details have first prompted a longing for the universal ("above the particulars the immense tinted pity, the waste, of being at one little place instead of everywhere, at every time"). That longing ultimately leads to the question of physical death. But death's vision is countered by more details—not necessarily transcendent in Christian fashion, but celebrated nonetheless as transcriptions of a creator's art. By the volume's end the narrative spokesman, now grown to resemble the real John Updike in the most personal of details, thinks of this celebratory technique as part of his own writer's art, of every little squib of life "all set sequentially down with the bald simplicity of intrinsic blessing, thousands and thousands of pages; ecstatically uneventful; divinely and defiantly dull."

The endings of both "Pigeon Feathers" and the fragment quoted above, "The Blessed Man of Boston," confirm Updike's moral stated in the volume's Foreword: "*We are rewarded unexpectedly.*" Of course David will not live forever; nor would any such manically unselective book be a useful work of art. But Updike is in full control of each

self-conscious irony, for the boy's and the author's innocent intentions have successfully challenged death. A relish for detail helps, for
as another fragment states, "we have no gestures adequate to answer
the imperious gestures of nature"; transitory as we are, we must improvise with what we have. By assembling a catalogue of existence
Updike locates what he calls the "thin point" of "piercing survival."
"Details are the giant's fingers," these stories tell us. Or, as one of
Updike's rare writer-narrators answers when asked the point of all he
has written, "We in America need ceremonies."

    We are rewarded unexpectedly. Fifteen years later this moral and
motto is transformed, in the pages of *Too Far To Go*, as "all blessings are
mixed." Within those 15 years of American life can be found the
aftermath of President John F. Kennedy's "Camelot," the experiences
of Vietnam and Watergate, and then another half-decade of change in
world economics. The very first stories are brought back from the
even earlier years of Eisenhower's presidency and Kennedy's thousand days; every one of the 17 stories and fragments re-collected here
is stamped by its evolving historical time. But once more Updike's
personal scheme of things and his own sense of language are the
collection's true subjects. The three-stage narrative structure of the
individual Olinger pieces (initial sensitivity/challenge by rearrangement/triumph over death) is reflected in many of the Maples stories,
and the second volume is reassembled and chronologically arranged
just like the first. The initial stories of *Too Far To Go* overlap in matters
of character, theme, and biographical reference with the fragments
near the end of *Olinger Stories* and with the little correspondences to
Updike's own life (such as makes of cars, personal habits, and even
home addresses). The volumes are indeed companions, and just as
Updike told an interviewer in 1968 (the comments are reprinted in his
Picked-Up Pieces) that "if I had to give anybody one book of me it would
be the Vintage [edition of] *Olinger Stories*," so his similar creation of a
new work from the Maples stories makes *Too Far To Go* a good clue to
his manner and methods of more recent years.

    A typical Maples story will, like an Olinger piece, begin with a
reference to or demonstration of the protagonist's sensitivity. But with
ripening age and a deteriorating marriage there comes a change in
attitude, for Richard Maple's aesthetic judgments are sometimes
wasted on frivolous or farcical details: a supermarket cabbage, overwrought art or tasteless racial parodies. The narrative scheme of
sensitivity, challenge, and triumph becomes at times more heavily

ironic, especially when the references to *Olinger Stories* are kept in mind. At the book's end, when the Maples are in court for their no-fault divorce, the presiding judge is noted to have "a polished pink face" which "declared that he was altogether good, and would never die"—a sad diminishing of David Kern's illusion of triumph at the end of "Pigeon Feathers." At one point Richard becomes a victim of his creative memory, letting his imagination sentimentally rewrite the history of his marriage and then sealing it with a kiss. Throughout *Too Far To Go* details of American life are less sublimely celebratory and more sardonically diminished. The promise of a sheltered boyhood— of anyone's boyhood, Updike seems to say—is not fulfilled by an unlimited future of blessed moments. All blessings, our older American man of 1979 reports, are mixed.

If *Olinger Stories* explains much of what goes on in Updike's early novels, *Too Far To Go* helps one understand his major works which followed: *The Centaur* (1963) and his transitional novel *Of the Farm* (1965). The fate of married men and women in America is of course central to his novel *Couples* (1968), but even *Rabbit Redux* (1971) and *A Month of Sundays* (1975) are more heavily dependent upon the subject of sexual relations than the sense of shelter (and more rari-fied aesthetic longing) so integral to the earlier books. And with *Marry Me* (1976) and the closing stories of *Problems* (1979) Updike begins what may be the next saga in his fiction: remarriage. Yet the seeds of his full-grown interest in marriage and divorce predate even the first Olinger novel, *The Poorhouse Fair* (1959). The earliest of the Maples stories, "Snowing in Greenwich Village," appeared in *The New Yorker* on January 21, 1956, with the Maples (and the Updikes) not yet two years married; but already outside interests are in the air, as figured by the attractively threatening character named Rebecca. By the fourth story, "Twin Beds in Rome" (February 8, 1964), Richard and Joan are already discussing separation; and even in the two stories in between, Updike's narrator is regretting that "Once my ornate words wooed you" and acknowledging that "Romance is, simply, the strange, the untried."

The strange and the untried are Updike's new variation on the rearrangement scheme of *Olinger Stories*, for which an eager and heightened sensuosity is the perfect tool. Joan Maple is challenged by a need to redefine her identity—"housewife" must be replaced by some more dignifying role and name for it—but Richard is the true slave of words. "Mistress," "nakedness," and the like haunt him, all the more so because his childhood's America has become "this nation of temporary arrangements" which nevertheless lacks institutions and even gestures to accommodate his plainly sensuous interest in any woman not his wife. Divorce is regretted and is in fact experienced as a death for him and for Joan because happy marriage is a myth his childhood taught him. His and Joan's gesturings as they vacillate between divorce and reconciliation are meaningfully pathetic, for as fraudulent as their relationship has become, it is the only thing they really have. "He saw through her words to what she was saying," a narrator sympathetic to Richard notes, "—that these lovers, however we love them, are not us, are not sacred as reality is sacred. We are reality. We have made children. We gave each other our young bodies. We promised to grow old together." Though the marriage crumbles, "her gestures would endure, cut into glass," an image which Updike's own respect for fine creation (reestablished by careful imagery earlier in this same story) leads the reader to accept as sincere.

The larger structure of *Too Far To Go* eclipses its obvious history and is formed instead by the patterns of Richard and Joan's language: words which alternately tear them apart and knit them together as they discuss their marriage. Once more, despite the sometimes contradictory hints of a larger plan for life, carefully noted details are the most one can have, and Updike is the master of those details. In 1960 Rabbit had worried that his life amounted to no more than the tacky particulars of his shabby life and so tried to compensate by creating a life of superior aesthetics (harking back to the successful creative plan of his high school basketball career). In 1971 (the year of *Rabbit Redux*) one of Updike's stories later transposed into the voice of Richard Maple finds the narrator shuffling about the house his family has just vacated for another and feeling guilty "that we occupied it so thinly," that although the 300-year-old colonial home has offered archaeological treasures from America's past, "Of ourselves, a few plastic practice golfballs in the iris and a few dusty little Superballs beneath the radiators will be all for others to find." Like so many of the Olinger stories, this Maples episode ends with a moral: "All around us, we are outlasted." Natural details, elevating and enriching in the boyhoods of *Olinger Stories*, no longer do their job so rewardingly; by necessity, they have been replaced with the intimate details of a 20-year marriage. These shared associations have bred a private language, and when the relationship ends, the language and composite details do not disappear. Remarriage is a new lease on creative life, but it is not a simple and entire rebirth as the inconclusive turmoils shown among the couples of *Marry Me* make clear. As the last story of *Problems* more confidently concludes, experiences from a previous marriage form a lost Atlantis of stored memories, a part of one's self, once shared, which is now submerged but still really there. And though harder to reach, they are no less persistent, no less valuable.

"Life goes on; stray strands are tucked back," Updike wrote in his "Introduction to the 1977 Edition" of his first novel, *The Poorhouse Fair*. He maintains this optimism despite his younger writer's pessimism that "All is flux; nothing lastingly matters." For John Updike, of contemporary America's writers probably the one most deeply read in theology and religion, the details of existence are the makings for a love-hate relationship with the world. Death and immortality have been the contrary poles of his writing career. But against the conventional wisdom of what he calls the death-oriented futurism in H. G. Wells's *The Time Machine* and George Orwell's *1984*, Updike declares his visionary faith in the creative powers of language—his characters', and his own. In the second of his Maples stories, a piece first published in 1960 during the high promise of a still-young Maples marriage, a narrator finds words in James Joyce's *Ulysses* to woo his wife:

> Smackwarm. That was the crucial word. Smacked smack-warm on her smackable warm woman's thigh. Something like that. A splendid man, to feel that. Smackwarm woman's. Splendid also to feel the curious and potent, inexplicable and irrefutably magical life language leads within itself.

Seventeen years later a poetic voice vaguely but in a deliberately suggestive way resembling Richard Maple's dedicates a book titled *Tossing and Turning* (1977) to a woman soon to become his second wife:

> When first he saw. Alas!
> Full tup. Full throb.
> Warbling. Ah, lure! alluring.
> Martha! Come!
> Clapclop. Clipclap. Clappyclap.
> —*Ulysses*

Words have been the saga in John Updike's life of fiction. And the words of any day's creation, unlike their fleshy promise, are never eclipsed or effaced.

Bibliography

By John Updike:

Novels

The Poorhouse Fair. New York: Knopf, 1959; reissued with a new introduction, 1977.
Rabbit, Run. New York: Knopf, 1960.
The Centaur. New York: Knopf, 1963.
Of the Farm. New York: Knopf, 1965.
Couples. New York: Knopf, 1968.
Rabbit Redux. New York: Knopf, 1971.
A Month of Sundays. New York: Knopf, 1975.
Marry Me: A Romance. New York: Knopf, 1976.
The Coup. New York: Knopf, 1978.
Rabbit Is Rich. New York: Knopf, 1981.

Stories Collected in Hardcover Editions

The Same Door. New York: Knopf, 1959.
Pigeon Feathers and Other Stories. New York: Knopf, 1962.
The Music School. New York: Knopf, 1966.
Bech: A Book. New York: Knopf, 1970.
Museums and Women. New York: Knopf, 1972.
Problems. New York: Knopf, 1979.

Paperback Originals of Re-collected Stories

Olinger Stories. New York: Vintage Books, 1964.
Too Far To Go: The Maples Stories. New York: Fawcett, 1979.

Poetry Collections

The Carpentered Hen and Other Tame Creatures. New York: Harper & Brothers, 1958.
Telephone Poles. New York: Knopf, 1963.

Mindpoint and Other Poems. New York: Knopf, 1969.
Tossing and Turning. New York: Knopf, 1977.

Collected Non-fictional Prose

Assorted Prose. New York: Knopf, 1965.
Picked-Up Pieces. New York: Knopf, 1975.

About John Updike:

Atlas, James. "John Updike Breaks Out of Suburbia." *New York Times Sunday Magazine,* 10 December 1978.

Hamilton, Alice and Kenneth Hamilton. *The Elements of John Updike.* Grand Rapids, Michigan: William B. Eerdmans, 1970.

Howard, Jane. "Can a Nice Novelist Finish First?" *Life,* 4 November 1966.

Markle, Joyce B. *Fighters and Lovers: Theme in the Novels of John Updike.* New York: New York University Press, 1973.

Vargo, Edward P. *Rainstorms and Fire: Ritual in the Novels of John Updike.* Port Washington, New York: Kennikat Press, 1973.

James Baldwin: Dialogue and Vision

Calvin C. Hernton

A few years before the stock market crash of 1929, James Baldwin, second child in a rather large family, was born in New York City in the largest black community in the Western world, Harlem, U.S.A. Like his father who was a part-time minister and pastor of a small Harlem church, Baldwin experienced religious "salvation" and became a preacher at the early age of 14. But the ministry did not altogether satisfy the craving in the young Baldwin for exploration, creativity, and self-expression. Eventually he abandoned the ministry, moved from Harlem to New York's famous Greenwich Village of artists and began to practice the craft of writing. Though Baldwin left the formal ministry, the Christian philosophy remained firmly implanted in him and would constitute the basis for many of the views expressed throughout his writing. The years he spent in Greenwich Village, or "The Village," as it is called, were dedicated completely to the pursuit of writing, but he did not meet with much immediate success. Frustrated (and Baldwin was a rather restless young man), he left New York and flew to Paris where, within a few years, he wrote his first novel, *Go Tell It on the Mountain*, which was published in America in 1952 and which brought Baldwin his first recognition as a writer of talent.

Today Baldwin has published over 15 books, novels, plays, essays, and countless articles. He is known throughout the world. Editions and translations of his works exist in virtually every country in the world, including places in which Baldwin has lived and worked— England, France, Turkey, Africa, Switzerland as well as others. The quality and treatment of subject matter have earned Baldwin the reputation of being a highly controversial writer. Books and articles have been, and are still being, written about his work.

His novels and other fiction aside, the books which first elicited the highest controversy and praise were those of a social, cultural, and often political nature. These were his essays, the first among which was *Notes of a Native Son* (1958) and, as of this writing, the last being *No Name in the Street* (1972). The reaction to *Notes of a Native Son* (including the other essay books, *Nobody Knows My Name* and *The Fire Next Time*) as well as to *No Name in the Street*, was, to say the least, utter amazement.

The essays deal with the situation of black and white people in the United States, and often in the world at large. "Controlled anger," "brutally frank," "incredibly honest," "devastatingly passionate" are typical of the reception of these essays. During the 1960s, the heyday of black-white confrontation in America, Baldwin's photograph appeared on the cover of *Time* magazine, and the *New York Post* ran a five-day feature series on him. He was hailed as a spokesman and interpreter of the mood of the Negro people; many referred to him as a "leader" of the Blacks. But Baldwin was weary of these pronouncements and experienced a conflict with them, of which he wrote: "The conflict was simply between my life as a writer and my life as—not spokesman exactly, but as public witness to the situation of the black people."*

More than anything else, Baldwin's essays constitute a compassionate dialogue on the part of no one but James Baldwin himself vis-à-vis the vision of the country in which he was born and which he loves, but with which he is at passionate odds. "Whoever is part of whatever civilization," he states, "helplessly loves some aspects of it, and some of the people in it. One would much rather be at home among one's compatriots than be mocked and detested by them."

Throughout his writings, Baldwin reiterates that America is his home. Then, in writing in Charlotte Pomerantz's *A Quarter Century of Unamericana*, he defines and distinguishes himself as a Black American, "I . . . does not refer so much to the man called Baldwin as it does to the reality which has produced me, a reality with which I live, and from which most Americans spend all their time in flight."

The "reality" that Baldwin refers to is the historical situation of racial hatred and repression that he and his race have suffered at the

---

* Unless otherwise specified, all quotations are from *The Fire Next Time* and *No Name in the Street*.

hands of at least half of the white people in America. It is to this situation that he is a "public witness." In a piece entitled "A Letter to My Nephew on the One Hundredth Anniversary of the Emancipation," Baldwin explains to his nephew:

> ... the root of my dispute with my country. You were born where you were born and faced the future that you faced because you were black and *for no other reason*. The limits of your ambition were, thus, expected to be set forever. You were born into a society which spelled out with brutal clarity, and in as many ways as possible, that you were a worthless human being.

Baldwin's dispute, or more correctly his dialogue, with his country pierces beneath the surface of the reality of the black-white situation; his interpretation penetrates behind the mere manifestations of racial hatred and injustice to the roots of the matter. He states, "It has been vivid to me for many years that what we call a race problem here is not a race problem at all. . . . The problem is rooted in the question of how one treats one's flesh and blood, especially one's children."

Baldwin, it must be noted, is a family man—that is, he assumes the patriarchical responsibility for his brothers and sisters, nephews and cousins, various ones of whom travel with him and engage in every manner of mutual support. Likewise, his views and feelings about Blacks and Whites in America are largely in terms of the family—the blood, flesh, labor, and sweat of its members having been mingled and fused over three or more centuries. Thus, he is able to write:

> To be an Afro-American, or an American black, is to be in the situation . . . of all those who have ever found themselves part of a civilization which they could in no wise honorably defend . . . and who yet spoke out of the most passionate love, hoping to make the kingdom new, to make it honorable and worthy of life.

To wit: black Americans belong to a family which uses and exploits and then rejects and detests them. Of this situation Baldwin writes, "The Negro came to the white man for a roof or for five dollars or for a letter to the judge; the white man came to the Negro for love. But he was not often able to give what he came seeking." Thus,

Baldwin speaks of an "emotional poverty" in America, a "terror"
of human life and of human touch, on the part of too many white
people:

> White people in this country will have quite enough to
> do in learning how to accept and love themselves and each
> other, and when they have achieved this—which will
> not be tomorrow and may very well be never—the Negro
> problem will no longer exist, for it will no longer be need-
> ed.

When Martin Luther King was killed, Baldwin stated that the
manner of King's death caused "something to alter in him," which
forced him into a "reluctant judgment," one aspect of which was that
"there are no American people yet."

Of course, the American people referred to here are the kind of
Americans whom poet Walt Whitman predicted would surely come
into being—O pioneers! An American people who would work and
struggle and love as separate groups, or ethnics, and yet exist as a
unified people. This is the vision of the American dream. As it was the
vision of Whitman, so is it the vision of James Baldwin.

Despite the despairing one (concerning the black-white confrontation during the 1960s) after King's death, and Kennedy's death,
and Malcom X's death, Baldwin wrote that that confrontation was
"obviously crucial, containing the shape of the American future and
the only potential of a truly valid American Identity."

In other words, for Baldwin the future of America hinges
imperatively on the working out of the relations between Blacks and
Whites. Baldwin's view of the situation is that although Blacks are
victims of white mockery and rejection, the Whites are even more the
victims of their own emotional poverty and ignorance, and therefore, the terrible weight of lifting the veil of history rests significantly
upon the shoulder of the Blacks. In his letter to his nephew, Baldwin
wrote:

> The really terrible thing, old buddy, is that *you* must accept
> *them*. And I mean that very seriously. You must accept
> them with love . . . for these innocent people have no hope.
> They are, in effect, still trapped in a history which they do
> not understand; and until they understand it, they cannot
> be released from it.

Baldwin goes on to say that whatever Whites do not know about Blacks reveals that which they do not know about themselves. The caption for his book of essays, *Nobody Knows My Name*, reads: IF YOU DON'T KNOW MY NAME, YOU DON'T KNOW YOUR OWN! In the final analysis, though Blacks may never live to become equal Americans, they are nevertheless an integral part of the nation and, as such, can precipitate chaos and "bring down the curtain on the American Dream." At the same time, Baldwin recognizes that the final analysis could well be the "final solution" for us all. Ridden with despair after the death of Dr. King, he expressed at once both sides of the paradoxical nature of human life and the human being:

> Ironically ... most people are not ... worth very much; and yet, every human being is an unprecedented miracle. ... One tries to treat them as the miracles they are, while trying to protect oneself against the disasters they've become ... and yet one was compelled (as an act of faith!) to demand of Americans ... a generosity, a clarity and a nobility. ...

His despair notwithstanding, Baldwin urges his vision upon us, to the effect that those both Black and White who are conscious must, "like lovers, insist on ... the consciousness of the others— handful that we are, to end the racial nightmare, and achieve our country, and change the history of the world." Only then, only when Blacks and Whites have come through the "dizzying height of tension," will Americans know what has been made of us all. He further believes that "we," the Blacks, "cannot be free until they," the Whites, "are free."

What Baldwin is calling for is not only a new species of Whites but a new generation of Blacks as well. The forging anvil of this new quality of human being is *love*. After having issued a warning that "the vision people hold of the world to come is but a reflection, with predictable wishful distortions, of the world in which they live," Baldwin reflects on the purpose of his "salvation" when he became a minister: "... if it did not permit me to behave with love toward others, no matter how they behaved toward me, what was the point?" He states further that "the unexamined life is not worth living." At the peak of his vision, he writes:

> ... in order to survive as a human, moving, moral weight

> in the world, America and all the Western Nations will be
> forced to reexamine themselves and release themselves
> from many things that are now taken to be sacred, and to
> discard nearly all the assumptions that have been used to
> justify their lives and their anguish. . . .

From the foregoing it is obvious that James Baldwin is a deeply spiritual man, a humanist and an existentialist, and a person who loves his country and loves humanity—all in the tradition of Walt Whitman. Elsewhere I have written that Baldwin, although having left the church critical of many of its hypocrisies, is a religious man, and his writings will continue to be informed by religious faith in human life and human potential. Baldwin writes within the frame of reference of *sin* and *redemption*. He is, in the existential sense, *condemned* to the battery of beliefs that holds faith as triumphant over doubt, hope over despair, struggle over failure and, most of all, love over hatred.

In his first novel, *Go Tell It on the Mountain*, which was almost straight autobiography, he not only experienced triumph through a deep spirituality, but this very spirituality served the execution of an excellent and masterful methodology of storytelling in the tradition of the black-sermon fused with, according to Baldwin himself, the scope and depth of human concern found in the works of Charles Dickens. But what is remarkable, in comparison with other white and black American writers, especially black ones, both in the carnal and in the spiritual or universal senses, is that Baldwin is the only secular writer who is literally, a Messenger of Love. Spinoza is said to have been "intoxicated" with God. Baldwin is "intoxicated" with love. Variously, he writes:

> . . . if love will not swing wide the gates, no other power will
> or can.
>
>   * * *
>
> To be sensual, I think, is to respect, and rejoice in the force
> of life, of life itself, and to be *present* in all that one does,
> from the effort of loving to the breaking of bread.
>
>   * * *
>
> I love a few people and they love me and some of them are
> white, and isn't love more important than color.

* * *

> It is the responsibility of free men to trust and to cele-
> brate what is constant—birth, struggle, and death are
> constant, and so is love. . . .

Speaking of Western civilization, he writes:

> . . . if we could accept ourselves as we are, we might bring
> new life to the Western achievements, and transform them.
> The price of this transformation is the unconditional free-
> dom of the Negro. . . . He is *the* key figure in this country,
> and the American future is precisely as bright or as dark
> as his. . . . It is for this reason that love is so desparately
> sought. . . . Love takes off the masks that we fear we cannot
> live without and know we cannot live within. I use the
> word "love" here not merely in the personal sense but as a
> state of being, or a state of grace . . . in the tough and
> universal sense of quest and daring and growth.

Early in Baldwin's life he stated his ambition to be a "good writer and an honest man." To my mind, there is no question that James Baldwin is one of the great writers of our time, a master essayist similar to Ralph Waldo Emerson; and similar to James Joyce, Baldwin is a painstaking unearther of the tangled emotions that beset the animal we call the Human Being. His second novel, *Giovanni's Room*, for example, is a masterpiece of literary style, eloquence, and finesse; at the same time, it is also a conquest of the nameless fears that lurk in the hearts of men and women, the dark, existential riddle (Bald-win's favorite word is "conundrum") of our nature that make us tremble with ontological terrror when we are in the arms of those we dare love.

It is amazing, moreover, to read *Go Tell It on the Mountain* and *Portrait of the Artist as a Young Man* together and experience the identical triumph of two different men of different times, countries, and circumstances, the triumph of the humanity of the human being over despair and human entrapment. For Baldwin, perhaps the role that love plays in the affairs of nations as well as individuals is most cogently illustrated by a statement he made in his letter to his nephew:

> But these men (white) are your brothers—your lost younger
> brothers. And if the word *integration* means anything, this

is what it means; that we, with love, shall force our brothers to see themselves as they are, to cease fleeing from reality and begin to change it. For this is your home, my friend, do not be driven from it; great men have done great things here, and will again, and we can make America what America must become.

Before he died, the British writer Colin MacInnes remarked to me that the writing of James Baldwin was a beacon for us all, if we would but cast a glance in Baldwin's direction.

Bibliography

By James Baldwin:

Go Tell It on the Mountain. New York: Knopf, 1953. (Novel)
Giovanni's Room. New York: Dial Press, 1955; London: Joseph, 1957. (Novel)
Notes of a Native Son. Boston: Beacon Press, 1955; London: Mayflower, 1958. (Essays)
Nobody Knows My Name. New York: Dial Press, 1961; London: Joseph, 1964. (Essays)
Another Country. New York: Dial Press, 1962; London: Joseph, 1963. (Novel)
The Fire Next Time. New York: Dial Press, 1963; London: Joseph, 1963. (Essays)
With Richard Avedon. *Nothing Personal.* New York: Atheneum, 1964; London: Penguin, 1964.
Blues for Mister Charlie. New York: Dial Press, 1964; London: Joseph, 1965. (Play produced in New York in 1964, in London in 1965.)
Going to Meet the Man. New York: Dial Press, 1965; London: Joseph, 1965. (Short fiction)
Tell Me How Long the Train's Been Gone. New York: Dial Press, 1968; London: Joseph, 1968. (Novel)
No Name in the Street. New York: Dial Press, 1972; London: Joseph, 1972. (Essays)
If Beale Street Could Talk. New York: Dial Press, 1974; London: Joseph, 1974. (Novel)

About James Baldwin:

Bone, Robert. "The Novels of James Baldwin." *Tri-Quarterly*, Winter 1965.
Coles, Robert. "Baldwin's Burden." *Partisan Review*, Summer 1964.
Hernton, Calvin. "Blood of the Lamb: The Ordeal of James Baldwin." In *Amistad*.

Vol. I. Edited by Charles F. Harris and John A. Williams. New York: Vintage
    Books, 1970.
Podhoretz, Norman. "In Defense of James Baldwin." In *Doings and Undoings*. New
    York: Farrar, Straus & Co., 1964.

William Burroughs on Writing

I am told that when Anthony Burgess was teaching a writing course, a student asked him: "Why should you be up there teaching writing and not me?" A good question; and I wish I could give as definite an answer as can be given in regard to other subjects where the technology is more clearly defined. No one, unless he is himself an experienced pilot, asks why the pilot of an airliner should be in the cockpit and not him. The answer is that he knows how to fly the plane and you don't. Nor would a student of quantum mechanics, engineering, or mathematics ask such a question; the teacher is there because he knows more about the subject than the student. To say he knows more presupposes that there is something definite to know, that a technology exists and can be taught to qualified students.

How many writers have taken courses in creative writing? Some of them certainly. James Jones, for one, who took a course with some literary lady who had her students imitate the styles of well-known writers . . . write Hemingway for a month, Graham Greene for a month, and so forth. A good exercise I think. But there are certainly, I think, more writers who have not taken courses in writing than writers who have. How many pilots have taken courses in flying? All of them, we hope. How many physicists have taken courses in physics? All of them. Which brings us to the question I intend to raise: Is there a technology of writing? Can writing be taught?

As soon as we ask the question, we realize that there is no simple yes-or-no answer, since there are many technologies of writing and a technique that is useful for one writer may be of no use to another. There is no one way to write. So we will begin looking for *answers*, not *the* answer. A pilot must possess certain qualifications before he starts flying lessons. A degree of coordination, steady nerves, a certain level of intelligence. A student of physics must have a considerable aptitude for mathematics. The qualifications for a writer are not so definable. The ability to sit at a typewriter for many hours without distraction is certainly useful. The ability to endure solitude is useful but not essential. An ability to empathize with others, to see and hear what is in their minds, is useful—but some very great writers like Beckett have only one character and need no others.

In general, the more observant a writer is, the more he will find to write about. I recommend an exercise I have practiced for years: when walking down any street, try to *see* everyone on the street before he sees you. You will find that if you see others first, they will *not* see you, and that gives you time to observe, or file for future use. I learned this exercise from an old Mafia don in Columbus, Ohio. If a writer is seen first, he won't necessarily get shot, but he may miss a set or a character. Someone glimpsed in passing may be used as a character years later; some doorway or shop front may serve as a set. An absent-minded writer closes the doors of perception.

Jean Genêt said of a French writer who shall here be nameless: he does not have the courage to be a writer. What courage does he refer to? The courage of the inner exploration, the cosmonaut of inner space. The writer cannot pull back from what he finds because it shocks or upsets him or because he fears the disapproval of the reader. Allied to this courage are persistence and the ability to endure discouragement. Any writer must do a great deal of bad writing and he may not know how bad it is at the time. Writers are not always good critics of their own work. Sinclair Lewis said, "If you have just written something that you think is absolutely great and you can't wait to show it to someone, tear it up, it's terrible." I have certainly had the experience of writing something I thought was the greatest and reading it over a few days later said "My God, tear it into very small pieces and put it in someone else's garbage can." On the other hand, something that I did not think much of at the time may stand up very well on rereading. What I wish to point out is that a writer must be able to survive an uneven performance that would be disastrous in another profession. An actor or a musician must put on a certain level of performance, whereas a writer has time to edit and choose what he will eventually put out as the finished product.

I have never known a writer who was not at one time an avid reader. I believe it was T. S. Eliot who said that if a writer has a pretentious literary style, it is generally because he has not read enough books. Some knowledge of what *has* been done in writing is, I think, essential—just as a doctor or a lawyer must be conversant with the literature in his field. A full-time professional writer does not as a rule get much time to read, so it is well to get your reading in early.

To recapitulate qualifications which are useful but not essential: the ability to endure the physical discipline of writing, that is, to sit at a typewriter and write; the ability to persist and to absorb the discouragement of rejection and the even deadlier discouragement that comes from your own bad writing; insight into the motives of others; ability to think in concrete, visual terms; a grounding in general reading. Now assume that the student has at least some of these qualifications. What can he be taught about writing?

It is of course easier to tell someone how not to write than how to write. Remember, for example, that a bad title can sink a good book or a good one sell a bad book. But it can sink a film faster and deeper, because a film has just one shot to make it. A book with a bad title or a slow beginning may make a comeback—a film just gets one chance. Here again there are no absolute rules; but there are guidelines. A good title gives the reader an *image* and arouses his interest in the image. Bad titles convey negative images, refer to images which the audience cannot understand until they see the film, or convey no image at all. Titles of more than three words are to be avoided—such turn-off titles as "The Marriage of a Young Stock Broker." "The Conformist" is a turn-off title. Those of you who have seen the film will know it is about a fascist who ends up denouncing his blind friend as a fascist when Mussolini falls. "The Survival Artist" would have been a better title.

There is a definite technology for the negative use of words to cause confusion, to create and aggravate conflicts, and to discredit opponents. This is the opposite of what a writer does. Here, the more abstract words and meaningless statements, the better. This technology has been developed in the mass media by Hearst and others, refined in *Life* and *Time*, and carried still further by the C.I.A. in such subsidized periodicals as *Encounter*. This technology for writing a turn-off review is so definite that one sentence will tell you when it is being used—and it is much more complicated than just saying derogatory things about the book. It is very important for any writer to be able to absorb unfair criticism calmly and, when given the opportunity, to reply to it. It is also good practice to write book reviews.

To return to the matter of a technology, let us consider first the question of our materials: words. Korzybski's book, *Science and Sanity,* is a great time-saver. The fact that word is *not* the object it represents—that this desk, whatever it may be, is not the label "desk"—fully realized, will save the student a lot of pointless verbal arguments. Look at abstract words that have no definite referent—words like Communism, materialism, civilization, fascism, reductivism, mysticism. There are as many definitions as there are users of these words. According to Korzybski, a word that has no referent is a word that should be dropped from the language and, I would say, certainly from the vocabulary of the writer. For example, take the word "fascism"; what does it mean? What is the referent? Consider the phenomenon of Nazi Germany—military expansion of an industrialized country; now consider South Africa—oppression designed to maintain a status quo; are these both fascism?

In short, we have so many different phenomena lumped under this word that the use of the word can only lead to confusion. So we can drop the word altogether and simply describe the various and quite different political phenomena. I have been accused of being an arch-materialist and a bourgeois mystic. What do these words mean? Virtually nothing. And because they mean nothing, you can argue about them for all eternity. Any words that have referents cannot be argued about; there it is—call it a desk, a table, call it whatever you like, but no argument is possible. All arguments stem from confusion, and all arguments are a waste of time unless your purpose is to cause confusion and waste time.

I have learned a lot about writing by writing film scripts. As soon as a writer starts writing a film script—that is, writing in terms of what appears on screen—he is no longer omniscient. He cannot for example inform the reader that "It was a clear bright day in May of 1923, St. Louis, Missouri." How does the film audience know that the month is May, the year 1923, the locale St. Louis? This information must be shown on screen, unless the writer falls back on the dubious expedient of the offstage voice. Or: "As he left his house and turned onto Euclid Avenue that morning, he felt a chill of foreboding." Did he indeed—and how is this to be shown on screen? Some incident must be presented that gave him this chill; perhaps someone passing him on the street who mutters something that may be or may not be directed towards him—or he intercepts a malignant expression as someone passes on a bicycle. And such phrases as "words cannot convey," "indescribable," "unspeakable," cannot be shown on screen. You cannot get away with an indescribable monster. The audience wants to *see* the monster. That's what they are paying for. The ability to think in concrete visual terms is almost essential to a writer. Generally speaking, if he can't see it, hear it, feel it, smell it, he can't write it.

The impact of the mass media is more directly felt in films than in books. In the 1920s gang war was box office year after year, but remember that there were no television pictures of gang war on screen. There were only still pictures and newspaper accounts. It was front-page news, and people were interested because it was something going on which they could not see directly. Had they seen it day after day, like the terrorist activity in Belfast, they would have lost interest. Image loses impact with use. Anyone like to try making a film about the IRA in Belfast? Or writing a book on the subject for that matter? People are fed up with the IRA in Belfast. Or how about the Arab terrorists? Call it "Death in Munich"? World War II—there were of course films on location, but not all that many, and no TV cameras at the front. There have been a lot of successful films made since then, and at least two books: *From Here to Eternity* and *The Naked and the Dead*. But who has written a bestseller about the Vietnam war?

Dreams are a fertile source of material for writing. Years ago I read a book by John Dunne called *An Experiment with Time* (1924). Dunne was an English physicist, and he observed that his dreams referred not only to past but also to future events. However, the future material, since it often seems trivial and irrelevant, will not be remembered unless it is written down. This got me in the habit of writing dreams down, and I have done this for about 30 years. I began writing dreams down long before I started to write. I have, over a period of years, turned up a number of future references; but much more important is the number of characters and sets I have obtained directly from dreams, and at least 40 percent of my material derives from dreams. When I contact a character, I start building up an identikit picture. For example, I meet a character in a dream; then I may find a photo in a magazine that looks like the character, or I may meet someone who looks like him in some respect. Usually my characters are composites of many people—from dreams, photos, people I know, and quite frequently characters in other writing. Over a period of years I have filled a number of scrapbooks with these identikit pictures.

Bibliography

By William Burroughs:

Junky. New York: Penguin Books, 1977. (First published as *Junkie* under the name
of William Lee by Ace Books [New York] in 1953; also as *Junkie* in 1964.)
Naked Lunch. New York: Grove Press, 1962; London: John Calder, 1964. (First pub-
lished as *The Naked Lunch* by Olympia Press [Paris] in 1959.)
The Soft Machine. Paris: Olympia Press, 1961; New York: Grove Press, 1966; London:
Calder and Boyars, 1968.
The Ticket That Exploded. Paris: Olympia Press, 1962; revised edition, New York:
Grove Press, 1967; London: Calder and Boyars, 1968.
Nova Express. New York: Grove Press, 1964; London: Cape, 1966.
The Last Words of Dutch Schultz. New York: Seaver Books/Viking Press, 1975. (First
published as a transcript of a 1965 reading, by Cape Goliad [London] in
1970.)
With Brion Gysin. *The Third Mind.* New York: Grove Press, 1970; reissued, New
York: Seaver Books/Viking Press, 1978.
The Wild Boys: A Book of the Dead. New York: Grove Press, 1971; London: Calder and
Boyars, 1972.
Exterminator! New York: Viking Press, 1974; London: Calder and Boyars, 1974.
Cities of the Red Light. New York: Holt, Rinehart and Winston, 1981.

About William Burroughs:

Goodman, Michael B. *A Study in Contemporary Literary Censorship: The Case History
of "Naked Lunch" by William S. Burroughs.* Metuchen, New Jersey: Scarecrow
Press, 1981.
Mikriammos, Philippe. *William Burroughs: La vie et œuvre.* Paris: Seghers, 1975.
Mottram, Eric. *The Algebra of Need.* London: Marion Boyars, 1977.

Literary Criticism

A Conversation among Ihab Hassan,
Jerome Klinkowitz, Richard Kostelanetz, and John Simon

Kostelanetz: By "criticism" I mean considered writing about literature, and with me are three of America's very best literary critics: Ihab Hassan, whom I rank among our most important literary theorists (his latest book, published in 1980, is *The Right Promethean Fire*); Jerome Klinkowitz, who has authored several books about contemporary fiction including *The Life of Fiction* and most recently *The American 1960s*; and John Simon, whom I consider among America's most serious reviewers, not only of books but of plays and films as well. His recent titles are *Paradigms Lost: A Reflection on Literacy and Its Decline* (1980), and *Singularities* (1976).

Now how would you, Mr. Klinkowitz, characterize your critical enterprise?

Klinkowitz: My critical enterprise would really be that which hasn't been described before and for which there are really no adequate tools on the shelf to pick up and use. My academic experience as a student was studying 18th and 19th-century American literature. I began teaching in 1969, I was asked to teach contemporary literature and soon found out that the contemporaries I liked best just did not fit into any of these pigeon holes—all these historical labels that I had learned to assign. Furthermore, even though I had been taught New Criticism as an undergraduate at Marquette, followed by conventional literary history in graduate school at the University of Wisconsin, I found out that, for so many of the contemporary American writers, these methods did not seem to yield too much.

I remember back in 1969 I began teaching Kurt Vonnegut simply because I enjoyed him, but that's all I knew: that I enjoyed him. I didn't know why, and so I began to try to invent some new tools, to improvise critical practice. I couldn't do it myself. I got together with a group of friends and tried to divide up many aspects of Vonnegut into different assignments, and about 12 of us put together a book called *The Vonnegut Statement.*

Kostelanetz: So you're taking contemporary literature as seriously as you would take classical literature?

Klinkowitz: Definitely. And all of us trying to do our job in it. Eventually we found that if we just involved ourselves in every aspect of Vonnegut's life, the way he writes fiction, but also some of the doggerel poetry he'd written, television scripts he'd written in the 1950s, odd hack journalism he'd done for money, if we divided this up—one of our colleagues went back and studied his collegiate writing when he was editor of the student daily at Cornell—and took all of these different aspects of Kurt Vonnegut and tried to mesh them together, we could somehow get a sense of the man's life as a writer.

Kostelanetz: Is there a problem in the fact that Kurt Vonnegut is still alive and still writing?

Klinkowitz: That was the problem.

Kostelanetz: It's almost as if you're putting him in a grave.

Klinkowitz: No, not at all, because, as we published this book, new work was coming out. And we made no pretense of summing up the man's life. You see, in graduate school I had been told you could not write on a subject unless the person was dead, all the memoirs and letters were published—everything safely under glass. And this had nothing to do with the literature I was enjoying, even loving. So we decided to enmesh ourselves in all aspects of the person's life, the life on the page, the life on the telephone, wherever it would be, and somehow try to find a synthesis.

Kostelanetz: Now that you've done this with Vonnegut, have you gone on to other contemporaries?

Klinkowitz: Yes, what I eventually found out is that there was a truth in the method itself. We would have boxes and boxes of odd reviews we'd dug up by the person, tape recordings from the telephone, from just meeting the person in a bar, things people had told us. Eventually we decided to explore the truth of the method, and so I put together this book called *The Life of Fiction*, which is basically a collage—no pretense at some superior intelligence organizing all of this, just putting it together. One negative reviewer said it looked like a vaudevillian's scrap book. But after all, what are our lives, except a scrap book of memories?

Kostelanetz: Why did the reviewer say that? Most books don't look like vaudevillians' scrap books.

Klinkowitz: No, we set it up with a snatch from a letter that the author wrote me, then some overheard conversation, someone else talking, then we would put together a little graphic design which represented an aspect of his career and just lay it out graphically on the paper.

Kostelanetz: But is this *criticism*?

Klinkowitz: I think so. The criticism takes place when the reader reads the book in the space between one unit and the other. The criticism happens when the reader reacts in the space between.

Kostelanetz: You have, in effect, chosen subjects new to literary criticism and then approached them in different ways as well.

Klinkowitz: Definitely. Just because a novelist writes novels, that doesn't mean that those books are the sum total of his identity. If he writes a hack review for $75, I think we should read it because he is revealing himself. He published it with his name. I think it counts, and so let's play with it—let's stick it on a page next to his fiction. Let people read both, and maybe something will happen.

Kostelanetz: You assume that all kinds of so-called "extraneous" material will illuminate his writing.

Klinkowitz: Perhaps. I can't judge. Perhaps.

Kostelanetz: Mr. Hassan, how would you describe your critical evolution?

Hassan: I would say there may be three phases to that evolution. The first and earliest one, which centered on the book called *Radical Innocence* in 1961, was really an appraisal of the new postwar American novelists. At that time there had been very little work on these novelists. I think that John Aldridge's book, *After the Lost Generation*, was perhaps the first one. I was very interested then in the generation of Bellow, Mailer, Capote, Styron, and so forth.

Kostelanetz: Were you interested in them because they were contemporaries of yours or because they hadn't been done before in the same sense that Mr. Klinkowitz is interested in virgin territory, so to speak?

Hassan: Yes, very much so, on both of those points. That is, they were contemporaries of mine, and I am interested in the new and the live and the problems of change. I am struck again and again by the fact that so many critics write their best work only about the generation of their youth and somehow or other don't develop after that.

They find it very difficult to relate to later generations. In any case, that was one phase. The second phase, I would say, with *The Literature of Silence* in 1967 and *The Dismemberment of Orpheus* in 1971, dealt with the question of post-Modernism—that is, a kind of literature that was attempting to distinguish itself from the great Modernist classics of Yeats and Joyce, Eliot and Faulkner, Rilke and Thomas Mann, Proust and Valéry, among others.

Kostelanetz: If those last people represent high Modernism, who were the writers you wrote about?

Hassan: They go against the grain of that high Modernism. The best example would be someone like Samuel Beckett, who stands in a very interesting contrast to Joyce. Joyce wanted always to master a language completely. Beckett masters language by undercutting it, by minimizing it, by moving toward, asymptotically toward something that we might call metaphorical silence.

Kostelanetz: And who else would be in this second Modernist wave?

Hassan: In this second, post-Modernist phase I would put people like Genêt, and possibly some plays of Brecht, but particularly the younger writers, people like Barthelme and Barth, Sukenick and Federman. The third phase, beginning with *Paracriticisms* in 1975 and *The Right Promethean Fire* in 1980, is an attempt to recover cultural criticism in its widest sense, and so I'm very interested in questions of science, of how the imagination takes or does not take power in society. The feature of these books that is disturbing is their attempt to explore or recover the form of the essay in what I call paracritical ways, using materials that are not usually included in logical discourse.

Kostelanetz: Such as?

Hassan: Such as dreams, anecdotes, travel notes.

Kostelanetz: Your own as well as others'?

Hassan: Yes, but my own a good deal. Also montage and collage effects, quotations from various people, and odd juxtapositions, and simply a way of dislocating a little bit the form, format, and logical structure of the page.

Kostelanetz: For what purposes?

Hassan: Well, that's an interesting question. I'm not quite sure. Some would say for the purpose of opening up certain spaces between these various kinds of statements so that you do not yourself impose a total structure. Since post-Modern literature itself is very interested in opening these spaces and creating these lacunae it might be an interesting way to deal with alternate methods of presentation.

Kostelanetz: Can you describe to me one form of alternate presentation that you've used?

Hassan: Well, for instance, a page would have 10 to 15 lines of logical argumentation or criticism or description of a particular writer.

Kostelanetz: What we would call straight, conventional critical exposition.

Hassan: Exactly. And then I would simply shift to two or three quotations taken from very disparate sources: some of them might be from the *Journals* of Marco Polo, some of them might be from Heisenberg's journals or autobiography.

Kostelanetz: What would the subject of the original passage be?

Hassan: Well, let us say the nature of mental or spiritual travel. And so I would try to create some kind of association or connection or contrast between a spiritual journey in a work of literature and the idea of spiritual discovery from the point of view of a physicist, and then for the traditional traveler like Marco Polo, the traditional explorer like Vasco da Gama, or Columbus, or whoever it may be. Then the third part would be perhaps an anecdote dealing with my own travel that casts another perspective on the same question.

Kostelanetz: Mr. Simon, how would you define what you have done as a critic?

Simon: Well, I guess my function as a critic is to stand in opposition to the previous two speakers. I am a conservative and unashamed about it. I don't divide literature into Modernism, and second Modernism, and post-Modernism, and post-post-Modernism. I see a continuous flow. I'm interested in relating the new to the old. I'm interested in maintaining standards. I'm interested in using old, tested, and still viable techniques in an unbroken continuum with the past as much as possible. I stand against what I consider foolish innovation.

Kostelanetz: In what form do you work? What is your medium?

Simon: My medium is the same medium that critics for centuries have used. It's expository prose. It does not use any visual devices; there's no layout technique to speak of.

Kostelanetz: I meant "medium" in the sense that your work has been mostly in reviews.

Simon: Yes, if you want to call them reviews, fine. I like to think of them as criticism.

Kostelanetz: I don't mean that as a derogatory term. I mean the shorter essay that appears regularly.

Simon: Right. Actually in the *Hudson Review*, where I also write, I can use as much as 10 or 12 fairly capacious pages for discussion of one or two works. It's shorter compared to a book, but it's longer compared to what reviewing usually consists of.

Kostelanetz: How many works do you review in the course of a year?

Simon: Well, I don't know. As a film critic, I see maybe as many as 200 films a year. As a drama critic, I see probably somewhere between 150 and 175 plays a year.

Kostelanetz: That's one film or play a day on the average.

Simon: Just about. Fewer books because I don't have a regular book reviewing post, although I may take one on in the near future.

Kostelanetz: And your reviews tend to run 1,000 to 2,000 words?

Simon: It depends on the publication. In something like *New York Magazine* it's 1,400 to 2,000.

Kostelanetz: You review plays now for it, though you have reviewed films there in the past.

Simon: Occasionally books, too, but rarely. And for something like *The Saturday Review* it might be around 1,500 to 2,000 words. For the *Hudson Review* it's usually around 4,000 to 5,000, but that might cover several works. It depends on the publication. For *The New Leader*, where I do a lot of book reviews, it tends to be 2,500 words.

Kostelanetz: It always struck me that one of the tests of the serious reviewer as opposed to an unserious one is whether or not he would collect his work, because then readers would be able to see the critic's work as a whole—whether it comes together, whether or not it makes sense, whether or not there's a position taken or whether the reviews are really opportunistic in going with the various tides. Are your books as important to you as your reviewing?

Simon: Well, my books and my reviewing are really the same thing because, with the exception of my book about Ingmar Bergman and one or two anthologies of other people's work, they're all collections of my reviews. When I print my essays, I usually make some improvements, but I don't make any substantial changes.

Kostelanetz: Now, you characterize yourself as a conservative.

Simon: Yes.

Kostelanetz: Jerry Klinkowitz, how would you characterize yourself?

Klinkowitz: I try not to characterize myself. I try to keep my ego completely out of my work, and that's why I'm more happy about a book like *The Life of Fiction* than, say, *Literary Disruptions,* which did try to interpret things in terms of earlier standards and did try to make historical judgments. It sickened me when I did it; I was ashamed of myself. I finally decided that I'm just going to deal with the process of reading this work and collecting this information and let the readers make the judgments. I'll just give them all the materials.

Kostelanetz: And so, therefore, "egolessness" is a virtue for you.

Klinkowitz: For me, yes.

Kostelanetz: Mr. Hassan?

Hassan: It's very difficult to characterize oneself with these terms, but I have been called sometimes a "radical Tory" or an "elitist anarchist." Of course, these are contradictions. But to be a little more specific, I have absolutely no difficulty, for instance, with the stance that Mr. Simon has taken. In fact, I do admire it. I think that it is very important to write in a scrupulous style, and I think it is important to use our intelligence in the most exacting and exigent way. But, having done so and having insisted on standards in whatever enterprise, there is a great deal of leeway then, room for different temperaments to manifest themselves with equal integrity. For me, I see history as a strange combination of both continuity and discontinuity. It is precisely that dual claim on our attention of the discontinuous and the continuous that makes for the problems of change that we experience.

Kostelanetz: There's a question also among us of stance, of distance. It seems to me that Mr. Simon's in the front line, seeing an incredible amount of fresh work and observing it scrupulously; and Mr. Klinkowitz is in the next line; and that, Mr. Hassan, you're in the third line, yet further back, looking at things with greater distance and theoretically seeing a larger scope. Would you accept this characterization?

Hassan: Yes, I think this is fair, but this would describe my distance, as you put it, in the last five or seven years, in my recent phase, in the sense that I do not deal with specific works anymore; and I think, both Mr. Simon and Mr. Klinkowitz are doing a great deal with that.

Kostelanetz: You deal with issues.

Hassan: Issues, cultural problems, things like the divergences and the convergences of imagination and science, problems of change, problems of literary theory.

Kostelanetz: Whereas it seems to me that Mr. Klinkowitz centers on individuals—individual writers, individual mentalities.

Klinkowitz: Yes, because it is the only thing I can hope to know.

Kostelanetz: It is the individual corpus.

Klinkowitz: Yes.

Kostelanetz: And, Mr. Simon, you center on the work at hand?

Simon: Yes, generally speaking, when I do what you call, correctly I think, front-line criticism, but sometimes, of course, one works with other things. For example, if I review the letters of Flaubert, I'm obviously not a front-line critic any more; so it's a little bit of rear-guard action, too.

Kostelanetz: Why, John Simon, do you write criticism rather than other kinds of writing?

Simon: Well, I suppose I could answer with the old classic tag line: "Just lucky, I guess!" I happen to enjoy it. I don't know why a plumber gravitates toward plumbing or a painter toward painting. I happen to have written poetry when I was younger, and while I did it, I liked it, but when the poetry somehow stopped—perhaps mysteriously, perhaps not—it became criticism instead. It chose me more than I chose it. I've been with it ever since. The marriage works; it has resisted the American divorce rate, and here I am.

Kostelanetz: Mr. Klinkowitz, where does your best criticism appear?

Klinkowitz: I try to do a little bit of everything. I try to produce the kind of work I see the writers I like producing. I figure that if they can be judged on the full range, maybe I'd better extend myself. So I'll do Sunday reviewing for the *Chicago Sun-Times,* occasionally the *Tribune,* once in a while *The Washington Post.* I will work in very traditional scholarship for the academic organizations, but. . . .

Kostelanetz: Very traditional scholarship meaning?

Klinkowitz: Descriptive bibliography.

Kostelanetz: You've done that?

Klinkowitz: Two books of it. I will work on the staff of *American Literary Manuscripts,* going out and counting up manuscripts in libraries here and there. I will also work for people like Ishmael Reed in *Yardbird Reader,* doing "little" magazine, "little" press stuff.

Kostelanetz: So you try to maintain a great spectrum of activity, ranging from reviews to head-counting and manuscript-counting.

Klinkowitz: Yes, but when I have the chance to do a book, I try to pull that all together from *American Literature,* to the *Yardbird Reader,* to *The Washington Post*.

Kostelanetz: So the book brings your "variousness" together, and therefore, the book is the sum of your activities?

Klinkowitz: It tells me what I have been doing for the last two years.

Kostelanetz: Mr. Hassan, where does your criticism appear?

Hassan: It tends to appear in quarterlies, in literary journals perhaps more specialized than I would like: periodicals like *New Literary History* or *Diacrtics* or *The Georgia Review*.

Kostelanetz: *New Literary History* and *Diacritics* are publications we would characterize as theoretical journals—journals interested in the theory of literature.

Hassan: Yes, that's correct. And a new periodical that is associated with the Center for the Humanities at the University of Southern California, *Humanities in Society*. What I would like to do sometime soon is to write a short, simple book—simple, that is, in style, no experimentation in typography—that could reach a wider audience.

Kostelanetz: A book about what?

Hassan: Ah, that's difficult to say, but it's something about autobiography, something about travel and journeys of different kinds, spiritual and physical, and something about the humanities, what it means to be a human being, but also the particular dilemma and perplexity of the disciplines of the humanities at this time.

Kostelanetz: How does American literary theory differ from European?

Hassen: This is a complex question, but I think I can give a brief answer in the following way. When the influence of the New Criticism receded. . . .

Kostelanetz: By the "New Criticism" you mean?

Hassan: I mean the formalist kind of criticism that's associated with Cleanth Brooks, Robert Penn Warren, R. P. Blackmur, Allen Tate, and John Crowe Ransom, which flourished in the 1940s and 1950s particularly. When its influence began to recede, I think there was some kind of vacuum in academic theoretical circles. That vacuum has been filled by various waves of Continental criticism and philosophy. The first wave may have been existentialism and phenomenology. That particular one did not prove as strong or as influential as some others that came after. Then came structuralism and post-structuralism.

Kostelanetz: We're talking now about the late 1960s.

Hassan: Now we're talking about the late 1960s right through the 1970s: structuralism, but particularly post-structuralism, the kind of work that's associated with Jacques Derrida, the French philosopher, and the later work of Roland Barthes. That kind of work found eager, in fact, avid disciples in various American universities, notably Johns Hopkins and Yale, but also Cornell and the University of California at Irvine. Now the differences are difficult to characterize because I think that whenever you have a kind of transmigration of ideas, there's always something lost in that movement and also something gained in terms of a fanaticism that does not exist in the original.

Kostelanetz: You mean the disciples are fanatics the way their fathers are not.

Hassan: That's my view. The followers seem to be even more dogmatic than the originators. I think this is true of Marxists and Freudians and many others. It has created a climate of tension and of excitement and of exasperation and of exhilaration and of a great deal of cant and jargon in the journals that on the stylistic level I personally detest.

Kostelanetz: To get back to the question, how does American literary theory today differ from European?

Hassan: In one way, I would have to say that it does not really differ, that the most important ideas come from France at the current time. And the people who have been influential are people like Lévi-Strauss, and Saussure with the structuralists, and later people like Derrida, Foucault, Roland Barthes, Gilles Deleuze, and Lacan. So I would say that that's the main theoretical impulse. On the other hand, I would say that the part of American criticism that I respond to personally tries to marry or to bring a native Romantic or native transcendentalist tradition—namely, the work of Emerson, Whitman, and Thoreau—into the concerns of the post-structuralists.

Kostelanetz: John Simon, how does American front-line criticism differ from European?

Simon: I'm not quite so *au courant* with various European schools of criticism and practice at the moment as I would like to be, but as far as I can tell, the difference a few decades ago was that the Europeans were tougher minded than we were, that the standards were a little higher, that the expectations were a little more exalted, and that irony and destructive criticism were a little freer flowing in Europe than they were here.

Kostelanetz: It seems to me you have a paradox in that statement, Mr. Simon, in that, in general, American reviewing is rather flaccid; on the other hand, the kind of tough-mindedness that you represent has succeeded, at least for yourself.

Simon: I was going to say, though, that the difference between European and American reviewing, or whatever you want to call it, is now very slight, perhaps nonexistent. What little I see of foreign reviewing strikes me as equally tepid, not to say insipid, as what I see around me in this country. Now the answer to your next question is that there is always room for one maverick, even on television. There's always been one person in the terrible, tepid, amorphous, permissive and lowbrow world of television, there's always been room for one Oscar Levant.

Kostelanetz: And are you the one?

Simon: I guess, without my necessarily aspiring to this mantle, it has descended on me. Mind you, I like the fact that among the characters in the *commedia dell'arte*, I can play more than one. I'm not always Arlecchino, I'm not always Pierrot. I mean, I can do various *shticks*. Obviously in *Hudson Review* I speak to a more demanding and more intellectual, even academic, readership than the kind of readership I speak to in *New York Magazine*.

Kostelanetz: But obviously there are other stringent critics who have not succeeded as you have. Why not? Because they weren't as good?

Simon: I think it's a question of style. Well, there are two things involved. Luckily for me, I write very fast, which a lot of my colleagues do not. So that speed is really an advantage in being able to turn out certain kinds of weekly reviewing. I could do it even daily if I had to, but thus far I've been spared that. On the other hand, I think the matter of style can be defined in my case as a style that combines a kind of highbrow, slightly allusive, slightly sesquipedalian, slightly arrogant, elitist condescension if you wish, sometimes sarcastic with a kind of punning, joking bonhomie, a kind of jollity that the middlebrows, at least the upper middlebrows, can appreciate.

Kostelanetz: In other words, as the boys in slick journalism say, it's readable.

Simon: Yes, it's readable. So that I have highbrow tastes, but I can express them in a fairly middlebrow, jokey way, shall we say. Not that I necessarily prefer that style but I don't hate it either. So I can do it when that's called for, and when I can be more serious, I am more serious.

Kostelanetz: Is there a serious criticism of contemporary litera-ture in other countries?   If so, how would you contrast it with American?

Klinkowitz: I think there has been a very serious tradition in France, in Germany, in many of the South American countries, but what disenchanted me with the European scene is that it seemed the theory came first, the writers responded to it and created works, and then the critics went back full circle and said, "*Voilà*! It's now been produced." I don't think that situation happens in America. I disagree with Professor Hassan.   There does not seem to be a valid critical theory in America. Our best works have been written naïvely.

Kostelanetz: Best critical works or best literary works?

Klinkowitz: Best literary works. So what I'm trying to do is keep the criticism self-effacing to respond to the naïve genius that we see in these works.

Hassan: Well, I was referring, of course, to the critical schools, that is, the schools of criticism, the writers, and the theoreticians of criticism.   They are the ones that have a very strong and dogmatic outlook, and they can be characterized as post-structuralists or neo-Marxists or neo-Freudians and so forth.   But if I may make just a slightly different comment along the same lines that Mr. Simon and Mr. Klinkowitz made a moment ago, I think that what strikes me about the Europeans, in addition to what has been said, is that they still think of the essay as a very fluid and large statement of mind and they do not simply associate it with criticism in the narrower sense. And it's really wonderful to see how some European writers like Sartre or Camus or Butor could cover a very wide range of topics like bull fighting or painters or sometimes a literary work or sometimes a political subject or sometimes fashions of dress.   All of these are treated with such vivacity of mind that they compel attention.   To me, this is a very healthy manifestation: we should not identify the essay with criticism only. In fact, when you go back to its origins, you find that the essay treated a great many things, from how to go fishing in Izaak Walton to what is the meaning of truth in Bacon and to all the essays of Charles Lamb and Hazlitt.

Kostelanetz: So what you're suggesting is that criticism is really a sub-category of the essay as a genre?

Hassan: A special category, yes. A very fine one, but a special category.

Klinkowitz:　　And I disagree. I think criticism should be a response to the fiction. It breaks my heart when I see fiction writing following the essay. I'd like to turn that completely around.

Hassan:　　Once again we don't have any disagreement here because what I'm talking about is that if you are going to write criticism, by all means, do what you are saying. But not every one of us should write criticism.

Klinkowitz:　　No, not at all. But in Europe, especially in France, we have these marvellous literary intellectuals who write essays. In the United States, thankfully, we've been spared that. I think our fiction is the better for it.

Simon:　　I think our criticism is the better for it, too. I have to disagree with Mr. Hassan. I find people like Lacan and Derrida and Barthes and the rest of the boys unreadable in varying degrees— Barthes perhaps a little less unreadable than Lacan and Derrida. But all sufficiently unreadable and all sufficiently overintellectualized and sufficiently masturbatory to be of absolutely no use to the average reader who, I think, is still the man or woman for whom literature— or whatever the art form is—is being created.

Kostelanetz:　　"Overintellectualized" meaning?

Simon:　　Well, with Michel Foucault, for example, one feels it particularly: the critic assuming an adversary position to the man of ordinary common sense. If the man of common sense thinks that sex is such and such, then Foucault will prove that sex is really the opposite. And Derrida will take an obvious point and belabor it in the most esoteric and most vague way and write in the most arcane terminology until that obvious point no longer even retains its obviousness but is argued out of existence.

Kostelanetz:　　Well, I've always thought there was an Anglo-American tradition of empiricism in critical discourse, and that the New Critics extended it. I myself find this kind of European criticism to be terribly *foreign*; it doesn't seem like the kind of thing my mind relates to best.

Simon:　　May I just say this: I think that this kind of overcerebral, European literary criticism is really a form of one-upmanship and that American criticism, on the whole, tries to maintain contact with the readers and not to outsmart them, not to show them what fools they are, but tries to summarize, to epitomize their voices in the most palatable, the most pregnant, the most available yet lapidary form.

Hassan: I can see very clearly that the style of the post-structuralists and the people particularly that Mr. Simon mentioned can be difficult, perhaps even repulsive, certainly overelaborated, manifesting a kind of Byzantine Gongorism or involution that can be very offputting.

Simon: Hear, hear.

Hassan: What I do want to say is something else: that in Europe—and this is true not only of France but of the rest of Europe—there is a tradition of essay writing that the great writer himself or herself explores and exploits at the same time. So we have a figure like Thomas Mann writing some of the most marvelous essays on various subjects. You have figures like Camus and Sartre writing on many different subjects. It's very seldom that you see an American writer of stature like Hemingway or Faulkner writing in this fashion. This was, I think, the point I was trying to make.

Simon: That is true. I don't think one can disagree with that. It has to do with the fact that the American writer very seldom has the kind of broad culture that the European writer has. I mean, if Vonnegut's life depended on writing an essay on some speculative philosophical, scientific subject (other than, let's say, some narrow aspect of science that might interest him), some sociological or theological subject, he'd be lost, totally lost.

Kostelanetz: Is it a failure?

Simon: Well, it doesn't mean failure; it just means a different approach to literature. It is a more monomaniacal, more blinkered, more narrow-minded, more intense approach having to do with insufficient culture, insufficient education, but it produces very interesting results. I mean, race horses profit from wearing blinkers, and maybe writers to some extent and in some ways do, too. But you can't get that kind of contemplative play of ideas that Matthew Arnold advocated so eloquently and that people like Thomas Mann and Camus and others put to action.

Klinkowitz: When I look at the kind of essays Kurt Vonnegut has written, I think he's very smart that he didn't try to write an essay on phenomenology. But do we need an essay on phenomenology by Kurt Vonnegut? What have we had from him? An essay on the Maharishi, an essay on the Apollo 11 launch, an essay on the nation of Biafra, which back in 1971 he covered as a journalist. One person would say the way he writes is a blinkered approach; I would say it's a rather humble approach. He's an average guy. He experiences this, writes what it feels like to experience this.

Kostelanetz: I would say that it would be a more empirical, less theoretical approach.

Klinkowitz: Yes, total, utter empiricism.

Kostelanetz: And curiously one of the greatest essayists in modern American literature, to my mind, is Henry Miller.

Klinkowitz: For the same reason.

Hassan: And Norman Mailer. I think there are exceptions in America.

Kostelanetz: But it is a different kind of essay.

Hassan: Yes, it's a cultural essay; it's not a theoretical essay. I think there are a few writers that do take advantage of that, but not as many as you would find on the Continent.

Kostelanetz: What other American critics do you particularly respect? Mr. Simon?

Simon: Well, in my school of criticism, let's say, which is no school at all, people like Dwight Macdonald; like Robert Brustein; with grave strictures but nevertheless Eric Bentley.

Kostelanetz: By your school, do you mean drama critics or front-line men?

Simon: Yes, I mean front-line men. Wilfrid Sheed, for example; Stanley Kauffmann, with even graver strictures; and in an even more narrow sense—just as a film critic—Pauline Kael.

Kostelanetz: These are honest reviewers.

Simon: Yes, some of them. I think some of them go beyond that. Surely, Dwight Macdonald does.

Kostelanetz: Whose work initially appears in magazines.

Simon: Yes, usually.

Kostelanetz: Mr. Klinkowitz?

Klinkowitz: I admire Mr. Hassan immensely. He has been one of my finest teachers. Every book of his I read, I am retaught. I admire Robert Scholes. But what I am most interested in is a whole new crop of very young critics who are coming along. The book I'm reading this weekend, *John Barth*, by David Morrell, in which he studies every aspect of John Barth, his books, how he wrote them, when he wrote them, why he wrote them, talking to agents, publishers, editors. There is a young critic who has studied black American literature this way, John O'Brien. In Poland Jerzy Kutnik, who's doing this; in Hungary Zoltán Szilassy, who is doing this with American 1960s drama. It just seems to me an immensely fruitful involvement in the entire life of art, life of drama—all actions, not just what happens on the page but what happens in the reviews, what happens when someone gives a performance of their work, what do they do, how do they change it. It's covering every single base in artistic creation.

Kostelanetz: Mr. Hassan, who are the American critics that you particularly respect today?

Hassan: I'm very eclectic in my tastes and heterodox rather than orthodox. I think that schools of criticism or of thought have both their limitations and their strengths. Their strengths are obvious: they provide a form of reinforcement and of intensity of mind that has been used for centuries, back to the salons of the 18th century. But also such schools, such cliques if you wish, have their limitations because they make for a kind of blindness rather than insight, and they make for a parochialism.

Kostelanetz: They also have their own dynamics of people inspiring one another rather rapidly and energizing each other.

Hassan: Yes, that's the positive side. The negative side is the self-insulation that comes from this, so that you feel that you really haven't been recognized unless you are discussed by one in that particular group and not outside. So I'm very heterodox, and all the names that have been mentioned I do admire. I could add, for instance, people as different as Harold Bloom, Leslie Fiedler, and Susan Sontag, as well as all the people that have been mentioned.

Kostelanetz: How would you speak of Kenneth Burke?

Hassan: Now, he's coming back in a very interesting way in literary circles, and that is a phenomenon in itself. That is, he is very often perceived or re-visioned as one of the founders of current post-structuralist theories on native American grounds. I think that it's very difficult to give a final appraisal of Kenneth Burke because he is appropriated by different groups and seen in different ways by each one of these groups. But the man obviously has a great range and a body of ideas that is really very interesting and diverse.

Kostelanetz: Would you consider him a uniquely American phenomenon?

Hassan: Yes, definitely, very definitely.

I would like to ask about how the various critical vocations perceive each other and to what extent they can encourage a dialogue that is not flaccid, as you pointed out earlier, but at the same time that is not necessarily agonistic? What would be the relationship between the various modes of discourse, critical discourse in the country and the culture?

Simon: I would really like to see a bit of agonistic critical discourse. I think one of the things that I miss in our culture is the critical debate. There is very little of this.

Kostelanetz: Too many people talking too much to their friends.

Simon: Yes. There is, of course, such a thing as unfavorable reviews coming out, but usually that's it. Sometimes the author writes a little letter to the editors, rather lamely protesting the review he got. But there isn't the sort of thing that even *The Times Literary Supplement* used to generate in the old days in England where Robert Graves and whoever it was would have an extraordinarily long exchange of lengthy letters, tearing each other apart, which, I think was useful in stirring up excitement. The nearest thing we had to it in this country was the Nabokov-Wilson debate mostly in the *New York Review of Books*, but it spread to other publications.

Kostelanetz: Why do you think this is?

Simon: Because we have a kind of timidity and politeness that are very American about discussion, about offending other people, about hurting other people's feelings. It has something to do obviously with American history, with the pioneer spirit, which is not to attack one another but to stick together and conquer the frontier, holding hands as it were, not fighting one another, only the Indians, poor things. Whatever it is, it's some kind of terrible cameraderie.

Kostelanetz: I know you haven't met Mr. Klinkowitz and Mr. Hassan before. And you and I see each other no more than once every three years although we both live in New York. Yet we all engage in criticism.

Simon: Well, I would say that if this were France or England, one would meet in London or in Paris, but since this country is really half a continent, I guess, we don't meet one another. Even if we live in New York, the city may be too big and too busy to allow for that. And even in New York there are no cafés, for example. I mean the nearest thing we've got is Elaine's, but that is really a place where tourists go to catch a glimpse of Woody Allen or something like that. We don't have the Viennese literary café; we don't have the Café Royal that London had, or whatever. We don't have salons either. We don't have any sort of Old World, European graciousness that can be extended to the literary scene and can then give rise to interesting debates.

Kostelanetz: Would you say conversely that there's a virtue in perhaps not knowing people?

Simon: Well, every virtue has its other side, which is a vice, and every vice has its other side, which is a virtue.

Klinkowitz: I think too many American critics—and I include myself—are like 13-year-olds; we're great except when we congregate in groups of larger than three. Every time I see critics getting together to debate things, the most obnoxious type of schools form. I try to figure out why this is. We don't have a legitimate American academy, but we have the university structure, and we have Hollywood. They're the two places where writers can work, the two places where they're read.

Now, look what happens in the academy. John Gardner, who is a writer and a professor, puts out a book called *On Moral Fiction* in 1978. John Barth described it as an exercise in literary kneecapping. What this book adds to our knowledge of the world of art escapes me. We have professors who do this. Gerald Graff published a book, *Literature Against Itself*, which just pushes the argument out of fiction into styles of criticism. And where is something good or useful being produced in this? I fail to see it. I think we're best when we're left alone as servants. If we're daily reviewers, we stand between the work and the readers of the paper who will rely on this review: Should I go see the work? Should I buy the book? If we are scholars, I think again that we *serve* our students. We present the material and do not make judgments, especially preliminary judgments. When we get together in groups of more than three or four, it's just mayhem.

Simon: I would like to put in a good word for Gerald Graff's book. It's a very interesting book. It doesn't go far enough, but at least it combats some of the more sinister influences in American criticism.

Kostelanetz: What is his argument?

Simon: Well, his argument is against the people whom Mr. Hassan admires: against Harold Bloom, against the entire Yale school. . . .

Kostelanetz: On what grounds?

Simon: On grounds pretty much the same, I think, as mine: that they are too esoteric, that they're too overcerebral and simply lose contact with the reality of the work and the reality of living.

Hassan: I think that Graff's uneasiness about these new waves of criticism is, from my point of view, based not only on objections to style, which might be legitimate, but on an epistomology of realism that is a nostalgia not only for realism in fiction but a realism in all forms of discourse, so that there is an ascertainable relationship between the object out there in the world and the language that we use.

Kostelanetz: That we would call empiricism.

Hassan: Well, it is realistic in that it is associated with the great tradition of the 19th-century novel, in which novelists thought that they were dealing with reality outside there and not simply with problems of language. I am a great admirer of that tradition, but I also believe in history. And to believe in history is to believe in the possibility of change.

Kostelanetz: So what you're suggesting is that a 20th-century criticism should have the qualities of 20th-century literature?

Hassan: Well, if both of them are part of the larger climate of culture, I don't see how they can avoid that. On the other hand, they cannot imitate one another: that has been called the mimetic fallacy. So that you cannot, for instance, write a piece of criticism of a Mallarmé poem, let us say, and try to write another Mallarmé poem to do that.

Klinkowitz: Can I get back to Gerald Graff? What I regret about his work is not simply that he knocks down the critics, whose work I don't like myself, but that he takes the fiction with them. He talks about overcoming the Cartesian split. He dislikes the critics who do this. Well, he winds up dismissing the fiction writers who are trying to do that as well. I just noticed in the most recent edition of *American Literature* that Graff reviews a scholarly book by Robert Scholes called *Fabulation and Metafiction*. Now here Scholes is talking about writers who try to overcome the Cartesian split, and Graff says: "As somebody who likes to keep his objects pretty firmly out there and other, where I can keep an eye on them, I was mystified by this point [the point that Scholes makes as a critic] though I gathered that it has something to do with Love and Peace." He just completely dismisses the whole style of fiction.

In the *MMLA Bulletin* (the Midwest Modern Language Association) he begins a statement by saying: "Let me begin by making clear my own position. I believe that literature, or at least eminent literature, does make truth claims and it makes them in the precisely same way that non-literature makes them." The man is not simply a realist. He wants *War and Peace* to speak to him the way his bank statement speaks to him. Truth is truth, whether a fiction writer says it or whether an accountant says it. There is no difference between the two. Now this throws a lot of criticism out the window. It also throws all of the art of our time out the window. It's more than simply 19th-century realism.

Simon: All I can say is that I don't always agree with Graff, but at least he's not a fuzzy thinker and a bad writer like Robert Scholes, whom I consider deplorable in every way. That's all I am prepared to say about it here.

Kostelanetz: One fact that distinguishes America from other cultures, I think, is the sheer number of people writing and publishing literary criticism. I'm thinking not only of reviewers but of professors who have mastered the discipline of literary criticism. One result of abundance is variety. So that even among the best, as we have here, there are distinct differences, not only in subject and concern, but in critical approaches.

On Becoming a Pop Critic:
A Memoir and a Meditation

Leslie A. Fiedler

I have never known anybody who became a literary critic deliberately. Certainly I—after I gave up dreaming of becoming a cowboy, a fireman, a garbage collector, a revolutionary, an actor, a foreign correspondent, and a mouthpiece snatching gangsters from well-merited punishment—settled for thinking of myself as a poet-novelist and a teacher: a teacher who wrote, a writer who taught, I was never quite sure of the order. But I never think of myself as the critic-pedagogue I have become to most readers who know me at all. I have never ceased writing poetry and fiction; and even in the field of criticism I have remained an amateur, a dilettante, a "specialist" in nothing, preferring approximate insights to documented "facts" and passion to precision or rigor. I have said over and over in print and from the public platform that criticism is a kind of "literature," fiction about fiction, or it is nothing at all.

But there is much left unsaid even when I have added that I deal primarily not with "texts" but with the myths that underlay them, particularly the myth of the Outsider. For me "myths" are the opposite of "ideology": world views in the form of fables, entertained below the level of conscious belief and, indeed, sometimes in opposition to it. I read stories and poems, therefore, *cryptanalytically*, seeking revelations not only of the secret psyche of the writer but of the culture to which he belongs: the general culture, the communal dreams which bind us all together, however sophisticated or naïve we may be. Consequently, I have felt obliged (and this I have always known) not only to deal with popular as well as "high" art, but also (as I have just recently come to realize) to address, like a popular artist rather than an elite one, the mass audience rather than my professional peers.

I should have been aware of this earlier, since I began my career with an irreverent piece of pop criticism called "Come Back to the Raft Ag'in, Huck Honey." Even more confused about it than I was Philip Rahv, the editor who first accepted it for publication in *The Partisan Review*, only because, he insisted years later, he was convinced that it was a joke, a put-on of the academic community. And in this opinion the writers of the first fan letters it occasioned concurred—referring to it (troubled elitists turning always to French) as a *boutade*, a *canard*, a *jeu d'esprit*. But I was of course, in earnest; though the title was a booby trap, suggesting to the unwary—some of whom wrote me much less flattering letters, after searching in vain through the novel—that it was a direct quotation from *Huckleberry Finn* rather than an extrapolation, a not-quite-serious attempt to add a line of my own to a book I have always wished I might have written. And the jest has been consummated by John Seelye, who in *The True Huckleberry Finn* ironically rewrote that perfect novel to suit its caviling critics; so that not only do Huck and Nigger Jim in his version cuss more broadly than Twain let them and smoke pot on the raft, but Jim speaks my pseudo-quotation twice over.

More than three decades later, that article, rejected by the academic establishment and misunderstood even by some who thought they loved it, has entered the public domain, becoming part of a secondary myth larger than the book itself. Within the past couple of weeks, for instance, I have been sent a clipping from a Seattle newspaper which recommends a new dramatic production of *Huckleberry Finn* as "good family entertainment," then adds, "Apologies to Leslie Fiedler"; while in another from *The New York Times* a middle-aged commentator recounting his difficulties with his son writes, "and then he went off on a raft with Nigger Jim or Leslie Fiedler." Both clearly assume a response from many more people than have ever read my article or, indeed, the novel to which it refers.

What that larger audience believes, however, is that Fiedler (whoever the hell he is!) once claimed that Mark Twain's Huck and Jim (whom everyone knows from movies and television) were a pair of faggots buggering each other as they drifted down the Mississippi. What I actually contended, referring not just to *Huckleberry Finn* but other American classics like *The Leatherstocking Tales, Moby-Dick* etc., etc., was that, oddly enough in a society characterized on the conscious level by fear and distrust of what I called then "homoerotic love" ("male-bonding" has since become the fashionable euphemism), and by mutual violence between white and non-white Americans—there has appeared over and over in books written by white American authors the same myth of an idyllic anti-marriage: a life-long love, passionate though chaste, and consummated in the wilderness, on a whaling ship or a raft, anywhere but "home," between a white refugee from "civilization" and a dark-skinned "savage"—both of them male.

What is revealed in this archetypal story, I argued, is an aspect of our psycho-social fantasy life quite different from the nightmare of miscegenation and sexual jealousy which has cued most of our past history and a cause therefore for modest hope in the future. This hope has seemed justified (however slow the actual changes in the political arena) by the persistence of the myth since 1948, when my essay first appeared, in a score of movies like *The Defiant Ones*, *The Fortune Cookie* and the belated film version of Ken Kesey's *One Flew Over the Cuckoo's Nest*; as well as numerous television shows, ranging from *I Spy* to *Tenspeed and Brown Shoe*. And I am especially pleased that as we prepare for our entry into deep space and our first encounter with "aliens," we are taking with us that old American myth, embodied in the relationship of the very white Captain Kirk and his green-blooded Vulcan buddy, Mr. Spock, as portrayed in the cult television series *Star Trek*—one early review of which was quite properly headed: COME BACK TO THE SPACE SHIP AG'IN, SPOCK HONEY!

Encouraged by the early response to that little essay, at any rate, and eager to make clear that I really meant what I was saying, I fleshed out my original insights in three substantial volumes, *Love and Death in the American Novel* (1960), *Waiting for the End* (1964), and *The Return of the Vanishing American* (1968); then began to gather what I considered illustrative texts in our literature in a multi-volumed anthology only the first of which, called *O Brave New World*, ever appeared. That critical trilogy, however, turned out to be so thick and allusive and, I fear, so formidable and solemn, despite my frequent use of hyperbole and my occasional bad jokes, that it lost much freshness and consequently some of the large audience. It helped only a little when, conscious of this, I tried in a second edition (1966) to slim down the forbidding bulk of the first volume. I wanted also to illustrate it, figuring it high time to "show" as well as "tell" what was so fascinating about our tradition; but economics and a timid publisher stood in the way. Nonetheless, that volume has never gone out of print; and with the third, which coincided with the Indianizing mood of the late 1960s and actually became a kind of Youth Best Seller, particularly in French and German translations, I seem to have reached a new segment of the popular audience.

In that volume and more especially, perhaps, in the second edition, I tried to set my exploration of our homegrown myths in the context of that expectation of Apocalypse which has always possessed the American imagination: that endless waiting for the end of humanity, whether as a result of total atomic war, over-population, desecration of the environment, depletion of organic fuels, or—in the pop prophecy of science fiction—an invasion from outer space or the rapid mutation of our species into something no longer quite man. I had long read futurist fantasy; but only since realizing its connections with our chiliastic view of history, have I explored it in depth: compiling an anthology of my favorite stories with a long theoretical introduction under the title of *In Dreams Awake* (1976), reflecting on pioneers in the genre like Olaf Stapledon and Philip José Farmer, and writing such fiction myself, culminating in the most unread of all my books, *The Messengers Will Come No More* (1974).

Imagining the Future, however, is for me finally—as it is for most science fiction writers—just another way of discovering or inventing a useable past, which, as a vestigial Marxist, I believe is fate. Consequently, I have never used myth criticism as a way of denying history. For me, strange anti-Jungian Jungian that I am, the archetypes are not eternal but socially determined, changing as our relationship to the environment and each other changes. I have, therefore, traced the peculiarly American myths which concern me from the beginnings of our history to what really threatens to be its end: from the moment when ex-Europeans first encountered the nonwhite denizens of the New World wilderness to those fatal years during which we dropped the bomb on nonwhite Hiroshima and launched our last wilderness war in Vietnam. In the course of doing so, I have felt obliged to qualify the optimism of "Come Back to the Raft Ag'in, Huck Honey" by confronting what is negative and malign in our mythologies of race: especially the bad dream of genocide, and the implicit misogyny (specifically the hatred of white women) which complement and contradict the good dream of interethnic male bonding.

These concerns (obsessions, some have called them) inform my fiction as well, especially such studies of race and place as the novel *Back to China* (1965) and "The First Spade in the West," the third novella in a volume called *The Last Jew in America* (1966). And they appear not infrequently in the essays I have chosen to collect, all the way from the first book I ever published, *An End to Innocence* (1955), to *A Fiedler Reader* (1977). But they make perhaps their strangest most unexpected appearance in my long-postponed *The Stranger in Shakespeare* (1972), which I projected when I was young enough to know no better and finally wrote in grief and temporary exile.

I published in *Being Busted* (1970) a rather reticent account of the events which made me first an advocate of legalizing marijuana, which I do not smoke; then a felon, convicted of a crime which does   not exist; and at last led me to seek refuge in England, a country which I do not love, but where in self-defense, I began the required book on Shakespeare I swore I would never do. Divided into four sections, "The Woman as Stranger," "The Jew as Stranger," "The Black Man as Stranger," and "The New World Savage as Stranger," that book examines the way in which Shakespeare sometimes ironically undercuts, sometimes slavishly accepts the stereotypical attitudes of his time toward the relationships of male and female, Black and White, Jew and Gentile, Old World "culture"and New World "barbarism."

It ends, therefore, though it is, in fact, the only book I have entirely written abroad, by bringing me back home again; which is to say, to Prospero's island and that prototypical American, Caliban. Not only does that "Monster" in relationship to the "Master of Arts" represent the fate of the Indian under the yoke of European imperialism, but he foreshadows the plight of white Americans as well: those refugees from Europe whose consciousness was altered by the confrontation with an alternative way of being human into something new under the sun—different from and profoundly troubling to the European mind. "Ca-Ca-Caliban,/Have a New Master,/ Be a new man," D. H. Lawrence quotes from his chant, suggesting that it has remained the theme song of America ever since; and James Joyce in *Ulysses* refers snidely to the immigrant Irish as "Patsy Caliban, our American cousin"—both illustrating the persistence of that mythological figure at the heart of European anti-Americanism.

In part, no doubt, because of its concessions to pedantry, *The Stranger in Shakespeare* has been chiefly read by professional Shakespeareans, interested in *Othello*, *The Merchant of Venice*, and *The Tempest* as texts for classroom analysis, rather than general readers, more interested in what they have to say about misogyny, anti-Semitism, and xenophobia. And such scholars have responded in

the main—as they have in fact to all of my work—by publicly vilify-
ing it, while storing away its insights for future use, without acknowledgement, of course. It is a major mystery of my career (of
which I have been reminded recently by a young East Indian just
finishing a Ph.D. dissertation on my criticism) that I have come to be
regarded as a "seminal" though "controversial" critic, even though
almost everyone of my books has been more scorned than praised
in the academic and literary reviews; and I have graduated—in the
view of my critics—from the status of *enfant terrible* to that of "dirty
old man" without passing through decent maturity. I have long since
ceased reading such responses, but my best friends insist on telling
me all about them, and I have ended with a sense of needing to get
through or around the official critics to my proper audience: those
who return over and over (as I do) to popular authors like Twain and
Dickens, but never read anything labelled "criticism" which deals with
them.

It has occurred to me that one way to do this is to bypass print
by returning to the "archaic" public lecture, the Chautauqua—or even
better, by taking advantage of what persists of that older popular form
in the newer media, particularly the talk show on television. There
was a moment during the 1960s when the format of the Merv Griffin
Show, for instance, had come to include—along with an aging actress,
a current pop music star, and a stand-up comedian—a visiting "nut,"
at that point usually Allen Ginsberg or Norman Mailer, or occasionally, as it turned out, me. After all, I had learned to communicate, beginning at age 13 or 14, on a street-corner soapbox, and I have always
enjoyed lecturing to large classes inside the university, where the
sense of public speech lives on. Moreover, it seemed to me after
having published four or five books, that I was beginning (despite my
invariable practice of never writing down a sentence until I have
listened to it in my own head) to lose the sense of addressing a living,
listening audience. Not that I have ever ceased venturing outside the
classroom, addressing anyone who would invite me, book study
groups in Whitefish, Montana, for instance, or monthly meetings of
organizations with names like the "As You Like It Club," where
everyone in attendance was likely to be knitting furiously as I talked
about, say, *Finnegans Wake*.

But somehow television came closer to giving me the sense of
a connection with a responsive nonacademic audience that I had
experienced for the first time when someone in a heterogeneous group

of listeners (it was in a park, as I recall, on the South Side of Chicago)
screamed, "Now you're 'preachin,' brother. Go right on 'preachin.'"
But television ran out for me after a while; perhaps when some clown
clapped me on the back after I had sat hopefully for an hour backstage
in the Green Room, only to be cancelled out of the show because that
night's comedian had been especially hot, and said (I swear it), "Well,
that's show biz." Or maybe it was the obnoxious business agent who
bullied me into joining the American Federation of Television and
Radio Actors after my second appearance on prime time. Still, being
a member of AFTRA meant being paid "scale," so that before I quit I
was able to buy a large-screen color television for my kids, whom I
made promise in return (I was then still the victim of vestigial elitism)
that they would never watch me on it.

After a while, however, I stopped paying my union dues and,
though I never ceased entirely talking to the cameras, returned to the
college lecture circuit. At that point I had become incapable of
committing anything to paper which I had not previously tried out
viva voce several times; but I felt that the need of doing so before
auditors able and willing to talk back, as a studio audience typically
does not. Students and teachers, even when they do not really listen,
make responsive noises; and besides they, like me, are accustomed to
50 and 60-minute presentations rather than the three, four or five-
minute *shticks* television format demands. For such reasons among
others, I feel at home with university audiences, even in remote places
like Japan and India and Brazil, where more and more I have tended
to wander (Europe having somehow used up its cultural usefulness to
me) whenever I temporarily leave my own country.

That I had nonetheless not really escaped "show biz" I did not
realize until a couple of lecture agents recruited me, upping my fees
and making it possible for me to deliver my same old talks before
church groups, social workers, and dermatologists, as well as at
"star"-studded Symposia on the Urban Experience, Aging, Child
Abuse and the Influence of D. H. Lawrence—held often enough in
colleges, but subsidized by federal agencies, foundations, sometimes,
indeed, the C.I.A. Actually, I had written by 1963 a novel called *The
Second Stone* about a World Congress on Love held in Rome under
American auspices, which is doubly disrupted when the wife of the
theologian-organizer falls in love with an expatriate American loser,
a writer who does not write, and the deliberations of the assembled
critics, poets, shrinks, and gurus are drowned out by the shouts of

demonstrators, convinced by the Italian Communist Party that the whole thing is a C.I.A. plot. It turns out that American intelligence has indeed, without the knowledge of the organizers, picked up the tab for reasons which no one is ever able to understand—not even I who write the book.

What I was, however, beginning to understand then, and what has become clearer to me since is the equally ironic fact that one does not cease being an "entertainer" by leaving lowbrow talk shows for highbrow symposia. The television cameras grind away even there; since, however elitist in their aspirations, such assemblages are a part of that "popular culture" which, to be sure, sometimes these days they rather condescendingly discuss. Even before the fashion changed, I had been dealing with such matters, publishing in the 1950s what I fondly believe to be the first apology for the Superman comics. Yet like my colleagues then and now, I, too, condescended to, when I did not actually deplore or scold the producers and distributors of "commodity" art. To be sure, I made exceptions occasionally—for *ukiyoe*, for instance, the popular woodblock engravings of whores and actors mass-produced in Japan after the middle of the 18th century; and the best-selling novels of Richardson and Dickens and Mark Twain. But the latter I would not confess for a long time, even to myself, were as much "mass culture" as Class B movies, television sitcoms—and my own platform performances.

Nonetheless, I found myself dealing more and more with unequivocal, unredeemed printed "pop": pulp science fiction, hardcore pornography, the fairy tale, as well as fiction by novelists never accepted into the canon of o.k. art, like Conan Doyle, Bram Stoker, Rider Haggard, L. Frank Baum, and Margaret Mitchell. Nor have I ignored the post-Gutenburg "media," from the semi-iconic comics to Class B movies (celebrating, for instance, Russ Meyer's atrociously wonderful *Beyond the Valley of the Dolls*) and the day-time serials on television. It was during a public argument with Lionel Trilling on the "soaps" that I became fully aware: first, of how obsessed I had become with such uncanonical literature; second, of how I had passed from snide analysis to passionate apology; and finally, of how equivocal the position of elitist critics of the "media" had become, particularly if they were teachers in the mass American university. The occasion of my argument with Trilling was especially revealing, since we spoke side by side with a crew which included *inter alia* three Nobel Prize winners, a radical feminist, a black insurgent, and Truman Capote at a Symposium of the Future of Almost Everything, sponsored by I.T.T.—in the interests, I gathered, of real estate development in Florida.

I have written and talked all my life long under the sponsorship of anyone willing to let me publish what I believed at that moment (my not-so-secret motto being, "Often wrong, but never in doubt") and to pay me for my effort. Such sponsors have ranged from a magazine later revealed as subsidized by the C.I.A. to the magazine which revealed that fact; and from institutions funded with money left by America's robber barons to the Writers Union of Romania. I am not troubled therefore by the impurity of I.T.T.'s money or motives, only by my own long-term ignorance of what they were paying me for; which, quite simply put, is to allay boredom by making our country and culture seem more amusing and interesting than most academic accounts would have us believe. What has bugged me, however, ever since I came to realize this, is the fact that most of my readers are likely to have encountered, say, *Love and Death in the American Novel* on assignment in the classroom: a context which falsifies it as much as does reading *Huckleberry Finn* under similar circumstances.

Nor have I, alas, succeeded in breaking out of that trap with my fiction; yet surprisingly enough I have begun to do so with my last long nonfiction work, *Freaks: Myths and Images of the Secret Self* (1978): a book so equivocally "inter-disciplinary" that library cataloguers did not know whether to classify it under "psychology," "sociology," or "literary criticism." Actually, my model for it (a secret guessed by one acute reviewer) was Richard Burton's *Anatomy of Melancholy*, which would make it, I guess, what used to be called *belles lettres*; though it has, in fact, intrigued chiefly "soft" and semi-"soft" scientists, longing to rejoin the humanities. The last couple of times I have talked about it in public, at any rate, I did so at a meeting of the Association of Medical Schools and before a group of professional sociologists—with whom most of my own colleagues believe we have no language in common. Nonetheless, though it delighted me to have escaped the church of True Believers—English majors, fellow teachers, and literary critics—I am a little distressed by the fact that my auditors were academics still.

Before that, however—under the auspices of my super-hype, hardsell publishers—I had spoken about that same book on the Dick Cavett Show, the Today Show, the Tomorrow Show, the Phil Donahue Show (where I appeared side by side with actual freaks), plus God knows how many others on radio and television. There sweating in my make-up under the hot lights, I had to discuss what I had written with interviewers few of whom had read *Freaks* and some of whom did not even know my name, though they (or their more literate assistants) were aware that it had been reviewed not only in respectable literary journals like *The New York Review*, but in the more popular press, including *The New York Daily News*, *Penthouse*, *Hustler*, and *High Times*—the last, by the way, convincing my 15-year-old son for the first time that I was to be taken seriously as a writer. Moreover, it turned out that a fledgling writer-director-producer of a G-rated fantasy-romance was watching a local Los Angeles interview show in which I confessed that I had always thought of myself as an actor and was getting tired of the single role of professor I had been playing for 40 years; as a result of which I ended up joining this time not AFTRA but the Screen Actors Guild, and before my three weeks as a film actor were over, had been mentioned in the gossip column of the *Hollywood Reporter*.

The movie in which I play, appropriately enough side by side with a dwarf, has not yet been released and may remain bogged down in "post-production difficulties" forever. But what media attention my brief film career attracted has confirmed the worst fears of certain high-minded colleagues, who had already begun to think of me as an apostate from high art: a self-styled critic who had forgotten how to be "rigorous" (they are not amused when I remind them from time to time that the extreme form of rigor is *rigor mortis*), i.e., how to deal, in language accessible only to initiates, exclusively with "Great Books"—or even better, pure literary theory. Before publication, I had as a kind of try-out delivered a talk on freaks and their significance at Johns Hopkins University, where most of the audience ("post-structuralist" to a man) walked away afterwards mournfully shaking their heads and observing just loud enough for me to overhear that this is where they knew I would end up, writing *pop criticism!*

But that is, indeed, where I was headed from the start, though I had temporarily gone astray on the way to publication and tenure; and to get back to the mass audience I once dreamed of addressing, I realized that I must learn to deal with archetypes not as they are embodied in works like, say, Ezra Pound's *Cantos* and James Joyce's *Ulysses*, or even *Moby-Dick* and *Huckleberry Finn*. Justly or unjustly (but, in any case, largely through the efforts of teachers like me) such books have come to be thought of as remote and canonical, a part of "required" rather than optional literature—and they have therefore ceased to move ordinary men and women as myth moves them. Better, it seemed to me, to confront "images of the secret self" as they have been made flesh in congenital malformations, displayed for the profit of their exhibitors, as well as the edification and amusement of the mass audience, in sideshows, dime museums, at fairs and carnivals, and in popular movies made about such shows, like Todd Browning's extraordinary *Freaks*. Though never exhibited without words, printed or spoken, human anomalies have always been perceived visually first of all; and I determined consequently that my *Freaks* would be—at long last—an illustrated book; or rather one with an alternative iconic text side by side with the printed one: a kind of gloss or translation for the benefit of the many in our culture who read pictures better than Gutenberg type-face.

It is, therefore, possible to look at nothing but the illustrations in my book and have a real sense of what it is all about. Indeed, some—as I have been learning recently—have done precisely this; like the group of ten to twelve-year-old boys who, a librarian in South Philadelphia writes, come day after day to stare at my book, which she has exhibited under glass, turning—at their request—to a new picture daily. In light of this, it seems only just that *Freaks* is about to be reborn without any printed text at all; is—at this very moment—being translated into a full-length documentary film to be shown, if all goes well, at neighborhood theaters some time in 1981. There it will be seen by some who ordinarily do not read books at all, or for that matter willingly attend "documentaries," unless, as in this case, they are lured in by the aura of taboo, mystery, and magic, which clings to congenital malformations as it does to few things in our secular, neutralized world. Only *Mondo Cane*, the producers tell me, of all nonfiction cinema has made it at the box office, because of its subject matter, monstrous and grotesque to the point of pornography. If *Freaks* works in the same way, doubtless I will be (though I have no control over the script) accused of "exploitation" and "selling out." I will, however, have become a full-fledged pop critic at last, having made it into the movies, not as I had fondly hoped with one of my more scandalous stories ("Nude Croquet" was not only banned in Tennessee, it twice seemed on the verge of being filmed) but with a piece of socio-psychological nonfiction, an historical study of one of the oldest of the popular arts, "pop criticism," in short.

Post Script

I am presently at work on a long theoretical book exploring the implications of my new understanding of the literary arts, popular and elite. Called *What Was Literature?*, it extends earlier suggestions for subverting the distinction between high and low literature and changing the traditional ways we have taught "English" which have already moved certain of my stuffier colleagues to call for my resignation from the profession. Some of the directions in which I propose in light of all this to open up the canon of American literature are sketched in a just-published essay (first delivered as a series of lectures over Canadian radio) called *The Inadvertent Epic*, in which I reassess a series of popular books including *Uncle Tom's Cabin*, *Gone With the Wind*, and Alex Haley's *Roots*.

Clearly *What Was Literature?* will be my last critical book; after which I will return full time to poetry and fiction, especially, I think, to the oldest of popular forms, the fairy tale. (I am awaiting the publication at the moment, in fact, of my doggerel English version—intended for children—of the Japanese *märchen*, *The Little Peach Boy*, and a story, "What Used to be Called Dead," that begins like a fairy tale and ends as science fiction.) Or maybe instead I will renew my membership in SAG and AFTRA, perhaps even try to qualify for the Screen Writers Guild. After all, I have never written a film script. Not yet, anyhow.

Bibliography

By Leslie A. Fiedler:

An End to Innocence: Essays on Culture and Politics. Boston: Beacon Press, 1955.
Love and Death in the American Novel. New York: Criterion Books, 1960; revised edition, New York: Stein and Day, 1966; London: Cape, 1967.
Waiting for the End. New York: Stein and Day, 1964; as *Waiting for the End: The American Literary Scene from Hemingway to Baldwin*, London: Cape, 1965.
Back to China. New York: Stein and Day, 1965. (Novel)
The Last Jew in America. New York: Stein and Day, 1966. (Short stories)
The Return of the Vanishing American. New York: Stein and Day, 1968; London: Cape, 1968.
Being Busted. New York: Stein and Day, 1970; London: Secker & Warburg, 1970.
The Collected Essays of Leslie Fiedler. New York: Stein and Day, 1971.
The Stranger in Shakespeare. New York: Stein and Day, 1972; London: Croom Helm, 1973.
The Messengers Will Come No More. New York: Stein and Day, 1974. (Novel)
A Fiedler Reader. New York: Stein and Day, 1977.
Freaks: Myths and Images of the Secret Self. New York: Simon and Schuster, 1978.

About Leslie A. Fiedler:

Kostelanetz, Richard. "Leslie A. Fiedler." In *Twenties in the Sixties.* Westport, Connecticut, and London: Greenwood Press, 1979.
Krim, Seymour. "Leslie Fiedler's Bronco Ride from Pocahontas to Marjorie Morningstar." In *Shake It for the World, Smartass.* New York: Dial Press, 1970.

The Voice of America and the
Voice of Eric Bentley

VOA: Do you think of yourself as Eric Bentley the critic? Or Eric Bentley the playwright? Or under some third or fourth heading? Your work has been in more fields than one, but do you think of yourself as mainly one thing?

Bentley: Yes: a writer. The term is broad enough to embrace several kinds of writing. My non-writing activities, even teaching, I would consider for me, subordinate. Performing—yes, I have sung in nightclubs, and have recorded Brecht songs and the like—was subordinate. So was stage directing.

VOA: Would you divide up for us—or join together, if you prefer—the different kinds of writing you have done? We see for ourselves—glancing at the list of your publications*—what they are. You have been a theater reviewer for a magazine and a critic and historian of the drama on a fairly grand scale. You gave the Norton Lectures at Harvard and published them as *The Life of the Drama*. You've translated European playwrights—Brecht, Pirandello. Then, in the 1970s, we began to see plays of your own on stage: *Are You Now Or Have You Ever Been* (1972) at Ford's Theatre in Washington, D.C.— and hasn't that play recently been published and produced in West Germany?

Is this all one person?

Bentley: Or do I have ghost writers on my payroll? No. On the contrary, I myself sometimes write under another name.... Whatever shows up in a person in later life has been there all along. The public may not have known but the person himself couldn't avoid knowing. Well, I'm what today's students would call a theater nut. Stage struck, if you will. Yes, even after everyone has proved that the theater is

---

* At the end of this dialogue.

finished, that the future is with television or whatnot! Does the future interest me? Possibly. Does the theater interest me? Definitely. That's the difference. Some people have to imbibe peanuts all the time. Others have to do endless crossword puzzles. I have to *make theater*.

VOA: But such a compulsion, surely, doesn't inevitably make a person both a critic and a creator?

Bentley: Then let me tell how all that evolved. As an infant, one sees performers and picks up the art of acting—in my case it was seaside "Pierrots" on a beach in North Wales. So I didn't begin as a writer. I began as an actor. But then so did many other theater writers. . . . Then comes education. School gave me the chance to do somewhat more mature acting but, more importantly, shifted my interest somewhat from *acting* to—not yet *writing* but certainly to *conceiving* and *comprehending* not to mention a certain degree of *knowing*. School and university. I went all the way through with that—to the Ph.D. And my earliest publications reflect the process directly: me informing myself—and passing the information on.

VOA: Turning again to this list of your publications, are the early, scholarly titles on the lines of graduate papers, doctoral dissertations?

Bentley: Oh, yes. A master's thesis I wrote at Oxford never saw the light except as a couple of essays in a review. My Yale doctoral thesis, revised, became my first published book, *A Century of Hero Worship* (1944), a study in the history of ideas.

VOA: Then came a book still in print which many of us read in college days, *The Playwright as Thinker*(1946). Was that your first book written for others and not as part of your own education?

Bentley: I hope others find it properly addressed to them and their interests, but in the first instance I did the work on that manuscript, yes, in order to inform and educate myself. And you're getting warm now. I had at last got to what was always going to be my subject: theater. This was my first book about it. For I had discovered my ignorance. Theater was my subject, but I knew nothing about it. I must find out. My job at the time was teaching at Black Mountain College. May I teach drama? I asked. I had been teaching history. And it was the kind of college where they gave a teacher his head. I got all the drama books out of the library, took notes, talked, listened to student discussion, then wrote *The Playwright as Thinker*.

VOA: The book came out of books, then, not out of theater, not out of performance?

Bentley: Unavoidably.

VOA: You would have preferred it otherwise?

Bentley: I didn't say *that*. I just said (in effect) that I didn't *get* it otherwise. And Nietzsche taught me to try to love my fate. Well, my fate has been to miss out on . . . so many things. But there was always a book in my hands. Several books. I like to live surrounded by books, and I do live surrounded by books.

VOA: Not surrounded by actors?

Bentley: Huh? Come right out with it!

VOA: As a dramatic critic, are you over-literary? Some people after all wouldn't concede that theater is primarily literary. Or even verbal.

Bentley: Things of mine have even been quoted to that effect, but I don't believe I want, here and now, to endorse them. If I'm outlining the evolution of my own consciousness, I should, instead, readily concede that, as its title suggests, *The Playwright as Thinker* did propose a literary theater.

VOA: Playwrights primarily as thinkers?

Bentley: No. Does the title suggest *that*? The book does not go that far. Doesn't say "only thinkers" or even "primarily thinkers," only that even playwrights think, drama is not mindless.

VOA: Did someone say it was?

Bentley: You bet your life. Everyone was saying it was at the time. Especially George Jean Nathan—himself the best mind, the brightest intellect among the drama critics of the day.

VOA: But were you *anti*-theatrical?

Bentley: Absolutely not. I was just saying theater needn't be mindless.

VOA: But, for you, the script was always the heart of the matter, was it not?

Bentley: The play's the thing? Ye-e-es, I have generally been happiest with theaters where the play was the thing: where the inspiration radiated outwards from the playwright—a Molière, an Ibsen, a Brecht.

VOA: So that the others are judged as interpreters of the playwright and condemned if they "misinterpret" him?

Bentley: I was happiest in a theater where that was the assumption, yes. But I also had occasional "happiness" from something different: the idea of a silent theater—mind, silent film. Dance as a theatrical art in its own way. Opera which, however dramatic it may become, does not give the librettist the place of honor. . . .

VOA: All of which is discussed in *The Playwright as Thinker*?

Bentley: Much of it is. But I hadn't finished putting my views together at that time. I mean that my views would develop a bit *after* that time.

VOA: The emphasis changed, didn't it? From thinkers and from literature to executors—is that the word?—and performance? Your next books—as of the early 1950s—reflect this change even in their titles: *In Search of Theater* (1953), *The Dramatic Event* (1954), *What is Theater?* (1956).

Bentley: And I had indeed been moved, in the meanwhile, from the library stacks to the critic's seat on the theater aisle.

VOA: You *were* moved—you didn't just go?

Bentley: I was placed there by editors who asked me to review shows. I accepted—to get free seats, yes, to get paid for writing, yes—but above all to get into the next phase of my life. What I needed before was educational background: first in history and languages; second, book knowledge of dramatic literature. Now I needed to see those dreams acted out. I needed to learn what acting was like—any acting, to begin with. Then I would need to find out how far the art of acting can go—what the best actors can manage to achieve.

VOA: You say "acting." Is that a good synonym for "theater"? What about directing, stage design, choreography, music?

Bentley: Indeed! Sometimes I think music is the key to all the rest. Especially rhythm—it's everything. When I work in the theater, I feel that my theatrical sense is underpinned chiefly by my sense of movement as I know movement from music. Wagner said his operas were endless melody, and I think that is perhaps what any of the temporal arts should be. . . .

VOA: Yet, when you said drama, you spoke of writers; and when you say theater, you at once speak of actors.

Bentley: Yes. The musicians are not the principal people in the dramatic theater; the actors are. My only qualifier is that an actor should be a musician too in a profound sense—not the player of violin, necessarily, but the possessor of a rhythmic sense as fine as a violinist's. Or a dancer's.

VOA: For the sake of his gestures? Body movement?

Bentley: For everything. When Ina Claire spoke a comic line, it had a rhythmic subtlety and precision like that of Horowitz playing Chopin.

VOA: So you made it your business to see actors. Ordinary but also *extra*ordinary actors. This was in the late 1940s, early, middle 1950s?

Bentley: And, when I could, ever since.

VOA: You made yourself an expert on the texts early on? Then you spent at least ten years becoming expert on the *performance* of texts? From *In Search of Theatre*, I note that this "search" took you outside the U.S. back to your native Britain and thence to France, Germany, Italy? Is acting equally bad—or good—in all countries?

Bentley: Countries with a strong theatrical tradition have a marked advantage: Sweden, Germany. . . . But I was not making a comparative study nation by nation. Just looking for what was outstandingly good anywhere.

VOA: You were the discoverer of the Berlin Ensemble? Also Felsenstein's Komische Oper in East Berlin?

Bentley: Let's say I turned up at quite an early date. With Brecht I was already associated before he founded the Berlin Ensemble in 1949: I simply followed him to Berlin, where he told me the only other company worth seeing was the Komische Oper company. And Brecht introduced me to Felsenstein, who had just founded *that* company. Through Felsenstein I learned what opera could do with theater— what opera would be if it was not the more boring thing that it generally is. If not more boring, less dramatic.

VOA: And Brecht? Or is that the 64-dollar question for you?

Bentley: It's my fate anyway, to be asked that question, and as I say, I try to love my fate.

VOA: A vision of Jesus made clear to St. Paul what religion would be for him from then on. Did meeting with Bertolt Brecht make clear to you what theater would always be for you from then on?

Bentley: I did pick up more about theater from BB than from any other person I have ever met. Yes. Yes.

VOA: His celebrated theories?

Bentley: No. No. His savvy, his talent, his genius, *anything* but his theories. What's more: in Brecht—in my relationship with him— I lived that whole transition from theater as book to theater as performance. You see, I read him first. No one was performing BB back then. But I also talked with him. Then—last phase—I saw his work on stage, beginning with his own production of *Galileo* in

Hollywood in 1947, following through with his *Mother Courage* in Berlin, 1949. And when BB directed *Courage* in Munich, 1950, I assisted him and was at all rehearsals.

VOA: There's a notation on the desk here—one of our staff must have written it—"For Bentley nothing has happened *since* Brecht. Anything later he rejects on Brechtian grounds."

Bentley: Well, well, is that the younger generation knocking at my door? Scary. I am supposed to have rejected everything since BB's death in 1956? No, no, I seem to remember giving *Waiting for Godot* a rather favorable write-up, was not always unfavorable to Ionesco, Dürrenmatt, Frisch in the 1950s and 1960s . . . and today do not "reject" all of Pinter, Sam Shepard, Albee, Mamet. . . .

VOA: To use your own word *happy*, have you been as *happy* with any playwright since the 1950s as you were with Shaw and Brecht before that?

Bentley: A weighty question indeed! You are mentioning men who made the greatest possible impact on me as a youth. Can any later impact equal something of *that* sort?

VOA: Well, but did Brecht put you in blinkers and prevent you seeing the things that are invisible to Brechtianism?

Bentley: Obviously I have to hope not. But I see *some* force in your argument. When I glance back over my work of the past several decades, I do see that some writers took a beating from me mainly because they were not Brechtian enough: I did not do full justice to the non-Brechtians, to writers of, say, a surreal or subjectivist tendency. Today, I think some of my criteria were over-austere, Puritanic.

VOA: Too didactic?

Bentley: I'm not sure on that. What I do see is a certain prejudice against, say, Jean Cocteau, Christian Bérard, Cecil Beaton, a theater I too easily dismissed as decadent. . . .

VOA: Did you mean homosexual?

Bentley: Oh, dear, another weighty question!

VOA: Not to be too personal, but also in our notes is that, in the 1970s, you championed Gay Liberation in speeches, essays, songs, plays. . . . Not to mention your dramatization of the trials of Oscar Wilde.

Bentley: You are giving me too much to respond to all at once: Let me take one of the easier points. In the days before Gay Liberation, a lot of . . . well, especially the designers were gay and had a style that was even called gay—it certainly signalled the authors' gayness to their audience. I called it the Bonwit Teller Window style. Beaton, Messel, Bérard, Raoul Pène du Bois, many others. "Gay" colors, so-called, lavender, pink, yellow. Now these colors and that style were the opposite of "Brecht." And was I not a Brechtian, *the* Brechtian? A contradiction here then? Only if it is assumed that homosexuals as such are addicted to lavender, pink and yellow. I for my part had been seduced by BB's blacks, greys, and browns. So I wasn't exactly getting in position for Gay Liberation, was I? But then what's wrong with black, grey, and brown?

VOA: You were not a regular theater reviewer for very long, were you? On *The New Republic*?

Bentley: Only four years, '52 to '56.

VOA: What was the next step?

Bentley: Well, throughout these various periods in my life, I was teaching—mostly at Columbia University. And some of the writing I did reflected the teaching experience.

VOA: No longer just the learning experience?

Bentley: Perhaps I was *learning* to *teach*. Anyway, at the end of the 1950s Harvard asked me to give the Norton Lectures. I said: on what? They said: tell your students what theater means to you. Bull's eye! They had sent their arrow right at what had always been my own target! It was a challenge and today my attempt to meet it survives as the book *The Life of the Drama*, my main contribution to theory in my field. For those who are interested in how long things take, let me mention that such a theoretical book had been my project when first I got a Guggenheim Fellowship in '48. *The Life of the Drama* didn't come out till '64. Even theory takes a long time to mature, at least with me. Ideas are not what I start out from: they emerge, and rather reluctantly, from observation, from experience.

VOA: Is it possible to encapsulize such a large book for us here?

Bentley: I should hope not. What I can do is cite what surprised me most about it when it was done. My friends had said it would be an elaboration of Brecht's ideas. I myself thought it might be Aristotle's *Poetics* as rephrased by a Freudian—I was being "analyzed" in those years. What surprised me was that the philosophy of theater in the book was neither Brecht (my "father") nor Freud (my "guru" at the time) but Pirandello, one of a number of Europeans I had translated. He saw life as role-playing.

VOA: But by 1980 isn't that idea a commonplace of psychiatry?

Bentley: Except that the psychiatrists earn their money by promising *a release* from role-playing. You discover the real you, remember? Nothing different there from what you learned at mother's knee! The different thing in Pirandello was: *all* life is role-playing. No way out. "All the men and women *merely* players. . . ."

VOA: But is that true? Or perhaps we should only ask: Did you *take* it to be true?

Bentley: I took it to be an explanation of theater, or as near to such an explanation as we shall ever get. Theater provides an image of life, *the* image of life, because *life is a theater.*

VOA: "All the world's a stage." That's not Pirandello, it's Shakespeare.

Bentley: Shakespeare didn't mean it. Pirandello did. For Shakespeare, or maybe just for his Jacques who says the line, the notion is merely illustrative. At best a comparison: life reminds one of drama in one or two vivid ways. No problem is seen therein. In Pirandello it is all problem—even agony—that one cannot escape play-acting. If there is any truth in that, then theater embodies the profoundest pain and conflict—a whole destiny.

VOA: Then you do believe Pirandellianism is true!

Bentley: Obviously I am convinced there is something to it. Much. But what I was most convinced of was that it brought me to the center of my particular subject, the subject of my life's intellectual-spiritual effort.

VOA: Just Pirandello? No other helpers?

Bentley: I have written an essay—which perhaps should have been in *The Life of the Drama* but which I hadn't yet conceived at the time—about a latter-day Pirandellian, J. L. Moreno.

VOA: The founder of Psychodrama?

Bentley: Exactly. Terrible writer. Which is why so few have read him. If only he had wielded a more eloquent pen, either in German or English, I think he would today be regarded as one of the leading psychologists of this century.

VOA: But if he expressed himself badly, how do you know what he thought?

Bentley: Not just from his books, it's true. I knew *him.* I witnessed his group therapy sessions.

VOA: You don't mean you found some sort of "Final Answer" in Moreno, the way others have in some of the big-name gurus?

Bentley: No. Not at all. I was interested in confirmation for Pirandello, dramatist and philosopher of drama, in the work of a clinician with patients. Life is dramatic: that is a very general notion but there are many fascinating specifics to it—in the details of role-playing, of drama-building. Drama is important because all human beings dramatize all the time. It seems to be the only way to reach out, to try to grasp, to visualize oneself and others, to recapitulate the past, to plan the future. Scenarios. Enactments. A dramatist is just a man who makes a *work of art* out of constructs which all of us put together inartistically.

VOA: Hearing you say that, I do seem to be hearing a man arriving at a conclusion he has been seeking all his life.

Bentley: No, no, no, just a fruitful hypothesis congenial to the modern mind! Aristotle might have found it boring. Besides, my life hasn't ended yet. Or, just in case I die tonight, let me say: my life hadn't ended when I wrote about Pirandello and Moreno in the late 1960s.

VOA: You went on to become a playwright?

Bentley: Thank you. But I shan't venture to claim, either, that playwriting was the culmination of everything I had ever done. Just my attempt, at long last, to try my hand at the work I had long regarded as central in my chosen field.

VOA: Did this seem sudden when it came? I know some people thought it rather a . . . plunge.

Bentley: It wasn't. I had approached it gingerly, gradually. As a translator, mainly. Jerome Robbins told me once he had to dream himself the author when he studied a play he was going to direct. I always dreamed myself the author when I translated. That was why I translated—notable addition to my dream life! A sort of Walter Mitty fantasy when the author I translated seemed immeasurably greater than myself! Sometimes it was a relief to translate the less sublime authors. Or the less sublime works of the more sublime authors. And touch them up a bit. There's creativity for you! "Additional lyrics by. . . ." And that is how one injects oneself into the pages of Art. I must have been ambitious to do that, for I was becoming progressively more meddlesome. Translations were becoming adaptations. Next step my own name under the title and above the phrase "Based on . . ."! I was now a playwright.

VOA: You have written a well-known play, *Are You Now Or Have You Ever Been*, to which these remarks don't seem to apply.

Bentley: No? It is not quite "a play by Eric Bentley" because none of the dialogue is original. I took it all from the historical record. Just edited, arranged interpolated comment. Its first producer wanted to say "Collated by Eric Bentley," but I said a collation was a luncheon or at best high tea. . . .

VOA: Which plays of yours are definitely plays—and yours?

Bentley: Is *Measure for Measure* Shakespeare's?

VOA: How d'you mean?

Bentley: It is "based on" another play. And how about Brecht's *Threepenny Opera*?

VOA: Based on *Beggar's Opera*.

Bentley: But still Brecht's. His stamp unmistakably on it. Let others decide—don't ask me—which of "my" works has my stamp on it.

VOA: Does playwriting do anything for you which was not done for you by your other writing?

Bentley: Yes. It practically kills me. It's harder. Slower. So many drafts, so few pages to show after many months' work.

VOA: You're sustained by the ambition to be creative, to do the more difficult thing, to be at last at the center of theater art as you see it?

Bentley: Often I am not sustained. I throw up my hands. I scream. But there are seductions. For me, the writing of dialogue is seductive. I enjoy thinking up what people say—or should say.

VOA: So dialogue is a basic?

Bentley: What a person does when he doodles is his basic! And I am composing dialogue all the time! Second-guessing my friends: preparing their excuses, their witticisms. A natural ghost writer. When I am wakened from a dream at night, the wakener is always interrupting a torrent of (often awful) dialogue—pretentious, sometimes non-sensical, turgid double talk.

VOA: You are a Shavian playwright then: drama is dialogue?

Bentley: Wrong: here at any rate I am Brechtian. Although my doodling is dialogue, my doodles don't turn into plays. I have to plot and plan. In fact, that's how my playwriting differs from my other writing. The other stuff flows. Stream of consciousness. Compulsive chatter. But as for drama, I always think of Racine saying that, once he'd plotted the entrances and exits, the rest was easy. Oh, those entrances and exits—plot 'em right and you're Racine!

VOA: It's the entrances and exits that impose structure?

Bentley: For Racine. That's not actually how things come to me. The influence on me—as to this—was Brecht's *directing*. Tell the story, he said. Brecht the playwright had begun by telling it himself.

VOA: A play of yours—on Galileo, on Oscar Wilde—is full of ideas—dialogue at a rather high level of abstraction—

Bentley: I have room for all that. I hope I have room for all that. Even so, what I was mainly doing in both those plays—*The Recantation* and *Lord Alfred's Lover*—was threading my way from incident to incident. Telling what happened. Inwardly, sometimes: what happened *inside* my people. But never to the neglect of story in the most obvious and external sense. Galileo recanted. What chain of events led up to that? This was the urgent and ever-present question for the playwright, not what Galileo said in class.

VOA: Is there any way of recapping your remarks on this latest phase of your work?

Bentley: No need to make great claims for the development I've been outlining. I would hate it if my narrative followed the banal pattern of success story: I'm not that successful a playwright. I wasn't scaling ever-higher heights or even undertaking more and more complex tasks. For that matter, is playwriting more complex? I doubt that anything is harder than being a really good critic. And, conversely, one thing in one kind of playwriting that attracts me is simplicity. Naïveté. In plays I find I can expose more elemental parts of myself, things that sophistication would cover up in my scholarship and criticism. . . . One of my plays ends on the word "shameless," and I think that one great source of attraction to me, in the kind of playwriting that I do, is a certain *shamelessness*.

VOA: No fig leaf?

Bentley: No fig leaf.

Bibliography

By Eric Bentley:

Plays

Orpheus in the Underworld (opera libretto). New York, Program Publishing Co., 1956.
A Time to Live, and A Time to Die (first produced as *Commitments*, H. B. Playwrights,
    New York, 1967). New York: Grove Press, 1970.
The Red White and Black (La Mama, New York, 1979). In *Liberation* (New York, May
    1971).
Are You Now or Have You Ever Been (Yale Repertory, New Haven, Connecticut, 1972).
    New York: Harper & Row, 1972.
The Recantation of Galileo Galilei: Scenes from History Perhaps (Wayne State University
    Theater, Detroit, 1973). New York: Harper & Row, 1972.
From the Memoirs of Pontius Pilate (Buffalo, New York, 1976). Together with *Are You*
    and *Recantation* in *Rallying Cries: Three Plays*. New York: New Republic/
    Simon and Schuster, 1977.
Wannsee (Buffalo, New York, 1978). In *The Massachusetts Review* (Amherst, Autumn
    1979).
Lord Alfred's Lover (Gainesville, Florida, 1979). In *The Canadian Theatre Review*
    (Downsview, Ontario, Spring 1978).
The Fall of the Amazons (Buffalo, 1979).

Criticism

A Century of Hero Worship. Philadelphia: Lippincott, 1944; as *The Cult of the Super-
    man*, London: Hale, 1947.
The Playwright as Thinker: A Study of Drama in Modern Times. New York: Reynal and
    Hitchcock, 1946; as *The Modern Theater*, London: Hale, 1948.
Bernard Shaw: A Reconsideration. New York: New Directions, 1947; revised 1957; re-
    vised London: Methuen, 1967.
In Search of Theatre. New York: Knopf, 1953; London: Dobson, 1954.
The Dramatic Event: An American Chronicle. New York: Horizon Press, 1954; London:
    Dobson, 1954.
What is Theatre? A Query in Chronicle Form. New York: Horizon Press, 1956; London:
    Dobson, 1957.
The Life of the Drama. New York: Atheneum, 1964; London: Methuen, 1965.
The Theatre of Commitment, and Other Essays on Drama in Our Society. New York:
    Atheneum, 1967.
Theatre of War: Comments on 32 Occasions. New York: Viking Press, 1972; London:
    Methuen, 1972.
The Brecht Commentaries. New York: Grove Press, 1981.

As Editor-Anthologist

The Importance of "Scrutiny." New York: G. W. Stewart, 1948.
From the Modern Repertoire (3 volumes). Bloomington: Indiana University Press, 1949-56.
The Play: A Critical Anthology. New York: Prentice-Hall, 1951.
Shaw on Music. Garden City, New York: Doubleday, 1955.
The Modern Theatre (6 volumes). Garden City, New York: Doubleday, 1955-60.
The Classic Theatre (4 volumes). Garden City, New York: Doubleday, 1958-61.
Let's Get a Divorce, and Other Plays. New York: Hill & Wang, 1958.
The Storm over "The Deputy." New York: Grove Press, 1964.
The Genius of the Italian Theatre. New York: New American Library, 1964.
The Brecht-Eisler Song Book. New York: Oak Publications, 1966.
The Great Playwrights (2 volumes). Garden City, New York: Doubleday, 1970.
Thirty Years of Treason. New York: Viking Press, 1971.

As Editor-Translator

Seven Plays, by Bertolt Brecht. New York: Grove Press, 1961. Also other volumes in the Grove edition of Brecht.
Naked Masks: Five Plays, by Luigi Pirandello. New York: Dutton, 1952.
The Wire Harp, by Wolf Biermann.
Filumena, by Eduardo De Filippo.

Record Albums

"Bentley on Brecht"—performer (Riverside 1963; Folkways, 1965).
"Brecht before the Un-American Activities Committee"—commentator/editor (Folkways, 1963).
"A Man's a Man"—adapter/lyricist (Spoken Arts, 1963).
"Songs of Hanns Eisler"—performer (Folkways, 1965).
"The Elephant Calf/Dear Old Democracy"—adapter/lyricist/narrator (Folkways-Asch, 1967).
"Bentley on Biermann"—translator/performer (Folkways-Broadside, 1968).
"Eric Bentley Sings The Queen of 42nd Street"—performer (Folkways, 1969).

About Eric Bentley:

Borklund, Elmer. "Eric Bentley." In *Contemporary Literary Critics.* New York: St. Martin's, 1977.
Fuegi, John. "Eric Bentley." In *Contemporary Dramatists.* New York: St. Martin's Press, 1977.
Kostelanetz, Richard. "Critics of Contemporary Literature." In *Twenties in the Sixties.* Westport, Connecticut, and London: Greenwood Press, 1979.
Rogoff, Gordon. Review of *The Life of the Drama,* by Eric Bentley. *Virginia Quarterly Review,* Winter 1973.

Sylvia Plath: Beyond the Biographical

Rochelle Ratner

The mere mention of the name Sylvia Plath conjures up the image of the tortured woman poet in America. This image comes more from the biographies about her and from her *Letters Home* (1975) than from her poetry. Certainly Plath was not the first American poet to commit suicide. But has this image really helped us in the long run? My feeling is that the tortured, suicidal image has done her more harm than good: we're so fascinated by the myth that when we do read the work, we lose sight of critical standards, and for that reason I want to take a closer look at the work itself.

The details of her life are still necessary to any reading of her work: born in Massachusetts on October 27, 1932, she was the daughter of an Austrian mother and a German father. Her father died in 1940, a few days before her eighth birthday. Though her widowed mother was not wealthy, Sylvia managed to attend Smith, a prestigious women's college, on a full scholarship from 1950 to 1955. She missed a semester in 1953 after a suicide attempt which led to hospitalization and shock treatment. To judge from her writing, this suicide attempt seems to have been provoked by a brief summer job as a student editor at *Mademoiselle* magazine and her first experience of the New York literary life. Throughout college she won several prizes for her poems and stories, and in 1956 and 1957 she attended Newnham College of Cambridge University, England, on a Fulbright Scholarship. She married the British poet Ted Hughes in 1956 and had two children by him: a daughter, Frieda, in 1960, and a son, Nicholas, in January of 1962. She and Hughes separated in October of that year, and she committed suicide on February 11, 1963, at the age of 30.

Only two books were published during her lifetime: *The Colossus and Other Poems* (1960 in England, 1962 in America) and *The Bell Jar* (a "confessional" novel published under the pseudonym "Victoria Lucas" in 1962, just before her death in England). Her finest works, the poems written just before her death, appeared in *Ariel* in 1966. But once her publishers realized that American readers wanted more Plath, they were quick to provide it: *Winter Trees* (1972), which consists of poetry written between *The Colossus* and *Ariel; Crossing The Water* (1971), poems written at the same time as those in *Ariel,* but omitted from that collection because Hughes (rightly) considered them inferior; *Letters Home,* letters written to her mother, edited by her mother; a book of selected prose, *Johnny Panic and the Bible of Dreams* (1979). Countless biographical and critical studies have appeared in the past few years, and while it may be interesting to scholars and voyeuristic housewives my feeling is that it would have been best to leave well enough alone. Let the audiences read *Ariel* and not clutter the market with work of inferior quality. Ted Hughes says as much in his introduction to the selected prose:

> Reading this collection, it should be remembered that her reputation rests on the poems of her last six months. . . . In other words, this collection does not represent the prose of the poet of *Ariel,* any more than the poems of *The Colossus* represent the poetry of the poet of *Ariel.* But it does give glimpses into the early phases of the strange conflict between what was expected of her and what was finally exacted.

The stories, written mostly during her college years and aimed at the women's magazines, have undertones of death, woman's beastliness, and inhumanity. In "The Day Mr. Prescott Died" a young woman is dragged by her mother to comfort a recently widowed friend. Plath's narrator views the situation with piercing irony:

> Mrs. Prescott didn't look as if she had been through much of anything. Mrs. Mayfair began sobbing in her handkerchief and invoking the name of the Lord. She must have had it in for the old guy, because she kept praying, "Oh, forgive us our sins," like she had up and killed him herself.

In "Superman and Paula Brown's New Snowsuit," a group of fifth graders all gang up to blame the narrator unjustly for pushing another girl in the mud. As the story implies, this is just the beginning; nobody is going to believe anything the narrator says from now on.

The most valuable part of *Johnny Panic and the Bible of Dreams* is Hughes's introduction, which is to date the best insight I've read into Plath's work and her poetic writing process. Writing 15 years after her death, he is able to speak of her with an enormous amount of tenderness, love, and respect.

Plath has been slapped with the catch-all label of a "confessional" writer. Much of this mistaken label has been the result of Robert Lowell's introduction to the American edition of *Ariel*, where he says:

> Everything in these poems is personal, confessional, felt, but the manner of feeling is controlled hallucination, the autobiography of a fever.... This poetry and life are not a career; they tell that life, even when disciplined, is simply not worth it.

Lowell, like all too many excellent poets, can view Plath's work only in relation to his own, and this approach entirely misses her value as a poet. The inappropriateness of the label became obvious when critics, in their over-zealous attempts to come to terms with Plath, have ended up contradicting each other, often even contradicting themselves. The respected British critic A. Alvarez, for example, writing in March 1965, perceptively comments that *Ariel* "has an originality that keeps it apart from any poetic fads. It is too concentrated and detached and ironic for confessional verse, with all that implies of self-indulgent cashing-in on misfortunes." Unfortunately, in his voluminous other writings on Plath, especially *The Savage God*, Alvarez has contributed to her being labeled a confessional writer.

My own understanding, rather, is that the early poems in *The Colossus* are overly concerned with craft; she was searching to find what she really had to say, struggling to relate the words to her life. Vividly bleak images give a hint of the power to come, but the anger is too often forced onto distant or inanimate figures, and thus the poems feel false and academic. Plath herself referred to *The Bell Jar* as a "pot boiler." It is essentially a poorly written novel which Plath dashed off in the hopes that she could make some money from it. She had only her own life to draw from and wisely decided to publish it under a pseudonym. Twelve years later, when her *Letters Home* was published, the relationship *The Bell Jar* had to her own life during her college years became clear. For the sake of sensationalism, the novel overplays the experiences, just as her letters underplay them. I view *Letters Home* as even more of a "fiction" than some of her more serious writing. These letters speak of love in the same way that her stories geared to the slick women's magazines do. And just as she studied the magazines to see what they would want, so she studied her mother to know what she would want.

It would seem as if the retrospective torment she portrayed in *The Bell Jar* freed Plath to deal directly with the negative and often overwhelming circumstances of her life as a single mother. But the poems of *Ariel*, while they contain personal elements, are anything but confessional. How can one "confess" to suicide, death, and resurrection? They are, rather, deep visions, mystical experiences, prayers.

What Plath took from her life were images, not facts. This becomes clear when reading the precisely detailed journal entries in her selected prose. Hughes's introductory comments make sure the reader will not overlook this important point:

> What is especially interesting now about some of these descriptions is the way they fed into *Ariel*. They are good evidence to prove that poems which seem often to be constructed of arbitrary surreal symbols are really impassioned reorganizations of relevant fact.

Judith Kroll, in her book *Chapters In A Mythology*, gives an even clearer picture. Commenting on drafts of a poem later omitted from *Ariel*, she implies that similar examples can be cited for drafts of other poems:

> The drafts of "The Other" include a number of apparently literal biographical details about Plath's rival. These are typically absent from the final poem. If she were writing "confessional" poetry, there would presumably be a premium on including precisely those juicy, convincingly specific, "real life" details which, when they find their way into her poems, she almost invariably and routinely eliminated *if they do not also serve a more mythic and general purpose*—which, because of her extraordinary sensibility to correspondences with myth, they often do.

While studying at Cambridge, Plath had a deep interest in tragedy, and I view the poems in *Ariel* as a series of dramatic monologues, a cycle of birth/death/rebirth. Near the beginning of the book, "Lady Lazarus" sets the stage for what is to come. The persona is 30 now, as was Plath then. It is time to attempt her third suicide, convinced that "like the cat I have nine times to die." With the marvelous irony that is Plath's trademark in her best poems, she describes a suicide attempt which "the peanut-crunching crowd shoves in to see":

(Fourteen stanzas,
each three lines in length,
excluded at the publisher's request.)

It's important to see *Ariel* as an integral book, rather than as a collection of individual poems. The images of the poems build upon one another and clarify each other. "The pure gold baby/That melts to a shriek," which is the narrator's image of herself in "Lady Lazarus," reflects back to the first poem in the book, "Morning Song," a poem written for Plath's daughter: "Love set you going like a fat gold watch." A few lines later, the child cries and "the clear vowels rise like balloons"—a celebration. But near the end of the book, in the poem "Balloons," the shreds of the broken balloon symbolize the child's view of death. It's important to remember that many of the images in a particular poem become symbols when read in the context of the book.

With its "Herr Doktor" and "Herr Enemy," "Lady Lazarus" also contains references to the Nazis. Plath saw herself as a political person, if not a political writer. Though she was gentile, she identified with the cruelties done to the Jews and often created a Jewish persona for a self whose immediate enemies (father, husband, etc.) she saw as Nazis. Her intentions were to give a larger resonance to her own suffering. An early fiction, "The Shadow," states that when she was growing up there was suspicion that her father was a Nazi simply because he was German. With her opening paragraph, she sets *The Bell Jar* in a more worldly context by speaking of the electrocution of the Rosenbergs, and this image becomes even more powerful later when Esther Greenwood describes being given electric-shock treatments. Her first reaction was: "I wondered what terrible thing it was that I had done."

By the time she began writing the poems that later formed *Ariel*, Plath had craft at her fingertips. Poems were written at record speed, often two a day. She rose at 4 a.m., wrote until her baby cried, and let her duties as a mother take up the rest of her day.

Near the middle of *Ariel* is the long sequential poem, "Berck-Plage." This poem is an outsider's view of an old-age home where men are dying. Her observations are precise; from the specific to the imaginative is just one giant step. As always, Plath takes that step so smoothly that her images startle the reader who hasn't been paying close attention. The old-age home is by the beach, which in earlier poems Plath saw as her refuge. With her refuge gone, she feels threatened:

> (Six lines, beginning
> "Why would I walk"
> excluded at the publisher's request.)

By the end of the poem, however, she is drawn in. She is forced to the awareness that at least this man's death is final, he will not resurrect: "For a minute the sky pours into the hole like plasma./There is no hope, it is given up."

Following "Berck-Plage" is the title poem, "Ariel"; and it is her reaffirmation of life by challenging it directly in a display of bare-back riding. (Ariel was the name of the horse Plath used to ride, though the relation to Shakespeare's Ariel, the tortured fairy slave of *The Tempest*, cannot be ignored.) Life-affirming or not, the poem ends with the fact that behind this desire to face life so squarely in the face is a desperate death wish. It is a challenge:

> (Six lines, beginning
> "And I"
> excluded at the publisher's request.)

"Daddy" is Plath's most famous poem. In many ways, it embodies all the concerns of this book and her work in general: the love-hate of the father, loss of (betrayal by) father, the self as afflicted Jew, suicide and death, husband as father's surrogate. Its short lines and playful rhymes make it technically a companion poem to "Lady Lazarus." It's an exorcism in the truest sense, but (and this is what her feminist supporters have been careful to overlook) it's also a poem of intense love. Possibly, it's her own death wish she is trying to exorcise, and here more than ever, the irony comes from two conflicting elements deep within her: her fear of death and her desire for death. Plath has described this poem as written in the persona of "a girl with an Electra complex. Her father died while she thought he was God." Like the poetry of Theodore Roethke, which she greatly admired, she creates a rhythm of pure madness, epitomized by the need to return to the womb-like security of early childhood. She begins with a vivid image of the child's conception of the father, echoing the nursery rhyme "There was an old woman who lived in a shoe":

> (Five lines, beginning
> "You do not do,"
> excluded at the publisher's request.)

She then goes on to describe the search for this absent father who kept "chuffing me off like a Jew./A Jew to Dachau, Auschwitz, Belsen." The poem gains momentum as it moves toward her present situation. I quote the entire second half:

> (Eight stanzas,
> each five lines in length,
> excluded at the publisher's request.)

In *Letters Home* she writes of deciding to become a bee-keeper (her father was an expert on bees) and the five-poem bee-sequence in *Ariel* is her attempt to replace her father by assuming his identity. The bees, locked in their box or coffin, become metaphors for the oppressed, the imprisoned, the insane. She is their keeper, she loves them, she will set both them and herself free. The ending of "Stings" contains echoes of both "Lady Lazarus" and "Ariel":

(Two stanzas,
each five lines long,
excluded at the publisher's request.)

Another important symbol for Plath is that of flowers. In the wonderful long poem "Tulips," early in *Ariel*, the flowers have been given only to torment her: "Their redness speaks to my wound, it corresponds." And "They come from a country far away as health." The ironic, simplistically trivial poem "Kindness" ends with: "You hand me two children, two roses." But the image here is seen in a much more serious light when in "Edge," two pages later, she describes the dead woman with:

(Four stanzas,
each two lines long,
the first beginning "Each dead child coiled,"
excluded at the publisher's request.)

One has to agree with Kroll when she states that Plath's dying heroines "have little in common with stereotypes of suicidal women (in whose actions a sense of the meaning of death does not even figure) and have a great deal in common with tragic heroines who die calmly and nobly."

The book ends with a short poem called "Words," presumably the last poem Plath wrote. Many critics have casually dismissed this poem, but I see it as extremely important. If the entire book is viewed as a tragedy in the classical sense of the word, then this is the poem spoken by the narrator after the characters have left the stage. It's almost a denial of all that has gone before it, as in old age many artists will deny their early works as being invalid. "Years later I/Encounter them on the road,/Words dry and riderless," picks up images used earlier in *Ariel* and turns them on themselves, while the poet/narrator lives on despite her death in words. It is not something about which, in the end, she has any choice, since: "From the bottom of the pool, fixed stars/Govern a life."

It's important to remember that Plath was only 30 when she died. Though in one sense her work was just beginning to find its mature voice, her early death also links her with the great Romantic poets: Byron, Shelley, and especially Keats. One could call her a Romantic poet working within the classical tradition.

Bibliography

By Sylvia Plath:

The Colossus and Other Poems. New York: Knopf, 1962.
Ariel. New York: Harper & Row, 1966.
The Bell Jar. New York: Harper & Row, 1971.
Letters Home: Correspondence 1950-1963. New York: Harper & Row, 1975.
Johnny Panic and the Bible of Dreams. New York: Harper & Row, 1979. (Selected prose, short stories, and diary excerpts.)

About Sylvia Plath:

Kroll, Judith. *Chapters in a Mythology.* New York: Harper & Row, 1976.
Lane, Gary, editor. *Sylvia Plath: New Views on the Poetry.* Baltimore: The Johns Hopkins University Press, 1979.
Newman, Charles, editor. *The Art of Sylvia Plath.* Bloomington: Indiana University Press, 1971.

The Poetry of Robert Lowell

Allen Grossman

Robert Traill Spence Lowell (1917-1977) was the central poet of the first post-Modernist period in Anglo-American poetry. His literary generation, born in the second decade of the century (including Randall Jarrell, John Berryman, Delmore Schwartz, Charles Olson, Robert Duncan, Elizabeth Bishop, Dylan Thomas), took in hand the question of the continuity of the culture after the Second World War, as Eliot and Pound had taken in hand the continuity of culture after the First World War. Lowell was a great worker at his art and, after 1946, a famous man in American letters. But, like the rest of his generation, he left a less determinate answer to the questions which poetry addresses than did his high Modernist predecessors.

The literary masters whom Lowell encountered on the American ground, and whom he acknowledged, formed a heterogeneous group of singular and, on the whole, nativist practitioners, among whom were Allen Tate (b. 1899), Hart Crane (b. 1899), William Carlos Williams (b. 1883), Theodore Roethke (b. 1907), Robert Frost (b. 1874), and, by an accident, Ford Madox Ford in Ford's later years. From these men and others Lowell took his meticulous, severe, and arduous sense of the poet's craft. He did not, however, take from them a sense of the poet's role that, as in Yeats or Stevens, supplanted the social identity of the writer. For Lowell a particularly complex and marked social identity was always the primary allegory of his meanings.

Born into an insecure collateral branch of a family unmistakably identified with the political and social domination of American Protestantism and with the moral ambiguities of American industrialism, Robert Lowell struggled not with the absence of identities but with their stigmatizing unexchangeability, their bewildering superfluity, their demonic constraints—the gifts of the God, Jehovah, which could not be put off. Assigned a name borne at once by an American

city, a president of Harvard, and two earlier American poets, Lowell
identified his personal nature with history at a catastrophic moment
in history—the inheritor neither of power nor knowledge, but of a will
imprisoned among external and ungovernable energies. His last and
most ambitious poem, the song of his self, is called with bland but
relentless appropriateness just *History*. Hence, Robert Lowell's poetic
commission was from the beginning of a satiric and prophetic character, a national judgment and at the same time a personal rectification
of genealogies, modelled not on the high Modernist examples of Yeats
and Eliot, but on the nativist and formalist impulses that flowed, on
the one hand, from Tate and Crane and, on the other, from the New
Critical phase of American post-Modernism promulgated by John
Crowe Ransom. With these means Lowell, as poet and as disempowered inheritor, attempted to reconstruct symbolically a self whose
form was nothing less than the whole world—public, inescapable,
identified, insane, not the cultural "ruins" of Eliot but a brilliant rubble
of dead fact.

     Robert Lowell's first book, published at Cummington, Massa-
chusetts, in 1944, was called *The Land of Unlikeness*. The title is an
Augustinian phrase supported by an epigraph from Saint Bernard
(*Inde anima dissimilis deo/inde dissimilis est et sibi*) and is borrowed from
(or repeated in) a chorus at the end of Auden's Christmas Oratorio,
"For the Time Being" (published in the same year):

> He is the Way.
> Follow Him through the Land of Unlikeness;
> You will see rare beasts, and have unique adventures.
>
> He is the Truth.
> Seek Him in the Kingdom of Anxiety;
> You will come to a great city that has expected your
>   return for years. . . .

The Land of Unlikeness contains 20 poems, beginning with "The Park
Street Cemetery" ("The graveyard's face is painted with facts") and
ending with "Leviathan," in which the Protestant capitalist culture,
indistinguishable from the culture of war, is identified with the
lineage of Cain. Lowell took more than half of the poems in *The Land
of Unlikeness* into *Lord Weary's Castle* (1946), the book which established his reputation. Although they were strenuously revised for the
later volume, the basic analysis of history remains unchanged.

Such innocence as history can manifest is subverted (literally the Boston subway runs under the graves of the Old Granary burial ground) by the Protestant individualist and materialist innovation which founded and now rules America. Such are "The Children of Light" who "wrung their bread from stocks and stones/And fenced their gardens with the Redman's bones." This paternity is in itself unredeemable, or redeemable only by reference outside of history to the transcendental Mother, Mary, who will restore the genealogy disrupted by paternal violence. *The Land of Unlikeness* announces all the features of Lowell's later style. As redemption (not "meaning," but a nurturant and tranquil relationship between mother and son, a right ordering of the energies of love and trust) can only come from outside the present, so the *order* of language comes from outside of language in the form of measured traditional structures, pre-modern, archaic, in effect miraculous. In an introduction to *The Land of Unlikeness* Allen Tate speaks of Lowell's style as "bold and powerful . . . the symbolic language often has the effect of being *willed*; for it is an intellectual style compounded of brilliant puns and shifts of tone; and the willed effect is strengthened by formal stanzas, to which the language is forced to conform." This is correct. The "unlikeness" of the world to its right form is repeated in the *alienness of structure to experience*, leading to a style of violent imposition, the counter-violence of the will of the son directed against the paternal violence of fact and the presented civilization.

The figure of "unlikeness" in Lowell's *The Land of Unlikeness* announced his central trope, the meeting of the self as history with its own prior authenticity, the past, the ancestors, as in the mirror of an impossible paradigm, an encounter without recognition—the face of the speaker as child seen reflected in the glass of the portrait of a numinous predecessor. The result is sealed in the exclamation of "The Fat Man in the Mirror": "O it is not I." In Yeats, history can reverse itself. But in Lowell, encounter cannot become recognition by any process inherent in the self. Hence tragedy eludes him. Like the satirist in general, Lowell is a comic writer anticipating only apocalypse (at first) and then ironic endurance. It is the curing of the genealogy, the restoration as innocence of the energies of the past, and the sanctioning of love through the reconstitution of the family, which Lowell pursues, first by sacred and then by secular means, through three marriages and a score of volumes. In the end Lowell refused to regard poetry as healing—an inference from his experience of it, a reading of the meaning of his own practice. In the book published in the year of his death, 33 years after *The Land of Unlikeness*, he records— still in theological terms, still incomplete—the deepest penetration of his secular insight into the problem of setting in order the house of man:

> Is the one unpardonable sin
> our fear of not being wanted?
> For this, will mother go on cleaning house
> for eternity, and making it unlivable?
> Is getting well ever an art,
> or art a way to get well?

Lord Weary's Castle (1946) and the book which followed it, *The Mills of the Kavanaughs* (1951), describe first a conversion, the recapitulation and universalization of the discoveries of *The Land of Unlikeness*, and then repudiation of that conversion, a contraversion, the abandonment of a motif and a style. *The Mills of the Kavanaughs* ends with a poem the title of which is an announcement, "Thanksgiving's Over," which itself concludes upon a question and an answer: "*Miserere?* [pity?] Not a sound."

The self-characterization of the high Modern poet was in general atavistic (Yeats, the Druid master; Eliot, the Anglican; Pound, the reactionary Populist; Stevens, the Republican). Lowell literalized this formula. A radical satirist in a Protestant world, itself founded on dissent, Lowell represented himself, in effect, as an émigré from the archaic interior of American cultural space, emerging in the only posture possible to the rebel against a radical dispensation, the archaic intruder. Gothic, aristocratic, anachronistic, Catholic, the *epigone* as scapegoat who undertook by sacrificial self-transformation to recover the innocence of the world. The epigraph (in Latin) which precedes *Lord Weary's Castle* is a prayer for restoration of holy sanity: "Accept, Lord, gifts in remembrance of your Saints: so that, as their passion made them glorious, our devotion may restore our innocence." Here, indeed, the *willed* nature of Lowell's style, joined with the Christian idea of the cosmic efficacy of the choices of the person, produces a speaker central to the well-being of the race—an Agamemnon, Prometheus, or Hamlet, on whose right relationship to the gods depends the fertility of the field, the health of the kingdom.

The primary sentiment in Lowell's world is fear, its color his pervasive yellow. In the form of evangelical and redemptive anxiety in *Lord Weary*, that fear has meaning; and the obsessive deliberateness of his style has appropriateness in his early work, as it does not in his later, as the gesture of a mind responding to sacramental obligations. *Lord Weary's Castle* begins ("The Exile's Return") with the homecoming of the prophetic wanderer to postwar Belgium, a world of disrupted lineage ("Ancestral house/Where the dynamited walnut tree/Shadows a squat, old, wind-torn gate")—a world therefore of unredeemed fact. This is a world, like the *Inferno* (*Voi ch'entrate*), but where redemption is still a power of the will. *Lord Weary's Castle* ends ("Where the Rainbow Ends") with the announcement of the sacrament of the Eucharist as a promise of peace: "What can the dove of Jesus give/You now but wisdom, exile? Stand and live,/The dove has brought an olive branch to eat." As we have observed, the sense of cosmic centrality which sacramental privilege gives Lowell as a poetic speaker justifies the immense scope of this book. The moral implications of right choice in a Christian universe make sense of Lowell's stylistic insistence, his obsessive enactment of choice as technique.

Lord Weary's Castle* begins in 1945, announcing the postwar world with the same monumental deliberation with which Eliot announced the Modern world (also postwar) in *The Wasteland*. Lowell's method is however not the "mythic method" of Eliot and Yeats (which implies after all, a fittedness of past and present, an effective continuity of lineage); but neither is it in any new way immanentist or strictly secular. The past as "history" which speaks through and agonizes Lowell's personae amounts to a sort of poetic demonism which does not succeed either in revising Modernist poetic impersonalism or in continuing and developing it in significant ways. The agonistic courage of Lowell's procedure results from the laborious and painfully unmistakable persistence of his poetic speaking in the absence of a formal idea intrinsic to his subject. ("History" for Lowell in itself has no form.) Intensity of style and monumentality of project (the centralization of an historical self without its mythic amplification or cognitive illumination) produces as subject a victimization of the self precisely at the point at which the self becomes visible, becomes the subject of his art. Hence, all spaces in Lowell's poetic world, like all occasions of his speaking, are the same in so far as they are enabled by the one crisis which speaks for him—the moment of terror when the two images, the self and its ancestor, the present and the past confront one another. This is the moment of "madness" and of art.

There is no private space in Lowell, hence in a strict sense no "confession," no recuperation, and no absolution. The self is identical with history and history both remembers and is incapable of using its own powers and images. "The Lord survives the rainbow of his will."

Published in 1951, *The Mills of the Kavanaughs* is the most experimental of Lowell's books. It consists of seven poems (apparently his whole output since *Lord Weary's Castle*), all of them dramatic narratives in which the world becomes manifest through the narrow aperture of an extremely specific station of consciousness. The title poem, for example, is preceded by a note which reads in part: "An afternoon in fall of 1943; a village north of Bath, Maine. Anne Kavanaugh is sitting in her garden playing solitaire. She pretends that the Bible she has placed in the chair opposite is her opponent. . . ." Lowell is not an obscure writer, because he is not in the philosophical sense profound. Rather he is *difficult*, and that difficulty arises from and repeats the paralyzing specificity with which he experiences the world. Identity is the cage in which his persons are displayed, and that captivity which keeps them in representation keeps them from joy. "Life's a cell," as the girl screams in "Thanksgiving's Over." The only possible principle of organization in Lowell's world is the person. The person, however, always a captive in consciousness, is like an inhabitant of Dante's *Inferno*, both inextinguishable and overwhelmed by the alien facts (the intruder is always an alien) of which consciousness consists in an unredeemed world. Only violence can make the connection. Like the electric chair of "West Street and Lepke" in *Life Studies* the poem becomes an "oasis" in the "air of lost connections."

In *Lord Weary* Catholicism provides a supplement to the inadequate mediations of mere conscious life. In *The Mills of the Kavanaughs* Lowell undertakes to become human by a transformation less dependent on transcendental certitude than the Eucharist, namely dramatization. The female soul which is the principal speaker of that book endures, in several forms, bereavement of the empowering grammar of male relationship (genealogical intelligibility). The obsessive tightening of the form, the notable and extreme archaizing of discourse in *The Mills of the Kavanaughs* fails to compensate the bridegroom's violent betrayal of hope; for Lowell's poetic dramatizations lack the freedom of the difference between actor and role. They have no true alterity as his early Eucharistic imagination had no true sacredness.

At the end of the different but related transformative efforts of *Lord Weary* and *The Mills* Lowell abandons strict metricality together with the adoration of the Virgin. The self overwhelmed from without in his first three books becomes the self-describing soul in *Life Studies*. Lowell at this crucial moment ceases to construct the poem as a supplement to experience. He now undertakes to gain access to experience through its repetition.

In the literary community of the 1950s Lowell seemed the only poetic writer capable of meaningful self-revision. *Life Studies* (1958) offers a new style for a new reality, the new reality announced in the refusals and impossibilities of *The Mills of the Kavanaughs*, but left there unperformed. "Much against my will/I left the City of God where it belongs." Thus in the opening poem of *Life Studies* Lowell's speaker announces the "bodily assumption of the Virgin Mary." The impersonality and transcendental experiments of Lowell's earlier poems had left undecided the question whether there was to be found in the scope of his genius any alternative to poetic Modernism. *Life Studies* was Lowell's effort to settle the issue by producing in effect a truly secular art such as Modernism could only, as it were, imagine.

Life Studies itself consists of four parts of which the second is a prose memoir. The first part addresses the implications of the secularization of the object of love, the "bodily assumption of the Virgin." Indeed, Lowell's development as a whole consists of a lifelong struggle to assimilate the implication of that secularization, and *History* in the end becomes merely the late stage of a vital process first stated in *Life Studies* and never concluded. Lowell's conception of this process can be seen in another poem early in *Life Studies* called "The Banker's Daughter." In this poem Lowell's speaker is identified with the sexual woman, a mother out of shape ("such a virtuous ton/of woman only women thought her one."), out of shape and engulfing—the self-generating female soul of Lowell's open-form poetry—who drives out the king (Henri IV). The banishing of the same king, the good soldier, and his supplanting by the promises and powers of the woman, the desire for form, and the exploitation of its terrible elusiveness—these themes of the opening of *Life Studies* come to a climax in a poem called "A Mad Negro Soldier Confined in Munich": "I had her six times in the English garden/Oh mama, mama, like a trolley-pole/sparking at contact, her electric shock—/the power-house! . . ."

Part II of *Life Studies* is a strong autobiographical prose piece which accounts in a clear narrative style for the anxiety of a mind seeking its relationship to its own style and the imaginative wealth of its world in the absence of a central principle of order which, if it existed, could make that mind and wealth accessible by giving it a determinate structure. "91 Revere Street" is the story of Lowell's failed warrior father ("the Commander") who has to go to school to learn to cut meat. Correlatively "91 Revere Street" is the account of a mother in search of a style of self-presentation in the world the father has left disorderd, the female soul once again doing the whole work of civilization. In this family the child is indeed an intruder who seeks mastery by the arraying of archaic resources, by an alliance, as it were, with the dead for the purpose of rescuing the intelligibility of the living.

It should not therefore be surprising that Part III of *Life Studies* consists of a set of poems which effect the substitution of a literary genealogy for a natural one—George Santayana, Delmore Schwartz, Hart Crane, Ford Madox Ford. Ford Madox Ford is the true warrior, author of *The Good Soldier* ("Was it war, the sport of kings, that your *Good Soldier,*/the best French novel in the language, taught/those Georgian Whig magnificos at Oxford,/at Oxford decimated on the Somme?") whose mortal pathos embodies the ambiguities of the prose model which Lowell has accepted. Throughout Lowell's life his politics, insofar as politics enters his poetry, consists of the search for the *real* Commander, as absurdly in "For Eugene McCarthy": "I love you so . . . Gone?"

The fourth part of *Life Studies* bears out the title of the book and identifies Lowell's meaning, the drawing from the naked life, the body. Of these poems two are most distinguished, "West Street and Lepke" and "Skunk Hour." In the former we see a poem constructed from the zero point of coincidence between the language of the ordinary life of the world and the language of poetry. The poem begins in the leisure of casual repose and mounts toward that oasis of significance where meanings arise, that violent threshold where experience yields its meanings, in this case the electric chair. The indistinguishability in Lowell of representation and overwhelming sensation here marks the strange failure of this masterful poet to give an account of the reconciled state which should be the fruit of his new stylistic discovery. In the same way, "Skunk Hour" records the failure of the older strategies of order, and finds the moment of self-discovery in the parodic ancestral mirror of the animal eye, as before in earlier poems a similar confrontation without recognition was registered in the mirror glass of the human portrait.

For the Union Dead (1962) and Near the Ocean (1967) are paired works marking the end and outcome of Lowell's stylistic experimentation. Thereafter poetic structures function in Lowell as neutralized principles of the mere endless speaking of a world whose only conceivable forms are either smaller or larger than the scope of the lyric poem and by implication of the individual self. For the Union Dead enacts the project of Life Studies, as Life Studies puts in place the project rendered inevitable by The Mills of the Kavanaughs. Now the fallen world in which discourse and experience approach one another is imperiled by the experimental indistinguishability of those two great principles. It is for this reason that For the Union Dead contains many of Lowell's most difficult poems, poems of hallucinated lostness of the cognitively empty space between meaning and experience. This is a realm of "suffering without purgation." As in "Eye and Tooth," the field of perception becomes itself a space of suffering. The endings of the poems of this period manifest a world which cannot be shut out and cannot be made sense of—a world which has no closure except the exhaustion of the mind which experiences it.

> Nothing! No oil
> for the eye, nothing to pour
> on those waters or flames.
> I am tired. Everyone's tired of my turmoil.

The most progressive discovery in this book is the consciousness of the desirability of sentiment even in the face of overwhelming threat ("Fall 1961"):

> A father's no shield
> for his child.
> We are like a lot of wild
> spiders crying together,
> but without tears.

In the title poem of the book, "For the Union Dead," the absence of formality leads to a sense of inversion, the reversal of inside and outside, a drowned and subverted world—precisely that deluge against which the formal will in Lord Weary's Castle asserted precarious dominance. The hero's "angry, wrenlike vigilance," "his lovely,/

peculiar power to choose life and die" is now lost in the no-difference of a world where outside and inside, up and down, are indiscriminable. This is captivity.

The title poem of *Near the Ocean,* returning to formality, is a dream of escape. The book divides in half, the first six poems being original in the ordinary sense of the word, and the last six being translations (Lowell's term is "imitations") of Horace, Juvenal, Dante, Quevedo, and Góngora. The poems in this volume of greatest interest are the first two parts of the title poem and "The Vanity of Human Wishes," a version of Juvenal's Tenth Satire (a poem to which Samuel Johnson's imitation gave large standing in English letters.)

The first section of "Near the Ocean" is called "Waking Early Sunday Morning" and is a parody of Wallace Stevens's monument of early modern secular confidence, "Sunday Morning" (1915). "Near the Ocean" begins:

> O to break loose, like the chinook
> salmon jumping and falling back,
> nosing up to the impossible
> stone and bone-crushing waterfall—
> raw-jawed, weak-fleshed there, stopped by ten
> steps of the roaring ladder, and then
> to clear the top on the last try,
> alive enough to spawn and die.

These octosyllables cast the mind of Lowell's reader back to one of his earliest poems, appearing both in the *Land of Unlikeness* and *Lord Weary's Castle,* called "The Drunken Fisherman." In that poem Christ was the "rainbow" trout hunted by the mortal heart betrayed by history. In "Near the Ocean" the apocalyptic fish is more remote, being a secular metaphor neither as accessible as the Eucharist nor as truly a part of nature. The sense of history motivating the old desire to "break loose" is laid out at the beginning of Lowell's imitation of Juvenal later in the volume:

> In every land as far as man can go,
> from Spain to the aurora or the poles,
> few know, and even fewer choose what's true.
> What do we fear with reason, or desire?
> Is a step made without regret? . . .

The singularity of "Waking Early Sunday Morning" is its fidelity to and captivity in the hyperbolic impressionism which marked his early dramatic monologues and is now made to serve the desolate scepticism of a lyric speaker:

> I watch a glass of water set
> with a fine fuzz of icy sweat,
> silvery colors touched with sky,
> serene in their neutrality—
> yet if I shift, or change my mood,
> I see some object made of wood,
> background behind it of brown grain,
> to darken it, but not to stain.

The desire for escape (from the skull, the lyric "cell," the "world") still throws the speaker back upon the transcendental model ("When will we see Him face to face?"), and the meter of the poem mirrors the hymn structures ("stiff quatrains shovelled out four-square—") which at least "gave darkness some control."

The structure of the poem is itself a retrospect upon unworkable solutions. It is the counter-truth to the windowless simultaneity of life and art in "For The Union Dead," but it is inefficacious in the face of the world of fact:

> No weekends for the gods now. Wars
> flicker, earth licks its open sores,
> fresh breakage, fresh promotions, chance
> assassinations, no advance.
> Only man thinning out his kind
> sounds through the Sabbath noon, the blind
> swipe of the pruner and his knife
> busy about the tree of life. . . .

As always Lowell's speaker is interrupted by history in his reflective self-discovery. The speaking is pitched forward by the speaker's unwillingness to penetrate either history or the self. Lowell has no psychology as he has no politics, only the truth-bearing sentiment of fear in the presence of forces inside and outside the self, forces which are out of human scale and beyond "control." The archaic intruder is not at home, having been incarnated against his nature, and like the old model of his God dying in the incarnation, in the prison of the skull, the private Golgotha, the Golgotha of privacy.

The second section of the title poem of "Near the Ocean" is a parody of Yeats's "Prayer for My Daughter" called "Fourth of July in Maine." It is dedicated to an aged "cousin" Harriet Winslow (the mother's family name) after whom Lowell named his daughter. About this figure as about the daughter there hangs an air of exemption from the terror. In the figure of Harriet is wrapped up all Lowell's competent imagination of ease and satisfaction in the world. The two Harriets clearly know in their several ways both sentiment and its place in the world. They stand as delegates toward a future in which Lowell cannot find himself and for which he has a voice scarcely used. In the effective genealogy of those women whose names are inside one another lies obscured a future for poetry which Lowell has bequeathed unexplored to his successors—the space which he has left unentered, to which his voice scarcely reached, as all the spaces which he filled with his voice can only be entered in imitation of him, in service of his desolating mastery.

After *Near the Ocean* the work of Lowell shatters into 500 or so satiric epigrams in sonnet-like form, the fragments of a shattered mirror all of which reflect only the one face. These compose all the works of the 1970s, except the last (*Day by Day*). They constitute *Notebook, For Lizzie and Harriet, The Dolphin,* and *History*. Lowell has now come to assert the unexchangeability of immanent fact for any meaning. His large late work is therefore a parody of epic, the premise of which is the inherent structure of the whole human world. What is true is only the voice. Lowell had chosen poetry, as I think, for its atavistic promise of authenticity—a genealogy outside of history, a lineage which included the Holy Spirit—by which to repair the guiltiness and disability of the life he remembered. In the end the passion for genealogy and authenticity remains, but the expectation of its actualization as transcendental order has been lost. Only the self that speaks is real. Lowell experienced his honesty like a disease, and his disease as a form of honesty. His integrity consisted in lifelong endurance of an externally enforced collision between the irreducible "unlikeness" he perceived and his monumental desire for a world in which to be at home. His late and endless sequences of short sonnets—assertions of the momentary relationship of things actualized in the picture of a person, of the disparate elements of experience bound together, if at all, by the insufficient knowledgeless fact of "the same voice"—enact the treadmill of a powerful will without an intelligible truth. He cannot stop, stay married, affirm anything except himself. Seldom in the history of representation has so powerful a voice found in the end so little to say. There is both magnificence and waste in the spectacle.

  Notebook, first published in 1967 and revised in 1970, contains in its revised form 309 of Lowell's sonnet-like poems. It announces the most marked discontinuity in the sequence of works Lowell so deliberately laid upon the line of his life. In Lowell, as we have seen, mind and the world are never "fitted" to one another, as they become, for example, in Lowell's younger contemporary A. R. Ammons. Though Lowell was as acute an observer of nature's regime as ever wrote English poetry, natural process for him lies only on the perceptual field as a failed allegory for the processes of personal acknowledgement, love, and fame. The difference between minds (the sentiment of love's imperfection and also of its natural triumph) in Lowell is madness—the madness of the mind disempowered by its great models in love, mother and father, and at the same time driven by an energy which, because it contemplates no good outcome in the social world, seems bound in guilty fidelity to an "unlike" personhood not in human scale. The scale of this energy in Lowell is potentially sublime. *Notebook* (and its shaped sequel *History*) is, as I have indicated, an epic project in the scale of a great motive, actualized from the shattered perceptual outlook of the natural man not exempt from the body of flesh and reason which the true sublime, as Kant reminds us, interrupts. Lowell's man cannot, as Yeats hoped, embody truth. It would destroy his body. Nor can he exempt himself, as Stevens proposed, by an art which makes a difference from life, which relieves the "pressure of reality." Art is bound to life and therefore baffled by experience.

  Though Lowell from first to last is a poet the substance of whose art is the person, he cannot engage persons or make sense of relationship as a form of knowledge. He either identifies with persons (his pseudo-dramatic inhabitation of the lives of the great) or combats them by insisting on their unreachable otherness. (The poem wholly in quotation marks seems his characteristic invention.) In 1973 he split the *Notebook* into three parts. *For Lizzie and Harriet* contains the poetry memorializing the former beloved, as it were the natural person past and future (Elizabeth Hardwick and their daughter Harriet); *The Dolphin* (mostly new poems) records the unstable and largely allegorized new marriage, another version of the symbolic bride. What remains, his story, becomes *History*. In this manner he separates the beloved from his central poem and finds *within* the beloved a dichotomy which portends, if life permitted it, an endless fragmentation.

The split between the mortal and the immortal beloved, "Lizzie and Harriet," on the one hand, and "The Dolphin," on the other, is a traditional procedure in Modernism. The development, in Yeats for example, is from the allegorized woman to the immanent body of the world. Lowell's singularity is the severity with which both are judged as incompletely realized, incompletely taken into life. The scene of *For Lizzie and Harriet* is "the mind which is also flesh." The restlessness of Lowell's speaker with the mortal marriage, the "Dear Sorrow," seems accounted for by the implicit severity of her criticism of the Gothic hyperbole by which he exchanges life for style even at the moments of greatest intimacy. Here in the clarity of her challenge to acknowledgment, his style evacuates its qualities:

> Lizzie, I wake to the hollow of loneliness,
> I would cry out *Love, Love,* if I had words:
> *we are all here for such a short time,*
> *we might as well be good to one another.*

Lowell has no style of repose, no way to live both as a poetic speaker and as a reconciled, morally acknowledged, and conceded social and sexual person. "Man," he says in the second of his "Dear Sorrow" sequences, "cannot be saved outside the role of God." And in the fourth:

> Do I romanticize if I think that I
> can be as selfish a father as Karl Marx,
> Milton, Dickens, Trotsky, Freud, James Mill,
> or George II, a bad son and worse father—
> the great lions needed a free cage to roar in. . . .

If it is part of Lowell's heroism and accomplishment to press art hard against the life lived, then it must be concluded that he does not obtain a credible account of life under the pressure of the motive to art. He remains the Gothic intruder whose life is hallucinated by "the role of God." *For Lizzie and Harriet* begins with the birth of Harriet, the daughter, in "Summer" and ends just beyond "Late Summer" with an "Obit" for the marriage from which the child came. This child is the future beyond his ability to experience a future consistent with his motive to art, not a possible occasion of art for him but perhaps the best inference his art awakens.

The counter-work of 1973 to *For Lizzie and Harriet* is *The Dolphin*. Its subject is not the mortal love and genealogy, the immanent destiny, the birth of the daughter, but a return to the dynastic conception, a re-symbolization of an earlier state of the Lowell self—not, in other words, the birth of an other, the daughter, but of the self-mirroring son. The Lizzie of the counter-volume speaks in *The Dolphin* wholly in quotation marks. Her utterance is separated and distinguished by the terms of its remote mediation: "Records," "Communication," "Voices," "In the Mail," "On the End of the Phone." It is the voice not his own that loves him. By contrast, the lyric voice in *The Dolphin* is vagrant, searching for its lost authority. The singular apparition of Racine in *The Dolphin's* last and best poem mocks the interminable patrol:

> . . . Racine, the man of craft,
> drawn through his maze of iron composition
> by the incomparable wandering voice of Phèdre.

In his early writings Lowell's demon was his madness. It is now his sanity. Always a demonized writer, the compelled activity of self-record is now seen as a betrayal of life rather than an instrument of its redemption. "Everything's real until it's published" is a characteristic sentiment of the poetry in *The Dolphin*. It declares the end of the confessional enterprise. Indeed, with the exception of some few vitally symbolized stanzas, the poetry of *The Dolphin* is inept and casual, compromised by the posture of a man who does not speak the truth to either lady—"the hangman's-knot of sinking lines." The sense is of scribal automatism, a keeping on with writing that is a postponement of the truth. The dead end of the confessional mode is the identification of art with consciousness, and the disabling of consciousness by identification with art. The empty endlessness of self-awareness without recognition becomes what Lowell in his culminating work calls *History*.

Lowell began as the poet of New England, not in the way of Frost the *genius loci* but in the manner of the Jeremiad preacher, the disturbed conscience of the place. At the end of his career the genealogy of the catastrophe he saw around him had become coterminous with the totality of history, and at the same time somehow specified within the implications of the names and persons of history rather than its processes. *History*, his major work—his story, a satiric dismemberment of epic—is accordingly a mere sequence of re-perceptions (more than 360) of the same moment of aberration, viewing through the same window of personal obliquity not a calculus of forces articulated in ideologies (e.g., the Protestantism and Catholicism of *Lord Weary*) but the endlessly repeated deformation of personal energies, the energies of individuals all of whom are, in the captivity of his unmistakable voice, himself. If there is a point of intersection between lyric structure (the account of a self by a self) and the structure of *History*, it lies in an implication similar to that of Neitzsche when he said: "At bottom, I am all the names in history." For example:

Caligula 2

My namesake, Little Boots, Caligula,
tell me why I got your name at school—
Item: your body hairy, badly made,
head hairless, smoother than your marble head;
Item: eyes hollow, hollow temples, red
cheeks roughed with blood, legs spindly, hands that leave
a clammy snail's trail on your scarlet sleeve,
your hand no hand could hold . . . bald head, thin neck—
you wished the Romans had a single neck.
That was no artist's sadism. Animals
ripened for your arenas suffered less
than you when slaughtered—yours the lawlessness
of something simple that has lost its law,
my namesake, not the last Caligula.

The Lowell who speaks in *History* constructs (confesses) a story beginning in the primordial pre-texts of the culture ("Man and Woman," "Bird?" "Dawn," "In Genesis," "Our Fathers"), and rotating at its center on the discovery of the moral uselessness of a past in which he is himself always present, and always the same. The central poem of the vast sequence is "Mother and Father 1": "I hit my father." The structural device which characterizes this sequence—a device touching the syntagmatic relationship of elements rather than the prosody of representation—is what Lowell called "Surrealism," which is to say the juxtaposition of the contents of consciousness (and therefore experience) without securing the meaning of their relationship—once again a strategy of confrontation without recognition:

Mother and Father 2

This glorious oversleeping half though Sunday,
the sickroom's crimeless mortuary calm,
reprieved from leafing through the Sunday papers,
my need as a reader to think celebrities
are made for suffering, and suffer well. . . .
I remember flunking all courses but Roman history—
a kind of color-blindness made the world gray,
though a third of the globe was painted red for Britain. . . .
I think of the ill I do and will;
love hits like the *infantile* of pre-Salk days.
I always went too far—few children can love,
or even bear their bearers, the never forgotten
my father, *my* mother . . . these names, this function, given
by them once, given existence now by me.

The gathered events of memory are displayed without assessment of their interrelation, hence without the entailment of tragic conclusiveness. Such a habit of consciousness sustains the on-going of representation in the mode of comic or satiric registration rather than the shaped riskiness of judgment. The self-absolving tone of Lowell at this point serves only its own prolonged presence in the world, rather than the penetration by art of cause on behalf of life. Lowell's scepticism, at bottom the decision by which he is characterized by his own hand, seems a willful postponement of majority. In this sense the "realism" of Lowell's *History* is inferior to the imagination of Yeats's *A Vision* (another sorting of a world of names), or to the extravagant and costly over-determination of Crane's *The Bridge*. In the motiveless inclusiveness of Lowell's dis-obligated structure (his sequences of rhetorically colored sonnets) the terrors which arise seem arbitrary, as they are found to be uncaused.

The difference between *Notebook* and *History* (aside from the strenuous revision of many of the stanzas) is the chronologizing of the elements. Lowell's last book, as it turned out, was called *Day by Day* (1977). At the beginning of this book the myth of Odysseus' return articulates the sentiment of "coming home," and also of a life posthumous of emergence, a life capable of the conciliation of past and present because it is no longer obligated to act. There is here a marked seriousness about the thinking through of experience and a greater intelligence about structure than in the other works since 1967—less mere representational opportunism and more struggle with the resistance of the world to meaning. *Day by Day* is at once elegiac and clear-

sighted, a profounder secularization of the motifs of mother and son—
son and the loves which the mother has permanently shattered into
multiplicity. In *Day by Day* Lowell gives an account of his latest style
as if it were felt by him to be an instrument no longer responsive to his
purpose and not yet replaced by a more powerful means. As in
"Shifting Colors":

> But nature is sundrunk with sex—
> how could a man fail to notice, man
> the one pornographer among the animals?
> I seek leave unimpassioned by my body,
> I am too weak to strain to remember, or give
> recollection the eye of a microscope. I see
> horse and meadow, duck and pond,
> universal consolatory
> description without significance,
> transcribed verbatim by my eye.
>
> This is not the directness that catches
> everything on the run and then expires—
> I would write only in response to the gods,
> like Mallarmé who had the good fortune
> to find a style that made writing impossible.

This nostalgia at the end for a style which resists discourse, for a
structure which opposes rather than conspires with experience, *for an
effective intention*, declares the exhaustion of a motive which began in
Lord Weary's Castle, and before in *The Land of Unlikeness*, to see the
world transformed, made innocent, aggregated in a Holy Family
through which as a just inheritance the good promise of life could
flow.

    Lowell's last poems are the end of a transit of styles which
began with *Life Studies* as a disencumbering of mediations, an empowering of the self toward the object of desire. What he learned
(though the inference he draws from what he learned is not clear)
is that experience represented at the point of coincidence between
world and mind really has no meaning and no end; it confers no consolation—yields no story but the account of its own production as
story. And that is not a story adequate to human hope. For Lowell, I
think, the great Moderns—Yeats and Eliot—had exhausted the implications of transcendental fidelity without healing the pain of life he
felt so keenly—a pain which now awaits a new poetic insight, the pos-

sibility of which he kept alive by the patience of his labor at utterance but the truth of which he left to be found again by another.

Bibliography

By Robert Lowell:

The Land of Unlikeness. Cummington, Massachusetts: Cummington Press, 1944.
Lord Weary's Castle with *The Mills of the Kavanaughs.* New York: Harcourt Brace, 1964.
        (First published 1946, 1951, respectively)
Life Studies with *For the Union Dead.* New York: Farrar, Straus and Giroux-Noonday,
        1967. (First published 1959, 1964, respectively)
Near the Ocean. New York: Farrar, Straus and Giroux, 1967.
Notebook 1967-1968. New York: Farrar, Straus and Giroux, 1969; augmented edition
        1970.
For Lizzie and Harriet. New York: Farrar, Straus and Giroux, 1973.
History. New York: Farrar, Straus and Giroux, 1973.
The Dolphin. New York: Farrar, Straus and Giroux, 1973.
Selected Poems. New York: Farrar, Straus and Giroux, 1976.
Day by Day. New York: Farrar, Straus and Giroux, 1977.

About Robert Lowell:

Axelrod, Steven Gould. *Robert Lowell: Life and Art.* Princeton, New Jersey: Princeton
        University Press, 1978.
London, Michael, and Robert Boyers, editors. *Robert Lowell: A Portrait of the Artist
        in his Time.* New York: David Lewis, 1970.
Plimpton, George, editor. "Interview with Robert Lowell." In *Writers at Work: The
        Paris Review Interviews.* Second series. New York: Viking Press, 1963.
Williamson, Alan. *Pity the Monsters.* New Haven, Connecticut, and London: Yale
        University Press, 1970.

Adrienne Rich: The Evolution of a Poet

Wendy Martin

In her poem "Toward the Solstice" Adrienne Rich has written, "I am trying to hold in one steady glance all the parts of my life." Her life has been sufficiently varied and complex that it is indeed difficult to comprehend it in a single, encompassing vision. Born in 1929, Rich grew up in Baltimore, Maryland; her father was a pathologist at Johns Hopkins Medical School and her mother had studied music at Juilliard. She attended Radcliffe College, Harvard's undergraduate school for women, and then married Alfred Conrad, an economist teaching at Harvard. In the decade following their marriage Rich and Conrad had three sons—David, Paul, and Jacob—and lived in Cambridge, Massachusetts, until 1966 when they moved to New York City. During the late 1960s Rich was actively involved in the protests against the Vietnam war. During the decade of the 1970s Adrienne Rich and her husband were separated and divorced, and she became increasingly involved in the feminist movement.

An articulate proponent of the need for social, economic, and political equality for both women and men, Rich has dedicated herself to "the struggle for self-determination of all women, of every color, identification or derived class...." Rich delivered this statement at the National Book Award Ceremony in 1974 at which her volume of poetry *Diving into the Wreck* (1973) was honored as the best volume of poetry to be published that year.

Many of the poems in this volume lament the failure of communication between men and women on both a personal and cultural level. For example, in the poem "Waking in the Dark" Rich writes: "The tragedy of sex/lies around us, a woodlot/the axes are sharpened for." In the title poem the poet explores the wreck of an old ship submerged beneath the sea. The ship is a metaphor for the poet's personal past as well as past history. The poet wants to confront the past directly. In order to do so she must undertake a treacherous journey into the ocean depths to see "the thing I came for:/the wreck and not the story of the wreck/the thing itself and not the myth." Once beneath the sea, the poet must "learn alone/to turn my body without force/in the deep element." Having arrived at the origin of the social and psychic systems which have denied her a voice, the poet reclaims her energies and recognizes that women need a new mythology which will enable them to share equally with men the task of building an egalitarian civilization. The creation of this new mythology, Rich feels, requires that women separate themselves from male values in order to create a community based on the truths of female experience:

> Outside the frame of his dream we are stumbling up the hill
> hand in hand, stumbling and guiding each other
> over the scarred volcanic rock

This conviction has remained central in her work since the publication of *Diving into the Wreck*.

During her career Adrienne Rich's poetic vision has become increasingly woman-centered. An analysis of her work reveals that she has gradually evolved a feminist poetics and politics. In her early work Rich mastered the craft of poetry and tended to conceal her deepest feelings behind a screen of carefully wrought words. After her poetic skill and power were acknowledged, she dared to articulate her deepest feelings in later poems.

As a young poet, Adrienne Rich was praised for her artifice. W. H. Auden observed in his foreword to *A Chance of World*, her first volume of poems in 1951: "Miss Rich, who is, I understand, twenty-one years old ... [has] a love for her medium, a determination to ensure that whatever she writes shall, at least, at last, not be shoddily made."

Randall Jarrell admired Rich's deft metrics in a review of her second book, *The Diamond Cutters and Other Poems* (1955), which won the Ridgely Torrence Memorial Award of the Poetry Society of America: "Her scansion ... is easy and limpid, close to water, close to air."

In spite of this early success, it wasn't until the publication of *Snapshots of a Daughter-in-Law* in 1963 that Rich developed a style and subject matter which were deeply personal. In this collection she writes for the first time from a female perspective; many of the poems explore the self-hatred and dependency experienced by women in patriarchal society:

(Ten lines, beginning
"Sigh no more ladies."
excluded at the publisher's request.)

In this poem the lilting cadences and precise rhymes of her earlier work are replaced by staccato rhythms of everyday speech. Now there is an effort to discover personal truths rather than to create highly polished surfaces: "Our blight has been our sinecure:/mere talent was enough for us—/glitter in fragments and rough drafts."

This volume concludes with a poem, "Prospective Immigrants Please Note," which declares the poet's intention to leave her old life and begin a new phase. Recognizing the dangers of this undertaking, she observes that the potential reward for leaving her old life behind is finding a more authentic self: "If you go through/there is always the risk/of remembering your name."

Necessities of Life (1966) reveals the poet's deepening conviction that the culture in which she lives is destructive. In several of the poems in this volume she expresses a need to separate herself from what she perceives to be the landscape of death:

(Seven lines, beginning
"I am gliding backward"
excluded at the publisher's request.)

These lines are written in the looser form of the poems in this volume; as Rich moves away from traditional subjects, her metrics become more flexible.

Like Emily Dickinson, who is portrayed in the poem "I Am in Danger—Sir," Adrienne Rich decides to "have it out at last/on [her] own premises." Dickinson separated herself from the world around her in order to write poetry. She persisted in her art in spite of the well-known critic Thomas Higginson's comment that her meters were "spasmodic." Unlike Dickinson, Rich has not cut herself off from public life, but she does share Dickinson's determination to survive as an independent and creative person.

During the years 1966-1976 Adrienne Rich taught in a wide range of colleges and universities which included Harvard, Swarthmore, Columbia, Brandeis, and the City College of the City University of New York. In particular, her work with the City University's remedial education programs for ghetto students convinced her that private and public life were profoundly interconnected. In *Leaflets*, which was published in 1969, Rich asserts her conviction that poetry is often written in the hope of re-integrating the political and the personal; as she writes in "Implosions," "I wanted to choose words that even you/would have to be changed by." The poems of this volume document the political turmoil of the 1960s: the destruction of the Vietnam war, the student unrest in France and the United States, the revolt in Algeria. In "Nightbreak" Rich writes of the interconnection of all people; her body becomes a battleground, a graphic metaphor for the horrors of war:

(Seven lines, beginning
"In the bed the pieces"
excluded at the publisher's request.)

In "The Demon Lover" the poet reiterates the need for social change: ". . . A new/era is coming in./Gauche as we are, it seems/we have to play our part."

The poems in *The Will to Change* (1971) continue to chronicle the anomie of modern life. The disjunctive character of this life is captured in "The Shooting Script," in which such words as "crack," "split," "broken," and "fracture" emphasize fragmentation:

(Two stanzas, the first beginning
"Now to give up"
excluded at the publisher's request.)

Again, this volume reiterates the poet's growing sense that personal
change and social change are interconnected, that she must change
herself as well as work for reforms in public life.

As we have seen, the poet explores the wreckage of personal
and public realities in her next volume, *Diving into the Wreck*. In an
essay that appeared in a 1973 issue of the critical journal *Parnassus*, the
noted critic Helen Vendler observed that "the forcefulness of *Diving
into the Wreck* comes from the wish not to huddle wounded, but to
explore the caverns, the scars, the depths of the wreckage." In *Poems:
Selected and New*, published in 1975, Rich searches for new patterns
and principles with which to structure her life. In a 16-part poem,
"From an Old House in America," she reviews the lives of the women
who were pioneers of the American frontier. Weaving the past and
present together, the poet discerns in these women's lives a pattern
which has, for the most part, not been recorded in official historical
records. Although the women in this poem have nurtured and
sustained their friends and families, they have not had the power to
express their values in a large social context. Instead, they have been
confined to the private sphere of domesticity while their men have
shaped public life:

(Four stanzas, the first beginning
"I am washed up"
excluded at the publisher's request.)

Rich explores the bifurcation of male and female social roles in her prose volume *Of Woman Born: Motherhood as Experience and Institution*, which was published in 1976. Reviewing the archeological and anthropological theories of James Mellart, Erich Neuman, Robert Briffault, J. J. Bachofen, G. Rachel Levy, and Elizabeth Gould Davis, Adrienne Rich discusses the growing control of women's bodies and the birth process by patriarchal societies. In this study the control of the birth process by men is analyzed not only as a social reality but it becomes a metaphor for male dominance in general. Concluding with a visionary statement, Rich outlines her ideal for a future society:

> We need to imagine a world in which every woman is the presiding genius of her own body. In such a world women will truly create new life, bring forth not only children (if we choose) but the visions, and the thinking, necessary to sustain, console, and alter human existence—a new relationship to the universe. Sexuality, politics, intelligence, power, motherhood, work, community, intimacy will develop new meanings; thinking itself will be transformed.

The poems in *The Dream of a Common Language: Poems 1974-77* (1978) frequently parallel the themes in *Of Woman Born*. Both works are concerned with the suffering of women separated from community and thus with the power of collective effort and the need to understand and name one's experience. In addition, *The Dream of a Common Language* celebrates female energy as it is expressed in both its domestic and public manifestations. The achievements of both Marie Curie and Elivira Shatayev and her team of women mountain climbers who died in their effort to scale Lenin Peak in August 1974 are acclaimed. In addition, the daily efforts of women to survive and to nurture life are also recognized.

At the heart of this volume is Rich's conviction that female energy has potential to transform the world. In "Hunger," for example, Rich envisions the power of the collective energy of women:

> (Six lines, beginning
> "of what it could be"
> excluded at the publisher's request.)

Rich is suggesting here that a nurturing ethos is a necessary antidote
to the excesses of patriarchal civilization; that female energies must
balance those of men.

The concluding poem of *The Dream of a Common Language*,
"Transcendental Etude," is one of Rich's finest lyric poems to date. In
addition to its extraordinary passages describing the complex plenitude of the New England countryside where Rich has spent her summers and now lives full-time, the poem once again underscores the
need for female insight in our culture:

(Example excluded at the
publisher's request.)

In 1979 Rich published *On Lies, Secrets, and Silence, Selected Prose 1966-
1978*. These essays document her evolution as a poet through the
phases of self-analysis, individual assertion and accomplishment,
rejection of patriarchal values, feminist activism, and finally to the
building of a woman-centered community. In one of her essays in this
book, "Disloyal to Civilization," Rich refers her readers to the following passage from Virginia Woolf's *Three Guineas* which can serve as a
touchstone:

> . . . Let us never cease from thinking, what is this "civiliza-
> tion" in which we find ourselves? What are these ceremo-
> nies and why should we take part in them? What are these
> professions and why should we make money out of them:
> Where in short is it leading us, the procession of the sons of
> educated men?

In this volume Rich asserts that "language is power," and she commits herself to writing the kind of poetry that will "dare to explore, and to begin exploding, the phallic delusions which are now endangering consciousness itself." According to Rich, feminism, like good poetry, is concerned with a transformation of individual and social consciousness. It is her hope that reformed social and personal mind-set will make possible the creation of a non-exploitative society. Her fundamental conviction is that society in the United States should be able to "meet the fundamental needs of all human beings." As Rich has observed, "We can give [people] a minimum standard of living, we can given them an education, we can create an environment which is more healthy to live in, and we can give people free medical care."

According to Rich, feminism is dedicated to the ideal of an egalitarian and deeply humane society based on a transformation of our present values. This shift in consciousness will require a re-visioning or re-forming both of our linguistic habits and traditional sex roles. In order to break the hold of patriarchal restrictions on women's lives, embedded habits of language must be changed, and Rich thinks poetry can help to create these linguistic reforms: "Poetry is, among other things, a criticism of language. . . . Poetry is above all a concentration of *power* of language, which is the power of our ultimate relationship to everything in the universe." According to Rich, this is where art and politics meet.

Bibliography

By Adrienne Rich:

A Change of World. New Haven, Connecticut: Yale University Press, 1951.
The Diamond Cutters and Other Poems. New York: Harper, 1955.
Snapshots of a Daughter-in-law: Poems 1954-1962. New York: Harper & Row, 1963; reissued, New York: W. W. Norton, 1969; London: Chatto & Windus, 1972.
Necessities of Life: Poems 1962-1965. New York: W. W. Norton, 1966.
Selected Poems. London: Chatto & Windus, 1967.

Leaflets: Poems 1965-1968.   New York: W. W. Norton, 1969; London: Chatto & Windus, 1972.

The Will to Change: Poems 1968-1970. W. W. Norton, 1971; London: Chatto & Windus, 1973.

Diving into the Wreck: Poems 1971-1972. New York: W. W. Norton, 1973.

Poems: Selected and New. New York: W. W. Norton, 1975.

Of Woman Born: Motherhood as Experience and Institution. New York: W. W. Norton, 1976.

The Dream of a Common Language. New York: W. W. Norton, 1978.

On Lies, Secrets, and Silence: Selected Prose 1966-1978. New York: W. W. Norton, 1979.

About Adrienne Rich:

Gelpi, Barbara and Albert Gelpi, editors. *Adrienne Rich's Poetry.* New York: W. W. Norton, 1978. (This volume contains essays by W. H. Auden, Randall Jarrell, Albert Gelpi, Robert Boyers, Helen Vendler, Erica Jong, Wendy Martin, and Nancy Milford.)

Kalstone, David. *Five Temperaments: Elizabeth Bishop, Robert Lowell, James Merrill, Adrienne Rich, and John Ashbery.* New York: Oxford University Press, 1977.

Martin, Wendy. "Adrienne Rich's Poetry." Monograph in the *American Writers Series.* New York: C. Scribner's Sons, 1978.

Literature in Languages Other than English

A Conversation among Joseph Brodsky, Raymond Federman,
José Ferrater-Mora, and Richard Kostelanetz

Kostelanetz: With me are three major writers—American citizens all—who write in languages other than English. The first is José Ferrater-Mora, born in 1912, who left his native Spain at the end of the 1936-39 Spanish Civil War, settling first in Cuba and then in Chile before moving in 1947 to New York and then to Philadelphia, where he has lived since 1949. Raymond Federman, born in France in 1928 and then a Jewish survivor of the Nazi occupation of France, is presently Professor of English at the State University of New York at Buffalo. The last is Joseph Brodsky, born in Russia in 1940 who emigrated to America in 1972 and is presently teaching at New York University.

It should not be forgotten that America has always been a country of immigrants, and among those immigrants have been poets, novelists, and critics who have continued to write in their native language as well as their new language. One historical example that comes to mind is O. E. Rölvaag, who emigrated from his native Norway in 1896 when he was 20 years old. After attending college in Minnesota, he wrote, initially in Norwegian, a series of novels which are still read, the most famous being *Giants in the Earth*, published in Norway in 1924-25 and in the United States in 1927 in Rölvaag's own translation. During World War II many of Germany's major writers lived in America, among them Thomas Mann and Bertolt Brecht, who returned to Europe after the war, while other Germans stayed here, including Hannah Arendt, Erich Auerbach, Paul Tillich, and Herbert Marcuse. Vladimir Nabokov came to America in 1940 and produced a series of novels in English that we regard among the very best contemporary American fiction. The Portuguese writer George de Sena lived in Santa Barbara until his death a few years ago, and the

Philippine writer Bienvenido D. Santos has for many years taught at
Wichita State University in Kansas. The French novelist Marguerite
Youcenar, the first woman ever elected to the august Academie
Française, is an American citizen who has lived most of the past 30
years in the state of Maine.

In a large American city like New York, there are newspapers
published in French, Russian, Italian, Greek, Yiddish, Ukranian,
among other languages; and wherever you have vernacular newspapers you have a place for poets and fiction writers to publish in their
native tongues. In fact, most of the fiction of Isaac Bashevis Singer, the
internationally known Nobel Prize winner, initially appeared in the
daily *Forward*, a Yiddish newspaper that has been published in
New York City since the beginning of the century.

Let me ask, Mr. Ferrater, how did you come to America and
then what kinds of writing have you done since you've been here?
Ferrater-Mora: Well, I came to America in 1947, and it was a
matter of chance, as most events in our lives. I was living in Chile,
and I was asked whether I would be willing to apply for a Guggenheim Fellowship. I said yes without thinking much of it; as a matter
of fact, I was quite pleased in Chile at the time. I got the Guggenheim
Fellowship, and I came to New York for a year. I was going to go back
to Chile or to Argentina when two very good friends of mine, a
Spanish poet, Pedro Salinas, who was teaching at the time in Baltimore at Johns Hopkins University, and the great Spanish historian,
Américo Castro, who was teaching at Princeton University, suggested
that I stay here where I would find obviously many more facilities,
particularly bibliographical facilities, for research.

I had at the time published a number of books in Mexico and
Argentina, as well as a book in Spain before I left, including the first
edition of a dictionary of philosophy which has been quite successful
in the Spanish-speaking countries.
Kostelanetz: Which you wrote by yourself?
Ferrater-Mora: Which I wrote by myself, yes. It has been expanding, and now the last edition, published last year in Spain, has
four big volumes of more than a thousand pages per volume.
Kostelanetz: So then it is a project that has been with you for 45
years.
Ferrater-Mora: Yes. Actually this is the only way of carrying on
such a project. Namely, if you see the book now, if you see these
enormous four volumes of more than a thousand pages each, and if

you ask the author, "Would you be willing to produce such a project?" the author obviously would say no. The possibility of producing such a book is that you produce first a tentative, imperfect, small, disgusting edition, and then later you learn and you refine. You learn by mistakes, and then at the end you come out with something that is much more acceptable than the first time. I also had produced by then a considerable number of articles, mostly in South American journals.

I came here in 1947, and by 1949 it was suggested that there was a vacancy in philosophy at Bryn Mawr College. I visited Bryn Mawr; I saw the president. At the time things were easier in hiring people in this country. Namely, today you go through many committees, which does not mean the selection is better necessarily. But the fact is that at the time it was quite sufficient to go have a visit, to see the president; and if the president liked you, if the dean of the gradaute school liked you, if the chairman of the department liked you, and if everybody else liked you, well, no matter how many committees there were, they hired you.

Kostelanetz: Then did you teach in English or in Spanish?

Ferrater-Mora: Well, in the beginning I taught one course in Spanish and two courses in English, and I've been teaching only in English ever since. As a matter of fact, as far as teaching philosophy is concerned, it is easier for me to teach in English than to teach in Spanish after 40 years of teaching.

Kostelanetz: Why?

Ferrater-Mora: Well, just as a matter of habit. I can teach in Spanish perfectly well. I taught a seminar in Madrid and another one in Barcelona two years ago.

Kostelanetz: Now the books you've written in America, are they in Spanish or English?

Ferrater-Mora: Both. I have five books in English, three of which I wrote directly in English, one on Unamuno, one on Ortega y Gasset, and one entitled *Philosophy Today*. And then there are two translations, which actually are my own books in a way, because I was not very pleased with the original translation so I rewrote the books in their entirety. These are *Men at the Crossroads* and *Being and Death*.

Kostelanetz: Now these are all books of philosophy?

Ferrater-Mora: Yes, as a matter of fact, I never published a literary book until last year when I published a book of short stories in Spain.

Kostelanetz: When did you write the stories?
Ferrater-Mora: I wrote the stories in the course of the last four or
five years.
Kostelanetz: And they're all in Spanish?
Ferrater-Mora: They're all in Spanish, yes, but as a matter of fact,
they happen in the United States. It is difficult to write something on
a place where you are not living. In one of the shorter stories I have the
example of a South American writer who comes to this country and
wants to be a novelist. He is teaching, but then he gives up teaching
and tries to write a novel. He has no ideas; he has writer's block.
Then he sees a number of things happening on the street, and that
becomes the subject matter of his novel. He has the problem of finding
the proper subject matter: something that happens in the country
where he is living, not in the country where he came from.
Kostelanetz: Raymond Federman, when did you come to the
U.S.?
Federman: I left France on October 1, 1947. I specify the date
because I have begun all my novels on October 1 by some curious
coincidence. I left in 1947 when it became clear to me that I had to
look for a future somewhere else.
Kostelanetz: You were 19 years old?
Federman: Yes, and it was obvious that my parents and sisters
were not coming back from Auschwitz where they had been deported.
I went to Detroit where my uncle was living, an uncle I didn't know
before I came, who incidently was working as an editor for the Jewish
daily *Forward* but the Detroit branch.
Kostelanetz: He was working for Detroit's Yiddish newspaper?
Federman: Yes. He brought me to Detroit, and two weeks after I
came to Detroit, I was working for Chrysler.
Kostelanetz: You worked in the automobile plants?
Federman: Yes, and attending some high school in the afternoon,
evening, whenever, trying to learn English, which I didn't know at all
when I came to this country.
Kostelanetz: Why had you chosen America?
Federman: The land of dream: cowboys, gangsters, paved with
gold on the streets. You know the dream that we got from American
movies in those days.
Kostelanetz: And you had the uncle whom you knew about?
Federman: I had my uncle, who died in 1960. It turned out that
my uncle didn't speak a word of English or a word of French; he spoke

only Yiddish. He also had come from Poland in a strange manner during the war. And we couldn't communicate. For many years we didn't speak to each other. Anyway, in two years in Detroit, I got involved with jazz, became a jazz musician, and then moved to New York in the fall of 1950. I was drafted into the army in 1951, and I found myself in Korea for a few weeks until I was called to Tokyo. They had a need for someone who spoke French to deal with the French, Swiss, Belgian troops, the United Nations forces that spoke French. I became an interpreter in Tokyo, where I stayed for a year and a half and where I became an American citizen. And, going on quickly, I came out of the army in 1954 and with the GI Bill started my formal education, you might say—I was a freshman at the age of 26 at Columbia University.

Kostelanetz: The GI Bill was a way that military veterans could go to college at government expense.

Federman: Right, and it paid for my education for four years. I did my B.A. at Columbia, where I began writing—in fact, two unpublished, unfinished novels while at Columbia University and all kinds of poetry, *oeuvres de jeunesse*, I suppose. They just poured out of me, most of it autobiographical. And then I had a choice between going on to write a novel that I really wanted to do or pursuing a Ph.D., which I did; and I went to UCLA to do a Ph.D. in comparative literature. From there on I've taught. I've been teaching since 1958, first in Santa Barbara and then at SUNY in Buffalo since 1964.

Kostelanetz: Now, what do you teach?

Federman: When I started teaching, it was French. For many years I taught French literature, contemporary literature, did some critical writing, mostly on contemporary French literature, but especially on Beckett—several books on the work of Beckett. In 1973, when the English department in Buffalo needed a novelist, they asked me to move from French to English. I was very happy with this move and became a novelist-in-residence.

Kostelanetz: So you're now a Professor of English, having been a Professor of French?

Federman: Yes, English instead of French.

Kostelanetz: What kinds of books have you written?

Federman: Well, I've written criticism, essays, some poetry but mostly in the last 15 years fiction. I've published five novels now.

Kostelanetz: Are they in English or French?

Federman: One is in French, three in English, and one is bilingual, working both with French and English in a kind of displacement system.

Kostelanetz: Joseph Brodsky, how did you get here?

Brodsky: In 1972 I was summoned by the local authorities in my home town in Russia, and I was told that in ten days I should get out.

Kostelanetz: Because?

Brodsky: As a result of some seraphical decision, without any cause being given. Well, in Russia you don't ask why.

Kostelanetz: No questions.

Brodsky: I said, "What if I say no?" Well, then I was going to have a hot time pretty soon, and by that time I knew what the hot time was all about. I had served three times in prison, twice in mental hospitals. So by that time I was sufficiently bored with the precedent. Besides it really wasn't a matter of choice. They bought me a ticket.

Kostelanetz: They gave you a ticket?

Brodsky: Yes.

Kostelanetz: To where?

Brodsky: To Vienna. Basically, I was supposed, in their minds, to go to Israel. That was part of a cleaning-up operation, the cause of which never became clear to me. The only thing I know was that Nixon was supposed to come to my home town. And they were just trying to clean out the city of all the hostile or dubious elements, I think. At any rate, I found myself in Vienna. The night before, I sent a telegram to a friend of mine, whom I knew from before—an American scholar from the University of Michigan, Carl Proffer—telling him what was happening to me. Well, the first thing I saw in Vienna was him at the airport.

Kostelanetz: He flew to Vienna?

Brodsky: Yes, he flew in.

Kostelanetz: You knew him before?

Brodsky: Through Nadezhda Mandelstam and some other people. We met as long ago as 1968 or even earlier. As an American scholar, he was frequently in Russia in those days. Now the Soviets deny him an entry visa. At any rate, I found myself on the tarmac in Vienna. He said, "Hi, Joseph, how are you? What are you going to do? Where are you going to?" And I said, "I have no idea whatsoever." And I really didn't have any idea indeed. He said, "What do you think about coming to the University of Michigan? The school suggested you take this kind of a chair." I said, "That's fine by me." And that was it. On

July 9 I landed in Detroit and ended up at the University of Michigan, being given this job. It's called poet-in-residence but, in fact, it means a regular teaching position.

Kostelanetz: So like Mr. Ferrater and unlike Mr. Federman, you had friends in America who knew of your work and were eager to have you come?

Brodsky: Yes, the University of Michigan, notably the Slavic department, was fairly eager. They did a great deal of leg work to get me in. They went to the Department of State and pleaded with Bill Rogers, the Secretary of State, to accelerate the process and get my papers.

Kostelanetz: What have you written since you've come here?

Brodsy: Just the same things I've been writing all my conscious life, that is, poems. Poems, and here, partly out of the necessity to make additional money and partly out of interest, I began to write essays on literary and other subjects.

Kostelanetz: Which you hadn't done before?

Brodsky: Not really, no. Chekhov said once about himself that he wrote everything in his life except poems and police reports. I say that I never wrote prose until I came here.

Kostelanetz: Is this prose in English?

Brodsky: Yes, most of it is in English.

Kostelanetz: Did you know English before you came here?

Brodsky: Not really. Well, I knew some. I'd got some English in high school or in the Russian equivalent of high school, but it was nowhere. I remember that I used to translate a great deal. I translated the metaphysical poets and others, but I did it with the dictionary. I hardly had any opportunity to speak English while in Russia, natur-ally. I remember the first English I knew by the time of my arrival in the United States was largely Elizabethan. Instead of saying "earthquake" I'd say "trepidations," and the students would be very puzzled.

Kostelanetz: Have you taught in English since you came?

Brodsky: Yes, I arrived on July 9, and on September 3, I was taken into the classroom by Mr. Proffer, who said, "This man is going to talk to you about poetry." And that was it. And I had to speak English from the very threshold.

Kostelanetz: Now the poems you've written here since you've come, are they in Russian or in English?

Brodsky: No, they're in Russian. Well, I've done two or three in

English, and they have even been printed to my amazement and
pleasure, but that was for other considerations . . . not for show-off. I
wrote one English poem of which I am quite proud—in memory of
Robert Lowell. I did it in English mainly because I wanted to please
his shadow. I could have done it in Russian, but then I thought that he
would like it that way better.

Kostelanetz: In modern literature we have two kinds of myth.
One I associate with Evgeny Zamyatin, the Russian novelist of whom
it is said that once he left Russia, he could not do as well again. And
the contrary myth is the one of Joseph Conrad, who had to come to
England from his native Poland in order to write books of literature.
Which myth do you identify with, Mr. Ferrater?

Ferrater-Mora: Well, I don't think I could identify with either of
those. There is a considerable discussion about Joseph Conrad's case:
how much English he knew. It was assumed that he knew exactly
nothing and that he learned English from scratch and then he became
a great writer. I think it's very dubious myself.

Kostelanetz: That might be true. I was talking more about the
myth.

Ferrater-Mora: First of all, I am not like Mr. Federman or Joseph
Brodsky, except for my little book of short stories. I am not strictly
speaking a writer but a philosopher, and, therefore, although language is still important, it possibly has not the crucial significance that
it has for a writer, particularly for a poet. Namely, in philosophy
you can without any great difficulty change languages or translate
much more easily than you do in poetry.

Kostelanetz: And there is a tradition of philosophers writing in
several languages whereas I know of no example of a poet writing in
several languages.

Ferrater-Mora: I think so. Let's take a case today. English has
become a kind of *koine*, a kind of international language for many
reasons, political and economic; and I think this is also due to the very
structure of the language, which gives it a certain flexibility which
makes it possible to say things in a very short manner.

Brodsky: Clarity.

Ferrater-Mora: Maybe. I don't know whether it's clarity. It may
be, but it's also the possibility of absorbing: taking a noun and making
it a verb, taking a verb and making it a noun, and then constructing
adverbs out of nouns and verbs very easily. It has the facility that
German has without imposing the structure that German syntax has.

Brodsky: It's simply hard to be fuzzy in English.

Ferrater-Mora: I would say yes and no because I could find examples for both cases. For instance, there is a French philosopher today who is greatly admired and talked about whom I find unreadable, Jacques Derrida. Well, I can't understand anything of what he writes and I doubt that anyone can; in fact, he is often praised because he is *illisible*, or unreadable. However, I've read something on him by Anglo-Saxon writers and American philosophers, and I don't know how, but they managed to make Derrida clear.

On the other hand, I can say that there are a lot of things that are written in English that are pretty fuzzy, that you wonder whether they have been actually written in England.

Brodsky: I've noticed that British academic writing is extremely fuzzy.

Kostelanetz: There's a different kind of fuzziness. It's not a French fuzziness but a kind of vagueness.

Brodsky: Yes, yes.

Kostelanetz: Imprecision through vagueness, with underkill rather than overkill—that is, the British academic way.

Joseph Brodsky, which myth is yours—Zamyatin's or Conrad's?

Brodsky: Neither really. Just as you say, they are myths. Because, in every particular case the development takes, it seems, a different turn. Well, I'll tell you a very brief story. Just two weeks or so after I came in 1972, I got a letter from a poet whom I consider a great poet, Czeslaw Milosz; he's a Pole and he's lived here in this country for a good 25 years.

Kostelanetz: Another major refugee writer.

Brodsky: That would be an understatement really to call him that. He said, among other things in that letter, "I know, Brodsky, that you are scared you won't be able to write here, that you will forget your language, etcetera. And such a thing is possible; I've seen it happen. If such a thing will happen to you, well, it will mark your value." I was very fortunate to get this kind of message at the very beginning.

Kostelanetz: It wasn't something you were afraid of.

Brodsky: Well, I was somewhat worried.

Kostelanetz: But indeed it hasn't happened.

Brodsky: Not to me.

Ferrater-Mora: It depends to a great extent on the kind of writing.

I suppose with poetry you can be more pure. Namely, you can stay in another country for years and years and write poetry in your native language and not be influenced. The evolution of the language in poetry in the country of your origin is not so considerable because poetry is already a highly formalized language.

Kostelantz: Are you thinking of Pedro Salinas?

Ferrater-Mora: I'm thinking of the difference between a poet and a novelist, a novelist who uses ordinary language, who sometimes tries to reproduce ways in which people talk—which change considerably, particularly at the present time. Change in language is constant.

Brodsky: Exactly. Because in prose, in the novel, there is at least one premise that a writer ought to reflect the existing verbal idiom of the nation. It happens quite often that writers fall into a trap in that the idiom creates the writer, whereas in poetry it is a slightly different situation: it is the poet who creates in a sense an idiom, or, at least, a mental idiom, spiritual idiom, because after all, poetry is the supreme form of the language, so to speak, yes? Well, again, this may sound demagogical, but today in Italy they speak Dante's Italian.

Kostelanetz: Raymond Federman, as a writer of fiction and criticism, how do you relate to these issues?

Federman: Let me start with a slight digression. Being French-born and therefore born into the French language, I should point out that the French have a different attitude towards language. In fact, the French who emigrate to America never consider themselves immigrants. There is no such thing as an ethnic French group in the U.S. as there are Italians, Germans, whatever. They remain French always, and I have many friends in America who have been here many years and who refuse to write in English in order to preserve the purity, so-called, of their French language. It is a problem that I had to face when I first came and for a good number of years. I immediately started to learn English and write in English, and I placed the French language aside. I didn't want to have that language corrupted by the English language.

Kostelanetz: So you grew up under the myth that a Frenchman should not write in English?

Federman: Exactly. English was merely a useful language since I was living here. However—this may be where I differ from most of my French friends and most of them are writers—I quickly began to use both languages to the despair of a lot of my friends who feel that you're going to corrupt the purity of the French language.

Brodsky: And which it deserves.

Federman: And which it deserves. And, of course, some of the great French writers or others who write in French have been able to corrupt that language. I think of people like Beckett and Cioran. . . .

Kostelanetz: And Céline.

Federman: Céline, and especially Cioran, who has done magnificent things with the French language.

Kostelanetz: But Cioran is Romanian, isn't he?

Federman: Yes, Romanian.

Brodsky: Although he regrets that he doesn't write in English. He expressed that regret more than once.

Federman: Being a bilingual writer raises different questions. For many years I would keep the two languages apart and write some texts in English, some in French.

Kostelanetz: What was the distinction? What did you do in French? Mr. Ferrater-Mora spoke about doing his fiction in Spanish but his philosophy sometimes in English.

Federman: I'd say that at first I wrote mostly criticism in French because that sort of French came back to me. Although I've continued to speak French for the many years that I've lived in this country, academic French came back to me while working on a Ph.D. and studying French literature. But it was when I sat down to write my French novel, *Amer Eldorado*, that I recovered what I call my original French. In fact, the novel is extremely slangish, very Célinian in many ways, and it is that language which was mine when I was young and not the academic French that I learned on top of that.

But the interesting thing for me was at which point—I can almost pinpoint this—I began to bring English and French together and, in fact, allowed the two languages to move into each other. My ambition is to write a totally bilingual book, but I don't mean just one page French, one English; it's where the languages shift back and forth into French and English. . . .

Kostelanetz: An example of that in Russian and English would be Anthony Burgess's *A Clockwork Orange*.

Federman: Except that that's a made-up language that he invented. It remains in a way a fabricated language whereas I would like my two languages to flow into each other freely, depending on the mood and the inspiration and so on.

Brodsky: I was going to say Le Bourget English or Kennedy

French or whatever.

Ferrater-Mora: I'm sorry. I don't see how this novel could be constructed. I mean, what do you have in mind—one language going into the other?

Federman: There are key sentences, of course, depending where the situation of the action is, but there are key terms in both languages that could serve as pivot.

Brodsky: That's a terrific idea, by the way. Well, suppose you have a novel in which one action takes place in Paris, another in London or wherever it is, so you write that chapter in the appropriate language.

Ferrater-Mora: Like editing in film when you take, for instance, an image as a point of departure. . . .

Federman: Sure, there is a lot of montage, but it is not just the situation but also the characters. There are characters who must speak English while others speak English. Or unless you do the old-fashioned thing and say, "He said in French. . . ." But then you're writing it in English.

Brodsky: But it is a very esoteric, very avant-garde idea basically. It is not the old idea of a novel, yes, but it's kind of a linguistic feat. That's what it is all about.

Kostelanetz: Except that his point is that it is also a reflection of his particular sensibility. . . .

Brodsky: Well, that's something else.

Federman: Which is bilingual. . . .

Kostelanetz: Which is also his linguistic experience.

Ferrater-Mora: But you're talking in terms of dialogue.

Federman: No, no, not dialogue. I mean that I as a bilingual writer, I live a bilingual language, culture; I live my life both as a Frenchman and an American. My children are bilingual, and we turn back and forth, French, English. We speak the two languages freely.

Kostelanetz: Now how does this reflect itself in your work?

Federman: I started writing the two books that are now called *Take It or Leave It* and *Amer Eldorado* at the same time simultaneously in French and English. Obviously they started departing from each other, and eventually I finished the French one and went back to the English one. But by the time I returned to *Take It or Leave It*, I had a kind of model in French, and what I did, I took this French text upon which I inscribed another book.

Kostelanetz: Inscribed another book?

Federman: In other words, *Amer Eldorado* is a 200-page novel. . . .

Kostelanetz: Which was published in France.

Federman: Yes, in 1974. And *Take It or Leave It* is about 500 pages. The same story was moved into it, and I wrote a second inscription on top of it. *Amer Eldorado*, as it finds it way into this book, was turned into English, and I complicated the text by adding to it an English dimension.

Kostelanetz: Now how do the novels differ from each other aside from their linguistic difference?

Federman: In terms of structure, in terms of tone. *Amer Eldorado* in a way works on the principle that the narrator is addressing a group of listeners, and those listeners in the French novel are definitely French intellectuals, including Derrida and company, to whom the book is addressed. The English novel is addressed also to a group of listeners, but they are not French intellectuals, they are New York Jewish intellectuals. And so the direction of the book goes somewhere else.

Kostelanetz: Mr. Ferrater, you spoke similary about writing a book of philosophy in Spanish and having a translation made. You decided the translation was not good and so you rewrote your book in English.

Ferrater-Mora: But I find in that case that I differ from Mr. Federman's opinion, probably because of temperament, maybe because of a lack of literary invention. I find it easier to be linguistically schizophrenic.

Kostelanetz: Either/or.

Ferrater-Mora: Yes, either/or. Namely, when you use one language, then you use that language, and you forget about the other one. I think the language commands a great deal what you are going to say and the way in which you are going to say it. Of course, this is not a literary work that I am talking about.

Kostelanetz: But Mr. Federman implied that this would be true in his novels which start in the same place but go in two different directions. The language moved them in different directions.

Ferrater-Mora: But then I don't see how—probably it will be a very interesting work—but I don't see how it works practically.

Federman: It does something else. You see, I translate myself.

Ferrater-Mora: And you say you are not going to coin any new terms or vocabulary like in the case of Anthony Burgess.

Federman: No. Let me perhaps explain it this way. When I write a text in French or English, immediately I will need to transpose that text into the other language, whether it's a poem or a novel, though I haven't done it with novels except in the case of these two novels. But I find something interesting in the process when I translate or adapt, from one language into another, is that the second text is not really an adaptation, a translation; it is a continuation of the text. The text wants to go on into that other language.

Ferrater-Mora: Suppose that you find the following case: you have one page written either in French or in English, and you want to translate this page either in English or French. Do you find there is an important, a remarkable difference, or no?

Federman: There is a great difference.

Ferrater-Mora: There is a great difference. Sometimes it doesn't look like the same thing.

Federman: But it doesn't matter.

Brodsky: Mr. Federman merely regards the writing or the text as the novel. That is the main distinction. We regard the novel as something that has a plot, well, that is mostly interesting because of the plot, so to speak—this is an old-fashioned idea, the normal idea.

Ferrater-Mora: Which will come back eventually.

Brodsky: Well, which still survives in biographies, etcetera. They're the last bastion of realism. His idea is more avant-garde or more inventive, as simple as that.

Federman: But it is central to my existence as someone who has been displaced from one place to another, displaced into another language. What is central to my work is the notion of displacement. Everything I do is a form of displacing something from one language to another. That's how I can explain what I am doing.

Ferrater-Mora: For instance, when you write in French, you try to avoid Anglicisms.

Federman: Not necessarily. I use them or abuse them if necessary.

Ferrater-Mora: Well, there are some Anglicisms that are used consciously and purposely, but. . . .

Kostelanetz: Esoteric Anglicisms.

Ferrater-Mora: Yes, but some others are not, they are simply just sloppiness.

Federman: Oh, if you're not conscious or in control of what you're doing, that's something else. But even a writer like Céline was deliberately using Anglicisms in his writing, and so does Beckett.

As you know, writers, especially those who write so-called creatively, need always to gain a kind of distance from their own writing, especially if they are writing from their own experience. The use of two languages, for me, gives that distance. A friend of mine made an interesting comment once when I published a book of poems in Paris in English and French. (Some poems are written in French, some in English, and some poems are translations.) He was reading the book and pointed out to me that this poem was written first in English and then translated in French or vice versa.

Kostelanetz: How could he tell?

Federman: He could tell because, he said, the translation or the adaptation always carries an element of irony which is not as visible in the original text.

Kostelanetz: Let me ask, Mr. Ferrater, about your fiction. What kind of tradition lies behind your recent books of stories?

Ferrater-Mora: My fiction is a little ripple on a more important sea or river or whatever body of water, which is the philosophical one.

Kostelanetz: True. But it was not written for nothing.

Ferrater-Mora: No, it was written a little bit because. . . . The present situation in philosophy is rather complex, and now is not the time to express it, but there has been a general diffidence in the philosophical undertaking from every quarter. I think I am doing nothing but what everyone else is doing in philosophy—namely, trying to find other ways aside from the traditional philosophical one.

Kostelanetz: So therefore your fiction is meant to be philosophical fiction as Unamuno wrote philosophical fiction?

Ferrater-Mora: No, it's not meant to translate into fiction a philosophical idea. What I am saying is something of a different character: it's that the philosophical enterprise as we have known it for 2,000 years may come to an end or has come to a dead end.

To come to a dead end doesn't mean necessarily to finish. It means that it has to change considerably or transform itself considerably from the inside. And so I think it is quite normal that philosophers do try to find other ways of doing other things aside from philosophy. I suppose that this is one of the reasons why, aside from my general interest in literary affairs, I have written these short stories.

Kostelanetz: Could you please read a sample?

Ferrater-Mora: No, I don't have a sample of the short stories at

all. I'll just read one paragraph from a book of mine entitled *Being and Death*, in Spanish entitled *El Ser y la Muerte*, which I wrote originally in Spanish, and then I rewrote it in English.
Kostelanetz: When?
Ferrater-Mora: The original version in Spanish was in 1950, and then there was a new version, quite different, in 1965. The English edition was in 1967. So I will read in Spanish this paragraph which refers to the experience of the death of a person:

> La muerte del familiar, precisamente por hallarse éste tan «prójimo,» no lograba producir por entero esa sensación de soledad completa ante la muerte que en otras ocasiones suele revelarnos el morir humano. En este respecto me resultó más alleccionadora la muerte de un hombre que sólo en el sentido corriente, y harto vago, del término, podía llamarse «un prójimo.» Así me ocurrió un día cuando, en el curso de una jornada sangrienta, vicaer, segado por una bala, el cuerpo de un hombre. No hubo aquí dolor ni—excepto en un sentido muy general—congoja. Parcecía que la *muerte* ajena era una muerte *ajena*— algo acontecido «fuera,» algo, por así decirlo, «objetivo,» un «mero hecho»—. ¿No era por lo pronto, sólo el cuerpo de un semejante el que caía, como un muñeco a quien le fallaran de súbito los resortes, con un ruido sordo y seco, sobre el duro empedrado de la calle? Contribuía a esta impresión la patética escenografía sobre la cual se montaba el hecho: la luz incierta de la alborada, los secos restallidos de los disparos, la calle solitaria, y, bajo el foco de la mirada, como alumbrado por un resplandor invisible, el aspecto final de estatua del caído.

As a matter of fact, it is a philosophical piece, but it is quite literary because it is a description.

And then I tried the English translation—and I don't know how faithful or unfaithful it is. I'll just read a couple of sentences from the end of this.

> Was it not, to begin with, only the body of an unknown fellow creature that fell, like a marionette whose strings had suddenly been cut, with a dull and muffled thud, on the stone covered field? Enhancing this impression was the somewhat dramatic setting in which the event occurred: the dim light of dawn, the abrupt crack of rifle fire, the desolate landscape, and, within my gaze, as if lit by an invisible projector, the quiescent shape of the fallen man.

Brodsky: What about that "pathetic scenography"?

Ferrater-Mora: I beg your pardon.

Brodsky: You have that expression about the "pathetic scenography," *patética escenografía* or whatever it is. How does it go in English?

Ferrater-Mora: Yes. Well, I don't know whether I have it in the English text. As a matter of fact, it changed a good deal here and there. Yes, you're right that there are some places where the word "pathetic" is in Spanish and it's not in the English text.

Brodsky: That's a terrific image, terrific verbalization.

Kostelanetz: Mr. Brodsky, has your poetry changed in sound now that you've lived in America?

Brodsky: Well, I think it did because writing is subject to change like anything else, but I wouldn't really know what to ascribe those changes to: either myself moving to a different linguistic milieu or just getting older. It hasn't changed in sound, not really. The prosody underwent certain alterations. I am writing, I would say, in a somewhat less regular meter. That is, it is more accentuated or quantitative verse rather than. . . .

Kostelanetz: Which is the Anglo-American tradition as distinct from a Russian tradition?

Brodsky: No, meters are meters regardless. That's what there are meters for. So my poetry is essentially the same although it sounds presently less like, say, Hart Crane and more like MacNeice or Auden.

Federman: Has the American experience of living here had an impact on your poetry at all? The material of it, I mean.

Brodsky: I don't think so. I don't think there is any. . . . Look, it is impossible. Such a thing is unthinkable. Such a thing is nonexistent—that kind of an impact. There's Karl Marx's famous dictum that one's being determines one's conscience, or something like this. Well, I never bought it really because I think it's true up to a certain point after which conscience determines one's being, well-being or poor-being or whatever it is, welfare. Well, to a certain extent, there are some thematical introductions or entries that wouldn't be thinkable if I lived at home: for instance, a description of Venice, or—I don't really know—of Cape Cod, etcetera, those things. Aside from that, what you're trying to do about any material world, any material phenomenological world, be it American or Russian, is basically the same: you're trying to make sense out of it.

Federman: Let me ask you then another question, which may be unfair. When you were writing in Russia, in Russian of course, you had in a way a sense of a reader out there. Do you still have? Or do you feel you're writing in a kind of vacuum because you have lost it? I don't say you've lost it, but you know what I am saying, abstractly.
Brodsky: No, I understand that. I had always, I had not exactly a vague but a fairly limited notion of my reader, really.
Kostelanetz: Because of the nature of the Russian literary scene?
Brodsky: Not so. Not only because of that. The best answer to this sort of question has been given by the late Stravinsky. When asked by Robert Craft for whom does he write, he said, "For myself and for the probable alter ego." This is what it's all about, and it really doesn't change. You can flatter or deceive yourself by small things. You can tell yourself that I have this kind of a readership or that kind, big or small, or whatever it is. The nation listens to me or two people listen to me. But basically you are not writing for them, for either quantity. You're writing for that ideal, perhaps angelic audience, yes?
Federman: That's the kind of reader I meant, the ideal reader.
Kostelanetz: Your ideal reader has to be bilingual.
Federman: Of course.
Brodsky: My angel should speak Russian.
Kostelanetz: Would you please read for us a poem that you've written?
Brodsky: Ты забыла деревню, затерянную в болотах
залесенной губернии, где чучел на огородах
отродясь не держат — не те там злаки,
и дорогой тоже все гати да буераки.
Баба Настя, поди, померла, и Пестерев жив едва ли,
а как жив, то пьяный сидит в подвале,
либо ладит из спинки нашей кровати что-то,
говорят, калитку не то ворота.
А зимой там колют дрова и сидят на репе,
и звезда моргает от дыма в морозном небе.
И не в ситцах в окне невеста, а праздник пыли
да пустое место, где мы любили.

Kostelanetz: That does not sound like Anglo-American poetry.
Brodsky: Well, it's a Russian poem.

Federman: Can you give us the title in English?

Brodsky: It's a short poem from the cycle which is called *A Part of Speech,* and it's a very simple poem. It's addressed to a supposedly beloved, and it charges her with forgetting. It says, you forgot that village lost in the wooded provinces of such-and-such region where there are no scarecrows in the orchards because there are not that kind of crops there to keep scarecrows. The roads have a very bad surface. And that old man and that old woman who just gave us shelter presumably by now are dead, or if the man is alive, he's drunk in his cellar or he fixes a gate or wicket from the headboard of our former bed. In winter people chop wood, firewood, and eat turnips. And a star winks from the smoke in the frozen sky. There's no bride in brocade in the window but a holiday of dust and an empty place where we loved.

Kostelanetz: So even in its content that is a Russian poem. Raymond, can you illustrate, or demonstrate, your conception of bilingual literature?

Federman: There are several passages I could read in *Take It or Leave It.* The book is basically in English but there are some passages where the two languages come together. Let me preface this and tell you why in *this* passage it was essential to write this. The protagonist of the novel, a young Jewish Frenchman, arrives in New York. This   is not the first time, but he's returning to New York, and upon returning, in his mind appears the image of the arrival of Bardamu in Céline's *Voyage au Bout de la Nuit.* He identifies with Bardamu and therefore allows the language of Céline—it's not my French, it's Céline's French —to work its way into his own vision of New York. So that. . . .

Kostelanetz: Céline's French was an argot, a slang.

Federman: And it's straight out of the language of *The Journey to the End of Night.* Let me pick it up a little before that.

> ah New York at this time of evening in February in the rain
> the fog the mist incredible windows all the way up to the
> sky glass walls all over huge walls of glass up to the sky and
> even higher corridors of walls up to the sky even beyond
> skyscrapers my ass skyfuckers all the way up and you walk
> inside that labyrinth of corridors like a little bug flattened
> against the asphalt a guy must look ridiculous seen from
> above and the wind blows in there screams and the wind
> pushes you against the walls ah I love it I love it especially

when the streets are deserted at night when the garbage
flies in your face ah New York what a tough city you can die
right there on the sidewalk and who cares no one will stop
to look at you to touch you to take your hands and lift you
up physically or morally but doesn't matter you die when
it's time to die in New York City who needs an audience
better die here than far away over there

and the broads the elegant broads on Fifth Avenue Madison Park Avenue on the Eastside with their gorgeous
bodies and legs silk legs that drive you insane here go back
and reread the arrival of Bardamu in New York in le
Voyage then you'll see what I mean by elegant long supple
svelte legs that keep going up and up under the skirts to
where it's all warm in there warm and furry where it's all
cozy in there but where only your imagination can enter to
feel it!

Here   simultaneously
let me quote you a little passage   just a few sentences
to refresh your memory page 193 in my Pléiade Edition (he
said to my astonishment)   because me too like
a jerk (he had found the place in his book) j'attendis une
bonne heure or more after the phone call à la même place
and then de cette pénombre in this gray rain de cette foule
en route discontinue morne surgit around 10:00 p.m. une
brusque avalanche quite unexpected de femmes abso-
lument belles gorgeous stunning out of nowhere quelle
découverte quelle Amérique quel ravissement was I lucky
to be here je touchais au vif de mon pélerinage and if je
n'avais pas souffert en même temps des continuels rappels
the loud gurgling in my stomach de mon appétit wow was
a I hungry suddenly je me serais cru parvenu à l'un de ces
moments de surnaturelle and of surrealistic révélation
esthétique les beautés que je découvrais just like that
incessantes m'eussent avec un peu de confiance et de
confort and a bit more self-confidence ravi à ma condition
trivialement humaine

It goes on and on.

Ferrater-Mora: There is one question here. This very good passage, which you have just read now, it's mostly descriptive; I mean, it's
not conceptual. The difficulties that there are—when we compare one
language to the other and when we want to say something in one
language that we assume can or cannot be said in another language—
occur mostly on the conceptual level, I think. I have an example.

Brodsky just asked me whether I found in English anything like the expression *patética escenografía,* and I found it. In English it reads *dramatic setting.* What happens here? I heard a number of times the Argentinian writer Borges being interviewed. He always makes the same claim that you cannot say much in Spanish. He always deplores that he is not an English writer, and he always claims that you cannot say in Spanish a number of things that you can say in English. Well, I would say that he is right but you reverse the case. You cannot say in English a number of things that you can say in Spanish. And that particular passage, I think, is interesting. I mean, it is an insignificant passage, but I think it is linguistically interesting. There is something you can say in Spanish here and it's perfectly well and it's quite ordinary, *patética escenografía,* which in English would be ridiculous. So in English you have to say something like *dramatic setting.* On the other hand, in Spanish it continues *sobre la cual se montaba el hecho;* in English you have to say something to translate the concept—I am not talking about description but to translate the concept—something like *the dramatic setting in which the event occurs,* which is literally not interesting at all. My experience is that sometimes it goes both ways. I mean sometimes I find something in English which I find absolutely impossible to say in Spanish with the same degree of vividness and color, but also the other way around. And that happens always on the conceptual level rather than on the descriptive level. So I think that your passage is magnificent, but I think that if it succeeds, it's mostly because it's maintained on a stylistic level.

Federman: Let me relate to you an anecdote to point out to you this problem of concept if we are saddled with two languages—we live in two languages, all of us. In 1958 I went back to France after 11 years, for the first time after coming to America, and one afternoon I was going to pick up a friend at the airport, an American friend, and I called a taxi, "Place Denfert-Rochereau." The cab opens the door and I get in. The taxicab driver says to me, "4 Rue Louis Rolland"—that's the address where I used to live when I was a kid. I was dumbfounded. He says, "But don't you remember me?" He was speaking French to me and using the *tu. "Tu bien parles.* We were in school together. You remember, you used to live around the corner. You lived there. Oh, I worked for 15 years in a factory, but I was fed up. Now this is my cab. I own this cab." He goes on with his life. He had lived his entire life in this little square. Finally, he turns to me, "*Et toi?*" I hesitated, "Well, I live in America." "Come on, you're kidding me." "No, no, I've

been there for ten years." And I go on, and we talk while he's driving
me to the airport in the *tu* form. I say, "Wait for me." I go pick up my
friend; we get back in the cab, and now we're speaking English
because this friend doesn't speak a word of French. And suddenly the
gap was opened. And my schoolmate switched back, but hesitantly,
and addressed me with the *vous*, "*Vous allez où?*" And it's in that shift
from the *tu* to the *vous* that something very central appeared. And
after he left us wherever we were going, he said—and this was so
crucial, and I'm using that in a book I'm writing now—(I'm going to
say it in French) "*Viens quand même diner un soir.*"—Come and have
dinner with us *in spite of* all. These are crucial linguistic problems. If
I write this in English, I am losing it. I have to work with this *tu* and
this *vous* and this *quand même*. And that's conceptual for me. That's no
longer descriptive. That's getting into the core of the gap that exists
between the two languages.

Kostelanetz: Well, how did you handle that in your new book?
Instead of writing an English or a French book as you have in the past,
you've now written a bilingual book.

Federman: *The Voice in the Closet* was a different problem for me.
It was a way to get back to a very original experience which I first wrote
in English and decided that I needed to go back to it in French. And
so I basically wrote the same text twice, although it is not the same text;
one sort of overlaps and displaces the other and so on. But this incident
that I related I am working with it now in terms of allowing the French
to come in any time it needs to come in. Or the English.

Kostelanetz: Are there other non-English writers working in
America now who you greatly admire, Mr. Ferrater?

Ferrater-Mora: Well, it happens that at present none, but there
have been a number of very distinguished poets in the United States.
Jorge Guillén, for instance, was here for many years. And Salinas was
here for many years. This is the Generation of 1927, and this generation is now either back in Spain or they simply died.

Kostelanetz: Generation of '27—people who left in '27?

Ferrater-Mora: No, in Spain there is a tendency, which comes
from a German tradition, of calling a generation a certain number of
people who flourished, had their acme, as they say in Greek, at a
certain period, and for this group it was in 1927. There was Ramón
Sendor, a great novelist who was very old and went back to Spain. I
think there are really very few people now.

Kostelanetz: So the phenomenon of Spanish writers coming to this country has passed.

Ferrater-Mora: Yes, I think so. As a matter of fact, most of the Spanish writers that were not living in Spain were living in South America rather than in the United States.

Kostelanetz: Joseph Brodsky?

Brodsky: Certainly the Russians that I have in mind. . . . Well, for one, there is obviously Solzhenitsyn. There are Poles and Czechs and Hungarians. Milosz, for instance: he's the best poet of the Polish language in this century.

Bibliography

Brodsky, Joseph. *A Part of Speech.* New York: Farrar, Straus and Giroux, 1980.

Federman, Raymond. *Double or Nothing.* Chicago: Swallow, 1972.

—. *Take It or Leave It.* New York: Fiction Collective, 1976.

—. *Voice in the Closet.* Madison, Wisconsin: Coda, 1979.

Ferrater-Mora, José. *De la materia a la razón.* Madrid: Alianza Universitaria, 1979.

Zyla, Wolodymyr T., editor. *Ethnic Literature Since 1776.* Two volumes. Lubbock: Texas Tech University Press, 1978.

Donald Hall on His Poetry:
Looking for Noises

Beginning

When I was 12, I was a loose aggregate of ambitions with no direction to them. I wanted to be an actor, a politician, a writer. At 14 I decided to be a poet. Although I have since taught at a university, advised publishers, edited magazines, and written prose—fiction, biography, journalism, children's books, plays—poetry has remained at the center of my life.

When I was 16, I published free verse poems in small magazines like *Trails, Experiment,* and *Matrix.* I thought of the poet as alienated from middle-class culture and therefore innovative. At 17, I discovered metrics. It was the mid-1940s, then, when the dominant American poets wrote rhymed stanzas, and I studied at a boarding school where the English teachers formed a coven of Robert Frost worshippers. Although Frost was a good poet, my teachers admired him for silly reasons—because he was not T. S. Eliot—and, alas, they looked upon Stephen Vincent Benét as Frost's heir apparent.

If Eliot would not do, Ezra Pound and E. E. Cummings were unmentionable, and no one had heard of William Carlos Williams. At Harvard my poetry teachers dedicated themselves to discovering irony, complex textures, and the iambic foot. By the time I was graduated, "I knew the way to write poems."

And so did many poets of my generation; I have changed as others have.

At Harvard during my four years I knew other undergraduate poets: Peter Davison, L. E. Sissman, Adrienne Rich, Frank O'Hara, Kenneth Koch, John Ashbery, and Robert Bly. Robert Creeley had dropped out the year before and lived nearby in New Hampshire; I met him at the Grolier Book Shop in 1949, and we talked poetry for an hour. John Hawkes was beginning to write fiction; John Updike arrived as a freshman when I was a senior. Richard Wilbur was a graduate student, later a Junior Fellow. John Ciardi was my first writing teacher; two others with me in that class were O'Hara and Edward Gorey. Archibald MacLeish arrived as Boylston Professor in my junior year; Bly and I took his class. Robert Frost lived nearby in fall and winter; T. S. Eliot visited every spring.

But it was the other undergraduates who mattered most. We were serious about our writing and hard on each other. Many of us worked together on a student magazine, *The Harvard Advocate*, and we would argue until four in the morning about printing a particular poem. I suppose we were self-important—as if our decisions *mattered*; yet I learned more in these arguments than I learned in classrooms.

When I left Harvard and spent two years at Oxford, I was appalled by the amateurishness of the young English poets. (There were exceptions: Geoffrey Hill was at Oxford, Thom Gunn at Cambridge.) Oxford was poetry-crazy—it was the only place I know where writing poems was a form of social-climbing—and in a variety of publications Oxford printed more than 400 student poems a year. At Harvard our one magazine grudgingly printed 20 or so.

Most young English poets of 1951 were sloppy indeed, sub-Georgian, without skill or brains or talent for verse—and I hurled the word "amateurish" at them. In my American way, it never occurred to me to doubt "professionalism." But my view of poetry was distorted by notions borrowed from businessmen, from professionals like doctors and lawyers and engineers—and from the universities which manufacture and accredit them. It took years before I could see that by "professionalism," which emphasized academic craft or technique, I wedded myself to safe old ways which precluded change or growth.

Entrepreneurship

Once a good poem is made—with its sweet sounds, its miseries and joys, its spirit and shapeliness, its *new word*, its luck—it enters the marketplace. People do not like to hear this. Many poets avoid public appearances in the marketplace, although their poems appear there. There is always a marketplace apart from oneself—publishing houses, magazines, anthologies—and someone else will always run the store.

From my years at college on, as editor of magazines and anthologies, as advisor to publishers and sometimes to foundations, I have judged other people's poems, printed them, reviewed them, rewarded them. I have tried to persuade others of my taste.

In small part I have concerned myself with older poets. I interviewed Eliot, Pound, and Moore for the *Paris Review* and later wrote reminiscences of Dylan Thomas, Frost, Eliot, and Pound. For the most part I have tried to judge and discriminate among the poets of my own generation and the generations that follow. In 1957, I co-edited (with Robert Pack and Louis Simpson) an anthology called *The New Poets of England and America*. This was the anthology which became known as "academic," as opposed to Donald Allen's *New American Poetry*, three years later, which became known as "beat." Our book included good poets, but it became known for the poets it left out, an astonishing list: Frank O'Hara, Kenneth Koch, John Ashbery, Robert Creeley, Denise Levertov, Robert Duncan, Gary Snyder, Allen Ginsberg et al. For the most part, we had not read the poets we omitted: sometimes we missed them from provinciality, and sometimes from preconceptions. But that is another story. Although it was not our intention, our omissions proved useful; it drew Donald Allen's counter-anthology out of the air, which presented an array of alternative poetries. No longer would it be easy to think that one "knew the way to write poems."

A few years later, in 1962, I made an eclectic anthology for Penguin called *Contemporary American Poets*. By this time I loved Creeley's work, Gary Snyder's, Denise Levertov's, Robert Duncan's. . . . I am glad that by this time I could see past my own *atelier* because many people took from this anthology their sense of American poetry after the war. But as a literary event, the more biased an anthology is, the more powerful it is; and my Penguin suffered from the blandness of eclecticism.

In the meantime, I was a member of the editorial board of the Wesleyan Poetry Series, to which I brought books by Bly, Wright, Simpson, Dickey, and others. Then I became an advisor to Harper & Row. I edited poetry for the *Paris Review*, I wrote book reviews, gave lectures and interviews. . . . And I continue—although I have learned with age that even my most passionate prejudices are subject to change.

Changing

As my taste in poetry changed, so of course did my poems. Here is a poem I wrote in 1954 at 25, when I had been working with Yvor Winters.

My Son, My Executioner

My son, my executioner,
    I take you in my arms,
Quiet and small and just astir,
    And whom my body warms.

Sweet death, small son, our instrument
    Of immortality,
Your cries and hungers document
    Our bodily decay.

We twenty-five and twenty-two,
    Who seemed to live forever,
Observe enduring life in you
    And start to die together.

Meter, rhyme, paradox, irony, abstraction. I no longer quite know the person who wrote this poem, though I remember him dimly, as if recalling not a person but a photograph. In 1957, I began to write poetry which I associated with surrealism; the first was "The Long River," finished in 1958:

The musk ox smells
in his long head
my boat coming. When
I feel him there,
intent, heavy,

the oars make wings
in the white night,
and deep woods are close
on either side
where trees darken.

I rowed past towns
in their black sleep
to come here. I rowed

by northern grass
and cold mountains.

The musk-ox moves
when the boat stops,
in hard thickets. Now
the wood is dark
with old pleasures.

Although this poem is 22 years old now, it does not feel alien to me. I no longer use this sound—a short, slow, enjambed, percussive line with emphatic monosyllabic assonance—but I can still hear myself in it.

There were a number of reasons for changing. And as I changed, so did the poets with whom I talked poetry. We had written iambic stanzas; now we seemed to feel that we had come to the end of something. Independently and simultaneously, we moved into free verse, following various masters, and most of us began to incorporate fantasy in our poems. In my metrical verse I had come to feel limited by my associations of subject and structure with metrical form. Now I felt free, loose, improvisational, excited, and a little frightened.

We changed, I think, independently—but of course we spoke to each other. About 1957, I talked about the poetry of fantasy with Robert Bly and later with James Wright. Bly and Wright translated Georg Trakl, and Bly among others did Pablo Neruda. I learned from these poets and from others of Spain and Latin America. A little later, I found another source of change. In 1960, I met the English sculptor Henry Moore, when I interviewed him for a magazine. In the early 1960s, I spent much time with him and wrote a book about him. Several poems came directly out of his work.

"Reclining Figure"

Then the knee of the wave
turned to stone.

By the cliff of her flank
I anchored,

in the darkness of harbors
laid-by.

Moore told me, paraphrasing Rodin, "Never think of a surface except as the extension of volume." I wanted to write a poetry with an articulated surface under which one could sense a volume of emotion pressing upwards.

In the 1930s both constructivism and surrealism thrived briefly in London. Of course, they were at war—the poles of Modernism— but Moore showed sculpture in both camps. While I wanted for my poetry the emotion provided by expressionist distortion, I wanted as well the resolutions of a constructed object. Thus the small poem above improvises formal resolution by drumbeat and assonance. As Henry Moore never abandons reference to the human form, I never intend—in the pursuit of resolution—to leave behind intensity of feeling. For me, the extremes seem to touch in a poem's sound—as vowel and consonant both "rhyme" and provide the catalyst to feeling.

Noises

As my writing has changed, I have noted that changes announce themselves first as changes in sound. It seems as if, when my mouth begins to make a new noise, something inside me begins to speak, something that was dumb before. When a new noise begins, I feel full of energy and ideas; everything I look at blooms with poetry: I write and write. Over years, the energy drains from the new noise— not all at once, and by no means with a steady decline. Eventually I feel as if I had painted myself into a corner, as if the new noise—at first mysterious and undefined—became more restrictive the more I knew about it. Knowledge or self-consciousness erects rules. About 1970 or 1972 my poems could *only* be short-lined, monosyllabic, assonantal, and fantastic; of course such a rulebook restricts subject matter.

For a number of years I flailed about, writing in several manners without settling into any. I wrote prose poems; I revisited meter and felt the old grievances rise again. Then in the autumn of 1974 a new sound started—and I wrote the poems of *Kicking the Leaves* (1978): long-lined poems, asymmetrical, various in intensity, with many flat passages, less "constructed" in the intimate collision of syllables, perhaps more inclusive and architectural in the large scale. These poems are longer and more various—in detail and in tone—than anything I

have written before. They differ from each other, but having room
only for one, I pick "The Black Faced Sheep":

Ruminant pillows! Gregarious soft boulders!

If one of you found a gap in a stone wall,
the rest of you—rams, ewes, bucks, wethers, lambs;
mothers and daughters, old grandfather-father,
cousins and aunts, small bleating sons—
followed onward, stupid
as sheep, wherever
your leader's sheep-brain wandered to.

My grandfather spent all day searching the valley
and edges of Ragged Mountain,
calling "Ke-*day*!" as if he brought you salt,
Ke-*day*! Ke-*day*!"

* * *

When a bobcat gutted a lamb at the Keneston place
in the spring of eighteen-thirteen
a hundred and fifty frightened black faced sheep
lay in a stupor and died.

* * *

When the shirt wore out, and darns in the woolen
shirt needed darning,
a woman in a white collar
cut the shirt into strips and braided it,
as she braided her hair every morning.

In a hundred years
the knees of her great-granddaughter
crawled on a rug made from the wool of sheep
whose bones were mud,
like the bones of the woman, who stares
from an oval in the parlor.

* * *

I forked the brambly hay down to you
in nineteen-fifty. I delved my hands deep
in the winter grass of your hair.

When the shearer cut to your nakedness in April
and you dropped black eyes in shame,
hiding in barnyard corners, unable to hide,
I brought grain to raise your spirits,
and ten thousand years
wound us through pasture and hayfield together,
threads of us woven
together, three hundred generations
from Africa's hills to New Hampshire's.

* * *

You were not shrewd like the pig.
You were not strong like the horse.
You were not brave like the rooster.

Yet none of the others looked like a lump of granite
that grew hair,
and none of the others
carried white fleece as soft as dandelion seed
around a black face,
and none of them sang such a flat and sociable song.

* * *

In November a bearded man, wearing a lambskin apron,
slaughtered an old sheep for mutton
and hung the carcass in north shade
and cut from the frozen sides all winter, to stew in a pot
on the fire that never went out.

* * *

Now the black faced sheep have wandered and will not return,
though I search the valleys
and call "Ke-*day*" as if I brought them salt.

Now the railroad draws
a line of rust through the valley. Birch, pine, and maple
lean from cellarholes
and cover the dead pastures of Ragged Mountain
except where machines make snow
and cables pull money up hill, to slide back down.

* * *

At South Danbury Church twelve of us sit—
cousins and aunts, sons—

where the great-grandfathers of the forty-acre farms
filled every pew.
I looked out the window at summer places,
at Boston lawyers' houses
with swimming pools cunningly added to cowsheds,
and we read an old poem aloud, about Israel's sheep
—and I remember faces and wandering hearts,
dear lumps of wool—and we read

that the rich farmer, though he names his farm for himself,
takes nothing into his grave;
that even if people praise us, because we are successful;
we will go under the ground
to meet out ancestor collected there in the darkness;
that we are all of us sheep, and death is our shepherd,
and we die as the animals die.

Making a Living

From 1957 to 1975 I taught at a university. At first it was
good, as I learned by speaking what I did not know I knew; but
repetition was inevitable, and when I spoke what I knew I would
speak, I learned nothing. In 1975 I moved to the New Hampshire farm
where my family had lived since 1865, and I support myself by writing
prose, by editing, and by reading my poems aloud.

But most days, now, I write all day.

Bibliography

By Donald Hall:

The Alligator Bride. New York: Harper & Row, 1969.
The Town of Hill. Boston: Godine, 1975.
Kicking the Leaves. New York: Harper & Row, 1978.
Goatfoot Milktongue Twinbird. Ann Arbor: University of Michigan Press, 1978.
Remembering Poets. New York: Harper & Row, 1978.

About Donald Hall:

Bly, Robert. "Donald Hall." In *Contemporary Poets*. Second Edition. Edited by James Vinson. New York: St. Martin's Press, 1975; London: St. James Press, 1975.
Mills, Ralph J. "Donald Hall's Poetry." In *Cry of the Human*. Urbana: University of Illinois, 1975.
"Donald Hall Issue." *Tennessee Poetry Journal*, Winter 1971.

The Poetry of Gary Snyder

Thomas Parkinson

Gary Snyder was born in San Francisco in 1930. Shortly after his birth, his family moved to a small farm outside of Seattle, where he early acquired his proficiency with tools and with animals. When he graduated from high school, Reed College in Portland wisely gave him a scholarship, and his senior thesis, *He Who Hunted Birds in His Father's Village*, exhibits his early professional interest in the anthropology and mythology of the American Indians. During his youth and in summers while in college, he worked with the Forest Service and in logging camps in the Pacific Northwest, increasing his knowledge of the remarkable Indians of that area at firsthand and further developing his expertise in the outdoor life. His primary experience has come from the Pacific Basin, that is, the three U.S. Pacific Coast states and Japan and India. After graduating from Reed, he broke that pattern by studying at the University of Indiana; his subject remained the anthropology and mythology of American Indians. He then returned to the Pacific Coast and enrolled at the University of California at Berkeley, where he studied Oriental Languages with special emphasis on Japanese. He completed all requirements for the doctorate except for a thesis, but he decided not to continue his formal studies because that would commit him to, or at least afford the temptation of, an academic career. His true vocation was poetry, and his cultural assumptions extended beyond the Far East to include the Far West in a vision of a Pacific Basin culture. His travels as a merchant seaman in the Pacific and Indian Oceans gave him some detailed geographical perceptions, and his several years spent in Japan, much of them in residence at Zen Buddhist monasteries, gave him a rather full knowledge of Japanese culture and language.

These preliminary biographical notes should indicate that Snyder's world view grew organically from his experience and his basic impulses. The fact that some aspects of his view should have been taken up by the unskilled and unknowing as fads and fashions should not diminish his hard-earned artistry and solidly based thinking, for Snyder is not interested in fad, fashion, or convention: he is interested in tradition, and he is concerned with constructing a valid culture from the debris that years of exploitation have scattered around the Pacific Basin.

RIPRAP is Snyder's first book. The title means "a cobble of stone laid on steep slick rock/to make a trail for horses in the mountain." In the last poem in the book he writes of "Poetry a riprap on the slick rock of metaphysics," the reality of perceived surface that grants men staying power and a gripping point.

> Lay down these words
> Before your mind like rocks,
>   placed solid, by hands
> In choice of place, set
> Before the body of the mind
>   in space and time:
> Solidity of bark, leaf, or wall
>   riprap of things:
> Cobble of milky way,
>   straying planets,
> These poems. . . .

The body of the mind—this is the province of poetry, a riprap on the abstractions of the soul that keeps men in tune with carnal eloquence. Snyder's equation is one of proportions: poetry is to metaphysics as riprap is to slick rock. Things and thoughts are not then in opposition but in parallel:

>   ants and pebbles
> In the thin loam, each rock a word
>   a creek-washed stone
> Granite: ingrained
>   with torment of fire and weight
> Crystal and sediment linked hot
>   all change, in thoughts,
> As well as things.

The aim is not to achieve harmony with nature but to create an inner harmony that equals the natural external harmony. There is not then an allegorical relation between man and natural reality but an analogical one: a man does not identify with a tree nor does he take the tree to be an emblem of his own psychic condition; he establishes within himself a condition that is equivalent to that of the tree, and there metaphysics rushes in. Only poetry can take us through such slippery territory, and after *RIPRAP* Snyder tries to find a guide in his *Myths & Texts*. *RIPRAP* was an engaging, uneven first book of poems. It is still in print and deserves to be so, but it lacks unity of impact and style, however proper its intentions.

Myths & Texts is a different matter. Although some of the poems were printed as early as 1952 and Snyder gives its date of completion as 1956, it is a world away from the first book. It has a genuine informing principle and the coherence of purposeful movement, and the line has a life that is particular to its subject. The first two sections of the book are on "Logging" and "Hunting," what men do to the earth; the third on "Burning," why they do it. In this book appear in complex form the issues that compel the verse at its base. Snyder wants to reach a prehuman reality, the wilderness and the cosmos in which man lives as an animal with animals in a happy ecology. This precivilized reality Snyder finds embodied in Amerindian lore, especially of the Pacific Northwest and of California, and in Buddhist myth. He occupies the uneasy position of understanding this mode of perception and of acting, as logger and hunter, against its grain. This realization is the dramatic core of the book and holds it from sentimentality, granting it a kind of tension and prophetic force (evident in the pro-Wobbly poems) that *RIPRAP* and much of his later work lacks. *Myths & Texts* is an elegy of involvement: to have witnessed, it was necessary to be one of the destroyers. His sense of involvement keeps him from invective, except against those exploiters who ordered the destruction of nature and at the same time denied rights to the workers who had the hard nasty labor. The world that Snyder treats is part of his total fabric, and he cannot falsely externalize it. He cannot point with awe to the objects of his experience because they have become attached to him through touch and action. It is not even necessary for him to lament this world which, through his poetry, he has preserved. He moves fluently through this world as a local spirit taking the forms of Coyote and Han-shan and a ghostly logger. In these poems action and contemplation become identical states of being, and both states of secular grace. From this fusion wisdom emerges, and it is not useless but timed to the event. The result is a terrible sanity, a literal clairvoyance, an innate decorum.

This poetry does not suffer from cultural thinness. The tools, animals, and processes are all interrelated; they sustain the man; he devours them. But the author of the book and the poet in the book are nourished by a web of being, a culture. To have the support of a culture you have to work in and respect your environs, not as one respects a supermarket (thanks for the grapefruit wrapped in plastic) but as one respects a farm, knowing what labor went into the fruit, what risks were accepted and overcome, what other lives (moles, weasels, foxes, deer) were damaged or slighted in the interests of your own.

One of the touchstone lines for modern poetry is Pound's "Quick eyes gone under earth's lid." It holds its unity partly through the internal rhyme of the first and final word, partly through the unstrained conceit of random association between eyelid and coffin lid, and the earth as dead eye and graveyard. Mainly, though, it has no waste, no void spaces, none of the flab that English invites through the prepositional phrase designs of a noninflected language. Solid poetry in English manages compressions that keep up the stress, and realizations from that motive have their justification in the larger poetic unit of poem or book. The temptation of composition in serial form, the method of *Myths & Texts*, is vindicating the relaxed line in the name of a higher motive: the world view of the poet, the personal relevance. Snyder doesn't fall back on such flimsy supports. Sometimes, straining to maintain the stress he loses control: ". . . fighting flies fixed phone line. . . ." This is not only pointlessly elliptical but meaninglessly ambiguous and far too clogged. But in its excesses it demonstrates the basic prosodic motive, full use of consonant and vowel tone as organizing devices, reduction of connective words having only grammatical function and no gravity.

Snyder himself thinks of this prosody as deriving from classical Chinese forms, and both he and Pound make severe and interesting variations on that line—but only variations—and after Pound's *Cathay* and the Chinese *Cantos*, people like Snyder are compelled toward Pound's brilliant invention using the Anglo-Saxon alliterative line in conjunction with a line of four and two main centers of stress divided by caesura or by line break.

I talk at such length of prosody because it is the main factor ignored in most recent discussion of poetry. Thanks to Donald Davie and Josephine Miles, attention has very rightly been turned toward poetic syntax, with fine results, and the extension to prosody is in-

evitable and right. New Criticism (old style) placed heavy weight on
suggestion and symbolic reference; now as our poetry stresses drama
and syntactic movement, vocality, it seems necessary to extend beyond the notion, and a pernicious one, that poetry functions mainly
through symbol. Language functions symbolically and metaphori-
cally, but poetry makes more precise and delimiting use of syntax
through its prosodic measure. This is after all what Pound and
Williams were agitated about: the dance of language. What poets like
Snyder, Duncan, and Creeley ask is that readers take the poem as
indicator of physical weight. Until the day, not far off, when poems
are related to taped performances as musical scores now are, the
poem on the page is evidence of a voice and the poetic struggle is
to note the movement of that voice so that it can be, as is music,
followed.

> The groves are down
>   cut down
> Groves of Ahab of Cybele
> Pine trees, knobbed twigs
>   thick cone and seed
>   Cybele's tree this, sacred in groves
> Pine of Seami, cedar of Haida
> Cut down by the prophets of Israel
>   the fairies of Athens
>   the thugs of Rome
>   both ancient and modern;
> Cut down to make room for the suburbs
> Bulldozed by Luther and Weyerhaeuser
> Crosscut and chainsaw
>   squareheads and finns
>   high-lead and cat-skidding
> Trees down
> Creeks choked, trout killed, roads.

The procedures of the line here are largely halving and coupling and
the variations are relaxations that reach out semantically to other
results:

> Crosscut and chainsaw
>   squareheads and finns
>   high-lead and cat-skidding
> Trees down
> Creeks choked, trout killed, roads.

The violence of these lines creates a tension that is cumulative; the dangers of the catalogue are diminished by the prosody so that it is not a simple matter of adding item to item but of seeing each item as part of design and pattern—a concert of yoked energies. The final line leaves a single word uncoupled, a result, a relaxation into barrenness. The poem is a perversion of religious ceremony, the text of life against the myth of natural sacredness.

In 1965 Synder published *Six Sections from Mountains and Rivers Without End*, part of a very long sequence of poems. The book has some fine matter in it, but much of it is taken up by poems that are not sufficiently concentrated, though they may serve a function in the whole sequence once completed. I shall concentrate on the poems that have power and represent important aspects of Snyder's world view.

Snyder has spoken often of the importance of the rhythms of various kinds of work for his poetry, and his sense of experience is largely a sense of work, of measured force exerted on the world. When he sees a second-growth forest, he wonders, looking at the stumps, what they did with all the wood; a city evokes in him the tough brutal labor involved, the carpentry and plumbing and simple excavating. His world is a world of energy constantly reformulating itself, and most often a world of human energy, exploited, misdirected, and full of pathos—he can't take it for granted but sees at its base the wilderness and fundamental man, and the products generated through history. This is why "The Market"—full of the dangers of sentimentality in tone, and mere cataloguing in technique—has an inner vigor that the hitchhiker poem lacks. This is not entirely a matter of mood but of conviction and of consequent drive. Technical considerations aside, poetry like all art comes out of courage, the capacity to keep going when reason breaks down. The equivalences established in "The Market" are equivalences of energy very roughly estimated.

> seventy-five feet hoed rows equals
> one hour explaining power steering
> equals two big crayfish =
>   all the buttermilk you can drink
> = twelve pounds cauliflower
> = five cartons greek olives = hitch-hiking
>   from Ogden Utah to Burns Oregon
> = aspirin, iodine, and bandages

```
= a lay in Naples = beef
= lamb ribs = Patna
                  long grain rice, eight pounds
equals two kilogram soybeans = a boxwood
                              geisha comb.
equals the whole family at the movies
equals whipping dirty clothes on rocks
    three days, some Indian river
= piecing off beggars two weeks
= bootlace and shoelace
       equals one gross inflatable
       plastic pillows
= a large box of petit-fours, chou-crêmes—
        barley-threshing
   mangoes, apples, custard apples, raspberries
= picking three flats strawberries
= a christmas tree = a taxi ride
carrots, daikon, eggplant, greenpeppers,
oregano      white      goat      cheese
   = a fresh-eyed bonito, live clams.
a swordfish
a salmon
```

And the close of the second section shows the melancholy and weariness that accompanies the breakdown of reason before all this relentless, pointless, back-breaking labor:

```
I gave a man seventy paise
in return for a clay pot
of curds
was it worth it?
how can I tell
```

The terrible concluding section leaves us with a vision of a totally human world, a world of monstrosity:

```
they eat feces
    in the dark
    on stone floors
one legged animals, hopping cows
    limping dogs    blind cats

crunching garbage in the market
    broken fingers
        cabbage
    head on the ground.
```

who has young face.
    open pit eyes
between the bullock carts and people
    head pivot with the footsteps
             passing by
dark scrotum spilled on the street
    penis laid by his thigh
        torso
turns with the sun

I came to buy
    a few bananas by the Ganges
        while waiting for my wife.

Contemporaneous with this long-projected series of poems like an enormous Chinese scroll are other poems, more lyric and brief, many of which were collected and published in 1968 by New Directions under the title *The Back Country*. Characteristically, the first two sections are called "Far West" and "Far East"; and Snyder's most re- cent essay is called "Passage to More Than India." The synthesis he is working toward, that obsesses his being, maintains its momentum:

We were following a long river into the mountains.
Finally we rounded a ridge and could see deeper in—
the farther peaks stony and barren, a few alpine
trees.
Ko-san and I stood on a point by a cliff, over a
rock-walled canyon. Ko said, "Now we have come to
where we die." I asked him, what's that up there,
then—meaning the further mountains.
"That's the world after death." I thought it looked
just like the land we'd been travelling, and couldn't
see why we should have to die.
Ko grabbed me and pulled me over the cliff—
both of us falling. I hit and I was dead. I saw
my body for a while, then it was gone. Ko was
there too. We were at the bottom of the gorge.
We started drifting up the canyon, "This is the
way to the back country."

This poem provides the title for Snyder's *The Back Country*, an inclusive collection, the longest and in many ways most representative book of Snyder's poetry. It includes poems written after the publication of *Myths & Texts* in 1960 and some earlier poems that did not fit the design of the three earlier collections. The book is carefully structured, with sections treating Far West, Far East, Kali (goddess of creation and destruction), Back (return), and translations of Mivazawa Kenji. The book is dedicated to Kenneth Rexroth, and many of the earlier poems have an apprentice tone, in particular the lovely elegiac poem "For the Boy who was Dodger Point Lookout." The poem is a nostalgic evocation of a casual meeting between the anonymous boy, Snyder, and his wife in the Olympic Mountains of western Washington.

> The thin blue smoke of our campfire
> down in the grassy, flowery,
> heather meadow
> two miles from your perch.
> The snowmelt pond, and Alison,
> half-stoopt bathing like
> Swan Maiden, lovely naked,
> ringed with Alpine fir and
> gleaming snowy peaks. We
> had come miles without trails,
> you had been long alone.
> We talked for half an hour up
> there above the foaming creeks
> and forest valleys, in our
> world of snow and flowers.
>
> I don't know where she is now;
> I never asked your name.
> In this burning, muddy, lying,
> blood-drenched world
> that quiet meeting in the mountains
> cool and gentle as the muzzles of
> three elk, helps keep me sane.

The Back Country has the advantage both of variety and secure control of the medium of poetry. If it lacks the unified impact of *Myths & Texts*, it covers even more ground. The point of view remains constant, the wilderness as repository of possibilities and reminder of psychological richnesses that cities, notably "This Tokyo," pervert or destroy, the reality and importance of work, what a simpler age called the dignity of labor, while recognizing the horror of exploitation both of nature and of the working man.

Many of these poems come from a wandering man, wandering in his travels, wayfaring in his sexuality, solitary, exploratory, inconstant, seaman and bindlestiff, finding his true Penelope only in the world of poetry and thought. Like much of Snyder's work, these poems have the quality of a very good *Bildungsroman*. In my opinion, for narrative and description and characterization, they are far superior to the novels of the 1960s in this country. They are not tricked up or contrived; and in spite of their autobiographical content, they are not egotistical. They are articulations, not mere expressions. Their motivation is perhaps best expressed in essays written contemporaneously with the poetry: "Buddhism and the Coming Revolution," "Passage to More than India," and "Poetry and the Primitive," all reprinted in *Earth House Hold*.

> "Poetry" as the skilled and inspired use of the voice and language to embody rare and powerful states of mind that are in immediate origin personal to the singer, but at deep levels common to all who listen.

> * * *

> The mercy of the West has been social revolution; the mercy of the East has been individual insight into the basic self/void. We need both.

The prose in *Earth House Hold*, parts of *Turtle Island*, *The Old Ways*, and *The Real Work* should be read not only as partial explanation of the poetry but as the record of an evolving mind with extreme good sense in treating the problems of the world.

Regarding Wave is best thought of as two books. *Regarding Wave* is both the title of the book and the first 35 pages of text. It is a unified work of art with some of Snyder's best poems, for instance, "Not Leaving the House."

> When Kai is born
> I quit going out
> Hang around the kitchen—make cornbread
> Let nobody in.
> Mail in flat
> > Masa lies on her side, Kai sighs,
> > Non washes and sweeps
> We sit and watch
> > Masa nurse, and drink green tea.

Navajo turquoise beads over the bed
A peacock tail feather at the head
A badger pelt from Nagana-ken
For a mattress; under the sheet;
A pot of yogurt setting
Under the blankets, at his feet.

Masa, Kai,
And Non, our friend
In the green garden light reflected in
Not leaving the house.
From dawn til late at night
        making a new world of ourselves
        around this life.

Unlike some of the poems in the sections that succeed "Regarding Wave," this poem shows Snyder in the grip of a major principle, so that he becomes the agent of a voice, that of common experience, and the personal and superficially exotic change to the general and present.

Snyder's recent books, *Turtle Island* (poetry with some essays, notably "Four Changes") and *The Old Ways*, reiterate his chosen themes and methods. Some critics complain that Snyder does not develop or change in any major way. Why should he? He has chosen a substantial body of thought and experience to explore. Poets change not through fad and fashion but through a realization that their idiom no longer fits their experience. When that occurs, change is valid, but Snyder's wide and varied idiom is adequate to his intense and rich experience.

Snyder's work addresses major problems. He tries to see the world against the vast background of all human possibilities. At present, human power, pure brute controlled energy, threatens the entire planet. Some norms have to be found and diffused that will allow men to check and qualify their force. Snyder makes this large effort:

> As poet I hold the most archaic values on earth. They go back to the late Paleolithic: the fertility of the soil, the magic of animals, the power-vision in solitude, the terrifying initiation and re-birth, the love and ecstasy of the dance, the common work of the tribe. I try to hold both history and wilderness in mind, that my poems may approach the true measure of things and stand against the unbalance and ignorance of our times.

He is calling upon the total resources of man's moral and religious being. There is no point in decrying this as primitivism; it is merely good sense, for the ability to hold history and wilderness in the mind at once may be the only way to make valid measures of human conduct. A larger and more humble vision of man and cosmos is our only hope—and the major work of any serious person. In that work Snyder's verse and prose compose a set of new cultural possibilities that only ignorance and unbalance can ignore.

Bibliography

By Gary Snyder (in order of composition):

He Who Hunted Birds in His Father's Village. Bolinas, California: Grey Fox, 1979.
RIPRAP and Cold Mountain Poems. San Francisco: Four Seasons Foundation, 1966.
Myths & Texts. New York: New Directions, 1978.
Six Sections from Mountains and Rivers Without End. San Francisco: Four Seasons Foundation, 1970.
The Back Country. New York: New Directions, 1968.
Earth House Hold. New York: New Directions, 1969.
Regarding Wave. New York: New Directions, 1970.
Turtle Island. New York: New Directions, 1974.
The Old Ways: Six Essays. San Francisco: City Lights, 1977.
The Real Work: Interviews and Talks. New York: New Directions, 1980.

About Gary Snyder:

Almon, Bert. *Gary Snyder.* Western Writers Series. Boise, Idaho, 1978.
Geneson, Paul. "An Interview with Gary Snyder." *The Ohio Review,* Fall 1977.
Paul, Sherman. "From Lookout to Ashram: The Way of Gary Snyder." *The Iowa Review,* Summer and Fall 1970.
Steuding, Bob. *Gary Snyder.* U.S. Authors Series. Boston: Twayne, 1976.

Feminist Criticism and Literature

Sharon Spencer

The history of feminine, as well as feminist, criticism and literature is very long although somewhat obscure. The greatest lyric poet of antiquity was Sappho, who lived in the sixth century B.C. The first poet of note in the United States was Ann Bradstreet, born in 1612. Emily Dickinson's reputation as one of the greatest literary artists in the U.S. has never been challenged. The first major work of feminist criticism was written by Christine de Pisan, who was born in 1364. An active spokeswoman in the "querrelle des femmes," de Pisan criticized the description of woman's nature drawn by Jehan de Meun in the *Roman de la Rose*.

The adjective "feminine" when applied to literature nowadays customarily indicates the author's preoccupation with intimate human relationships, concern with the emotional aspects of life and with the dynamics of the psychic realm of experience. "Feminine" writing, which may, of course, be produced by men as well as by women, is usually nonauthoritarian in narrative point of view (the reader is allowed to draw his own conclusions about the characters); it often displays an unconventional literary structure or approach to language.

It is important to distinguish between "feminine" and "feminist"; the term "feminist" implies a political position: the conviction that "traditional definitions of women are inadequate" and that "women suffer injustices because of their sex."[1] Feminist literary criticism is prescriptive: that is, it attempts to set standards for a literature that is as free as possible from biased portraits of individuals because of their class, race, or sex.

In the United States the women's movement of the 1960s and onward represents a renewed attempt to establish social and legal equality for women. The present wave of feminist criticism may be said to have been born with the appearance in 1970 of Kate Millett's powerful polemic, *Sexual Politics*. In the same year the Modern Language Association, a professional organization of more than 28,000 professors of literature and modern languages, held its first workshop on "Feminist Literature and Feminine Consciousness." The most basic purpose of feminist criticism is to eliminate what Mary Ellmann in her much-quoted book of 1968, *Thinking About Women*, has called "phallic criticism": the automatic assigning of inferior status to books because they have been written by women or because they display "feminine" characteristics of substance, structure, or style. In an articulate article titled "Critical Revision" Josephine Donovan states that feminist critics "propose a critique of the literary and social structures that have held women in a condition of lesser reality in both the past and the present." Denying the possibility of the "masculine" ideal of "objectivity" in judging literature, feminist critics "pose a challenge to the assumption that any scholar is free from ideological bias or value preference." To recognize one's bias is at least to come to the act of criticism in good faith." Donovan concludes: ". . . the immediate work in feminist criticism must be to develop more fully our understanding of what a female perspective or vision includes. . . . We must begin to articulate criteria of judgment that are consonant with the wisdom and experience of womankind, as developed and transmitted through the ages."[2]

Feminist criticism may be said to have four specific tasks: the identification of women's works that are out of print or have been neglected or misunderstood; analyses of the image of woman as she appears in the existing literature; the examination and reinterpretation of the existing criticism of women writers' books; the creation of a body of new work, imaginative as well as critical, based upon the egalitarian vision of humanity that is the fundamental basis of feminist thought.

The reclamation of lost or undervalued writers has been carried out with considerable success. A particularly striking rescue is that of *The Awakening* by Kate Chopin, a writer who has been traditionally dismissed by academic critics as a "regionalist." Because *The Awakening* explores a married woman's rebellion against the restrictions of her life, the book was damned by reviewers when it first appeared in 1899 and virtually disappeared from literary history in spite of its artistic distinction. The economic mainstay of a family of six, Chopin was denied membership in the Fine Arts Club of St. Louis because her novel was considered "immoral." Today, however, many good articles on this book have been published, including "The Treatment of Chopin's *The Awakening*" by Priscilla Allen.[3] Typical titles of recent articles focused on the rediscovery of neglected writers are "Who Buried H.D.?" (Susan Friedman); "Constance Fenimore Woolson: First Novelist of Florida" (Evelyn Thomas) and Tillie Olsen's Afterword to The Feminist Press's 1972 reprint of Rebecca Harding Davis's work *Life in the Iron Mills* (first published in 1861 in the *Atlantic Monthly*).[4]

A great deal of work has also been done on images of women in literature, especially as they appear in books written by men. Analyses have uncovered such stereotypes as the virgin and the whore; the mother (angel or devil?); the submissive wife, the domineering wife; the bitch; the seductress; man's prey, the sex object; the old maid; the bluestocking; the castrating woman.[5] One critic wittily asks, "What If Bartleby Were a Woman?" Another studies the presentation of the pioneer woman: "Eve Among the Indians," while a third re-examines the often-heard charge that Hemingway's women are inadequately characterized ("*A Farewell to Arms*: Ernest Hemingway's 'Resentful Cryptogram'").[6]

Closely related to the analysis of images of woman is the examination from a feminist perspective of existing criticism of women authors' books. Feminists strive to persuade critics to discuss books without regard for their writers' gender, to turn their attention toward new or neglected writers, and, most important, to check the tendency to generalize about human experience on the basis of male experience. Annette Kolodny, who has written one of the most lucid theoretical essays on feminist criticism, states the problem:

> In unquestioningly accepting a literature largely of male making and of male concerns as its given, excluding women's materials from anlaysis and investigation, a largely male-dominated academic establishment has, for the last seventy-five years or so, traced men's writing as though it were the model for *all* writing. In other words, the various theories on the craft of fiction, and the formalist and structuralist models that have been based on this closed tradition, but which have been offered up as "universals" of fictive form or even (under the influence of the psycholinguists) as emanations of yet deeper structures within human cognitive processes, may in fact prove to be less than universal and certainly less than fully human.[7]

Demonstrating the power of logical thinking, that women are often said not to possess, Margaret Andersen unmasks Henri Peyre, elder statesman among American critics of French literature:

> Henri Peyre speaks in his excellent study, *French Novelists of Today*, of the "striking flowering of French feminine fiction." . . . Peyre adds that "easily half of the talents in French fiction and short story, since 1930 or so, have been women." However, only one of the 12 chapters of Peyre's book deals with the writings of women, altogether 30-40 pages. Fourteen of these pages furthermore deal with Simone de Beauvoir only, which does not leave much space for other authors. We must conclude that Peyre needs only 15 pages to deal with "half the talents" since 1930, the female half, and that the male half of the talents is dealt with much more fairly.[8]

The creation of a body of new work is the fourth task of feminist criticism. Many writers have addressed this subject, among them Annette Kolodny, in the article already cited, and Annis Pratt in a piece titled "The New Feminist Criticism." She states that feminist critics need to develop two skills: "The *textual analysis* necessary to determine which works are novelistically successful, and the *contextual analysis* which considers the relevance of a group of works, even if artistically flawed, as a reflection of the situation of women." Continuing, Pratt adds: "The new feminist critic should be a 'new critic' (in the aesthetic rather than the political sense) in judging the formal aspects of individual texts; she should be 'feminist' in going beyond formalism to consider the literature as it reveals men and women in relationship to each other within a socio-economic *context*, that web of role expectations in which women are enmeshed."[9]

Pratt's distinction between the aesthetic and the political dimensions of literature is articulately opposed by Lillian S. Robinson, whose Marxist orientation insists upon the inherent political significance of all ideas. Reacting to Pratt's position as stated in "The New Feminist Criticism," Robinson accepts only the category of the contextual. She protests that "it is not something 'old-fashioned' or stuffy about traditional criticism that [she] objects to, but rather its use in the service of class interests." Robinson denies that feminist critics can work successfully with established approaches and techniques. She asserts: "New feminism is about fundamentally transforming institutions."[10]

In the decade since critics such as Pratt, Kolodny, and Robinson developed theories of feminist criticism, most of the work produced has been a combination of the textual and the contextual. Two characteristic titles are "Humanbecoming: Form and Focus in the Neo-Feminist Novel" by Ellen Morgan and "The Need To Tell All: A Comparison of Historical and Modern Feminist 'Confessional' Writing" by Kathleen Dehler.[11] Some of the outstanding works that embody the combined textual and contextual analyses of books by women are: *The Madwoman in the Attic: The Woman Writer and the Nineteenth Century Literary Imagination* (Sandra Gilbert and Susan Gubar); *Reaching Out: Sensitivity and Order in Recent American Fiction by Women* (Anne Z. Mickelson); *The Female Imagination* (Patricia Meyer Spacks); *Literary Women* (Ellen Moers); *Madness and Sexual Politics in the Feminist Novel* (Barbara Hill Rigney); and *A Literature of Their Own: British Novelists from Brontë and Lessing* (Elaine Showalter).

The two most profound issues that have been restated by feminist writers involve the related questions of innate differences between men and women, if any, and the effect of these differences on the psychology and the language employed by men and women respectively in life and in the arts. Inevitably, the body of thought created by C. G. Jung and his associates and followers is both stimulating and problematic for feminists. It is stimulating because the complicated concept of the Self that Jung proposed endows the principle of the Feminine with the dignity and status that are firmly denied it by the Freudian model. In Jung's thought the Masculine and the Feminine principles are polarities, opposite but equal. Jung regards psychological bisexuality, or the integration of one's contrasexual qualities as an ideal of self-realization. (Most feminists prefer the term "bisexuality" to "androgyny," a word whose structure embodies the primacy of the male.) In principle, then, Jungian psychology presents not only an ideal vision of a mature Self in which the Feminine is accorded equal weight with the Masculine but also a description of a process through which members of both sexes can integrate characteristics that have been given the labels of genders in an overall striving for the greatest degree of unity and wholeness.

In practice, however, Jungian thought presents problems. For one thing, the terms in which the Feminine is defined repeat the stereotypes of female passivity (a Jungian would use the term "receptivity"), emotional orientation to experience unpredictability, and bondage to the realm of the senses. Although Jung's view of women is, on the whole, less insulting than Freud's, it comes no closer to describing an authentic psychology of women.

Nevertheless, feminists do find value in the process of human growth that Jungians have described and have documented by references to mythology, the arts and the dreams of patients in psychotherapy. It is necessary to bear in mind that the Anima, as Jungian thinkers describe it, expresses the male's experience of the Feminine, not the female's. This authentic sense of what feminity feels like to women has never been fully expressed and remains, therefore, the elementary task of women's literature and other forms of cultural expression. In a journal called *Anima*, founded in 1975, authors of both sexes have been exploring woman's authentic experience of the Feminine in a context that preserves Jung's description of the process of self-realization while questioning his statements and assumptions about the Anima. Representative titles are "Feminism and Jungian Theory," "The Iconography of Heroic Womanhood," "Jungian Theory: A Reply to Feminists," and "Problems with Jungian Uses of Greek Goddess Mythology."[12]

In "The New Feminist Criticism" Annis Pratt identified the archetypal as a necessary critical approach to describe "the psycho-mythological development of the female individual in literature."[13] Calling for an attempt to discover the "myth of the heroine," Pratt raised the related question of the nature of the muse for the woman poet. She has been answered by Pamela Di Pesa in an essay titled "The Imperious Muse: Some Observations on Woman, Nature, and the Poetic Tradition."[14] During the 1970s a great deal of fine archetypal criticism has been written. Most of it is focused on the relationship of modern woman to the goddesses of pre-patriarchal antiquity. This is an area in which two men authored pioneering books: Robert Graves, who wrote *The White Goddess*, 1948, and Erich Neumann, whose study *The Great Mother*, published in 1955, remains the best book on matriarchal consciousness and its symbolism. In a recent article Diane F. Sadoff explores "Mythopoeia, The Moon and Contemporary Women's Poetry." The special mission of the woman artist has been studied in relation to Emily Dickinson, Sylvia Plath, Anne Sexton, and other writers. "The Female Faust" is the topic of an essay by Ann Ronald.[15] However, the richest source of materials on the archetypal aspects of woman's experience are the nine issues of *Anima* published so far.

The concept of bipolar gender implicitly alludes to the question of male and female language. This question, in turn, implies the possibility of different feminine and masculine aesthetics. If it is true that women and men write differently (and this has not yet been established), why is this the case? On this issue feminists are as sharply divided as on the question of innate sexual differences. Some accept male being and male achievement as the human ideal and wish to change the conditions in which females are raised so that they, too, can attain the "transcendent" position of the male; this, for example, is the basic position of Simone de Beauvoir, who takes great pains in *The Second Sex* (1949) to show that biology alone cannot account for the differences in the life situations and the achievements of men and women. Other feminists accept the definition of the feminine as it has been articulated by men, but reinterpret it, endowing it with positive significance, even exalting qualities that men regard as weaknesses (i.e., intuition, spontaneity, intense feeling, close bond with nature, and even passivity).

An inherent part of the question of authentic femininity is the related inquiry whether women writers ought to master the literary language invented by males or whether, instead, they should devote their energy to the discovery or to the creation of a specifically "feminine" literary aesthetic. Tillie Olsen, author of *Silences*, addresses this dilemma in a passage on the differences between Anaïs Nin's *Diary* and her fiction, the latter written from an avowedly "feminine" philosophy of style and structure: "So Anaïs Nin: . . . Dwelling in the private, the inner; endless vibrations of mood; writing what was muted, exquisite, sensuous, subterranean. That is, in her fiction. In her *Diaries* (along with the narcissistic), the public, the social; power of characterization, penetrating observation, had intellect, range of experience and relationship; different beauties." Olsen adds, "Qualities and complexities not present in her fiction—to its impoverishment."[16] Tillie Olsen laments the absence in Nin's fiction of "masculine" qualities, but it is possible to argue that Nin's "feminine" fiction is not inferior to her *Diaries* but different. In giving voice to a "feminine" aesthetic, Nin was a pioneer.

Unique in the literature of North America, the French-born Nin developed an approach to writing that she unashamedly associated with female reproduction:

> ... woman's creation far from being like man's must be exactly like her creation of children, that is it must come out of her own blood, englobed by her womb, nourished with her own milk. It must be a human creation, of flesh. ...
>
> ... most women painted and wrote nothing but imitations of phalluses. The world was filled with phalluses, like totem poles, and no womb anywhere. ... My work must be the closest to the life flow. I must install myself inside of the seed, growth, mysteries. I must prove the possibility of instantaneous, immediate, spontaneous art. My art must be like a miracle. Before it goes through the conduits of the brain and becomes an abstraction, a fiction, a lie. It must be for woman, more like a personified ancient ritual, where every spiritual thought was made visible, enacted, represented.[17]

In her attempt to discover an authentic philosophy of writing for herself as a woman, Nin may be grouped with the English novelists Dorothy Richardson, May Sinclair, and Virginia Woolf, as well as with the Russian-born French writer Nathalie Sarraute. Without being directly influenced by one another, these women have applied themselves to the search for a mode of verbal expression that would reflect the psychic life that is hidden beneath the surface of "reality." In a larger literary context, this search is an aspect of modernism and has been the goal of prominent male writers as well as female. Richardson, Woolf, and Nin have claimed the subjective as the feminine, while Sarraute formulated her ideal of *sous-conversation* as a reaction against the superficiality of literary realism.[18]

The related issues of the authenticity and the desirability of a "feminine" aesthetic are, of course, extremely complex. Some research does, indeed, indicate that the brain is utilized differently by men and women; females tend to have greater verbal fluency than males, while males are superior in certain visual-spatial tasks. It is not yet known whether these differences are transcultural, and they do not affect all individuals. Mary Ritchie Key, author of *Male/Female Language*, concludes: "Today, the concepts of masculinity and feminity are being challenged and in many cases are being rejected as unworkable and destructive."[19] Although it seems safe to conclude that the time has passed when a woman writer felt complimented when told she "writes like a man," it is still too soon to assert that all, or even most, women writers feel proud of being told that they "write like women." We are experiencing a period of profound cultural change. Nearly all writers who have undertaken to formulate the goals of feminist literature—whether imaginative or critical—agree that the eventual goal is a unity of "masculine" and "feminine" capabilities: mental bisexuality. This ideal was eloquently stated by Virginia Woolf in a book whose arguments still form the center of feminist inquiry, *A Room of One's Own* (1929):

> One has a profound, if irrational, instinct in favour of the theory that the union of man and woman makes for the greatest satisfaction, the most complete happiness. But the sight of two people getting into the taxi and the satisfaction it gave me made me also ask whether there are two sexes in the mind corresponding to the two sexes in the body, and whether they also require to be united in order to get complete satisfaction and happiness. And I went on amateurishly to sketch a plan of the soul so that in each of us two powers preside, one male, one female; and in the man's brain the man predominates over the woman, and in the woman's brain, the woman predominates over the man. The normal and comfortable state of being is that when the two live in harmony together, spiritually cooperating.[20]

Stimulated and encouraged by the atmosphere of intellectual excitement and inquiry that I have sketched in this brief essay, women today are pursuing careers in literature with greater confidence than ever before. In *A Room of One's Own* Woolf predicted that it would take a century before the world produced a woman writer equal to the genius of Shakespeare. We have a half century still before us.

Notes

[1] Agate Nesaule Krouse, "Toward a Definition of Literary Feminism," *Feminist Criticism: Essays on Theory, Poetry, and Prose*, editors Cheryl L. Brown, and Karen Olsen (Metuchen, New Jersey: Scarecrow Press, 1978), p. 282.

[2] Josephine Donovan, "Critical Revision," *Feminist Literary Criticism: Explorations in Theory*, editor Josephine Donovan (Lexington: University Press of Kentucky: 1975), p. 76, 77.

[3] Allen's essay is printed in *The Authority of Experience*. For more precise details, see the bibliography.

[4] Friedman's and Helmick's articles may be found in *Feminist Criticism*. Olsen's Afterword, "Rebecca Harding Davis: Her Life and Times," is reprinted in *Silences* (New York: Delacorte Press/Seymour Lawrence, 1978).

[5] For studies of the image of woman in literature, see Mary Anne Ferguson, editor, *Images of Women in Literature* (New York: Houghton Mifflin, 1973); Susan Koppelman Cornillon, editor, *Images of Women In Fiction* (Bowling Green, Ohio: Bowling Green University, 1972); Arlyn Diamond and Lee R. Edwards, editors, *The Authority of Experience: Essays in Feminist Criticism* (Amherst: University of Massachusetts Press, 1977).

[6] Again, see *The Authority of Experience*.

[7] Annette Kolodny, "Some Notes on Defining a 'Feminist Literary Criticism,'" *Feminist Criticism*, pp. 51-52.

[8] Margaret Andersen, *Mother Was Not a Person: Writings by Montreal Women* (Montreal, Canada: Content Publishing Co., 1972), p. 89.

[9] Annis Pratt, "The New Feminist Criticism," *Feminist Criticism*, p. 12.

[10] Lillian S. Robinson, "Dwelling in Decencies: Radical Criticism and the Feminist Perspective," *Feminist Criticism*, pp. 27-28, 35.

[11] Morgan's and Dehler's essays are in *Feminist Criticism*.

[12] *Anima: An Experiential Journal* is published by Conococheague Associates, adjacent to the campus of Wilson College, 1053 Wilson Avenue, Chambersburg, Pa., 17201.

[13] Pratt, p. 18.

[14] Once again, see *Feminist Criticism*.

[15] These essays are included in *Feminist Criticism*.

[16] *Silences*, p. 43.

[17] See *The Diary of Anaïs Nin: 1934-1939*, editor Gunther Stuhlmann (New York: Harcourt, Brace and World, 1967), pp. 231-236; Sharon Spencer, *Collage of Dreams: The Writings of Anaïs Nin* (Chicago: Swallow Press, 1977), pp. 109-113, 115, 120, 127-128, 138-139; Margaret Andersen, "Critical Approaches to Anaïs Nin," *The Canadian Review of American Studies*, Vol. 10, No. 2, Fall, 1979, pp. 255-265.

[18] See Nathalie Sarraute, *L'Ere du Soupçon: essais sur le roman*. Paris, 1956. Translated by Maria Jolas as *The Age of Suspicion: Essays on the Novel* (New York, 1967).

[19] Marie Ritchie Key, *Male/Female Language (with a Comprehensive Bibliography)* (Metuchen, New Jersey: Scarecrow Press, 1975), p. 28.

[20] Virginia Woolf, *A Room of One's Own* (New York: Harcourt, Brace, and World, 1929), pp. 101-102.

Bibliography

General Theory:

Brown, Cheril L. and Karen Olson, editors. *Feminist Criticism: Essays on Theory, Poetry and Prose*. Metuchen, New Jersey: Scarecrow Press, 1978.
Diamond, Arlyn and Lee R. Edwards, editors. *The Authority of Experience: Essays in Feminist Criticism*. Amherst: University of Massachusetts Press, 1977.
Donovan, Josephine, editor. *Feminist Literary Criticism: Explorations in Theory*. Lexington: University Press of Kentucky, 1975.
Ellmann, Mary. *Thinking About Women*. New York: Harcourt Brace Jovanovich, 1968.
Gould, Carol C. and Marx W. Wartofsky. *Women and Philosophy: Toward a Theory of Liberation*. New York: Putnam, 1976.

Outstanding Books Combining Textual and Contextual Analyses:

Cornillon, Susan Koppelman, editor. *Images of Women in Fiction: Feminist Perspectives*. Bowling Green, Ohio: Bowling Green Popular Press, 1972.
Ferguson, Mary Anne, editor. *Images of Women in Literature*. New York: Houghton Mifflin, 1973.
Fetterley, Judith. *The Resisting Reader: A Feminist Approach to American Fiction*. Bloomington: Indiana University Press, 1978.
Gilbert, Sandra M. and Susan Gubar. *The Madwoman in the Attic: The Woman Writer and the Nineteenth Century Literary Imagination*. New Haven, Connecticut: Yale University Press, 1979.
Mickelson, Anne Z. *Sensitivity and Order in Recent American Fiction by Women*. Metuchen, New Jersey: Scarecrow Press, 1979.
Miles, Rosalind. *The Fiction of Sex: Themes and Functions of Sex Difference in the Modern Novel*. London: Vision Press, 1974.
Showalter, Elaine. *A Literature of Their Own: British Novelists from Brontë and Lessing*. Princeton, New Jersey: Princeton University Press, 1977.
Spacks, Patricia Meyer. *The Female Imagination*. New York: Knopf, 1972.

Archetypal Criticism and the Feminine:

Anima: An Experiential Journal. Chambersburg, Pennsylvania: Conococheague Associates, Inc., 1st issue (Spring 1975).
Harding, M. Esther. *Woman's Mysteries Ancient and Modern: A Psychological Interpretation of the Feminine Principle as Portrayed in Myth, Story, and Dreams*. New York: Putnam, 1971. (First edition 1935.)
Neumann, Erich. *Amor and Psyche: The Psychic Development of the Feminine: A Commentary on the Tale by Apuleius*. Translated from the German by Ralph

Manheim. Princeton, New Jersey: Princeton University Press, 1973. (First edition 1956.)

—. *The Great Mother: An Analysis of the Archetype*. Translated from the German by Ralph Manheim. Princeton, New Jersey: Princeton University Press, 1972. (First edition 1955.)

Rank, Otto. "Feminine Psychology and Masculine Ideology," *Beyond Psychology*. New York: Dover Publications, 1958. (First edition 1941.)

Language and the Feminine Esthetic:

Butturff, Douglas and Edmund L. Epstein, editors. *Women's Language and Style*. Studies in Contemporary Language and Style, University of Akron, Akron, Ohio (No. 1, 1978). See essays by Sydney Janet Kaplan on Katherine Mansfield and by Carolyn Allen on *Nightwood* by Djuna Barnes, as well as Robin Lakoff's essay.

Donovan, Josephine. "Critical Response: Feminism and Esthetics," *Critical Inquiry*, III, 3 (Spring 1977).

—. "Feminist Style Criticism," *Images of Women: Feminist Perspectives*. Edited by S. K. Cornillon. Bowling Green, Ohio: Bowling Green Popular Press, 1972.

Duras, Marguerite. "Smothered Creativity" and "From an Interview." In *New French Feminisms: An Anthology*. Edited by Marks and de Courtivon. Amherst: University of Massachusetts Press, 1980. See also articles by Forrester, Chawaf, and Rochefort.

—. "An Interview by Susan Husserl-Kapit," *Signs: Journal of Women in Culture and Society* (Winter 1975).

Landy, Marcia. "The Silent Woman: Towards a Feminist Critique." In *The Authority of Experience*. Edited by Arlyn Diamond and Lee R. Edwards. Amherst: University of Massachusetts Press, 1977.

Nin, Anaïs. *The Diary of Anaïs Nin: 1931-1934*. Edited by Gunther Stuhlmann. New York: Swallow Press and Harcourt, Brace and World, 1967.

Richardson, Dorothy M. "Foreword" to *Pilgrimage*. Vol. I. New York: Popular Library, 1976.

Stanley, Julia Penelope and Susan J. Wolf (Robbins). "Toward a Feminine Aesthetic." *Chrysalis*, Vol. 6.

Woolf, Virginia. *A Room of One's Own*. New York: Harcourt Brace Jovanovich, 1963. (First edition 1929.)

Literary Translation

A Conversation among Guy Daniels, Charles Doria, Richard Kostelanetz, Barbara Stoler-Miller, and Robert Payne

Kostelanetz:　Our subject today is literary translation, and with me are four American writers who have done distinguished work in this field:

Guy Daniels was born in 1919 in Gilmore City, Iowa. He has translated over 50 books from both Russian and French, including works of poetry and fiction and nonfiction.

Barbara Stoler-Miller was born in New York in 1940, and she has translated poetry and plays from Sanskrit and from Spanish. She is presently a professor of Oriental Studies at Barnard College and Columbia University.

Charles Doria, born in Cleveland in 1938, has translated poetry from Latin and Greek. He coedited the anthology *Origins* (1976) and collaborated with Jerome Rothenberg in editing and translating an anthology called *A Big Jewish Book* (1978).

Robert Payne is one of the directors of the Translation Center at Columbia University and coeditor of its magazine, *Translation*. He was born in England in 1911 and came to America in 1946. He has translated both poetry and prose from German, Russian, and Danish, and was the chief translator, as well as the editor, of the most familiar American anthology of Chinese poetry, *The White Pony*. He has also written over 100 books, including biographies of Gandhi, Mao Zedong, Stalin, and Hitler.

My first question is a general one: How did you get into literary translation, and what have you done?

Daniels:　Well, I began in the way that I think is possibly most understandable. After having come to love certain poems—and this has to do with French poetry to begin with—and wanting very badly to make them available to people who didn't know the language, I started by doing some French poets. Then the same feeling caught hold of me with Russian poetry, and I realized that you couldn't expect too many people to learn Russian. So I quickly dropped the French—with the idea that people should go ahead and learn it for themselves if they wanted to read Mallarmé, for example, whom you cannot translate—and I have since then concentrated, except for prose books, mostly on Russian.

Kostelanetz: Were you in college at this time?

Daniels: No, this was afterward. I first started publishing my own work. My first book was my own poetry. This was about the same time that I began to have this feeling about French poetry.

Kostelanetz: Who are the poets that you have particularly specialized in?

Daniels: Well, mostly Russian classical poets—Lermontov, Krylov, Mayakovsky; those are my three chief book translations of classical Russian poetry. Others are in anthologies.

Kostelanetz: Barbara Stoler-Miller, how did you get into translation, and what have you done?

Miller: I was a philosophy student at Columbia, interested in languages and had intended to go to graduate school in philosophy when I began to study Sanskrit. I was writing at the time.

Kostelanetz: Writing poetry?

Miller: Yes, poetry mainly. I encountered translations of Sanskrit poetry in Oriental humanities courses taught by Burton Watson and Donald Keene, who I think are very good translators and have brought an enormous amount of attention to both Chinese and Japanese literature.

I was fascinated by the content of Indian literature but dismayed by the quality of the Sanskrit translations. I rather boldly decided to pursue the study of Sanskrit philology. One of my professors quickly presented me with the challenge of preparing translations of Sanskrit poems for the Oriental humanities course. I enjoyed this work so much that I had no choice but to continue.

Kostelanetz: What works of Sanskrit have you done?

Miller: My first work was the poetry of Bhartrihari, who lived in the 5th century. He was a monk and a scholar who was notable because he couldn't decide which career to pursue and vascillated between the court and the monastery. He composed a series of short poems, and those were my first translations. From that, I turned to an 11th-century Sanskrit poet, Bilhana, known as the "Love-thief."

Bilhana composed a series of short poems called the *Caurapañcāśika*, which I translated as *Phantasies of a Love Thief*. For this work it was necessary not only to translate the text but, first, to edit it because the manuscripts were so dispersed. There has in general been great difficulty in editing Sanskrit manuscripts critically.

Kostelanetz: Editing means establishing a definitive edition.

Miller: A critical edition, if not a definitive edition.

    The next thing is probably the most important work I've translated, a religious erotic poem of the 12th century, the height of Indian medieval devotional literature called *Gītagovinda*, which is still sung in India today. I've translated that as *Love Song of the Dark Lord*. The poet was born in eastern India, and the poem was probably composed at a temple that is still a living temple in India the Jagannath Temple at Puri. And one can walk in the streets of Puri and still hear this poem being sung.

Kostelanetz: Where did you find that text?

Miller: I heard it sung in India the first time, and it stuck in my head. Eventually I virtually memorized all the verses and the 24 songs of the *Gītagovinda*. I had to establish my contact with it. At first, I found it somewhat cloying, and I had to come to appreciate the sweetness that was central to its aesthetic. In India they have a notion of *rasa*, or juice, of a work, and in a sense this work is one of the high points of Sanskrit literature because it incorporates into its vocabulary, its music, its meaning, the sweetness of *rasa*, this essence of erotic and religious emotion. I think I just had to mature enough to understand India even better, before I could hope to translate it.

Kostelanetz: But when you edited your definitive text, where did you find it?

Miller: It has been printed, but the printed versions vary tremendously. The most interesting thing is that the most common printed version is a 16th-century version edited by a cult that wished to de-eroticize the poem somewhat, and so they added refrains that almost neutralized the eroticism of the poem. When I investigated the manuscript traditions, it was quite clear at what point in the tradition of the poem, which dates to the 12th century, these *maṅgala ślokas*, or auspicious verses, had been added at the end of each section. Needless to say, these are now in the footnotes.

Kostelanetz: You had to get rid of them.

Miller: And when one eliminates them, the poem has a very different total impression. My text is very much a part of one or more of the living Indian traditions of the poem. It is not as though I recreated a text that doesn't exist anywhere in India. It's just that a particular and most popular version in northern India that was most often printed included these kinds of verses. So that's part of the adventure.

Kostelanetz: What about languages other than Sanskrit?

Miller: As you mentioned earlier, I've recently done a book of Spanish poetry. This is because the poet, a friend of mine, was influenced by my translations from Sanskrit, and she incorporated into her Spanish poetry the compounding of words, which Borges says is really inimical to the Spanish. I think she did it very successfully. The title of the book will give you a hint of what she did. It's *Sombraventadora*, which I translated as *Shadowwinnower* in English. I had the challenge to reproduce in English *Shadowwinnower*, which was inspired by these marvelous composite words in the Sanskrit.

Kostelanetz: Have you done any poetry influenced by your translations?

Miller: I have, but I don't publish it. I'm so absorbed in the task of bringing these ancient poets to the attention of an English-speaking audience that translation has been my major effort.

Kostelanetz: Are these poets who have been translated before?

Miller: Some have been translated before but very badly, I think, either by people who didn't know the original language or by people who knew the original language but had no literary sense and no concern with the audience in English. Ruckat, the German poet, did a very beautiful translation of the *Gītagovinda* into a rather archaic German so it's not very available to an English-speaking audience.

Kostelanetz: Charles Doria, how did you get into translation, and what have you done?

Doria: Well, my story is similar to Ms. Miller's in the sense that I was trying to become a poet. I was interested in writing poetry, and I was reading a lot of it, particularly French and German poetry, when I was in high school and college. And I was unhappy with the translations. I guess it's curious that the first translations that I tried were of the French writers—particularly Mallarmé and Baudelaire.

Kostelanetz: The same writers that got Guy Daniels into translation?

Doria: Right, yes, but who, I believe he said, were untranslatable, and, yes, I think I do agree with that.

But in terms of my own work with Greek and Latin, I'd have to say that I was more interested in the material that hadn't been translated before, particularly in what one might call the folk element—in the vast bodies of writings that are left over by the Gnostics, the Orphics, the Neo-Platonists, plus others who worked in no known tradition or school.

Kostelanetz: We always thought that since classics have been the cornerstone of Western humanities education, everything must have been translated.

Doria: No, that's not true. By and large, there has been a great deal of attention focussed on the 4th and 5th centuries B.C., which is to say on Athens—on Thucydides, Aeschylus, Plato, people like that—and also on the first centuries, B.C. and A.D., in Rome—Propertius, Virgil, Cicero, Catullus. And, then, with regard to the material that comes after, it's almost like a bell curve; there's a shading off of interest the further one gets from the highlighted area.

Kostelanetz: Well, why wasn't the other work translated before?

Doria: I really don't know, although this is something that I've often thought about. For example, Maximian, or Maximianus, a very important elegist and contemporary of Boethius, from the 7th century A.D., has never been translated into English or, so far as I know, into a modern language, except perhaps in German. One of the things I've been working on—since 1971, to be precise—is a translation of his six elegies. Maximian, a writer who was read well into the Middle Ages, was an important part of the medieval and humanistic curriculum.

Kostelanetz: How did you discover him?

Doria: Simply by reading many medieval references to him and discovering him in Diehl's *Minor Latin Poets*. Maximian was so minor that in this particular edition there was no index for him, and you just had to simply know where his work was by finding a reference elsewhere and looking it up.

Kostelanetz: Do you have problems in establishing definitive editions as well?

Doria: Well, let me talk about that in terms of my Orphic "Sacred Stories" translation from *Origins*. This poem was originally, as I understand it, as long as Homer's Iliad or Odyssey—that is, in 24 books, ranging between 500 and 1,000 lines each. All that remains of this epic (if it even existed in as long a form as we're told) is something like 200 miscellaneous citations preserved usually because of their grammatical peculiarities.

Kostelanetz: When you say "all that remains," where does it remain? In one place?

Doria: Just scattered around. Classicist grammarians, for example, are fond of quoting ancient poets to illustrate linguistic oddities—e.g., "This is a genitive you'll never see except here." So you'll get a line or a line and a half to illustrate a strange genetive. Notice the line is quoted not because it tells us anything about the play or the myth, but just simply to illustrate a point that it was of interest to a scholar some 1600 years ago.

Kostelanetz: So you had to collect the text then from various sources?

Doria: Yes, exactly. In reconstructing the "Sacred Stories," I had these 180-200 citations—that is to say, short passages quoted for random reasons by later writers—and from that, I tried to reconstruct a coherent text.

Kostelanetz: Now this piece is in *Origins*.

Doria: Yes. The complete title of the book is *Origins: Creation Texts from the Ancient Mediterranean*. It contains about 200 creation texts from six or seven languages, from Egyptian, Hebrew, Sumerian, Akkadian Ugaritic, as well as Greek and Latin.

Kostelanetz: Did you do all those languages?

Doria: No; I did the Greek, the Latin, and most of the Egyptian, and then my coeditor did the others.

Kostelanetz: And in *A Big Jewish Book*, what was your contribution?

Doria: There I worked by area, principally in Hellenistic and Gnostic Judaism. There the problem of authorship and text is even more difficult to determine because what we are trying to do is recover a lost tradition, since most of the Hellenistic texts remain buried, except for obvious people like Philo. But most of the others remain only as items quoted in later writers; for example, this happened with one piece that I did, the Naasene cosmology.

Kostelanetz: Naasene?

Doria: Naasene, yes, from Greek. It's the Greek translation of the Hebrew word *nahas* meaning snake or serpent—in other words, worshippers of the snake, a form of Gnosticism. I had to take this particular text from two Christian writers, Eusebius and Hippolytus,

who compiled scrapbooks of heresies so that various missionaries and
priests of the time could recognize a heresy when they saw it. In other
words, the Naasene cosmology had already been taken from folk
religion by Gnostics with vaguely Jewish and/or Hellenistic roots,
moved by Christians into heresy, and then just quoted or garbled in
almost cartoon form in a preacher's Cliff notes.

Kostelantz: And so you picked it as a special text, isolated it, and
then translated it?

Doria: Yes, it's one of these texts that Gnostic scholars often refer to;
I mean, the text in this case is the major surviving witness to the
religion, the tradition.

Kostelanetz: Robert Payne, what was your first translation?

Payne: The first was a book in Russian by Yuri Olesha, and I found
him by accident in a library in Liverpool University where I was more
or less free to do nothing except learn and read Russian. I also found
a man called Rozanov and a man called Pasternak, and as far as I knew
at the time, they were completely unknown in English. So I decided
that those were the three people I would translate. My translation of
Envy (*Zavist'*) by Olesha came out in 1936 or '37 with the Hogarth
Press; the novel was an absolute masterpiece of ribaldry and fun, with
tremendous, scathing, almost invisible between-the-lines attacks on
Stalinism. As a result of this book and other books, he got into very bad
trouble. He was thrown into the hinterland and not allowed to be
anything but a journalist.

Kostelanetz: What about Pasternak?

Payne: I translated the short stories of Pasternak, which were then
completely unknown. I say I translated them, actually, what I did was
just have a great deal of fun with them—I wasn't thinking of publishing them at that time. I'd just come out of working in a shipyard, and
I was rather fresh at Liverpool University and didn't know what to do.
So I translated them as well as I could.

But Rozanov was the one who impressed me the most. It took
about 30 years to get that one published. It was published two years
ago. He did a diary over a period of about 20 years, from about 1900
to 1917, in which he put all of his most intimate thoughts and his
own philosophy. The last part of the diary, which is called *The
Apocalypse of Our Time*, was written in enormous poverty in 1917, with
the Bolsheviks suddenly taking power and himself completely pow-
erless. He went on publishing his books on a little press in a monastery. So we got all of these things together, finally. There are four or

five volumes. One was called *Solotaria,* another was called *Fallen Leaves,* and another was called, as I said, *The Apocalypse of Our Time.* I think it's a tremendously important book; it's still reasonably un- kown because these volumes were never properly published in America.

I find Pasternak absolutely enthralling. He wrote some short stories—only about five or six in his whole lifetime—and they were simply wonderful. They were really poems in prose. And the most important of them was called *The Childhood of Lyuvers,* which is a very odd title for one of the most wonderful evocations of a girl growing up that I have ever come across.

Well, I finally finished it in 1939. At that time, I was an armament officer in the Singapore naval base, which is a very odd place to try to publish anything. But I got it published; I printed it myself on the *Singapore Times* press. We had 250 copies, and there was just time to send a copy to the Bibliothèque Nationale and to the Library of Congress and the British Museum; then, of course, the Japanese came in, and I went off to China.

So, basically, right up to 1941, which was when all this hap- pened, my translations were from Russian. Then I left Russian behind when I went to China. I was sent by the British. I never learned why I was sent, but I ended up in the Chinese universities for most of the war.

Kostelanetz: Teaching?

Payne: I was teaching there, yes. I had a very curious title; I was Professor of English Poetry and Lecturer on Naval Architecture. And I liked that very much! I had learned some Chinese in Singapore, though not terribly well. And then when I got to China and got into the universities, very early on, I started collecting translations of Chinese poetry and doing some myself. I had an enormous advantage later when I got to Kunming, which is in southwest China, and where all the major universities had trekked right across China, somewhere near the Tibetan border. There we had all of the best scholars in the whole of China in one little town. So I got them to help on the translations. That was quite wonderful because we had all this available talent around.

Kostelantz: That work became *The White Pony.*

Payne: That became *The White Pony,* and it also became a few other books of translations that I got these scholars to do or tried to do myself. I think there were about four volumes, including one on contemporary Chinese poetry.

Kostelanetz: Whereas you did the Russian by yourself, here you're translating in collaboration with Chinese-speakers.

Payne: It was not so much collaboration as I would make a rough draft and then they would tell me where I went wrong. I mean, it wasn't collaboration in the sense they do it now, where they get a pony and then somebody puts it into English.

Kostelanetz: So you did your first draft and then went back to a native speaker.

Payne: Very often. In some cases, they did the whole thing.

Kostelanetz: And your translations from the Danish and German, how were they done?

Payne: Well, as for the Danish ones, I got terribly fascinated by Kierkegaard. At that time in the 1930s, there were no translations of Kierkegaard available. So I did two of his books: *Fear and Trembling* and *Repetition*. And that was sheer selfishness. I just wanted to know what he was saying. Again I didn't expect to get it published, but the Oxford University Press very kindly published it.

Kostelanetz: And your new book is a collection of Hölderlin's poems.

Payne: Not a book really: it is coming out in *Translation* magazine; it's the last poems of Hölderlin. I worked on them during the war. They are very ancient translations.

Kostelanetz: Now, Guy Daniels, how do you prepare for a translation? And then how do you do it? Do you work directly— transcription to typewriter? Do you collaborate with others such as the author? Do you do one draft or several?

Daniels: Well, it depends obviously upon the nature of the material. In the case of a serious work of literature, and especially a poet, you of course have to soak yourself in it for a long time. I will not recite the biographies of my favorite authors nor indeed anything about the redaction of the text. But yes, in this case, you need a long exposure, living with the poet for a long time, reading biographies, memoirs, and so on, and obviously reading and rereading the poetry until you get to a certain point, until you feel like you're ready to go.

Kostelanetz: How long is "long"? You said "a long time."

Daniels: Oh, the Lermontov book was about 10 years. The Krylov book was a number of years, and it's only 15 little poems. The Mayakovsky was a little shorter because I had been familiar with it before, Mayakovsky's complete plays. But it matters also how much background you have. When I did the Lermontov books, I didn't have that much background so that took a longer time. But with any decent size volume of poetry, it takes years.

Kostelanetz: Now how do you do it? Do you work at a type-writer?

Daniels: Well, for poetry, no. Only for a second draft, not a first draft. I am not like T. S. Eliot. I don't tap out poetry on a typewriter. It's wonderful when you get to that stage, and you can see it on the page—that's fine. With other things, again, it depends on the materials: I've had to do certain books very rapidly, one draft only. I did Sakharov's second book in five days—that was, of course, one draft— and then I got sick immediately thereafter.

Kostelanetz: But that was a prose book.

Daniels: Yes. So again this depends a great deal on the material, but sometimes, it's a terrible strain. There are deadlines that require you to work almost like a simultaneous interpreter except that you have to have a better style, you are not dealing with bureaucratic prose. Even in books, the style of which is not particularly distin-guished—let's say, for example, Sakharov—you still have to come up with something better than what's passed around at the United Nations. So in other words, you have to work the way they do but come up with something a lot better.

Kostelanetz: Because you're going to be in print, and their stuff just goes up in the air.

Daniels: Exactly.

Kostelanetz: I think, in contrast to the others here, you have a more varied translating activity in the sense that you do poetry, plays, and prose, and therefore, you probably have different techniques for each genre.

Daniels: That's right. And one has to be a bit of an actor. There's the question of elective affinities: there are some people that one shouldn't do, simply because they're not one's kind of person. It's not going to come out well, so you shouldn't even do it.

Kostelanetz: And so at times you turn down jobs that are offered you.

Daniels: Yes, quite a few times.

Kostelanetz: Because you know you're not the best person.

Daniels: Well, Mr. Payne once told me—it was about Aleksandr Blok—I said I did like certain things of his. And he said, "Well, you could never translate Blok." And Payne's quite right; there isn't the proper affinity there.

Kostelanetz: Barbara Miller, you talked before about how you had first to edit a text before you did it. How long does this take?

Miller: The editing can take a great deal of time, depending on the availability of manuscripts. But it's a very good way of traveling to remote parts of India and meeting people, scholars—traditional scholars. This is something that I think is a unique aspect of working in India; that one can still work with the traditionally educated with whom one must converse in Sanskrit. It still is spoken among scholars in India, being similar to what medieval church Latin was, or Latin still is in the Vatican. You can communicate in Sanskrit with a pundit from a remote part of South India who may not speak anything but Tamil (a Dravidian language) and maybe a little bit of book English, but that is hardly a Sanskrit medium of communication.

Kostelanetz: But since you know Sanskrit, you have, so to speak, an entrée to this world.

Mille: Yes, and it's been a tradition, particularly in American scholarship, for students to study Sanskrit, at least for a year, at one of the traditional schools in India. I think this has been a great benefit and opportunity. There has been much fruitful collaboration, particularly in critical work, with these traditional Indian scholars. I myself have worked extensively with a young pundit at the Mysore Oriental Research Institute, with whom I discuss a lot of my work to get his criticism in terms of traditional commentaries.

Kostelanetz: Does he know English?

Miller: Yes.

Kostelanetz: So he becomes, therefore, your principal editor, or your first editor, your first reader.

Miller: Yes. We often would sit with commentaries from different traditions, particularly in the case of the *Gītagovinda*. Because it is a religious text, it has been interpreted variously by different schools. We often discussed controversial passages in Sanskrit, though he knew English, because it would have meant translating the commentaries, so we would discuss them in the original. This is part of the immersion process.

Kostelanetz: Have you written a commentary, too?

Miller: Yes, but I've written commentaries in English, not in Sanskrit.

Kostelanetz: Nevertheless, you've written your commentary after reading the poem and consulting the earlier commentaries.
Miller: Right. Often one draws on those.
Kostelanetz: Charles, have you used any other similarly esoteric sources to find a text that no one else has translated?
Doria: There is my Moses chant, which is in your anthology *Text-Sound Texts*, that I came across in the most accidental way. I was reading a book by Marie-Louise von Franz, in English. She's a Jungian critic; the book is called *The Eternal Boy*. She said more or less, "And then they talk about a goddess whose name of 49 letters I can't pronounce, so I'm not going to bother you any more with it." Then in her usual fashion she shoots on to something else. I thought, well, now, that's interesting—divinities running around with 49-letter names. Finally, I located this collection of magic texts.
Kostelanetz: Where did you find it?
Doria: I found it in the *Greek Magical Papyri*, which was another one of these collections that was never completed thanks to World War II. Only two of the projected three volumes ever came out, so there's no index to it. This was a book whose publication, I think, was stopped during the Nazi period.
Kostelanetz: Published where?
Doria: Published in Germany.
Kostelanetz: In what language?
Doria: That's an interesting question. What language are these texts actually in? The original texts, at any rate, are in Greek and Coptic, and there's a running German translation provided, and a short commentary by the editor Karl Preisendanz. I found the Moses chant by just simply paging through the book until I found a text that more or less matched the description in the Marie Franz book. This turned out to be in "Papyrus 13." More precisely "Papyrus 13" contains two very long creation texts and the Moses chant. I did the creation texts first, which, like the Moses piece, are also based on vowel chants, and they went in *Origins*. Then I did the Moses chant later as a kind of sidebar to the work I was doing on *A Big Jewish Book*. What I discovered was a long magic chant or performance, untranslated into English, which, except for the running German translation (more designed to help you to read the original than anything else) remained unknown in any modern language.
Kostelanetz: How long did it take you to translate it?
Doria: That particular piece took me about three years.

Kostelanetz: And did you show it to anyone, or did you have collaborators?

Doria: No, I did that alone.

Kostelantz: Now this work, your translation—is it meant to read like an original, or is it meant to read like a translation that gives you a sense of the original?

Doria: I don't know that there's really too much difference between these two possibilities or directions. To me translation means translation of the whole, not just translation as a kind of English guide or entry into texts in other languages. I guess I'm automatically assuming that most people aren't going to be reading in the original, that they are not going to learn Sanskrit or Classical Greek, Russian or whatever. I mean we actually do live, as Pound said, in an era of translation. This is both a blessing and a curse, however.

So you have to consider, "What is the whole like? What is its nature and extensions?" And then you try to translate something of the form and impact of the original.

Kostelanetz: Willard Trask, a great American translator, said that poetry can only be translated into prose, that it can't be translated into poetry, and therefore, a prose translation can only give you a sense of what the poetry was about. Do you agree with that?

Doria: No. If that's true, it must follow then that good prose can only be translated into poetry. I don't believe the function of translation is transformation—turning the text into something it's not: poetry into prose or whatever. There are poetic resources in English, as in any other language, and as I say, if we're interested in translating the whole, we need to view translation as totality. The translator additionally has to use or learn to use some of the same poetic resources that any poet or literary artist commands.

Miller: I think I disagree with Trask, as you do. There's a leap there that leaves out the enormous effort that goes into the choice one makes to try to bring something over into English as poetry, simultaneously remaining as faithful as you can to the original and still creating something that is a literary work with its own resonance. I think people are only beginning to realize the enormous effort that goes into this, perhaps living with the work for ten years. The play I'm translating now is one that I had read when I was a student, but only 15 years later did it occur to me that I might be ready to begin to translate it, that I had matured into it. When you were talking earlier, Charles, you said that you memorize. I often find that a work that I end up choosing to translate is a work of which I have virtually memorized great quantities so that it has been in my head and in my subconscious for longer than even I realize.

Kostelanetz: Do you translate in your head?

Miller: Oh, yes, I often walk around in a daze translating or writing.

Kostelanetz: No, but I mean, all of a sudden, is your head saying Sanskrit words and then suddenly it's saying English words?

Miller: Well, I'm not sure it's so clear-cut. I think it goes on; a little bit is done in dreams, a little bit is done while you're walking around; a little bit is done in the shower; and suddenly, you may have a scene of a play. Then you sit at the typewriter, and there it is surprisingly.

Kostelanetz: Does anyone want to defend the Willard Trask position?

Payne: I don't think it's defendable. I remember he'd talk about it at length, but I think he was quite incapable himself of writing poetry—and that was the reason.

Daniels: I would say that Dante's translation "*Nessun maggior dolore, che ricordarsi del tempo felice nella miseria . . .*" was rather good poetry and quite close to the original Boethius. I don't really think there is any argument there at all. I think that Dante worked hard. I think that, as Barbara said, you've got to work awfully hard, and that people who think that you can't write or do a translation that—not always, but very often—is quite close and at the same time good, readable English poetry, simply don't work hard enough.

Kostelanetz: But Robert was introducing another notion: that you would have to be a poet to translate poetry.

Payne: Trask was an extraordinary stylist in prose. And he was an awfully good translator, right from his very earliest books. His first book was a translation of parts of the trial of Joan of Arc. He did it when he was about 24. And so he went on, absolutely gripped by this business of translation, and always, as far as I know, every single line of verse would be transformed by him into a line of prose. It was rather sad in a way.

He was, I think, by any kind of definition we can provide, the greatest of modern translators of his generation. He was one of the most quirky, sometimes most disagreeable people we had ever come across. If we made a misprint, then we'd get a tremendous telephone call saying what in the world were we doing, and we'd be told in very, very definite terms that we were just the lowest of the low. We had a long, long fight, and it didn't matter because we loved the man very much.

But the thing that I find now in retrospect, because we'd been so close to him for so long, was the enormous range and courage of the man. He would take on languages in the way that Arthur Waley took on languages. Waley learned Ainu just to translate one poem which he thought was worth translating. In much the same way, Willard Trask learned—or tried to learn with the help of his friend Margolies—a Nigerian language, I think, which had some poetry attached to it.

And the thing that I find absolutely astonishing about this— and translation itself is a sufficiently astonishing thing—is the enormous range that some translators have, and I think it's due very much to an incredible dedication. What Trask was dedicated to was not literature so much as the translation of literature. He lived until he was 80, and I think he was translating from the age of about 20 right up to the time of his death.

Kostelanetz: What's extraordinary, too, about Trask is that he did major books which involved great problems, such as Erich Auerbach's *Mimesis*, where he not only had to translate Auerbach's commentary in German but the original passages from different periods of literature in several languages, or Curtius' *European Literature in the Latin Middle Ages*, where, again, he not only had to translate the critical commentary but all the quotations within it as well.

But he was a translator of prose, not poetry, as we pointed out before.

There is one of Trask's books which I have not read, and maybe you could describe it to me—*The Anthology of Primitive Poetry*?

Payne: That was primitive poetry, basic poetry of Africa, Australia, whatever he could pick up in any kind of primitive. . . .

Kostelanetz: With translations done by himself in prose.

Payne: Well, not really by himself. Sometimes he did use a French crib. It is a very strange mixture, but what is most amazing was the fact that he managed to make it look as if he'd sat there and read 30 different languages.

Kostelanetz: You mean, he used a French translation of the original language, and. . . .

Payne: In some cases, he did.

Kostelanetz: And then worked from that to translate into English?

Payne: Sure.

Kostelanetz: Charles, didn't you do something similar in *A Big Jewish Book*?

Doria: Yes, in the sense that we often had to work from a translation first. However, I wasn't thinking so much of that book as *Origins*, where we did a passage on Wisdom the Creatrix from *Ecclesiasticus*, first in Greek. Then later we discovered the Hebrew, which had to be reconstructed and in part retranslated from the Greek, itself a translation from a Hebrew original that got lost somewhere along the line.

Kostelanetz: Going back to Trask, I should note that he got the first gold medal from the Translation Center at Columbia University. And looking through his bibliography, I was struck by the fact that he didn't publish books until he was well into his 30s. The Joan of Arc book, it seems to me, came out in 1935, when he was 35. He seemed to have taken a long time to warm up, as we say.

Payne: Well, actually, he was bumming around; he was terribly poor for a long time. And there's a wonderful story about how he got his first translation. He was a waiter in, I think, Greenwich Village in New York, and he heard a publisher talking about a translation. They wanted a translator very badly. So he said, "Excuse me, but I'm also a translator as well as being a waiter." And that's how it all started.

Translators are terribly important, and I think the wonderful thing about Trask was that he realized this importance and covered such a vast field.

Kostelanetz: What makes one translation better than another?

Payne: It's very much what Barbara Stoler-Miller was talking about: it's this living with it. We know that Arthur Waley lived with *The Tale of Genji* for something like 15 years. And his *Genji*, in one sense, is an inaccurate translation. I mean, the words are not exactly the words in Japanese. What he's done is regurgitated *The Tale of Genji*, and it works.

Kostelanetz: By giving us an authentic but inaccurate *Genji*?

Payne: No, the word inaccurate has to be redefined.

Kostelanetz: Inaccurate in detail, but authentic in speaking.

Payne: Inaccurate in minor, minor things. He obviously did not follow the text because what he was doing was absorbing it into himself. That, I think, is the important word—the absorption; that's what Ms. Miller was talking about.

Waley would talk about regurgitating; it's like a bird regurgitating for its children. And if you translate accurately, word by word, the game is up. It just doesn't work at all.

Kostelanetz: Should poetry be published with the original across from it, *en face*, as they say in French? Guy Daniels, in your Voznesensky translations, the Russian originals are published across from your translation. Is that useful?

Daniels: Well, it depends on the audience. I liked it because I worked awfully hard to keep the translation close to the original and, at the same time, to make it stand on its own in English. I'm proud of how close it is, and so I'm happy to have people see it. Again, it's the old question of how hard you work at it. I am sure that lots of people don't want the other text there at all. It's very embarrassing.

Miller: I don't think it's just a matter of that. The first two books of Sanskrit that I did had a transliterated text of the original.

Kostelantz: Transliterated?

Miller: Meaning that the Sanskrit script, Devnagari, was put into roman script. The script was transliterated so that the Sanskrit words were spelled with roman letters. I thought it would give people a sense of the sound of the original, but, oddly enough, it was a deterrent. People felt obliged to leave the book where it was because of the obstacle of this language to which they had no access. Subsequently, I've decided that translations from a language that so few people would have access to should be published independently of the original text. If you want the text for scholars, then put it in the back, in the original script. Whereas with the Spanish book, it was absolutely essential to keep the original because I wanted people to be directed toward the original. I think it depends on the language. There will be more justification with Greek or with Latin because one can assume that more people know them; whereas, if I were publishing things exclusively in India, for people who know English and enough Sanskrit to be able to follow the text, I would definitely want the translation and text to be on facing pages. I think it depends on circumstance.

Daniels: Well, that's what I meant when I said it depends on the audience.

Kostelanetz: Is it fair to say that people have different translating styles? Does Waley have a different kind of style of translating than you three, or are differences simply a matter of quality or excellence of immersion?

Payne: I think it's entirely a matter of excellence. If you get into the style of translation, there are all kinds of pitfalls that are best avoided.

Kostelanetz: In the translations of classics, Christopher Logue had a different style of translating from the Greek than William Arrowsmith.

Doria: But particularly if you are talking about his translation of *The Patrocleia*, it's clear what Logue is trying to do is assimilate Homer to Pound and T. S. Eliot, particularly the Pound of the *Cantos*, so that I'm not sure that one can talk about Logue's translation of *The Patrocleia*, except as an adjunct to a kind of encyclopedic, informational style which has grown up among some of the writers of this century, as in Pound's *Cantos* and William Carlos Williams's *Paterson*.

And this gets us into another question: To what extent does translation mirror the literature that's currently going on?

Kostelanetz: So then it's really a question of what kind of English the translator chooses to use.

Doria: Well, Pope, of course, would hear Homer in heroic couplets, because that was the style of the period. No one then apparently could consider narrative or expository poetry without the couplets, without hearing rhymes at the line's end.

Kostelanetz: Then how would you characterize your translating style? Obviously, it's not Pope's.

Doria: No, it's obviously not Pope's. I don't know that I can very succinctly or coherently characterize it. What I think I am most interested in doing is to reproduce in English what I finally have come to believe is the poem or the text that I'm working on, what I have finally internalized it to be, and to try to reproduce something of what I have seen or glimpsed of the original, in the original.

Kostelanetz: But then you're also telling me that you've internalized it in terms of your sense of poetry today.

Doria: Yes. I think one has to make use of one's position in time, even take advantage of it. I mean, I don't think one can work in a consciously archaic vein and insist on a particular style for translation or for translating any particular text. Nor do I think we can become ahistorical and say, "Well, we'll simply do it a way that's never been done before," because then I think nobody can read it. There will be no contemporary access to either original or translation.

Kostelanetz: Barbara Miller, what English poets did you hear in your translations from Sanskrit?

Miller: I've often found an English poet as a companion. For instance, when I was working on Bhartrihari, I read a great deal of John

Donne. I was very anxious to find the right tone to bring out the irony of the poetry, and Donne was a very appropriate companion. I've chosen other companions for other books of poetry.

Kostelanetz: So your immersion process included not only the original poet but some English-speaking companion.

Miller: Bicultural immersion, bilinguistic immersion. I was thinking of the comparison between Burton Watson's and Gary Snyder's Han Shan, as being something I often use for students. Both translated the Chinese poet Han Shan, and by just presenting those two translations, I think one can see a lot about what someone has chosen as a voice or what one hears as a voice.

Payne: But they're very different though.

Miller: Very different—that's part of the point—but contemporaries.

Daniels: But this is an extremely important point, and I'm awfully glad to have heard Ms. Miller say this, because there has been a lamentable tendency to use slang, like "cool," "yeah, yeah," "dig," for Homer. It just does not work. If you're a decent translator, you're supposedly rather well read, and you do, in fact, live in the company of people from Chaucer on down to the present. If you echo some other language, you do not modernize to the point of saying, "yeah, yeah, I really dig ya, man." I'm sorry. This is not to be done. I think I know more black English than most white Americans, and I like it very much—especially the black English that has never been picked up by the press!

Doria: But one does not do this. Barbara is absolutely right: you live in the company of lots of poets. And then again, the term "magic" comes up, and somehow you're picking up from here and there all at once. But it's certainly not a question of chaining yourself to the cant of your own day. For God's sake, no! That's terribly important.

Kostelanetz: Mr. Payne, in translating from the Chinese, what kinds of models were in your head?

Payne: Oddly enough, the chief model we had in mind was Ezra Pound. We knew very well that Ezra Pound's Chinese was terribly flawed. He just didn't know Chinese, and he spent his whole life pretending that he did. So he translated Confucius, and he translated a lot of poets. But what he did do was something quite miraculous. Again we come to this magic business and the immersion process that we were talking about; this is not literary language, this is magical language. And immersion, particularly, is a magical language.

Somehow, by some mysterious process, Pound reproduced a Chinese feeling, a brightness in verse, which simply didn't exist in all the other translations.

Remember that up to about 1929, except for Waley, absolutely no one had translated Chinese into English with any kind of real sense of what Chinese was about. We had rhymed translations of Chinese poetry, written by people who obviously belonged to the Victorian era, and these had somehow survived into the 20th century. What Pound had was an extraordinary feeling for words and an extraordinary imagination of what it would have been like to have been a Chinese poet. He had the whole feeling of that, and so what we did was study Pound's translations rather carefully and try to find out what this magical process was. Basically what we discovered was that his rhythms were very close to Chinese rhythms; his choice of words was closer to Chinese, and yet he would translate a whole poem, and every single word would be wrong. Possibly, two words would be right.

And it didn't matter.

Kostelanetz: Did Pound have helpers?

Payne: He had a manuscript by a man named Fenollosa, which was given to him, and it was a word by word translation. And what he would then do was try to imagine what the words meant, on the basis of the design of the words. I mean, a Chinese word would have something that looked a little bit like a house and two legs sticking out of it. And so he put in a house and two legs.

He did everything unimaginably wrong, but in a most extraordinary way he got the spirit. This is something that one has to think a great deal about in translation—reviving mysteriously the spirit, say, of *Genji*. And it's not done by any obviously textual method; it's done simply by an enormous emotion.

Kostelanetz: And you think of Pound as one of the great translators?

Payne: No, I don't. I think he was enormously useful, but I don't think he was a translator because he didn't translate. He made versions rather as Robert Lowell made versions, but he did them much better.

Doria: Much better.

Kostelanetz: Who are the great translators living today, in your mind?

Payne: Living today? I don't know. Trask just died, and Ivan

Morris is dead, and Waley is dead, and so far as China and Japan are concerned, I don't think there are any. Ivan Morris was an extraordinary translator, and he did it in a way which was entirely different from Waley. He would painstakingly go ahead and make ten versions; Waley would make one, and that would be the end.

Ivan Morris would spend a whole week on one page of one of the Japanese texts he was doing. I've seen his manuscripts, and it's extraordinary, incredibly painstaking. Finally he'd throw all the versions away, and you'd get something in absolutely wonderful English.

Kostelanetz: So he went through many drafts, literally?

Payne: Oh, drafts and drafts and drafts.

Kostelanetz: He was your colleague at the Translation Center at Columbia and on *Translation* magazine?

Payne: Yes.

Kostelanetz: How do you describe their function?

Payne: What we're trying to do is assemble a large number of very good translations from all possible languages, and we're not having too much success because what we really want is to cover the whole world. So far we haven't covered very much of the Arab literatures or the African literatures. We've done quite well in Chinese, Japanese, and some of the European languages. But it seems to me that the European languages are the least important for us to deal with because publishers will publish them anyway. We're trying very hard to get the stuff that is not usually published.

Kostelanetz: Where do you find such translations?

Payne: This is a very great problem, and we're faced with it all the time. All we can do is to say to everyone, please send more translations to us at 307-A Mathematics Building, Columbia University, New York, New York 10027, and in any language and whatever form you can, and we do need them. If you write to the Executive Director, you will get a very prompt reply.

Kostelanetz: Well, then how would a non-English writer living today establish contact with likely translators in the U.S.?

Miller: In Italy this past summer people were asking me who in America would be interested in translating certain writers; and that seems to be an equally great problem for writers and scholars in other countries—finding Americans, English-speakers, to translate works of importance.

Kostelanetz: And what advice did you give them?

Miller: I told them that the Translation Center or American PEN were very good places to send suggestions and to send works.

Kostelanetz: Of course, another way is for the writer desiring translation to simply do some research and find out who in America is translating your language and then send your books blindly, send them care of the translator's publishers or directly to the translator's address, if you can find it from *Who's Who* or any of the other indices, or get it from the Translation Center. That would be the best way to introduce oneself, it seems to me, to an American translator.

Now, Guy Daniels has done books for both commercial and noncommerical publishers. Barbara Miller's books have come entirely from university presses. Charles Doria, what kinds of publishers have you had?

Doria: Well, I've used Doubleday and Swallow Press, and this year I think is the first time I've been with a university press. The Ohio University Press is doing an anthology of mine called *Tenth Muse, Classical Drama In Translation,* a collection of Greek and Latin plays. It's unique in that it unites poets and traditional scholars working without intrusive editorial supervision on every type of ancient drama—tragedy, comedy, satyr plays.

By and large, I've found the university press to be much more helpful and forthcoming in every way than the commercial publisher. I don't know how that tallies with anyone else's experiences here.

Kostelanetz: I wanted to ask your sense of major translators in America today. Whom would you identify?

Doria: Well, I guess I would identify Ezra Pound, for the "Homage to Propertius," but particularly for his version of *The Women of Trachis* because I know the original well and I find what he did both amazing and suggestive.

Kostelanetz: Why?

Doria: For reasons I mentioned earlier: that Pound had carried over a great many of the qualities of the original. I also hear things going on there, particularly in the choruses, that make me think his version is poetry—that if one didn't know the Greek original, had simply read this, one would find it interesting on its own terms, not as a reminder or a replica of the Sophocles original.

But I'd have to say that beyond Pound and his influential example, I really can't think of anyone who has consistently translated in a way that I would call "great," whatever that means here. There are a lot of interesting translators working nowadays. I am thinking of

Guy Lee, who did a version of Ovid's *Amores*, or *Love Elegies*. I don't know what else he's done, but that's a very interesting book which should be better known. I should also mention Jerome Rothenberg for his theories on total translation and for his "reworkings" of sacred texts in *Technicians of the Sacred* and *A Big Jewish Book*.

Kostelanetz: Guy Daniels, who are your heroes in America or otherwise?

Daniels: Well, I would include, certainly, Pound's earlier work with Provençal and Italian; I think some of those are excellent. I'm quite a Pound fan; I've lost so much of my Latin, and I never have known Chinese, so I'm not much of a judge of that. I love what he did in *The Seafarer*, for example—what he called "stretching" English, which I think was marvelous.

But I don't think there's anyone around, really, that you could call great today. I would be great if they would let me live and give me time and money to do something great, but so far that hasn't happened!

Kostelanetz: How are you paid?

Daniels: Miserably! Mostly fees and some royalties obviously for anything in the public domain, royalties with certain living authors, but mostly fees.

Kostelanetz: Fees meaning a specific price for. . . .

Daniels: A fee slightly below the level of the average Manhattan doorman, I would say, in terms of income. But then, if one works as I have for seven years without a vacation, and during weekends, one can almost catch up with the doorman.

Kostelanetz: Do you do other writing besides?

Daniels: I used to. And occasionally I just say, "The hell with it," and sit down and write something of my own. But then I pay for it later. It comes out in literary magazines for ten dollars.

Kostelanetz: How many words a year do you translate?

Daniels: Oh, I don't even want to think about it—awful!

Payne: How many pages?

Daniels: Hundreds.

Kostelanetz: Barbara, how are you paid?

Miller: By the university; I teach.

Kostelanetz: You're a subsidized writer then.

Miller: Yes. As far as earning a living from the kind of translation that I do, it would be impossible. I occasionally get a grant which gives me the opportunity to devote my time to translation and editing.

Kostelanetz: So it is subsidized. And Charles Doria?

Doria: Well, when I teach, I would regard that as Barbara said, a subsidy. Otherwise, I have to make it on grants, advances, doing free-lance work.

John Barth:
Writing Fiction in an Age of Criticism

Jerome Klinkowitz

If American critics were to follow the practice of their Spanish and Latin American colleagues, John Barth and certain of his contemporaries would be called "the Generation of '31"—a helpful term which has thus far escaped us. Give or take a few years on either side of that date, one can list the birthdates of a whole constellation of fiction writers who for the lack of a better word have been consistently called "young" and "new," even as still newer and fresher ways of writing fiction have come along: John Barth (1930), Donald Barthelme (1931), Ronald Sukenick and Robert Coover (1932), and Jerzy Kosinski (1933), to name only the most commercially prominent. Just a few years older are Raymond Federman, John Hawkes, and William H. Gass; and even fewer years younger are Thomas Pynchon, Clarence Major, Imamu Amiri Baraka, Steve Katz, and Ishmael Reed.

Though their differences are more numerous than their similarities, all have taken part in the trend which, for a time in the late 1960s and early 1970s, brought an emphasis on anti-realism to mainstream American fiction. Often against their will, they have been grouped together as a school of Metafiction, Superfiction, Surfiction, Disruptive Fiction, and the like. Joe David Bellamy's *The New Fiction: Interviews with Innovative American Writers* (Urbana: University of Illinois Press, 1974) and Jack Hicks's anthology *Cutting Edges: Young American Fiction for the '70s* (New York: Holt, Rinehart & Winston, 1973) are symptomatic of the critical habit of calling these writers collectively "new" and "innovative," tacitly assuming that "youth" (however inappropriate to a writer 44 years old at the time, or even 51) is superior to "age" and that "innovative" means "better," in the sense of a new and improved product. But virtually no critic or literary historian of these years, including the author of this essay, can evade responsibility for such over-enthusiastic label making. If indeed there was any sort of breakthrough in fiction, never—as many of these same critics now admit—was it so sloppily described.

Quite unhappily at the center of this critical mess stands John Barth, the American fictionist probably most responsible for the boom anti-realistic fiction enjoyed for a time among the large commercial publishers. What does Barth truly have in common with his collectively unwilling colleagues, besides sharing their desire to be treated individually and not as part of some critically regimented group? For one thing, and most importantly, he is a member in good standing of American academe. Even before publishing his first novel in 1956 he had earned a graduate degree from Johns Hopkins University and was teaching as a member of Pennsylvania State University's Department of English. Subsequent novels and growing critical fame, enhanced by his reputation as a brilliant teacher, have propelled him from increasingly distinguished professorships at the State University of New York at Buffalo and Boston University to his present post as Alumni Centennial Professor of English and Creative Writing at his alma mater, Johns Hopkins. Virtually every other member of our improvised Generation of '31 is graduate-school trained or oriented and boasts a long (if not continual) association with universities. Most, like Barth, have published significant critical work. In previous literary epochs American fiction writers have been preachers, plumbers, able bodied seamen, or workaday journalists, but rarely conventional academics. If for Herman Melville a whaling ship was his Harvard and his Yale, Yale and Harvard (and their sister institutions) have been the whaling ships of a great many writers of the Generation of '31.

Other correspondences are just as easy to note. Women are conspicuously absent, though the popularity of Anaïs Nin which crowned her later years and the example of Englishwoman Doris Lessing have inspired critical attention for anti-realistic work by American women writers in more recent years. And although few of the Generation of '31 have been consistently anti-realistic throughout their careers, the prominence of their self-reflective fictions in the minds of critical adversaries has led to a violent backlash against the style. This reaction was articulated most comprehensively for fiction in John Gardner's *On Moral Fiction* (New York: Basic Books, 1978) and for critical theory in Gerald Graff's *Literature Against Itself* (Chicago: University of Chicago Press, 1979). Succeeding generations of writers, particularly the M. F. A. graduates of programs such as the University of Iowa's Writers' Workshop, have tended on the whole to turn away from self-conscious innovation as sternly as the Pop Art and Hard Edge painters of the 1960s rejected the "action painting" of the Abstract Expressionists dominant in the 1940s and 1950s—simply as a gesture of creative independence, perhaps for fresher fields of economic gain, and most certainly because the ground floor opened by the higher education boom had been filled up and closed.

What becomes clear in terms of simple historical observation (something much easier from the distance of 1980) is that the self-reflective innovationists of the Generation of '31 wrote their fiction under tremendous critical pressure: having been told that because of realism's eclipse the novel was dead, they felt compelled to challenge and hopefully reinvent conventions of fiction which in terms of the mainstream had been fairly stable since the days of Fitzgerald, Hemingway, and Faulkner. But the very success of their work—artistically, commercially, and philosophically—served many contrary interests. Like the "Boom in Spanish American Literature" described with no small irony by one of its participants, José Donoso, in his book of that name (New York: Columbia University Press, 1977; first published in Spanish as *Historia personal del "boom"* by Editorial Anagrama, Barcelona, 1972), America's momentary boom in anti-realistic fiction has been more useful as a descriptive tool for its enemies. For its writers, the effects have been at times debilitating. Writing novels in an age of criticism, when the very life of fiction is a matter of hot and often vicious debate, has been no easy pleasure.

"In a sense, I am Jacob Horner," proclaims the narrator of John Barth's second novel, *The End of the Road* (1958). Sentenced to a self-consciously absurdist therapy of teaching college English, Barth's narrator reminds us of the dispensation under which Barth himself felt he must write. It was 1958, not 1851; Melville's "Call me Ishmael" was part and parcel of another time, just as Kurt Vonnegut's invocational "Call me Jonah" for *Cat's Cradle* (1963) would entertain the same heartbreaking paradox of having to (yet being unable to) write a Great American Novel for our times, an era which, as Barth saw it, had rejected the Cartesian definition of ego so central to traditional novelistic design. A hero could no longer speak with confidence and coherence and so define himself since under contemporary philosophical pressure the old "cogito, ergo sum" had become a farcically

painful lie.

    The End of the Road and Barth's first novel, *The Floating Opera* (1956), were written in the same burst of creative energy during the mid-1950s, when the promise of commercial publication drove Barth to a frenzy of literary production he has not since matched (as noted by David Morrell in the most complete study of this novelist to date). That first work was not to have been a novel at all—"a philosophical minstrel show" is how Barth describes his plans, not wanting to write a novel yet hoping to make it "a work of literature" nevertheless. In form both books turned out to be rather conventional novels in the then-popular style of André Malraux, Albert Camus, and other such thinkers. Each was heavily philosophical, and the first brushed so close with absolute nihilism that its original publishers insisted on a different, more humanistically acceptable ending. (Barth's preferred text is found in the revised and restored edition published by Doubleday in 1967.) But these initial works won Barth the beginnings of a substantial following: not among the reading public (for Morrell estimates less than 5,000 copies of the two books were sold), but with John Barth's colleagues in the profession of English. A knowledge of literary and philosophical tradition complemented by the life-experience of teaching these verities were the qualifications of Barth's ideal reader.

    "My Uncle Mike, the Zen Philosopher, says it wouldn't make any difference to him if he was *dead or alive!*" reads a popular children's cartoon of the 1960s, showing two little kids sitting in a treehouse with their scuffed sneakers and baseball cards, tossing this Zen wisdom back and forth. "Well, if he feels *that* way," one kid argues, "why don't he *kill* his self?" The other kid's answer is the same as John Barth's: "He says 'cause it *wouldn't make any difference!*" This attitude, so easily satirized in the Sunday comics, was more somber stuff in the 1950s when Barth wrote *The Floating Opera* and *The End of the Road*. Todd Andrews of the first novel lives with a heart which any moment might stop ticking, or so his doctor tells him; Jake Horner of the second book teaches English as medically prescribed therapy for his crisis of identity. Barth fleshes out their intellectual problems with—to a man of his generation and profession—the most salaciously flirtatious of actions: the invitation from a consenting husband to bed the latter's wife, in both cases a seeming triumph of the cultured mind over the messy limits of emotions. To some extent life has bored each protagonist, but neither is willing to risk it. Others take that risk for them: in the second novel a woman dies, and a whole boatload of persons in the first are saved only by the most whimsical chance. Emotional casualties litter each novel, but the narrator-protagonists survive to walk full circle back to their novels' beginnings, themselves unchanged by the entire catastrophic experience. All that's been confirmed are their own initial suspicions (about time in the first book, about identity in the second), which started things rolling in the first place. The most sterling survivor is tradition, for in both novels it has been left perfectly intact.

John Barth's work in fiction has been to one end: the employment of literary exhaustion as a device against itself. Barth's eloquent justification of this technique was published as "The Literature of Exhaustion" in *The Atlantic* for August 1967; but nearly a year before, in the pages of *Commentary* (for October 1966), critic Robert Garis had perceived just what Barth was doing. *The Floating Opera*, Garis noted, was "modeled on *Tristram Shandy* (amusing inability to get down to telling the story)," while *The End of the Road*, he might have added, was an almost perfect rehearsal of forms and themes prominent in postwar European Existentialism. (In fact, Garis argued that the Jake Horner novel was an excellent dramatization of Barth's academic times.) Garis did proceed to check off Barth's next two novels as further self-apparent literary exercises—*The Sot-Weed Factor* (1960) being "an 806-page literal imitation of every picaresque novel from Rabelais to *Fanny Hill* and *Giles Goat-Boy* (1966) as "a 710-page pseudo-adaptation of the Swift of *Gulliver's Travels* and the narrative sections of *A Tale of a Tub*." But unlike Barth's other academic endorsers, Garis was strongly critical of this tactic. "I call what Barth is doing Baconianism," he complained:

> ... because, as the length itself of the two latter books might suggest, one sees here a heartbreakingly obsessive patience and persistence; and yet, it doesn't work. Just as the Baconians in the end tell us nothing about Shakespeare, so Barth's laborious imitations fail to produce interesting or important works of art. An extremely talented novelist has, for motives one can only guess at, deliberately turned himself into a kind of mad graduate student in English literature.

John Barth's motives were clarified in his "Literature of Exhaustion" essay published in *The Atlantic* ten months later, and a sequel called "The Literature of Replenishment" for the same magazine's January 1980 issue added further commentary pertinent to his book-length works of the intervening years: *Lost in the Funhouse: Fiction for Print, Tape, Live Voice* (1967), *Chimera* (1972), and *Letters: A Novel* (1979). Why should a contemporary American novelist use the form of Henry Fielding in 1960? Or of Samuel Richardson in 1979? Should the literary aspirations of our age be "*Tom Jones* by Samuel Beckett? Saarinen's Parthenon, D. H. Lawrence's *Wuthering Heights*, *The 1001 Nights* by John Barth?" as the first essay's subhead playfully asked? Barth the critic went on to explain that any educated writer in this day and age was faced with "the used-upness of certain forms or exhaustion of certain possibilities—by no means necessarily a cause for despair." In his 1980 sequel Barth adds that any writer, in any age, faces such exhaustion, as disclaimers from the earliest Egyptian scribes suggest. The literary work of John Barth, however, employs these ultimacies against themselves. In the years since Barth published his first essay, a panoply of theories to explain such authorial practice have flooded America, from the "anxiety of influence" operative upon writers to the "reception theory" which might describe the role of any natural reader. But if we are to trust the teller before the tale (something most traditional critics tell us not to do), we must take Barth's word that he has been writing this way to counteract the tendencies he sees in other contemporary art, which he insists falls short of genuine aesthetic achievement.

The Sot-Weed Factor and *Giles Goat-Boy* employ various 18th-century conventions to make their own 20th-century artistic statements. In the former, the secret journal of a character named Henry Burlingame is framed within the narrative adventures of the poet, Ebenezer Cooke; and all of the familiar Fieldingesque techniques, so tedious themselves in the hands of anyone else but their inventor, are interesting and entertaining because they must be read not as the product of a third-rate contemporary but instead as the studied parody by a brilliant scholar of Fielding's art. In similar manner *Giles Goat-Boy* takes what it can from Swift, substituting an allegory of mid-20th-century academic politics as a comment on the state of the world ("University" for "Universe," "Twelve-Term Riot" for "World War II," and so forth). As technique, the transpositions from Fielding and Swift are flawless; but as Robert Garis and others have complained, they are only technique, offering no new perspective at all and telling readers nothing they do not already know. *Lost in the Funhouse* and

Chimera are more deliberate investigations of narrative itself, including a cut-out Moebius strip, a series of quoted quotes successively swallowed up by the necessary punctuation marks, a story which narrates its own inception and dissolution, and various retellings of ancient myths. *Letters* functions as a coda to Barth's entire literary career so far, for its seven epistolary authors who exchange correspondence among themselves are either characters from the previous six books or are John Barth himself and his fresh creations.

This seven-book canon, no small achievement for a writer born in 1931, would be the perfect index of a literary age except for one fact, which its author keeps repeating in his influential essays: he does not sympathize with the spirit of his times. "The Literature of Exhaustion" opens with a playfully sarcastic dismissal of a style of work then being produced by a young writer/publisher outside the conservative academic community: Dick Higgins and his Something Else Press (Higgins's own essay, "Intermedia" [1966], is reprinted in Higgins's *foew&ombwhnw* [New York: Something Else Press, 1969], and in Richard Kostelanetz's *Esthetics Contemporary* [Buffalo, New York: Prometheus Books, 1978]). Within this style Barth included a good sample (but not all properly attributed to their best practitioners) of literary, theatrical, musical, and artistic work unlike his and his academic colleagues' own, including the assemblage novels of Robert Filliou, the Happenings of Allen Kaprow, the non-predictable music of John Cage, and the Pop Art of Robert Rauschenberg. All were whimsically degraded as lacking seriousness, discipline of effort, and achievement of stable form, as if these were the prime requisites of artistic success—which Barth indeed believed they were. "The New York Correspondence School of Literature," as he called them, were capable of interesting ideas for beer drinking conversation. But they were fully incapable of producing great art.

What Barth overlooked, and what he overlooked more deliberately in his sequel essay of 1980, was nothing less than the history of 20th-century art. That history, according to even the most conservative of critics, has been the steady effacement of represented action from works of art in all disciplines—whether literary, dramatic, musical, or graphic. Disfavor for such history may be a valid excuse for any person granted an advanced degree before the late 1960s and continuing to teach in the same discipline, since most American graduate schools until then insisted that the subjects of scholarly inquiry be deceased, all pertinent texts established, and all letters and memoirs published or at least open to study. For academic scholarship, such a rule may have merits. But it is hardly an excuse for anyone professing to be on the leading edge of creative achievement.

The aesthetic of mid-century America is traced most easily by the work of artists Barth dismisses as impertinent to his own High Art. The Abstract Expressionist painters active in New York during the 1940s and 1950s (deKooning, Pollock, and Kline, for example) established, in critic Harold Rosenberg's words, that for this time and place the canvas of one's work (in any medium) was to be less "a surface on which to represent" than "an arena in which to act." The work's own action, and not a representation of an action, would be art's subject. The predictable reaction to this aesthetic by succeeding generations of creative artists did not negate Rosenberg's truth; Pop Art, Hard Edge, Minimal, and Conceptual Art (all products of the years when John Barth has written fiction) simply established new ways of non-Aristotelian expression which could not be merchandised either as imitations of a now-saleable style or as portable objects in themselves. Foremost was the integrity of the unaligned artist, even though those strategies of non-alignment could later be described as movements of their own; "anti-movement" art was the period's capstone. During all these years, however, John Barth was solidly aligned with a tenured academic community and a succession (following a trail of job promotions of his editors) of mainstream commercial publishers; each establishment maintained a vested interest in representational literary art, as eminently teachable and saleable.

The words of approbation which course their way through John Barth's "Literature of Exhaustion" and "Literature of Replenishment" essays are "heroic," "salvation," "apotheosis," "virtuoso," and the like—terms which admittedly stand against the style of creative artists not aligned with either the academic or commercial entertainment industries of contemporary America. In his 1980 sequel Barth recalled that his first essay was conceived and written on a university campus besieged by the challenging forces of demonstrating students and the reactions of tear-gassing police. It appears that he himself was quite uncomfortable in these circumstances, which others saw as genuinely revolutionary in terms of both curricular and aesthetic change. The key to Barth's personal aesthetic is back in that original essay written during the hectic days of the American 1960s, where he states his admiration for writers atypical of those times—that is, for writers who replace the representation of one action (an Aristotelian mimesis of behavior within the social world) with another: the act of writing a novel. *How that act is performed*, as an action in itself or as the representation of an action, is the key distinction in finding where Barth stands. Each of his examples, which include conventionally Modernist works by Nabokov, Beckett, and Borges, are similar to his own, in that the typical suspension of disbelief in what one reads need not itself be suspended (as opposed to the anti-Aristotelian style of work the non-academic writers were doing). "Novels which imitate the form of the Novel, by an author who imitates the role of the Author" are the books which Barth appreciates and writes himself. These booklength fictions—*Pale Fire, Labyrinths,* and *Giles Goat-Boy* are the cited examples—are written by admittedly good Modernist writers who have held tenured positions in their own respective literary establishments. And each follows Aristotle's aesthetic belief that art imitates, rather than creates.

Literary works which suspend the suspension of disbelief, which in anti-Aristotelian fashion include the act of writing by the author and the act of reading by the reader as integral parts of their aesthetic, are excluded from John Barth's pantheon. He much prefers fictions which represent something already existing in the world— fictions in which the things that happen are metaphors for something else, not something in themselves. For Barth, it seems, fiction should forever be an imitation of an action, and not an action in itself.

This exclusion has unnecessarily complicated the history of late 20th-century American literary art, for even among the Generation of '31 can be found excellent writers who alternately accept or reject the critical canon enshrined by received academic theory. The history of exhaustion and replenishment, however, has been a decidedly Aristotelian affair, and hence escapes the true spirit of our times. Yet Barth, like several other members of his literary generation, is capable of surprise; and his novel *Sabbatical* (New York: Putnam's, 1982), which follows his intellectual desk-clearing in *Letters* and "The Literature of Replenishment," is just the style of trans-mimetic work he had earlier resisted.

Sabbatical is aptly titled. Supposedly about a vacation retreat during which its man-and-wife narrators, after seven years of a second marriage, will take stock and determine future directions, the novel is in fact a reconstitution of Barth's technique in the wake of his first seven novels. As fiction in an age of criticism, it is productively self-conscious, with none of the awkward posing which marked *Giles*

Goat-Boy and the works which followed. Its narrative situation comfortably accommodates talk about fiction writing without turning into self-reflexivity: co-narrator FennTurner had tried to be a novelist twenty years before, enrolling himself in the old-fashioned practices of authorship complete to a year holed up in Europe on a shoestring budget with nothing to do but write. But with nothing to do, nothing has resulted beyond metafiction of the most ill-considered type: "It was supposed to be about the politics of political journalism," Fenn recalls, "but it had taken an autobiographical turn and was more and more about a frustrated writer and a marriage strained by its first reciprocal adulteries." "The story, bogged down in self-concern, of a story bogged down in self-concern" is a deliberate parody of the Moebius strip style of fiction which obsessed Barth in his *Lost in the Funhouse* exercises. For *Sabbatical*, however, these memories have a more salutary effect, and his unfinished novel remains "the story of the story that taught me I couldn't write stories"—in the conventional sense, that is—and therefore it becomes a valid part of the new style of novel being composed before our eyes.

Fenn the failed novelist had become a CIA man, deciding to live a story because he feels he can't write one; but this very life of fiction offers the key to Barth's *Sabbatical*. As Fenn and his young wife, Susan, complete their half-year's cruise through the Caribbean and return to home port in Maryland, they shape their experiences into a story—a necessarily artifical act with its principles of composition and exclusion. By doing so, they recall adventures and fill each other in with their own memories, in the process treating the reader to a fully natural workshop session on narratology. Susan tells the story of her sister's torture and rape; Fenn fills in scenes from his first marriage; the happy circumstances of their meeting are recalled as well, so by novel's end the reader knows everything needed to appreciate their lives. They debate the contrary virtues of realism and fantasy, seeing the need for each. Myths and dreams are introduced for their structural services, and several of Barth's own stories and favorite notions (including the sperm-swim of "Night-Sea Journey" and the notion that "the key to the treasure is the treasure") are entertained.

What is being created, however, is their own narrative as their lives revolve about it, and in this case the key to the story is the story. As Fenn admires in Cervantes, the road is more comfortable than the inn. And as Susan, a scholar of nineteenth-century American literature and a descendent of Edgar Allan Poe (as Fenn is of Francis Scott

Key) can explain a compellingly interesting story such as *The Narrative of Arthur Gordon Pym* derives its effect from the fact that although the tale itself ends with the character's disappearance into the texture of narrative itself, its very telling testifies to his survival in its transmission. This life of fiction is what Susan and Fenn eventually find for themselves, amid the shambles of abortion, family dissolution, and vexing career decisions. As with *Pym*, "It is not that the end of the voyage interrupts the writing, but that the interruption of the writing ends the voyage"—and in an endless repetition of the tale, their writing never ends, since they "begin it at the end and end at the beginning." In this formulation, there is no imitation of imitation of reality. The fiction is most clearly and productively itself, making John Barth once more a timely representative of his literary age.

Bibliography

By John Barth:

The Floating Opera. New York: Appleton-Century-Crofts, 1956; revised edition, Garden City, New York: Doubleday, 1967.
The End of the Road. New York: Appleton-Century-Crofts, 1958; revised edition, Garden City, New York: Doubleday, 1967.
The Sot-Weed Factor. Garden City, New York: Doubleday, 1960; revised 1967.
Giles Goat-Boy. Garden City, New York: Doubleday, 1966.
"The Literature of Exhaustion," *The Atlantic*, August 1967.
Lost in the Funhouse. Garden City, New York: Doubleday, 1968.
Chimera. New York: Random House, 1972.
Letters: A Novel. New York: Putnam, 1979.
"The Literature of Replenishment," *The Atlantic*, January 1980.
Sabbatical. New York: Putnam, 1982.
The Friday Book: Essays and Other Nonfiction. New York: Putnam, 1984.
Tidewater Tales. New York: Putnam, 1987.

About John Barth:

Garis, Robert. "What Happened to John Barth?" *Commentary*, October 1966.
Morrell, David. *John Barth: An Introduction.* University Park: Pennsylvania State
University Press, 1976.
Tharpe, Jac. *John Barth: The Comic Sublimity of Paradox.* Carbondale: Southern Illinois
University Press, 1974.
Weixlmann, Joseph. *John Barth: A Descriptive Primary and Annotated Secondary Bib-
liography.* New York: Garland, 1976.

Thomas Pynchon

Joseph W. Slade

In Thomas Pynchon's *V.* (1963) one of the characters, caught up in a "conspiracy" variously described as "The Plot Which Has No Name" and "The Situation as an N-Dimensional Mishmash," says to the reader as much as to his fellows that "We are all spies in this together." Real or imagined conspiracies and the paranoia with which characters respond to them are the trademarks of Pynchon's other two novels, *The Crying of Lot 49* (1966) and *Gravity's Rainbow* (1973), and of most of his half-dozen short stories as well. As elements drawn from middlebrow literature, the conspiracies help to explain the broad base of their author's appeal, for it is his style effortlessly to graft mandarin themes onto popular genres. Although the zany cabals amuse and fascinate, Pynchon employs them principally to engender a sense of community and to restore a sense of mystery to a cultural waste land desiccated by Western commerce and secularized by historical rationalization. As these terms suggest, the conspiracies illuminate one of the great intellectual currents of 20th-century letters as they both parody and extend the insights of Pynchon's three largest influences—T. S. Eliot, Max Weber, and Henry Adams. Their ideas and those borrowed from many other thinkers emerge as encyclopedic allusion from behind the historical vignettes—the accounts of private postal systems, the premiere of a Stravinsky opera, the colonization of South-West Africa, the currency debacles of Weimar Germany—that appear in Pynchon's global narratives.

Eliot, who himself adopted *The Education of Henry Adams* as source for his own poetry, is the prophet of the wasteland, a topography that recurs in Pynchon's fiction in the form of literal junkyards (the short story "Low-lands"), the sterile rock of Malta (*V.*), the absurd landscape of southern California (*The Crying of Lot 49*), or the ravaged Europe of World War II (*Gravity's Rainbow*). In Pynchon's work as in

Eliot's, humans suffer from loss of love, loss of faith, loss of vitality; they feel isolated from one another and from their environment. For Eliot and for Pynchon the affliction is spiritual impoverishment, but here, despite superficial similarities, the two writers diverge. Eliot charged modern science with diminishing man by divorcing him from nature; as correctives he advocated Anglo-Catholic mysticism and a reawakened awareness of tradition. Pynchon is sympathetic to these claims, but his perspective has been sharpened by his superior understanding of science.

An afficionado of technology, Pynchon is enamored of the aesthetics of science and invention although he is careful to distinguish between achievements themselves and their perversions. Embedded in the texts of his novels are learned passages on engineering, ballistics, or plastics, sometimes coupled with laments on their use to oppress or destroy but just as often celebrated—along with other human endeavors like music, film, or painting—as examples of creativity. In our time technology is more than art or science; it is the cultural end product of a linear history. The First Industrial Revolution, during which machines came to do the work of human muscle, has given way to the Second, in which systems do the work of human senses and intelligence. Both Revolutions resulted from the rationalization of the environment described by Max Weber in *The Protestant Ethic and the Spirit of Capitalism* and elaborated upon by writers like Jacques Ellul, Lewis Mumford, and Herbert Marcuse. Rationalization fragments nature in order to control her and recombines her elements in order to erect artificial institutions. It is an irreversible process that has transformed society on a vast scale by enlarging, concentrating, and connecting human labor into new aggregates of energy. In acquiring the power to refashion his world, however, man has paid a Faustian price. Rationalization has alienated him from nature and from his fellows. It has eroded the organic ties of family, friends, and folk by subordinating them to contractual bonds and abstract, anonymous relationships. Rationalization has shattered ritual, dogma, and tradition—the older props of culture—by emphasizing new ideals of production and commerce. Rationalization has reduced the fruitful dialectic between ancient dualities like life and death, illusion and reality, determinism and freedom, and in the process has converted humans themselves into what Marcuse calls "one dimensional men." The fault lies not with the specific invention or discovery but with the systemization of man's tools and knowledge into interdependent networks.

In short, the Second Industrial Revolution has overlaid the world of nature with comprehensive artifice. Its networks are so pathologically complete, its operations so thoroughly synthetic, that we no longer understand the dimensions of human freedom or the meaning of the human condition. To call the condition mechanical is to mislead, for the machine model is a metaphor belonging to the First Industrial Revolution, and, in a sense, Thomas Pynchon's career can be construed as a search for an appropriate metaphor for its successor. As he remarks in *Gravity's Rainbow*, "We have to look for power sources . . . and distribution networks . . . [;] we have to find meters whose scales are unknown in the world, draw our own schematics, getting feedback, making connections, reducing the error, trying to learn the real function . . . zeroing in on what incalculable plot?"

According to the narrator of *The Crying of Lot 49*, a metaphor is "a thrust at truth and a lie." The ambiguity, especially as it cloaks science and technology, is central to Pynchon's purpose and one of the reasons he has altered his metaphors from novel to novel. In his first book he seems to condemn technology with a vigor T. S. Eliot would applaud, in large part because he tries to make use of the machine as symbol for human degeneration. The shadowy V., seeking reification, turns herself into a metal and plastic apparatus, a darkly comic version of Henry Adams's Virgin transformed into Dynamo. A Venus in transit toward death, V. embodies the sterility of the wasteland. Herbert Stencil, who "stencilizes" events to fit his own psychic templates, puts V. at the center of "The Plot Which Has No Name"—the cause, he thinks, of crisis after apocalyptic crisis in Europe and Africa. In his third novel, however, Pynchon sketches a different conspiracy: "Them," the multinational corporations (which have superseded the rationalized national states of Weber's scheme), who rule through economic supremacy and bureaucratic privilege. Acting in concert, these cartels shape the destinies of men and nations through webs of interlocking industrial alliances. Since they buy and sell expertise and information, the ingredients of technical prowess, they suborn even the most wonderful of man's technological achievements. "The Firm"— as "Their" conspiracy is sometimes called in *Gravity's Rainbow*—serves as a suitably advanced industrial metaphor: to account for the distribution of technological power in our culture is to account also for the political, social, and psychological forces that devolve upon the individuals who live within the matrices of networks.

Pynchon believes that society reproduces its cultural norms in its citizens. "The Firm" is thus the beneficiary of a mind-set derived from rationalization, which is, after all, linked to creativity and to the human propensity for taking the world apart and putting it together in new ways. Thinking, for example, requires language; and language, the most primal of technologies, is a tool of rationalization, though often used for irrational ends. Language, says the paranoid narrator of *Gravity's Rainbow*, has affinities with science; it is a form of "name-giving, dividing the Creation finer and finer, analyzing, setting namer more hopelessly apart from named, even to bringing in the mathematics of combination, tacking together established nouns to get new ones, the insanely, endlessly diddling play of a chemist whose molecules are words." Given the extent of its psychic roots, the urge toward rationalization can Balkanize consciousness and prevent the individual from seeing the world whole. Lacking large perspective, the individual endorses determinism because he is persuaded that his well-being rests on the need for control and that his personal security depends on the stability of the systems in which he lives. To be inside artificial systems is to lose freedom, but to be outside is worse.

Cultural norms reinforce personal disposition with discipline and conditioning. Tyrone Slothrop, the protagonist of *Gravity's Rainbow*, is a paradigm for modern man in that he has been literally conditioned in infancy by a Pavlovian, betrayed as a child by his parents, and placed under surveillance as an adult by "The Firm." The "Counterforce" of the novel, whose members oppose "Them" and try to rescue Slothrop, fail because they are infected by rationalization themselves. "The Firm," says the novel's narrator, "has a branch office in each of our brains." The web-like constraints of the metaphor would seem to close off possibilities for freedom, dignity, spirituality, or understanding. If control is so rigid and far-reaching, so internalized and assimilated, then humans cannot escape their limitations.

To this metaphor, however, Pynchon weds another borrowed from Henry Adams: thermodynamic entropy as an emblem of cultural decline. *The Education of Henry Adams* adopts the Second Law of Thermodynamics as historical metaphor to explain the disintegration of 12th-century religious unity into 20th-century democratic multiplicity. For Adams, chaos was overtaking civilization; entropy signalled the eventual heat-death of human systems and the end of history, a prognosis that made his thought attractive to T. S. Eliot. Fortunately, Pynchon understands the metaphor better than his predecessor, and knows that random events—a sign of entropy—are not necessarily threatening.

For Pynchon, "the entropies of lovable but scatterbrained Mother Nature" are aspects of Creation at its most inexplicable; aleatoric events are reminders of continuous evolution and mystery. Nature's operations and structures sustain themselves; human institutions and systems, on the other hand, require conscious effort, constant maintenance, and unremitting labor to remain in orderly repair. In a complex artificial world the ultimate horror is the collapse of systems, but the chaos that can indicate the approach of collapse, says Pynchon, can also promise hope. The zone of war in *Gravity's Rainbow* attracts motley characters seeking freedom and fresh starts in a place where conflict has swept away labyrinths and bureaucracies. The characters also seek spiritual redemption amid the anarchy. When rationalization falters, opportunities for "grace" arise.

Just as Henry Adams conceived of history as a process of spiritual decay, as a shifting away from religious touchstones, so Max Weber thought of rationalization as a process of increasing "disenchantment" of the world, as a diminishing of reverence for the magic of creation. Ironically, the original impulse toward rationalization was religious, growing out of the Protestant need to impose order on chaos, an impulse that led inevitably to the "demystification" or "desacralization" of nature. The Protestant prefers to be certain about the world; he wants it determined, Newtonian, predictable. By contrast, the first principle of Pynchon's theology is that the unpredictable is the holy. Anything that deepens mystery—random events, surprises, paradoxes—can be a manifestation of the sacred.

Paradox is inherent in the Second Law of Thermodynamics. The more ordered a system—be it the universe or human society—the greater the tendency toward entropy. Precisely because human institutions do exercise rigid control, entropy can ensue as the result of overorganization. Order succumbs to disorder, as manifest in random occurrences, over time. Since Pynchon identifies randomness as an attribute of nature, the implication is that human institutions, no matter how powerful, cannot wholly supplant natural processes, and that nature herself endures in all her majesty as "another world," the substratum of our own. When random events occur, their frightening aspect can trigger "an odd, religious instant" like the "epileptic moments" experienced by Oedipa Maas in *The Crying of Lot 49*. In these moments Oedipa senses the "intersection" of worlds at cosmic synapses. Only primitive, non-Western, incompletely rationalized peoples such as the Kirghiz of *Gravity's Rainbow* and the Hereros of that novel and *V.* can apprehend the rhythms of nature directly, but Oedipa and other Westerners with vestigial religious feeling can still sense nature's fits and starts.

This aspect of Pynchon's metaphysics meshes perfectly with information theory, which holds that entropy is a measure of information: the more unpredictable a message, the more information it carries, and the more it *reveals*. "Communication is the key," says John Nefastis of *The Crying of Lot 49*. If modern corporate society has made a fetish of information and treats it as an article of trade, even as currency, it is also true that real information, which stems from a recognition of disorder, is the source of genuine understanding of culture, of nature, and of man's place in both of those worlds. Such reflections lead Pynchon into considerations of epistemology, a subject on which he can be learned and comic. The dilemmas of perception and knowledge typically plunge his characters into hapless solipsism, from which they can be redeemed only by faith, which is a condition that few attain. Being sensitive to chance is one thing; knowing how to use this "information" as a basis for action is quite another.

Judged superficially, Pynchon's explorations of these areas seem to recap the philosophical debates of the 1920s, when Bertrand Russell and others seized on the Heisenberg Principle of Indeterminacy as a sanction of free will in a determined world. Actually Pynchon has completed a circle: he has invested Adams's metaphor of entropy with the luminousness of Weber's charisma, a spiritual diversion that can on occasion redirect (but not end) the progression of rationalization, in order to establish the possibility of redemption for Eliot's wasteland. Pynchon's syncretic metaphor contains two difficulties for those of his characters inclined to adopt it as a spiritual guide. The first is that the limitations of perception make it impossible for humans to know whether chance events really are random. A belief in the validity of chance is thus in some measure an act of faith although as such it is no more suspect than the Protestant faith in certainty. An assumption that chance really does exist leads to the second difficulty. While random events may provide authentic religious revelation, or even on a more prosaic level indicate a healthy rebalancing of an overorganized system, they may also be harbingers of disaster—of the system's collapse. Apocalypse is always just over the horizon in Pynchon's world, its imminence made more probable by the proliferation of lethal technologies like the V-2 rocket. However gratifying the visions of annihilation may be to certain characters and many readers of the novels, Pynchon's warnings of doom are clearly designed to promote life, if only because they should remind us of the fragility of human existence and of the need to live it. The dangerous ambiguity that fuels his fiction should serve to quicken the pulse of a palsied culture. At the very least, Pynchon suggests, a proper response to mystery so profound would be religious awe. With only a few exceptions, however, his characters allow the perceptual difficulties to push them into paranoia.

"There is something comforting—religious, if you want—about paranoia," says the narrator of *Gravity's Rainbow*: it is the beginning "of the discovery that everything is connected, everything in the Creation, a secondary illumination—not yet blindingly One. . . ." "A Puritan reflex," paranoia resembles the original Protestant shrinking from chaos. Since chaos is deadly to any human endeavor, even a quasi-religious defense is better than none. Paranoia is certainly preferable to what Pynchon calls "anti-paranoia, where nothing is connected to anything, a condition not many of us can bear for long." Besides encouraging a belief in unity and continuity, paranoia has the virtue of educating the individual to patterns of control that explain determinism. But if a little paranoia is not a dangerous thing, total paranoia is, for it can submerge areas of real human freedom in a false gestalt of absolute determinism. There are other drawbacks as well. By convincing himself that everything that happens is directed against himself, the paranoid invites a solipsism that robs him of full participation in the human community. By attributing menace to forces beyond his control, the paranoid indulges in a passivity that forestalls action. Worse, by insisting that nothing that happens to him is accidental, the paranoid denies chance and cuts himself off from surprise and the wonder of authentic revelation.

Even Oedipa Maas, who comes closest to bearing the weight of Pynchon's theology, suffers to an extent from this affliction. Oedipa is one of three improbable Messiahs (one in each novel) or would-be redeemers of the wasteland. Two of them, Benny Profane of *V.* and Tyrone Slothrop of *Gravity's Rainbow*, are losers, comic incompetents for whom their creator nevertheless has obvious affection. They fail in their quests partly because they prefer immobility to hard work and partly because they cast themselves as victims in order to evade responsibility. Their paranoia isolates them from the human community they might otherwise join. By contrast, her active love and enormous sympathy for the "disinherited" drive Oedipa on a search for clues to the Trystero "conspiracy." Her America is a culture over-stuffed with material goods unequally distributed, deranged by commercial vulgarity, drained of energy by a managerial class that is infatuated with realpolitik. The Trystero may be a secular attempt to restore a balance between order and disorder in America through an alternate postal system, the most primitive of communications networks. On the other hand, the clues Oedipa gathers may have sacred significance as the leading edge of a spiritual revelation about the relationship between America and nature. At any rate, Oedipa does not allow what she admits may be paranoid fantasy to deter her from sorting the information she has. To sort information with courage and love is to achieve humanity, and in this respect Oedipa approaches nobility. For her labor Oedipa is rewarded at the novel's climax with the imminence of revelation. She reaches the antecham-ber of the temple, where she sits across the aisle from the protagonist of Eliot's *The Waste Land*. Oedipa is Pynchon's finest character, superior to Benny Profane, who concludes his search for meaning with the words "Offhand I'd say I haven't learned a goddam thing," and to Tyrone Slothrop, who ends his by literally dissolving back into nature.

If Oedipa Maas is the most admirable of these three, Slothrop is the most interesting. The product of Pynchon's maturity, Slothrop is the most sustained of the writer's parodies of his influences. Slothrop is chance personified, a "sudden angel," a "thermodynamic surprise." More humorously, he is startlingly potent—a hilarious reversal of the condition of Eliot's males—and his penis erects, by chance, in the midst of the death wrought by rocket strikes on London in 1944. Although his ability to oppose life to death can be understood in terms of the statistical probabilities that describe the operations of nature herself, no one in the novel can comprehend Slothrop's charismatic function—which is to redirect a rationalized culture. He is supposed to reveal Eliot's themes: that life without spiritual meaning is a form of death and that death, when natural, can be redemptive. Slothrop's fate is linked to the equally charismatic rocket, the pinnacle of human technology, man's means of escape from the planet he has blighted, and to the plastics, fuels, and automatic systems that make up the missile's being. Born of the earth that supplied all of its components, the rocket loses its potential to the human passion for destruction. Captain Blicero tries to give the rocket life by enclosing Gottfried in the iconic V-2, but the gesture is a mockery of its rationalized purpose: death. It would be foolish to deny that human inventions have spiritual presence. After all, Pynchon implies, any technological achievement represents human dreams, human labor, and—to some degree—human understanding of nature. These qualities notwithstanding, technology is still just "the impersonation of life"; ingenuity can plumb organic mysteries but synthesizing does not result in "resurrection." To trespass on the precincts of the organic is not forbidden; the crime is "taking and not giving back"—the violation of the natural life-and-death rhythms of the world, which is "a closed thing, cyclical, resonant, eternally-recurrent." Looting nature for energy to keep calcified systems running is bad enough, but to make those systems nonbiodegradable is worse. Rationalization returns nothing. If debased artifice is eternal, then human existence can only end in sterile death. One of the more outrageous conceits of *Gravity's Rainbow* is a bureaucracy of ghosts—a suggestion that rationalization would render even death artificial. In returning to nature, Slothrop symbolizes life in death. As is usually the case with Messiahs, hardly anyone notices. If he could articulate a message, few would hear it; most of his colleagues are demoralized by their own interior wastelands.

The prodigality with which Pynchon peoples his novels, the comic distortion with which he draws the figures, and the delightful names he gives them combine to offset the solemnity of his themes. Despite their grotesqueness virtually all of his characters yearn for spiritual fulfillment. The weakest wish to jettison uncertainty, usually by means of exhaustive sexual perversions, lunatic obsessions, or narcotic binges. The wisest put their trust in Fortune, Godel's Theorem, statistical probability, or Murphy's Law. The best cleave to those social relationships like love and friendship that rationalization has not completely overwhelmed. Love does not conquer all in Pynchon's wasteland, so it can be fertile. Still other characters achieve minor triumphs of the spirit through reliance on ancient mythologies, rituals, or magic. The most engaging, however, are those like V. and Blicero who confront the frustrations of rationalization directly. They grapple with boundaries, interfaces, and limitations in their lust for an escape through a transcendence that they can never engineer. Super-romantics, they hurl themselves at barriers and launch themselves at void. When the "screaming comes across the sky," it is their cry as much as the rocket's.

Pynchon's credo rests on moral imperatives. Humans need not worship the world as divine; rather they should celebrate it as creation. They should hold themselves open to chance as a source of surprise if not revelation. They should sort information in order to understand their fellows, their systems, their world. Finally, they should love when that is possible, and "keep cool but care" when that is all they can manage.

These axioms are delivered as idiom, with the wit and imagination for which Pynchon is already famous. Each of his novels has increased his mastery of his craft; his third far outstrips his first, and his second is slim but brilliant. Since he is young and productive, he will surely write others: he has world enough, and time.

Bibliography

By Thomas Pynchon:

V. Philadelphia: Lippincott, 1963.
The Crying of Lot 49. Philadelphia, Lippincott, 1966.
Gravity's Rainbow. New York: Viking Press, 1973.

Pynchon has published a half-dozen short stories in several periodicals.

About Thomas Pynchon:

Cowart, David. *Thomas Pynchon: The Art of Allusion.* Carbondale: Southern Illinois
    University Press, 1980.
Levine, George, and David Leverenz, editors. *Mindful Pleasures: Essays on Thomas
    Pynchon.* Boston: Little, Brown and Co., 1976.

Siegel, Mark Richard. *Pynchon: Creative Paranoia in "Gravity's Rainbow."* Port Washington, New York: Kennikat Press, 1978.
Slade, Joseph W. *Thomas Pynchon.* New York: Warner Paperback Library, 1974.

Visual Poetry

A Conversation among Alain Arias-Misson, Richard Kostelanetz, Tom Ockerse, and Mary Ellen Solt

Kostelanetz: Our subject today is visual poetry, by which I mean, simply, language whose principal means of enhancement is visual rather than syntactic or semantic. With me are three of America's most prominent visual poets: Alain Arias-Misson, Tom Ockerse, and Mary Ellen Solt.

Arias-Misson was born in Brussels in 1936, grew up in America, and graduated from Harvard University with a degree in classics. He presently lives in New Jersey and works mostly as a polylingual simultaneous interpreter. The best collection of his work is *The Public Poem Book*, which was published in Italy in 1978. He also wrote a novel entitled *Confessions of a Madman, Murderer, Rapist, Bomber, Thief, or a Year from the Journal of an Ordinary American* (1975).

Tom Ockerse was born in The Netherlands in 1940, and he emigrated to the United States in 1957, taking his degrees in visual communication and design. He's presently Associate Professor of Graphic Design and Chairman of Design at the Rhode Island School of Design in Providence, Rhode Island.

Mary Ellen Solt, born in Iowa in 1920, is the author of *Flowers in Concrete*, a book of concrete poems published in 1966, and most recently of a paperbound book called *The Peoplemover* (1978). She has also edited and introduced the anthology *Concrete Poetry—A World View* (1968). She is presently Associate Professor of Comparative Literature at Indiana University.

Alain, will you tell me how you came to visual poetry—and where your work has gone since you began?

Arias-Misson: Yes, first of all, I should make it clear that, for me, visual poetry does not include concrete poetry. The early work that I did in the early 1960s—like everybody else who was working in the

1950s and early 1960s, I guess—was the spatialization of text really. . . .

Kostelanetz: Spatialization?

Arias-Misson: Spatialization of text: typographical space or words in the space of a page, basically. This, for me, was really derivative work, and I don't consider it as my visual work. But in the second half of the 1960s especially—and I think this happened to many people in Europe: Jean-François Bory and Julien Blaine in France, Paul de Vree in Belgium, and Jiri Valoch in Czechoslovakia, and a number of others—political events impinged so strongly on our work that the pure universe of concrete poetry, for me and for many of them, exploded under the impact of media. At this point— and this is what I understand as visual poetry from my own work and the group that I work with—the written language invaded the image: first, the media image from newspaper photographs to publicity posters, and—what I'm particularly interested in now—television imagery. Written language erupted into this kind of imagery. So the work I'm interested in was created on the model of mass media, mass media being essentially text-image production. The visual poem uses the same kind of text-image combinations.

Kostelanetz: So you would use, therefore, an image from the mass media, a taken image, a found image, a stolen image. . . .

Arias-Misson: Yes, really what we call a parasite poetry.

Kostelanetz: And then write over it? Write on it? Write next to it? Where would the writing go?

Arias-Misson: First of all, it should be clear that visual poetry is characterized by a very strong cross or complementarity of text and image. So the text has various ways of integrating or disrupting the image. I think that at the beginning words were simply placed or written across the contours. Then, as it became a little more sophisticated, there were more integrative approaches, such as disruption, for example, of the two-dimensional image through tearing or other manual operations on the image and the introduction of text there. Most of the people working in visual poetry were initially writers or poets or critics. But the image is privileged in this kind of work; these are very much visual objects or visual products and were mostly seen in galleries and museums as well as in book form.

Kostelanetz: Mary Ellen Solt, in addition to making her own poetry, edited and introduced what is still the most elaborate survey we've had of this kind of work, the anthology *Concrete Poetry—A*

World View.

Solt: I was introduced to concrete poetry by Ian Hamilton Finlay, who's a Scottish poet, and at that point he had not really written a concrete poem, but he had an anthology of concrete poetry from Brazil. This was 1961, in Edinburgh. I was living with my family in England that year. Ian had done—I guess you could say it was *one* concrete poem—a fold-out poem called "Accordion." Ian worked with an artist. The poem had a butterfly image painted on, and the language was the current idiom: "Thisaway, thataway, thisaway, thataway. . . ."

Kostelanetz: Now you said this was his "first" concrete poem to distinguish it from his earlier poetry.

Solt: I had gone to see him because of his earlier poetry. Cid Corman had just brought out the issue of *Origin* featuring Ian Hamilton Finlay. However, this poem was visual, you see. It was visual and it was kinetic.

Kostelanetz: Because of the accordion or folded-paper format?

Solt: Because of the motion.

Kostelanetz: Was there also a different sense of language, a different way of using language?

Solt: Yes, there was only that one phrase: "Thisaway, thataway, thisaway, thataway. . . ." It was very minimal word material.

Kostelanetz: Such language is semantic, but it isn't syntactically organized.

Solt: In a way it was a found linguistic image like Alain was talking about. But you can't say the visual image of the butterfly was "found," because it was created by another artist. I myself was very much involved with William Carlos Williams's poetry at the time and with Louis Zukofsky's. I really didn't know quite where to go from there, but the minute I saw this new poetry I was excited by it. I sent for the Brazilian anthology, and in the process of studying it with a dictionary (because I don't know Portuguese) I suddenly, without planning to, made a concrete poem, a visual poem. In that poem the page just went round and round and round as I was writing it.

Kostelanetz: What was the verbal content?

Solt: I looked out the window and saw some yellow crocuses, and I started making an anagram: Y, E, L, L, O, W, C, R, O, C, U, S. Then for the next set of words, I picked up on the last letter of each word I had used previously: like the word *yellow*. Imagine these words were in columns (only they were going around in circles). I had a column with YELLOWCROCUS; then in the next column I would have to begin the column with the last letter, say, the W of yellow, the S of crocus, and so forth. The minute I finished the poem I sort of liked it, but I felt that the visual image was incongruous to the subject. Somehow I knew immediately that was wrong, that if you are going to do a visual poem, the visual image has to have a meaning related to what you're talking about. There has to be meaning in the visual image, in other words. So then I used the same form and wrote a poem, "White Rose," because a rose does grow out that way from the center in a circular way. That was my first really concrete poem. Somehow I felt very much liberated by it. I had never felt so free as a poet. I had been struggling for ten years or more, trying to find my way of doing it; and something really happened there. I sent the poem off to Ian Hamilton-Finaly, who was editing the magazine *Poor. Old. Tired. Horse.* He had not yet brought out his first concrete issue when I was in Edinburgh. I sent it to him just to show him, but he liked it and he said he was going to print it. That's how I got started.

Kostelanetz: This led to your first book of poems called *Flowers in Concrete*, which came out in 1966. What I find interesting about that work was this: although your tradition was working with books (you had done critical writing on William Carlos Williams), in those poems you immediately went into a large graphic form.

Solt: No, my first version was printed in a very small edition in 1964. I actually did the poems calligraphically by hand.

Ockerse: They are quite beautiful.

Solt: And this was terribly important to me—that I used my hand. But a professor of design at Indiana University, George Sadek, liked them very much. Only he said that I should really do them in type, which, of course, at that point I couldn't have done. A student named John Dearstyne in the Master of Fine Arts/Design Program copied the design in type for the 1966 edition. He did a really beautiful job.

Kostelanetz: Was the original form 8 1/2-by-11-inch sheets?

Solt: Yes, on typewriter paper. And at that point I had never had an art lesson in my life. After that, I did study design and I had a good many courses with Tom Ockerse.

Kostelanetz: This is now a memoir of Indiana University in the early 1960s.

Solt: Somehow the concrete poetry movement was sort of a group thing wherever it happened. That is, the Brazilians were intermarried, they were interrelated, they were brothers. Alain, you worked in a group in Europe, didn't you?

Arias-Misson: Yes.

Solt: Then we had a group in Bloomington.

Kostelanetz: So what looks like a leap, in retrospect, of getting out of 8 1/2-by-11-inch sheets, which is a standard writer's medium in America—(the approximate equivalent of the European A 4), into the larger format of the graphic prints, was done by joining this university design situation.

Tom Ockerse, how has your work evolved?

Ockerse: I came to concrete poetry/visual poetry from the visual end of it, as an artist-designer. That might appear somewhat unusual since visual poetry (I consider concrete poetry to be within visual poetry) is linked mostly with the literary field and most of its practitioners come to it from that direction. My intentions were always toward the "visible" end of it, with language (or perhaps linguistic) interests developing via my studies and practices in graphic design. As a graphic designer I am involved primarily as a problem solver in visual communication, which results in a product I call "visual language"—that is, language in the ordinary sense (verbal, spoken, signed) but marked or "written" through visual forming and structuring.

Kostelanetz: Now, when you came to America in 1957, did you immediately go to college here?

Ockerse: No, I was still in high school, after immigrating with my family. In 1959 I entered the Ohio State University where my studies were directed toward "commercial art."

Kostelanetz: So this means advertising, packaging, graphics, magazine design, things like that?

Ockerse: Exactly, although I add that in general it has only an apparent regard for visual aesthetics which, if any, are usually in a cosmetic, trendy sense. I mention this because this set of principles differs greatly from those of "graphic design," an issue being hotly debated in the field. Somewhat derived from commercial art, graphic design assumes a position which places its emphasis on the word *design*, which refers both to the aesthetic functioning of visual form and structuring as well as to the professional practice of problem solving and objective creation.

After Ohio State I entered the graduate program of graphic

design at Yale University. There I began to broaden (or is it focus?) my interests in the "designing" of language expression, i.e., the presentation of information and "written" communication. The potentials of language made visible and the expressive possibilities of the visual in marriage with language intrigued me, and I experimented, researched, and began to define alternative attitudes toward the more traditional concepts of presenting language.

Looking back, I might add that perhaps one of the major encouragements I gained during these studies was through the presence of the German artist Dieter Roth, who came to Yale during my last year there. As you know, Dieter is one of the outstanding contributors to visual/concrete poetry. I had been working on my thesis project, a book which used cut-outs and fragmented pages, a technique similar to some of Dieter's own works. Obviously it promoted our interaction, and I especially value the attitude Dieter was able to expose me to in terms of visible language and visual experiment. Perhaps also important was that we never discussed this attitude as having a reference to either art or literature; it was more universal in its objectives. By the way, the thesis project I mentioned is better known now as *The A-Z Book*, a very simple alphabet book which contains only the 26 letters of our alphabet in black and white.

Kostelanetz: Your characterization underestimates the book, since it is a rather complex visual sequential work.

Ockerse: Of course, I realize that now, but I did not at the time. And then only several years later did I realize its reference to concrete poetry. What became evident was that at the time I created the book I was intuitively tuned in to concrete poetic concepts. The book is very concrete, being obviously self-referential, with the letters "speaking" about themselves (and one another).

Kostelanetz: Can we describe the book?

Ockerse: Yes, I will try. The pages present the letters of the alphabet, but not in the normal A, B, C, sequence (although the book starts with A and ends with Z). The first page A is followed on the reverse side by the letter W; the W is created partly out of the letter A, which has the legs or inverted V die-cut out and a black bar printed between. When you turn the page, you see that to the inverted V two black diagonal bars are added to make the W.

Kostelanetz: It's really an extraordinary book, but hard to describe in words. The letter A is not composed on a single sheet of paper but partly printed black on white paper and partly cut-out of the white page to reveal the black on the page underneath.

Ockerse: Yes. The letter M follows W and in a similar fashion creates the letter V on the other side. Then the E shows up, and the two upper bars are die-cut to create the letter F on the other side, which then continues to create in part the T. The upper curve of the letter S is die-cut to reveal a portion of the letter P on the other side of the page, to which two quarter-sized pages are added which create the letters B and R. And so forth.

Kostelanetz: So that visually all the letters evolve out of one another in one way or another as you turn the pages.

Ockerse: Right. And the sequencing is derived from their basic formal structures as letterform designs. Originally the book was intended for children as an alphabet book, to speak of letters in a simple and straightforward approach. The book was to be a playful process of discovery while learning the formal relationships of the letters.

Although the subject of visual or concrete poetry was not so much apparent to me at the time, not even when I made *The A-Z Book*, I was introduced to it through its attitude as expressed by Dieter Roth. I also had another influence, namely a book titled *Schrift Und Bild*, which was a catalogue of an art exhibition held in 1963 in both Germany and Holland.

Kostelanetz: *Schrift Und Bild*—what does that mean?

Ockerse: "Writing and Picture." It's important to note that the book/exhibit was about the visual arts and not considered in a literary context. It was especially exciting because of the variety of works displayed which in some manner reflected visual writing: from calligraphic arts to typography, and from graphic designs to painting. Unfortunately my German was not good enough to get much out of the text, but I immediately felt the excitement in the attitude expressed by the works. Interestingly enough, many of the better known concrete poets were included (e.g., Ferdinand Kriwet, Franz Mon, Dieter Roth, Arno Schmidt, Emmett Williams).

After college and two years as a full-time professional graphic design practitioner (I continue to free-lance even today), I began a teaching stint at Indiana University. I taught graphic design for four years, and visual poetry came to me in full blast. Mary Ellen Solt had already exposed the graduate program to concrete poetry by sharing some of the visitors to the university who often came through her efforts. The contact with Mary Ellen was expanded (she even took one of my typography courses, in which she produced her ZIG-ZAG poem), and to a large extent our campus became a center for visual poetry activities in America. Later Mary Ellen's anthology was designed in our department and published by Indiana University Press.

Kostelanetz: You had at that time not done any visual poetry, aside from *The A-Z Book*?

Ockerse: Which I did not consider to be poetry, of course.

Kostelanetz: Which you still thought was a children's book.

Ockerse: Seeing now the existence of the visual poetry as a subject of specialized activity, I began to connect the literary idea with the typographic potential and visual expression. The influences I had received at Yale became more fully appreciated, and the languages game became more focused.

Kostelanetz: How would you characterize your work in this period in relation to the work other people were doing—not only in America but Europe?

Ockerse: Well, let me put it this way: I was frequently confronted by Mary Ellen Solt on the notion of whether my works were indeed "poetry" (by which, I suppose, she meant "literary"). While she enjoyed the work, she felt it was lacking the literary reference. We could not quite come to an agreement, but then this was exactly the issue debated heavily throughout the literary (and even some of the visual) world. I can now say that I am much more confident in defining and distinguishing the quality of such works and I am probably not much apart from Mary Ellen. (I should note, by the way, that during a visit I had to Emmett Williams in 1968, he expressed great enthusiasm for my work *as* visual poetry; Emmett, as we know, is often considered the "father" of concrete poetry in America.) But quite frankly, my interests even now are least concerned with whether my works are "literary," or even "art" for that matter. At Indiana I was interested in "expanded typography," which I later dubbed "language experiments" and "concrete language," and which I now prefer to call "visible language." Obviously the visual element remains important, which is where my expertise is; but I am combining this visual language with our "written" language. My concerns are with the semantic potentials of visual time and space structuring and the semantic potentials of materials, form, and any visual matter. I play games: visually, semantically, typographically.

Kostelanetz: Well, did you begin with a particular word? Or did you begin with certain ideas? Or is that not a meaningful distinction?

Ockerse: It was developing an attitude toward language and how visual elements could take on symbolic significance—an equation of words and images. I can't remember with which word I started.

Kostelanetz: Let's take the word *GOD*, which you've used in several formats.

Ockerse: God. Yes. The word *GOD* became a *G?D* in one poem; the question mark in the middle was carefully designed to suggest the shape of O, and you could almost immediately see the word *GOD*, but it wouldn't be there. At the same time, there would be two other elements, the G and the D, an abbreviation for *God Damn*. That contradiction was again contradicted by the same question mark. So there was recognition as well as damnation, but the question mark itself then created questions about both. This was a very simple presentation of three typographic elements, which then dealt with all sorts of elements of communication that the reader would simply add as part of the reading.

Kostelanetz: What is your distinction between concrete and visual poetry, Alain?

Arias-Misson: I would like to follow my friend, Klaus Peter Dencker, where he says that it is the quality, dominance, and function of nonlinguistic means that distinguish visual poetry from concrete poetry.

Kostelanetz: That would mean a picture. . . .

Arias-Misson: The eruption of that which is not language, which can assume different forms. It can also be actions, as in my Public Poems.

Kostelanetz: Therefore, the presence of the image other than language makes it visual poetry.

Arias-Misson: That's what I would say.

Kostelanetz: Mary Ellen Solt, do you go with that?

Solt: I think the term "concrete" poetry is probably an unhappy term, but in the very beginning it was adopted by the Brazilians—the de Campos brothers, Haroldo and Agusto, and Decio Pignatari.

Kostelanetz: And then by Gomringer in Switzerland.

Solt: Although Gomringer retained the term "constellations" for his own poetry to distinguish his practice technically. But the term "concrete poetry" was originally adopted to establish a relationship to concrete art.

Kostelanetz: That is, the painting of Max Bill, a Swiss artist.

Solt: Max Bill and that group whose work is basically a form of constructivism based on mathematical systems.

Kostelanetz: And also it's a nonsymbolic, nonrepresentational, abstract art. So the idea was to use language nonsymbolically and abstractly as well. Therefore, if you were representing something in language, that is, describing something outside of language, it was by definition not concrete poetry.

Solt: We got into trouble with this, too, because it is very difficult to use a noun and not have it refer to something.

Kostelanetz: Let's go back to this distinction: What is the difference then between concrete and visual?

Solt: Well, I think the pure concrete poetry has a system; it's very much related to constructivist art. You can very often apply a numerical system. That is, you can very often substitute numbers for separate letters or for words. Now, visual poetry, as Alain does it and others in Europe do it, is, as you said, more expressionistic. I guess they began to talk about *constructivist*-concrete and *expressionist*-concrete.

Kostelanetz: Let me pursue this distinction about concrete and visual poetry, if I can, with Tom Ockerse.

Ockerse: Well, I think that concrete poetry really was foreclosed around 1968, and everything that has been done after this is more or less repetitive.

Arias-Misson: Derivative.

Ockerse: Concrete poetry was intended by its participants to break away from tradition and convention; but visual poetry seemed to be more tolerant toward such possibilities and opened new doors and saw broader horizons.

Kostelanetz: Let me work with the distinction, if I can, which is that *concrete* is an attitude to language—that is, the nonsyntactic, nonsymbolic language we spoke about before—and that visual qualities were indeed an attribute of this concrete poetry—that is, it was to be seen—but they were not the principal attribute.

Solt: No, I wouldn't agree with that entirely because it was terribly important that concrete poetry be seen in the right type face. What concrete poetry did was make us realize how visually beautiful letters are, that language isn't just a bearer of meaning, that it is an object. The word is an object.

Kostelanetz: And that process in itself is making poetry of the word. In the case of your classic work in the *Flowers in Concrete*, let's take "Forsythia." What you did there was to take the word *forsythia*, put the letters on the ends of stems which were made of lines that were composed of the Morse code for those letters. That is, the letter F is dot-dot-dash-dot. So those dots and dashes become the stems of letters as they "flower" above the base, which is also composed of the word *forsythia*.

Solt: And the text reads like a telegram.

Kostelanetz: Now, to me, you were a poet because you did something visually to enhance the word *forsythia*. Now, in the case of Alain's work we get an image and a text which comment upon each other, and the measure of poetry is the richness of the commentary between the two elements, is that right?

Arias-Misson: The complementarity. The "poem" is the complementary character of the text/image.

Kostelanetz: Now in both these kinds of visual work after-image is very important, and that is why they resemble painting—you want

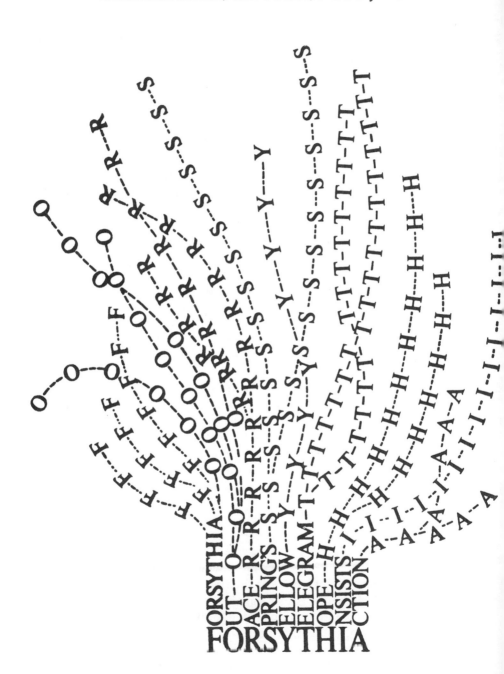

to put in the head of the viewer an image with a word that will stick. As a traditional poet might have used rhyme to make the word stick, we use visual devices to make the word stick.

I find it curious that everyone here has discovered something in Europe to form their own work. But that suggests a contrary question: How does American visual poetry, or American work in the genres we're talking about today, differ from European?

Solt: I have a theory about this. I think it related to where painting was in this country. Constructivist art never got off the ground here like it did in Europe. Our dominance in painting was abstract expressionism. At the time that concrete poetry was developing in Europe, our poetry was much more confessional. This was the time of the Beat Generation, the New York School of poets, and so forth. Therefore, I don't think concrete poetry could have happened here, even though we were so close to it so many times before. You see, our earlier modern poets—Cummings, Pound, particularly Pound— were the major influences on the creation of concrete poetry in Brazil. William Carlos Williams is cited by Gomringer. These poets are so close to concrete poetry already.

Ockerse: To a large extent the difference has to do with appreciation by all concerned, the poets as well as the public. This appreciation was much stronger in Europe as there was more of an understanding of the fundamental objectives and a respect for the breaking of traditional concepts. One would expect that to have been true for America, but for some reason it was not. Mary Ellen's theory is probably correct. Perhaps also European poets maintained more consistently a kind of structuralist attitude and the inherent discipline of the literary heritage, which helped to maintain relationship and recognition of quality and value. In America this poetry was largely misunderstood. It was often considered frivolous and juvenile, and probably still is. These misconceptions were fueled by an apparent inability of the participants (poets, artists) to agree on fundamental objectives, and parochial and self-indulgent attitudes often undermined any sort of action. In Europe activity was much more unified and there it was considered a movement.

Kostelanetz: Here the kind of thing we did was also very quickly dismissed as being both "not poetry" and "not art."

Mary Ellen, where has your work gone in the past decade?

Solt: I've been moving, as I think many poets have, more toward the semiotic—more toward signs and less discursive language, less like linear poetry. I guess the best thing to do is talk about poems themselves. I did a poem in 1968 called "The People Mover—A Demonstration Poet." I simply couldn't deal with events of 1968, which was a very political year, in any way except to make a demonstration poem. I made two-sided posters. On one side I had very minimal linguistic material—perhaps just the word *Vietnam* combined with an image suggesting the flag disintegrating. Or I used Humphrey's campaign logos and made a pun: "Ho, Ho, Hum, Free Election." Then on the back of each poster, I extended the carrying stick up and made a sign. On the back of the Vietnam poster it was a combined jet bomber and peace symbol. The back of the Nixon-Humphrey posters were voters' X's.

Kostelanetz: So you're mixing highly resonant visual and verbal images.

Solt: Yes. This was meant to be performed, and it was performed first with people just carrying the posters to the Souza march "The Stars and Stripes Forever." Then a text evolved.

Kostelanetz: Performed where? Outside? On the street?

Solt: Outside. It was a demonstration out in the middle of the country which nobody saw.

Ockerse: I did.

Solt: You were in it, Tom, yes. We had a club called Fiasco. Then I did it later with about a 10-minute text and still later with a 20-minute text, which was made up of quotations from American history. And now in its published form the text is over a hundred pages: a montage, a collage of quotes from American history, commenting upon—some of them taken from—1968.

Kostelanetz: Now, therefore, semiotics to you means visual and verbal signs in an equal universe?

Ockerse: Semiotics is the theory of signs, and a sign, in simple terms, is understood as anything which communicates something to somebody. However, it is not an object, it is actually a process.

Kostelanetz: So a picture of a place is the same as a word.

Solt: Yes.

Ockerse: Well, it can be; but as I said, a sign is a process involving the interpretation of a thing which stands for or refers to something else.

Solt: Yes. My last poem is a semiotic poem called "Marriage—A Code Poem." It consists of a very complex visual image, which is made up of over a hundred individual signs, and you have to read the code that goes with the poem. It's a memorable image, but in order to really understand what I'm saying you have to relate the separate signs to the code and there are eight sets of signs. Now this was a challenge to me. The composer Iannis Xenakis said in a class lecture one time that he didn't think poetry could deal with a complex subject matter such as music. So I wanted to make a really complex subject.

Kostelanetz: There is a translation mechanism here in that images must be read as words, but it's not a natural, let's say immediate translation.

Solt: No, it's not immediate. You have to sit down and spend time with this poem.

Kostelanetz: You must look at the code.

Solt: But the original image is very beautiful and can be comprehended as a suggestion, say, of a quilt, or rug, or wallpaper, or something domestic, which relates to marriage.

Kostelanetz: Tom, how have you been working since the early collection of poems which you called *T.O.P.*, or the Tom Ockerse Project?

Ockerse: Right, *T.O.P.* was a convenient label for my file on this book project and the works the book was to contain. So, when I was looking for a title, the initial P seemed to be symbolic of a number of references meaningful to the book and the *T.O.P.* initials seemed to be as appropriate as any.

Kostelanetz: You call it a book even though, I should point out, it was published as a box.

Ockerse: It's a box with loose pages—a collection of poems/works produced in a three-year period. I was working on other things as well, which were leading me further into newer territories. Yet, the selection chosen for *T.O.P.* seemed worthwhile to do even though many of them were only ideas and sketches. Especially the three-dimensional poems were only developed as prototypes. Therefore, *T.O.P.* allowed me to collect them and share them instead of leaving them in a drawer as ideas.

Kostelanetz: Although the sculptures appear in the book as photographs, of course.

Ockerse: Yes, as documents of monumental sculptures.

Kostelanetz: And because of the nature of photography in book form, it's hard to tell from the photographs themselves how big the things being photographed are, unless, of course, your hand is also in the picture, as it is in the case of the God sculpture, which is different

from the one mentioned earlier. I think it is very special. Let me see
if I can describe this. Here you pull out of a round egg, not an egg but
a truly circular object, the letters G and D, so that when placed against
the O in the middle form the round object to become GOD.
Ockerse: Again, what I have been dealing with mostly is the
visual potential in language expression. This is likely to be considered
"literature," and, of course, it includes the sense of poetry, the narrative
of "reading." However, when we consider the means for communication in relation to the semiotic term "signs," then possibilities for such
poetic expression open up tremendously, and they easily fall outside
the established conventions and definitions of literature.

        My more recent work has been operating with a more "docu-
mentary" approach. For example, when I was in Scotland, I planned
three walking trips and made statements on each which I plan to
publish in book form. One walk was through a part of the city of
Edinburgh, the second through the countryside near central Scotland,
and the third was on one of the western isles, Barra. My intention was
to produce some sort of concrete poetic statement about the environments, which I did by extracting a series of visible signs by means of
some system. One set of signs came from having documented a group
of city blocks in Edinburgh, the only section of town built on a rectangular grid plan. I photographed each corner on that grid, and
extracted certain elements, fragments, which were essential, in my
opinion, in reference to the corner.
Kostelanetz: Both visual and verbal.
Ockerse: Yes. This residue of signs was placed on a page and
became a text.
Kostelanetz: Is there one page for each corner?
Ockerse: Yes.
Kostelanetz: So it becomes a symbolic extraction or a symbolic
residue, as you said, of your perceptions in the course of the walk.
Ockerse: Yes. I called these activities "documentracings," since
tracing is part of the method. I document fragments as I pass through
the experience at that particular moment of time. They are walks,
although not necessarily in its literal sense, since I have done this also
with the television screen and magazines.
Kostelanetz: What fascinates me, as we're talking, is that you're
talking about poetry that is very externally stimulated. So is Alain, but
in a different way. And so is Mary Ellen, also in a different way. It
sounds to me as though visual poetry has become public or, let's say,

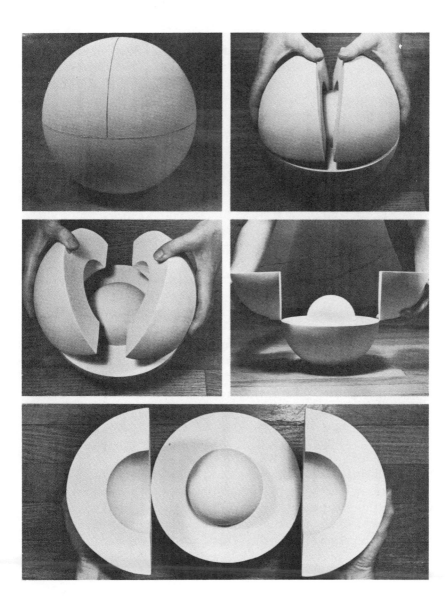

sociological or societal in a way that's quite contrary to the traditions of poetry as very much about personal experiences, personal consciousness, and the materials of language.

Arias-Misson: A word might be said here also on the difference of the personality between the concrete/visual poet and the traditional poet. Traditional poetry is a personal vision, a personal interpretation of a world-view, whereas I think that visual poetry is closer to a sort of an engineering of language and of image—or, to put it in more modest terms, a craftsmanlike approach. And, in fact, the very use of the word *experimental* is good here because there is a possibility of repetition, of control, of the elements that are being used.

Solt: I don't think that we should perpetuate the idea that visual poetry is a new thing, because they had schools of visual poetry about four centuries before Christ in Greece. There was a long tradition of it in India. We had it in the Carolingian period in France, in the 16th and 17th centuries in England, and then the Dadaists, the Futurists. . . .

Kostelanetz: I've edited an anthology called *Visual Literature Criticism* (1980), which included critical essays on precursors going back to the Greeks. On the other hand, I think there are certain new developments within the tradition that are strictly contemporary, and our sense of what we do as something radically different from most poetry is certainly distinctly contemporary. Some of these new developments are the reflections of the electronic media, as Alain has pointed out, or of mass-production printing, which is very much of the 20th century.

Arias-Misson: I just want to say, in answer to Mary Ellen, that you could also look back historically to an archeology of concrete and visual poetry, and see two parallel developments: one of a kind of concrete precedence, such as numbers in Kostelanetz's work, and Baroque and Christian medieval texts. In visual poetry—in other words, in text-image dialectic—there are the magic papyri, Greek bucolic, Latin poems, the Old French, Spanish, English sources, Russian mannerism, carmina cancelate, grave inscriptions and so on.

Kostelanetz: Sure. But it seems to me, Alain, that a precursor in American literature to the kind of work you do is Kenneth Patchen, whose works are really very special and sadly neglected.

Arias-Misson: There is a tendency today in some publications to claim an archeology, as kind of aesthetic justification, of what is essentially marginal work. I think our work is marginal to the established literary mode and current artistic convention. It is just that marginal quality which I find very exciting and provocative about what we're doing. I wouldn't want to cancel it by laying claim to a kind of archeology or historical justification.

Solt: But the marginal possibility has been there for centuries, and it's popped up on the margin over hundreds and hundreds of years.

Arias-Misson: Agreed. And the sociological analysis of why this marginal work has always existed would be very interesting.

Solt: Yes.

Kostelanetz: Marginal work has always existed because some people don't play in the mainstream. But also one of the great truths in Modernism is that in the current margins is where the next new art has traditionally been.

Ockerse: Well, as I consider poetry to be the potential of human expression, I am interested in this more universal viewpoint. Its universality is not limited to medium, or space, or one's focus, whether as video artist, architect (conceptual architects have been involved with spatial definition through semantic definitions), poet, musician, or performer.

The whole notion of conceptualism contains the idea of after-image which you mentioned before, and this requires the participation of the viewer in the process of interpretation. I am glad to see that this participatory attitude is prevalent in all areas of contemporary endeavors, as it has been in concrete and visual poetry.

Kostelanetz: But you also spoke before about the varieties of poetry in America today or the varieties of even our kinds of works; so that to pretend exclusivity is false—we all exist in tangential relationship to each other.

Ockerse: Definitely.

Kostelanetz: But on equal footing, and thus visual poetry and sound poetry, for another, and conventional verse and rhymed poetry, and confessional poetry are just different ways of doing it. And even in our own cases, they are approaches equally available to us. We can do one or another kind of work.

Bibliography

Gross, Ronald, and George Quasha, editors. *Open Poetry*. New York: Simon and
        Schuster, 1973.
Kostelanetz, Richard, editor. *Visual Literature Criticism*. Carbondale: Southern
        Illinois University Press, 1980.
—, editor. *Image Words & Worded Images*. New York: Outerbridge, 1970.
Ockerse, Tom. *T.O.P.* Bloomington, Indiana: Privately Published, 1971.
—. *The A-Z Book*. New York: Colorcraft-Brussel, 1969.
Solt, Mary Ellen, editor. *Concrete Poetry—A World View*. Bloomington: Indiana Uni-
        versity, 1969.
—. *The Peoplemover 1968: A Demonstration Poem*. Reno, Nevada: West Coast Poetry
        Review, 1978.
Williams, Emmett. *An Anthology of Concrete Poetry*. New York: Something Else
        Press, 1967.

Hispanic Literature in the United States

Bruce-Novoa

The literature of Hispanic peoples in the United States is certainly not a recent development; it was the first literature in a European language to be written on the continent. Before any permanent English settlement appeared on the American shores, Cabeza de Vaca had wandered from Florida to Mexico and then written his famous account of the journey. In the mid-1500s Coronado and De Soto led expeditions into the territory now occupied by the United States, producing more chronicles; and by that time, the eastern seaboard, later the site of the English colonies, had already been explored and named in Spanish—and naming your environment is perhaps the most elementary form of poetry. That English names came to replace the Spanish is an accurate sign of the conflictive relationship that has persisted between the two groups of settlers and their respective written expressions.

In other parts of the continent the Spanish presence was more permanent. In the second half of the 16th century, the Oñate expedition to settle New Mexico produced not only another of the many epic poems composed by the Spanish conquistadors everywhere from North America to Tierra del Fuego but also the first performance of a European drama within what is now the United States of America. Through the years, in spite of the isolation and the rather primitive conditions of the northern provinces of Nueva España (later Mexico), the Spanish-speaking population maintained a rich oral tradition of stories, poetry, and drama. Specialists, such as Aurelio Espinosa and Arturo Campa, began gathering this material during the first half of our century; their studies, besides showing a mere presence of a literary tradition, proved that this material was the direct heir to Spanish peninsular literature, such as the medieval ballads and religious dramas. This is not unusual. Similar phenomena can be found—or could be until recently—in most Latin American countries where technology or non-Spanish migrations have not wiped out the traditional culture. In the U.S. Southwest, the Hispanic inhabitants of New Mexico were anxious to maintain their language as an essential foundation of culture; thus the first book printed in the area, shortly before the take-over by the United States, was a manual of grammar and spelling.

Since 1848, when the states of Arizona, California, Nevada, Utah, New Mexico, Texas, and half of Colorado passed from Mexican to U.S. ownership, a continuous Spanish journalistic tradition existed in the Mexican communities that survived in that area. Some strictly literary pieces appeared from time to time, and now it is becoming clear that the Hispanic writers living in the United States were not totally unaware of the literary trends in Latin America. However, official literary history—both U.S. and Mexican versions—ignored this activity and still does for the most part. In Puerto Rico, which has been occupied by the United States since 1898, literature has continued within the traditions of a Latin American country. The U.S. presence has affected Puerto Rican literary expression certainly, but the literature that is culturally comparable to Chicano (Mexican American) literature is that written by Puerto Ricans living on the mainland, mostly in the northeastern coastal region. Wherever Hispanic immigrants or migrants have settled for any length of time, there has usually appeared some form of journalistic media, and literature has been produced.

In addition, there exists a steady and highly significant outpouring of writing by Latin American visitors to the United States. Authors like Sarmiento, José Martí, Mariano Azuela, Martín Luis Guzmán, Pedro Juan Soto, Carlos Fuentes, Octavio Paz, Jorge Luis Borges, and many others have spent time in this country; and it, in turn, has entered into their writing. Yet they were visitors; their writings, though pertinent to the comprehension of the U.S. American experience, belong more legitimately to Latin American letters and should not be mistaken for that which this essay treats. Space does not allow me to differentiate thoroughly between these two bodies of writing. Suffice it to say that there is a centuries-old tradition of Hispanic writing done in and about the United States, written by Latin Americans deeply concerned with the implications of the United States and who viewed the country and its people from the perspective of temporary sojourners. Moreover, they usually wrote for readers in their home countries. The literature which concerns us here was written by permanent residents of this country, insiders in spite of being an ethnic and linguistic minority often excluded from the mainstream; and their literature is, for the most part, directed at and read by other permanent residents of the United States.

Racial and ethnic awareness surged to prominence during the 1950s and 1960s with the rise of the black civil rights movement. Following closely behind, and greatly influenced by the black example, came the efforts by Hispanics, Orientals, and Native Americans (Indians) to win the same civil rights. These easily recognizable minorities overshadowed other ethnic groups, such as the Poles, Italians, Irish, and others, who, though apparently assimilated into the general society, still maintain traditions and, in some cases, their own language and feel themselves to be distinct and separate from those of English (and Protestant) extraction. The decade of the 60s shattered the ideal of a national cultural homogeneity that some had believed realized during World War II. The citizenry of the United States is still, *de facto*, a conglomerate of many national groups that immigrated to this country in the recent past (the last 150 years) and some—very few—who were here prior to that. It really should not shock anyone that in 200 years, a relatively brief period on the historical scale, a country which has steadily embraced such huge numbers of immigrants of widely divergent origins has not managed to meld them into a single cultural character. Much older countries with less influx have not done so either. Within this setting of unrest, division, and shattered ideals, there arose the literary activity of Hispanic groups living in the United States, predominantly Chicanos and Puerto Ricans, with an as yet ambiguous Cuban presence.

We can eliminate immediately from our discussion the Cuban literary production in the United States. Their main literary activity comes from writers who consider themselves exiles more than U.S. citizens or permanent residents. The journal *Escandalar* (New York) is an example. The editorial board includes major Latin American writers; its content is completely in line with the latest trends in Latin America; the literature published neither treats nor engages the U.S. experience. This is not to say that it is less valid or undesirable, but only that as literary production it is still essentially Latin American; the journal could be published in Mexico City without any significant change in orientation. Perhaps this derives from the fact that the

Cuban literati still think of themselves as among that distinguished group of sojourners mentioned above, with every intention of returning someday to their mother country.

Although it is convenient for government agencies—as well as some leftist organizations—to lump Chicanos and Puerto Ricans (and any other Hispanics) together under any of several rubrics, this is as much an illusion as that of a monolithic U.S. and national character. The groups are diverse and their literature cannot be reduced to simple generalities without doing each violence. It is more instructive to compare and contrast them to understand the reasons why they differ and how the differences affect the literature. Ironically, one can take the supposed common denominators, which outsiders utilize to unite Chicanos and Puerto Ricans, and identify points of divergence: Spanish heritage, Latin American historical roots, miscegenation, minority status in the United States as immigrants, a common language.

Both groups acknowledge antecedence in Hispanic culture, but its significance certainly is not the same. This is closely tied to their history as Latin Americans. Mexican culture underwent a strongly anti-Spanish period after independence in 1821 and again during the Revolution in 1910. The Mexican nation developed a non-Spanish identity. Puerto Rico remained a Spanish colony until the end of the 19th century and then passed directly into the U.S. sphere of influence, never developing the same independent identity as Mexico. One could say that, to date, Puerto Rico has not achieved independence and remains a colony. Some Chicanos claim that the Southwest of the U.S. is also colonized territory; but even so, it was independent for almost 30 years. And Chicanos who have come from Mexico since 1848 bring with them a sense of independent nationality.

More significant is the fact that Chicano culture derives from northcentral Mexico, while Puerto Rican culture is part of the Caribbean region. If Chicanos were influenced to any great extent by the southeastern coastal cultural patterns of Veracruz or Yucatán, they might be closer to the Puerto Ricans and Cubans; but the fact is that Mexico itself is not Caribbean in its national ethos. Thus Chicanos may well feel closer to a Columbian from Bogotá or an Argentine from Mendoza than to a native of San Juan. In addition, the Chicano movement has inherited—or chosen to appropriate—much of the agrarian ideology from the Mexican Revolution. This produces a much stronger preoccupation in Chicano literature with the recuperation of land—in the sense of farms and small-property ownership as well as a national territory—than in Puerto Rican literature.

This difference was reinforced through the immigration patterns that, until recently, led Puerto Ricans to the northeast coast and Mexicans to the southwestern states. Although both groups are concentrated in cities and urban areas, in general terms the Puerto Ricans are urban oriented, while Chicanos tend to retain a rural quality. Chicano literature is full of *campesinos* and migrant workers; one of the prime proponents/protagonists of the literature, the Teatro Campesino of Luis Valdez, began as the propaganda arm of the United Farm Workers Union. Puerto Rican literature is more concerned with the urban ghetto and the New York style of life. Moreover, the western United States traditionally has signified the dream of land acquisition, while the eastern cities have come to represent the renters' ghetto. Add to this the ideology propagated by much Chicano literature that the southwest belongs to the Chicanos because it was taken from Mexico through an illegal invasion, and one can understand how Chicano literature would contain a proprietary vein absent in Puerto Rican writing.

Both groups are considered minorities of mixed racial backgrounds. However, the predominant non-Spanish element differs in each case. Chicanos see themselves as Indian and Spanish; Puerto Ricans emphasize their black heritage. Thus Miguel Méndez, a Chicano from Arizona, calls for a close association with Native Americans, and Alurista utilizes pre-Columbian mythology as the basis for the projection of a Chicano identity. Piri Thomas, on the other hand, struggles with being black but not a Black in *Down These Mean Streets*. This difference is compounded by the fact—suppressed in public— that there is anti-black prejudice in the Chicano (and Mexican) community, as well as a lingering resentment over what is perceived as pro-black favoritism in the government circles. This mistrust and envy is projected onto Puerto Ricans when they emphasize their blackness. In literature the black influence is most obvious in Puerto Rican poetry written in English, with its black rhythm and penchant for repetitive words and facile rhyme. Some Chicano poets, like the above-mentioned Alurista, have deliberately cultivated a black voice which they sprinkle into their usual style; but these usages are recognized and classified as an extraneous element. Chicano *pinto* (prison) writers sometimes show more similarity to black styles because of a predominant black presence within the prison system; but cultural and ethnic divisions seem to be spreading behind the prison walls as well, and recent *pinto* poetry shows much more influence from Chicano writers outside the walls than from Blacks within.

In terms of miscegenation, what is shared is a status of less than full-fledged racial identification with the non-Spanish group to which each relates. Neither Blacks nor Native Americans consider Puerto Ricans or Chicanos, respectively, completely theirs.

The government often unites the groups under the rubric of Spanish-speaking people. Yet the Spanish spoken is quite different, both phonetically and in vocabulary. Once again, the difference between Caribbean and non-coastal origins is a significant factor. Moreover, the literary usage of Spanish differs. One is more apt to find Spanish and English used in the same text in Chicano writing than in Puerto Rican. Code switching was legitimized by the best Chicano poets in the 1960s—José Montoya, Alurista, and Ricardo Sánchez use it extensively. "Hoy enterraron al Louie / and San Pedro o san pinche / are in for it," reads the beginning of Montoya's classic poem "El Louie"; "la canería y el sol / la mata seca, red fruits / the sweat / the death / el quince la raya / juanito will get shoes," are typical verses from Alurista's collection *Floricanto en Aztlán*. Certainly not all Chicano literature is written in this interlingual form—much is in Spanish or English, sometimes published in bilingual editions with translations from the original language. Puerto Rican writers are much more liable to remain in one language, although younger poets—Victor Hernández Cruz, Pedro Pietri, and Miguel Algarín—are utilizing code switching more and more in their writing. Both groups use anglicisms, but not the same ones, just as the Spanish slang they employ is not the same; at times the same word has completely different meanings for the two groups. Thus, ironically, it is exactly the usages which characterize the speech of Puerto Ricans and Chicanos within the family of Latin American speech patterns that also distinguish them from each other.

It could be added that in literature both groups preoccupy themselves with the injustice suffered by Hispanic people within the U.S. sphere of influence. However, the self-appraisals of their status as a people differ considerably. Chicano literature has produced several epic-like books which attempt to create historical and mythological overviews of a Chicano nation. Works like Rodolfo Gonzales's *I Am Joaquín*, Sergio Elizondo's *Perros y antiperros*, Alurista's *Floricanto en Aztlán*, and Miguel Méndez's *Los Criaderos humanos* provide an ideological base for cultural cohesion and purpose. Nothing similar has appeared in mainland Puerto Rican literature.

Chicano literature, in addition, has created archetypes of cultural survival despite assimilatory pressures—the Pachuco and the *campesino*. The former came to prominence in the 1940s when U.S. military men attacked them on the streets of Los Angeles. Writers like José Montoya and Luis Valdez have transformed the Pachucos into percursors of the Chicano Movement. As a literary image they represent militant resistance to both U.S. and Mexican society, and thus symbolize the intercultural synthesis of Chicanismo. *Campesinos*, or migrant farm workers, have come to represent the exploited labor force utilized by the dominant society to maintain a high standard of living for the middle class at the expense of underpaid workers; yet they also represent Mexicans willing to leave Mexico and change their way of life for a better standard of living in the United States. Puerto Rican literature has produced no comparable archetypes.

Immigration and deculturation are favorite subjects of both groups. René Márquez's *La Carreta* compares well with Ricardo Vásquez's *Chicano* or even Ernesto Galarza's *Barrio Boy*. Families leave their rural home in the mother country to move to the urban United States, where the younger members begin to adopt new ways; the family unit suffers and the older generation longs for the lost past. Both literatures have explored the *bildungsroman* within the milieu of immigration, though Chicanos give it more emphasis. Piri Thomas's *Down These Mean Streets* relates a young Puerto Rican's struggles with blackness and then with prison; Pedro Juan Soto's *Hot Land, Cold Season* explores a mainland youth's return to Puerto Rico, where he discovers alienation. In Chicano literature José Antonio Villareal's *Pocho*; Rudy Anaya's *Bless Me, Ultima*; John Rechy's *City of Night* and *The Fourth Angel*; Tomás Riera's *. . . y no se lo tragó la tierra*; and Oscar Zeta Acosta's *The Autobiography of a Brown Buffalo* all fall within the genre to some extent, exploring Chicano rites of passage in a variety of social settings. What distinguishes the Chicano *bildungsroman* is the inclusion of writing itself as an essential factor in the process of maturation. Several of the most important Chicano novels can be read as portraits of the artists as young men. Writing becomes the means of preserving culture and, at once, a way of redefining it within the new situation of the United States. This concern is not present in Puerto Rican literature to any great extent.

Chicano literature manifests, in spite of the great variety of thematic concerns and stylistic tendencies, a unifying paradigm: to a perceived threat to the existence of the culture the work itself responds, becoming a proof of survival. Within this paradigm there functions what Ramón Saldivar calls the dialects of difference. Chicanos in literature choose to be other than U.S. American or Mexican. They reject the chaos of deculturation, but in the act of defining themselves they discover a non-Mexican identity as well. The literature is the production of a space of difference, an intercultural synthesis between dialectical forces, be they United States vs. Mexico, urban vs. rural, English vs. Spanish, or even rock 'n' roll vs. polkas. To choose one over the other is to cease to be Chicano, because Chicanismo is the product/producer of synthesis. Therefore, the literature proposes an alternative, an "inter" space for a new ethnic identity to exist.

Mainland Puerto Rican literature, while doing the same thing, still tends to advocate unity with the island and to disparage the creation of a new cultural synthesis not centered in the homeland. Militant *independistas* discourage the idea of a separate identity for Puerto Ricans residing on the mainland. Yet there already exists a different cultural manifestation, sometimes pejoratively called Nuyorican. Writers like Miguel Algarín (*Nuyorican Poetry*) and Jaime Carrero (*The FM Safe*) utilize the term with a new pride in a similar fashion to what Chicano writers did with the previously disparaging word *Chicano* in the late 1960s. This redefinition of one's hybrid state is the first step towards an ideology of difference.

The next logical step would be to synthesize the Nuyorican and Chicano identities into a Latino or Hispano ethnicity. In the Chicago area, where Puerto Ricans and Chicanos live side by side, the effort has begun. The *Revista Chicano-Riqueña* is a forum for the two groups. However, to date, very little synthesis has occurred. Ethnicity is not a matter of rational planning. The two groups share a similar situation, and perhaps they will come to share the paradigm of resistance to chaotic destruction through the creation of a different, alternate identity. But at present the cultural differences between them are still stronger than the will to unify; their writing reflects those differences as much as it constitutes a literature different from the mainstream writing of the United States.

Bibliography

Chicano Literature:

Alurista. *Floricanto en Aztlán*. Los Angeles: Chicano Studies Center, University of California Los Angeles, 1971.
Anaya, Rudolfo. *Bless Me, Ultima*. Berkeley, California: Quinto Sol, 1972.
Arias, Ron. *The Road to Tamazunchale*. Reno, Nevada: West Coast Poetry Review, 1975.
Bruce-Novoa. *Chicano Authors: Inquiry By Interview*. Austin: University of Texas Press, 1980.
Gonzales, Rodolfo. *I am Joaquín*. New York: Bantam, 1972.
Jiménez, Francisco, editor. *The Identification and Analysis of Chicano Literature*. New York: Bilingual Press, 1979.
Méndez, Miguel. *Los Criaderos humanos (épica de los desamparados) y Sahuaros*. Tucson, Arizona: Editorial Peregrinos, 1975.
—. *Peregrinos de Aztlán*. Tucson, Arizona: Editorial Peregrinos, 1974.
Rivera, Tomàs. *. . . y no se lo tragó la tierra*. Berkeley, California: Quinto Sol, 1970.
Valdez, Luis. *Actos*. San Juan Bautista, California: Cucaracha Publications, 1971.
Valdez, Luis and Stan Steiner, editors. *Aztlán, An Anthology of Mexican American Literature*. New York: Vintage Books, 1972. See in particular José Montoya's "El Louie."
Villanueva, Tino. *Hay otra voz poems*. Staten Island, New York: Mensaje, 1972.
—. "Sobre el término 'Chicano'." *Cuadernos Hispanoamericanos*, junio 1978.
Zamora, Bernice. *Restless Serpents*. Menlo Park, California: Diseños Literarios, 1976.

Puerto Rican Literature:

Algarín, Miguel. *On Call*. Houston: Arte del Pueblo Press, 1980.
—, editor. *Nuyorican Poetry*. New York: Morrow, 1978.
Babín, María Teresa and Stan Steiner, editors. *Borinquen, An Anthology of Puerto Rican Literature*. New York: Vintage Books, 1974.
Hernández Cruz, Victor. *Mainland*. New York: Random House, 1973.
—. *Tropicalization*. New York: Reed & Cannon, 1976.
Kanellos, Nicolás and Jorge A. Huerta, editors. *Nuevos Pasos: Chicano and Puerto Rican Drama*. Gary, Indiana: *Revista Chicano-Riqueña*, 1979.
Laviera, Tato. *La Carreta Made a U. Turn*. Houston: Arte del Pueblo Press, 1980.
Márquez, René. *La carreta*. Río Piedras, Puerto Rico: Editorial Cultural, 1963.
Muckley, Robert F. Introduction to *Notes on Neorican Seminar*. San Germán, Puerto Rico: Inter American University, 1972.
Pietri, Pedro. *Puerto Rican Obituary*. New York: Monthly Review, 1974.
Soto, Pedro Juan. *Hot Land, Cold Season*. New York: Dell Publishing Co., 1970.
—. *Spiks*. Río Piedras, Puerto Rico: Editorial Cultural, 1973.
Thomas, Piri. *Down These Mean Streets*. New York: Knopf, 1967.

Dick Higgins on His Work

I began as a composer; in fact, when I was about six, in 1944, my grandmother asked me what I wanted to do when I grew up, and I said, "Write symphonies." My work is still mostly musical—even when it is word or image-based.

I went to boarding school at eight and did such things as hanging up all the heavy junk from the school dump into the trees, where the wind caused it to make lovely percussion music. Visiting back there 25 years later, I found the junk still lying below the trees, ready to be hung up again.

In high school I edited the school literary magazine but read orchestration books on the side. Composition was not taught there, so I concentrated instead on arranging and learning instruments. I let nothing stop me, even waking up the poor old reverend from his afternoon nap in order to get access to the old chapel organ at odd hours—that kind of thing.

But quite early in the game I learned the necessity to identify power sources and to work around their guardians. Astronomy fascinated me; and for years I struggled to get access to our prep school's

observatory, even going so far as to organize an astronomy club. No luck. No
matter what I did, it was kept locked.
However, I noticed, on a plaque outside
the structure, the name of the woman who
had donated it in memory of her dead son.
So in a fit of frustration I got her address
from the alumni office and wrote her a sad
and humble letter: "Dear Mrs. X, I am a
student here, and (blah blah blah) we
have not been able to use the observatory...." A week later I happened to walk
past the headmaster's office, and he came
running out the door at me. "Young man,"
he said, purple-faced, "you have *no idea*
what you've done! I've been on the phone
all day with practically every member of
the board of trustees about this observatory, and never have I experienced such a
hornet's nest!" "Sir, can we use the observatory?" I asked. "Yes," he sputtered, "but
if only you had come to me and asked!
This is *not* the way we do these things—
not the way at all...." So *he* said, and I kept
my mouth shut; I had learned my lesson.
It became my paradigm experience for
later years, for my publishing. It *is* how I
do things.

At Yale College there was no way to find
out about really modern music. So I ignored the official courses, got myself a
radio program on the student station, and
wrote letter after letter to record compa-
nies on the radio station letterhead, re-
questing review copies of avant-garde
records. Boxes upon boxes of samples
were sent to me, and these I played and
commented on over the air waves. In that
way I became familiar with the music of

John Cage, Lou Harrison, Henry Cowell, and, of course, Charles Ives, whose papers were in the Yale Library but whose music then was seldom, if ever, played in concert, although Yale had been his alma mater.

One day after a geology lecture by a dapper professor named "Rocky" Flynt, I realized that I was learning more about glaciation than I wanted to know about the subject. His wry jokes about the "P test"—pissing onto the walls of deep holes in the glaciers in order to detect how compressed the snow was and thus how old the glacier might be—these jokes left me cold. So I left Yale.

I dropped out, but dropped into a famous public relations firm, Ruder & Finn, where I was shown not only how to write press releases, but also how to research information out of libraries; courses in this area should be required for *all* arts students of all kinds. But in my case, it also led to my first published pamphlet—a history of roast beef (cuisine, folklore, and literary mentions) in the English-speaking world.

The public relations firm paid for its employees to take courses at the New School in downtown New York. I saw that John Cage was teaching there, so I decided to take his course. In the first class he stuck a match book into the piano strings, altering their sounds. "Nice," he said—I agreed and knew I had come home.

Cage said that musical notation systems all said: "So much space equals so much time." Cage felt that, since Einstein was concerned with space and time, it was an appropriate area of inquiry—"makes me feel we're in the right century" was his phrase. I disagreed, feeling that Cage allowed too little room for subject matter. For instance, why not make a notation system that said: "The more space, the angrier the performance, and the less space, the calmer"?

Cage seemed to imply that one could make music with words, compose poems with visual materials, make sculpture with sound—for me this was his most important teaching of all.

I formalized this notion as "intermedia," a term I revived from Coleridge, for works which fell conceptually between media that were previously recognized, creating new fusions, no longer separable into their component media. Operas mix media—one knows what's the music, what's the libretto, what's the mise-en-scène. Happenings are intermedia—the life of the work is lived *among* the sight, the sound, and the sense, where they fuse.

I also studied at Columbia with Cage's own former music teacher—Henry Cowell. He noticed how my music never looked like it sounded, and encouraged me to explore this phenomenon and all other aspects of notation. Thus Cage and Cowell set me onto doing my *Graphis* series of compositions (1958-   ), which includes

many works that are non-musical, and to
which I am still adding nearly 25 years
later.

My friends in intermedia were doing
"happenings." I performed in the first of
these in New York, including the very
first—fragments by Allan Kaprow and
by myself on the Henry Morgan Show
on television. But I felt the happenings
group was naïve, assuming as it did that
all art must produce a catharsis or strong
effect. I felt the happenings crowd had too
much baggage left over from their visual
art days—working through art galleries, painting or sculpture departments,
museums, and other academic sites. They
insisted that each work must be unique,
could not be repeated, etc. I took my cues
from music, where works are *meant* to be
repeated and part of the pleasure is the
comparison of different performances,
or from literature, which is usually designed for re-reading. This set me strongly at odds with the happenings bunch,
and it set me outside their scene from
the outset; I realized I could not automatically follow their line but must make my
own scene apart from the fashionable
line.

When I graduated from Columbia, I decided to go to printing school so I could
avoid dependence on the fashion world's
milords. I did so, loved doing color sepa-
rations, and learned type design, not as art
students learn it (by doing subtle tissue
overlays) but by designing bank checks
for, among others, Elvis Presley and by
"faking" book designs of established de-

signers for cost-conscious printers and publishers.

Word-art seemed (and seems) to me to be virgin territory—so little progress has been made in it! Thus, around this time, 1961, I cut down on my performances and began to concentrate on the making of texts, never forgetting, however, my performance art or intermedial experience.

There was insufficient continuity, so far as the public was concerned, in the work of the intermedia artists. Each performance, each printed thing seemed sui generis, unclassifiable, separate from all known quantities and thus inaccessible to a normal audience. We who were doing such works needed a common rostrum.

We found it in "Fluxus." I won't repeat the history of that non-movement, but George Maciunas was editor of a magazine of intermedia, *Fluxus*, and to publicize it he organized a series of festivals in Europe (1962-63) and the United States (1964-65) which caused a great sensation and led to our being called "the fluxus people," which was sort of okay with us.

We were a very disparate lot, but Maciunas tried to use surrealism as his paradigm in organizing us, with himself as pope. It didn't work. At various times he read most of us out of Fluxus, but we didn't accept his judgments and kept the offending members aboard the ship in spite of him.

Actually, Fluxus was a formal tendency—
minimal and intermedial—not a historical movement at all; anyone can be a Fluxus
artist, even now. Just study Fluxus work
and do something in that format and
spirit.

>Maciunas was supposed to do a collection
>of my texts but kept putting it off. Finally
>I took back my manuscript, got drunk in a
>bar, and staggered home to Alison
>Knowles, herself a Fluxus artist. "Alison,"
>I said, "we've started a press." "Really,"
>she said, "what's it called?" "Shirtsleeves
>Press," I answered. "That's no good," said
>she. "Call it something else." So I did—
>*Something Else Press*.

The phrase "something else" seemed to
define just what I *did* want to publish—
something else from what the fashion
fakers were grinding out. And let it be
fine, as in the admiring slang phrase, "Oh,
that's something else!" Something else
from what was known and charted and
accepted.

>We did my book of texts, *Jefferson's Birth-
>day*, bound back-to-back with a short his-
>tory of happenings and Fluxus as I then
>saw them, *Postface*. Next we did Ray
>Johnson's *The Paper Snake*, the first book of
>"mail art." Then along came *The Four
>Suits*, non-Fluxus work by Fluxus artists.

Many of our books were too expensive for
a good number of our friends, and so in
1965 we began our Great Bear Pamphlets,
named for our favorite brand of spring
water (very refreshing during that sum-

mer when the series began, in 1965). By 1968 the series included works by Knowles, Oldenburg, Kaprow, myself, Vostell, Cage, af Klintberg, Emmett Williams, Filliou, and many others. They were cheap and went places the larger books couldn't. We liked it that at the Berkeley Coop they were sold at the end of the fresh vegetable counter.

Concrete poetry was then a widespread intermedial form, largely unknown in egocentric America. So we opened an art gallery where we did the first substantial New York show of concrete poetry—the Something Else Gallery (1966-69, 1972). We also published Emmett Williams's *Anthology of Concrete Poetry* (1967), which was utterly international (though it also had many omissions) and which was reviewed in *Newsweek* and *Vogue*, among other places. It made the term famous in the United States, and the anthology sold some 18,000 copies, not bad for a tiny publisher like us, or for *any* avant-garde anthology.

To deepen our context, we also reprinted avant-garde works from the past. Most people who attacked us or Fluxus, saying "Oh, the Dadaists did it all before you," had no idea what the Dadaists had done; so we reissued the German *Dada Almanach* (1921) in facsimile. Those who saw my work as deriving from Gertrude Stein missed the subtlety of that relationship—I adored Stein and had once even organized a year-long program of reading her complete works aloud. So now I set out to republish her works that were in the public domain: *The Making of Americans, Lucy Church Amiably, How to Write, A Book Beginning With As A Wife Has A Cow*, and *Geography and Plays*.

> Once, when Alison Knowles went into a store, she saw a young man gesturing feebly at the shelf where the Something Else Press books were displayed, evidently telling his girl friend to look at one. She did and looked puzzled, asking him "What is it?" The young man said, "I don't know, but they're *all* like that!"

Obviously this young man had no way of understanding our books, so when Alison told me the story, I made up my mind that I should do something about theory, in order to give the public some appropriate keys to the understanding of us, of the Something Else Press, of intermedia, of Fluxus—so they wouldn't be puzzled because we weren't doing what traditionally was expected of the arts. Thus we did a series of *Something Else Newsletters* and sent them free by the thousands to our mailing lists. They included my "Indermedia" essay and about twelve other theoretical texts, initially collected into a collection of my own works, *foew&ombwhnw* (1969), which was bound as a prayer book to suggest the irony of a new canon, and which was later revised and supplemented by other theory texts in *A Dialectic of Centuries: Notes Towards a Theory of the New Arts*, published by Printed Editions. Taken in sum, the essays add up to a usable theoretical system, though as yet I haven't written the whole system into one single or unified essay.

Besides the new poetry (Eugen Gomringer, Emmett Williams, Jackson Mac Low,
and others) we also did new fictions
(Daniel Spoerri, Toby MacLennan, and
the Richard Kostelanetz anthology *Breakthrough Fictioneers*), along with books on
music and music theory, gardening and
wild mushrooms.

But by 1973 there were too many time
conflicts between myself as organizer and
myself as artist. Too many people were
seeing me as a business-person before
all else, and I was spending too much
time fund-raising for our books. So I
turned Something Else Press over to a
young editor, Jan Herman. I'd left him a
list of appropriate cigars to go light if he
wanted to get funds, but he went nowhere, lit no cigars. His idea of doing
business was wrapping and mailing
books—so the serious executive work went
undone, and in 1974 the Something Else
Press went into bankruptcy—much
mourned.

Even before that, at the suggestion of my
friend Nelleke Rosenthal, I had started a
new small press for works that didn't fit
the Something Else Press emphasis on big
books. We called it "Unpublished Editions." I liked the paradox of the name—
the idea being that these were small editions which could serve as prototypes for
later, larger ones.

For me the important thing was to make
my work available; as a composer I felt
no work existed until it was performed,
and as a writer I feel no text exists until

it is shared with a public. Thus in 1972, when I began Unpublished Editions, I consciously set out to cover my ground and create my world—poetry (*amigo*, *classic plays*, *Modular Poems* and *some recent snowflakes*), drama (*The Ladder to the Moon*), fiction (*Legends & Fishnets*), theory (*A Dialectic of Centuries*), graphics (*of celebration of morning*) and, of course, music (*Piano Album*), etc. That conscious program is now complete (1980), and my publishing can now slow down.

Unpublished Editions worked so well for me, as a program, that it was then opened up to others; thus it became a cooperative, each of whose members produces sher (his or hers) own books, and each is then paid back as the books are sold via our catalog and distribution network. In 1978 the group changed the name to Printed Editions, and the members are currently John Cage, Philip Corner, Geoffrey Hendricks, myself, Alison Knowles, Jackson Mac Low, Pauline Oliveros, and Jerome Rothenberg. Except for Oliveros, all had been Something Else Press authors, so there is still considerable continuity with our older intermedial publishing tradition.

I feel no conflict as a polyartist (one working in many media)—one area of concern seems to lead to another, and, so long as I have the technical skills necessary to realize the potential of each work as it confronts me with its necessities, I am happier following my nose instead of the demands of my presumed self-image or of my Official Career.

I have been looking for flexibility in my forms. In music, graphic notations continue to fascinate me. In poetry, I've found myself interested in making verbal analogues to the musical "cancrizan," popular in Renaissance and again today —cancrizans proceed up to a fulcrum point at which they reverse themselves and go exactly backwards back to their beginning. My verbal cancrizans I call "snowflakes" because they are visual and symmetrical and have some resemblance to the snowflakes that school-children cut in paper. Is the snowflake the first clearly defined visual poetic form? I wonder.

Right now I am writing no theory and almost no criticism. I would like to make about a dozen "movies" that are slide shows, where the sequences are crucial, along with the timing and the musical accompaniment, but where there is no illusion of movement. I have just bought a church in the Hudson Valley, and there I will organize a musical and verbal ensemble. Where once my music came to center upon words, now I would like to see if my poems want to include more musical sounds.

Bibliography

By Dick Higgins:

foew&ombwhnw. New York: Something Else Press, 1969. This is a collection of works
     from the 50s and 60s—theoretical, poetic, performance, Fluxus, graphic
     notations, etc.
A Book About Love & War & Death. Barton, Vermont: Something Else Press, 1972.
     This is the complete version of Higgins's longest aleatoric work—a chance
     novel.
classic plays. West Glover, Vermont: Unpublished Editions, 1976. This is Higgins's
     most ambitious poetic work, partly visual and partly anticipating his
     "snowflake" form. It constantly interfaces (and puns between) French and
     English, with a little Latin thrown in for good measure.
A Dialectic of Centuries: Notes Towards a Theory of the New Arts (second edition). New
     York: Printed Editions, 1979. Here Higgins's theoretical articles are col-
     lected in final form, including the "Exemplativist Manifesto." These estab-
     lish a historical and philosophical position which centers on the viewer or
     reader, and which cuts the present avant-garde free of the outmoded
     assumptions that are often used to condemn it.
some recent snowflakes (and other things). New York: Printed Editions, 1979. This col-
     lection of short pieces can be used to provide examples and illustrations of
     the ideas in *Dialectic of Centuries* (above).

About Dick Higgins:

Chase, Gilbert. "New Content for Old Shells." *Arts in Society* (Madison, Wisconsin,
     1970).
Frank, Peter, et al. *Dick Higgins and the Something Else Press*. New Paltz, New York:
     Documentext, 1983.
Graffi, Milli. "Diario su Quattro." *Tam Tam* (Modena Italy, 1974).
Kostelanetz, Richard. "Dick Higgins." In *Twenties in the Sixties*. Westport, Connec-
     ticut, and London: Greenwood Press, 1979.

Writing and Performance

A Conversation among Linda Mussmann, Richard Foreman, Robert Wilson, and Richard Kostelanetz

Kostelanetz: With me are people who represent new developments in American dramatic writing and theatrical performance: Richard Foreman, the founder-director of the Ontologic-Hysteric Theater, whose plays are collected in a book entitled *Plays and Manifestos* (1976). Linda Mussmann, the artistic director of Time & Space Limited in New York. In her early 30s, she has both written and directed theater events, many of which are based on non-dramatic texts. And the last is Robert Wilson, the author of *Einstein on the Beach* (1976) and *Death, Destruction in Detroit* (1979) among other productions that have been prominently presented in both Europe and America.

Richard Foreman, may I ask you first: What are your scripts like? And how do they differ from traditional theater texts?

Foreman: My texts these days are rather strange, and they are rather different from the kinds of texts I wrote when I began ten years ago. Ten years ago I would work from an outline, and the writing was the task of sort of deconstructing that outline, trying to attack the outline. If in the outline I had said, oh, "Ben enters and complains that he doesn't like his job," I would, keeping that outline unit in mind, try to lie about it—try to write in response to that outline, lying about it.

Kostelanetz: Lying about it? How?

Foreman: I would have Ben say, "I love my job." It was a matter of a kind of spiritual discipline, keeping in the mind what I knew was supposed to be the content of the scene according to the outline, and then perversely trying to put on the page all the negative, the reverse sides. . . .

Kostelanetz: To charge the detail or to invert the detail with respect to your original scheme.

Foreman: Yes. Now writing plays in that way, I found that every couple of months I would write a play. Before that period in which the writing went well, day after day I would sit down, start to write the play, and there would be a false start of one sort or another, and I would throw it out.   At a certain point—I suppose in the middle 1970s—I decided, "Why should I throw out all this material? These false starts express the real energies of my life, the real frustrations and successes of my life, and I began staging this day-by-day effort to write.

Kostelanetz: Your *own* effort to write?

Foreman: Yes. And philosophically at this point I cannot conceive, for the theater, of staging, of writing anything other than these kind of day-to-day notions of my struggle to write. It seems to me that building a more coherent, consistent structure, a more unified structure, is a lie. It's a lie about what my life here in New York City in this moment of the 20th century is about. Now when you look at my texts these days, not only are there page-by-page radical changes of locale, of idea, of what-have-you, but there are no characters indicated. I am not writing lines. I am writing information. There is no indication of the context in which this information occurs.

Kostelanetz: Now doesn't this relate to what Gertrude Stein was doing in her theatrical texts, which likewise by and large eschew character, setting and all specific connection between particular lines and certain characters?

Foreman: Yes. My work began specifically under the influence of a French philosopher, Gaston Bachelard, and I began with the notion, suggested by Bachelard, that my writing would be the registration of a certain level of activity. In my case, I decided in my first plays only to talk about what was physically experienced by the body, to wipe the scripts clean of any ideas, any conclusions; only sensory impact went into my scripts. About two years later I started reading Gertrude Stein for the first time and became very influenced by the notion of writing exclusively in the present and in response to present stimuli when you were writing. These days—I am remembering Stein's original statement in one of her lectures that the thing that always bothered her about the theater was that what you were watching was always ahead of or behind the time of what was going on stage.

Kostelanetz: What does that mean?

Foreman: Well, it means that it is not like a book, reading a book, where you control your own time, control the rhythm of your own esthetic experience. It means that you are always leaping ahead, anticipating what the character is going to do next and Character B, responding to the statement of Character A, is either saying after you imagined the response or before you imagined the response, so it's a syncopation in time.

Kostelanetz: Isn't that one of the things that makes theater interesting?

Foreman: Yes, well, I was about to say that Stein, of course, created what she called a kind of "landscape" theater because this bothered her. I tended to do the same thing for a while, but in the last few years, if I've done anything, it has been to exploit all the more radically, I think, the nervousness of that not being together as spectator and stage life. And I am exploiting the fact that I, as a writer, when I am writing, am always ahead or behind my own writing. And I am allowing the normal stumbling, the normal difficulty, the normal incoherence that results from that split time to interpenetrate my text and to disrupt my text.

Kostelanetz: But then your writing is in part about the perceptual experience of writing—about the perceptual experience of understanding and manipulating language.

Foreman: My writing is about taking dictation in terms, well, I think that was most cleary enunciated by the American poet, Jack Spicer—just taking dictation. At a certain point lines start to come from somewhere; *but* not letting it come through purely, allowing the failure of my own mechanism as this radio that is receiving dictation to interfere with the text. There is a collision between the spirits, the muse, and the fellow that's sitting here with a heavy pen, with a tired hand, with a tired brain.

Kostelanetz: Linda Mussmann, what are your texts like?

Mussmann: The texts that I write are linguistic studies of the thinking process. Ideas associate—they repeat, they sound, they do not mean, they list, and they comment on themselves and the moment of being on the page and in the theater. The relationship to the written work and to the theater are directly related to me as a process and a way of working and thinking.

The relationship to my writing and the theater is directly connected—my whole existence evolves with theater as an art form. Theater as it is perceived by the general public is everything my work and writing is *not*. I work with language and theater simultaneously. I return to the simplest form of theater and language with my writing. As a theater artist who also writes, I see my work as a composer who works from theater/performance as a primary source.

For example, my first text was about space—my approach with language was compositional, architectural. There were three pieces, a "triptych." "Room/Raum" discussed space. The text was written in English, then, translated into German, then translated to English clichés/slang. Then it was translated to the clarinet as musical abstraction. The use of the clarinet was to explore the sound of the text via the language. The player of the clarinet used an abstract method of thinking since the mouth issuing information was abstract—the space of the word could be filled with music; therefore verbal meaning was successfully abandoned and a pure language was established.

Kostelanetz: Was the original text something you wrote?

Mussmann: I wrote the text in English. The purpose of writing and performing "Room/Raum" is to define—to be concrete, to be exact. Language (even though it is a communicator) does not assist in being clear, precise. Therefore a new language is necessary. The creation of this text was done through German and the speaker of a mysterious language. None of the performers knew German, which was a freedom. I understood that meaning which our own language provided usually abused the performer and listener.

Kostelanetz: What was perceived?

Mussmann: Language (English) communicates by meaning. The speaker/reader is hindered by constantly translating to the definition of the word, then the circumstances of the word in relation to the sentence, then the situation and attitude of the speaker at the time of the saying of the word or sentence. The conditions are too inaccurate and the chances of the definitive are impossible. Therefore, the abuse is rendered and the ultimate freedom was in the language that none of us knew, "German." This piece was composed for an American audience. The reader/listener is asked to listen for sound outside of meaning. The entire performance was based on the language of mystery and a language that sounds definitive to my American ear.

So I found that in working and evolving that text for a particular performance point of view that I relied mostly on things that I knew very little about. In fact, I preferred to know less about the text than more, which relates to Mr. Foreman's earlier response. Both of us have been influenced by Gertrude Stein and have approached the text in the different ways that she talks about in her experiments.

A lot of the texts that I write, they are unedited. They come out of my ideas, thought-patterns, and they are brought to the paper, and then they are brought to the theater, to a space apart from the page that is also comparable to theater space. They're brought to the theater, and then the actor or performer brings his/her relationship, as he/she perceived the page, to the work and the work then starts to evolve by erasing, sort of taking away. . . .

Kostelanetz: Erasing. So you start out with a text. Now the first text you described to me seemed to me about the same experience in several languages: English, German, cliché and clarinet. Or the same verbal material in several languages, shall we say? Do your other texts work that way as well?

Mussmann: In working and preparing this text I approach the work from a "sound" point of view and rely on the ear for information rather than reason/logic.

The pieces that I write evolve from ideas—thought-patterns that are graphed on the page—and then transferred to the stage. The performer then translates from the page to the stage in a verbal and physical pattern to then transfer the ideas to the watcher/listener.

The next text I wrote was "Door." It functions as an associative text and uses percussion as a supportive form. Percussion in this performance functioned as sound not music—it shows how language moves, how it is sculpted and how it maintains its own space by defining its limits which are visual and verbal.

Percussion is to sound as studs are to walls as writing is to language. Percussion, studs and writing support the ideas of sound, walls and language.

Kostelanetz: "Supports"—in what sense?

Mussmann: If language attempts to do something, it seems that everything needs to help it: like the effort of the body to express the language needs to move the hand or the arm or the body. Then the vocal cords can percuss. They'll make sounds that sound like or pretend to be like music. The problem is that music came after language. One of the ideas of these texts is to return to language and to make the language primary instead of secondary. So that out of the language emanates everything: gesture, movement, picture, form. All of the work is taken from the text.

Kostelanetz: So you do not write in your scripts any gestures.

They evolve only in performance, only in rehearsal.

Mussmann: The texts are a series of words or pictures indicating a visual form. But there are no instructions as to how to proceed and "do" these writings—the texts are and will be different for each set of performers and readers. The texts present formulas not answers.

Kostelanetz: Bob Wilson, what kind of text do you write?

Wilson: When I write a text, I work on the walls of my studio. I cover the walls with paper and then I start writing different lines. As I'm writing the lines, I don't think about who's going to say them, whether it's a man or woman, a child or an older person. Sometimes I put colors in the margins besides the lines to indicate the themes.

Kostelanetz: Colors to indicate the themes in what sense?

Wilson: In that the text is arranged architecturally, and there will be a theme or a motif that can be introduced and can later reappear, and it can be larger or more developed in one scene and less developed in another or diminishing. . . .

Kostelanetz: A motif in terms of language, character, visual materials?

Wilson: Well, I consider all those things. One reason I work on the walls is because I can stand far away from the text and see it in one glance. When it's in a book, I only look at it page by page. When it's all up on the walls, I can see where the text is very dense and where it's very thin. Also I go close and read the content, what the words are saying, and then I arrange them. But I am also concerned with the visual aspect, of how words look printed on the page.

Kostelanetz: The page of the text page?

Wilson: Yes, the text page. I usually work with a certain predetermined size of page. Sometimes the decision to put a word on the page or a line on the page is determined by the width of the page or the length of the word.

Kostelanetz: Which is to say that you have at the beginning this mural, sort of, on your studio wall and you compose on the mural.

Wilson: That's right.

Kostelanetz: And from that composition on the mural you extract pages.

Wilson: Well, I can cut the text up and rearrange it.

Kostelanetz: Then you physically go to the paper on the wall?

Wilson: And I type it, eventually it's typed, and I look at the arrangement of the words. A text doesn't tell one story; usually it tells many stories, and so it's arranging these stories. But I'm not primarily concerned with the narrative form—or I haven't been so much in the past. I'm more concerned with the musical arrangement.

Kostelanetz: The musical arrangement of the material on the wall?

Wilson: The architectural arrangement and the musical arrangement.

Kostelanetz: So your script then looks like what: lines and drawings? Or just lines?

Wilson: Well, in the beginning it looks just like typed lines.

Kostelanetz: Just typed lines.

Wilson: And then I go through another period where, instead of thinking about the text or about various themes in the text that I might be interested in, I select a group of people that I'd like to work with. They, in themselves, seem to tell a certain kind of story, just by looking at who the people are naturally. Then, in rehearsal, I decide which actor gets what line or sometimes they choose them on their own and eventually all the lines are given away. Thus far I've always assigned the characters numbers: they don't necessarily have names; they have a number. I write in the margins beside the lines the numbers of the characters. Sometimes I work with that pattern of numbers and the rhythms that it establishes or I can make.

Kostelanetz: Okay, so, therefore, the lines are assigned to characters in the course of rehearsal. They're not preassigned; you don't think of this line as written for a young woman or this line for an old man when you write them. That assignment turns up in rehearsal.

Wilson: That's right. For example, I'm working on a play now. It's dealing with 19th-century Japan, and it also concerns the Civil War in America. Various other themes are included, and different locales. But when I'm writing the text and even when I'm casting the play, I don't think about those things. The text is really an audio score, yet it's not *the* most important element in the play. It's important, but other elements are just as important.

Kostelanetz: Richard Foreman, how do you realize your texts?

Foreman: These days there's a text that is simply a series of lines with no character indicated. The first thing I do is to design a set. It's difficult to say how I decide to design a set, how I decide what form the set will take. When the time comes to produce a play, I have many, many texts that I've *generated* (I prefer to say rather than written) over the past few years. I very casually pick one. I pick them on the basis of a very casual reading of the text, you know, just skimming through it. Then to design the set, I may just skim through it—really, a 20-page play I might look at over the period of a minute and a half, just getting the feel of what some of the scenes are like, some of the pages are like—and then I start to make sketches and just sort of doodle my notion of articulating a kind of space. As the set proceeds, it sort of takes on a life of its own in a certain sense, in a way similar to the way that Cage and Cunningham, the American composer and dancer, work when they're creating dances where Cage will perform a musical score that Cunningham doesn't listen to while he is creating the choreography.

Kostelanetz: Except that you are both the author and the stage designer here. Are you trying to separate your functions so that they both function autonomously?

Foreman: What I'm saying is that when I'm designing the set, I don't go back and refer to the play very often to make sure that I'm doing the right thing. The set gets built. Then rehearsals start. And when rehearsals start, my task is to find a way to make my text exist 'in the world of this set in much the same way that the various animal species on this planet have to find the way through natural selection to adapt to the circumstances of this planet.

Kostelanetz: But then you're competing against yourself literally, or one part of you is competing against another part of yourself, or one expression of yourself. . . .

Foreman: We're not competing. We're falling over each other. Because I believe that in mistakes, in falling-downs, in these collisions, unexpected collisions, there alone arises the opportunity for invention, arises the opportunity for creation. So I try to create situations where things will collide and fall over each other, and get into trouble in that way.

Now I suspect that as a writer, most people think of me as a director and say, "Oh, well, you have an ability to manipulate space, to be an effective theatrical director, and your texts, of course, are sort of nonsense in a neo-Dadaist tradition." I feel that that is absolute nonsense and an absolute misunderstanding. I think of myself as a writer. I feel that in all kinds of ways my writing is much more adventurous than my staging, which, I fear, tends to take these rather exploratory texts and turn them into a more classical kind of theater than I'm totally satisfied with.

Kostelanetz: In what sense do you mean the writing is more exploratory? It's less conventional, less immediately accessible?

Foreman: I would like to discover, to build for myself, a way of staging plays that exploits this same kind of disassociated, daily note-taking, that exploits and uses these false starts, that is very honest about what comes up in my fallible human life. I would like to stage in a similar way. I find it very difficult to do. I find myself invariably making it work better in classical theatrical terms.

Kostelanetz: Linda Mussmann, we were discussing before the unusual ways that your work evolves in rehearsal with people. Now how do you realize them in the end? Do you have a permanent company?

Mussmann: I work with different types of performers: those who are physically and vocally skilled, those who have previous theatre/performance work with me, and those who are new to the work and to me.

The more the performers are trained and informed the more precise and polished is the performance. But the writing sustains new and old performers as well.

My texts, in opposition to Mr. Foreman's work, create an open quality, and from listening to what he's been talking about, his texts create a closed operation.

Kostelanetz: Be more precise about "open" and "closed."

Mussmann: I am looking for a kind of writing form that is comparable to music. The writing gives a set of possibilities, a group of possible combinations; and the probabilities are infinite, changeable—similar to a geometric jazz which has mathematical sound patterns that create concrete forms out of abstract concepts. I work in reverse—from abstract to reality. I am looking for a field—a landscape within which to operate. It is closed in that the limits are visible, and yet it is open because I can define the limits. This understanding of field and boundary is scientific and mathematical, for example: the process of addition shows me how to add an infinite number of amounts. It is a device that helps me obtain answers—many answers. It is always mysterious and yet provides me with right answers and wrong answers—it is functional, creative, and flexible. I write texts that resemble a kind of field similar to math or music. In other words, his work sounds to me as if he's providing a stage before he puts that actor upon it.

Kostelanetz: The setting comes first.

Mussmann: For me, the physical requirements for each piece are open—any number of performers and any space. The conditions of each situation will dictate how each piece will look. The field/landscape is open until rehearsal begins—then objects and spatial dimension take shape. These texts, "Room/Raum, Door, Window," are meant to be performed in different spaces—not the same environment. Also the work has been recorded/video-taped/filmed/sung/read/sculpted and painted. These are works that ask to be formed and performed by all arts and especially by multiple art forms. The pieces are reflective (thinking). The writing represents a non-restrictive format—an open scape or white ground. In other words, when I work at the Cooper-Hewitt Museum in a space, "Door" takes on other proportions than it has in the storefront where we usually work.

Kostelanetz: The distinction is that Richard Foreman's plays have largely been done in theaters of his own creation, is that true?

Foreman: Yes.

Kostelanetz: Your plays have been toured through various spaces, where you respond to the differences in the space.

Mussmann: I am working from a theatrical background in traditional spaces—museums, churches, lofts, storefronts, galleries. Many times the form of a theater piece requires a number of limitations—sets, actors, lights. In working formally with theater I find too many limits. The design for my own writing is to use the idea of "installation"—that the work would adapt to any given space at any given time. Theater/plays do not always have that freedom—I take the text and work from a sculptural point of view with the given images that are on the page and the given images make a performance for each different space. The written text could be considered an instruction sheet—a map or a plan of "how to do *Room-Window-Door.*"

Kostelanetz: How reflective then, of the text, is the performance? Is it useful to read the text—to have a copy of the text in hand while one sees your performance?

Mussmann: The performance follows the order of the written words—knowing the text before would be an advantage and a disadvantage. I have forecast the images which work all ways depending on the intent of the project. I prefer working in the present tense with the images.

Kostelanetz: Would the text be distracting?

Mussmann: I have presented the text on tape recorder, video, writing on the wall, on paper—in general all methods work to prepare the audience for the piece. Now I remove any approach that distracts the watcher. Again I want an open system of operation.

Kostelanetz: Did that recording device work?

Mussmann: The recording method works to make the audience more of an authority—perhaps more closed. The recording tells what is to come, which works to the advantage and disadvantage of the performance. The most effective use of recording is simultaneous dialogue of different texts—it tends to create three *times* (past-present-future) at once. The most successful texts and performances use Gertrude Stein's notion of the "continuous present." The less distinct time is the more effective. I find the most immediate time is the most useful—an "all time" in transmitting the ideas. Therefore, the movement of the writer's mind to the page is first, then movement to the performer, then to the listener.

Kostelanetz: So your argument would be that it is useful for theatrical experience to see the text before one sees the performance of the text?

Mussmann: There is no argument—the text functions on several levels. It can be read or looked at—but it remains independent from the performance and vice versa. The text is a house plan—it provides the directions of "How to make" but it must be translated by the performer who has particular translating skills. The texts I write function outside of meaning—they use the form of writing or literature—but they function as units with their own rules and conditions—they are well-made and work at every turn—the performance shows this concept to the reader/listener.

Kostelanetz: Richard Foreman, would it help to have a text of your play while seeing it? Would that give the language more emphasis?

Foreman: Lord, I have no idea. I can't possibly say because I'm not thinking very much of my audience when I am making this stage a theatrical object. I'm trying to create a device, a machine, that will have a certain effect upon me when I see it, and then it is up to other people to use this machine or not to use this machine as they see fit. I must say that in staging my work, I do all kinds of things to make it more difficult for the audience to perceive the text. For instance, let's say that there is a line of dialogue in the text that during rehearsals we have determined that Rhoda, who is my leading character in all of my plays for the last ten years or so, says, "I'm going to the store to buy some whole wheat bread." I will record on tape four different voices, one of them Rhoda, three of them other actors, each of them will have one word from that sentence—I'm . . . going . . . down . . . the . . . street— each of those words by a different actor. Each of those four actors has their own loudspeaker.

Kostelanetz: Since you have four-track tape. . . .

Foreman: There's a loudspeaker in each of the four corners of the audience, so you hear this line word by word, the first word coming from lower right, the second word from lower left, and so on. At the same time this is coming over the loudspeaker, on stage the real live Rhoda will be repeating that same line at a different rate of speed from the words coming from the loudspeakers. Now, why? Not simply for the music, though partially for the music of such a sound. I'm interested in the theater, in freeing individual elements, freeing the individual word, freeing individual gestures, freeing individual noises in much the same way modernist poetry since Rimbaud tends to free the word on the page. So that in the third sentence there is a word that is a little loosened from its moorings, so you can relate that word to a word back at the beginning of the poem and not read it in a direct narrative line as it comes up. Now it does make it difficult, therefore, for the audience to keep on top of what exactly is being said. I have profound faith that on some unconscious or semi-conscious level an awful lot comes through, even though we may not really be aware of it.

Kostelanetz: Because of the strength of the language or the strength of the articulation with the tape machine and the live performance?

Foreman: Because of the strength of the articulation of the entire space-object, which is the performance.

Kostelanetz: Robert Wilson, are you always the director of your own play?

Wilson: Yes, I am. But once I did a very long play. It was seven continuous days and there were various people within the company that directed sections of the material. And I did another play that was 24-hours long in Paris, France, and different portions of that play were written and directed by members of the company, but for the most part, I organized it. I just finished doing a performance in Torino, Italy, with Christopher Knowles. It was actually a text that he had written; the decor was his, and even the choreography, our positions on the stage, were predetermined by Christopher, but I realized it.

Kostelanetz: Could somebody else realize your text?

Wilson: They could. My texts have no indication as to stage direction or as to character development or, as I said, who the characters are, whether it's a man or a woman. Someone could take the text and make whatever play they wanted with it.

Kostelanetz: Let me ask Richard Foreman the same question. Could somebody else realize your text?

Foreman: Oh, yes, as a matter of fact, I think there have been, what, five people that I know of, five different productions of my works that I have not directed. I'm not too happy with them.

Kostelanetz: How were they different from what you would do?

Foreman: Well, I thought they weren't different enough. I would hope that some day someone would take my texts and do a production radically different from anything I could have imagined for them. These productions were too close to what I could imagine for them.

Kostelanetz: Was it because they tended to favor in their settings your characteristic browns and your blacks—the kinds of color you use and the kinds of stage abstractions you use?

Foreman: To a greater or lesser extent, although I must admit that one of them—one of the directors—had never seen any of my productions, so perhaps there was more in the text than I thought.

Kostelanetz: Linda Mussmann, could anyone else realize your texts?

Mussmann: Definitely. Anyone can realize the texts. It does not matter how they create the performance. They would have to create a new approach and a new form. I hope they do not mimic my performance ideas, because my concepts were circumstantial, for a particular time and place, and were created with and for performers that make my work unique and non-repetitive. Difference is the point—I am breaking traditions, not making more rules. My work is to encourage new ways of thinking.

Kostelanetz: But you want your text to be suggestive in a way that it would require people to do things differently from what they normally do.

Mussmann: Definitely. They could not possibly do a normal theater performance with those pieces. They would have to evolve their own approach to them outside of any other known forms. My texts

ask one to think in non-linear ways. You cannot act the work: there are
no characters, no story, no chairs, no sets. The work is stark—it is all
voice and movement. Anyone who works with these forms of non-
literary texts must re-think every motion, gesture, attitude, word. All
must be scrutinized—nothing is taken for granted. The whole point
of the work is to be innovative and unique. The performance can be
by musicians, dancers, actors. The work can be placed in any space.
The texts can be musical scores, graphs, maps, lists, plans: they are
"open toes."

Kostelanetz: Robert Wilson, are your texts published?

Wilson: No, for the most part, they haven't been published. In fact,
I still haven't had a work copyrighted as a play. They've been rejected
in Washington by the copyright office because I guess, they just don't
look like plays. "Patio" probably had, in one year, as much exposure
as any contemporary American play. It toured all over Europe for a
year and was seen here in New York and toured the U.S. and three
times it's been rejected as a play. I can copyright it as dramatic poetry,
but not as a play.

Kostelanetz: What else in contemporary theater or contemporary
theatrical writing do you find particularly interesting? We spoke
before about Gertrude Stein as an antecedent we all find interesting.
Richard Foreman?

Foreman: Oh, dear. I suppose probably most of this table would
say that we're not that interested in the theater in general, even though
we make theater and we make theater in reaction to the theater that
exists. For myself, when I grew up, from the age of 15 to the age of 26,
all I thought about was Brecht. Trying to copy Brecht in every
conceivable way. I'm sure that still shows in my work though at this
point I'm not nearly as interested in Brecht as I once was. I am
interested in contemporary literature. I'm not aware of any literature
in a theatrical context that I'm that interested in. I'm interested in
contemporary American poetry for instance, which I think is going
through one of its glorious periods.

Kostelanetz: Linda Mussmann, why make theater rather than
film or write books? I mean, what's special about theater to you?

Mussmann: For me, the theater has all the problems and possibilities that no other art form contains. One can make theater under
any circumstances. There is always a way. There are no limits in
theater because there is every limit—at least from my point of view.

Kostelanetz: "Limits" such as?

Mussmann: I can make theater in a shoe box. I can make it at the Metropolitan Opera. I can make it in great spaces or small spaces. I can make it in New York City. I can do it outside of the city. Theater /performance limits are based on people—full of variables and not controllable or everlasting. The rate of success and failure is about the same, and none of it can ever be repeated—it is in and of itself.

Kostelanetz: Is there something about live performance that you find special as opposed to a filmed or videotaped performance?

Mussmann: The point about live performance is that it never repeats. The idea of having to repeat on a day-to-day basis is overwhelming enough, and in theater that repetition is no longer there. I've watched my work for years. I've gone through endless hours of rehearsal of the same play even in traditional form; it's never boring to me. Life is always tediously overwhelming, and theater always has an endless, continual response that keeps going and going and going and never is it a sure thing, never does it resolve itself. It always opens doors and continuously baffles and has endless opportunity to perceive that which is outside of it in reality very difficult to perceive. In theater you can establish a particular time, place, zone that you can't establish in any other format. To face the paper is indeed an isolation that is very hard on my particular person. The theater is an open *room*.

Kostelanetz: So therefore your pages themselves are comparable to your theatrical form in being evolving and open-ended?

Mussmann: Definitely. They try not to limit themselves. Even paper is a problem. In writing things down on paper, it's a disturbance to have to use paper or be committed to a particular size or format. When I went to high school, I remember we used to write on our hands, we wrote on our shoes and clothes. We wrote on ourselves and objects. And that seems to be an instinctual process to write on the walls. One is punished for writing on walls as well; yet one sits for years facing the blackboard in the process of learning, or in the institutional process. We look at a wall where someone writes something or sentences are diagrammed on this or numbers added. It seems that all of those processes are somehow abandoned when we sit down to become a writer or a theatrical something. The visual and physical are absent.

Kostelanetz: It sounds to me that you're trying to make a theater that corresponds to this writing process that you grew up with.

Mussmann: It sounds like the theater's asking for the walls to be
shoved out, too, to get rid of the walls (physical and mental walls) and
the prosceniums and all the limits that go with theater. To close the
theaters perhaps is the first step and then we can open spaces and
allow the processes to evolve without all the limitations of Brecht and
Stein and all of the other people who have gone before us.

Kostelanetz: Robert Wilson, why do you make theater rather than
other arts?

Wilson: Well, when I first came to New York and went to the
theater, I wasn't interested in it. I started going to the ballet and I saw
George Balanchine's work. I was very interested in what he was
doing. What interested me, first of all, was seeing an architectural
arrangement in time and space, and watching architectural patterns
and listening to music, and that the event didn't necessarily involve
itself in a narrative form of telling a story. I thought that was enough.
So initially I started working with theater because I was concerned
about those two aspects, about visual arrangements architecturally in
time and space and then perhaps hearing music or sound. My texts
now are really like audio scores that can accompany the visual arrangement or can stand independent of it.

Kostelanetz: Then you are making live theater in response to
ballet—in other words, to do with your own material the kinds of
things ballet does?

Wilson: I don't think it's in response to ballet. I mean, I call it a play
or theater, but my primary concern is not in telling a story, but in
watching a visual pattern and then listening to something.

Kostelanetz: On a live stage.

Wilson: In a live situation, yes.

Kostelanetz: Richard Foreman, why theater?

Foreman: Oh, I've always had very ambivalent feelings towards
the theater. I started making theater when I was a very young kid
because I was a very shy kid, and it enabled me to live a less shy, more
active life. So when I was ten years old, I started making my own plays.
As I grew up, I grew more and more unhappy with the medium that
I found myself placed it. I harbor tremendous distrust for the theater
in the sense that the theater classically and almost unavoidably is an
art form that is made for a group of people together to respond to.
There is one thing on this planet that I don't trust: it's the response of
any kind of group of people. If I could take the individual members
of my audience and work with them, I'm sure I would find them

to be more intelligent and more sensitive than they're going to be as a group.

I do lust and do love the kind of three-dimensional manipulation in space of all the elements. I theorize a great deal about the writing of texts and the implication of texts; however, putting actors on a stage and manipulating them in three dimensions with scenery I have no theories about, because it's something I just love to do and I do it very easily.

Kostelanetz: What other media are you working in?

Foreman: I have made some television pieces. I've recently made my first feature film, and I expect to make a second. After making my own Ontological Hysteric Theater for about ten years now, I would be happy to stop making theater and start making something else simply because, whether people like or dislike what I do in the theater now, I can do it. I must admit that it does not have the same degree of risk to me that it had when I began, and I do admit that I find it difficult to conceive of new strategies for myself and the theater which would entertain a similar degree of risk. For that reason, I'm moving into other areas.

Kostelanetz: Do you plan to do any books?

Foreman: I tell you, logically, I should either write books and /or paint. The problem is that I am such an anti-social person that if I wrote books or painted, I would never see anybody, and I think that would be bad for me. Forcing myself to work in the theater or in film forces me to have some social contact, which I think is necessary.

Kostelanetz: Robert Wilson, what other media have you worked with, what other kinds of work have you done?

Wilson: Well, I've worked as a painter, I've designed furniture, and most recently I've made a series of 30-second television episodes.

Kostelanetz: Where were those made?

Wilson: They were made in France and shown in Germany and throughout most of Europe and the Middle East and South America now. So I've started working in television, and I'm now working on a six-and-a-half-hour television program that's broken down into 20- and 40-second segments.

Kostelanetz: Forty-second segments?

Wilson: Yes. When all put back together it comprises six and a half hours of material.

Kostelanetz: When you say "working" are you the author or the director?

Wilson: What I've done is that I've made drawings, story boards, for the visual aspect. Each movement of the actor and each movement of the camera is predetermined and drawn. Then, separately, I've written an audio text, or score, or indicated what sounds or music will accompany the images. I will also realize it as a director.

Kostelanetz: Linda Mussmann, what other media do you work with or what other kinds of work to you do?

Mussmann: Most of my work is in the theater. I've worked with mostly traditional scripts and non-dramatic texts—in other words, novels, essays, poetry.

Kostelanetz: What do you mean by "non-dramatic"?

Mussmann: Non-dramatic. Right now I am working on "Danton's Death" by George Buchner in a new translation that was done for us by Hedwig Rappolt. I have used the structure of opera, all the speeches are designed, and the text functions from a pure linguistic, language point of view.

Kostelanetz: What does that mean—"linguistic, language point of view"?

Mussmann: That everything emanates from language and the text; all the movement, all the positions come out of the language. This is totally new for the theater.

Kostelanetz: You mean that they are implicit in the language or that you don't do anything that isn't in the language?

Mussmann: I work primarily from the language. In other words, the language dictates everything that I do with the script and have the actors do. Therefore, it is an entire process. (I took the idea from boxing—that if you hit the boxer in the stomach long enough, the head will fall.) And most of my work up until the Japanese play that I did three years ago—"The Bandit Princess" by Kikue Tashiro, which was all Eastern forms, Kabuki, Noh, Bunraku, which I transformed into a Western version. Up to that point everything I did within theater (as conceptual) was from movement and gesture—then language evolved into the new phase of my development. I mean, I decided to go away from movement and work only from a vocal point of view, I designed the vocal patterns for the actor that the body would then have to reform itself to satisfy the voice rather than the reverse, which is usually the way theater works.

Kostelanetz: So you've worked not only with your own texts but with classical texts as well?

Mussmann: Most of my history comes out of 40 or 50 classical plays from Ibsen, Strindberg, Buchner, Brecht, Becket, and on and on to work with Japanese texts—all traditional, classical points of view. It is a matter of training to keep myself out of habitually doing the same text, the same work over and over, to go and look for new challenges. And most of these have come recently in language, which is why I have been writing because I cannot find the texts to satisfy my needs—no one has written them, so I decided that I would write them.

Kostelanetz: Now, Richard and Bob, you've both been involved with opera as well—as director of your own texts, in Richard's case, and the Brecht text of "Threepenny Opera" as well. How is opera writing different from theatrical writing?

Foreman: I've only done opera in the context of more commercial, more entertainment-oriented theater than the work that I do for my own Ontological Hysteric Theater; and, therefore, the difference for me is that when I work in opera, there is narrative content. When I work in my own theater, there is really no narrative content, especially for the last six years or so. I would say the only thing that interests me in working on opera—indeed I'm doing another opera this fall for the New York City Opera—is that I direct to the music rather than to the text, which I hope makes things a little less obvious.

Wilson: I think it's difficult to hear and see at the same time. Frequently when I go to the opera, it's difficult to hear because I'm visually distracted. I became interested in opera because I was concerned about this problem: the possibility of hearing and seeing at the same time.

Kostelanetz: How did you resolve it?

Wilson: In that what we see doesn't necessarily illustrate what we hear, and that these things are thought about separately, although sometimes what we see can illustrate what we hear. I didn't start out to serve the music or to serve the text but to think about the visual aspect as something separate. It had its own construction, and they were thought about separately. In the case of working with Philip Glass on "Einstein on the Beach," although I knew what Phil was doing with the structure of the music, I chose to do something different with the structure of the imagery or the action of the actors. Sometimes we worked together, but for the most part we worked independently, and they were put together like a sandwich.

Kostelanetz: In the operas you've done, you've controlled what
we see and what we hear in the language but not the music?
Wilson: Well, in the case of "Einstein" I didn't do the music. But it's
always been difficult to put a label on some of my work—whether it's
really a play or is it an opera, or is it a dance, or what is it? When
I was in France in 1971, they said my work was more or less like
a silent opera, structured silences. Since then, I've started, as I've
said, working with words, but really the words are arranged in
the same way that music is arranged. They are arranged architecturally.
Kostelanetz: Do you ever plan to write the music?
Wilson: Well, I have used music from other sources, music from
the past, almost the way you would go to a juke box and select different
songs.
Kostelanetz: So you've become an editor of the music for your
own theater.
Wilson: In the last play that I did in Europe, I used sound effects
that are put together like a collage, sometimes as many as 14-16
different tapes running simultaneously. So I'm working with the
density of the sounds.
Kostelanetz: Richard Foreman, you've collected your texts in a
book, *Plays and Manifestos*. Is that book useful to people? How should
it be read? Is it just documentation or is it indeed scenarios that can be
performed?
Foreman: Well, there are scenarios that can be performed. I
believe it's literature also. I'm primarily concerned, I would have to
reiterate, not with the theater, or not with film. If I make film, I'm
concerned with a kind of activity, a kind of activity that has something
to do with my experience when I am thinking and get ideas. When I
get ideas, that little gap is jumped by my head and by my whole
physiology. Something happens in my body, and I am concerned with
trying to make an object—make a machine that evokes, is a metaphor
for—that somehow operates in a similar way.
Kostelanetz: And so a book of your texts can be this kind of
machine?
Foreman: Yes, and I wouldn't say the book. You see, I didn't
design the book, not that I have any objection to the design of the book,
but I would only say that because I didn't design the book, I can only
speak for the texts, and the texts, I think, do operate that way, yes.
Kostelanetz: Linda, I know right now that you're making a book

about your theater. How is that book going to work?

Mussmann: I'm making a book about the text of "Room/Raum," "Door," and "Window"—a triptych. I'm putting those three pieces in a book and dealing with the spatial problems of the page and how that reflects (not documents) what we did on the stage, but how it would occur on the page that would suggest how the language works and can form movement, gesture, design, landscape for anyone who would like to pick it up. So it is not a book of content, it is a book of form. If you want to evolve form and content, you have to get up and do it. That brings my two ideas together.

Kostelanetz: What will the pages look like?

Mussmann: They will have drawings on them that evolve from the words. So, for the word "dooooooor," O's might curl around. It seems very simple, but in that curling around and the expression of the O will evolve another sound that comes out. And it will be diagramed, much like you would read how to make a house, how to read the floor plans for a house, an architectural design to make something. So it puts forth the idea of "how to" something; whatever that something would be and however it would occur, that information could be gotten from the page similar to the way we work in the theater to put it forth on the stage. So it is a *form* point-of-view to bring to the texts.

Kostelanetz: So if Richard Foreman's texts are perhaps primarily to be read, your texts are primarily to be performed.

Mussmann: And looked at.

Bibliography

Brecht, Stephen. *The Theatre of Visions: Robert Wilson.* Frankfurt: Suhrkamp, 1978.

Foreman, Richard. *Plays & Manifestos.* New York: New York University Press, 1976.

Kostelanetz, Richard, editor. *Scenarios.* New York: Assembling, 1981.

Mussman, Linda. *Room/Raum.* New York: T S L Press, 1981.

Beyond Poetics

Jerome Rothenberg

In a "personal manifesto," circa 1968, I wrote: "I think of myself as making poems that other poets haven't provided for me and for the existence of which I feel a deep need." It seemed then, as now, important to situate myself in relation to the life and work of those "others": to set my own work against that of a generation or an even broader time span. That generation was post-World War II American; the broader span, at least to start with, was the 20th Century, a time that seems still more pressing and more poignant now that its end is drawing near. What we're looking back at, then, though still inside it, is an age of revolutions—real and pretended—in politics and art, consciousness and language: to reverse (as one consequence) the progression of several centuries of Euro-American domination that came before us.

"A specter is haunting Europe" (1848)—and it was, and it is.

And just as *they* were writing that, the specter was both what they said it was—viz "communism" as a basic human longing, also as a terror—and more: a sense of the industrial west's vulnerability, its stirring up of old forces, even chthonic powers, that would someday pull it down. Alongside which, to bring it nearer home, I would set a second specter: the recent brief emergence of America as the culmination, on the one hand, of biospheric imperialism (i.e., the greatest of the European settler states), and on the other, as the catalyst for "New World" culture that might even be a new "world culture."

In such a setting, American poets of my generation have followed their European and American predecessors in a two-fold work: the invention of counter-modes and strategies, along with the recovery of lost and despised modes drawn from territories long dominated by the west—not third world only but, equally, in poet Robert Duncan's formulation, "the female, the proletariat, the foreign;

the animal and vegetative; the unconscious and the unknown; the criminal and failure," etc. In the face of which, my statement for my own work must also be the larger statement: POETRY, AS WE ATTEMPT TO MAKE IT, IS AN INHERENTLY POLITICAL AND SUBVERSIVE ACT: THE EXPERIMENTAL GROUND FOR A QUESTIONING AND RE-DEFINITION OF ALL HUMAN IMAGES AND VALUES.

* * *

*From an Interview**

Rothenberg: It was my intuition early along (and the basis for what I came to call "ethnopoetics") that the avant garde wasn't so much obliterating traditions as expanding our whole sense of the human past. For example, an early avant garde poet like Tristan Tzara makes his manifesto statement that "there is a great negative work of destruction to be done," while at the same time (still during the dada period) he's beginning to compile a kind of proto-*Technicians of the Sacred* he calls "poèmes nègres": his gatherings, out of anthropological books of that time, of ritual poetry from Africa and the Pacific. Blaise Cendrars was involved in a similar work and his was actually published in the 1920s whereas Tzara's wasn't until a few years ago—but the point is that even though Tzara was a Dadaist, he was perfectly serious about this. People used to take it as a put-on, the juxtaposition of all that "primitive" work, its being given equal status with the European "classics." But my sense of it is that it was no put-on at all, that it was very real for him: a positive work of recovery he was involved in. Like, so to speak, a second renaissance for Europe: building a new paradigm and finding something like it in the past.

Higgins: Marxists put this kind of exploration down as being essentially nostalgic, a way of trying to get away from the issues of revolution. . . .

Rothenberg: Though the anthropologist Stanley Diamond assures me that Marx himself was not putting it down.

Higgins: Furthermore, the kind of research that's involved in this kind of thing is similar to what Engels did in his *History of the Family*

---

* Interviewer: Dick Higgins. May 2, 1977. Previously unpublished.

anyway, yet the normative Marxist approach is to attack this. . . .
Rothenberg: . . . to view it as nostalgic. . . .
Higgins: How do you deal with that kind of objection?
Rothenberg: Well, the point is that it isn't absent from Marx's thinking but may be central to it. Because what the "primitive"—in political or social terms a classless, stateless society—offers is a basic human model in which people aren't presumably as we know them in capitalist or highly industrialized society. When Marx and Engels use Morgan and Rousseau and so on, they're identifying with and trying to clarify a critique of civilization that sets it in opposition *not* to an *imagined* set of human potentialities but to something that has previously existed and still exists. A kind of basic communalism as the fundamental form of human society. And aspects of that—the sacred and so on, as I understand it—is part of their projection: a creative human potential, again not as a projection out of nowhere but in *those* lives, *those* cultures, day by day—and which resulted, according to anthropologists like Radin and Diamond, in a normative experience of the real world under red hot/white hot conditions: as a "blaze of reality." Or to be fancy about it in a kind of Marxist way, it resulted in a form of dialectical thought and behavior throughout those cultures, that can hold and deal with contraries, oppositions—even as we try to, from Blake and so forth on. That recognition made of something like surrealism a political movement, and the idea was to unify experience again (including, for them, the dark side of the "primitive" as well)—like, not just "intermedia" but a step beyond that into inter-everything. And that was in the tribal model too, that blurring of the boundaries between art and life (which is a dialectical proposition right at the core and really what we're after). But the political Marxists—the ones who always get control—are as much into the overmechanization, the regimentation, the anti-"primitive" in Diamond's sense of "primitive" as anyone. Even more so. And the rest of us *are* susceptible in turn to a nostalgia for the sacred, when the question is how—given industrial conditions and so on—can any viable communalism still be re-established.
Higgins: Further, it's obvious from your work that it has gone way beyond any naive or popular nostalgia for a simple life, and also beyond any novel search for exotic color.
Rothenberg: Because it's more complicated than that, and it's important too not to confuse this basic communalism with the actual lives of, say, third world peoples, or to impose the ideal image on the

realities of those lives. There's a tremendous American Indian re-
luctance, for example, to be decontextualized, and a strong sense of
the implications of what that means when it comes back into the
Indian culture. But Indians can decontextualize and romanticize as
well as whites, and I think my own intention, if understood, has
been to see it from a different, radically different point of view—
and with no pretense, I would hope, to more than I can say as a poet.
Higgins: And yet the question in anyone's mind has to be what
happens, anyway, when you take a religious ceremony and translate
it and perform it entirely in a secular context. It's as if one should stage
a Holy Communion service in the theater for the benefit of people
who would like to see a Holy Communion service of the Christian
ritual.
Rothenberg: Well, many churches feel more secular to me than
many theaters. And the theater, after all, for Grotowski and people
like that, becomes itself a sacred place . . . really returns again to an
early sense of theater as god-place, sacred precinct. It isn't in any
significant way a question of staging a Holy Communion service or a
Sun Dance but of re-establishing the conditions of "communion" as a
most general proposition about all our work. The problem, after all,
is largely western, because in the west there was this historical con-
signment of great areas of human experience to the domain of something called the secular—like dance, like comedy, like the natural
world itself to take a really major instance. Drama to a great degree.
Most of what we can now recognize again as poetry. And so on. And
we look to re-discover that wherever we can find it—that communion,
ritual—but not to pick it up whole and make a show of it. Like with
the "gift event" at the Judson Church:* there was a use, a derivation
from a Seneca ritual structure that incorporated a number of different
activities; and that was the extent of it. But even where it goes further,
there's always been that kind of learning and adoption—like some
instances, for example, of a group or tribe taking over songs from
another tribe and in a language they don't even understand, which
then becomes a "sacred language." Or, closer to home, look how much
was ripped off (to use a term that's often used here) from the Jews.

---

*Refers to a performance, circa 1967, of a work by Jerome Rothenberg, loosely based
on the Seneca Indian Eagle Dance and including Dick Higgins among its performers.
(See *Technicians of the Sacred*, page 376.)

Even by Christian *Indians*. And still—or just because of that—the Jews
have muddled through.

Higgins: I heard the daughter of a friend of ours sing the prayers
connected with the Bar Mitzvah while she herself, although she's
Jewish, isn't religious at all. They sounded very strange, so completely
out of context, as we were driving along in a car. Does this shift of
context ever bother you? Or does it modify the ways you present the
materials you're working with?

Rothenberg: No, it doesn't bother me. Not something innocent
like that . . . and sometimes it can be very funny, very crazy . . . which
it may be in my own work as well, like seeing the Baal Shem at the end
of *Poland/1931* as a kind of cowboy (which he pronounces *cock*-boy)
and the locals, because he's got a *shtreimel* on (the big hat that the
Hasidic Jews wear), figure he's from Mexico, and so on. *Poland/1931*
is full of such things, but so is *A Seneca Journal* in a different way. The
displacement has a lot in fact to do with my work and the questions of
loss and separation that run through it.   Which brings up even
memory questions, taken on both a personal and on a kind of group
memory, cultural memory, basis. Partly one is dealing with a reading
of material from which a separation has occurred.   You remember
some thing, you don't remember every thing.   You can't delude
yourself that you're in, or even want to be in, the identical situation
from which those memories come. So, in *A Big Jewish Book* I preface it
with a story about the Baal Shem and his followers: that the Baal Shem
had everything down perfectly, the prayers, the place to say the
prayers, the meaning of the prayers, the place in the woods to go for
the appropriate ceremony. (The woods are important there because
he was also doing a kind of modified return to "nature" or "wilderness.") In the second generation the place in the woods was remembered and the prayers, but the ritual was forgotten.   In the third
generation only the place in the woods was remembered and, at
present, nothing is remembered but the story, and yet (the poet tells
us) "that too proved sufficient." So, there's a kind of distancing and the
distancing is what we *really* know and have to know to get our
bearings. In other words you work out of the circumstances in which
you find yourself.

* * *

Manifesto and Collage (1980)

The tradition I identify with has tended to be experimental in both poetry and life.

Blake and Whitman are its founders in the English language. The poets of Dada are, literally, the Fathers.

Poetry and art form an area of relative freedom in which to experiment with alternative forms, with new or radical processes and structures.

This is the domain of poetic licence, whose end, whose aim, wrote the Jewish mystic Moses Porges, 1794, "is liberation from spiritual and political oppression." And William Blake: "Poetry fetter'd fetters the Human Race."

The tragic side of which, at this point in the century, is the suppression of poet-revolutionaries not only by the old tyrannies and powers but by the new tyrannies of political revolution.

Human rights are at the heart of our poetics.

("Il faut aboutir a une nouvelle déclaration des droits de l'homme."—Slogan on the masthead of *La Révolution Surréaliste*, December 1924.)

If the question is then raised of a possible reconciliation between the poet/artist and the state, the answer must be that it is not only impossible but not even desirable.

("No more masters, no more slaves.")

("No more gurus, no more disciples.")

For the poet must remain what he or she has been from the beginning: the primitive, non-state oriented spokesman for man and nature.

We must continue our avant garde and ancient function of disruption, and must not be seduced into settling for an easy status as patronized exceptions who prove the rule of an as yet unrealized liberation for all.

(Thus even to subscribe to the present volume is to risk the loss of poetic identity and freedom. *These words are written at risk.*)

I see a poetics of liberation as not only mystical and metaphysical, not only linguistic and structural, but as inseparable from the poet's use of his or her own presence (if not the poetry *per se*) to oppose large and small outrages against humanity and life itself.

The present and future of poetry involve the revival of a genuinely prophetic tradition that frees us (or forces us) to see/say things that would otherwise be concealed, left silent.

"When a man has a reason to scream, and cannot though he wants to—he has achieved the greatest scream." (Menachem Mendel of Kotsk, per Abraham Heschel.)

"The voice of Honest Indignation is the voice of God." (W. Blake.)

Bibliography

Poems for the Game of Silence. New York: Dial Press, 1971; New York: New Directions, 1975.
Poland/1931. New York: New Directions, 1974.
A Seneca Journal. New York: New Directions, 1978.
Vienna Blood. New York: New Directions, 1980.
6 Horse Songs for 4 Voices. New York: New Wilderness Audiographics, 1978.
Technicians of the Sacred. Garden City: Doubleday-Anchor, 1968.
Shaking the Pumpkin. Garden City: Doubleday-Anchor, 1972.
A Big Jewish Book. Garden City: Doubleday-Anchor, 1978.
Pre-Faces, & Other Writings. New York: New Directions, 1981.
That Data Strain. New York: New Directions, 1983.
Symposium of the Whole. Berkeley: University of California Press, 1984.
New Selected Poems 1970-1985. New York: New Directions, 1986.
Khurbn & Other Poems. New York: New Directions, 1989.

Albert, Barry, editor. *Vort*, 7 [A special issue devoted to David Antin and Jerome Rothenberg]. Silver Springs, Maryland: Vort Works Ink, 1975.
Kostelanetz, Richard. "Jerome Rothenberg," *The Old Poetries and the New*. Ann Arbor, Michigan: University of Michigan Press, 1980.
Paul, Sherman. *In Search of the Primitive: Rereading David Antin, Jerome Rothenberg and Gary Snyder*. Baton Rouge and London: Louisiana State University Press, 1986.
Polkinhorn, Harry. *Jerome Rothenberg: A Descriptive Bibliography*. Jefferson, North Carolina, and London: McFarland Publishing Company, and *American Poetry* Contemporary Bibliography Series, 1988.
Rothenberg, Jerome. "A Dialogue on Oral Poetry with William Spanos," *Boundary* 2, III/2 (Spring 1975).

Reading Modern American Science Fiction

Samuel R. Delany

The first World Science Fiction Convention in 1939 was attended by less than 50 science fiction readers, science fiction writers, and science fiction artists. In 1978 at the World Science Fiction Convention in Phoenix, Arizona, over 6,000 readers, writers, and artists filled up two large luxury hotels.

In 1951 some 15 texts were published in the United States which could be called science fiction novels. These included several magazine serializations published over several months and some books of science fiction short stories which, because the stories were related to one another, were labeled by the publisher as "SF novels." In 1979 there were 1,291 science fiction books published in the United States; of these, 689 were books appearing for the first time. The rest were reprints or reissues of older work. Approximately 15 percent of all new fiction published in the United States in 1979 was science fiction.

These figures are, of course, points on a growth curve. But if you study the whole of the curve, not just these highly contrasting points, you will be struck by how smooth that growth is. We might expect that certain pop-cultural phenomena, such as the extraordinary success in 1968 of Kubrik's film *2001: A Space Odyssey* (in its first three months, despite intially bad reviews, it outgrossed *The Sound of Music*, till then the biggest money-making film of the time) or the even more successful *Star Wars* of 1977 (the biggest money-making film in history, period), to cause the curve to cease its steady slope and go soaring.

But the slope remains constant through both years. It rises, but it rises smoothly, propelled by its own autonomous and coherent forces. The suggestion seems to be that the steady growth of the science fiction field of writers, readers, and texts from time to time causes a big growth jump in related fields, such as science fiction film or science fiction television shows—but not the other way around.

We can ask, then, what causes this steady, autonomous growth in science fiction. We can also ask what this growth can tell us about the overall "scene of writing," as the post-structuralist critics sometimes call it.

To answer these questions, we start with the observation that science fiction seems to be a kind of fantastic narrative. But then, what is the nature of the fantastic in matters narrative anyway?

If we step back from the tradition of "realistic fiction" ("bourgeois fiction" those same post-structuralists would designate it) that is local to Western Europe and the colonized strata of society in the Americas after 1700, we can say that, historically speaking—and in world terms rather than Western terms—the *vast* majority of human narrative production is fantastic rather than realistic in much the same way that the vast majority of human art production is abstract and aspect-emphasizing rather than representational and reproductive. Bounded by the Western cultural horizon, we forget the limitations that must be placed on the myth, the folk-tale, the fairy-tale, the tall story, or the entertaining lie, to reduce it to the particular kind of lie whose entertainment value comes solely from the fact that, when read with the eyes at the proper squint (we call it "the suspension of disbelief"), it might possiby be mistaken for a true account.

But again: What marks a narrative as fantastic?

Most human narratives describe some kind of thinking being moving, and acting and reacting *in a world*—which is to say, there is a figure *and* there is a ground.

What identifies the fantastic, and distinguishes it from the realistic, is that the world (or ground) against which the thinking being (or figure) moves, acts and reacts, operates differently from the immediate world of the hearer/speaker or, indeed, the reader/writer.

Take the Tsimshian Indian myth that the French anthropologist Claude Lévi-Strauss somewhat ironically titled *La Geste d'Asdiwal*. In this myth, bears turn into women, birds turn into men, humans can talk underwater, seals and mice can communicate with humans, and a single rotten berry can feed two women for a whole winter. As well, birds have children by human women and the sun is a god whose daughter marries a man. Arguably the last set of propositions are "believed" by the Tsimshians, on some level or other, as "true." *I* do not believe that any Tsimshians believe the former set encompasses occurrences they will encounter in the course of their own lives. The Tsimshians are much too familiar with mice, seals, birds, berries, and bears, as well as drownings in the Skenna and the Nass rivers— more familiar with them than you and I—to expect such goings on from nature: the *world* of the Tsimshian *geste* operates by notably different rules than their day-to-day world, though Asdiwal's mother-in-law, his wife, Asdiwal himself, and his child seem more or less identifiable with the average Tsimshians mother and daughter, father and son.

The assumption has always been, at least in the West, with its local tradition of realistic fiction, that the different machinations of the fantastic world (or ground) are, *vis-à-vis* the real world of the teller/hearer, the writer/reader, arbitrary. Even the occasional attempt to psychoanlayze the fantastic in various western narrative texts presupposes that the fantastic elements are simply the unconscious detritus of desire—rather than useful and autonomous responses (with both conscious and unconscious aspects) to a specific cultural reality.

But what could be useful in the specific fantastic response of our society to science fiction? Why would a writer pursue the creation of the fantastic, in science fiction, seriously?

One of the ways that all narratives make their point is by presenting characters who undertake various endeavors. These characters either succeed or they fail. If the narrative is realistic, then the ground against which the success or failure occurs presumably operates by the laws governing our real world. But to the extent the ground (or world) effects that success or failure, the character will be seen as having adjusted to the world in some way in the case of success, or as not having adjusted to it in the case of failure. In short, realistic fiction has a subtle and insidious way of consigning all humans to one of two categories: slaves, who adjust to the real world, or madmen and madwomen who are defeated by it and are mad by the fact that, indeed, they have not adjusted.

If, however, the narrative world operates in some way *differently* from the way the real world is perceived to operate, then the failure or success of the character no longer implies the one-to-one correspondence with adjustment or lack of adjustment to the real. Indeed, it would seem that to talk about true human freedom of an existential order, the world itself must be seen as free and capable of change, of options, of alternatives; and change, options, and alternatives are, of course, what science fiction is about.

If the fantastic narrative is to be a useful, conscientious, and sensitive response to society, then we cannot be surprised when the fantasies of one culture differ from another. The fantasies of the Tsimshian Indians, in a rural society that must deal with seal hunting, candlestick fishing, periodic famines, and floods of the Skeena and the Nass, are not going to be the fantasies of a people living in a high-technology, urban-oriented society—not if both fantasies are going to be useful, coherent, autonomous responses to the particular societies.

We can, if we want, view the growth in science fiction, from practically zero percent to 15 percent of the national fictive production of the United States as a *sui generis* eruption at odds with the prevailing tradition of realism, in the same way we can view the growth of abstract painting in the West as a *sui generis* revolt against an earlier, prevailing realistic tradition. But a more historically sensitive view must take cognizance in the history of Western painting, for example, of the famous 1907 visit Picasso made with Apollinaire to the Trocadero, where he first became aware of the tremendous aesthetic force of African masks. Matisse had already been profoundly impressed by similar African sculptural works; and though there were always elements of abstraction in even the most representational Western art, the impetus toward the Western abstract movements of the 20th century, such as Cubism and Futurism, grew out of this specific encounter with an extra-European, older, and, in world terms, far more pervasive artistic tradition. The pioneering abstract artists of this century took that extra-European tradition and contoured it specifically to their local Western cultures. Nevertheless, the abstract movement that today dominates Western painting is much better seen, in world-historical terms, as the encroachment of a pervasive world aesthetic tradition on the local realistic tradition of Western painting, and which has, in many ways, by now almost swamped that realistic tradition. Similarly, the growth of science fiction may best be seen as an encroachment of a world narrative tradition on the local tradition of "bourgeois" fiction—specifically contoured by the particular social forms of our culture, yet nevertheless only completely comprehensible in light of the world tradition of fantastic narrative.

We have spoken of coherence as an aspect of these fantastic responses. In science fiction the principles of Western science supply that coherence, just as the particular Tsimshian principles of hunting, fishing, and even architecture and family organization supply the coherence to the Tsimshian mythology, or as other similar principles supply them to the mythologies of other non-Western cultures. In the words of the Australian science fiction critic John Foyster, "The best science fiction does not contradict what is known to be known." But what is known to be known in the West is a very small part of what may be the case in the world, the cosmos, and it is in this much larger field—which contains many possibilities both for coherence *and* contradiction—that science fiction spreads its wings . . . or fires its jets.

The particular kinds of alterations in the machinations of the world that science fiction endlessly suggests seem to be useful, or at any rate highly pleasurable, to more and more people; and the steady growth in the number of readers, writers, and texts seems to represent, more than anything else, the growth in the number of people who are learning how to respond to, recognize, and enjoy these alterations.

And it very much is a matter of learning.

No matter how seriously I talk about science fiction here, we all know there are people who simply *won't* read science fiction. These people suffer only from snobbism and their affliction doesn't really interest me. But there are many people who honestly *can't* read science fiction, which is to say that they have picked up several science fiction stories and tried to read them, only to find that much of the text simply didn't make sense. From time to time, these readers have been very sophisticated readers of literary texts. Several times now I have had the chance to work with such readers, reading science fiction texts slowly, phrase by phrase, sentence by sentence, checking on what has been responded to and what has not. When you read science fiction texts in this manner with such readers, it is clear that their difficulty is almost entirely in their failure to create for themselves the alternate world—the different ground—that gives the story's incidents their sense. While these readers may have no trouble imagining a Balzac provincial printing office, a Dickens boarding school, or a Jane Austen sitting room, they are absolutely stopped by, say, the most ordinary contemporary science fiction writer's "monopole magnet mining operations in the outer asteroid belt of Delta Cygni." And the stoppage, the failure is not so much a failure of the imaginative faculties as it is a failure to respond word by word to the text. Let's examine that failure with this particular textual fragment.

Monopole magnet. . . . First of all, most of the readers I worked with had no idea what monopole magnets might be. Monopole magnets do not exist—at least as far as we know. All magnets that we have ever discovered or created on Earth are dipole: they have two poles, a north and a south pole. If you put like poles together, the poles push each other apart; if you put unlike poles together, they attract one another. For this reason the mention of monopole magnets means that in this universe a completely new kind of magnet has been discovered. And this suggests , in turn, that there may be a whole new branch of electromagnetic technology (every electrical motor, electrical generator, or transformer would be an example of current electromagnetic technology), which would then have to be reconceived in the world, or worlds, of this particular science fiction story.

Monopole magnet mining operations. . . . I had one reader who, besides not knowing what monopole magnets might be, assumed that whatever they were, the mining was done *with* the magnets rather than *for* the magnets, even though a term like "gold mining operations" or even "uranium mining operations" would not have created the same confusion. (This reader had read the phrase according to the model of "strip-mining operations" or "pellet-mining operations." Note that this reading is actually somewhat *more* technical than the writer's intended one. The point is that we are dealing primarily with a failure to respond to language, not a failure to know facts about the world. Many scientists cannot read science fiction either.) Needless to say, this reader would be perfectly lost in any further mention of the goings-on in these mines.

Monopole magnet mining operations in the outer asteroid belt. . . . Another reader, already as confused as the others over *monopole magnet mining,* thought that an asteroid belt was "a ring of stones around a world." Well, if you substitute "sun" for "world," you might describe it that way. When I questioned this reader further, I discovered the mental picture the reader had was that the stones "were not very big, maybe a few feet or so across," and that they were "packed together" so that they were only "a few feet or few inches apart." For this reader the mines were "probably tunnels that went from stone to stone. Maybe the stones were even in the tunnels." And what about the word "outer"? Over half these readers thought "outer" meant that the mining took place on the outside of this wall of stones rather than inside it. And Delta Cygni? Maybe that was "an area of space" or "a planet." Patiently and repeatedly I had to explain to these readers, several of whom incidentally had published books and/or articles on various literary subjects, that the asteroid belt in our own solar system was a ring of stones that went around the sun at a greater distance than the Earth and that, though a few of the stones were as large as a mile or even ten miles in diameter, most of them were much smaller, pea-size or dust-size. I also had to reiterate that even the dust-size ones were hundreds, or even thousands, of miles apart. They had to be told that Delta Cygni was a star, a sun, in the constellation of Cyegnus (the Swan), the fourth star named in the constellation. "How do you know that it's the fourth one named?" Because *delta* is the fourth letter of the Greek alphabet and there's an astronomical naming convention (i.e., a language convention). . . .

Nor was it a matter of simply saying these things once. They had to be repeated and questioned and repeated again. "What do you mean, a sun? I thought you said a star?" Star and sun are two words in the language of astronomy for the same class of object, i.e., still another language convention. They had to be told that "outer asteroid belt" was the writer's stenographic method for, first, re-minding you that our sun has only *one* asteroid belt and at the same time suggesting that Delta Cygni might be a star with *two* asteroid belts—one farther out than the other. "Well, how much farther out?" There is no way to be sure, of course, but one can make a guess that it will be many millions of miles. "Many *millions* of miles?" They had to be told that it was in this outer asteroid belt rather than in the inner one that these mining operations were going on. "But how does the writer *know* there are two? How do *you* know?" The writer does not know. This is a language convention for *saying* that there are. This is a fictive text, and there is no constraint on what is said in fiction to be true.

These particular readers were perfectly capable of negotiating the 19th-century novel, whether it was written by a Russian count on a family estate outside Moscow, or by a tubercular parson's daugh-ter living with her sisters on the edge of an English moor, or by an ex-printer in Paris who, having penned nothing but pot-boilers till age 30, decided to write something more ambitious. Yet for these same readers a sentence like "The stars are suns, many with planets like our own" did not call up a clear concrete visualization laid out to the proper scale of the planetary, stellar, and galactic organization of the universe. Rather, it was simply a muzzy and confusing statement associated with the vast and impossible complexities of "all that scien-tific stuff" which they had tried to avoid all their lives.

In the 19th century Sir Arthur Conan Doyle, whose Doctor

Challenger stories are some of the clearest examples of proto-science fiction, was surprisingly aware of the factual side of this problem. In one Sherlock Holmes story—the same one, incidentally, in which we learn that Holmes takes cocaine—Dr. Watson is astonished to learn that his friend Holmes, who can infer so much from cat-hairs, heel-prints, and the like, does not know that the Earth moves around the sun—that he is ignorant, in the good doctor's words, of "the entire Copernican theory of the solar system." Holmes explains, however disingenuous that explanation reads today, that while cat-hairs, heel-prints, etc., affect his present life and livelihood, it makes absolutely no difference to him at all whether the Earth moves around the sun or the sun moves around the Earth. Therefore he doesn't have to know such facts, and what's more, even though Dr. Watson has informed him of the truth of the matter, he intends to forget it as quickly as he can. If Holmes's explanation is true, what we can say with certainty is that Holmes would be as lost in the monopole magnet mining operations of that outer asteroid belt as any of our 19th-century novel readers.

But the inability to visualize scenes on the astronomical level does not exhaust the language failure of these readers. Though perfectly comfortable following the social analysis of a Balzac, a Jane Austen—or even a Durkheim, Marx, or Weber—they are completely at sea when they come across the description of a character who, upon going to the drugstore to purchase a package of depilatory pads, "inserted his credit card in the purchasing slot; his bill was transferred to the city accounting house to be recorded against the accumulated credit from his primary and secondary jobs." Such a sentence suggests a whole reorganization of society along lines of credit, commerce, computerization, and labor patterns. Certainly, from a single sentence no one could be expected to come up with the details of that reorganization, but one should be able to see at least the shadow of its general outline. And that shadow should provide the science-fictional *frisson* that is the pleasure of the science-fiction vision. The readers I worked with, however, were likely to respond to such a sentence: "But why didn't he pay for it with the money in his pocket?" And they were very surprised when I told them that the character probably carried no money. "But how do you know?" Such readers, used to the given world of mundane fiction, tend to overlay the *fabulata* (the fantastic elements in the narrative) of science fiction on top of that given world and see only confusion. They do not yet know the particular syntactical rules by which these *fabulata* replace, displace, and reorganize the elements of the mundane world *into new worlds*. All the practice they have had in locating specific areas of the given world that mundane fiction deals with has given them no practice at all in creating imaginative alternatives. The hints, the suggestions, the throwaways, and even sometimes the broadest strokes by which the skilled science fiction writer suggests the structure of the alternate world do not come together for them in any coherent vision, but only blur, confuse, and generally muddy the vision of the given world of mundane fiction they are used to. Reading science fiction texts with these readers, I was able to bring them to a point of understanding for the particular texts we read. But any feeling that they were now better prepared to read more science fiction texts was about equally mixed with the feeling that the complexities of science fiction were even more daunting than they had thought till then.

Science fiction is a sub-language of the greater language it is written in. Like most languages, it is best learned early, by repeated exposure. That it must be learned in the way languages are learned is perhaps the greatest steadying influence on that rising growth curve we began with. When a *2001* or a *Star Wars* in film, or a *Star Trek* on television, becomes a great success, this language-like aspect of science fiction is what prevents millions of people from simply running into their local bookstore, picking up any paperback with a picture on its cover similar to some scene in the film (and, yes, publishers frequently try to make their science fiction bookcovers suggest successful films, even when there's no real connection), and discovering the wonder, the adventure, and the stimulation science fiction's many alternate worlds provide. Certainly the wonder, the adventure, and the stimulation are there; but access to them, if one has had no real experience *reading* science fiction, may turn out to require a daunting struggle with a text where a string of words such as "her world exploded" is not a metaphor for a lady's emotional state (but means, rather, that a planet, belonging to a woman, blew up); where "he turned on his left side" does not indicate insomniac tossings at night (but rather that a man activates with a switch the circuitry in his sinistral flank); where "he rinsed his face with the trickle from the fresh water tap" is the writer's subtle way of explaining that in this world the apartments have not only fresh-water taps but salt-water taps as well, and that in this world the fresh-water supply is low; or where "the door dilated" is the writer's way of suggesting a specific level of technology capable of constructing mechanically operable iris-aperture doorways.

I have written here about science fiction in the most general terms possible (its relation to the larger tradition of world narrative production) and in the most specific terms possible (science fiction's particular use of language). Much of what is most interesting in science fiction to the general reader, however, takes place somewhere between these two extremes. This essay began with a mention of the World Science Fiction Convention—usually held in early September in some large American or, occasionally, European city. But there are over 70 science fiction conventions given in various cities of the United States each year, where a hundred to 2,000-3,000 readers will get together for parties, programs and panels, and talks, formal and informal, with whatever local science fiction writers happen to be living in the area. Though there is usually an entrance fee, these conventions are strictly non-commercial ventures. If a writer has to travel to get to the convention, the convention committee may reimburse the writer for expenses, but that is the end of any payment for the writer's time and talk. The conventions are traditionally organized by groups of enthusiastic readers who want to provide a formal structure where that enthusiasm can be shared. These science fiction conventions, incidentally, should *not* be confused with the frequent conventions based on the television show, *Star Trek*, or some of the successful science fiction films, conventions inspired by the real science fiction conventions. These, of course, are highly commercial and charge high entrance fees; they feature actors rather than writers—actors well-paid for their appearances. They are put on by businessmen who want to make money. And the most important part of the *real* science fiction convention, the mingling of writers and readers on a pretty even footing, is not to be seen at these commercial conventions at all.

Science fiction conventions have been part of the genre since 1936. Because of them, the reader-writer relations in science fiction is rather different from the relation between reader and writer in most other areas of writing. Besides conventions, there are many hundreds of amateur "fanzines" (magazines) published each year by science fiction readers, containing articles on aspects of the genre, the work of individual writers, sometimes book reviews, and for the most part letters from other readers, frequently responding to what was in the last issue. Often professional science fiction writers will write articles in the fanzines (for no pay); as I said, these fanzines exist by the hundreds. Most are more or less clearly mimeographed, with from five to 75 pages, though some are merely a page or two of pale purple hectography. A very few are printed with elegant art work and shiny covers. But the overall effect of the conventions and fanzines on the genre is that science fiction writers have a specific sense of an involved and committed audience to a degree that very few other genres of writing can provide for the writer.

Any standard history of modern American science fiction talks a great deal about editors. To know that modern American science fiction *has* a history is to know that editor Hugo Gernsback more or less began modern American science fiction with pulp magazines in the 1920s, and that editor John W. Campbell made vast changes in the field when he took over *Astounding Magazine* in 1937. But the fame of these two editors is only an emblem of the fact that, just as the writer-reader relation in science fiction is unique, so is the writer-editor relation.

Something as simple as magazine-production schedules versus book-production schedules has made the critic-writer relation very different in science fiction from the critic-writer relation in the rest of American fiction. With most realistic fiction, publishers go to a great deal of effort to coordinate the appearance of reviews with the appearance of the books themselves. A good review in a wide-circulation newspaper can significantly affect the sales of an ordinary novel—if that review appears the week that novel arrives in the bookstores. Whether they revel in it or abhor it, professional reviewers are aware of this. Both the writers and the critics know that the critics may have a significant effect on the writers' livelihood. And it colors the criticism throughout. Large-circulation newspapers, by and large, ignore most science fiction; the professional science fiction magazines, where most new science fiction is reviewed, all have a three to five-month printing schedule, which means that reviews always appear three to five months after the science fiction book has been published. Reviewed or unreviewed, a new book's sales tend to reach its peak in the first six to 12 weeks, after which those sales level off. This is true both of the best-seller and the rank failure, of any genre. But once that peak has passed, very little any reviewer says will have much effect on actual sales. This means that, by comparison with the rest of American fiction, the professional science fiction critic has little or no power to affect actual sales. And this means that the professional science fiction critic can be at once more passionate *and* more disinterested. The passion and disinterest gives professional science fiction criticism a very different flavor from most journalistic criticism, and contours the writer-critic relation in the way we mentioned above. The critic-reader relation is also different for science fiction. By and large, the critics of ordinary fiction see themselves as tasteful arbiters of what their readers will or will not spend money on. In science fiction, since the money has been spent well before the criticism appears, the science fiction critics tend to see themselves as educators to the vast number of young amateur writers who write for the hundreds of fanzines published around the country.

But all of these differences will make more sense to a reader who has a grip on the central field, an axis whose poles—one in the world tradition of fantastic narrative and one grounded in the actual sentences of the science fiction text—I have written of here.

Some Modern Science Fiction of Interest

Niven, Larry. *Ringworld*. New York: Ballantine Books, 1970.
Disch, Thomas M. *334*. New York: Avon Books, 1974.
Malzberg, Barry N. *Galaxies*. Moonachie, New Jersey: Pyramid Publications, 1975.
Russ, Joanna. *The Female Man*. New York: Bantam Books, 1975.
Pohl, Frederik. *Man Plus*. New York: Bantam Books, 1976.
Russ, Joanna. *The Two of Them*. New York: Berkley Books, 1978.
Coover, Arthur Byron. *An East Wind Coming*. New York: Berkley Books, 1979.
Disch, Thomas M. *On Wings of Song*. New York: St. Martin's Press, 1979.
Bishop, Michael. *Catacomb Years*. New York: Berkley Books, 1980.
Wolfe, Gene. *The Island of Doctor Death and Other Studies*. New York: Pocket Books, 1980.

Book Art

A Conversation among Jamake Highwater, Richard Kostelanetz,
Lucy Lippard, and Paul Zelevansky

Kostelanetz: Our subject today is book art, which is to say the book is not just a vehicle for information or for literary representation but as an art object in itself, usually because the form of the book has been treated in a rather distinctive, original fashion. With me are three people who have been involved with book art in different ways: Lucy Lippard, who has published fiction and art criticism, most recently about a phenomenon that she calls "artists' books," in addition to producing exhibition catalogues and highly innovative books of her own; Jamake Highwater, a writer on music and American Indian art and also a novelist, who produced and designed *Rock and Other Four-Letter Words* (1969), which I regard among the masterpieces of recent book design; Paul Zelevansky who has, among other things, produced two extraordinary books that combine visual image and written words. The first is *The Book of Takes* (1976); the second is called *Sweep* (1979). Book art is something I do as well.

The three people who are with me today approach the subject of bookmaking from radically different directions. So perhaps it is best to begin, Jamake Highwater, with a basic question: What is the subject here, and how have you handled it?

Highwater: I dealt with this subject about a decade or more ago, as you say, but it is still very fresh in my mind. My interest in bookmaking was brought about by looking at codices, the books of old that were made by ancient peoples, in which the notion of successive pages was not so important as the entire surface of the object being engraved or painted. So I regarded the surface of the page and the succession of the pages, the very edge of the page, as a kind of continuity like a Japanese fan and to reveal something in terms of succession and of overall momentum which had not really been very much the emphasis or focus of the Western concept of bookmaking.

Kostelanetz: That's probably because of limitations in the conventional technology of book manufacture. It is very easy for a printer to print in signatures of 16 or 32 pages, which are then cut apart and bound together. A book in the form of a fan or an accordion is harder for the printer's machinery to do. But then in *Rock and Other Four-Letter Words* you dealt with notions of the images in succession.

Highwater: Not only images in succession but the way in which the eye is affected and how images are implemented by the eye. I feel that reading is not just an activity of absorbing words but is also a process of actually *seeing* them. I think that there is a direct relationship between the word as it is seen and the image that is seen. In other words, I think that books are a little like looking at painting.

Kostelanetz: In the *Rock* book you mixed photographs with graphic drawings and charts, as well as written text and all kinds of typography. Do you regard these as individual units that were then pulled together under the theme of rock music in the 1960s?

Highwater: Well, not really. The most basic answer to that question is that I was dealing with a subject, rock music, which I felt was ineffable. I didn't feel that it was well-suited to normal syntax. I thought that rock music needed something else, and when I sat down with the notion of writing a definitive work on rock, I realized it was quite impossible. I thought that rock was a very important movement, and I thought that there were all kinds of elements and attitudes that I just simply couldn't convey through realistic syntax. So I began to collect materials in much the way that an artist who is making a collage begins to collect materials related in some way to me or to the people I had talked to (and I talked to just about everyone in the field). As I assembled them, I really thought I was going to assemble a normal, everyday book. But it wouldn't work.

Kostelanetz: But is your book then like a visual art exhibition?

Highwater: No, the book is more like a succession of ideas that make themselves visible through whatever materials best express those ideas. It worked like this: if I found that 1900 typography suggested something to me in relationship to some photographs that either Linda Eastman had taken or that I had found along the way, I assembled these things so that they would have an interaction that expressed an idea that couldn't be expressed simply through written words.

Kostelanetz: Lucy Lippard, you have written books of criticism, such as *Changing* (1971) and *Six Years* (1973), in addition to writing about artists' books. What is your conception of what is inventive in bookmaking today?

Lippard: Well, maybe the most inventive thing that could happen in art bookmaking is to get people to read the books. I think that an awful lot of books about art and by artists are illegible, unreadable, and self-indulgent.

Kostelanetz: Jamake spoke about how he made his book readable, so to speak, by introducing pictures along with text as well as inventive typographies. How do you make your books more readable?

Lippard: I like to leave a lot up to the reader in the sense that I think when anybody looks at art or reads a book, an awful lot of the reader/spectator goes into it and fills in the gaps. I like the notion of a book with a lot of spaces for the reader to really fall into with her or his own experience so what the writer is trying to do is amplified and the book becomes a kind of collaboration. I see the book as a kind of dialogue. And that can be done in endless different ways. It doesn't have to be merely verbal or visual in a sense.

Kostelanetz: How have you done it?

Lippard: It depends on whether I'm writing my own things or about other people's work. *Six Years* is not that interesting physically as a book, though its structure is peculiar. It's simply a bibliography; I used to make a living doing bibliographies and indexes. So instead of writing a book *about* the art, I decided an equally important critical function would be to let the art speak for itself.

Kostelanetz: It's a critical book in the form of a bibliography.

Lippard: An annotated bibliography filled with original material—actual works, interviews, and comments. I was actually dying to put *everything* into it, but the publisher turned down about two-thirds of the book. They just said, "You must be kidding. We can't publish a 900-page book." So it went back down to a more selective thing. I wanted people to see the way the art object had, from 1966 to 1972, literally dematerialized and come closer to a book. There was a final meeting point where my book met the art, at the end of the last chapter, coming full circle. Art became criticism and the critical format became art.

Kostelanetz: In the book was a chronology with lots of examples and with commentaries—some commentaries of your own and

commentaries by others that you quoted. The book was a grand
mosaic.

Lippard: Yes, it was a collage. I am a great believer in collage as
perhaps the only way an artist in this day and age can communicate
everything that is there, because we live in the midst of such a weird
juxtaposition of values and objects and information coming at us so
fast that we can only see in fragments. For instance, I find it a very
surrealist or Dada experience to be here as a woman in this particular
patriarchal society, or as a socialist in this particular capitalist society.
My life seems to be a sort of collage.

Kostelanetz: And therefore your novel is a collage as well.

Lippard: Very much so.

Kostelanetz: Now how did you do those exhibition catalogues?

Lippard: That was again the idea that the reader ought to be able
to choose, to throw out what she or he didn't want to keep. I did a series
of exhibitions, beginning in 1969, in which the catalogues were five-
by-seven-inch cards; each artist designed a card of her or his own
which might be a piece in itself. At the beginning I did a few cards of
my own where I just played textual games because they were not
meant to be sequential. I didn't number them. If you read *this* card
first, it's okay; if you read *that* card first, it's okay, and so forth. A
change in sequence would change the content.

Kostelanetz: You've also written about the phenomenon of "artists' books." How do you conceive of this activity?

Lippard: When artists' books first appeared in the late 1960s, I saw
them as a marvellous way for visual artists, who usually make
expensive objects, to make things that were cheaper and more accessible to a broader public—where if someone didn't have $20,000 to buy
your painting, you could still offer them your aesthetic ideas through
some other medium. In the book, the pages might be seen as walls of
an exhibition—or as pages of a letter to the viewer. It's an intimate
medium, and less intimidating.

Kostelanetz: Paul Zelevansky, you have produced two extraordinary books that combine visual image and written word.

Zelevansky: I think I come to this from a different place than
either Jamake or Lucy; that is, I have been a practicing painter so my
relationship to looking at the page of a book is not an exclusively
literary one. I'll explain what I mean by that: to approach a blank
canvas (and by extension a blank page) is a process of working and
seeing through the edges of the frame. Therefore, the white space is

an open space with potentially unlimited scale. Depending on what you put on it and how you work with the edges of it, it becomes a solid ground, or an open, floating space, or anything you want to make of it. Whereas in a traditional book, which has a block of type on it which you read from left to right or from right to left depending on what the language is, there is no essential space on the page; it's simply a plate for the type to lie on and there is no reference to the edges of the page except in terms of where the page numbers are. So this was never an issue with me because I always saw the pages as if they were paintings. So that's the place I started from, and that is the place I start from every time I approach putting together a book: that the page is a completely flexible space and I'm always aware of what the edges are doing in relation to what's inside them.

Kostelanetz: But in a book the pages go in sequence.

Zelevansky: The sequence of the pages is another problem, which has to do with the description of time, moving from page to page or from event to event. But the essential problem, the thing I think I am interested in more than anything else, is the opening up of the space of that page.

Kostelanetz: Opening up—in what sense?

Zelevansky: If you place a very simple image on top of or even behind a block of type on a standard page, you change almost every relationship on the page except the literal content. I see all these things very concretely; I have a very physical sense of where each element is placed. In essence, you can create a hole in the page where things can float free and attach themselves to other things. And if you happen to be talking about a hole or happen to be talking about movement in a direction, you can literally and kinetically describe it visually as well as through the words. I'm interested in creating the fullest possible expression of that: a working integration of words and images where each element is capable of reflecting and responding to the others.

Kostelanetz: But the book is still a sequential medium. Can your books be read from any point in both directions or must they be read from front to back?

Zelevansky: I suppose that because I started as a painter, part of me is very traditional in relationship to books. Whatever complexity I create on the page or whatever complexity is involved in the sequence of pages, I'm not as interested in changing the sequential form of reading. Going from page to page is fine with me. There may be many structures within the book which repeat and enclose it, many interconnecting themes, but the essential reading is from page to page. This is true even though many pages are visually resolved and complete in themselves. For me there's enough to deal with on a single page without also opening that box up. In many ways, the fact that a book is made up of pages that must be turned sequentially is its least significant detail. The process of reading is a good deal more subtle than that.

Kostelanetz: So we agree then that our subject is dealing with the book in a different, innovative artistic way. Do you find that there is a limit to what printers can do? Do you find that there is a limit in the medium itself—that you wanted to make books that are very large— let's say, four feet by three feet—and that are very hard to print? Did you want your book, Jamake, to be in a larger format as well as a pocketsized paperback format?

Highwater: I had wanted it to be in a larger format, and it was supposed to be in a larger format, but the publishers became frightened. They were very enthusiastic about the book at first. It was a good time to do this kind of book, late in 1969, when publishers felt we authors knew something they didn't. (Now publishers are quite sure they know something we don't.) So it was easier to convince publishers to do things that were slightly unusual, but then they became confused, I think, because I constantly told them, "What I want to do is sensualize the book." And they'd look at me like: "What does that mean?"

Kostelanetz: You wanted to give your book a quality that books traditionally hadn't had.

Highwater: Yes. Even in the case of illuminated Bibles or when books were created by hand, there were still the restrictions of Western mentality. Implicit in the West was the notion that each page is separate and that each page is part of a syntactical activity in which words mean things and if things can't be named, they don't have meaning. I disapprove of that. As I said, because of my interest in codices and the painted books that were part of oral traditions rather than written traditions, I was very anxious to make Western ideas fit into an alternatively opened, sensual notion of communication.

So I wanted to change even the photographs I used. I don't like photographs per se, because they are a statement of a Western kind of reality, and I feel this kind of reality is arbitrary. So in the book I cut apart the photographs and opened them up and closed them down and even had photographs continue from page to page so that the edge of the page became part of the photograph. I just wanted to reexamine the whole notion of space and time in books.

Lippard: One of the books that best accomplishes this is a mass-produced book and not a small press "artist's book," which is interesting. But to go back briefly, one of the limitations on books that Richard didn't mention was money. I don't think that a three-foot-by-four-foot book makes much sense. It's no longer a book you're making. I like my books all to be paperback, cheap, and pocketable, portable, disposable. But the book I'm talking about is Judy Chicago's *The Dinner Party* (1979). Judy Chicago is trying to go back to illumination, but within a mass-production situation. She has a very large audience, she has a big publisher and so forth. But the book is literally an illuminated manuscript—both volumes, but especially the second one.

Kostelanetz: Now *The Dinner Party* is about an exhibition—to be more precise, about the origins of an exhibition with a particular theme.

Lippard: The exhibition and the book are about the same thing. They simply treat the subject two different ways. The theme of the exhibition is the history of womankind from scratch, from the Great Goddess right on through to Georgia O'Keeffe. It's a huge triangular table sculpture, each wing is 50 feet long, and there are 39 women represented with plates and table settings—each one on a needlework runner with the woman's name. And another 999 women are represented on floor tiles. The book takes up that historical/visual theme. Like the books we're all talking about, this book is a thing in itself; it is self-referential. The experience you get out of the book is the experience you get out of the book, not a second-hand experience of the sculpture/exhibition. What fascinates me, too, is why more artists don't work with this kind of mass-produced conception and why, when artists do, they are generally very unimaginative about it. I am talking about visual artists who have been through the whole art school trip.

Highwater: I liked *The Dinner Party* very much, by the way—but I got the feeling from it that we're right back to the Western concept of illustrating words.

Zelevansky: To go back to our discussion of your *Rock* book and how it worked, to me it was filmic in quality, something that is very much a Western development.

Highwater: But I feel film is, despite all its technology, an extremely primal approach to the way in which the mind works. I feel that film is about as close to oral tradition as you can get.

Kostelanetz: One of the themes of 20th-century literary criticism has been the impact of film on literature, critics usually citing the shifting points of view in William Faulkner's *As I Lay Dying* or the montage in John Dos Passos's *U.S.A.* as being an echo of cinematic form. What you're also suggesting now is that there are other ways that books can use cinematic form. The shift from image to image that you see in film or even from perspective to perspective in a single scene is comparable to your turning from page to page.

Highwater: Right.

Lippard: The turning of pages interests me very much, too. I work with a collective that publishes a magazine called *Heresies*, and we are constantly trying to figure out how the hell people *read* a magazine. The one fascinating thing about a book that film doesn't have is that you can go backwards and forwards; you can make different combinations. I mean, you put this element next to that one and it means one thing, then you put something else next to it and it means something else. You can jump back and forth. And a lot of people apparently read magazines from the back to the front. I do myself. So when you're structuring a magazine, you try to figure out: Should this go next to this, go next to that, go next to a third thing, or should this go over here? Are people going to read it that way or this way? Or do they go to the center? Or do they look at the pictures? And so I think books and magazines have much more possibility for variation and for innovation than film does, in a curious way, although I agree with you about the oral tradition and so forth.

Highwater: There are other things about film, too. When we talk about succession, I think it is terribly important to realize that index cards can do the same thing that film does. There's no binding, for instance, and, therefore, there's more opportunity for arbitrary succession. But when you think of Ingmar Bergman's films in which he admits that you're looking at a film, showing flash frames—3, 2, 1, and so on and so forth—that's like showing the edge of a page, admitting that a book is a book, admitting that one page follows another.

Kostelanetz: But there is also the notion as well that one of the powers of film and visual art is the after-image, the image that stays fixed in your head and makes this work of art different from other works of art. One of the things that book artists have scarcely gotten into is after-image, because after all the standard image of a book is the gray rectangle of horizontal lines with even, perpendicular edges. One of the things that I have tried to do, at least in my own book-art books, is to make a single image that will stick in your head. I think Paul Zelevansky has done that, too. This purpose is, of course, a visual art aesthetic transported into the book medium.

Lippard: One of the most popular things at Printed Matter, which is a little, nonprofit artists' book distribution company which I helped found in Manhattan, is flip books. People come in all the time wanting flip books. That is exactly the cinematic thing.

Kostelanetz: Can you describe a flip book in case someone doesn't know?

Zelevansky: A flip book is a series of images that change slightly from one to another.

Kostelanetz: They're usually printed on just one side of the two-page spread—just on the right-hand pages, say, so you can take the book in one hand, bend it with your thumb and let the pages flip across your thumb very rapidly to create the illusion of movement.

Zelevansky: You can take any book which has something close to the edge of the page and just flip it to see what happens in a flip book. It's a very primitive animated cartoon, in essence.

Lippard: And it was in fact the origin of movies.

Zelevansky: I wanted to mention a topic we began before—about money and readership. That is what I have found to be the greatest problem. There are certainly plenty of people doing things and there are distributors like Printed Matter and the Franklin Furnace (which is also in New York), and of course similar places across the country; but the general public and, I would think, even the general university-educated public is not really aware that people are doing books other than standard typographic books. I've had dealings with people who were in the book business, and they don't know anything about it at all.

Kostelanetz: My sense of our art is this: think of circles within circles. First, an artist communicates his idea, particularly a different idea, to his immediate friends, who become the first circle of communication. If those people still like it, they'll tell their friends, and so on. It grows like ripples. Indeed, the fact that lots of people are doing something in art, even though few people buy it, is usually an

indication that lots more people are going to buy it sometime soon.
That is, the word spreads that this new work is a legitimate art form,
that it should be taken seriously and purchased. The audience for it
increases. We know this from looking at the history of recent art. In
fact, one of the things we're doing now in this conversation is increasing the circumferences of circles, so to speak.

Lippard: Little ripples don't work too fast. You've got to have a
really good distribution system. One reason Printed Matter started
was the fact artists' books had no ways of getting out of studios and
galleries.

Kostelanetz: Well, the reason for that, which you pointed out, was
that the commercial publishers tend to do things in hardback editions
of at least 5,000 and in paperback of at least 10,000. Jamake Highwater's book was done in 50,000 by Bantam Books ten years ago. The kind
of books we're talking about are done mostly in much smaller editions;
therefore, the distribution system for small-edition books must be
developed in this country. This is the principal theme of what I call
"alternative publishing," which we've spoken about elsewhere in this
series.

Writing Extended

Richard Kostelanetz

From the beginning I decided that it would be better to do not
one thing but many things. Just out of college, I published reviews and
then critical essays. One of the latter became the occasion to edit an
anthology. And then came more reviews, more essays and more
anthologies, as well as the annual *Assemblings*. Around 1967 I began
a streak of creative work which I continued along with everything
else. Some people tell me that they prefer my criticism to my creative
work, while others prefer the anthologies or the *Assemblings*. More
than once I have heard admirers of one activity ask me why I "waste"
my time with the others; but since my career-advisers disagree with
one another, their advice has never been taken. It is my own opinion,
as a sometime critic of contemporary art, that my critical writing is
distinguished mostly by courage in discriminating among new works
and then a certain prognostic power; that my anthologies and *Assembling* are, in sum, a singular contribution, though collecting per se is
scarcely a major activity; and that the creative work is more remarkable and most likely to survive.

My intention has been to extend poetry and fiction into alternative formats and then into media other than printed pages and,
conversely, to discover how these other media could best be used for
publishing poetry and fiction. These two motives are obviously
related, if not entwined; and they extend as well from certain perceptions I had as a critic about the increasing limitations of commercial
book-publishing, especially for unconventional, experimental writing.

My first creative activity was visual poetry, where language is
enhanced visually, rather than syntactically or semantically. An
example is "Disintegration" that has appeared in many anthologies, as
well as my own *Visual Language* (1970). My initial aim was the creation

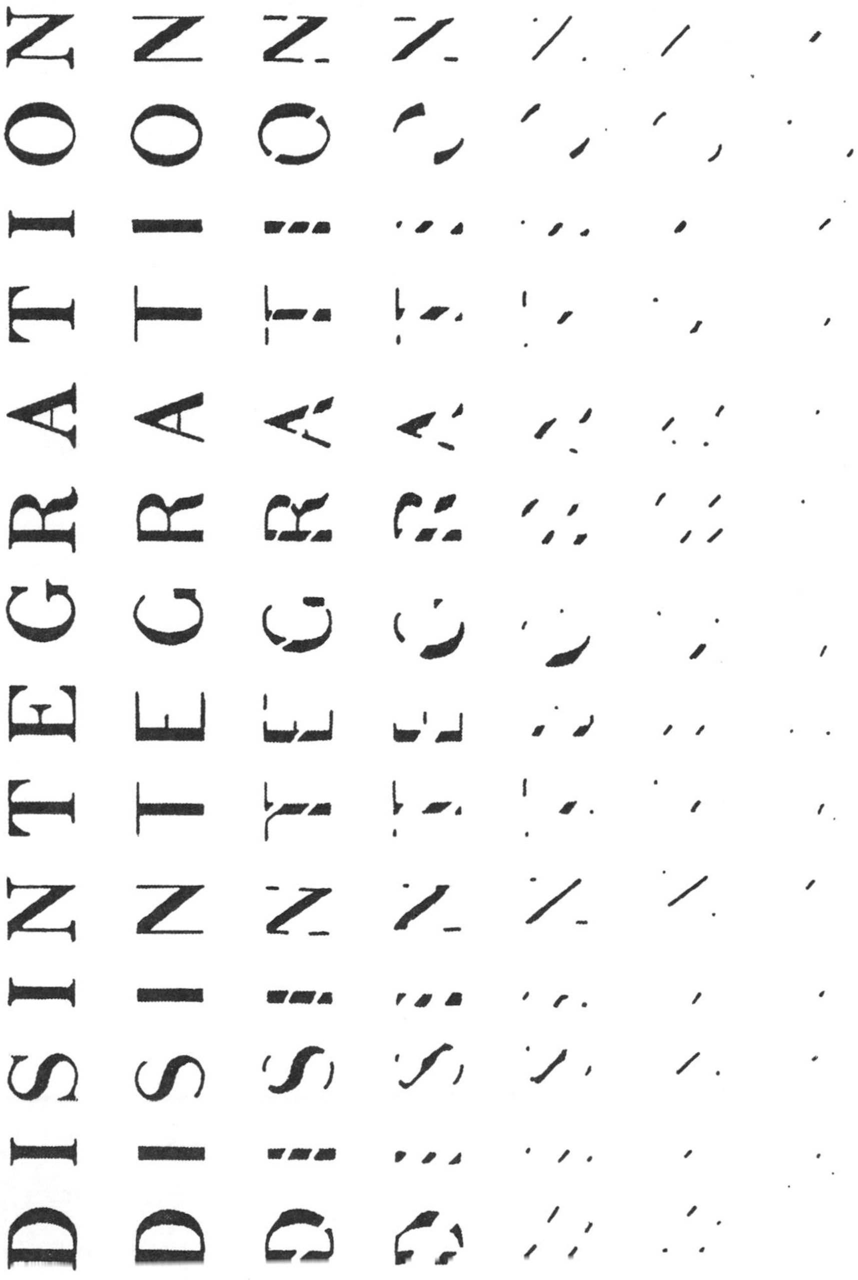
DISINTEGRATION

of a visual form so appropriate to a certain word that the whole would make an indelible impact—an after-image that would remain in the viewer's mind long after he or she "read" the poem.

Once my earliest poems were collected, I was obliged to do something else. One alternative was the poem composed of synonyms visually arranged, such as the "Live-Kill" pair (1972).

See pages 542-543.

Although these two images originally appeared in a book, I enlarged them not only for unique canvases that are 46" x 32 1/2" but also for a series of silkscreened prints (1975) that are 26" x 40", thinking not just to publish them in another way but also to increase their after-image capabilities.

Another alternative was handwritten visual poems, such as those comprising "The East Village" (1970-1971). In these works I wanted to get away from the centered space and simple perceptual perspective of my earlier work. Since I am scarcely able to invent a situation from scratch—or, to be precise, since I tend to be more inventive with materials than imaginative with situations—I chose a familiar subject, the New York neighborhood in which I then lived. My theme was the variousness of the individual side streets, each of which has its own characteristic spatial qualities, its own details and its own sounds. In doing for each block-long street a one-page portrait in language and space, I wrote a long poem that was eventually incorporated into my second collection, *I Articulations* (1974). A later, longer handwritten poem, "Portraits from Memory," appeared as an entire 35-page book (1975) in which each page contains a verbal-visual portrait of a woman I might have known. Here, as elsewhere in my work, the titles of individual pieces tend to be rather explicit.

My most recent visual poems, those done in 1979, involve a strict geometric structure—a form perhaps even more rigorous than the Japanese Haiku (with which they are sometimes compared). In the initial series, only four words could be used for each poem, and they were placed at four different angles in the corners of an invisible rectangle floating in the sapcae of a larger page. The words tend to relate to one another in a variety of ways. Sometimes they reenforce one another through complementary relationships; other times, one word becomes a contrast to the other three, perhaps as an antonym

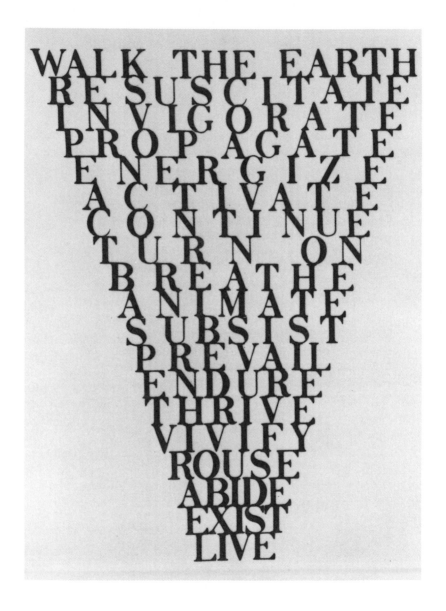

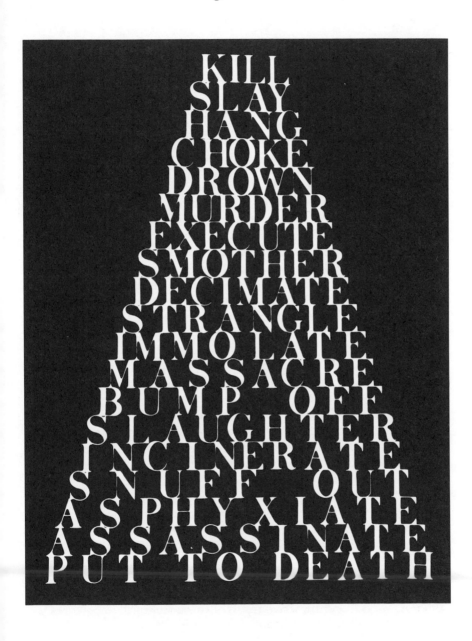

or as a critical contrast. If four spatially separated words could become more than the sum of their parts, I calculated, then *poetry* would arise among the words.

I later made two more sets of poems—one with eight words to a rectangular frame (the four additional ones, likewise set at four different angles, forming a compass in the middle) and then another with sixteen words to a frame (with the initial form divided into quarters). In these as well, the words within each poem resonate in various ways. While I feel, on one hand, that four words to a page might be too sparse for poetry, I'm not entirely sure that these more populous poems are necessarily more poetic.

In doing poetry I had already discovered the idea of a constraint so severe that it would prevent me from using language in familiar forms; and that primary restriction was the use of only one word that would then be visually enhanced. An imposed constraint, I discovered, serves to force the creative imagination to resist convention, if not cliché; and like meter in traditional poetry, the constraints I chose also encouraged puzzle-solving and other forms of linguistic playfulness. Early in 1968, I began to think about a similarly severe constraint for writing fiction; and after a few abortive experiments, I hit upon the hypothesis of writing a story with no more than two words to a paragraph. For a subject, I chose the conveniently familiar one of boy meets girl. This plot appears frequently in my fiction, not because I have anything particularly profound to say about heterosexual encounters but because a familiar, transparent subject makes both myself and my readers more aware of the formal issues that really interest me. Once the two-word paragraphs of "One Night Stood" were drafted, I typed them out, indenting alternative lines; and the following winter I realized that each two-word phrase could take up the entire page of a book, thereby expanding the story into a minimal novel (that was not published until 1977). Subsequent verbal fictions are similarly skeletal—"Excelsior," with only one word to a paragraph; "Milestones in a Life," in which chronological numbers are followed by just a single word or sometimes two; and "Dialogue," which is composed of only two words, "yes" and "no," repeated in different ways. One attractive result of these technical departures is a fluid, indefinite sense of fictional space and time.

In the summer of 1969, I discovered how to make *visual* fiction, realizing an implication of my much-reprinted "Football Forms"— that images in sequence could tell a story whose temporal rhythm is based upon the time a typical reader takes to turn the page. That perception informed not only my alphabet novella, *In the Beginning* (1971), but also my initial abstract fictions—those consisting only of lines, lacking words, save for their titles. That summer I also drafted the theoretical statement, "Twenty-Five Fictional Hypotheses," that even a decade later is still reprinted for its radical possibilities. It suggests, among other notions, that anything can be used to tell a story, not only nonsyntactic language but visual materials as well; and, of course, I practiced what I preached. I also noticed a fundamental difference between poetry and fiction: Whereas the former tends to concentrate both image and effect, fiction creates a world of related activity.

A further development in my story-telling is the work composed of sequential four-sided symmetrical line-drawings that metamorphose in systemic sequence. Begun in 1974 these "Constructivist Fictions," as I call them, presently include not only two published collections of short stories, *Constructs* (1974) and *Constructs Two* (1978), but two more unpublished collections, in addition to two full-length novels, "Symmetries" and "Intermix," that are both still unpublished. A variation on this Constructivist theme is *And So Forth* (1979), in which the geometric images, by contrast, are *not* perfect symmetries and their order is *not* fixed.

In the summer of 1970, I drafted another verbal fiction, "Openings & Closings," which remains in one crucial respect the most conventional imaginative piece I have ever written—it contains full sentences! Nonetheless, it resembles my other verbal fictions in observing a truncating constraint; for whereas the earlier stories had one or two words to a paragraph, here I decided to suggest, within single sentences, either a story that might follow or one that could have gone before. The isolated sentences were literally either the openings (of hypothetically subsequent stories) or the closings (of hypothetically previous stories). These could be considered incomplete stories, it is true; yet it was my aim to make a single sentence be artistically sufficient (and let readers imagine the rest). As there is no intentional connection between any particular opening and any closing, I thought that the stories should be set in two different styles of type—italics for the openings, roman for the closings—with plenty of white space between them; a book of them, in this form, appeared in 1975. Invited, in 1976, to exhibit "Openings & Closings" in a gallery, I typed the sentences out on individual cards—one card to a sentence—again using italics for the openings and a roman typeface for the closings. These cards were then scattered in no particular order, initially over a display board and later around a gallery's walls.

For a long time I doubted if I would ever do a fiction of sentences again, but in 1979 I found myself writing "Epiphanies," which I conceived as single-sentence stories that would represent the epiphany, in the Joycean sense, again of a larger hypothetical fiction. Parts of this project, which is not yet complete, have appeared in literary magazines (that represent the foundation of our culture), while other parts have been put on audiotape and videotape; but I am not yet entirely sure of the form(s) in which it will be published.

In my first numerical work, "Accounting," drafted early in 1969, I wanted to see if numbers could be used in lieu of words or letters; and that numerical fiction was also the first of its kind to appear in print, initially in my anthology *Future's Fictions* (1971) and then as a separate booklet (1973). Late in 1972 I set everything else aside to see how far I could take my growing interest in numbers—to see whether I could create a Literature composed of numerals alone. I thought at the time that I was making a book of "poems and stories," remembering my earlier distinction. However, by the following year, I realized that these works were actually becoming something else—a "numerature," perhaps; a "numerical art," to be sure. My aim in working with numbers was no longer the writing of poems and stories but the creation of a numerical field that is both visually and numerically coherent, with varying degrees of visual-numerical complexity. These works do not merely incorporate numerals within visual concerns, like, say, certain Jasper Johns paintings; my pieces are literally about the language of numbers.

My initial arrangements were numerically simple. "1024," for instance, incorporates both the parts and the factors of that variously divisible number, while "indivisibles" is a field of visually unrelated numbers whose common property is that nothing can be divided into any of them (except, of course, themselves and one). As before, titles in my works tend to be explicit. Realizing that my aim was arithmetical patterns that could be appreciated again and again (like art, but unlike puzzles), I then tried to create numerical fields whose relationships were more multiple and less obvious. In works like *Exhaustive Parallel Intervals*, I began, I think, to approach the levels of complexity that I admire in serial music and *Finnegans Wake*, for numbers were more conducive than words for my penchants for rigorous systems, structural complexity and geometric order. (Simply because one number can go next to any other number, arithmetic syntax, unlike that of words, is also infinitely permissible.)

See page 548.

In addition, these numbers realize the ideal of an esthetic empiricism that, though heretical, has long haunted me, for all the artistic activity that one identified in the work could be verified by another observer and yet be rich enough to be appreciated again and again.

In the spring of 1974 I completed *Recyclings*, the third and most successful of my initial series of experiments with continuous non-syntactical prose. The individual *Recyclings* were made by subjecting earlier essays of mine to selective processes that destroyed their original syntax, while retaining their characteristic language. The pages of *Recyclings* can thus be read both horizontally, like normal prose, or vertically, as the eyes, moving down and around the page, can perceive not only consistencies in diction but repeated words that usually reveal an identifiable ulterior source or subject.

Considering how to declaim this work aloud, I hit upon a structure that could aurally incorporate both the horizontal and the vertical. I recruited a chorus of readers each of whom would speak the text horizontally, which is to say continuously to the right. However, rather than read in choral unison, these readers would go in staggered succession, each new one beginning to declaim the opening word approximately one line behind the previous reader. Since I was not aiming for any specific vertical juxtapositions, but just for constant vertical counterpoint, each reader could go at his own pace, and in his own manner. I assumed that an audience listening carefully would hear serendipitous vertical relationships—words spoken simultaneously, much like chords in music—amid the continuous horizontal polyphonic declamation. When invited to be a guest artist at the new radio studios of WXXI-FM, in Rochester, New York, in 1975, I realized a seven-track version in which all the declamatory voices are my own, each one amplified differently from the others.

My other initial audiotapes are largely straight declamations of my truncated stories, amplified and enhanced in various comparatively modest ways. For *Openings & Closings* I put the opening

0
2   4
4   0   2
5   2   4   1
1   3   0   3   5
3   5   1   5   1   3
1   3   0   3   5
5   2   4   1
4   0   2
2   4
0

sentences on one side of a stereo system and the closing sentences on the other. In *Foreshortenings* (1978), a later verbal fiction, a voice clearly identifiable as mine swaps single-sentence lines with a chorus of my voice, both sides repeating the same repertoire of eighty-four simple sentences in increasingly different ways. More recently I have favored familiar religious and political texts, such as the Declaration of Independence or the Lord's Prayer, electronically modified in ways that might make them aurally incomprehensible to most ears, were not the texts already familiar. Indeed, religious materials strike me as especially suitable for electronic enhancements that generally increase the suggestion of sacredness. Otherwise, the main distinguishing characteristics of my audiotapes so far have been the use of inventive, uncommon language structure, whether truncated lines or nonsyntactic prose, and then the realization of aural experiences that would be unfeasible, if not impossible, in live performance. It makes no sense for me or anyone else to do in one medium anything that could be done better in another.

Late in 1975, I was invited to be a guest artist at the Synapse video studio of Syracuse University. Here I worked not with a single engineer-producer, as at WXXI-FM, but with an institutional staff of young instructors, graduate assistants and undergraduates. With their help, I realized video versions of four earlier texts. To do "Excelsior," a skeletal story in which two people make love in one-word paragraphs, I created a circular visual image for each character. As voices change, the screen flashes rapidly from one moving image to another. In "Plateaux," with its single-word paragraphs, each relating a different stage (or plateau) in the development of a love affair, we used video feedback to create kaleidoscopic moiré patterns that change slowly in no particular direction, complementing visually the pointless, ultimately circular development of the fiction's plot. For *Openings & Closings*, I instructed a large staff first to alternate between color cameras for the openings and black & white cameras for the closings and then to make each new image (mostly of me reading) as different as possible from the one before, thus realizing visually the leaps of time, space and tone that characterize the radically discontinuous prose text. Finally, whereas the audio *Recyclings* has nonsyntactic prose read by nonsynchronous voices (all mine), for the color video I hit upon the image of pairs of speaking lips (all mine again)— one pair of lips for the first *Recyclings*, two pairs for the second, etc. In this and subsequent video work, it was my aim to create not documentaries of live performances or dramatizations of stories but language-based works that could exist only on videotape, because they exploited the unique potentialities of the medium.

In 1976, I began to work with film, initially as an informal guest in a graduate animation course. With Barton Weiss, I made films composed entirely of words, which thus must be *read*, quite rapidly, in order to be "seen." The common joke is that these silent movies are "all titles, no action." What makes such entirely verbal films interesting to me are two complementary phenomena: the inordinate concentration required of the viewers, who realize that they must pay constant, strict attention if they are to see everything, and then the experience of reading in unison, with a crowd of strangers, in contrast to the conventional reading experience of perusing a text of one's own choosing, at one's own speed, by oneself. The second set of films, made in collaboration with Peter Longauer, shoot the Constructivist Fictions in negative, so that four-sided symmetries of white lines appear on the black screen, in sequences that are systematically composed (complementing the systematic composition of the drawings). Of all the media in which I have worked, film requires the most laboring time and seems to me, in terms of what I would ultimately like to do with it, the least developed.

In the summer of 1977, I completed my first photographs worth publishing. I had been thinking about the art of photography ever since doing my documentary monograph on *Moholy-Nagy* (1970), for the example of Moholy taught me that I could work in several arts at once and that, if I did photography, I should create images that would exist only as photographs—that would not be "moments" from films, say, or extensions of documentary reportage. After several abortive attempts I hit upon the idea of taking a single 8" by 10" photograph of myself, cutting it apart into eighty equally sized squares and then recomposing these squares into eighty new pictures, all likewise 8" by 10", which I called *Reincarnations*. Given my recent ambiguous feelings about exact systems, the geometric rearrangements of these photographs are only roughly, or incompletely, systemic, while the order of the images is not fixed. (The analogue in my Constructivist Fictions is *And So Forth*, which was done around the same time.) For the second sequential pieces, "Recall," each of the photographs is recomposed within scrupulously systemic principles, and the pictures are ordered into a fixed narrative (i.e., fiction).

The next step would take me into holography, a new technol-

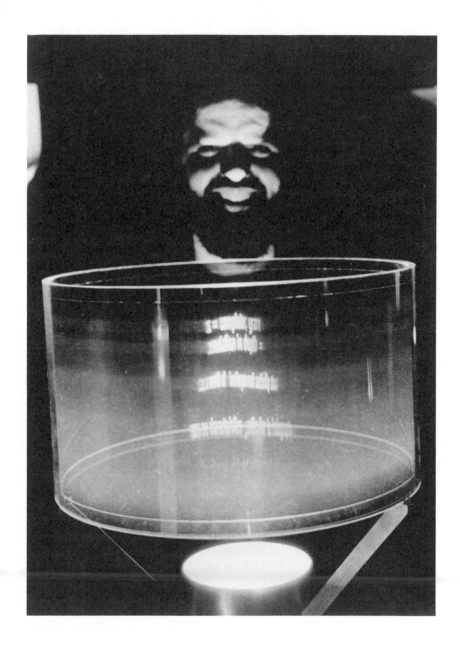

ogy for three-dimensional image-making that surpasses the stere-
oscope of photographic history. Once I saw a circular (360 degree)
cylindrical rotating hologram, I realized that its visual field could be
filled with five syntactically circular, grammatically seamless statements about holography, such as

> the hologram creates a world of incorporeal activity that
> exists only within

or

> the illusion not only of depth but of equal focus to all
> distances are characteristics peculiar to holography which
> creates

In my hologram, the ends of these lines are attached to each other,
making the statements visually circular and linguistically continuous.
For the initial exhibition of this work, I added a stereo audiotape of five
voices reading the same words on individually continuous, aurally
seamless audiotape loops; so that spectators could hear in five-voice
unison the same words that they see in five-line unison.

Books both authored and designed by me have been appearing
since 1970, when *Visual Language* was published; and an interest in
alternative forms of bookmaking goes back to critical essays I published in the late 1960s. Not until 1975, however, did I realize that book
art as such was a conscious interest of mine, and I soon published a set
of volumes that explore alternative book forms: the accordion books,
Modulations and *Extrapolate*; the handwritten book mentioned before,
Portraits from Memory; a chapbook with horizontal images spread over
two pages, *Come Here*; and then the cardbook, *Rain Rains Rain*; in
addition to a book that exists only on audiotape, *Experimental Prose*
(1976); the two-front book, *Prunings/Accruings* (1977); two mostly
blank books of 1978, *Tabula Rasa* and *Inexistences*; the looseleaf book,
And So Forth (1979); and the two newsprint books, *Numbers: Poems &
Stories* (1976) and *One Night Stood* (1977). That last title, *One Night
Stood*, also appeared as a small paperback book, 4" x 5 3/8"; for the
existence of both creates the illustrative contrast of reading the same
verbal text of two-word paragraphs in two radically different book
forms. That is, not until one reads both books together will he or she
realize how perceptibly different two formats of the same text can be.
See pages 554-555. In my creative work so far, there has been a

continuing concern with alternative materials for traditional literary genres, such as poetry and fiction, and then with alternative media for literature, such as audio and video and holography. I have worked in several media without becoming, say, "a filmmaker" or a "book artist," preferring to use such mediumistic categories to characterize work rather than people (such as me). I speak of myself as just an "artist and writer," wishing that there were in English a single term that combined the two, such as a weightier form of "maker."

Predisposed to invention, I had intended from the beginning to make literature that "read" like nothing else anyone knew; and since my reasons for doing creative work were quite different from those behind my critical essays, separate fundamental concerns insured that my professional functions were not confused. In doing things so differently, I have accepted the likelihood of losses with the gains; and should people complain, as they sometimes do, that certain qualities they like in my criticism are absent from my creative work, my reply is that the latter stems from different purposes in myself and hopefully exhibits certain qualities absent from my criticism.

Though superficially diverse, not only in media but in styles, my creative works still exhibit certain unifying qualities, such as riskiness, rigor, clarity, structural explicitness, variousness, empiricism, literary and conceptual audacity—qualities that might also characterize my critical writing, perhaps because they reflect my personal temper (and are thus as close as the work can be to representing me); and my creative concern with innovative structure is also a principal theme of my criticism and my anthologies. Two goals in mind for both my art and my criticism are that they be more complex and yet more accessible, if only to prove that these aims need not be contradictory.

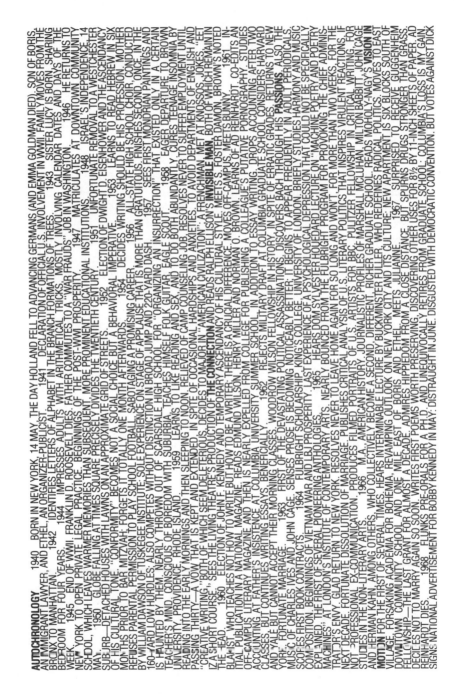

AUTOCHRONOLOGY 1940 BORN IN NEW YORK, 14 MAY, THE DAY HOLLAND FELL TO ADVANCING GERMANS (AND EMMA GOLDMAN DIED), SON OF BORIS, AN IMMIGRANT LAWYER, AND ETHEL, AN ORGANIZER-PUBLICIST. 1941 DECLARATION OF OFFICIAL U.S. INVOLVEMENT IN WWII. FAMILY MOVES FROM THE BRONX TO MANHATTAN. 1942 IDENTIFIES LETTERS OF ALPHABET IN THE BRANCH FORMATIONS OF TREES. 1943 SISTER LUCY'S BORN, SHARING BEDROOM FOR FOUR YEARS. 1944 IMPRESSES ADULTS WITH ARITHMETICAL TRICKS, MOSTLY INVOLVING CALENDAR DATES AND DAYS OF THE WEEK. 1945 END OF WWII. FRANKLIN D. ROOSEVELT DIES. FATHER COMMUTES TO A "WAR FRAUDS" JOB IN WASHINGTON. 1946 HE RETURNS TO NEW YORK TO OPEN PRIVATE LEGAL PRACTICE. BEGINNINGS OF THE POST-WWII PROSPERITY. 1947 MATRICULATES AT DOWNTOWN COMMUNITY SCHOOL, WHICH LEAVES WARMER MEMORIES THAN SUBSEQUENT, MORE PROMINENT EDUCATIONAL INSTITUTIONS. 1948 ISRAEL'S INDEPENDENCE. 14 MAY. 1950 GLOBE FALLING AT TIMES SQUARE PRECISELY DIVIDES THE TWENTIETH CENTURY. 1951 UNFORTUNATE REMOVAL TO A WESTCHESTER SUBURB—DETACHED HOUSES WITH LAWNS ON AN APPROXIMATE GRID OF STREETS. 1952 ELECTION OF DWIGHT D. EISENHOWER AND THE ASCENDANCY OF HIS CULTURAL TONE. "CONFORMITY" BECOMES NOT A SOCIAL CHOICE BUT A BEHAVIORAL IMPERATIVE. 1953 EARNS TO READ HEBREW IN SIX MONTHS PRIOR TO BAR MITZVAH; FORGETS IT TOTALLY ONE MONTH AFTERWARDS. 1954 DECIDES WRITING SHOULD BE HIS PROFESSION. MOTHER REFUSES PARENTAL PERMISSION TO PLAY SCHOOL FOOTBALL, SABOTAGING A PROMISING CAREER. 1956 ALL-STATE HIGH SCHOOL CHOIR, CONDUCTED BY WILLIAM DAWSON OF TUSKEGEE INSTITUTE: SOLE EXPERIENCE ON STAGE OF APPLAUSE THAT IS MORE THAN GRATUITOUS. FINISHES SECOND, ONCE, IN THE 160-YARD LOW HURDLES; ALSO COMPETES WITHOUT DISTINCTION IN BROAD JUMP AND 220-YARD DASH. 1957 SEES FIRST MONDRIAN PAINTINGS AND IS HAUNTED BY THEM, NEARLY THROWN OUT OF SCARSDALE HIGH SCHOOL FOR "ORGANIZING AN INSURRECTION" THAT EXISTED ONLY IN A CERTAIN TEACHER'S MIND. CONSCIOUS OF BOREDOM WITH SUBURBIA. TEACHES HIMSELF FOLK GUITAR. 1958 EAGER DEPARTURE TO BROWN UNIVERSITY, PROVIDENCE, RHODE ISLAND. 1959 LEARNS TO LIKE READING AND SEX, AND TO DO BOTH ABUNDANTLY. CURES TEENAGE INSOMNIA BY READING INTO THE EARLY MORNINGS AND THEN SLEEPING TO NOON. RELIEVED OF CAMP COUNSELING JOB, RESOLVES NEVER TO SUFFER EMPLOYMENT UNTIL PASSING THIRTY—A VOW THAT IS KEPT AND EXTENDED, IN SPITE OF OCCASIONAL HARDSHIPS AND ANXIETIES. TO AVOID DEPARTMENTS OF ENGLISH AND "CREATIVE WRITING," SEES THE LIVING THEATRE'S PRODUCTION OF THE CONNECTION AND READS RALPH ELLISON'S INVISIBLE MAN, BOTH OF WHICH REMAIN "ET ZA SHORT COURSE." BROWN'S NOTED 1960 ELECTION OF JOHN F. KENNEDY AND TEMPORARY ASCENDANCY OF HIS CULTURAL STYLE. MEETS FOSTER DAMON, THE HEAD. 1961 IN-BLAH-IST, WHO TEACHES "NO HOW TO WRITE." THERE'S A CRUCIAL MOVES OFF-CAMPUS. MEETS BUNNY. TIAL PUBLICATION IN A NATIONAL MAGAZINE. READS EDMUND WILSON. HENRY MILLER AND NORMAN O. BROWN. LEARNS OF AD REINHARDT. CO-EDITS AN OFF-CAMPUS LITERARY MAGAZINE AND THEN IS NEARLY EXPELLED FROM COLLEGE FOR PUBLISHING A COLLEAGUE'S PUTATIVE PORNOGRAPHY. STUDIES ACCOUNTING AT FATHER'S INSISTENCE AT COLUMBIA UNIVERSITY SUMMER SCHOOL. IN ADDITION TO ESSAY WRITING, DROPS ACCOUNTING AFTER TWO CLASSES, BUT CONTINUES WRITING ESSAYS. BENEFICIALLY. 1962 REJECTS MILITARY DRAFT AT COLUMBIA GRADUATE SCHOOL. CONSIDERS HARVARD AND YALE BUT CANNOT ACCEPT THEIR MORNING CLASSES. WOODROW WILSON FELLOWSHIP IN HISTORY. DISCOVERS BACH THROUGH HIS PASSIONS. ALSO THE MUSIC OF CHARLES IVES AND JOHN CAGE. SENSES PROSE IS BECOMING NOTICEABLY BETTER; IT BEGINS TO APPEAR FREQUENTLY IN ADULT PERIODICALS. RETURNS TO NEW YORK. FORTUNATE MARRIAGE. 1963 FULBRIGHT SCHOLARSHIP. KING'S COLLEGE. UNIVERSITY OF LONDON. BRIEFLY STUDIES HARMONY AND MUSIC. SCORES FIRST BOOK CONTRACTS. 1964 FIRST OF THE DEVASTATING POLITICAL ASSASSINATIONS. LAST EXPERIENCE OF A PSYCHOLOGICAL DEPRESSION THAT COULD NOT BE SPECIFICALLY COMPOSITION. BEGINNINGS OF SEVERAL PIONEERING ANTHOLOGIES. 1965 HEARS DOM SYLVESTER HOUÉDARD LECTURE ON "MACHINE" POETRY AND POETRY EXPLAINED. THE FIRST OF SEVERAL PIONEERING ANTHOLOGIES. NEARLY BOUNCED HOME FOR PROVOKING THE CHIEF ADMINIS- MACHINES," AT LONDON'S INSTITUTE OF CONTEMPORARY ARTS. LAST EXPERIENCE. FOR MORE THAN TWO WEEKS. FOR THE TRATOR'S ENVY. GLAD RETURN TO NEW YORK. RESOLVES NEVER TO LEAVE HOME AGAIN FOR SO LONG AND WON'T. FOR THE NEXT DECADE. FORTUNATE DISSOLUTION OF MARRIAGE. PUBLISHES CRITICAL ANALYSIS OF U.S. LITERARY POLITICS THAT INSPIRES VIOLENT REACTIONS. IF NOT PROFESSIONAL EX-COMMUNICATION. 1966 M.A., AMERICAN HISTORY. JOURNALISTIC PROFILES OF U.S. ARTISTS FOR BBC. PULITZER FELLOWSHIP IN CRITICAL WRITING. FOR STUDIES IN THE NON-LITERARY ARTS. PRODUCES FILMED PORTRAITS OF MARSHALL MCLUHAN. MILTON BABBITT. JOHN CAGE AND HERMAN KAHN, AMONG OTHERS. WHO COLLECTIVELY BECOME A SECOND, DIFFERENT, RICHER GRADUATE SCHOOL. READS MOHOLY-NAGY'S **VISION IN MOTION** FOR THE FIRST OF SEVERAL TIMES. HEARS INTERMINABLE LECTURE BY BUCKMINSTER FULLER, WHO REDEFINES RADICAL POLITICS. MOVES SOUTH OF VILLAGE. FORSAKING ACADEMIA FOR BOHEMIA. REVAMPING OUTLOOK ON NEW YORK CITY. AND ITS CULTURE: NEW APARTMENT IS SIX BLOCKS SOUTH OF DOWNTOWN COMMUNITY SCHOOL AND ONE MILE EAST OF BORIS. ADMIRES HIP IDIOM FROM A CLOSE DISTANCE. 1967 SURPRISED TO RECEIVE GUGGENHEIM FELLOWSHIP—THE LAST GRANT FOR ALMOST A DECADE. WRITES FIRST POEMS WORTH PRESERVING, DISCOVERING OTHER USES FOR 8½-BY-11-INCH SHEETS OF PAPER. AD DECIDES NOT TO MARRY AGAIN SO SOON. JULIANNE. BUT SPURNS DRUGS STRONGER THAN GRASS. REINHARDT DIES. 1968 FLUNKS PRE-ORALS FOR A PH.D. AND UNEQUIVOCALLY RETIRES FROM GRADUATE SCHOOL: COLUMBIA'S LOSS IS MY GAIN. SIGNS NATIONAL ADVERTISEMENT FOR BOBBY KENNEDY IN MAY: DISTRAUGHT IN JUNE. DISGUSTED WITH DEMOCRATIC CONVENTION, BUT VOTES AGAINST DICK

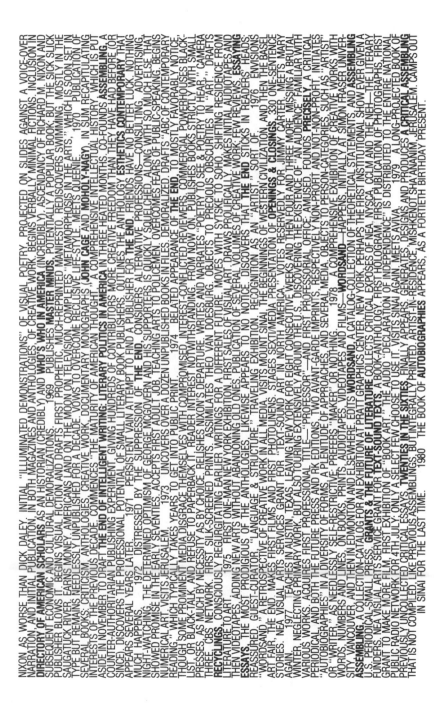

NIXON AS WORSE THAN DICK DALEY. INITIAL "ILLUMINATED DEMONSTRATIONS" OF VISUAL POETRY PROJECTED ON SLIDES AGAINST A VOICE-OVER NARRATION, AND INITIAL PUBLICATION, IN BOTH MAGAZINES AND ANTHOLOGIES, OF CREATIVE WORK. BEGINS VERBALLY MINIMAL FICTIONS. INCLUSION IN **DIRECTORY OF AMERICAN SCHOLARS** AS AN HISTORIAN (INCREDIBLY) AND **WHO'S WHO IN AMERICA** (INCREDIBLY), ASCENDANCY OF RICHARD M. NIXON AND SUBSEQUENT ECONOMIC AND CULTURAL DEMORALIZATIONS. 1969 PUBLISHES **MASTER MINDS**, POTENTIALLY A POPULAR BOOK, BUT THE SICK SLICK PUBLISHER BLOWS IT. BEGINS VISUAL FICTION AND DRAFTS FIRST PROPHETIC, MUCH-REPRINTED MANIFESTO. REDISCOVERS SWIMMING, MOSTLY IN THE SAUGATUCK RIVER. EARNS MONEY. AMERICANS LAND ON THE MOON ON TELEVISION. COMPLETES "METAMORPHOSIS IN THE ARTS," WHICH IS SOON SET IN TYPE BUT REMAINS NEEDLESSLY UNPUBLISHED FOR A DECADE. VOWS TO OVERCOME RECLUSIVE LIFE-STYLE. MEETS QUEENIE. 1970 PUBLICATION OF SEVERAL BOOKS: CRITICISM, ANTHOLOGIES, CREATIVE WORK, DOCUMENTARY MONOGRAPHS, (**JOHN CAGE** AND **MOHOLY-NAGY**), IN SUM RECAPITULATING INTERESTS OF THE PREVIOUS DECADE. COMMENCES "THE MATURITY OF AMERICAN THOUGHT," A COMPREHENSIVE INTELLECTUAL HISTORY WHICH IS PUT ASIDE IN NOVEMBER TO DRAFT **THE END OF INTELLIGENT WRITING: LITERARY POLITICS IN AMERICA** IN THREE HEATED MONTHS. CO-FOUNDS **ASSEMBLING**, A COUNTER-AUTHORITARIAN PUBLISHING EXPERIMENT GIVING HUNDREDS OF CONTRIBUTORS MORE CREATIVE FREEDOM THAN THEY HAVE HAD BEFORE (OR SINCE). DISCOVERS THE PROFESSIONAL POTENTIAL OF SMALL LITERARY BOOK PUBLISHERS. OUTLINES THE ANTHOLOGY **ESTHETICS CONTEMPORARY** THAT APPEARS SEVERAL YEARS LATER. 1971 PERSISTENT VAIN ATTEMPT TO FIND A PUBLISHER FOR **THE END**. FRIENDS HAVE NO BETTER LUCK. NOTHING MUCH HAPPENS. 1972 DISTRESSED BY THE SUPPRESSION OF **THE END**, CONSIDERS ALTERNATIVE PROFESSIONS—CONSULTING, ADVERTISING, NIGHT-WATCHING. THE DETERMINED OPTIMISM OF GEORGE MCGOVERN AND HIS SUPPORTERS IS QUICKLY SQUELCHED ALONG WITH SO MUCH ELSE THAT SHOWED PROMISE IN THE EARLY SEVENTIES. ACCEPTS FIRST ADULT JOB, TEACHING ARTS TO POLICEMEN. OVERCOMES FEARS OF PUBLIC-SPEAKING. BEGINS NUMERICAL ART. VISITS JERUSALEM. 1973 UNCOVERS OVER A DOZEN UNPUBLISHED BOOKS IN FILES. DEMORALIZED. DRAFTS "ABC OF CONTEMPORARY READING," WHICH TYPICALLY TAKES YEARS TO GET INTO PUBLIC PRINT. 1974 BELATED APPEARANCE OF **THE END**, TO MOSTLY FAVORABLY NOTICE, THOUGH SOME PROMINENT MEDIA DISGRACE THEMSELVES WITH COMPROMISED, INTEREST-CONFLICTED REVIEWERS. COMMERCIAL POWERHOUSES BLACK-LIST OR BLACK-TALK, AND REFUSE TO ADVERTISE, BY CHOICE. RELISHES NIXON'S DEPARTURE. WRITES AND NARRATES "POETRY TO SEE & POETRY TO HEAR," CAMERA THREE, CBS NETWORK. FIRST SILK-SCREENED PRINTS. ASSIMILATES THEO VAN DOESBURG. OBJECTS TO PRECIOUS OBSCURITIES IN "ART." DRAFTS **RECYCLINGS**, CONSCIOUSLY REGURGITATING EARLIER WRITINGS FOR A DIFFERENT FUTURE. MOVES WITH SYTSKE TO SOHO, SHIFTING RESIDENCE FROM LITERATURE TO ART. 1975 FIRST ONE-MAN NEW YORK EXHIBITION. FIRST SALES OF VISUAL ART. DRAWS PROLIFICALLY. MAKES INITIAL AUDIOTAPES AND THEN VIDEOTAPES. ADDING NEW ARTS WITHOUT ABANDONING OLD ONES. PUBLICATION OF SEVERAL VOLUMES OF CREATIVE WORK. FEW STICKS IN READERS' HEADS. **ESSAYING ESSAYS**, THE MOST PRODIGIOUS OF THE ANTHOLOGIES, LIKEWISE APPEARS. DISCOVERS THAT **THE END** STICKS IN READERS' HEADS. REASSURED. GUEST-CURATOR, "LANGUAGE & STRUCTURE," TRAVELING EXHIBITION. RECOGNITION AS AN "ARTIST," SORT OF. 1976 ENVISIONS "WORDSAND," A RETROSPECTIVE OF CREATIVE WORK IN ALL MEDIA. VISITS MOUNT SINAI. THE BEGINNINGS OF WESTERN CIVILIZATION, AND THEN THE BASEL ART FAIR. NEA VISUAL ARTS SERVICES GRANT FOR TEXT-SOUND ART IN NORTH AMERICA. VOTES RESERVEDLY FOR JIMMY CARTER. MEETS MARY. STAGES SIX MEDIA. PRESENTATION OF **OPENINGS & CLOSINGS**, 330 ONE-SENTENCE STORIES. NEA VISUAL ARTS SERVICES GRANT FOR "TEXT-SOUND" ART. FIRST FILMS AND FIRST PHOTO-LINENS. 1977 TEACHES IN AUSTIN, TEXAS. LEAVING NEW YORK FOR EIGHT CONSECUTIVE WEEKS AND THREE MORE. MISSING A BRUTAL WINTER. NEGLECTING PRIMARY WORK, BUT ALSO TOURING EXTENSIVELY AROUND THE U.S. DISCOVERING THE EXISTENCE OF "AN AUDIENCE" FAMILIAR WITH VARIOUS WORKS. ACQUIRES FIRST PROFESSIONAL TITLE—"PROFESSOR"—AND FIRST PROFESSORIAL OFFICE. AMUSED. FOUNDS **PRECISELY** A CRITICAL "AUTOBIOGRAPHIES" IN A DIVERSITY OF FORMS. A PLENITUDE OF APPROACHES. INITIATES FUTURE PRESS AND RK EDITIONS, TWO AVANT-GARDE IMPRINTS, RESPECTIVELY NON-PROFIT AND NOT-NON-PROFIT. OR "WRITER," AS NEEDLESSLY SELF-RESTRICTIVE. PREFERS "MAKER" OR SOMETHING. 1978 A COMPREHENSIVE EXHIBITION OF CREATIVE WORKS WITH WORDS, NUMBERS, AUDIOTAPES, VIDEOTAPES, AND FILMS—**WORDSAND**—HAPPENS. INITIALLY AT A SIMON FRASER UNIVERSITY, VANCOUVER, AND THEN IN EDMONTON AND ELSEWHERE. EDITS **WORDSAND**, A CATALOG-COLLECTION OF THEORETICAL STATEMENTS. AND **ASSEMBLING**, A COLLECTION-CATALOG FOR AN EXHIBITION AT PRATT GRAPHICS CENTER, NEW YORK. PERHAPS THE FIRST INSTITUTIONAL SHOW EVER GIVEN A U.S. PERIODICAL. SMALL PRESS. **GRANTS & THE FUTURE OF LITERATURE** COLLECTS CRITICAL EXPOSES OF NEA, NYSCA, CCM, AND THE NEH—THE LITERARY FUNDERS. NEA VISUAL ARTS SERVICE GRANT FOR **TEXT-SOUND TEXTS**, A BOOK-ANTHOLOGY. FIRST HOLOGRAM. FIRST PUBLICATION OF PHOTOGRAPHS. FIRST GRANT TO MAKE MORE FILM. FIRST EXHIBITION OF "BOOK ART." THE AUDIO "DECLARATION OF INDEPENDENCE" IS DISTRIBUTED TO THE ENTIRE NATIONAL PUBLIC RADIO NETWORK FOR 4TH JULY. ONLY A SELECT FEW CHOOSE TO USE IT. VISITS SINAI AGAIN. MEETS AVIVA. 1979 A LONG-PROJECTED BOOK OF PREVIOUSLY UNCOLLECTED CRITICAL ESSAYS, **TWENTIES IN THE SIXTIES**, FINALLY APPEARS. GENERATES, DESIGNS AND PRODUCES **A CRITICAL ASSEMBLING** THAT IS NOT COMPILED, LIKE PREVIOUS ASSEMBLINGS, BUT INTEGRALLY PRINTED. ARTIST-IN-RESIDENCE, MISHKENOT SHA'ANANIM, JERUSALEM. CAMPS OUT IN SINAI FOR THE LAST TIME. 1980 THE BOOK OF **AUTOBIOGRAPHIES** APPEARS, AS A FORTIETH BIRTHDAY PRESENT.

Bibliography

By Richard Kostelanetz (selected):

The Theatre of Mixed Means. New York: Dial Press, 1968.
Master Minds. New York: Macmillan, 1969.
Visual Language. Brooklyn, New York: Assembling, 1970.
I Articulations/Short Fictions. New York: Kulchur Foundation, 1974.
The End of Intelligent Writing. New York: Sheed & Ward, 1974.
Recyclings. Brooklyn, New York: Assembling, 1974.
Openings & Closings. New York: D'Arc Press, 1975.
Portraits from Memory. Ann Arbor, Michigan: Ardis, 1975.
Constructs. Reno, Nevada: West Coast Poetry Review, 1975.
Extrapolate. Des Moines: Cookie, 1975.
Come Here. Des Moines: Cookie, 1975.
Portraits from Memory. Ann Arbor, Michigan: Ardis, 1975.
Experimental Prose. Brooklyn, New York: Assembling, 1976.
One Night Stood. New York: Future, 1977.
Inexistences. New York: RK Editions, 1978.
On Holography. New York: RK Editions, 1978.
Tabula Rasa. New York: RK Editions, 1978.
Wordsand. Burnaby, BC: Gallery of Simon Fraser University, 1978.
Constructs Two. Milwaukee, Wisconsin: Membrane, 1978.
Twenties in the Sixties. Westport, Connecticut: Greenwood, 1979.
More Short Fictions. Brooklyn, New York: Assembling, 1980.
Exhaustive Parallel Intervals. New York: Future, 1980.
"The End" Appendix/"The End" Essentials. Metuchen, New Jersey: Scarecrow, 1979.
The Old Poetries and the New. Ann Arbor, Michigan: University of Michigan, 1980.
Reincarnations. New York: Future, 1981.
Autobiographies. Santa Barbara, California: Mudborn, 1981.

Edited by Richard Kostelanetz (selected):

On Contemporary Literature. New York: Avon, 1964; second edition, 1969.
The New American Arts. New York: Horizon, 1965.
Twelve from the Sixties. New York: Dell, 1967.
The Young American Writers. New York: Funk & Wagnalls, 1967.
John Cage. New York: Praeger, 1970.
Moholy-Nagy. New York: Praeger, 1970.
Possibilities of Poetry. New York: Delta, 1970.
Imaged Words & Worded Images. New York: Outerbridge & Dienstfrey, 1970.
Future's Fictions. Princeton, New Jersey: Panache, 1971.
Breakthrough Fictioneers. Barton, Vermont: Something Else, 1973.
Essaying Essays. New York: Out of London, 1975.
Younger Critics in North America. Fairwater, Wisconsin: Margins, 1976.

Visual Literature Criticism. Carbondale: Southern Illinois University, 1979.
Text-Sound Texts. New York: Morrow, 1980.
The Yale Gertrude Stein. New Haven: Yale University, 1980.
Scenarios. New York: Assembling, 1980.
Aural Literature Criticism. New York: Precisely-RK Editions, 1981.
The Avant-Garde Tradition in Literature. Buffalo, New York: Prometheus, 1982.

(Books no longer in print with their initial publishers can sometimes be obtained from RK Editions, P.O. Box 73, Canal Street, New York, New York 10013.)

About Richard Kostelanetz:

Augustine, Jane. "Richard Kostelanetz," *Contemporary Poets.* London: St. James, 1975 (and later editions).
Fox, Hugh. "Richard Kostelanetz," *West Coast Poetry Review,* 12 (Summer 1974).
Gigliotti, Davidson. "Just Plain Video and Video-Plus," *Soho Weekly News* (30 December 1976).
Myers, George. "Scavenger Art and Richard Kostelanetz," *An Introduction to Modern Times.* Grosse Pointe, Michigan: Lunchroom Press, 1982.
Powers, Thomas. "Conspiracy of Good Taste," *Harper's* (November 1974).

Poetry Prose Neo-Narrative Open Structure

Arlene Zekowski and Stanley Berne

From the late Renaissance on, *language*—which before printing had never differentiated between the written and spoken word—suddenly became *linear, one-dimensional*, where formerly it had been *plastic* and *multi-dimensional*. Line by line, sentence by sentence, subject verb predicate order virtually destroyed the free floating spontaneous images of speech into abstract rational analytic frozen and fixed standardized discourse. Soon the *metaphor* or *image*, the *neural* source of all creative thought (poetry or prose), was gradually buried and forgotten.

As Time was gradually blocked and circumscribed into units of cause and effect, *language* became limited to what the cause-effect sentence could do. No one questioned why sentences were said to express thoughts or whether logic was really true until our way of *seeing* changed again from words as synthetic pseudo-scientific abstractions back to images. This new way of seeing occurred first with the invention of the instantaneous photograph that revolutionized the classical traditional "grammar" of painting from reproduction of the *visible* linear flat plane, to creation of the *imaginative* multi-dimensional plastic interior-exterior world of the artist's own perceptions. Subsequently *the sentence* in literature was gradually rejected in part, or modified by Joyce, Woolf and Stein and their followers, for *the image*. As a result, cause and effect, invented by an earlier more deterministic age, became no more valid for relativistic post-Newtonian science than for painting or literature. *Exploration* and *possibility* became once more *limitless* in a finite but unbounded 20th century Einsteinian universe.

Although both Joyce and Stein experimented with language beyond grammar, they did not pursue this possibility as a solution to the dilemma of the artificial linear structure imposed upon English for the last 300 years. Virginia Woolf in emphasizing the eternal unit of the metaphor, somehow managed to skirt the ultimate ogre glaring in the distance of 20th century literary expression cutting off circulation: *the sentence* itself.

Sooner or later *the sentence* had to be confronted. This, we decided, was what we would have to do. Not consciously deliberately or arbitrarily as many seem to think, but instinctively inevitably, as it turned out to be.

We were fascinated with the play of language, not just in an intellectual and scholarly linguistic way, as was the case with Joyce's scintillating vision, or in the brilliantly analytical enigmatic way of Stein, or in the hauntingly musical poetic-prose of Virginia Woolf. We were concerned more with getting at a language that would extend the possibilities of both the *mind* and *sensibilities*, the multi-level consciousness of feeling, dreaming, sensation, thought, the areas of buried mystery and potential—a language that would speak to every human being regardless of time, place, circumstance, ethnic social mythic psychological milieu—of reaching into the immediate simultaneous spontaneous present as into the unknown potential of the future, as unbounded as defiant of encirclement as possible.

Exploring and experimenting with a more *goedetic* spatial form, more in harmony with the space-time dimensions of the twentieth century, we had to discard more and more, the traditional syntax of linear one-dimensional grammatic structure. In addition, *the sentence*, that vestigial anachronism of 18th century narrative vision, would likewise have to go. Just as there are roles we all must play, *there are different forms of language to meet different circumstances.* As far as we were concerned, *in art, a sentence was not a thought.*

In *Image Breaking Images: A New Mythology of Language,* a book of literary criticism on language, art, religion, feminism, psychology, science, literature, education, etc., with frequent passages in neo-narrative open structure dialogue, Zekowski had gradually come to realize that the artist in language affects not just the art form but eventually other forms of usage and application as well, and had to arrive at the inevitable conclusion that *the sentence was no more meaningful in everyday communication than it was in literary expression:*

> Why is it difficult to teach the sentence in grammar?
> Because in reality the thought continues. The unit of
> "thought" of perception, if you will, is not a "sentence" but
> a cluster of clauses or images. When does it end? Certain-
> ly not mechanically or arbitrarily with a period. The period
> is merely a mechanical device invented by the gram-
> marian's fanatic sense of logic and warped sense of
> truth. The thought which is a series of percepts, or clus-
> ters of images concepts constellating or elaborating upon
> or enlarging or exploring or probing or accentuating in
> any way or manner contributing to a state of being or
> motion or emphasis, what the totality of all these parts of
> which the sentence is a part, contributes to the entity or
> whole.
>
> (Zekowski, *Image Breaking Images*,
> 1976: 115-116)

A companion book of literary criticism by Stanley Berne, expressed the following, regarding *the sentence*:

> The enforcers of the Sentence are the enforcers of thought
> control: teachers, and the police. Both are noticeably little
> thought of.
>
> The Sentence is not organic to language. Only thought is.
>
> The Sentence has become, unhappily, an industry or fac-
> tory wherein youth are manufactured, if they allow it, into
> exact replicas of the demonstrated failure that the humani-
> ties have become.
>
> The Sentence is the argument of Dictators to read arbitrary
> law to the impenitent political prisoner about to be sent to
> the camps.
>
> (Berne, *Future Language*,
> 1976: 26-30)

Even in inflectional languages like Greek and Latin upon which English grammar was arbitrarily pretentiously and inorgani- cally based, *sentence word order did not originally exist*. According to Charlton Laird, there was "the strong suspicion that classical grammar was not the grammar of any living language, even in classical times." (*The Miracle of Language*, 1953: 143). The inflectional form or case ending was all that was needed. You could mix or scramble the word (verb, adjective, adverb, noun subject or noun object) according to its emphasis in the context. And that is most likely how Vulgar Latin and its adaptation into French, Spanish, Italian and Portuguese came about. People would not put up with seven case endings just as today school children avoid the lingering vestigial apostrophe of the Latin possessive, the only case ending left in English. (See Stanley Berne, *Future Language*, 83-87, on the frustrations of teaching the possessive to incoming college Freshmen).

Likewise with *ideographically* structured Chinese, which had even much earlier abandoned an inflectional case ending for the more economic more dynamic metaphoric image of distributive sequence and position usage. *Ming* or *mei* as noun, verb, adjective: "The sun and moon of the cup" (the cup's brightness) or "The cup sun-and-moons," "Sun-and-moon cup" reflect the comprehensive simultaneous concretion of the images. (Note these and other examples in: *The Chinese Written Character as a Medium for Poetry*, by Ernest Fenollosa, translated by Ezra Pound).

A similar conversion of *word as image* obliterating *word as syntax* Shakespeare observes throughout his work. As Simeon Potter points out:

> Shakespeare was probably the first to use *window* as a verb in the sense *to place in a window* ("Wouldst thou be win-dow'd in great Rome?": *Antony and Cleopatra*, IV. xii. 72) and *to make full of holes* ('Your looped and window'd raggedness": *King Lear*, III. iv. 30). Shakespeare used adverb as verb ("That from their own misdeeds askance their 'eyes'": *Lucrece*, 637), or as substantive ("In the dark backward and abysm of time": *The Tempest*, I. ii. 50) or as adjective ("Blunting the fine point of seldom pleasure": *Sonnet*, lii).
>
> (*Our Language*, 1954: 57)*

These are only a few of the myriad possible examples from the nature and structure of language as organic to the *word* and not to any superimposed arbitrary symbolic logic of syntax or grammar and the sentence.

---

* See also: "Notes On The Neo-Narrative," "The Word As Creation And As Thought," in *Abraxas*, 1964: 28-29, by Arlene Zekowski.

Soon after the appearance of *A First Book of the Neo-Narrative* with excerpts from *Bodies & Continents* by Stanley Berne and *Grounds For Possibilities* and *Hemispheres* by Arlene Zekowski, our *neo-narrative* was described by Robert Martin Adams of *The Hudson Review* as: "A device for responding directly to reality without the clumsy intervention of grammar," and referred to thereafter as *the grammarless language*. With the appearance of *Future Language* by Stanley Berne and *Image Breaking Images* by Arlene Zekowski (our latest books of literary criticism), we tended to incorporate as theory what we had heretofore largely only suggested in our earlier collaborative work of 29 essays: *Cardinals & Saints*, but of course expressed in separate and individual creative works of short story, novel, poetry and drama (*The Dialogues, The Multiple Modern Gods, The Unconscious Victorious, The New Rubaiyat*, Stanley Berne; *Concretions, Abraxas, Seasons of the Mind, The Age of Iron*, Arlene Zekowski). That is, *the reduction of 300 or more rules of English syntax in a work of literature to no more than two*: the *period* and the *comma*, each of which we had adapted to our own particular style: the *periodic* (Zekowski) and the *kommatic* (Berne).

In our *periodic* and *kommatic* expression we have acknowledged the legacy of Joyce, Woolf and Stein, perpetuating a new a more open 20th century structure of writing which not only supersedes 18th century grammar and the sentence, but furthermore—in a language based on the *word* as *image—no longer separates poetry from prose*.

––––––––––––––

There are many variations of both the Berne *kommatic* and Zekowski *periodic* in each of our works, with combinations of both forms.

In his "Forward," Berne describes *Bodies and Continents* as follows:

> *Bodies and Continents* is a novel that uses the body itself as a point of departure from which to examine the external world. The novel attempts to show that body and external world are one, interacting on each other in a way that cannot separate one from the other ... seeks to express the simultaneous existence of all things, as they exist to our perceptions, and as they lie hidden also, but are part of our consciousness.
>
> (Berne)

Sight, sound, touch, feel, smell, all seem to converge upon the exultant aliveness that transcends body into soul and back to body again as mind and spirit soar and transpose person and place, as in this opening passage from chapter II of *Bodies and Continents*:

> AWAKE
> To sing (hours stolen).
> Are fill. Hear.
> What cries are far as ferret.
> Eye round. Slow to feel there lie and wait as all grace and pay and for their area of veldt as mountain high are to swing to, . . . soul, that hunger throat that moves of feel and nest as hair and short are fall and spread as all the sea shakes and feels of liquid moving as the tempt, out, smell, shall rise, vast, shall reach, as eye the doze and shape—
>
> > (Berne, *Bodies and Continents*,
> > *A First Book of the Neo-Narrative*,
> > 1954)

The theme of *Bodies and Continents* continues in *Legs and Crevices* (Berne), with the body in coitus, defeating death by copulating into immortality:

> I seed, I fat, I grow and enter at the moments of her limbs and lips and spread and dancing and hollow of her parts and music as the wind that spread and legs and entrance there with my points unthinking to enter and spit and leave and soak and withdraw, defeating time, invigorating life, catching death, *defeating it!*
>
> > (*The Fault*, 1975 Berne)

With *Teeth and Tongue* (Berne), the human body and the body of earth finally merge as one:

> Short as I am.
> I need the well.
> The water of blue color (Beneath the earth. Gurgling round and licking over the rocks.) I have never seen, but want for the lips. Want fall and ask and around and envelop and warm. Want as the love of the plants that deep as their roots are people living.
>
> > (Berne, *Intermedia*, 1976)

As Berne states in his "Note About The Title," in *The Unconscious Victorious and Other Stories,* life and history coalesce in the ironies of the unconscious defeating the conscious of man's will:

> And beyond this, is the future, always hidden, somewhat menacing, . . . yet approaching, inevitable, uninvited, "unconscious"—and always victorious over man's will: always devastatingly victorious over his dreams, prayers and hopes.
> The "Unconscious Victorious" is the future.
>
> (Berne)

In "Brown Earth as Medium," from *The Unconscious Victorious* (Berne), the Roman wars become the principal theme:

> of Alva who loved to kill, . . . of 45,000 in battle slaughter lying for the men to come at night and steal the money, jewels, swords, . . . killing for ideas mistaken, for leadership by deviates . . . the feeling that it is hopeless, that the mad world is right, . . . small experiments sweated, perfected, given to the world as a bouquet of flowers—
>
> (Berne, *The Unconscious Victorious and Other Stories,* 1969)

Berne's recent work: *The Great American Empire* (1982), develops Roman themes as the major mirror images of today's America:

> The vogue for hair was well on then, before the next phase of shaving, shaving of the shagpot, so to speak, the scalp now carefully cut and shaved and polished, both men and women, the whiskers gone, sideburns, mustaches, even eyebrows for both sexes, smooth as billiard balls and very smart and modern indeed, quite suitable to the people whose style of life had brought them colonies on the moon and on mars—
>
> (Berne, *First Person Intense,* 1978)

Though in Zekowski's writing the unit of thought has always been the liberated *word,* which is structured in clusters of *images* basic to all literary form, past, present and future, there is a difference in the style from the fifties against the writing of the sixties and seventies. In *The Sudden Testimony, Salt From Sacraments, Lazarus: Book I*, written around the time of *Grounds for Possibilities* and *Hemispheres*, the images are radically compact, the emphasis a multi-faceted reverberation where the shock of language seems to exult in a wild almost intoxicated abandon from traditional more conventional patterns. The following, from Chapter XXVII of *The Sudden Testimony*, emphasizes the rich marine decay of the barrier reef, its symbiotic life/death aspect where nothing is wasted:

> Who tastes. Who sends to seas. And weeds. And salt. And fatted globuled seaweed. And the jellied muck. The first sting of arms. The fish in star. The octopus in rain. And streamered bone. And wired eel. All these. All wastage. Wampum. To the reef which grows. And stones. And offers lime. To stay. Secures the kill.
>
> (Zekowski)

Also, where each structure and moment of art, of nature, of the universe, has its own season its growth maturity and purpose, as in this final motif of the work:

> A loom looms. Blankets. In a cloud. A mountain gathers snow. Each thing to seasons. Seasons what it grows.
> (Zekowski, *Kayak* 26, 1971
> and *Delirium* 4/5, 1979)

Lazarus: Book I, was conceived as a composite portrait, a kind of moral allegoric fable of every sentient person's awakening to the conflicts tensions shocks surprises of mind body experiences, the murky confused hovering awareness of the self, family and others, shadowy reflections of fate and struggling spirit:

> The strands he straddled. Then now when. A boy man. His fin ribs. Fishing for the rib that quaked and caulked. Caked with his salt fears. Bobbed over in the bob-cut hair. Buster-browned as his shoes. As his suit of ulster. Blue. Collaring the cut keel of his sail-end tie. Shadowing the man.
>
> (Zekowski, *Lazarus: Book I,*
> *Intermedia*, 1976)

At this time, absorbed in the reading of the Book of Genesis, Zekowski found herself writing a neo-narrative prose fiction in which she tried to recreate a kind of verbal orchestral lyrical choreographic topographic bas-relief of those remote times people and events. Here is an excerpt from *Salt from Sacraments*, Chapter XIII on David and Bathsheba:

> Off spring. Of kind. Warblings. Where the brook trout swam. Bathsheba breasted. To the window. From. Where David saw. And feasted. Drinking. After.
>
> As before. The waiting. To be known. Makes. Made. Where music was. As rain beat days of rain. And other days. To be.
>
> Moves the cloud. The burst. The rain. Bowed out from under. On the colors. Is. As positive. To hue. And cry. The God.
>
> (Zekowski, *Salt from Sacraments,*
> Chapter XIII, *Kayak* 18, 1969)

In Chapter V of *The Sudden Testimony* there is also a spillover of the energy and preoccupation with those remote times, the bucolic simplicity, harmony of people and nature:

> As so. A chapter falls. To tombs. Lie hidden. Covers between. The pages of the written afternoon. When there these every very ones to say. Said all. A monument in mausoglyph encyclopedias.
>
> As full. They lived. These ours. Ancestried. To none except themselves. The first fruits. From no first fruits. Fallen. Angels were. The only. After. Towards reward. A seeming. Necessary for. Necessitied.
>
> (Zekowski, *The Sudden Testimony,*
> Chapter V, *Delirium* 4/5, 1979)

In our most recent critical volumes we decided to write a small critique of each other's writing as well as our own. This is how Stanley Berne described the following segment from Chapter XIII of *Grounds for Possibilities*, by Zekowski.

> All the blazon. And the flags.
> That summers. Birds. And feathers.
> In their under. Leaves. The tree.
>
> (Zekowski)

> What Zekowski is saying here is that original language
> was a picture, not an abstraction. "Birds." is a separate
> picture and does exist apart from specie detail, while, "
> And feathers." returns that knowledge of the structure of
> birds to its separate common characteristic. But the conclu-
> sion, "The tree." gives us the ongoing process in which it,
> the tree, "summers" the feathered birds: and all taken
> together, the birds, their plumage, the full leafed tree, and
> the shelter afforded by the tree to the, "Birds." are the flags
> and blazon of the glorious moment "That summers." or IS
> Summer.
>
> (Berne, *Future Language*: 61-63)

Some of the themes in *Seasons of the Mind* (Zekowski) contrast *Man thing* versus *Man thinking*: "My country 'tis of thee!/Sweet land of profitry./Let junk-heaps pile!"; Western druidic kinship of peoples: anglo, Spanish, Navaho, Zuni, Hopi, mingled with adventurers, fur trappers, hunters, scouts, pioneers, conquistadores, against modern man's buried ancestor-indifferent soul; History and Religion as "fictions" and "lies" versus Art as . . . "life-loving and life-giving"; and Reality, the "evolution . . . flux and flow of our feeling moments, the one true progress of the soul":

> And so we say goodbye to all the past. To all the pain and
> hate and horror and confusion. And wait in never resting.
> Restless expectation. For the flux of life within us. Each
> and all. Continuous and becoming. To be part of. In all our
> courage. And our fear. The glory of it all. Unknown. As
> all true glory. Of the true life. Always is. But must be in
> its full aliveness. Being what it is. In full becoming.
> Flowering and alive.
>
> (Zekowski, *Seasons of the Mind*,
> 1969: 111)

In addition, *Seasons of the Mind* (Zekowski), and the two works of the 1970's, *The Age of Iron and Other Interludes* and *Histories and Dynasties* (Zekowski) all explore and further develop one of the motifs introduced in *Abraxas*: the settling of the American continent as a myth of nature and of human history. Here is a selection from the book, *Histories and Dynasties* (Zekowski) to be published in 1981:

> So blessings on you. Wild Bill Hickock. Calamity Jane. Kit Carson. Coronado and Cortez. And Buffalo Bill. The friend of kings and presidents. Pony Express Rider, Buffalo Hunter, Frontiersman, Army Chief of Scouts. America's and the world's greatest huckster. Barnum of the West. And your Wild West Show.... And the whole darn breed of America's bummy seedy dustgrit greedy seething whiskey-bellied cowpoke huckstering lily-livered puritan hell-fired purgatoried god-fearing bible-toting man hating indian killered bushwacker mine and cattle stealer desperado, hired-gun vigilante justice rough and ready roistering bite the dust, hangman rail-road gangman and the whole glamor bag of smart-aleck frontier get-with-it success or succumb philosophy of exploit or be exploited. And carry the white man's burden. Which happens to be a bag of gold. And not his sins be hanged. Be hanged if you do. And be hanged if you don't.
>
> (Zekowski, *Histories and Dynasties,*
> *Voices from the Rio Grande,* 1976: 80)

In *Seasons of the Mind* (Zekowski) and in *The Unconscious Victorious and Other Stories* (Berne), we included, along with transcripts of several radio interviews, and the Sir Herbert Read correspondence, our most ambitious essays to date on language rhythm and texture, poetry and prose, the novel and short story, literature and science, high art and low art, etc.: above all, a *new kind of story*, a "fiction" based on the authenticity of experience, not on the old traditional literal "fiction" of a predetermined plot, constitutes our view of *literature for the year 2000*:

> ... The critics of literature seem to set their jaw in the stubborn direction of forcing writing to serve the cinema, by insisting there is but one kind of narrative, and that is cinematic narrative.
> ... the short story can do the things that only language itself can do, which the camera cannot do, ... operating within the frame of the action of language itself.
> (Berne, "The Short Story," *The Unconscious*
> *Victorious and Other Stories:* 1969)

> Story means simply a telling of something. The concept of story has become cliché because the telling of something has been reduced in the novel to an arbitrary

form known as plot.

Plot as we know it must be destroyed because in this form the reader does not experience anything new.

.... Story then simply means exposure to a new frame of reference in the form of a narrative which does not follow any familiar recognizable sequence but which creates its own. . . .

.... Every man and every woman who constitute the readers of the new narrative become, if you will, the "characters" where the responsibility of being exposed to an experience is no longer at last a fiction but the truth.

Only with the New Narrative will the old saw take on its true old and new meaning: "Truth is stranger than fiction." And only with the encouragement of what is true, can literature breathe authenticity now and in the future.

(Zekowski, "Questions And Answers,"
Seasons of the Mind: 1969)

Bibliography

By Stanley Berne:

The Multiple Modern Gods and Other Stories. New York: Wittenborn, 1964.
The Unconscious Victorious and Other Stories. New York: Wittenborn, 1969.
The New Rubaiyat of Stanley Berne. Portales, NM: American-Canadian, 1973.
Future Language. New York: Horizon, 1976.
The Great American Empire. New York: Horizon Press, 1982.

By Arlene Zekowski:

Abraxas. New York: Wittenborn, 1964.
Seasons of the Mind. New York: Wittenborn, 1969.
The Age of Iron and Other Interludes. Portales, NM: American-Canadian, 1973.
Image Breaking Images. New York: Horizon, 1976.
Histories and Dynasties. New York: Horizon, 1982.

About Stanley Berne & Arlene Zekowski:

Sutherland, Donald. "Preface to *Grounds for Possibilities*," in *A First Book of the Neo-Narrative*. Stonington, Connecticut: Metier Editions, 1954.

Everman, Welch D. "Mapping the Neo-Narrative and the Grammarless Language: An Interview with Stanley Berne & Arlene Zekowski," *X: A Journal of the Arts*, 6/7 (Winter, 1979).

—. "Berne and Zekowski: A Language Beyond Grammar," *The Review of Contemporary Fiction*, IV/3 (Fall 1984).

Miller, Walter James. "The Ego and Id and the Word," Preface to Zekowski's *Histories and Dynasties*. New York: Horizon Press, 1982.

Text—Sound

A Conversation among Charles Dodge, Bliem Kern, Richard Kostelanetz, and Jackson Mac Low

Kostelanetz: By "text-sound" I mean language that is enhanced primarily in terms of sound rather than syntax or semantics. An elementary example in English would be this tongue twister: "If a Hottentot taught a Hottentot tot to talk 'ere the tot could totter, ought the Hottentot be taught to say ought or naught or what ought to be taught 'er?" That ditty is obviously not about education or about African tribes, but about the sounds ôt and ŏt and how they can relate to each other in English. That is an elementary or *folk* example of text-sound art.

With me are three of America's finest text-sound artists: Bliem Kern, born in 1943 in Philadelphia, whose first book of poems was actually a paperbound book and a tape cassette put together in a square box, entitled *Meditationsmeditationsmeditations* (1973); Jackson Mac Low, born in 1922 in Chicago, who has been producing text-sound of various kinds for over four decades; and Charles Dodge, born in 1942 in Ames, Iowa, who has done extremely sophisticated computer voice-generation for his language pieces. I should mention that I also practice this art and that I edited the anthology *Text-Sound Texts* (1980).

Bliem Kern, would you describe the evolution of your work?
Kern: Well, as I began in college to write poetry, I wrote straight poetry, traditional poetry, consisting of nouns, verbs, adjectives, and adverbs, and so forth. I carried it down to its simplest essence through study of William Carlos Williams and of Bashō. I tried to make it as succinct as possible—say the most with as few words as possible. Then I broke the words up into syllables and letters. So then I had to voice these symbols—these letters, syllables, vowels, and consonants. And that's how my sound poetry evolved from that departure, from

the nouns and verbs to parts of words.

Kostelanetz: But it was a radical step to take apart the whole word. After all, the whole word is considered to be the sacred element in literature, the element that should never be violated.

Kern: True, but I think that sounds are perhaps more sacred. Ancient cultures used sound to convey messages orally. Before books were created or written texts, everything was memorized and passed on. So it was the sound. . . .

Kostelanetz: What kind of sound do you mean? Do you mean a language sound as though you were listening to a foreign language?

Kern: Well, certain sounds have meanings. This ties into the philosophy and religious beliefs of the Hindus and the Egyptians; they both had certain sounds for certain *chakras* within the body.

Kostelanetz: What are *chakras*?

Kern: These are areas in the body which align in the nerve channels up through the spine, and certain sounds open up these nerve channels.

Kostelanetz: When you hear them or when you say them?

Kern: Both, but you have to say them, such as *Om*, pronounced "aum."

Kostelanetz: *Om* is the sound in Hindu mythology that God made when he created the universe.

Kern: Yes, right. And the Christian Bible says, "God said, let there be light." So my philosophy, my whole belief, is that the world began in sound: "From vibration in the air we have light on the stair. Out of the darkness first time saw you standing there." That's a phrase from my "Nuclear Prayer." I say from vibration of matter we have sound and from vibration of matter we have light.

Kostelanetz: When did this evolution happen for you?

Kern: In the late 1960s. That's when I started to depart from traditional poetry.

Kostelanetz: What did your work sound like when you developed this?

Kern: Here's a typical piece. It's entitled "jealousy," [spoken from the following score]:

See page 573.

Kostelanetz: Here, in performing your poem, you have taken that

jealousy

liefinillusionofbeliefinillusionofbeliefinillusionofbeliefinil]

liefinillusionofbeliefinillusionofbeliefinil]

word *jealousy* and pared it down to its parts and into its sounds and
then brought it back into the recognizable word.
Kern: Right. Take it into chaos and then pull it back out of chaos
into order.
Kostelanetz: Jackson Mac Low, how has your work evolved?
Mac Low: I began writing poetry in 1937. I had studied music since
I was four, and in 1937 I began writing both poetry and music and
continued writing them parallelly until I began working with chance
operations and indeterminacy in 1954. At that point, those two arts,
along with theater—previously I'd written a few plays—and also
visual art, came together in the work that I began doing then. After
that time, I worked for the first few years primarily with words,
silences, and word groups.

Why don't I give you an example of that type of piece? This is
a recent one but it is very similar to my earlier chance-operational
work. It's called "Stoveblack." It's derived from a word list by a lady
named Leona Bleiweiss, who used to run a game in the New York *Post*
called "Word Power." The basis for this is the list of words she found
that can be spelled with the letters of the word *stoveblack*. Two strophes
should give you the patterning of this:

> above skate covet close ascot cable
> black cloak caste stole vocal store stoke
> slave covet eclat stale sable
> store
> close stalk cable
> covet
> eclat store sable beast besot beast
> stack besot slack slack
>
> stoke salve ovate beat baste block
> salve stoke vocal ovate cable beast bloke
> blast cable stale cable stole
> eclat
> store black beast
> scale
> stock stork stove stale costa slate
> stead costa cable stake

Kostelanetz: So your vocabulary is a collection of words found in
the word *stoveblack*.
Mac Low: Yes. And words were "randomly selected" from that
collection and so arranged as to constitute a repetitive structure by

means of chance operations involving random digits.

Kostelanetz: In that work you moved out of syntactical poetry, as we understand it, and also in a certain way out of semantical poetry.

Mac Low: Yes, this is characteristic of my work between 1954 and 1960 especially.

Kostelanetz: How are the words in "Stoveblack" organized?

Mac Low: Well, having decided to use Ms. Bleiweiss's list as a source, I then chose to employ random digits to determine both the poem's verse pattern and the specific words that would "fill" the "places" in the pattern. The verse pattern comprises the number of stanzas, of lines in each stanza, and of words in corresponding lines of stanzas. Thus this poem comprises eight eight-line stanzas, in each of which the successive lines comprise six, seven, five, one, three, one, six, and four words, respectively. The first random digits gave me the pattern; subsequent digits "filled the places." These methods yield two types of organization. The first—and, I think, the more impor- tant—is that constituted by the irregular recurrences of the limited number of English phonemes that may be represented by the letters in the word *stoveblack* and of the small number of five-letter words com- posed of those phonemes that appear in Ms. Bleiweiss's list and were brought into the poem by systematic chance. The second type of organization—more obvious but less basic—is that brought about by the chance-determined repetitive verse pattern. The second—the regular pattern—is arbitrarily associated with (or even "imposed upon") the first: the irregular repetition of a small number of meaning- ful sound groups.

Kostelanetz: So they are organized in terms of larger structures, rather than point-to-point structures.

Mac Low: Exactly. Up to 1961 I only used whole words, silences, and word groups, as in my book *Stanzas for Iris Lezak*. That is, I used as units in poems, not only single words but phrases, or even full sentences, everything from single words through phrases through larger sentence fragments to whole sentences. But then I began making a kind of piece in 1961 that I called "Gathas." This is a Sanskrit term used for versified sections of Buddhist sutras, and Dr. Daisetz Teitaro Suzuki also used the term when referring to the little verses that Zen masters and students wrote for each other, as when one would write: "The mind is like a mirror. Keep it cleaned off." And another would write in answer: "What mirror? What mind? What

dust?" And since at first I used Buddhist mantras as bases for my
pieces (later on, I also used other materials), I came to call them Gathas,
since I thought of them as Buddhist poems. However, they're organized on graph paper, and in them repetitions of a mantra are set forth
by chance operations to form a unique configuration.

Kostelanetz: On a horizontal and vertical grid.

Mac Low: Yes, exactly. On what they call quadrille paper. But in
performing them, the performer—and they can be performed either
by an individual or a group of any number—each follows a path of his
own or her own choosing by starting at any point on the grid and going
from point to point, horizontally, vertically, and/or even diagonally,
saying the names of letters, sounds of letters, syllables, whole words,
and/or the whole mantra.

Kostelanetz: So it exists as a score in which individuals can move
around in various ways.

Mac Low: Exactly. This is one that I wrote in 1976 and have used
as a beginning of every reading and concert that I have presented since
then. It's based on the mantra of Milarepa, who is one of the founders
of Tibetan Buddhism. And his mantra is *Je mila zhädpa dorje la sölwa
debso*. It's a Tibetan utterance in praise of Milarepa and contains, in
some sense, the spirit of Milarepa.

Kostelanetz: So what you have here is a set of words or, let's say,
collections of letters that you could read as words or as individual
letters or as phonemes.

Mac Low: Not only "sounds." On this particular grid, the mantra
is written vertically, starting at a different number of squares from the
top in each file, so the configuration that you get then forms, horizontally and diagonally, any number of combinations including English
words such as "road," "lad," "law," "as," and so on.

Kostelanetz: Charles Dodge, how has your work with language
evolved?

Dodge: Unlike my colleagues Bliem Kern and Jackson Mac Low,
I had a period of time in which I worked strictly in instrumental and
electronic music. In fact, most of my adult life has been spent using
digital computers to make electronic music. I had the good fortune to
be associated with one of the founders of computer music, Max
Mathews, who is the Director of Acoustical Research at the Bell
Telephone Laboratories. For a period in my life in which I was
blissfully on a grant, I was able to spend my evenings at the Bell Labs
making music with computers which had been designed and pro-

grammed for speech research. The Bell Telephone Company is very involved in research on the acoustics of speech, and as part of their speech research facilities they have computers which are programmed to analyze and synthesize voices. It was one such computer system that I used to make my *Speech Songs*.

I became experienced in what is called speech-synthesis-by-analysis. This method begins with a tape recording of the passage to be synthesized. The recording is first digitized and then analyzed by the computer. The analysis program extracts the frequency content of the voice as it changes with time and presents the results in such a way that the original speech may be reconstituted from the analysis. Of more interest to the musician, however, is that the analysis may be "edited" as it is reconstituted. For instance, if the pitch of the voice is, say 100 Hertz, or cycles per second, and that is not what I want, I can change it to 440 Hertz.

Kostelanetz: Why use the computer to make tape rather than traditional electronic tape recording techniques?

Dodge: The major advantage of computer voice synthesis, as compared with manipulation of the recorded voice with a tape recorder, is the possibility of altering the time base of the speech independently of its frequency content. For example, after you record something on tape, if you play it at half-speed and therefore elongate it, you also shift all the frequencies which constitute the vocal sound by one octave. This results in a distortion of the speech so that the speech will sound unnatural at best, and unintelligible at worst. With computer speech synthesis it is possible to change the speed of the speech a great deal but to retain the frequency content of the speech at the original level. This preserves the quality of the speech and retains its intelligibility.

Using the speech editing facility on the computers at Bell Labs, it was also possible to replace the recorded pitch contour of the speech without changing the speech speed. This feature enables the sort of "pitched but not sung" quality of the *Speech Songs*. Perhaps at this point we should give an illustration of how I did one speech song for my record *Synthesized Speech Music* (1976). I first made a tape of my voice speaking "live" a short poem by Mark Strand.

> The days are ahead
> 1,926,346 to 1,926,345
> Later the nights will catch up.

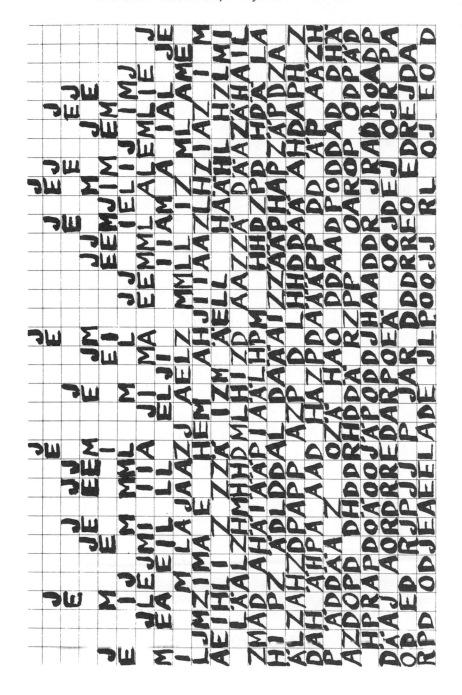

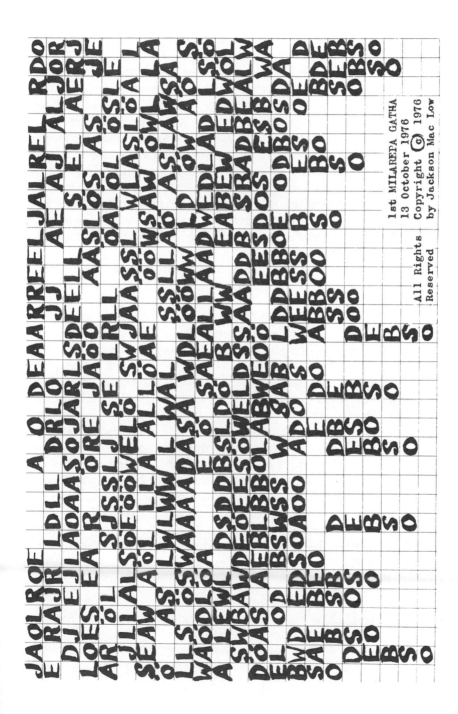

Once that rendition was stored in the computer, it was analyzed and presented at the computer console in a form to be edited. It is a feature of the Bell Labs system that the editing can be performed in either of two ways. You can communicate the edits in numerical form by means of typing at the system teletype or in graphical form by drawing patterns on a TV screen with a light pen. After the edits were made, the actual synthesis of the speech was computed and then the results were played through loudspeakers located right at the user's console. The speech song was created out of the single reading of the poem by editing the pitch contour of the speech into melodic patterns, by editing the time base of the original speech into rhythmic patterns, and by overdubbing. Overdubbing is the mixing of the voices together to make polyphonic textures. All overdubbing on the Bell Labs system was done digitally.

Kostelanetz: Digitally—you mean you didn't need to mix tape with a live voice?

Dodge: Exactly.

Kostelanetz: How long did that take you to make?

Dodge: The song took two months to produce working three or four nights a week—at night, because they were using the machines for speech research in the daytime. The reason that such a short piece takes so long is that each moment is "hand-crafted," that is, each moment of each voice has to be specified and edited separately and then, if necessary, mixed digitally with others.

Kostelanetz: The most extraordinary thing to me about your tape is how the language is enhanced by your computer-assisted method. The difference between your original straight reading of it and the tape realization is stunning and enormous. Is the language enhanced partly because the rendition is something that you cannot do live—there's no way that any human being could sound like that live? Is that what makes it so special?

Dodge: Partly that, I think, and also something else. The interesting thing about computer speech synthesis is that it has the tone quality and acoustics of speech, but the pitch and the rhythm of music. It does not sound "sung." To me that produces a very nice contradiction in terms.

Kostelanetz: You mean you are expanding the sound of the spoken voice without introducing melody.

Dodge: You do have melody; that is, you have pitch successions that people might think of as melodies, but you don't have that sort of bright and somewhat artificial sound that comes from singing. You have something that sounds quite relaxed and natural in its articulation.

Kostelanetz: Bliem Kern, have you worked with audio tape?

Kern: I've worked with it, but I like to do everything with my voice. I don't manipulate anything in the studio. I'm a purist. I don't think all these techniques add anything to my work. I remember back in November of 1971 I pre-recorded an hour-long broadcast at WBAI-FM Pacifica Radio. I worked for two hours recording my work and after I was through I found that the engineer had added all sorts of echoes, boops, and bleeps. They seemed to me to be quite unnecessary and inappropriate to my work. Besides he never asked me if he could do that to my poetry. It destroyed the purity of it. So, I came back the next day and did the whole show over again.

Kostelanetz: It seems to me, Bliem, that you have a sense of sound poetry as being rooted in the body, in the sounds the body can make, which would be a position quite different from Charles Dodge's position.

Kern: Truly, yes.

Kostelanetz: Jackson Mac Low, how have you used audio tape for your kinds of work?

Mac Low: A number of different ways. One, of course, is in recording performances. Another is producing multiple performances superimposd on each other. For example, one tape produced in Germany by S Press comprises four simultaneous performances of a group of my pieces called "The Black Tarantula Crossword Gathas." That is, the whole set of four performances was copied on both tracks of a dual stereo tape after having been recorded separately on a quadraphonic machine, and the two copies were started about 20 seconds apart from each other, so that they form a four-against-four canon. I have frequently worked with canonic devices of that sort. One superimposition is called *Counterpoint for Candy Cohen*, where I took a little fragment of speech. I rerecorded it, with randomly-placed silences, as a loop and then repeatedly rerecorded the loop on four different tracks of tape. Next I dumped all four tracks on both tracks of a dual machine and continued this process, going back and forth, until I had something like 360 superimpositions by the last stage.

Kostelanetz: By running the nuclear tape between machines, you can build it up through many generations of voices.

One of the more interesting American tape sound poets is

Charles Amirkhanian, and he has yet another way of working with tape loops and other kinds of superimposition, for example, the piece "Just" (1972) on his record *10 + 2; 12 American Text Sound Pieces* (1750 Arch, 1974).

Dodge: That's right. First he records his voice, then edits it into passages that he likes. He ties the tapes end to end and runs what I assume to be very long loops, possibly from one tape recorder to another, and then back around, and uses a mixing panel, a device that enables you to vary the gain on more than one signal at a time.

Kostelanetz: To make one or another louder than the other.

Dodge: That's right. To fade one in....

Kostelanetz: And fade another element out. But how would you characterize that kind of technique in contrast to your own technique?

Dodge: Well, that technique takes the recording as it comes out of the microphone and uses that as a fixed entity, albeit with editing. Mine takes what comes out of the microphone, analyzes it, and enables me to alter it in ways that we mentioned before, in pitch and time, before committing the results finally to tape.

Kostelanetz: So these are kinds of text-sound that could not have been done prior to the invention of. the tape machine, which is basically a post-World War II phenomenon. But then there are two traditions: one which is concerned with machinery and another which is concerned only with live performance. The live tradition, of course, goes back to primitive times and primitive kinds of speech communication.

Whom do you identify as your precursors for what you do?

Mac Low: I would say Gertrude Stein, Kurt Schwitters, and in the use of chance operations, John Cage and our predecessor among the earlier people, Marcel Duchamp. I would say that they were the strongest influences on my own work of this kind.

Kostelanetz: Stein in what sense?

Mac Low: In the sense that she often composed nonsyntactically.

Kostelanetz: And therefore was a clear precursor to some of your earliest poetry.

Mac Low: Oh, yes. She was a great inspiration to me from the time I was very young, and I started writing poetry of that sort as early as 1946.

Kostelanetz: And Schwitters?

Mac Low: Well, he composed pure sound poetry, pure phoneme poetry, and poetry composed solely of numbers. He also was a great master of the collage technique. For me, more than his sound poetry and his number poetry, his collage technique as a visual artist—what he called his Merz collages—were a great inspiration to my work.

Kostelanetz: So there is Schwitters and there is Stein. But John Cage? He is someone we associate with modern musical composition.

Mac Low: Well, yes. As I said, I was composing music and always interested very deeply in music since I was a child. I got acquainted with Cage's work as early as the late 1940s and came to know him personally in the early 1950s. I was very much interested in his use of chance operations in the composition of music, which he began around 1950. Undoubtedly, the most direct inspiration to using these then-unusual means—chance operations and composition of pieces that are different at each performance, which are called indeterminate pieces—was Cage's work. I wanted to see what could be accomplished using these methods with verbal material, not using the same methods that John did, but methods using the principles of chance and indeterminacy.

Kostelanetz: What do you mean by chance?

Mac Low: "Chance" means that the composer or poet does not decide the details or sometimes even the structure of the work.

Kostelanetz: In the same sense that, in your reading before, you said that the text could be read in any of several directions.

Mac Low: Well, that is another stage, but in the sense of the earlier kind of piece, where I have a definite repeating structure that was determined by random digits. That's a kind of a table that's produced now by computers for use by statisticians, physicists, and others to get digits, or numbers, that are not determined by any principle, but literally by chance. John Cage, however, uses a method associated with the *I Ching*, the ancient Chinese *Book of Changes*, which is consulted by chance operations involving coins or yarrow stalks.

Kostelanetz: Cage's method is an anti-structure structuring.

Mac Low: Yes. I tend to structure more than Cage. Often, I think John doesn't want to have structure at all. I make chance-determined structures in many works. But in the way I proceed in this other kind of work—we've only touched on a few kinds—in composing the other kind of work of which I gave an example, the Gatha, I produce a performance score by chance methods. When I composed the "1st Milarepa Gatha," chance determined where on the grid the mantra was repeated in each vertical file. But the score is then subject to the immediate impulses of the performer. It is not a matter, then, of impersonal chance, which is the case with the other kinds of work I've done, but rather, there, spontaneously using a chance-given structure to make a performance: one moves around on it as impulse directs.

Kostelanetz: It becomes then, an improvisatory structure.

Mac Low: Yes, it becomes an improvisatory structure. In performing such pieces, I try to relate to all the sounds that are audible at the time; and when there are a number of people working, they also relate to each other, so no single ego determines the total performance.

Kostelanetz: Charles Dodge, who are your precursors in terms of what you do?

Dodge: Well, I think I was highly influenced by Luciano Berio and, curiously, Arnold Schönberg, because of his *sprechstimme* technique for using the voice in a non-singing manner. I was also very interested in the work of the Swedish text-sound composers: Lars-Gunnar Bodin, Bengt Emil Johnson, and Sten Hanson. I became aware of their work at about the same time I became aware of the work of a Swedish speech acoustician, Gunnar Font, a physicist who has postulated an accurate acoustical model of the voice.

Kostelanetz: Bliem, who do you identify as your precursors?

Kern: Well, the poets I feel have influenced me the most are the ancient poets: Homer, Shakespeare—he's not ancient—Moses, Hermes Trigmegistus.

Kostelanetz: Is there a more particular influence in your case?

Kern: Particular influence? Well, there was my dear friend Norman Pritchard whom I studied with at The New School in 1968-1969. He encouraged me to voice my poems of letters, parts of words, vowels, and consonants. Norman pushed me beyond the limits of traditional poetry as we know it today into an old tradition of oral poetry from which I believe we will see the birth of a new tradition in literature. Books will need to be heard as well as seen. Books will be read aloud once again with new and beautiful forms created by artists and poets of the future. I also feel that it is more of an intuitive sense on my part to return to childhood, to babble, and to make meaning out of the babble.

Kostelanetz: So you feel you're really writing poems about childhood sensibility?

Kern: No, not about childhood sensibility. As children, we were freer and not as condensed and uptight about what we say as we are now. We didn't think too much.

Kostelanetz: So therefore, by bursting out of syntax you're getting back to childhood freedom?

Kern: In a sense getting back to childhood freedom; but I think, as a child, we're more intuitive and more unconscious about what we do. For me, my poetry is more an intuitive sense in trying to express beauty and truth intuitively rather than copying someone who did it before me. I mean, I became aware of these poets that are doing the same things that I am all over the world long after I had already gotten into it for several years.

Kostelanetz: Now we've heard two kinds of phrases used for this art: sound poetry is one, and text-sound is another. Which do you prefer and why?

Kern: I would prefer sound poetry because I am more of a purist. I was schooled in how to write a well-crafted poem, and from that I went into sound poetry.

Mac Low: Well, I don't tend to use either of the terms. People have been kind enough to call some of my work sound poetry or text-sound. I feel that it is just poetry and/or music. I tend not to be a purist. I'm probably the most impure of the group here in that sense, and as my friends here know, in the performances I often have used instruments that translate the letters of my poems and pieces into tones.

Kostelanetz: So that your letter scores can be translated into musical notes?

Mac Low: Yes, there is a way to translate the letters of some of my pieces into tones. There are a number of scores I call "Vocabularies," where a number of words, spelled with the letters of a person's name, are arrayed on a large sheet as a kind of a drawing, and people can either read them or play them. Usually these days, my "simultaneities"—Gathas, Vocabularies, etc.—are performed by speaker-instrumentalists.

Kostelanetz: So you consider yourself as freely relating to either language or musical sound and mixing them freely as well?

Mac Low: Yes, sometimes . . . often.

Dodge: I think text-sound composition was something that came to my work rather than the other way around. I was blissfully, or otherwise, unaware of much of the activity in this country until my speech songs began to be circulated on tape and made their way onto records. Now I am just as blissfully aware of the great profusion of activity of very different sorts which may be called "sound poetry" or "text-sound" composition and which is very interesting to listen to. That is what seems to interest me most.

Kostelanetz: I prefer the term text-sound myself. My anthology is
called *Text-Sound Texts* because much of the work is not poetry but
prose at base. The measure of the art is how it is enhanced, what it is
enhanced in terms of, and if it is enhanced in terms of sound, then it
is text-sound.

Kern: Let me say this. Poetry originally was an oral tradition and
it was primarily sound. It was passed from father to son through
memory of the particular sound and the order of the sounds. Since
the Gutenberg press, it's been written down, and now we've more or
less mucked it up. I think that sound was the essence of language in
the beginning and we have to find that essense that's been lost,
I think.

Mac Low: Every poem is as much meaning as sound and as much
sound as meaning.

Kostelanetz: But there is certainly a distinction between a Shake-
spearean sonnet and the kind of thing that you did earlier today.

Mac Low: A lack of syntax. A lack of intended meaning on the
utterance level, on the level of sentences, of larger, connected meanings. Yes, there is *that* distinction, but I shy away from the distinction
on the basis of whether sound is emphasized or not, because it seems
to me that meaning is a very important part of what is often called
sound poetry, and at the same time, that sound is always equally
important with the semantic meaning of the more "traditional" kinds
of poetry (although, as Bliem says, what is called "sound poetry" was
probably the first poetry).

Kostelanetz: Also we have these names in part because we're
aware of a particular tradition that people before us were not aware
of—tradition that leads to ourselves, needless to say. That's one
reason why a symposium on this subject is being done now, in 1980,
where it would not have been done 20 years ago, because 20 years ago
there was no sense of a tradition of sound poetry or text-sound as a
distinct literary form.

Bibliography

Dodge, Charles. *Synthesized Speech Music*. New York: Composers Recordings, Inc., 1976.

Kern, Bliem. *Meditationsmeditationsmeditations*. New York: New Rivers, 1973.

—. *Nuclear Prayer*. New York: La Maison de la Bleame, 1978.

Kostelanetz, Richard, editor. *Text-Sound Texts*. New York: Morrow, 1980.

Mac Low, Jackson. *Stanzas for Iris Lezak*. Barton, Vermont: Something Else, 1972.

—. *The Pronouns—A Collection of 40 Dances*. Third edition, revised. Barrytown, New York: Station Hill, 1979.

Bibliography

Richard Kostelanetz, with Jerome Klinkowitz

The literature about post-World War II American culture is plentiful and various; and much as this concluding chapter initially aimed to be exhaustive, it is finally incomplete and inevitably selective. In addition to mentioning important books about the history and nonliterary culture of the period, it acknowledges general works about large areas of recent literature (macro-criticism) as distinct from monographs (micro-criticism) which, only for those authors included in this book, are listed after their essays here. No doubt other commentators on this macro-criticism might list different books or organize them differently, or comment upon them in different ways. At base, two writers who have each produced several books on the period are here sharing their sense of the literature that they have read.

The most comprehensive cultural history of America's past 50 years remains William Manchester's massive *The Glory and the Dream* (1974), which is a panoramic, richly detailed survey in the tradition of Frederick Lewis Allen's books on earlier American eras. John Brooks's *The Great Leap* (1966) is more narrowly a social history of 1940 to 1965, while William Frank Zornow's *America at Mid-Century* (1959) is a strictly political history of 1945 to 1958. For the entire post-World War II period, the most up-to-date text is William Leuchtenberg's *A Troubled Feast* (revised edition, 1979). Geoffrey Perrett's *A Dream of Greatness* (1979) deals only with 1945-63 and thus with the triumph of American hegemony. *A History of the United States Since 1945* (1965), by Oscar Barck, Jr., covers the same period in a more perfunctory, superficial way. Eric F. Goldman's *The Crucial Decade and After—America, 1945-60* (1961) is slighter, if more stylish and interpretative. Joseph Goulden's *The Best Years* (1975) is a social history of the postwar boom of 1945-50. *The Fifties* (1977), by Douglas T. Miller and Marion Nowak, draws upon encyclopedic research mostly into manners and mores; *A Giant's*

Strength: America in the 1960s (1971), by David Burner, Robert D. Marcus, and Thomas R. West, is a textbook largely of political history, while Godfrey Hodgson's *America in Our Times* (1976) deals primarily with the 1960s, occasionally glancing backward at relevant earlier episodes. *The Sixties* (1977), edited by Lynda Rosen Obst, is an oversized, impressionistic anthology of memoirs and photographs. Richard Kostelanetz's *Master Minds* (1969) is a collection of comprehensive profiles of first-rank postwar culture figures.

For the Truman presidency, see Cabell Phillips's book of that title (1966), Truman's own *Memoirs* (1955-56), and Merle Miller's remarkably revelatory "oral biography," *Plain Speaking* (1974). T. R. Fehrenbach's *This Kind of War* (1963) is an anecdotal, prophetic military history of the Korean conflict; I. F. Stone's *A Hidden History of the Korean War* (1952) is a political critique. On the Eisenhower years, the basic books are Emmett John Hughes's *The Ordeal of Power* (1963) and Richard Nixon's memoir from the Vice-President's perspective, *Six Crises* (1962). For the Kennedy administration, the most comprehensive intimate memoir in Arthur M. Schlesinger's richly detailed *A Thousand Days* (1965); for his successor, the comparably intimate books are Eric F. Goldman's *The Tragedy of Lyndon Johnson* (1969) and Doris Kearns's unusually profound "psychobiography," *Lyndon Johnson and the American Dream* (1976). For Richard Nixon's career, four remarkably different books are Gary Wills's *Nixon Agonistes* (1970), Bruce Mazlish's *In Search of Nixon* (1972), J. Anthony Lukas's *Nightmare: The Underside of the Nixon Years* (1976), and Henry Kissinger's *The White House Years* (1979). Richard Reeves's *A Ford not a Lincoln* (1975) deals with Nixon's successor. Richard Rovere's *Senator Joe McCarthy* (1959), Alex Haley's *The Autobiography of Malcolm X* (1965), and Edward Jay Epstein's *Legend: The Secret World of Lee Harvey Oswald* (1978) are classic books on major "outsiders" of the period.

The principal sociological studies of American life in the early postwar years are David Riesman and collaborators' *The Lonely Crowd* (1950), William H. Whyte's *The Organization Man* (1956), Samuel Lubell's *The Future of American Politics* (1956), C. Wright Mills's more acerbic *White Collar* (1951) and *The Power Elite* (1956), Edgar Z. Friedenberg's *The Vanishing Adolescent* (1958), and Paul Goodman's *Growing Up Absurd* (1960). For the 1960s and after, the comparable books are Daniel Boorstin's *The Image* (1962); Marshall McLuhan's works, beginning with *Understanding Media* (1964); Kenneth Keniston's *The Uncommitted* (1965); Ben J. Wattenberg and Richard M. Scammon's *This*

U.S.A. (1965), which is sub-titled "An Unexpected Family Portrait of 194,067,296 Americans"; Tom Wolfe's books, beginning with *The Electric Kool-Aid Acid Test* (1968); Charles Reich's *The Greening of America* (1970); and Alvin Toffler's *Future Shock* (1970).

Major books on consequential episodes of postwar American life include Theodore Caplow and Reece J. McGee's *The Academic Marketplace* (1958), Herman Kahn's *On Thermonuclear War* (1960), Daniel Bell's *The End of Ideology* (1960), Theodore H. White's *The Making of the President 1960* (1961), Allen Weinstein's *Perjury: The Hiss-Chambers Case* (1978), and Martin Mayer's series of studies of the professions in America today—advertising, law, teaching, and banking. For the Kennedy assassination, see William Manchester's *Death of the President* (1967), Jim Bishop's *The Day Kennedy Was Shot* (1968), and the Warren Commission's *Report* (1964); the exemplary critiques of the last book are Edward Jay Epstein's *Inquest* (1966) and Sylvia Meagher's *Accessories After the Fact* (1967).

Both Laura Fermi's *Illustrious Immigrants* (1968) and *The Intellectual Migration: Europe and America 1930-1960* (1969), edited by Donald Fleming and Bernard Bailyn, identify the immigrant contribution to American culture. For a sense of post-World War II American historiography, see John Higham's anthology, *The Reconstruction of American History* (1962), and then the book he coauthored with Leonard Kriegel and Felix Gilbert for the Princeton Studies on Humanistic Scholarship in America, *History* (1965). For American historiography in the 1970s, see Michael Kammen's anthology, *The Past Before Us* (1980). For U.S. philosophy and anthropology, see two more books in the Princeton series, respectively Roderick M. Chisholm, et al., *Philosophy* (1964), and Eric R. Wolf's *Anthropology* (1964); for intellectual history per se, see John Higham and Paul K. Conkin's anthology, *New Directions in American Intellectual History* (1979).

The best introductions to major American painting and sculpture in the initial postwar period are two books by Irving Sandler, *The Triumph of American Painting* (1970) and *The New York School* (1978); Dore Ashton's *The New York School: A Cultural Reckoning* (1972); Wayne Anderson's *American Sculpture in Process, 1930-1970* (1975); and Brian O'Doherty's *American Masters* (n.d.). Barbara Rose's *American Art Since 1900* (1967), her *American Painting: The Twentieth Century* (second edition, 1977), and Sam Hunter's *American Art in the 20th Century* (1972) are three comprehensive histories that include elaborate, perceptive sections on postwar art. The two most influential critics of this period's visual art were Clement Greenberg and Harold Rosenberg, the former collecting his crucial essays in *Art and Culture* (1961) and the latter in several volumes. For the next period of American visual arts, the key texts are Lucy R. Lippard's *Pop Art* (1967) and Lawrence Alloway's *American Pop Art* (1974) and for the period after that, Lucy R. Lippard's *Six Years* (1973), Calvin Tomkins's *The Scene* (1976), Robert Pincus-Whitten's *Post-Minimalism* (1977), and Edward Lucie-Smith's *Art of the Seventies* (1980), in addition to several anthologies of arts criticism edited by Gregory Battcock.

The concluding chapters of John Burchard and Albert Bush-Brown's *The Architecture of America* (1961) contain the most descriptive and encyclopedic survey of the modernist tradition on native shores. For the first postwar decades, see especially William Jordy's *American Buildings and Their Architects* (1972) and then John Jacobus's *Twentieth Century Architecture 1940-65* (1966), in addition to Paul Heyer's comprehensive collection of interviews, *Architects on Architecture* (1966). The most enlightening books on the more recent period are Robert A. M. Stern's *New Directions in American Architecture* (1969), C. Ray Smith's *Supermannerism* (1977), and several provocative, witty volumes by Charles Jencks. Useful comprehensive introductions to postwar American "classical" music appear in Eric Salzman's *Twentieth Century Music: An Introduction* (1967) and Virgil Thomson's informative, if biased, *American Music Since 1910* (1970), as well as *Contemporary Composers on Contemporary Music* (1967), an anthology edited by Elliott Schwartz and Barney Childs. William Austin's *Music in the 20th Century* (1967) is both more scholarly and broader in scope, as it includes jazz. For the last alone, see Martin Williams's *Jazz Masters in Transition, 1957-1969* (1970). For understanding recent American modern dance, the best books are Edwin Denby's *Looking at the Dance* (1949) and *Dancers, Buildings and People in the Streets* (1965), Don McDonogh's *The Rise and Fall and Rise of Modern Dance* (1971) and *The Complete Guide to Modern Dance* (1976), and Sally Banes's *Terpsichore in Sneakers* (1979).

The most complete history of pre-1955 commercial film is Arthur Knight's *The Liveliest Art* (1957); Andrew Sarris's *The American Cinema* (1968) contains comprehensive notes on a large number of directors who worked between 1929 and 1968. Donald Bogle's *Toms, Coons, Mulattoes, Mammies & Bucks* (1973) is a brilliant history of Blacks in American films. The surest critical guides to the noncommercial film in America are Sheldon Renan's pioneering *An Introduction to the*

American Underground Film (1967) and P. Adams Sitney's more thoughtful *Visionary Film* (revised edition, 1979). Charlie Gillett's *The Sound of the City* (1970) is a sensitive and sensible history of the rise of rock and roll music, and Jan Ried's *The Improbable Rise of Redneck Rock* (1974) is a broad survey of sophisticated "country and Western" music. The best books about the 1960s boom in popular music are Lillian Roxon's awesomely comprehensive *Rock Encyclopedia* (1969, revised edition, 1979); Jim Miller's anthology, *The Rolling Stone Illustrated History of Rock & Roll* (revised edition, 1980); and David Pichaske's *A Generation in Motion* (1979), which relates changes in popular music to other cultural developments. The great history of "vernacular dance" in America is Marshall and Jean Stearns's *Jazz Dance* (1968). *The Smithsonian Collection of Newspaper Comics* (n.d.), edited by Bill Blackbeard and Martin Williams, complements Les Daniels's earlier, more stylish *COMIX: A History of Comic Books in America* (1971). The initial anthology of critical essays about *Mass Culture* (1957), edited by Bernard Rosenberg and David Manning White, remains in many respects the most various and profound.

Barry Ulanov's *The Two Worlds of American Art* (1965) is incomparably broad in its coverage of both "private" and "popular" arts. Richard Kostelanetz edited *The New American Arts* (1965), an anthology of essays by several hands on the post-1959 revolutions in literature, music, modern dance, painting, and film. *Metamorphosis in the Arts* (1980) is his critical history of the avant-garde in the fine arts in the 1960s—not only painting, sculpture, music, film and dance, but the new artistic intermedia. *Esthetics Contemporary* (1978) is his anthology of philosophical essays on recent arts.

The cultural histories of the postwar period can be divided into two groups—intentional and unintentional. Among the first bunch are four books on the 1960s that are so different in their emphases and approaches that they scarcely seem to be portraying the same period: Leslie Fiedler's *Waiting for the End* (1965), Ronald S. Berman's *America in the Sixties* (1968), Morris Dickstein's *Gates of Eden: American Culture of the Sixties* (1977), and Jerome Klinkowitz's *The American 1960s* (1980). Among the implicit histories are collections of one-person critical essays so unified in perspective and broad in scope that they finally succeed as cultural history: Edmund Wilson's *The Bit Between My Teeth* (1965); Leslie Fiedler's *Collected Essays* (1971); several collections of criticism apiece by Lionel Trilling, Irving Howe, and Dwight Macdonald; Ihab Hassan's *Paracriticisms* (1975) and *The Right Prom-*

ethean Fire (1980); and Richard Kostelanetz's *Twenties in the Sixties* (1979).

Most of the standard comprehensive histories and encyclopedias of American literature extend their coverage into the postwar period: Max J. Hertzberg's *The Reader's Encyclopedia of American Literature* (1962), James D. Hart's *Oxford Companion to American Literature* (1965), Sarah L. Prakken's *The Reader's Advisor* (1974), and *The Literary History of the United States* (fourth edition, 1973), edited by Robert Spiller, et al., where postwar writing is critically surveyed by Ihab Hassan, Daniel Hoffman, and Gerald Weales. Volume three of *The Penguin Companion to Literature* (1971) has an American section, edited by Malcolm Bradbury and Eric Mottram, that is culturally more up-to-date, if critically slighter, than the other books. No books cover as many individuals, American as well as British, as the massive, sporadically updated encyclopedias presently edited by James Vinson: *Contemporary Poets* (first edition, 1970; second edition, 1975; third edition, 1980), *Contemporary Novelists* (1972, 1976), and *Contemporary Dramatists* (1973, 1977). The essays in two encyclopedias, Jeffrey Helterman's and Richard Laymans' *American Novelists Since World War II* (1978) and Donald J. Grenier's two-volume *American Poets Since World War II* (1980), are longer, the cast of characters more selective.

There have been so far only three multi-genre surveys exclusively of post-World War II American literature; this book is the fourth. Daniel Hoffman's anthology, *The Harvard Guide to Contemporary American Writing* (1979) is ineptly organized, highly biased, and less current in its interests than Ihab Hassan's earlier, one-critic introduction, *Contemporary American Literature, 1945-72* (1972). Hans Bungert's anthology, *Die amerikanische Literatur der Gegenwart* includes articles by both European and American professors (all writing in German). Recent American literature in general, as well as many writers in specific, figure in Richard Kostelanetz's anthology of criticism of poetry, fiction and drama *On Contemporary Literature* (1964, 1969).

The first putatively comprehensive book on postwar American fiction was John Aldridge's *After the Lost Generation* (1951); and although subsequent literary history has made Aldridge's youthful, pioneering discriminations seem ever more embarrassing, he has since produced several more collections of essays on recent U.S. fiction. Malcolm Cowley's *The Literary Situation* (1954), by contrast, is the disparaging view of an older critic who likewise thinks he knows "what's happening" but who, 25 years later, seems equally wrong. It was not until the early 1960s that more definitive critical books appeared: Ihab Hassan's *Radical Innocence* (1961), Chester E. Eisinger's *Fiction of the Forties* (1963), Marcus Klein's *After Alienation: American Novels in Mid-Century* (1965), Jonathan Baumbach's *The Landscape of Nightmare* (1965), and David Galloway's *The Absurd Hero in American Fiction* (1966), in addition to Jack Ludwig's remarkably concise pamphlet, *Recent American Novelists* (1962), and three anthologies of extended critical essays: Joseph J. Waldmeir's *Recent American Fiction* (1963), Nona Balakian and Charles Simmons's *The Creative Present* (1963), and Harry T. Moore's *Contemporary American Novelists* (1964).

Later general books on postwar American fiction include Howard M. Harper's *Desperate Faith* (1967), Tony Tanner's *City of Words: American Fiction, 1950-1970* (1971), Helen Weinberg's *The New Novel in America: The Kafkian Mode in Contemporary Fiction* (1971), Arno Heller's *Odyssee zum Selbst* (1973), Josephine Hendin's *Vulnerable People* (1978), and Shigeo Hamano's *Konnichi No America Sakka Gun* (1978), in addition to Marcus Klein's anthology, *The American Novel Since World War II* (1969), Peter Freese's mostly German compilation, *Die amerikanische Short Story der Gegenwart* (1976), and Ira D. and Christine Johnson's collection, *Les Américanistes: New French Criticism on Modern American Fiction* (1978). Essays by Russian critics on several postwar writers are included, in English, in *Twentieth Century American Literature: A Soviet View* (1976, no editor credited), while *Forms of the American Imagination* (1979), edited by Sonja Bann and others, collects essays by both Austrians and Americans, in both German and English, on several aspects of recent American writing.

A second phase of critical literature deals mostly, if not exclusively, with those fiction writers who emerged in the 1960s: Robert Scholes's *The Fabulators* (1967), Raymond M. Olderman's *Beyond the Waste Land: The American Novel in the Nineteen-Sixties* (1972), Charles B. Harris's *Contemporary American Novelists of the Absurd* (1971), Max F. Schultz's *Black Humor Fiction of the Sixties* (1973), John Stark's *The Literature of Exhaustion* (1974), Manfred Pütz's *The Story of Identity: American Fiction of the Sixties* (1979), Ronald Wallace's *The Last Laugh* (1979), and two books on a yet newer group of writers who mostly emerged after 1967—Jerome Klinkowitz's *Literary Disruptions* (1975) and his *The Life of Fiction* (1977). One virtue of Jerry H. Bryant's *The Open Decision* (1970) is detailed coverage of many living novelists whom other critics neglect. New directions in both fiction and poetry, in addition to younger writers in general, are sketched in Richard Kostelanetz's *The End of Intelligent Writing: Literary Politics in America* (1974). Raymond Federman's critical anthology, *Surfiction* (1975), sets American experimental writing in an international avant-garde context. Mas'ud Zavarzadeh's *The Mythopoeic Reality* (1976) is an original study of the "Postwar American Nonfiction Novel."

Other critical books focus upon the postwar writing of only one or another minority group. Several books by Louis D. Rubin, Jr. follow literature in the American South: *The Faraway Country* (1963) was his early survey; the anthology *The American South* (1979), also published in this Forum Series, is the most recent. Other broadly conceived books on Southern literature are Louise Cowan's *The Fugitive Group* (1959), John M. Bradbury's *Renaissance in the South: A Critical History of the Literature* (1963), and John L. Stewart's *The Burden of Time* (1965). For Jewish-American writing, see Leslie Fiedler's *The Jew in the American Novel* (1959), Irving Malin's *Jews and Americans* (1965), Robert Alter's two collections of his essays, *After the Tradition* (1969) and *Defenses of the Imagination* (1977), Max F. Schultz's *Radical Sophistication* (1969), Allen Guttmann's *The Jewish Writer in America* (1971), Nathan A. Scott's 3 *American Moralists* (1973), and Irving Malin's anthology of critical essays by others, *Contemporary American-Jewish Literature* (1973). For contemporary black literature, see the concluding chapters of Robert Bone's *The Negro Novel in America* (1958), David Littlejohn's *Black on White* (1966), Edward Margolis's *Native Sons* (1968), Roger Rosenblat's *Black Fiction* (1974), Clarence Major's *The Dark and Feeling* (1974), and C. W. E. Bigsby's anthology, *The Black American Writer* (1969). For the writers customarily called "Beat," see John Tytell's *Naked Angels* (1976), Bruce Cook's *The Beat Generation* (1971), John Clellon Holmes's *Nothing More to Declare* (1967), and Lawrence Lipton's *The Holy Barbarians* (1959).

The essays of several regular reviewers of current fiction have been collected into books—not only the Irving Howe and Leslie Fiedler volumes mentioned before but Maxwell Geismar's *American Moderns* (1958); Herbert Gold's *The Age of Happy Problems* (1961); Elizabeth Hardwick's *A View of One's Own* (1962); Isaac Rosenfeld's *The Age of Enormity* (1962); Alfred Kazin's *Contemporaries* (1962) and *Bright Book of Life* (1973); Stanley Edgar Hyman's *The Promised End*

(1963), *Standards* (1966), and *The Critic's Credentials* (1978); Norman Podhoretz's *Doings and Undoings* (1964); three volumes apiece by Marvin Mudrick, Seymour Krim, and Benjamin DeMott; Theodore Solotaroff's *The Red Hot Vacuum* (1970); Granville Hicks's *Literary Horizons* (1970); Richard Poirier's *The Performing Self* (1971); William H. Gass's *Fiction and the Figures of Life* (1971) and *The World in the Word* (1978); John Leonard's *This Pen for Hire* (1973); Anatole Broyard's *Aroused by Books* (1974); Wilfrid Sheed's *The Good Word* (1978); and Philip Rahv's *Essays on Literature and Politics, 1932-72* (1978).

Several prominent authors of fiction have collected their fugitive essays into books that are partial and biased, and yet evocative and critically useful: Robert Penn Warren's *Selected Essays* (1958), Ralph Ellison's *Shadow and Act* (1964), Gore Vidal's *Homage to Daniel Shays* (1972) and his *Matters of Fact and Fiction* (1977), Mary McCarthy's *The Writing on the Wall* (1970), Kurt Vonnegut's *Wampeters Foma & Grandfalloons* (1974), Philip Roth's *Reading Myself and Others* (1975), Samuel R. Delany's *The Jewel-Hinged Jaw* (1977), and Ishmael Reed's *Shrovetide in Old New Orleans* (1978). Some of these writers, along with others, contributed to Granville Hicks's symposium, *The Living Novel* (1957). Michael Perkins's *The Secret Record* (1976) traces the development of a serious erotic literature in the wake of the 1960s evaporation of sexual censorship. James Burkhart Gilbert's *Writers and Partisans* (1968) is a history of general American "literary radicalism" as it funneled into the particular pages of the *Partisan Review*.

The surveys of postwar American poetry tend to be narrower than their subject, either by discussing only a particular group as putatively representative of the entire scene or by excluding whole groups of poets that the critic-author chooses not to accept. Stephen Stephanchev's *American Poetry Since 1945* (1965), M. L. Rosenthal's *The New Poets* (1967), Richard Howard's *Alone with America* (1969; expanded edition, 1980), Robert B. Shaw's *American Poetry Since 1960* (1973, an anthology of criticism), Robert Boyers's *Contemporary Poetry in America* (1975, also an anthology), David Kalstone's *Five Temperaments* (1977), Louis Simpson's *A Revolution in Taste* (1978), and Charles Altieri's *Enlarging the Temple* (1979) all share the common fault of acknowledging no poets more advanced than Allen Ginsberg or John Ashbery (the two current boundaries of academic acceptability), while Glauco Cambon's *Recent American Poetry* (1962), both Ralph J. Mills's *Contemporary American Poetry* (1965) and his later *The Cry of the Human* (1975), Robert Pinsky's *The Situation of Poetry* (1976), and

Jerome Mazzaro's *Postmodern American Poetry* (1980) are all yet more conservative. By contrast, Kenneth Rexroth's *American Poetry in the Twentieth Century* (1971) covers many of the radical figures whom the others neglect. (*Its* principal omissions are a table of contents and and index.) Paul Carroll's *The Poem and its Skin* (1968) is mostly about poets of his own generation (born between 1923 and 1927), while Ekbert Faas's *Toward a New American Poetics* (1978) is exclusively about poets in the Black Mountain tradition. William Everson's *Archetype West* (1976) surveys its scene with more historical depth than David Kherdian's *Six Poets of the San Francisco Renaissance* (1967). Samuel Charters's superficial "Studies in American Underground Poetry since 1945," *Some Poems/Poets* (1971) combines San Francisco and Black Mountain. Suzanne Juhasz's *Naked and Fiery Forms* (1976) examines a succession of mostly contemporary American women poets. James F. Mersmann's *Out of the Vietnam Vortex* (1974) documents the impact of a particular event upon certain U.S. poets. By contrast to all these, Karl Malkoff's *Handbook of Contemporary American Poetry* (1973) is the most comprehensive critical survey and, because of its introductory quality, initially the most useful.

Much of the serious criticism published in America about poetry comes from poets, and many of these essays are collected into books that are limited in interest, opinionated, and yet often critically informative about current activities: Allen Tate's *Essays of Four Decades* (1968) and *Memoirs and Opinions, 1926-1974* (1975), Howard Nemerov's *Fiction and Poetry* (1963) and then his *Reflections on Poetry and Poetics* (1972), James Dickey's *From Babel to Byzantium* (1968) and his *Sorties* (1971), Robert Creeley's *Contexts of Poetry* (1973), Stanley Kunitz's *A Kind of Order, a Kind of Folly* (1975), John Berryman's *The Freedom of the Poet* (1976), William Stafford's *Writing the Australian Crawl* (1978), Donald Hall's *Goatfoot Milktongue Twinbird* (1978), Dick Higgins's *A Dialectic of Centuries* (1978), David Ignatow's *Open Between Us* (1980), Diane Wakoski's *Toward a New Poetry* (1980), Robert Bly's *Talking all Morning* (1980), and Richard Kostelanetz's *The Old Poetries and the New* (1981). Among the anthologies of contemporary American poets writing about themselves are Alberta Turner's *50 Contemporary Poets: The Creative Process* (1977), William Heyen's *American Poets in 1976* (1976), Donald Allen and Warren Tallman's *The Poetics of the New American Poetry* (1973), and Howard Nemerov's *Contemporary American Poetry* (1966).

Several of the more consistent critics of current poetry have collected some of their longer reviews into their own books: Randall Jarrell's *Poetry and the Age* (1953) and *The Third Book of Criticism* (1969); Kenneth Rexroth's *Bird in the Bush* (1959), *Assays* (1961), and *With Eye and Ear* (1970); Karl Shapiro's *In Defense of Ignorance* (1962) and *To Abolish Children* (1968); Howard Moss's *Writing Against Time* (1969); Delmore Schwartz's *Selected Essays* (1970); Jonathan Cott's *He Dreams What Is Going on Inside His Head* (1973); Harold Bloom's *A Map of Misreading* (1975) and *Figures of a Capable Imagination* (1976); Lita Hornick's *Kulchur Queen* (1977); Lawrence Lieberman's *Unassigned Frequencies* (1977); Robert Boyers's *Excursions* (1977); Charles Molesworth's *The Fierce Embrace* (1979); and Donald Davie's *Trying to Explain* (1979). Robert Peters's *The Great American Poetry Bake-Off* (1979), Tom Montag's *Concern/s* (1977), and Hugh Fox's *The Living Underground* (1970) all cover many lesser-known "small press" poets.

The most comprehensive critical survey of postwar U.S., theater exists in two books by Gerald Weales: *American Drama Since World War II* (1961) and *The Jumping-Off Place: American Drama in the 1960's* (1969), as he mentions, at least, everything anyone ever considered important, from musical comedies to the "happenings" theater. Martin Gottfried's *A Theater Divided* (1967) dialectically separates the right-wing ("Broadway") from the left ("off-Broadway" and "off-off"), praying for a synthesis. Other useful, if partial, books include Eric Bentley's several collections of fugitive essays, Robert Brustein's continuing chronicle which has likewise been reprinted in several volumes, John Lahr's *Up Against the Fourth Wall* (1970), Richard Gilman's *Common and Uncommon Masks*, William and Jane Stott's *On Broadway* (1978), and M. C. Pasquier's *Le Théâtre américain d'aujourd'hui* (1978). Julius Novick's *Beyond Broadway* (1968) is a dated critical survey of the regional theater. More radical theatrical developments are represented in Stefan Brecht's *Queer Theatre* (1978), in Richard Schechner's *Public Domain* (1969), and in Michael Kirby's *Happenings* (1965) and *The Art of Time* (1969), as well as his anthology *The New Theater* (1974).

One form of writing about literature that has become increasingly popular in the past few decades is the published extended interview. The pioneers of this form were editors of the *Paris Review* who have so far collected their conversations with contemporaries into five volumes all entitled *Writers at Work* (1958, 1963, 1967, 1976, 1981). The Frenchman Pierre Dommergues reprinted his conversations with 40 American writers in *Les U.S.A. à la recherche de leur identité* (1967) and Bruce-Novoa did likewise with *14 Chicano Authors: Inquiry* by *Interview* (1980); Richard Layman edited *Conversations with Writers II* (1978); John O'Brien, *Black Writers* (1973); Frank Gato, *First Person: Conversations on Writers and Writing* (1975); Joe David Bellamy, *The New Fiction: Interviews with Innovative American Writers* (1974); William Packard, *The Craft of Poetry: Interviews from "The New York Quarterly"* (1974); George Garrett, *The Writer's Voice* (1973); and L. S. Dembo and Cyrena N. Pondrom, *The Contemporary Writer: Interviews with Sixteen Novelists and Poets* (1972), while David Ossman's *The Sullen Art* (1962) collects his radio interviews with 14 younger American poets. Richard Kostelanetz's book on the radical theater of the mid-1960s, *The Theatre of Mixed Means* (1968), consists largely of edited conversations with its major creators.

The following books are interdisciplinary symposia that, among other things, evoke the characteristic concerns of their subjects at each historical time: Allen Angoff's *American Writing Today: Its Independence and Vigor* (1957), Alan Pryce-Jones's *The American Imagination* (1960), John Fischer and Robert B. Silvers's *Writing in America* (1960), Elizabeth Janeway's *The Writer's World* (1969), Frank N. Magill's *The Contemporary Literary Scene 1973* (1974), Richard Kostelanetz's *A Critical Assembling* (1979), and then two thin, unedited paperbacks published by the Library of Congress—*The Little Magazine & Contemporary Literature* (1966) and *The Publication of Poetry and Fiction* (1977). Regarding the teaching of "creative writing," see two anthologies: Jonathan Baumbach's *Writers as Teachers/Teachers as Writers* (1970) and George Garrett's *A Craft So Hard to Learn* (1972).

Randall Jarrell characterized the postwar period as "an age of criticism," and one result of so much reflective literary preoccupation has been a series of critical books about American literary criticism itself. The pioneer here, Stanley Edgar Hyman's encyclopedic *The Armed Vision* (1948), contains definitive introductions to the characteristic procedures of Kenneth Burke, T. S. Eliot, Constance Rourke, Yvor Winters, and R. P. Blackmur, among others. Later books on contemporary Anglo-American criticism include William Van O'Connor's *An Age of Criticism* (1952), Murray Krieger's *The New Apologists for Poetry* (1956), Walter Sutton's *Modern American Criticism* (1963), René Wellek's *Concepts of Criticism* (1963), Elmer Borklund's *Contemporary Literary Critics* (1977), and Grant Webster's brilliant "History of Postwar American Literary Opinion," *The Republic of Letters* (1979). More recent books, such as Frank Lentricchia's *After the New Criticism* (1980), have critically analyzed the impact of European criticism upon

American practice. Phyllis Gershator did *A Bibliographic Guide to the Literature of Contemporary American Poetry, 1970-1975* (1976). John Somer and Barbara Eck Cooper compiled *Americans & British Literature, 1945-1975: An Annotated Bibliography of Contemporary Scholarship* (1979).

There are no doubt more books to be acknowledged here— some we missed and others that are presently appearing.

Notes About the Authors

John Ashmead (b. 1916) taught at Haverford College since 1947. His current title is Professor Emeritus of English. He has written on literature and film, as well as publishing a novel of his own.

Eric Bentley (b. 1916), a literary man in the theater, has written and directed plays, translated plays, edited anthologies of plays, in addition to teaching dramatic literature at Columbia, SUNY-Buffalo and Maryland. His latest books are *Monstrous Martyrdoms* (plays, 1985) and *Thinking about the Playwright* (essays, 1987).

Stanley Berne and **Arlene Zekowski** recently retired from decades of teaching at Eastern New Mexico State University at Portales. Books of their fiction are customarily published in tandem.

J. Bruce-Novoa, professor at the University of Texas at San Antonio, has authored *Chicano Authors: Inquiry by Interview* (1980). He has also published poems, stories and translations.

Richard Burgin, the editor and publisher of the semi-annual *Boulevard* (and before that of the *New York Arts Journal*), teaches at Drexel Institute in Philadelphia. Among his books are *Conversations with Jorge Luis Borges* (1969) and *Conversations with Isaac Bashevis Singer* (1985, paperback 1986), in addition to books of fiction.

William Burroughs (b. 1914) has by now overcome his controversial beginnings to become a distinguished man of American letters. Recently inducted into the Institute of Arts and Letters, he was also the subject of a recent full-length biography by Ted Morgan. He currently lives mostly in Lawrence, Kansas.

Lewis M. Dabney is Professor of English and American Studies at the

University of Wyoming. The author of *The Indians of Yoknapatawpha: A Study in Literature and History* (1974), he edited and introduced the *Portable Edmund Wilson* (1982).

Samuel R. Delany (b. 1942) has published many books of science fiction; among the larger are *Dhalgren* (1975) and the Flight from Neveryon series in four volumes. He has also written criticism of science fiction—*The Jewel-Hinged Jaw* (1978), *The American Shore* (1978) and *Starboard Wine* (1984).

Charles Doria (b. 1938), a classicist-at-large, received his doctorate from the State University of New York at Buffalo. He both coedited and cotranslated the anthologies *Origins: Creation Texts from the Ancient Mediterranean* (1976), *The Tenth Muse: Classical Drama in Translation* (1977), and *A Big Jewish Book: Poems and Other Visions of the Jews* (1978).

Irvin Faust (b. 1924) has worked since 1960 as director of guidance at a suburban New York City high school. Writing at night and on weekends, he has produced several novels and two collections of short stories, in addition to a sociological study. His most recent book is *The Year of the Hot Jock and Other Stories* (1985).

Leslie A. Fiedler (b. 1917) is Samuel Clemens Professor of English at the State University of New York at Buffalo. As well as lecturing widely, he has written many books of fiction, criticism and memoir.

Allen Ginsberg (b. 1926) has read and published his poetry around the world. Among his latest books are *Collected Poems* 1947-1980 (1984). He recently became Professor of English at Brooklyn College, CUNY.

Allen Grossman is the Paul E. Prosswimmer Professor of Poetry and General Education at Brandeis University. Among his books of poetry is *The Woman at the Bridge over the Chicago River* (1979).

Donald Hall (b. 1928), formerly a Professor of English at the University of Michigan, writes poems and prose full time at his farm in southern New Hampshire. His most recent books of poetry are *Poetry and Ambition* (1988) and *The One Day* (1988).

Ihab Hassan (b. 1925) is the Vilas Research Professor of English and Comparative Literature at the University of Wisconsin, Milwaukee. His writings include *Radical Innocence* (1961), *The Literature of Silence* (1967), *The Disememberment of Orpheus* (1971), *Paracriticisms* (1975), *The Right Promethean Fire* (1980) and *Out of Egypt* (1986).

Calvin C. Hernton, poet, critic and sociologist, is Professor of Black Studies at Oberlin College in Ohio. His books include *Sex and Racism in America* (1965), *White Papers for White Americans* (1966), *Coming Together* (1971), *Scarecrow* (1974) and *The Sexual Mountain and Black Women Writers* (1988).

Dick Higgins (b. 1938), the founder of the Something Else Press, has also published books of poetry, fiction and criticism. *Pattern Poems* (1987) is his major work in the last category. His music compositions and visual art have been presented around the world.

Jerome Klinkowitz (b. 1943) is Professor of English at the University of Northern Iowa. The author of such critical books as *Literary Disruptions* (1975), *The Life of Fiction* (1977), *The Practice of Fiction in America* (1980), *The American 1960s* (1980), *The Self-Apparent Word* (1984), *The New Novel of Manners in America* (1986), and *Rosenberg/Barthes/Hassan* (1988), he has also edited and contributed to *The Vonnegut Statement* (1973) and *Vonnegut in America* (1977), among other books. *Short Season and Other Stories* (1988) is a collection of his fiction.

Kenneth Koch (b. 1925) is a poet and Professor of English at Columbia University. In addition to many collections of poetry, he has written fiction and plays and books on teaching poetry writing to children and old people.

Richard Kostelanetz (b. 1940) has written books of and about poetry, fiction, criticism and art, as well as editing over two dozen anthologies of contemporary art, literature, criticism and thought. His art with words, numbers and lines in audio, video, books, films and holography has been exhibited around the world. He survives unaffiliated in New York.

David Madden has been writer-in-residence at Louisiana State University since 1968. A playwright, critic, novelist and editor, he has at various times taught English, dramatics and imaginative writing. His novels include *Bijou* (1974) and *The Suicide's Wife* (1978).

Karl Malkoff is Professor of English and American Literature at the City College of CUNY, where he has taught for over a quarter century. He is the author of *Theodore Roethke* (1966), *Muriel Spark* (1968), *Crowell's Handbook of Contemporary American Poetry* (1973) and *Escape from the Self* (1977).

Jay Martin is the Leo S. Bing Professor of English at the University of Southern California. His books include *Harvests of Change: American Literature, 1865-1914* (1967), *Nathanael West: The Art of His Life* (1970), and *Winter Dreams: An American in Moscow* (1979).

Wendy Martin is a professor of English at Claremont College. The founder and editor of *Woman's Studies: An Interdisciplinary Journal*, she also edited the anthology *The American Sisterhood: Feminist Writings from the Colonial Times to the Present* (1972).

Walter James Miller (b. 1918), Professor Emeritus at New York University, was for many years the host and producer of "Reader's Almanac" for the New York City municipal radio station. His books include a poetry collection, *Making an Angel* (1977); critical studies of Joseph Heller and Kurt Vonnegut; and annotated editions of such classics as *Catch-22* and *Twenty Thousand Leagues Under the Sea*.

Larry Neal (1938-1981) was a poet, critic, teacher and administrator. He taught at Lincoln, Yale and Harvard universities, among others, and was executive director of the Washington DC Commission on Arts and Humanities. With LeRoi Jones (Amiri Baraka), he coedited the anthology *Black Fire* (1968).

Thomas Parkinson (b. 1920) is Professor of English at the University of California at Berkeley. Besides publishing several volumes of his own poetry, he has written two books on William Butler Yeats and edited several more on modern literature, including *Hart Crane and Yvor Winters: Their Literary Correspondence* (1978).

Carl R. Proffer (1938-1984) was Professor of Slavic Literature and Languages at the University of Michigan. The cofounder of Ardis

Publishers, he also write books about Vladimir Nabokov and translated various 19th and 20th century Russian writers. *The Windows of Russia* (1987) is a posthumously published collection of criticism.

Rochelle Ratner (b. 1948) is a poet and fiction writer, as well as Executive Editor of *American Poetry Review*. *Bobby's Girl* (1986) is her first novel; *Practicing To Be a Woman* (1982) is her latest poetry book.

Jerome Rothenberg (b. 1931) has, after years of independence, become a Professor of English at the University of California at San Diego. Books of his poetry include *Poland/1941* (1974), *A Seneca Journal* (1978), *Vienna Blood* (1980), *That Dada Strain* (1983), and *New Selected Poems* (1986). He has also edited several distinguished anthologies.

Nathan A. Scott, William R. Kenan Professor of Religious Studies at the University of Virginia, also serves as Professor of English. Among his numerous books are *The Wild Prayer of Longing: Poetry and the Sacred* (1971), *Three American Moralists—Mailer, Bellow, Trilling* (1973), *The Poetry of Civic Virtue* (1976) and *The Poetics of Belief* (1985).

Joseph Slade is Professor of English at Long Island University in Brooklyn, New York, where he also heads the Communications Center. Besides editing *The Markham Review*, he authored *Thomas Pynchon* (1974) and numerous articles on technology, literature, film and American culture.

Sharon Spencer, Professor of English at Montclair State College in New Jersey, has published one novel, *The Space Between* (1973), and two books of criticism, *Space, Time and Structure in the Modern Novel* (1974) and *Collage of Dreams: The Writings of Anais Nin* (1977).

John Tytell (b. 1939), Professor of English at Queens College, CUNY, is also an associate editor of the *American Book Review*. Among his books are a biography of Ezra Pound and *Naked Angeles: The Lives and Literature of the Beat Generation* (1976), which has recently been reissued in paperback.